D0861779

COLLECTED PROSE

Also by Paul Auster

Novels

The New York Trilogy (City of Glass • Ghosts • The Locked Room) •
In the Country of Last Things • Moon Palace •
The Music of Chance • Leviathan • Mr. Vertigo • Timbuktu •
The Book of Illusions • Oracle Night

Nonfiction

White Spaces • The Invention of Solitude •
The Art of Hunger • Why Write? • Hand to Mouth •
The Story of My Typewriter (with Sam Messer) •
The Red Notebook

Screenplays

3 Films: Smoke, Blue in the Face, Lulu on the Bridge

Poetry

Unearth • Wall Writing • Fragments from Cold • Facing the Music •
Disappearances: Selected Poems • Collected Poems

Editor

The Random House Book of Twentieth-Century French Poetry •
I Thought My Father Was God and Other True Tales from
NPR's National Story Project

COLLECTED PROSE

Autobiographical Writings, True Stories, Critical Essays,
Prefaces and Collaborations with Artists

Paul Auster

Picador
Henry Holt and Company
New York

www.picadorusa.com

Picador® is a U.S. registered trademark and is used by Henry Holt and Company under license from Pan Books Limited.

For information on Picador Reading Group Guides, as well as ordering, please contact the Trade Marketing department at St. Martin's Press.
Phone: 1-800-221-7945 extension 763
Fax: 212-677-7456
E-mail: trademarketing@stmartins.com

For further copyright information see page 511

ISBN 0-312-42468-X
EAN 978-0312-42468-8

First published in Great Britain by Faber and Faber Limited

First Picador Edition: March 2005

10 9 8 7 6 5 4 3 2 1

This book could not have been done
without the remarkable assistance of Angus Cargill.

Contents

PREFACES

OCCASIONS

THE INVENTION OF SOLITUDE

Portrait of an Invisible Man

In searching out the truth be ready for the unexpected, for it is difficult to find and puzzling when you find it.

Heraclitus

One day there is life. A man, for example, in the best of health, not even old, with no history of illness. Everything is as it was, as it will always be. He goes from one day to the next, minding his own business, dreaming only of the life that lies before him. And then, suddenly, it happens there is death. A man lets out a little sigh, he slumps down in his chair, and it is death. The suddenness of it leaves no room for thought, gives the mind no chance to seek out a word that might comfort it. We are left with nothing but death, the irreducible fact of our own mortality. Death after a long illness we can accept with resignation. Even accidental death we can ascribe to fate. But for a man to die of no apparent cause, for a man to die simply because he is a man, brings us so close to the invisible boundary between life and death that we no longer know which side we are on. Life becomes death, and it is as if this death has owned this life all along. Death without warning. Which is to say: life stops. And it can stop at any moment.

The news of my father's death came to me three weeks ago. It was Sunday morning, and I was in the kitchen preparing breakfast for my small son, Daniel. Upstairs my wife was still in bed, warm under the quilts, luxuriating in a few extra hours of sleep. Winter in the country: a world of silence, wood smoke, whiteness. My mind was filled with thoughts about the piece I had been writing the night before, and I was looking ahead to the afternoon when I would be able to get back to work. Then the phone rang. I knew instantly that there was trouble. No one calls at eight o'clock on a Sunday morning unless it is to give news that cannot wait. And news that cannot wait is always bad news.

I could not muster a single ennobling thought.

Even before we packed our bags and set out on the three-hour drive to

New Jersey, I knew that I would have to write about my father. I had no plan, had no precise idea of what this meant. I cannot even remember making a decision about it. It was simply there, a certainty, an obligation that began to impose itself on me the moment I was given the news. I thought: my father is gone. If I do not act quickly, his entire life will vanish along with him.

Looking back on it now, even from so short a distance as three weeks, I find this a rather curious reaction. I had always imagined that death would numb me, immobilize me with grief. But now that it had happened, I did not shed any tears, I did not feel as though the world had collapsed around me. In some strange way, I was remarkably prepared to accept this death, in spite of its suddenness. What disturbed me was something else, something unrelated to death or my response to it: the realization that my father had left no traces.

He had no wife, no family that depended on him, no one whose life would be altered by his absence. A brief moment of shock, perhaps, on the part of scattered friends, sobered as much by the thought of capricious death as by the loss of their friend, followed by a short period of mourning, and then nothing. Eventually, it would be as though he had never lived at all.

Even before his death he had been absent, and long ago the people closest to him had learned to accept this absence, to treat it as the fundamental quality of his being. Now that he was gone, it would not be difficult for the world to absorb the fact that he was gone forever. The nature of his life had prepared the world for his death—had been a kind of death by anticipation—and if and when he was remembered, it would be dimly, no more than dimly.

Devoid of passion, either for a thing, a person, or an idea, incapable or unwilling to reveal himself under any circumstances, he had managed to keep himself at a distance from life, to avoid immersion in the quick of things. He ate, he went to work, he had friends, he played tennis, and yet for all that he was not there. In the deepest, most unalterable sense, he was an invisible man. Invisible to others, and most likely invisible to himself as well. If, while he was alive, I kept looking for him, kept trying to find the father who was not there, now that he is dead I still feel as though I must go on looking for him. Death has not changed anything. The only difference is that I have run out of time.

For fifteen years he had lived alone. Doggedly, opaquely, as if immune to the world. He did not seem to be a man occupying space, but rather a block of impenetrable space in the form of a man. The world bounced off him, shattered against him, at times adhered to him—but it never got through. For fifteen years he haunted an enormous house, all by himself, and it was in that house that he died.

For a short while we had lived there as a family—my father, my mother, my sister, and I. After my parents were divorced, everyone dispersed: my mother began a new life, I went off to college, and my sister stayed with my mother until she, too, went off to school. Only my father remained. Because of a clause in the divorce agreement which stipulated that my mother still owned a share of the house and would be given half the proceeds whenever it was sold (which made my father reluctant to sell), or from some secret refusal to change his life (so as not to show the world that the divorce had affected him in a way he could not control), or simply from inertia, an emotional lethargy that prevented him from taking any action, he stayed on, living alone in a house that could have accommodated six or seven people.

It was an impressive place: old, solidly built, in the Tudor style, with leaded windows, a slate roof, and rooms of royal proportions. Buying it had been a big step for my parents, a sign of growing wealth. This was the best neighborhood in town, and although it was not a pleasant place to live (especially for children), its prestige outweighed its deadliness. Given the fact that he wound up spending the rest of his life in that house, it is ironic that my father at first resisted moving there. He complained about the price (a constant theme), and when at last he relented, it was with grudging bad humor. Even so, he paid in cash. All in one go. No mortgage, no monthly payments. It was 1959, and business was going well for him.

Always a man of habit, he would leave for work early in the morning, work hard all day, and then, when he came home (on those days he did not work late), take a short nap before dinner. Sometime during our first week in the new house, before we had properly moved in, he made a curious kind of mistake. Instead of driving home to the new house after work, he went directly to the old one, as he had done for years, parked his car in the driveway, walked into the house through the back door, climbed the stairs, entered the bedroom, lay down on the bed, and went to sleep. He slept for about an hour. Needless to say, when the new mistress of the house returned to find a strange man sleeping in her bed, she was a little surprised. But unlike Goldilocks, my father did not jump up and run away. The confusion was eventually settled, and everyone had a good laugh. Even today, it still makes me laugh. And yet, for all that, I cannot help regarding it as a pathetic story. It is one thing for a man to drive to his old house by mistake, but it is quite another, I think, for him not to notice that anything has changed inside it. Even the most tired or distracted mind has a corner of pure, animal response, and can give the body a sense of where it is. One would have to be nearly unconscious not to see, or at least not to feel, that the house was no longer the same. "Habit," as one of Beckett's characters says, "is a great deadener." And if the mind is unable to respond to the physical evidence, what will it do when confronted with the emotional evidence?

During those last fifteen years he changed almost nothing in the house. He did not add any furniture, he did not remove any furniture. The walls remained the same color, the pots and pans were not replaced, even my mother's dresses were not thrown out—but stored away in an attic closet. The very size of the house absolved him from having to make any decisions about the things it contained. It was not that he was clinging to the past, trying to preserve the house as a museum. On the contrary, he seemed to be unaware of what he was doing. It was negligence that governed him, not memory, and even though he went on living in that house all those years, he lived in it as a stranger might have. As the years went by, he spent less and less time there. He ate nearly all his meals in restaurants, arranged his social calendar so as to be busy every night, and used the house as little more than a place to sleep. Once, several years ago, I happened to mention to him how much money I had earned from my writing and translating during the previous year (a pittance by any standard, but more than I had ever made before), and his amused response was that he spent more than that just on eating out. The point is: his life was not centered around the place where he lived. His house was just one of many stopping places in a restless, unmoored existence, and this lack of center had the effect of turning him into a perpetual outsider, a tourist of his own life. You never had the feeling that he could be located.

Still, the house seems important to me, if only to the extent that it was neglected—symptomatic of a state of mind that, otherwise inaccessible, manifested itself in the concrete images of unconscious behavior. The house became the metaphor of my father's life, the exact and faithful representation of his inner world. For although he kept the house tidy and preserved it more or less as it had been, it underwent a gradual and ineluctable process of disintegration. He was neat, he always put things back in their proper place, but nothing was cared for, nothing was ever cleaned. The furniture, especially in the rooms he rarely visited, was covered with dust, cobwebs, the signs of total neglect; the kitchen stove was so encrusted with charred food that it had become unsalvageable; in the cupboard, sometimes languishing on the shelves for years: bug-infested packages of flour, stale crackers, bags of sugar that had turned into solid blocks, bottles of syrup that could no longer be opened. Whenever he prepared a meal for himself, he would immediately and assiduously do the dishes—but rinse them only, never using soap, so that every cup, every saucer, every plate was coated with a film of dingy grease. Throughout the house: the window shades, which were kept drawn at all times, had become so threadbare that the slightest tug would pull them apart. Leaks sprang and stained the furniture, the furnace never gave off enough heat, the shower did not work. The house became shabby, depressing to walk into. You felt as if you were entering the house of a blind man.

His friends and family, sensing the madness of the way he lived in that house, kept urging him to sell it and move somewhere else. But he always managed to ward them off with a non-committal "I'm happy here," or "The house suits me fine." In the end, however, he did decide to move. At the very end. In the last phone conversation we ever had, ten days before he died, he told me the house had been sold and that the closing was set for February first, about three weeks away. He wanted to know if there was anything in the house I could use, and I agreed to come down for a visit with my wife and Daniel on the first free day that opened up. He died before we had a chance to make it.

There is nothing more terrible, I learned, than having to face the objects of a dead man. Things are inert: they have meaning only in function of the life that makes use of them. When that life ends, the things change, even though they remain the same. They are there and yet not there: tangible ghosts, condemned to survive in a world they no longer belong to. What is one to think, for example, of a closetful of clothes waiting silently to be worn again by a man who will not be coming back to open the door? Or the stray packets of condoms strewn among brimming drawers of underwear and socks? Or an electric razor sitting in the bathroom, still clogged with the whisker dust of the last shave? Or a dozen empty tubes of hair coloring hidden away in a leather travelling case?—suddenly revealing things one has no desire to see, no desire to know. There is a poignancy to it, and also a kind of horror. In themselves, the things mean nothing, like the cooking utensils of some vanished civilization. And yet they say something to us, standing there not as objects but as remnants of thought, of consciousness, emblems of the solitude in which a man comes to make decisions about himself: whether to color his hair, whether to wear this or that shirt, whether to live, whether to die. And the futility of it all once there is death.

Each time I opened a drawer or poked my head into a closet, I felt like an intruder, a burglar ransacking the secret places of a man's mind. I kept expecting my father to walk in, to stare at me in disbelief, and ask me what the hell I thought I was doing. It didn't seem fair that he couldn't protest. I had no right to invade his privacy.

A hastily scrawled telephone number on the back of a business card that read: H. Limeburg—Garbage Cans of All Descriptions. Photographs of my parents' honeymoon in Niagara Falls, 1946: my mother sitting nervously on top of a bull for one of those funny shots that are never funny, and a sudden sense of how unreal the world has always been, even in its prehistory. A drawer full of hammers, nails, and more than twenty screwdrivers. A filing cabinet stuffed with canceled checks from 1953 and the cards I received for my sixth birthday. And then, buried at the bottom of a drawer in the bathroom: the monogrammed toothbrush that had once belonged to my mother and which had not been touched or looked at for more than fifteen years.

The list is inexhaustible.

It soon became apparent to me that my father had done almost nothing to prepare himself for his departure. The only signs of the impending move I could detect in the whole house were a few cartons of books—trivial books (out of date atlases, a fifty-year-old introduction to electronics, a high school Latin grammar, ancient law books) that he had been planning to give away to charity. Other than that, nothing. No empty boxes waiting to be filled. No pieces of furniture given away or sold. No arrangements made with a moving company. It was as though he had not been able to face it. Rather than empty the house, he had simply willed himself to die. Death was a way out, the only legitimate escape.

There was no escape for me, however. The thing had to be done, and there was no one else to do it. For ten days I went through his things, cleared out the house, got it ready for the new owners. It was a miserable time, but also an oddly humorous time, a time of reckless and absurd decisions: sell it, throw it out, give it away. My wife and I bought a big wooden slide for eighteen-month old Daniel and set it up in the living room. He thrived on the chaos: rummaging among the things, putting lampshades on his head, flinging plastic poker chips around the house, running through the vast spaces of the gradually emptying rooms. At night my wife and I would lie under monolithic quilts watching trashy movies on television. Until the television, too, was given away. There was trouble with the furnace, and if I forgot to fill it with water, it would shut off. One morning we woke up to find that the temperature in the house had dropped to forty degrees. Twenty times a day the phone rang, and twenty times a day I told someone that my father was dead. I had become a furniture salesman, a moving man, a messenger of bad tidings.

The house began to resemble the set for a trite comedy of manners. Relatives swooped in, asking for this piece of furniture or that piece of dinnerware, trying on my father's suits, overturning boxes, chattering away like geese. Auctioneers came to examine the merchandise ("Nothing upholstered, it's not worth a nickel"), turned up their noses, and walked out. Garbage men clumped in with heavy boots and hauled off mountains of trash. The water man read the water meter, the gas man read the gas meter, the oil men read the oil gauge. (One of them, I forget which, who had been given a lot of trouble by my father over the years, said to me with savage complicity, "I don't like to say this"—meaning he did—"but your father was an obnoxious bastard.") The real estate agent came to buy some furniture for the new owners and wound up taking a mirror for herself. A woman who ran a curio shop bought my mother's old hats. A junkman came with a team of assistants (four black men named Luther, Ulysses, Tommy Pride, and Joe Sapp) and carted away everything from a set of barbels to a broken toaster. By the time it was over, nothing was left. Not even a postcard. Not even a thought.

If there was a single worst moment for me during those days, it came when I walked across the front lawn in the pouring rain to dump an armful of my father's ties into the back of a Good Will Mission truck. There must have been more than a hundred ties, and many of them I remembered from my childhood: the patterns, the colors, the shapes that had been embedded in my earliest consciousness, as clearly as my father's face had been. To see myself throwing them away like so much junk was intolerable to me, and it was then, at the precise instant I tossed them into the truck, that I came closest to tears. More than seeing the coffin itself being lowered into the ground, the act of throwing away these ties seemed to embody for me the idea of burial. I finally understood that my father was dead.

Yesterday one of the neighborhood children came here to play with Daniel. A girl of about three and a half who has recently learned that big people were once children, too, and that even her own mother and father have parents. At one point she picked up the telephone and launched into a pretend conversation, then turned to me and said, "Paul, it's your father. He wants to talk to you." It was gruesome. I thought: there's a ghost at the other end of the line, and he really does want to talk to me. It was a few moments before I could speak. "No," I finally blurted out. "It can't be my father. He wouldn't be calling today. He's somewhere else."

I waited until she had hung up the phone and then walked out of the room.

In his bedroom closet I had found several hundred photographs—stashed away in faded manila envelopes, affixed to the black pages of warped albums, scattered loosely in drawers. From the way they had been stored I gathered he never looked at them, had even forgotten they were there. One very big album, bound in expensive leather with a gold-stamped title on the cover—This is Our Life: The Austers—was totally blank inside. Someone, probably my mother, had once gone to the trouble of ordering this album, but no one had ever bothered to fill it.

Back home, I pored over these pictures with a fascination bordering on mania. I found them irresistible, precious, the equivalent of holy relics. It seemed that they could tell me things I had never known before, reveal some previously hidden truth, and I studied each one intensely, absorbing the least detail, the most insignificant shadow, until all the images had become a part of me. I wanted nothing to be lost.

Death takes a man's body away from him. In life, a man and his body are synonymous; in death, there is the man and there is his body. We say, "This is the body of X," as if this body, which had once been the man himself, not something that represented him or belonged to him, but the very man called X, were suddenly of no importance. When a man walks into a room and you shake hands with him, you do not feel that you are shaking hands with his hand, or shaking hands with his body, you are shaking hands with *him*. Death changes that. This is the body of X, not this is X. The syntax is entirely different. Now we are talking about two things instead of one, implying that the man continues to exist, but only as an idea, a cluster of images and memories in the minds of other people. As for the body, it is no more than flesh and bones, a heap of pure matter.

Discovering these photographs was important to me because they seemed to reaffirm my father's physical presence in the world, to give me the illusion that he was still there. The fact that many of these pictures were ones I had never seen before, especially the ones of his youth, gave me the odd sensation that I was meeting him for the first time, that a part of him was only just beginning to exist. I had lost my father. But at the same time, I had also found him. As long as I kept these pictures before my eyes, as long as I continued to study them with my complete attention, it was as though he were still alive, even in death. Or if not alive, at least not dead. Or rather, somehow suspended, locked in a universe that had nothing to do with death, in which death could never make an entrance.

Most of these pictures did not tell me anything new, but they helped to fill in gaps, confirm impressions, offer proof where none had existed before. A series of snapshots of him as a bachelor, for example, probably taken over a number of years, gives a precise account of certain aspects of his personality that had been submerged during the years of his marriage, a side of him I did not begin to see until after his divorce: my father as prankster, as man about town, as good time Charlie. In picture after picture he is standing with women, usually two or three, all of them affecting comical poses, their arms perhaps around each other, or two of them sitting on his lap, or else a theatrical kiss for the benefit of no one but the person taking the picture. In the background: a mountain, a tennis court, perhaps a swimming pool or a log cabin. These were the pictures brought back from weekend jaunts to various Catskill resorts in the company of his bachelor friends: play tennis, have a good time with the girls. He carried on in this way until he was thirty-four.

It was a life that suited him, and I can see why he went back to it after his marriage broke up. For a man who finds life tolerable only by staying on the surface of himself, it is natural to be satisfied with offering no more than this surface to others. There are few demands to be met, and no commitment is required. Marriage, on the other hand, closes the door. Your existence is confined to a narrow space in which you are constantly forced to reveal yourself—and therefore, constantly obliged to look into yourself, to examine your own depths. When the door is open there is never any problem: you can always escape. You can avoid unwanted confrontations, either with yourself or with another, simply by walking away.

My father's capacity for evasion was almost limitless. Because the domain of the other was unreal to him, his incursions into that domain were made with a part of himself he considered to be equally unreal, another self he had trained as an actor to represent him in the empty comedy of the world-at-large. This surrogate self was essentially a tease, a hyperactive child, a fabricator of tall tales. It could not take anything seriously.

Because nothing mattered, he gave himself the freedom to do anything he wanted (sneaking into tennis clubs, pretending to be a restaurant critic in order to get a free meal), and the charm he exercised to make his conquests was precisely what made these conquests meaningless. With the vanity of a woman he hid the truth about his age, made up stories about his business dealings, talked about himself only obliquely—in the third person, as if about an acquaintance of his ("There's a friend of mine who has this problem; what do you think he should do about it? . . ."). Whenever a situation became too tight for him, whenever he felt pushed to the verge of having to reveal himself, he would wriggle out of it by telling a lie. Eventually, the lie came automatically and was indulged in for its own sake. The principle was to say as little as possible. If people never learned the truth about him, then they couldn't turn around and use it against him later. The lie was a way of buying protection. What people saw when he appeared before them, then, was not really him, but a person he had invented, an artificial creature he could manipulate in order to manipulate others. He himself remained invisible, a puppeteer working the strings of his alter-ego from a dark, solitary place behind the curtain.

For the last ten or twelve years of his life he had one steady lady friend, and this was the woman who went out with him in public, who played the role of official companion. Every now and then there was some vague talk of marriage (at her insistence), and everyone assumed that this was the only woman he had anything to do with. After his death, however, other women began to step forward. This one had loved him, that one had worshipped him, another one was going to marry him. The principal girlfriend was shocked to learn about these other women: my father had never breathed a word about them to her. Each one had been fed a different line, and each one thought she had possessed him entirely. As it turned out, none of them knew the slightest thing about him. He had managed to elude them all.

Solitary. But not in the sense of being alone. Not solitary in the way Thoreau was, for example, exiling himself in order to find out where he was; not solitary in the way Jonah was, praying for deliverance in the belly of the whale. Solitary in the sense of retreat. In the sense of not having to see himself, of not having to see himself being seen by anyone else.

Talking to him was a trying experience. Either he would be absent, as he usually was, or he would assault you with a brittle jocularity, which was merely another form of absence. It was like trying to make yourself understood by a senile old man. You talked, and there would be no response, or a response that was inappropriate, showing that he hadn't been following the drift of your words. In recent years, whenever I spoke to him on the phone I would find myself saying more than I normally do, becoming aggressively talkative, chatting away in a futile attempt to hold his attention, to provoke a response. Afterwards, I would invariably feel foolish for having tried so hard.

He did not smoke, he did not drink. No hunger for sensual pleasures, no thirst for intellectual pleasures. Books bored him, and it was the rare movie or play that did not put him to sleep. Even at parties you would see him struggling to keep his eyes open, and more often than not he would succumb, falling asleep in a chair as the conversations swirled around him. A man without appetites. You felt that nothing could ever intrude on him, that he had no need of anything the world had to offer.

At thirty-four, marriage. At fifty-two, divorce. In one sense, it lasted years, but in fact it did not last more than a few days. He was never a married man, never a divorced man, but a life-long bachelor who happened to have had an interlude of marriage. Although he did not shirk his outward duties as a husband (he was faithful, he provided for his wife and children, he shouldered all his responsibilities), it was clear that he was not cut out to play this role. He simply had no talent for it.

My mother was just twenty-one when she married him. His conduct during the brief courtship had been chaste. No daring overtures, none of the aroused male's breathless assaults. Now and then they would hold hands, exchange a polite good-night kiss. Love, in so many words, was never declared by either one of them. By the time the wedding came, they were little more than strangers.

It was not long before my mother realized her mistake. Even before the honeymoon was over (that honeymoon, so fully documented in the photographs I found: the two of them sitting together, for instance, on a rock at the edge of a perfectly still lake, a broad path of sunlight behind them leading to the pine slope in shadow, my father with his arms around my mother, and the two of them looking at each other, smiling timidly, as if the photographer had made them hold the pose an instant too long), even before the honeymoon was over, my mother knew the marriage would not work. She went to her mother in tears and said she wanted to leave him. Somehow, her mother managed to persuade her to go back and give it a chance. And then, before the dust had settled, she found herself pregnant. And suddenly it was too late to do anything.

I think of it sometimes: how I was conceived in that Niagara Falls resort for honeymooners. Not that it matters where it happened. But the thought of what must have been a passionless embrace, a blind, dutiful groping between chilly hotel sheets, has never failed to humble me into an awareness of my own contingency. Niagara Falls. Or the hazard of two bodies joining. And then me, a random homunculus, like some dare-devil in a barrel, shooting over the falls.

A little more than eight months later, on the morning of her twenty-second birthday, my mother woke up and told my father that the baby was coming. Ridiculous, he said, that baby's not due for another three weeks—and promptly went off to work, leaving her without a car.

She waited. Thought maybe he was right. Waited a little more, then called a sister-in-law and asked to be driven to the hospital. My aunt stayed with my mother throughout the day, calling my father every few hours to ask him to come. Later, he would say, I'm busy now, I'll get there when I can.

At a little past midnight I poked my way into the world, ass first, no doubt screaming.

My mother waited for my father to show up, but he did not arrive until the next morning—accompanied by his mother, who wanted to inspect grandchild number seven. A short, nervous visit, and then off again to work.

She cried, of course. After all, she was young, and she had not expected it to mean so little to him. But he could never understand such things. Not in the beginning, and not in the end. It was never possible for him to be where he was. For as long as he lived, he was somewhere else, between here and there. But never really here. And never really there.

Thirty years later, this same little drama was repeated. This time I was there, and I saw it with my own eyes.

After my own son was born I had thought: surely this will please him. Isn't every man pleased to become a grandfather?

I had wanted to see him doting on the baby, for him to offer me proof that he was, after all, capable of demonstrating some feeling—that he did, after all, have feelings in the way other people did. And if he could show affection for his grandson, then wouldn't it be an indirect way of showing affection for me? You do not stop hungering for your father's love, even after you are grown up.

But then, people do not change. All told, my father saw his grandson only three or four times, and at no time was he able to distinguish him from the impersonal mass of babies born into the world every day. Daniel was just two weeks old when he first laid eyes on him. I can remember the day vividly: a blistering Sunday at the end of June, heat-wave weather, the country air gray with moisture. My father pulled up in his car, saw my wife putting the baby into the carriage for a nap, and walked over to say hello. He poked his head into the carriage for a tenth of a second, straightened up and said to her, "A beautiful baby. Good luck with it," and then proceeded to walk on into the house. He might just as well have been talking about some stranger's baby encountered in line at the supermarket. For the rest of his visit that day he did not look at Daniel, and not once, ever, did he ask to hold him.

All this, merely as an example.

Impossible, I realize, to enter another's solitude. If it is true that we can ever come to know another human being, even to a small degree, it is only to the extent that he is willing to make himself known. A man will say: I am cold. Or else he will say nothing, and we will see him shivering. Either way, we will know that he is cold. But what of the man who says nothing and does not shiver? Where all is intractable, where all is hermetic and evasive, one can do no more than observe. But whether one can make sense of what he observes is another matter entirely.

I do not want to presume anything.

He never talked about himself, never seemed to know there was anything he *could* talk about. It was as though his inner life eluded even him.

He could not talk about it, and therefore he passed over it in silence.

If there is nothing, then, but silence, is it not presumptuous of me to speak? And yet: if there had been anything more than silence, would I have felt the need to speak in the first place?

My choices are limited. I can remain silent, or else I can speak of things that cannot be verified. At the very least, I want to put down the facts, to offer them as straightforwardly as possible, and let them say whatever they have to say. But even the facts do not always tell the truth.

He was so implacably neutral on the surface, his behavior was so flatly predictable, that everything he did came as a surprise. One could not believe there was such a man—who lacked feeling, who wanted so little of others. And if there was not such a man, that means there was another man, a man hidden inside the man who was not there, and the trick of it, then, is to find him. On the condition that he is there to be found.

To recognize, right from the start, that the essence of this project is failure.

Earliest memory: his absence. For the first years of my life he would leave for work early in the morning, before I was awake, and come home long after I had been put to bed. I was my mother's boy, and I lived in her orbit. I was a little moon circling her gigantic earth, a mote in the sphere of her gravity, and I controlled the tides, the weather, the forces of feeling. His refrain to her was: Don't fuss so much, you'll spoil him. But my health was not good, and she used this to justify the attention she lavished on me. We spent a lot of time together, she in her loneliness and I in my cramps, waiting patiently in doctors' offices for someone to quell the insurrection that continually raged in my stomach. Even then, I would cling to these doctors in a desperate sort of way, wanting them to hold me. From the very beginning, it seems, I was looking for my father, looking frantically for anyone who resembled him.

Later memories: a craving. My mind always ready to deny the facts at the slightest excuse, I mulishly went on hoping for something that was never given to me—or given to me so rarely and arbitrarily that it seemed to happen outside the range of normal experience, in a place where I would never be able to live for more than a few moments at a time. It was not that I felt he disliked me. It was just that he seemed distracted, unable to look in my direction. And more than anything else, I wanted him to take notice of me.

Anything, even the least thing, was enough. How, for example, when the family once went to a crowded restaurant on a Sunday and we had to wait for our table, my father took me outside, produced a tennis ball (from where?), put a penny on the sidewalk, and proceeded to play a game with me: hit the penny with the tennis ball. I could not have been more than eight or nine years old.

In retrospect, nothing could have been more trivial. And yet the fact that I had been included, that my father had casually asked me to share his boredom with him, nearly crushed me with happiness.

More often, there were disappointments. For a moment he would seem to have changed, to have opened up a little, and then, suddenly, he would not be there anymore. The one time I managed to persuade him to take me to a football game (the Giants versus the Chicago Cardinals, at Yankee Stadium or the Polo Grounds, I forget which), he abruptly stood up from his seat in the middle of the fourth quarter and said, "It's time to go now." He wanted to "beat the crowd" and avoid getting stuck in traffic. Nothing I said could convince him to stay, and so we left, just like that, with the game going full tilt. Unearthly despair as I followed him down the concrete ramps, and then, even worse, in the parking lot, with the noise of the invisible crowd roaring behind me.

You could not trust him to know what you wanted, to anticipate what you might have been feeling. The fact that you had to tell him yourself vitiated the pleasure in advance, disrupted a dreamed-of harmony before a note could be played. And then, even if you did tell him, it was not at all sure that he would understand what you meant.

* * *

I remember a day very like today. A drizzling Sunday, lethargy and quiet in the house: the world at half-speed. My father was taking a nap, or had just awoken from one, and somehow I was on the bed with him, the two of us alone in the room. Tell me a story. It must have begun like that. And because he was not doing anything, because he was still drowsing in the languor of the afternoon, he did just what I asked, launching into a story without missing a beat. I remember it all so clearly. It seems as if I have just walked out of that room, with its gray light and tangle of quilts on the bed, as if, simply by closing my eyes, I could walk back into it any time I want.

He told me of his prospecting days in South America. It was a tale of high adventure, fraught with mortal dangers, hair-raising escapes, and improbable twists of fortune: hacking his way through the jungle with a machete, fighting off bandits with his bare hands, shooting his donkey when it broke its leg. His language was flowery and convoluted, probably an echo of the books he himself had read as a boy. But it was precisely this literary style that enchanted me. Not only was he telling me new things about himself, unveiling to me the world of his distant past, but he was telling it with new and strange words. This language was just as important as the story itself. It belonged to it, and in some sense was indistinguishable from it. Its very strangeness was proof of authenticity.

It did not occur to me to think this might have been a made-up story. For years afterward I went on believing it. Even when I had passed the point when I should have known better, I still felt there might have been some truth to it. It gave me something to hold on to about my father, and I was reluctant to let go. At last I had an explanation for his mysterious evasions, his indifference to me. He was a romantic figure, a man with a dark and exciting past, and his present life was only a kind of stopping place, a way of biding his time until he took off on his next adventure. He was working out his plan, figuring out how to retrieve the gold that lay buried deep in the heart of the Andes.

In the back of my mind: a desire to do something extraordinary, to impress him with an act of heroic proportions. The more aloof he was, the higher the stakes became for me. But if a boy's will is tenacious and idealistic, it is also absurdly practical. I was only ten years old, and there was no child for me to save from a burning building, no sailors to rescue at sea. On the other hand, I was a good baseball player, the star of my Little League team, and although my father had no interest in baseball, I thought that if he saw me play, just once, he would begin to see me in a new light.

Finally he did come. My mother's parents were visiting at the time, and my grandfather, a great baseball fan, showed up with him. It was a special Memorial Day game, and the seats were full. If I was ever going to do something remarkable, this was the moment to do it. I can remember catching sight of them in the wooden bleachers, my father in a white shirt with no tie and my grandfather wearing a white handkerchief on his bald head to protect him from the sun—the whole scene in my mind now drenched in this dazzling white light.

It probably goes without saying that I made a mess of it. I got no hits, lost my poise in the field, could not have been more nervous. Of all the hundreds of games I played during my childhood, this one was the worst.

Afterwards, walking to the car with my father, he told me I had played a nice game. No I hadn't, I said, it was terrible. Well, you did your best, he answered. You can't do well every time.

It was not that he was trying to encourage me. Nor was he trying to be unkind. Rather, he was saying what one says on such occasions, as if automatically. They were the right words to say, and yet they were delivered without feeling, an exercise in decorum, uttered in the same abstracted tone of voice he would use almost twenty years later when he said, "A beautiful baby. Good luck with it." I could see that his mind was somewhere else.

In itself, this is not important. The important thing is this: I realized that even if I had done all the things I had hoped to do, his reaction would have been exactly the same. Whether I succeeded or failed did not essentially matter to him. I was not defined for him by anything I did, but by what I was, and this meant that his perception of me would never change, that we were fixed in an unmoveable relationship, cut off from each other on opposite sides of a wall. Even more than that, I realized that none of this had anything to do with me. It had only to do with him. Like everything else in his life, he saw me only through the mists of his solitude, as if at several removes from himself. The world was a distant place for him, I think, a place he was never truly able to enter, and out there in the distance, among all the shadows that flitted past him, I was born, became his son, and grew up, as if I were just one more shadow, appearing and disappearing in a half-lit realm of his consciousness.

* * *

With his daughter, born when I was three and a half, it was somewhat easier for him. But in the end it was infinitely more difficult.

She was a beautiful child. Uncommonly fragile, with great brown eyes that would collapse into tears at the slightest prompting. She spent much of her time alone, a tiny figure wandering through an imaginary land of elves and fairies, dancing on tiptoe in lace-trimmed ballerina costumes, singing in a voice loud enough to be heard only by herself. She was a miniature Ophelia, already doomed, it would seem, to a life of constant inner struggle. She made few friends, had trouble keeping up in school, and was harassed by self-doubts, even at a very young age, that turned the simplest routines into nightmares of anguish and defeat. There were tantrums, fits of terrible crying, constant upheavals. Nothing ever seemed to go well for very long.

More sensitive to the nuances of the unhappy marriage around us than I was, her insecurity became monumental, crippling. At least once a day she would ask our mother if "she loved daddy." The answer was always the same: Of course I do.

It could not have been a very convincing lie. If it had been, there would not have been any need to ask the question again the next day.

On the other hand, it is difficult to see how the truth would have made things any better.

It was almost as if she gave off a scent of helplessness. One's immediate impulse was to protect her, to buffer her against the assaults of the world. Like everyone else, my father pampered her. The more she seemed to cry out for coddling, the more willing he was to give it to her. Long after she was able to walk, for example, he insisted on carrying her down the stairs. There is no question that he did it out of love, did it gladly because she was his little angel. But underneath this coddling was the implicit message that she would never be able to do anything for herself. She was not a person to him, but an angel, and because she was never compelled to act as an autonomous being, she could never become one.

My mother, however, saw what was happening. When my sister was five years old, she took her to an exploratory consultation with a child psychiatrist, and the doctor recommended that some form of therapy be started. That night, when my mother told my father the results of the meeting, he exploded in a violent rage. No daughter of mine, etc. The idea that his daughter needed psychiatric help was no different from being told she was a leper. He would not accept it. He would not even discuss it.

This is the point I am trying to make. His refusal to look into himself was matched by an equally stubborn refusal to look at the world, to accept even the most incontrovertible evidence it thrust under his nose. Again and again throughout his life he would stare a thing in the face, nod his head, and then turn around and say it was not there. It made conversation with him almost impossible. By the time you had managed to establish a common ground with him, he would take out his shovel and dig it out from under your feet.

Years later, when my sister suffered through a series of debilitating mental breakdowns, my father continued to believe there was nothing wrong with her. It was as though he were biologically unable to recognize her condition.

In one of his books R.D. Laing describes the father of a catatonic girl who on each visit to her in the hospital would grab her by the shoulders and shake her as hard as he could, telling her to "snap out of it." My father did not grab hold of my sister, but his attitude was essentially the same. What she needs, he would say, is to get a job, to clean herself up, to start living in the real world. Of course she did. But that was exactly what she could not do. She's just sensitive, he would say, she needs to overcome her shyness. By domesticating the problem to a quirk of personality, he could go on believing there was nothing wrong. It was not blindness so much as a failure of imagination. At what moment does a house stop being a house? When the roof is taken off? When the windows are removed? When the walls are knocked down? At what moment does it become a pile of rubble? She's just different, he would say, there's nothing wrong with her. And then one day the walls of your house finally collapse. If the door is still standing, however, all you have to do is walk through it, and you are back inside. It's pleasant sleeping out under the stars. Never mind the rain. It can't last very long.

Little by little, as the situation continued to get worse, he had to begin to accept it. But even then, at each stage along the way, his acceptance was unorthodox, taking on eccentric, almost self-nullifying forms. He became convinced, for example, that the one thing that could help her was a crash program in mega-vitamin therapy. This was the chemical approach to mental illness. Although it has never been proven to be an effective cure, this method of treatment has quite a large following. One can see why it would have attracted my father. Instead of having to wrestle with a devastating emotional fact, he could look upon the disease as a physical flaw, something that could be cured in the same way you cure the flu. The disease became an external force, a kind of bug that could be eradicated with an equal and opposite external force. In his eyes my sister was able to remain curiously untouched by all this. She was merely the *site* where the battle would take place, which meant that everything that was happening did not really affect *her*.

He spent several months trying to persuade her to begin this megavitamin program—even going so far as to take the pills himself, in order to prove that she would not be poisoned—and when at last she gave in, she did not take the pills for more than a week or two. The vitamins were expensive, but he did not balk at spending the money. On the other hand, he angrily resisted paying for other kinds of treatment. He did not believe that a stranger could possibly care about what happened to her. Psychiatrists were all charlatans, interested only in soaking their patients and driving fancy cars. He refused to pay the bills, which limited her to the shabbiest kind of public care. She was a pauper, with no income of her own, but he sent her almost nothing.

He was more than willing to take things into his own hands, however. Although it could not benefit either one of them, he wanted her to live in his house so that he could be the one responsible for looking after her. At least he could trust his own feelings, and he knew that he cared. But then, when she did come (for a few months, following one of her stays in the hospital), he did not disrupt his normal routine to accommodate her—but continued to spend most of his time out, leaving her to rattle around the enormous house like a ghost.

He was negligent and stubborn. But still, underneath it all, I know he suffered. Sometimes, on the phone, when he and I were discussing my sister, I could hear his voice break ever so slightly, as if he were trying to muffle a sob. Unlike everything else he ever came up against, my sister's illness finally *moved him*—but only to leave him with a feeling of utter helplessness. There is no greater sorrow for a parent than this helplessness. You have to accept it, even if you can't. And the more you accept it, the greater your despair becomes.

His despair became very great.

Wandering through the house today, without purpose, depressed, feeling that I have begun to lose touch with what I am writing, I chanced upon these words from a letter by Van Gogh: "Like everyone else, I feel the need of family and friendship, affection and friendly intercourse. I am not made of stone or iron, like a hydrant or a lamp-post."

Perhaps this is what really counts: to arrive at the core of human feeling, in spite of the evidence.

These tiniest of images: incorrigible, lodged in the mud of memory, neither buried nor wholly retrievable. And yet each one, in itself, a fleeting resurrection, a moment otherwise lost. The way he walked, for example, weirdly balanced, bouncing on the balls of his feet, as if he were about to pitch forward, blindly, into the unknown. Or the way he hunched over the table as he ate, his shoulders tensed, always merely consuming the food, never savoring it. Or else the smells that emanated from the cars he used for work: fumes, leaking oil, exhaust; the clutter of cold metal tools; the constant rattle as the car moved. A memory of the day I went driving with him through downtown Newark, no more than six years old, and he slammed down on the brakes, the jolt of it flinging my head against the dashboard: the sudden swarm of black people around the car to see if I was all right, especially the woman who thrust a vanilla ice cream cone at me through the open window, and my saying "no thank you," very politely, too stunned to know what I really wanted. Or else another day in another car, some years later, when my father spat out the window only to realize that the window had not been lowered, and my boundless, irrational delight at seeing the saliva slither down the glass. And still, as a little boy, how he would sometimes take me with him to Jewish restaurants in neighborhoods I had never seen before, dark places filled with old people, each table graced with a tinted blue seltzer bottle, and how I would grow queasy, leave my food untouched, and content myself with watching him wolf down borscht, pirogen, and boiled meats covered with horse radish. I, who was being brought up as an American boy, who knew less about my ancestors than I did about Hopalong Cassidy's hat. Or how, when I was twelve or thirteen, and wanted desperately to go somewhere with a couple of my friends, I called him at work to get his permission, and he said to me, at a loss, not knowing how to put it, "You're just a bunch of greenhorns," and how, for years afterward, my friends and I (one of them now dead, of a heroin overdose) would repeat those words as a piece of folklore, a nostalgic joke.

* * *

The size of his hands. Their callusses.

Eating the skin off the top of hot chocolate.

Tea with lemon.

The pairs of black, horn-rimmed glasses scattered through the house: on kitchen counters, on table tops, at the edge of the bathroom sink—always open, lying there like some strange, unclassified form of animal.

Watching him play tennis.

The way his knees sometimes buckled when he walked.

His face.

His resemblance to Abraham Lincoln, and how people always remarked on it.

His fearlessness with dogs.

His face. And again, his face.

Tropical fish.

Often, he seemed to lose his concentration, to forget where he was, as if he had lost the sense of his own continuity. It made him accident prone: smashed thumbnails from using a hammer, numerous little accidents in the car.

His absent-mindedness as a driver: to the point that it sometimes became frightening. I always thought it would be a car that did him in.

Otherwise, his health was so good that he seemed invulnerable, exempt from the physical ills that strike all the rest of us. As though nothing could ever touch him.

The way he spoke: as if making a great effort to rise up out of his solitude, as if his voice were rusty, had lost the habit of speaking. He always hemmed and hawed a lot, cleared his throat, seemed to sputter in mid-sentence. You felt, very definitely, that he was uncomfortable.

In the same way, it always amused me as a child to watch him sign his name. He could not simply put the pen against the paper and write. As if unconsciously delaying the moment of truth, he would always make a slight, preliminary flourish, a circular movement an inch or two off the page, like a fly buzzing in the air and zeroing in on its spot, before he could get down to business. It was a modified version of the way Art Carney's Norton used to sign his name on *The Honeymooners*.

He even pronounced his words a little oddly. "Upown," for example, instead of "upon," as if the flourish of his hand had its counterpart in his voice. There was a musical, airy quality to it. Whenever he answered the phone, it was a lilting "hellooo" that greeted you. The effect was not so much funny as endearing. It made him seem slightly daft, as if he were out of phase with the rest of the world—but not by much. Just a degree or two.

Indelible tics.

In those crazy, tensed-up moods he sometimes got into, he would always come out with bizarre opinions, not really taking them seriously, but happy to play devil's advocate in order to keep things lively. Teasing people put him in buoyant spirits, and after a particularly inane remark to someone he would often squeeze that person's leg—in a spot that always tickled. He literally liked to pull your leg.

Again the house.

No matter how negligent his care of it might have seemed from the outside, he believed in his system. Like a mad inventor protecting the secret of his perpetual motion machine, he would suffer no one to tamper with it. Once, when my wife and I were between apartments, we stayed in his house for three or four weeks. Finding the darkness of the house oppressive, we raised all the shades to let in the daylight. When my father returned home from work and saw what we had done, he flew into an uncontrollable rage, far out of proportion to any offense that might have been committed.

Anger of this sort rarely came out of him—only when he felt himself cornered, impinged upon, crushed by the presences of others. Money questions sometimes triggered it off. Or else some minor detail: the shades of his house, a broken plate, a little nothing at all.

Nevertheless, this anger was inside him—I believe constantly. Like the house that was well ordered and yet falling apart from within, the man himself was calm, almost supernatural in his imperturbability, and yet prey to a roiling, unstoppable force of fury within. All his life he strove to avoid a confrontation with this force, nurturing a kind of automatic behavior that would allow him to pass to the side of it. Reliance on fixed routines freed him from the necessity of looking into himself when decisions had to be made; the cliché was always quick to come to his lips ("A beautiful baby. Good luck with it") instead of words he had gone out and looked for. All this tended to flatten him out as a personality. But at the same time, it was also what saved him, the thing that allowed him to live. To the extent that he was able to live.

From a bag of loose pictures: a trick photograph taken in an Atlantic City studio sometime during the Forties. There are several of him sitting around a table, each image shot from a different angle, so that at first you think it must be a group of several different men. Because of the gloom that surrounds them, because of the utter stillness of their poses, it looks as if they have gathered there to conduct a seance. And then, as you study the picture, you begin to realize that all these men are the same man. The seance becomes a real seance, and it is as if he has come there only to invoke himself, to bring himself back from the dead, as if, by multiplying himself, he had inadvertently made himself disappear. There are five of him there, and yet the nature of the trick photography denies the possibility of eye contact among the various selves. Each one is condemned to go on staring into space, as if under the gaze of the others, but seeing nothing, never able to see anything. It is a picture of death, a portrait of an invisible man.

Slowly, I am coming to understand the absurdity of the task I have set for myself. I have a sense of trying to go somewhere, as if I knew what I wanted to say, but the farther I go the more certain I am that the path toward my object does not exist. I have to invent the road with each step, and this means that I can never be sure of where I am. A feeling of moving around in circles, of perpetual back-tracking, of going off in many directions at once. And even if I do manage to make some progress, I am not at all convinced that it will take me to where I think I am going. Just because you wander in the desert, it does not mean there is a promised land.

When I first started, I thought it would come spontaneously, in a trance-like outpouring. So great was my need to write that I thought the story would be written by itself. But the words have come very slowly so far. Even on the best days I have not been able to write more than a page or two. I seem to be afflicted, cursed by some failure of mind to concentrate on what I am doing. Again and again I have watched my thoughts trail off from the thing in front of me. No sooner have I thought one thing than it evokes another thing, and then another thing, until there is an accumulation of detail so dense that I feel I am going to suffocate. Never before have I been so aware of the rift between

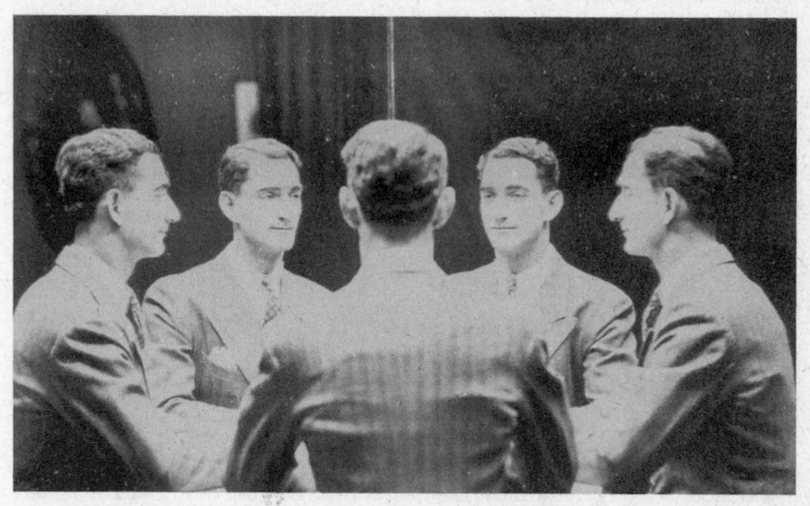

thinking and writing. For the past few days, in fact, I have begun to feel that the story I am trying to tell is somehow incompatible with language, that the degree to which it resists language is an exact measure of how closely I have come to saying something important, and that when the moment arrives for me to say the one truly important thing (assuming it exists), I will not be able to say it.

There has been a wound, and I realize now that it is very deep. Instead of healing me as I thought it would, the act of writing has kept this wound open. At times I have even felt the pain of it concentrated in my right hand, as if each time I picked up the pen and pressed it against the page, my hand were being torn apart. Instead of burying my father for me, these words have kept him alive, perhaps more so than ever. I not only see him as he was, but as he is, as he will be, and each day he is there, invading my thoughts, stealing up on me without warning: lying in the coffin underground, his body still intact, his fingernails and hair continuing to grow. A feeling that if I am to understand anything, I must penetrate this image of darkness, that I must enter the absolute darkness of earth.

Kenosha, Wisconsin. 1911 or 1912. Not even he was sure of the date. In the confusion of a large, immigrant family, birth records could not have been considered very important. What matters is that he was the last of five surviving children—a girl and four boys, all born within a span of eight years—and that his mother, a tiny, ferocious woman who could barely speak English, held the family together. She was the matriarch, the absolute dictator, the prime mover who stood at the center of the universe.

His father died in 1919, which meant that except for his earliest childhood he had no father. During my own childhood he told me three different stories about his father's death. In one version, he had been killed in a hunting accident. In another, he had fallen off a ladder. In the third, he had been shot down during the First World War. I knew these contradictions made no sense, but I assumed this meant that not even my father knew the facts. Because he had been so young when it happened—only seven—I figured that he had never been given the exact story. But then, this made no sense either. One of his brothers surely would have told him.

All my cousins, however, told me that they, too, had been given different explanations by their fathers.

No one ever talked about my grandfather. Until a few years ago, I had

never seen a picture of him. It was as though the family had decided to pretend he had never existed.

Among the photographs I found in my father's house last month there was one family portrait from those early days in Kenosha. All the children are there. My father, no more than a year old, is sitting on his mother's lap, and the other four are standing around her in the tall, uncut grass. There are two trees behind them and a large wooden house behind the trees. A whole world seems to emerge from this portrait: a distinct time, a distinct place, an indestructible sense of the past. The first time I looked at the picture, I noticed that it had been torn down the middle and then clumsily mended, leaving one of the trees in the background hanging eerily in mid-air. I assumed the picture had been torn by accident and thought no more about it. The second time I looked at it, however, I studied this tear more closely and discovered things I must have been blind to miss before. I saw a man's fingertips grasping the torso of one of my uncles; I saw, very distinctly, that another of my uncles was not resting his hand on his brother's back, as I had first thought, but against a chair that was not there. And then I realized what was strange about the picture: my grandfather had been cut out of it. The image was distorted because part of it had been eliminated. My grandfather had been sitting in a chair next to his wife with one of his sons standing between his knees—and he was not there. Only his fingertips remained: as if he were trying to crawl back into the picture from some hole deep in time, as if he had been exiled to another dimension.

The whole thing made me shake.

I learned the story of my grandfather's death some time ago. If not for an extraordinary coincidence, it never would have become known.

In 1970 one of my cousins went to Europe on a vacation with her husband. On the plane she found herself sitting next to an old man and, as people often do, they struck up a conversation to pass the time. It turned out that his man lived in Kenosha, Wisconsin. My cousin was amused by the coincidence and remarked that her father had lived there as a boy. Out of curiosity, the man asked her the name of her family. When she told him Auster, he turned pale. Auster? Your grandmother wasn't a crazy little woman with red hair, was she? Yes, that was my grandmother, my cousin answered. A crazy little woman with red hair.

And then he told her the story. It had happened more than fifty years before, and yet he still remembered the important details.

When this man returned home from his vacation, he tracked down the newspaper articles connected with the story, had them photocopied, and sent them to my cousin. This was his cover letter:

June 15, 70

Dear —— and ——.

It was good to get your letter, and altho it did look like the task might be complicated, I had a stroke of luck.—Fran and I went out to dinner with a Fred Plons and his wife, and it was Fred's father who had bought the apartment bldg on Park Ave from your family.— Mr. Plons is about three years younger than myself, but he claimed that the case (at that time) fascinated him and he remembered quite a few details.—He stated that your grandfather was the first person to be buried in the Jewish Cemetery here in Kenosha.—(Previous to 1919 the Jewish people had no cemetery in Kenosha, but had their loved ones buried either in Chicago or Milwaukee.) With this information, I had no trouble locating the plot where your grandfather is buried.—And I was able to pin point the date. The rest is in the copy I am forwarding to you.—

I only ask that your father should never learn of this knowledge that I am passing on to you—I would not want him to have any more grief than he already has suffered . . .

I hope that this will shed some light on your Father's actions over the past years.

Our fondest regards to you both—

Ken & Fran

The newspaper articles are sitting on my desk. Now that the moment has come to write about them, I am surprised to find myself doing everything I can to put it off. All morning I have procrastinated. I have taken the trash to the dump. I have played with Daniel in the yard for almost an hour. I have read the entire newspaper—right down to the line scores of the spring training baseball games. Even now, as I write about my reluctance to write, I find myself impossibly restless: after every few words I pop up from my chair, pace the floor, listen to the wind outside as it bangs the loose gutters against the house. The least thing is able to distract me.

It is not that I am afraid of the truth. I am not even afraid to say it. My grandmother murdered my grandfather. On January 23, 1919, precisely sixty years before my father died, his mother shot and killed his father in the kitchen of their house on Fremont Avenue in Kenosha, Wisconsin. The facts themselves do not disturb me any more than might be expected. The difficult thing is to see them in print—unburied, so to speak, from the realm of secrets and turned into a public event. There are more than twenty articles, most of them long, all of them from the

Kenosha Evening News. Even in this barely legible state, almost totally obscured by age and the hazards of photocopying, they still have the ability to shock. I assume they are typical of the journalism of the time, but that does not make them any less sensational. They are a mixture of scandalmongering and sentimentality, heightened by the fact that the people involved were Jews—and therefore strange, almost by definition—which gives the whole account a leering, condescending tone. And yet, granted the flaws in style, the facts seem to be there. I do not think they explain everything, but there is no question that they explain a great deal. A boy cannot live through this kind of thing without being affected by it as a man.

In the margins of these articles, I can just manage to decipher some of the smaller news stories of that time, events that were relegated to near insignificance in comparison to the murder. For example: the recovery of Rosa Luxemburg's body from the Landwehr Canal. For example: the Versailles peace conference. And on and on, day after day, through the following: the Eugene Debs case; a note on Caruso's first film ("The situations . . . are said to be highly dramatic and filled with stirring heart appeal"); battle reports from the Russian Civil War; the funerals of Karl Liebnecht and thirty-one other Spartacists ("More than fifty thousand persons marched in the procession which was five miles long. Fully twenty percent of these bore wreaths. There was no shouting or cheering"); the ratification of the national prohibition amendment ("William Jennings Bryan—the man who made grape juice famous—was there with a broad smile"); the textile strike in Lawrence, Massachusetts, led by the Wobblies; the death of Emiliano Zapata, "bandit leader in southern Mexico"; Winston Churchill; Bela Kun; Premier Lenine (sic); Woodrow Wilson; Dempsey versus Willard.

I have read through the articles about the murder a dozen times. Still, I find it hard to believe that I did not dream them. They loom up at me with all the force of a trick of the unconscious, distorting reality in the same way dreams do. Because the huge headlines announcing the murder dwarf everything else that happened in the world that day, they give the event the same egocentric importance we give to the things that happen in our private lives. It is almost like the drawing a child makes when he is troubled by some inexpressible fear: the most important thing is always the biggest thing. Perspective is lost in favor of proportion—which is dictated not by the eye but by the demands of the mind.

I read these articles as history. But also as a cave drawing discovered on the inner walls of my own skull.

The headlines on the first day, January 24, cover more than a third of the front page.

HARRY AUSTER KILLED
WIFE HELD BY POLICE

Former Prominent Real Estate Operator is Shot to Death in the Kitchen of the Home of His Wife On Thursday Night Following a Family Wrangle Over Money—and a Woman.

WIFE SAYS HUSBAND WAS A SUICIDE

Dead Man Had Bullet Wound in His Neck and in the Left Hip and Wife Admits That Revolver With Which the Shooting Was Done Was Her Property—Nine-Year-Old Son, Witness of the Tragedy, May Hold Solution to the Mystery.

According to the newspaper, "Auster and his wife had separated some time ago and an action for divorce was pending in the Circuit Court for Kenosha county. They had had trouble on several occasions over money. They had also quarreled over the fact that Auster [illegible] friendly with a young woman known to the wife as 'Fanny.' It is believed that 'Fanny' figured in the trouble between Auster and his wife immediately preceding the shooting. . . ."

Because my grandmother did not confess until the twenty-eighth, there was some confusion about what really happened. My grandfather (who was thirty-six years old) arrived at the house at six o'clock in the evening with "suits of clothing" for his two oldest sons "while it was stated by witnesses Mrs. Auster was in the bedroom putting Sam, the youngest boy, into bed. Sam [my father] declared that he did not see his mother take a revolver from under the mattress as he was tucked into bed for the night."

It seems that my grandfather had then gone into the kitchen to repair an electric switch and that one of my uncles (the second youngest son) had held a candle for him to see by. "The boy declared that he became panic stricken when he heard the shot and saw a flash of a revolver and fled the room." According to my grandmother, her husband had shot himself. She admitted they had been arguing about money, and "then he said,' she continued, 'there is going to be an end for you or me,' and he threatened me. I did not know he had the revolver. I had kept it under the mattress of my bed and he knew it."

Since my grandmother spoke almost no English, I assume that this statement, and all others attributed to her, was invented by the reporter. Whatever it was she said, the police did not believe her. "Mrs. Auster repeated her story to the various police officers without making any decided change in it and she professed great surprise when she was told that she was to be held by the police. With a great deal of tenderness she kissed little Sam good night and then went off to the county jail.

"The two Auster boys were guests of the police department last night sleeping in the squad room and this morning the boys were apparently entirely recovered from any fright they had suffered as a result of the tragedy at their home."

Toward the end of the article, this information is given about my grandfather. "Harry Auster was a native of Austria. He came to this country a number of years ago and had resided in Chicago, in Canada, and in Kenosha. He and his wife, according to the story told the police, later returned to Austria but she rejoined her husband in this country about the time they came to Kenosha. Auster bought a number of homes in the second ward and for some time his operations were on a large scale. He built the big triple flat building on South Park avenue and another one known as the Auster flats on South Exchange street. Six or eight months ago he met with financial reverses. . . .

"Some time ago Mrs. Auster appealed to the police to aid her in watching Mr. Auster as she alleged that he had relations with a young woman which she believed should be investigated. It was in this way that the police first learned of the woman 'Fanny'. . . .

"Many people had seen and talked with Auster on Thursday afternoon and these people all declared that he appeared to be normal and that he showed no signs of desiring to take his own life. . . ."

The next day was the coroner's inquest. My uncle, as the only witness to the incident, was called on to testify. "A sad-eyed little boy, nervously twirling his stocking cap, wrote the second chapter in the Auster murder mystery Friday afternoon. . . . His attempts to save the family name were tragically pathetic. Again and again when asked if his parents were quarrelling he would answer 'They were just talking' until at last, apparently remembering his oath, he added 'and maybe quarrelling—well just a little bit.' " The article describes the jurors as "weirdly stirred by the boy's efforts to shield both his father and his mother."

The idea of suicide was clearly not going to wash. In the last paragraph the reporter writes that "developments of a startling nature have been hinted by officials."

Then came the funeral. It gave the anonymous reporter an opportunity to emulate some of the choicest diction of Victorian melodrama. By now the murder was no longer merely a scandal. It had been turned into a stirring entertainment.

WIDOW TEARLESS AT AUSTER GRAVE

Mrs. Anna Auster Under Guard Attends Funeral of Husband, Harry Auster, Sunday.

"Dry-eyed and without the least sign of emotion or grief, Mrs. Harry Auster, who is held here in connection with the mysterious death of her husband, Harry Auster, attended Sunday morning, under guard, the funeral services of the man, in connection with whose death she is being held.

"Neither at the Crossin Chapel, where she looked for the first time since Thursday night upon the dead face of her husband nor at the burial ground did she show the least sign of weakening. The only intimation which she gave of breaking under the terrific strain of the ordeal was when over the grave, after the obsequies were finished, she asked for a conference this afternoon with the Rev. M. Hartman, pastor of the B'nai Zadek Congregation. . . .

"When the rites were completed Mrs. Auster calmly tightened the fox fur collar more closely about her throat and signified to the police that she was ready to leave. . . .

"After short ritualistic ceremonies the funeral procession was formed on Wisconsin street. Mrs. Auster asked that she also be allowed to go to the burial ground and the request was granted readily by the police. She seemed very petulant over the fact that no carriage had been provided for her, perhaps remembering that short season of apparent wealth when the Auster limousine was seen in Kenosha. . . .

". . . The ordeal was made exceptionally long because some delay had occurred in the preparation of the grave and while she waited she called Sam, the youngest boy, to her, and tucked his coat collar more closely around his neck. She spoke quietly to him but with this exception she was silent until after the rites were finished. . . .

"A prominent figure at the funeral was Samuel Auster, of Detroit, the brother of Harry Auster. He took as his especial care the younger children and attempted to console them in their grief.

"In speeches and demonstrations Auster appeared very bitter about his brother's death. He showed clearly that he disbelieved the theory of suicide and uttered remarks which savoured of accusations of the widow. . . .

"The Rev. M. Hartman . . . preached an eloquent sermon at the grave. He lamented the fact that the first person to be buried in the new cemetery should be one who had died by violence and who had been killed in his prime. He paid tribute to the enterprise of Harry Auster but deplored his early death.

"The widow appeared to be unmoved by the tributes paid to her dead husband. She indifferently opened her coat to allow the patriarch to cut a gash in her knitted sweater, a token of grief prescribed by the Hebrew faith.

"Officials in Kenosha fail to give up the suspicion that Auster was killed by his wife. . . ."

The paper of the following day, January 26th, carried the news of the confession. After her meeting with the rabbi, she had requested a conference with the chief of police. "When she entered the room she trembled a little and was plainly agitated as the chief provided a chair. 'You know what your little boy told us,' the latter began when he realized that the psychological moment had come. 'You don't want us to think that he's lying to us, do you?' And the mother, whose face has been for days so masked as to reveal nothing of the horror hidden behind it, tore off the camouflage, became suddenly tender, and sobbed out her awful secret. 'He isn't lying to you at all; everything he has said is true. I shot him and I want to make a confession.' "

This was her formal statement: "My name is Anna Auster. I shot Harry Auster at the city of Kenosha, Wisconsin on the 23rd day of January A.D. 1919. I have heard people remark that three shots were fired, but I do not remember how many shots were fired that day. My reason for shooting the said Harry Auster is on account of the fact that he, the said Harry Auster, abused me. I was just like crazy when I shot the said Harry Auster. I never thought of shooting him, the said Harry Auster, until the moment I shot him. I think that this is the gun I shot the said Harry Auster with. I make this statement of my own free will and without being forced to do so."

The reporter continues, "On the table before Mrs. Auster lay the revolver with which her husband was shot to death. As she spoke of it she touched it falteringly and then drew her hand back with a noticeable tremor of horror. Without speaking the chief laid the gun aside and asked Mrs. Auster if there was more she cared to say.

" 'That's all for now,' she replied composedly. 'You sign it for me and I'll make my mark.'

"Her orders—for a little moment she was almost regal again—were obeyed, she acknowledged the signature, and asked to be returned to her cell . . ."

At the arraignment the next day a plea of not guilty was entered by her attorney. "Muffled in a plush coat and a boa of fox fur, Mrs. Auster entered the court room. . . . She smiled at a friend in the crowd as she took her seat before the desk."

By the reporter's own admission, the hearing was "uneventful." But still, he could not resist making this observation: "An incident occurred upon her return to her barred room which furnished a commentary on Mrs. Auster's state of mind.

"A woman, held on a charge of association with a married man, had been brought to the jail for incarceration in an adjoining cell. Upon seeing her, Mrs. Auster asked about the newcomer and learned the particulars in the case.

" 'She ought to get ten years,' she said as the iron door clanged pitilessly. 'It was one of her kind that put me here.' "

After some intricate legal discussions concerning bail that were elaborately reported for the next few days, she was set free. " 'Have you any notion that this woman will not appear for trial?' the court asked the attorneys. It was attorney Baker who answered: 'Where could a woman with five children like these go? She clings to them and the court can see that they cling to her.' "

For a week the press was quiet. Then, on February 8th, there was a story about "the active support that the cause is being given by some of the papers published in the Jewish language in Chicago. Some of these papers contained columns arguing the case of Mrs. Auster and it is declared that these articles have strongly urged her defense . . .

"Friday afternoon Mrs. Auster with one of her children sat in the office of her attorney while portions of these articles were read. She sobbed like a child as the interpreter read to the attorney the contents of these papers . . .

"Attorney Baker declared this morning that the defense of Mrs. Auster would be one of emotional insanity . . .

"It is expected that the trial of Mrs. Auster will be one of the most interesting murder trials ever tried in the Circuit Court for Kenosha county and the human interest story that has been featured in the defense of the woman up to this time is expected to be largely developed at the trial."

Then nothing for a month. On March 10th the headlines read:

ANNA AUSTER TRIED SUICIDE

The suicide attempt had taken place in Peterboro, Ontario in 1910—by taking carbolic acid and then turning on the gas. The attorney brought this information before the court in order to be granted a delay in the trial so that he would have enough time to secure affidavits. "Attorney Baker held that at the same time the woman had endangered the lives of two of her children and that the story of the attempted suicide was important in that it would show the mental condition of Mrs. Auster."

March 27th. The trial was set for April 7th. After that, another week of silence. And then, on April 4th, as if things had been getting just a bit too dull, a new development.

AUSTER SHOOTS BROTHER'S WIDOW

"Sam Auster, brother of Harry Auster . . . made an unsuccessful attempt to avenge the death of his brother just after ten o'clock this morning when he shot at Mrs. Auster. . . . The shooting occurred just outside the Miller Grocery Store. . . .

"Auster followed Mrs. Auster outside the door and fired once at her. Mrs. Auster, though she was not struck by the shot, fell to the sidewalk and Auster returned to the store declaring according to witnesses, 'Well, I'm glad I done that.' There he calmly awaited arrest. . . .

"At the police station . . . Auster, entirely broken down nervously, gave his explanation of the shooting.

" 'That woman,' he said, 'has killed my four brothers and my mother. I've tried to help but she won't let me.' Then as he was being led down to the cell, he sobbed out, 'God's going to take my part though, I know that.'

"At his cell Auster declared that he had tried everything within his power to help the children of his dead brother. The fact that the court had refused to appoint him administrator for the estate because they declared that the widow had some rights in the case had preyed on his mind recently. . . . 'She's no widow,' he commented on that incident this morning. 'She is a murderer and should have no rights. . . .'

"Auster will not be arraigned immediately in order to make a thorough investigation of the case. The police admit that the death of his brother and subsequent events may have so preyed on his mind that he was not entirely responsible for his deed. Auster expressed several times a hope that he should die too and every precaution is being taken to prevent him from taking his own life. . . ."

The next day's paper had this to add: "Auster spent a rather troublesome night in the city lockup. Several times the officers found him sobbing in the cell and he appeared to be hysterical. . . .

"It was admitted that Mrs. Auster had suffered from a 'bad case of nerves' as a result of the fright which had attended the attack on her life on Friday, but it was declared that she would be able to be in court when the case against her is called for trial on Monday evening."

After three days the state rested its case. Contending that the murder had been premeditated, the district attorney relied heavily on the testimony of a certain Mrs. Mathews, an employee at the Miller Grocery Store, who contended that "Mrs. Auster came to the store three times on the day of the shooting to use the telephone. On one of those occasions, the witness said, Mrs. Auster called up her husband and asked him to come to the house and fix a light. She said that Auster had promised to come at six o'clock."

But even if she invited him to the house, it does not mean that she intended to kill him once he was there.

It makes no difference anyway. Whatever the facts might have been, the defense attorney shrewdly turned everything to his own advantage. His strategy was to offer overwhelming evidence on two fronts: on the one hand, to prove infidelity on the part of my grandfather, and on the other, to demonstrate a history of mental instability on the part of my grandmother—the two of them combining to produce a case of justifiable homicide or homicide "by reason of insanity." Either one would do.

Attorney Baker's opening remarks were calculated to draw every possible ounce of sympathy from the jury. "He told how Mrs. Auster had toiled with her husband to build up the home and happiness which once was theirs in Kenosha after they had passed through years of hardships. . . . 'Then after they had labored together to build up this home,' continued Attorney Baker, 'there came this siren from the city and Anna Auster was cast aside like a rag. Instead of supplying food for his family, her husband kept Fanny Koplan in a flat in Chicago. The money which she had helped to accumulate was being lavished on a more beautiful woman and after such abuse is there any wonder that her mind was shattered and that for the moment she lost control of her senses.' "

The first witness for the defense was Mrs. Elizabeth Grossman, my grandmother's only sister, who lived on a farm near Brunswick, New Jersey. "She made a splendid witness. She told in a simple manner the whole story of the life of Mrs. Auster; of her birth in Austria; of the death of her mother when Mrs. Auster was but six years of age; of the trip with her sister to this country eight years later; of long hours served as a maker of hats and bonnets in New York millinery shops; of how by this work the immigrant girl accumulated a few hundred dollars. She told of the marriage of the woman to Auster just after she reached her twenty-third birthday and of their business ventures; of their failure in a little candy store and their long trip to Lawrence, Kas., where they attempted to start over and where——, the first child was born; of the return to New York and the second failure in business which ended in bankruptcy and the flight of Auster into Canada. She told of Mrs. Auster following Auster to Canada; of the desertion by Auster of the wife and little children and how he had said that he was 'going to make way with himself' [sic] and how he had told the wife that he was taking fifty dollars so that when he was dead it might be found on him and used to give him a decent burial. . . . She said that during their residence in Canada they were known as Mr. and Mrs. Harry Ball. . . .

"A little break in the story which could not be furnished by Mrs.

Grossman, was furnished by former Chief Constable Archie Moore and Abraham Low, both of Peterboro county, Canada. These men told of the departure of Auster from Peterboro and the grief of his wife. Auster, they said, left Peterboro July 14, 1909, and the following night Moore found Mrs. Auster in a room of their shabby home suffering from the effects of gas. She and the children lay on a mattress on the floor while the gas was flowing from four open jets. Moore told of the further fact that he had found a vial of carbolic acid in the room and that traces of the acid had been found on the lips of Mrs. Auster. She was taken to a hospital, the witness declared, and was ill for many days. Both of these men declared that in their opinion there was no doubt but that Mrs. Auster showed signs of insanity at the time she attempted her life in Canada."

Further witnesses included the two oldest children, each of whom chronicled the family's domestic troubles. Much was said about Fanny, and also the frequent squabbles at home. "He said that Auster had a habit of throwing dishes and glass ware and that at one time his mother's arm had been so badly cut that it was necessary to call a physician to attend her. He declared that his father used profane and indecent language toward his mother at these times. . . ."

Another witness from Chicago testified that she had frequently seen my grandmother beat her head against the wall in fits of mental anguish. A police officer from Kenosha told how at "one time he had seen Mrs. Auster running wildly down a street. He stated that her hair was 'more or less' dishevelled and added that she acted much like a woman who had lost her mind." A doctor was also called in, and he contended that she had been suffering from "acute mania."

My grandmother's testimony lasted three hours. "Between stifled sobs and recourse to tears, she told the story of her life with Auster up to the time of the 'accident'. . . . Mrs. Auster stood the ordeal of cross questioning very well, and her story was told over three times in almost the same way."

In his summation "Attorney Baker made a strong emotional plea for the release of Mrs. Auster. In a speech lasting nearly an hour and a half he retold in an eloquent manner the story of Mrs. Auster. . . . Several times Mrs. Auster was moved to tears by the statements of her attorney and women in the audience were sobbing several times as the attorney painted the picture of the struggling immigrant woman seeking to maintain their home."

The judge gave the jury the option of only two verdicts: guilty or innocent of murder. It took them less than two hours to make their decision. As the bulletin of April 12th put it: "At four thirty o'clock this afternoon the jury in the trial of Mrs. Anna Auster returned a verdict finding the defendant not guilty."

April 14th. " 'I am happier now than I have been for seventeen years,' said Mrs. Auster Saturday afternoon as she shook hands with each of the jurors following the return of the verdict. 'As long as Harry lived,' she said to one of them, 'I was worried. I never knew real happiness. Now I regret that he had to die by my hand. I am as happy now as I ever expect to be. . . .'

"As Mrs. Auster left the court room she was attended by her daughter . . . and the two younger children, who had waited patiently in the courtroom for the return of the verdict which freed their mother. . . .

"At the county jail Sam Auster . . . while he cannot understand it all, says he is willing to abide by the decision of the twelve jurors. . . .

" 'Last night when I heard of the verdict,' he said when interviewed on Sunday morning, 'I dropped on the floor. I could not believe that she could go clear free after killing my brother and her husband. It is all too big for me. I don't understand, but I shall let it go now. I tried once to settle it in my way and failed and I can't do anything now but accept what the court has said.' "

The next day he, too, was released. " 'I am going back to my work in the factory,' Auster told the District Attorney. 'Just as soon as I get money enough I am going to raise a head stone over the grave of my brother and then I am going to give my energies to the support of the children of one of my brothers who lived in Austria and who fell fighting in the Austrian army.'

"The conference this morning brought out the fact that Sam Auster is the last of the five Auster brothers. Three of the boys fought with the Austrian army in the world war and all of them fell in battle."

In the last paragraph of the last article about the case, the newspaper reports that "Mrs. Auster is now planning to take the children and leave for the east within a few days. . . . It was said that Mrs. Auster decided to take this action on the advice of her attorneys, who told her that she should go to some new home and start life without any one knowing the story of the trial."

* * *

It was, I suppose, a happy ending. At least for the newspaper readers of Kenosha, the clever Attorney Baker, and, no doubt, for my grandmother. Nothing further is said, of course, about the fortunes of the Auster family. The public record ends with this announcement of their departure for the east.

Because my father rarely spoke to me about the past, I learned very little about what followed. But from the few things he did mention, I was able to form a fairly good idea of the climate in which the family lived.

For example, they moved constantly. It was not uncommon for my father to attend two, or even three different schools in a single year. Because they had no money, life became a series of escapes from landlords and creditors. In a family that had already closed in on itself, this nomadism walled them off entirely. There were no enduring points of reference: no home, no town, no friends that could be counted on. Only the family itself. It was almost like living in quarantine.

My father was the baby, and for his whole life he continued to look up to his three older brothers. As a boy he was known as Sonny. He suffered from asthma and allergies, did well in school, played end on the football team and ran the 440 for the track team at Central High in Newark. He graduated in the first year of the Depression, went to law school at night for a semester or two, and then dropped out, exactly as his brothers had done before him.

The four brothers stuck together. There was something almost medieval about their loyalty to one another. Although they had their differences, in many ways did not even like one another, I think of them not as four separate individuals but as a clan, a quadruplicate image of solidarity. Three of them—the youngest three—wound up as business partners and lived in the same town, and the fourth, who lived only two towns away, had been set up in business by the other three. There was scarcely a day that my father did not see his brothers. And that means for his entire life: every day for more than sixty years.

They picked up habits from each other, figures of speech, little gestures, intermingling to such a degree that it was impossible to tell which one had been the source of any given attitude or idea. My father's feelings were unbending: he never said a word against any of his brothers. Again, it was the other defined not by what he did but by what he was. If one of the brothers happened to slight him or do something objectionable, my father would nevertheless refuse to pass judgment. He's my brother, he would say, as if that explained everything. Brotherhood was the first principle, the unassailable postulate, the one and only article of faith. Like belief in God, to question it was heresy.

As the youngest, my father was the most loyal of the four and also the one least respected by the others. He worked the hardest, was the most generous to his nephews and nieces, and yet these things were never fully recognized, much less appreciated. My mother recalls that on the day of her wedding, at the party following the ceremony, one of the brothers actually propositioned her. Whether he would have carried through with the escapade is another matter. But the mere fact of teasing her like that gives a rough idea of how he felt about my father. You do not do that sort of thing on a man's wedding day, even if he is your brother.

At the center of the clan was my grandmother, a Jewish Mammy Yokum, a mother to end all mothers. Fierce, refractory, the boss. It was common loyalty to her that kept the brothers so close. Even as grown men, with wives and children of their own, they would faithfully go to her house every Friday night for dinner—without their families. This was the relationship that mattered, and it took precedence over everything else. There must have been something slightly comical about it: four big men, each one over six feet, waiting on a little old woman, more than a foot shorter than they were.

One of the few times they came with their wives, a neighbor happened to walk in and was surprised to find such a large gathering. Is this your family, Mrs. Auster? he asked. Yes, she answered, with great smiles of pride. This is —. This is —. This is —. And this is Sam. The neighbor was a little taken aback. And these lovely ladies, he asked. Who are they? Oh, she answered with a casual wave of the hand. That's —'s. That's —'s. That's —'s. And that's Sam's.

The picture painted of her in the Kenosha newspaper was by no means inaccurate. She lived for her children. (Attorney Baker: Where could a woman with five children like these go? She clings to them and the court can see that they cling to her.) At the same time, she was a tyrant, given to screaming and hysterical fits. When she was angry, she would beat her sons over the head with a broom. She demanded allegiance, and she got it.

Once, when my father had saved the huge sum of ten or twenty dollars from his newspaper route to buy himself a new bicycle, his mother walked into the room, cracked open his piggy bank, and took the money from him without so much as an apology. She needed the money to pay some bills, and my father had no recourse, no way to air his grievance. When he told me this story his object was not to show how his mother wronged him, but to demonstrate how the good of the family was always more important than the good of any of its members. He might have been unhappy, but he did not complain.

This was rule by caprice. For a child, it meant that the sky could fall on top of him at any moment, that he could never be sure of anything. Therefore, he learned never to trust anyone. Not even himself. Someone would always come along to prove that what he thought was wrong, that it did not count for anything. He learned never to want anything too much.

My father lived with his mother until he was older than I am now. He was the last one to go off on his own, the one who had been left behind to take care of her. It would be wrong to say, however, that he was a mother's boy. He was too independent, had been too fully indoctrinated into the ways of manhood by his brothers. He was good to her, was dutiful and considerate, but not without a certain distance, even humor. After he was married, she called him often, haranguing him about this and that. My father would put the receiver down on the table, walk to the other end of the room and busy himself with some chore for a few minutes, then return to the phone, pick it up, say something innocuous to let her know he was there (uh-huh, uh-huh, mmmmmm, that's right), and then wander off again, back and forth, until she had talked herself out.

The comical side of his obtuseness. And sometimes it served him very well.

I remember a tiny, shriveled creature sitting in the front parlor of a two-family house in the Weequahic section of Newark reading the *Jewish Daily Forward*. Although I knew I would have to do it whenever I saw her, it made me cringe to kiss her. Her face was so wrinkled, her skin so inhumanly soft. Worse than that was her smell—a smell I was much later able to identify as that of camphor, which she must have put in her bureau drawers and which, over the years, had seeped into the fabric of her clothes. This odor was inseparable in my mind from the idea of "grandma."

As far as I can remember, she took virtually no interest in me. The one time she gave me a present, it was a second- or third-hand children's book, a biography of Benjamin Franklin. I remember reading it all the way through and can even recall some of the episodes. Franklin's future wife, for example, laughing at him the first time she saw him—walking through the streets of Philadelphia with an enormous loaf of bread under his arm. The book had a blue cover and was illustrated with silhouettes. I must have been seven or eight at the time.

After my father died, I discovered a trunk that had once belonged to his mother in the cellar of his house. It was locked, and I decided to force it open with a hammer and screwdriver, thinking it might contain some buried secret, some long lost treasure. As the hasp fell down and I raised the lid, there it was, all over again—that smell, wafting up toward me, immediate, palpable, as if it had been my grandmother herself. I felt as though I had just opened her coffin.

There was nothing of interest in it: a set of carving knives, a heap of imitation jewelry. Also a hard plastic dress-up pocketbook, a kind of octagonal box with a handle on it. I gave the thing to Daniel, and he immediately started using it as a portable garage for his fleet of little trucks and cars.

My father worked hard all his life. At nine he had his first job. At eighteen he had a radio repair business with one of his brothers. Except for a brief moment when he was hired as an assistant in Thomas Edison's laboratory (only to have the job taken away from him the next day because Edison learned he was a Jew), my father never worked for anyone but himself. He was a very demanding boss, far more exacting than any stranger could have been.

The radio shop eventually led to a small appliance store, which in turn led to a large furniture store. From there he began to dabble in real estate (buying, for example, a house for his mother to live in), until this gradually displaced the store as the focus of his attention and became a business in its own right. The partnership with two of his brothers carried over from one thing to the next.

Up early every morning, home late at night, and in between, work, nothing but work. Work was the name of the country he lived in, and he was one of its greatest patriots. That is not to say, however, that work was pleasure for him. He worked hard because he wanted to earn as much money as possible. Work was a means to an end—a means to money. But the end was not something that could bring him pleasure either. As the young Marx wrote: "If *money* is the bond binding me to *human life*, binding society to me, binding me and nature and man, is not money the bond of all *bonds*? Can it not dissolve and bind all ties? Is it not, therefore, the universal *agent of separation*?"

He dreamed all his life of becoming a millionaire, of being the richest man in the world. It was not so much the money itself he wanted, but what it represented: not merely success in the eyes of the world, but a way of making himself untouchable. Having money means more than being able to buy things: it means that the world need never affect you. Money in the sense of protection, then, not pleasure. Having been without money as a child, and therefore vulnerable to the whims of the world, the idea of wealth became synonymous for him with the idea of escape: from harm, from suffering, from being a victim. He was not trying to buy happiness, but simply an absence of unhappiness. Money was the panacea, the objectification of his deepest, most inexpressible desires as a human being. He did not want to spend it, he wanted to have it, to know that it was there. Money not as an elixir, then, but as an antidote: the small vial of medicine you carry in your pocket when you go out into the jungle—just in case you are bitten by a poisonous snake.

At times, his reluctance to spend money was so great it almost resembled a disease. It never came to such a point that he would deny himself what he needed (for his needs were minimal), but more subtly, each time he had to buy something, he would opt for the cheapest solution. This was bargain shopping as a way of life.

Implicit in this attitude was a kind of perceptual primitivism. All distinctions were eliminated, everything was reduced to its least common denominator. Meat was meat, shoes were shoes, a pen was a pen. It did not matter that you could choose between chuck and porterhouse, that there were throwaway ball points for thirty-nine cents and fifty-dollar fountain pens that would last for twenty years. The truly fine object was almost to be abhorred: it meant that you would have to pay an extravagant price, and that made it morally unsound. On a more general level, this translated itself into a permanent state of sensory deprivation: by closing his eyes to so much, he denied himself intimate contact with the shapes and textures of the world, cut himself off from the possibility of experiencing aesthetic pleasure. The world he looked out on was a practical place. Each thing in it had a value and a price, and the idea was to get the things you needed at a price that was as close to the value as possible. Each thing was understood only in terms of its function, judged only by how much it cost, never as an intrinsic object with its own special properties. In some way, I imagine it must have made the world seem a dull place to him. Uniform, colorless, without depth. If you see the world only in terms of money, you are finally not seeing the world at all.

As a child, there were times when I became positively embarrassed for him in public. Haggling with shopkeepers, furious over a high price, arguing as if his very manhood were at stake. A distinct memory of how everything would wither up inside me, of wanting to be anywhere in the world except where I was. A particular incident of going with him to buy a baseball glove stands out. Every day for two weeks I had visited the store after school to admire the one I wanted. Then, when my father took me to the store one evening to buy it, he so exploded at the salesman I was afraid he was going to tear him to pieces. Frightened, sick at heart, I told him not to bother, that I didn't want the glove after all. As we were leaving the store, he offered to buy me an ice cream cone. That glove was no good anyway, he said. I'll buy you a better one some other time.

Better, of course, meant worse.

Tirades about leaving too many lights on in the house. He always made a point of buying bulbs with low wattage.

His excuse for never taking us to the movies: "Why go out and spend a fortune when it will be on television in a year or two?"

The occasional family meal in a restaurant: we always had to order the least expensive things on the menu. It became a kind of ritual. Yes, he would say, nodding his head, that's a good choice.

Years later, when my wife and I were living in New York, he would sometimes take us out to dinner. The script was always precisely the same: the moment after we had put the last forkful of food into our mouths, he would ask, "Are you ready to go?" Impossible even to consider dessert.

His utter discomfort in his own skin. His inability to sit still, to make small talk, to "relax."

It made you nervous to be with him. You felt he was always on the verge of leaving.

He loved clever little tricks, prided himself on his ability to outsmart the world at its own game. A niggardliness in the most trivial aspects of life, as ridiculous as it was depressing. With his cars, he would always disconnect the odometers, falsifying the mileage in order to guarantee himself a better trade-in price. In his house, he would always do his own repair work instead of hiring a professional. Because he had a gift for machines and knew how things worked, he would take bizarre shortcuts, using whatever materials were at hand to rig up Rube Goldberg solutions to mechanical and electrical problems—rather than spending the money to do it right.

Permanent solutions never interested him. He went on patching and patching, a little piece here, a little piece there, never allowing his boat to sink, but never giving it a chance to float either.

The way he dressed: as if twenty years behind the times. Cheap synthetic suits from the racks of discount stores; unboxed pairs of shoes from the bins of bargain basements. Beyond giving proof of his miserliness, this disregard of fashion reinforced the image of him as a man not quite in the world. The clothes he wore seemed to be an expression of solitude, a concrete way of affirming his absence. Even though he was well off, able to afford anything he wanted, he looked like a poor man, a hayseed who had just stepped off the farm.

In the last years of his life, this changed a little bit. Becoming a bachelor again had probably given him a jolt: he realized that he would have to make himself presentable if he wanted to have any kind of social life. It was not that he went out and bought expensive clothes, but at least the tone of his wardrobe changed: the dull browns and grays were abandoned for brighter colors; the outmoded style gave way to a flashier, more dapper image. Checkered pants, white shoes, yellow turtlenecks, boots with big buckles. But in spite of these efforts, he never looked quite at home in these costumes. They were not an integral part of his personality. It made you think of a little boy who had been dressed up by his parents.

Given his curious relationship to money (his desire for wealth, his inability to spend), it was somehow appropriate that he made his living among the poor. Compared to them, he was a man of enormous riches. And yet, by spending his days among people who had next to nothing, he could keep before his eyes a vision of the thing he most feared in the world: to be without money. It put things in perspective for him. He did not consider himself stingy—but sensible, a man who knew the value of a dollar. He had to be vigilant. It was the only thing that stood between him and the nightmare of poverty.

When the business was at its peak, he and his brothers owned nearly a hundred buildings. Their terrain was the grim industrial region of northern New Jersey—Jersey City, Newark—and nearly all their tenants were black. One says "slumlord," but in this case it would not have been an accurate or fair description. Nor was he in any way an absentee landlord. He was *there,* and he put in hours that would have driven even the most conscientious employee to go out on strike.

The job was a permanent juggling act. There was the buying and selling of buildings, the buying and repairing of fixtures, the managing of several teams of repair men, the renting of apartments, the supervision of the superintendents, listening to tenant complaints, dealing with the visits of building inspectors, constant involvement with the water and electric companies, not to speak of frequent visits to court—both as plaintiff and defendant—to sue for back rent, to answer to violations. Everything was always happening at once, a perpetual assault from a dozen directions at the same time, and only a man who took things in his stride could have handled it. On any given day it was impossible to do everything that had to be done. You did not go home because you were finished, but simply because it was late and you had run out of time. The next day all the problems would be waiting for you—and several new ones as well. It never stopped. In fifteen years he took only two vacations.

He was soft-hearted with the tenants—granting them delays in paying their rent, giving clothes to their children, helping them to find work—and they trusted him. Old men, afraid of being robbed, would give him their most valuable possessions to store in his office safe. Of all the brothers, he was the one people went to with their troubles. No one called him Mr. Auster. He was always Mr. Sam.

While cleaning out the house after his death, I came across this letter at the bottom of a kitchen drawer. Of all the things I found, I am happiest to have retrieved this. It somehow balances the ledger, provides me with living proof whenever my mind begins to stray too far from the facts. The letter is addressed to "Mr. Sam," and the handwriting is nearly illegible.

April 19, 1976

Dear Sam,

I know you are so surprised to hear from me. first of all maybe I better introduce my self to you. I'm Mrs. Nash. I'm Albert Groover Sister in law—Mrs. Groover and Albert that lived at 285 pine Street in Jersey City so long and Mrs. Banks thats my Sister too. Any way. if you can remember.

You made arrangement to get the apartment for my children and I at 327 Johnston Ave right around the Corner from Mr. & Mrs. Groover my Sister.

Anyway I move away left of owing a $40. rent. this was the year of 1964 but I didn't for get I owed this earnest debt. So now here is your money. thanks for being so very nice to the children and I at that time. this is how much I appreciated what you done for us. I hope you can recall back to the time. So you was never forgotten by me.

About 3 weeks ago I called the office but weren't in at that time. may the Good Lord ever to Bless you. I hardly comes to Jersey City if so I would stop by see you.

No matter now I am happy to pay this debt. All for now.

Sincerely

Mrs. JB. Nash

As a boy, I would occasionally go the rounds with him as he collected rent. I was too young to understand what I was seeing, but I remember the impression it made on me, as if, precisely because I did not understand, the raw perceptions of these experiences went directly into me, where they remain today, as immediate as a splinter in the thumb.

The wooden buildings with their dark, inhospitable hallways. And behind each door, a horde of children playing in a bare apartment; a mother, always sullen, overworked, tired, bent over an ironing board. Most vivid is the smell, as if poverty were more than a lack of money, but a physical sensation, a stench that invaded your head and made it impossible to think. Every time I walked into a building with my father, I would hold my breath, not daring to breathe, as if that smell were going to hurt me. Everyone was always happy to meet Mr. Sam's son. I was given innumerable smiles and pats on the head.

Once, when I was a bit older, I can remember driving with him down a street in Jersey City and seeing a boy wearing a T-shirt I had outgrown several months before. It was a very distinctive shirt, with a peculiar combination of yellow and blue stripes, and there was no question that this was the one that had been mine. Unaccountably, I was overcome with a feeling of shame.

Older still, at thirteen, fourteen, fifteen, I would sometimes go in with him to earn money working with the carpenters, painters, and repair men. Once, on an excruciatingly hot day in the middle of summer, I was given the job of helping one of the men tar a roof. The man's name was Joe Levine (a black man who had changed his name to Levine out of gratitude to an old Jewish grocer who had helped him in his youth), and he was my father's most trusted and reliable handyman. We hauled several fifty gallon barrels of tar up to the roof and got to work spreading the stuff over the surface with brooms. The sunlight beating down on that flat black roof was brutal, and after half an hour or so I became extremely dizzy, slipped on a patch of wet tar, fell, and somehow knocked over one of the open barrels, which then spilled tar all over me.

When I got back to the office a few minutes later, my father was greatly amused. I realized that the situation was amusing, but I was too embarrassed to want to joke about it. To my father's credit, he did not get angry at me or make fun of me. He laughed, but in a way that made me laugh too. Then he dropped what he had been doing, took me to the Woolworth's across the street, and bought me some new clothes. It had suddenly become possible for me to feel close to him.

As the years went by, the business started to decline. The business itself was not at fault, but rather the nature of the business: at that particular time, in that particular place, it was no longer possible to survive. The cities were falling apart, and no one seemed to care. What had once been a more or less fulfilling activity for my father now became simple drudgery. In the last years of his life he hated going to work.

Vandalism became such a severe problem that doing any kind of repairs became a demoralizing gesture. No sooner was plumbing installed in a building than the pipes would be ripped out by thieves. Windows were constantly being broken, doors smashed, hallways gutted, fires started. At the same time, it was impossible to sell out. No one wanted the buildings. The only way to get rid of them was to abandon them and let the cities take over. Tremendous amounts of money were lost in this way, an entire life's work. In the end, at the time of my father's death, there were only six or seven buildings left. The whole empire had disintegrated.

The last time I was in Jersey City (at least ten years ago) the place had the look of a disaster area, as if it had been pillaged by Huns. Gray, desolate streets; garbage piled everywhere; derelicts shuffling aimlessly up and down. My father's office had been robbed so many times that by now there was nothing left in it but some gray metal desks, a few chairs, and three or four telephones. Not even a typewriter, not one touch of color. It was not really a work place anymore, but a room in hell. I sat down and looked out at the bank across the street. No one came out, no one went in. The only living things were two stray dogs humping on the steps.

How he managed to pick himself up and go in there every day is beyond my understanding. Force of habit, or else sheer stubbornness. Not only was it depressing, it was dangerous. He was mugged several times, and once was kicked in the head so viciously by an attacker that his hearing was permanently damaged. For the last four or five years of his life there was a faint and constant ringing in his head, a humming that never went away, not even while he was asleep. The doctors said there was nothing that could be done about it.

In the end, he never went out into the street without carrying a monkey wrench in his right hand. He was over sixty-five years old, and he did not want to take any more chances.

Two sentences that suddenly come to mind this morning as I am showing Daniel how to make scrambled eggs.

" 'And now I want to know,' the woman says, with terrible force, 'I want to know whether it is possible to find another father like him anywhere in the world.' " (Isaac Babel)

"Children have always a tendency either to depreciate or to exalt their parents, and to a good son his father is always the best of fathers, quite apart from any objective reason there may be for admiring him." (Proust)

I realize now that I must have been a bad son. Or, if not precisely bad, then at least a disappointment, a source of confusion and sadness. It made no sense to him that he had produced a poet for a son. Nor could he understand why a young man with two degrees from Columbia University should take a job after graduation as an ordinary seaman on an oil tanker in the Gulf of Mexico, and then, without rhyme or reason, take off for Paris and spend four years there leading a hand to mouth existence.

His most common description of me was that I had "my head in the clouds," or else that I "did not have my feet on the ground." Either way, I must not have seemed very substantial to him, as if I were somehow a vapor or a person not wholly of this world. In his eyes, you became part of the world by working. By definition, work was something that brought in money. If it did not bring in money, it was not work. Writing, therefore, was not work, especially the writing of poetry. At best it was a hobby, a pleasant way to pass the time in between the things that really mattered. My father thought that I was squandering my gifts, refusing to grow up.

Nevertheless, some kind of bond remained between us. We were not close, but stayed in touch. A phone call every month or so, perhaps three or four visits a year. Each time a book of my poetry was published I would dutifully send it to him, and he would always call to thank me. Whenever I wrote an article for a magazine, I would set aside a copy and make sure I gave it to him the next time I saw him. *The New York Review of Books* meant nothing to him, but the pieces in *Commentary* impressed him. I think he felt that if the Jews were publishing me, then perhaps there was something to it.

Once, while I was still living in Paris, he wrote to tell me he had gone to the public library to read some of my poems that had appeared in a recent issue of *Poetry*. I imagined him in a large, deserted room, early in the morning before going to work: sitting at one of those long tables with his overcoat still on, hunched over words that must have been incomprehensible to him.

I have tried to keep this image in mind, along with all the others that will not leave it.

The rampant, totally mystifying force of contradiction. I understand now that each fact is nullified by the next fact, that each thought engenders an equal and opposite thought. Impossible to say anything without reservation: he was good, or he was bad; he was this, or he was that. All of them are true. At times I have the feeling that I am writing about three or four different men, each one distinct, each one a contradiction of all the others. Fragments. Or the anecdote as a form of knowledge.

Yes.

The occasional flash of generosity. At those rare times when the world was not a threat to him, his motive for living seemed to be kindness. "May the good Lord ever to Bless you."

Friends called him whenever they were in trouble. A car stuck somewhere in the middle of the night, and my father would drag himself out of bed and come to the rescue. In certain ways it was easy for others to take advantage of him. He refused to complain about anything.

A patience that bordered on the superhuman. He was the only person I have ever known who could teach someone to drive without getting angry or crumpling in a fit of nerves. You could be careening straight toward a lamp post, and still he would not get excited.

Impenetrable. And because of that, at times almost serene.

Starting when he was still a young man, he always took a special interest in his oldest nephew—the only child of his only sister. My aunt had an unhappy life, punctuated by a series of difficult marriages, and her son bore the brunt of it: shipped off to military schools, never really given a home. Motivated, I think, by nothing more than kindness and a sense of duty, my father took the boy under his wing. He nursed him along with constant encouragement, taught him how to get along in the world. Later, he helped him in business, and whenever a problem came up, he was always ready to listen and give advice. Even after my cousin married and had his own family, my father continued to take an active interest, putting them up in his house at one point for more than a year, religiously giving presents to his four grand-nephews and grand-nieces on their birthdays, and often going to visit them for dinner.

This cousin was more shaken by my father's death than any of my other relatives. At the family gathering after the funeral he came up to me three or four times and said, "I ran into him by accident just the other day. We were supposed to have dinner together Friday night."

The words he used were exactly the same each time. As if he no longer knew what he was saying.

I felt that we had somehow reversed roles, that he was the grieving son and I was the sympathetic nephew. I wanted to put my arm around his shoulder and tell him what a good man his father had been. After all, he was the real son, he was the son I could never bring myself to be.

For the past two weeks, these lines from Maurice Blanchot echoing in my head: "One thing must be understood: I have said nothing extraordinary or even surprising. What is extraordinary begins at the moment I stop. But I am no longer able to speak of it."

To begin with death. To work my way back into life, and then, finally, to return to death.

Or else: the vanity of trying to say anything about anyone.

In 1972 he came to visit me in Paris. It was the one time he ever traveled to Europe.

I was living that year in a minuscule sixth-floor maid's room barely large enough for a bed, a table, a chair, and a sink. The windows and little balcony stared into the face of one of the stone angels that jutted from St. Germain Auxerrois: the Louvre to my left, Les Halles off to my right, and Montmartre in the far distance ahead. I had a great fondness for that room, and many of the poems that later appeared in my first book were written there.

My father was not planning to stay for any length of time, hardly even what you would call a vacation: four days in London, three days in Paris, and then home again. But I was pleased at the thought of seeing him and prepared myself to show him a good time.

Two things happened, however, that made this impossible. I became very ill with the flu; and I had to leave for Mexico the day after his arrival to work on a ghostwriting project.

I waited for him all morning in the lobby of the tourist hotel where he had booked reservations, sweating away with a high fever, almost delirious with weakness. When he did not show up at the appointed time, I stayed on for another hour or two, but finally gave in and went back to my room where I collapsed into bed.

Late in the afternoon he came and knocked on my door, waking me from a deep sleep. The encounter was straight out of Dostoyevsky: bourgeois father comes to visit son in a foreign city and finds the struggling poet alone in a garret, wasting away with fever. He was shocked by what he saw, outraged that anyone could live in such a room, and it galvanized him into action: he made me put on my coat, dragged me off to a neighborhood clinic, and then bought the pills that were prescribed for me. Afterwards, he refused to allow me to spend the night in my room. I was in no condition to argue, so I agreed to stay in his hotel.

The next day I was no better. But there were things to be done, and I picked myself up and did them. In the morning I took my father along with me to the vast Avenue Henri Martin apartment of the movie producer who was sending me to Mexico. For the past year I had been working on and off for this man, doing what amounted to odd jobs—

translations, script synopses—things that were only marginally connected to the movies, which anyway did not interest me. Each project was more idiotic than the last, but the pay was good, and I needed the money. Now he wanted me to help his Mexican wife with a book she had been contracted to write for an English publisher: Quetzalcoatl and the mysteries of the plumed serpent. This seemed to be pushing it a bit, and I had already turned him down several times. But each time I said no, his offer had gone up, until now I was being paid so much money that I could no longer turn away. I would only be gone for a month, and I was being paid in cash—in advance.

This was the transaction my father witnessed. For once, I could see that he was impressed. Not only had I led him into this luxurious setting and introduced him to a man who did business in the millions, but now this man was calmly handing me a stack of hundred dollar bills across the table and telling me to have a pleasant trip. It was the money, of course, that made the difference, the fact that my father had seen it with his own eyes. I felt it as a triumph, as if I had somehow been vindicated. For the first time he had been forced to realize that I could take care of myself on my own terms.

He became very protective, indulgent of my weakened condition. Helped me deposit the money in the bank, all smiles and jokes. Then got us a cab and rode all the way to the airport with me. A big handshake at the end. Good luck, son. Knock 'em dead.

You bet.

Nothing now for several days. . . .

In spite of the excuses I have made for myself, I understand what is happening. The closer I come to the end of what I am able to say, the more reluctant I am to say anything. I want to postpone the moment of ending, and in this way delude myself into thinking that I have only just begun, that the better part of my story still lies ahead. No matter how useless these words might seem to be, they have nevertheless stood between me and a silence that continues to terrify me. When I step into this silence, it will mean that my father has vanished forever.

The dingy green carpet in the funeral home. And the director, unctuous, professional, suffering from eczema and swollen ankles, going down a checklist of expenses as if I were about to buy a suite of bedroom furniture on credit. He handed me an envelope that contained the ring my father had been wearing when he died. Idly fingering the ring as the conversation droned on, I noticed that the underside of the stone was smeared with the residue of some soapy lubricant. A few moments passed before I made the connection, and then it became absurdly obvious: the lotion had been used to remove the ring from his finger. I tried to imagine the person whose job it was to do such things. I did not feel horror so much as fascination. I remember thinking to myself: I have entered the world of facts, the realm of brute particulars. The ring was gold, with a black setting that bore the insignia of the Masonic brotherhood. My father had not been an active member for over twenty years.

The funeral director kept telling me how he had known my father "in the old days," implying an intimacy and friendship I was sure had never existed. As I gave him the information to be passed on to the newspapers for the obituary, he anticipated my remarks with incorrect facts, rushing ahead of me in order to prove how well acquainted he had been with my father. Each time this happened, I stopped and corrected him. The next day, when the obituary appeared in the paper, many of these incorrect facts were printed.

Three days before he died, my father had bought a new car. He had driven it once, maybe twice, and when I returned to his house after the funeral, I saw it sitting in the garage, already defunct, like some huge, stillborn creature. Later that same day I went off to the garage for a moment to be by myself. I sat down behind the wheel of this car, inhaling the strange factory newness of it. The odometer read sixty-seven miles. That also happened to have been my father's age: sixty-seven years. The brevity of it sickened me. As if that were the distance between life and death. A tiny trip, hardly longer than a drive to the next town.

Worst regret: that I was not given a chance to see him after he died. Ignorantly, I had assumed the coffin would be open during the funeral service, and then, when it wasn't, it was too late to do anything about it.

Never to have seen him dead deprives me of an anguish I would have welcomed. It is not that his death has been made any less real, but now, each time I want to see it, each time I want to touch its reality, I must engage in an act of imagination. There is nothing to remember. Nothing but a kind of emptiness.

When the grave was uncovered to receive the coffin, I noticed a thick orange root thrusting into the hole. It had a strangely calming effect on me. For a brief moment the bare fact of death could no longer be hidden behind the words and gestures of ceremony. Here it was: unmediated, unadorned, impossible to turn my eyes away from. My father was being lowered into the ground, and in time, as the coffin gradually disintegrated, his body would help to feed the same root I had seen. More than anything that had been said or done that day, this made sense to me.

The rabbi who conducted the funeral service was the same man who had presided over my Bar Mitzvah nineteen years earlier. The last time I had seen him he was a youngish, clean-shaven man. Now he was old, with a full gray beard. He had not known my father, in fact knew nothing about him, and half an hour before the service was to begin I sat down with him and told him what to say in the eulogy. He made notes on little scraps of paper. When it came time for him to deliver the speech, he spoke with great feeling. The subject was a man he had never known, and yet he made it sound as though he were speaking from the heart. Behind me, I could hear women sobbing. He was following what I had told him almost word for word.

It occurs to me that I began writing this story a long time ago, long before my father died.

Night after night, lying awake in bed, my eyes open in the darkness. The impossibility of sleep, the impossibility of not thinking about how he died. I find myself sweating between the sheets, trying to imagine what it feels like to suffer a heart attack. Adrenalin pumps through me, my head pounds, and my whole body seems to contract into a small area behind my chest. A need to experience the same panic, the same mortal pain.

And then, at night, there are the dreams, nearly every night. In one of them, which woke me up just hours ago, I learned from the teenage daughter of my father's lady friend that she, the daughter, had been made pregnant by my father. Because she was so young, it was agreed that my wife and I would raise the child after it was born. The baby was going to be a boy. Everyone knew this in advance.

It is equally true, perhaps, that once this story has ended, it will go on telling itself, even after the words have been used up.

The old gentleman at the funeral was my great uncle, Sam Auster, now almost ninety years old. Tall, hairless, a high-pitched, rasping voice. Not a word about the events of 1919, and I did not have the heart to ask him. I took care of Sam when he was a little boy, he said. But that was all.

When asked if he wanted anything to drink, he requested a glass of hot water. Lemon? No thank you, just hot water.

Again Blanchot: "But I am no longer able to speak of it."

From the house: a document from St. Clair County in the State of Alabama duly announcing my parents' divorce. The signature at the bottom: Ann W. Love.

From the house: a watch, a few sweaters, a jacket, an alarm clock, six tennis rackets, and an old rusted Buick that barely runs. A set of dishes, a coffee table, three or four lamps. A barroom statue of Johnnie Walker for Daniel. The blank photograph album, This Is Our Life: The Austers.

At first I thought it would be a comfort to hold on to these things, that they would remind me of my father and make me think of him as I went about my life. But objects, it seems, are no more than objects. I am used to them now, I have begun to think of them as my own. I read time by his watch, I wear his sweaters, I drive around in his car. But all this is no more than an illusion of intimacy. I have already appropriated these things. My father has vanished from them, has become invisible again. And sooner or later they will break down, fall apart, and have to be thrown away. I doubt that it will even seem to matter.

". . . here it holds good that only he who works gets the bread, only he who was in anguish finds repose, only he who descends into the underworld rescues the beloved, only he who draws the knife gets Isaac. . . . He who will not work must take note of what is written about the maidens of Israel, for he gives birth to the wind, but he who is willing to work gives birth to his own father." (Kierkegaard)

Past two in the morning. An overflowing ashtray, an empty coffee cup, and the cold of early spring. An image of Daniel now, as he lies upstairs in his crib asleep. To end with this.

To wonder what he will make of these pages when he is old enough to read them.

And the image of his sweet and ferocious little body, as he lies upstairs in his crib asleep. To end with this.

1979

The Book of Memory

"When the dead weep, they are beginning to recover," said the Crow solemnly.
"I am sorry to contradict my famous friend and colleague," said the Owl, "but as far as I'm concerned, I think that when the dead weep, it means they do not want to die."

Collodi, *The Adventures of Pinocchio*

He lays out a piece of blank paper on the table before him and writes these words with his pen. It was. It will never be again.

Later that same day he returns to his room. He finds a fresh sheet of paper and lays it out on the table before him. He writes until he has covered the entire page with words. Later, when he reads over what he has written, he has trouble deciphering the words. Those he does manage to understand do not seem to say what he thought he was saying. Then he goes out to eat his dinner.

That night he tells himself that tomorow is another day. New words begin to clamor in his head, but he does not write them down. He decides to refer to himself as A. He walks back and forth between the table and the window. He turns on the radio and then turns it off. He smokes a cigarette.

Then he writes. It was. It will never be again.

Christmas Eve, 1979. His life no longer seemed to dwell in the present. Whenever he turned on his radio and listened to the news of the world, he would find himself imagining the words to be describing things that had happened long ago. Even as he stood in the present, he felt himself to be looking at it from the future, and this present-as-past was so antiquated that even the horrors of the day, which ordinarily would have filled him with outrage, seemed remote to him, as if the voice in the radio were reading from a chronicle of some lost civilization. Later, in a time of greater clarity, he would refer to this sensation as "nostalgia for the present."

* * *

To follow with a detailed description of classical memory systems, complete with charts, diagrams, symbolic drawings. Raymond Lull, for example, or Robert Fludd, not to speak of Giordano Bruno, the great Nolan burned at the stake in 1600. Places and images as catalysts for remembering other places and images: things, events, the buried artifacts of one's own life. Mnemotechnics. To follow with Bruno's notion that the structure of human thought corresponds to the structure of nature. And therefore to conclude that everything, in some sense, is connected to everything else.

At the same time, as if running parallel to the above, a brief disquisition on the room. An image, for example, of a man sitting alone in a room. As in Pascal: "All the unhappiness of man stems from one thing only: that he is incapable of staying quietly in his room." As in the phrase: "he wrote The Book of Memory in this room."

The Book of Memory. Book One.

Christmas Eve, 1979. He is in New York, alone in his little room at 6 Varick Street. Like many of the buildings in the neighborhood, this one used to be nothing but a work place. Remnants of its former life are everywhere around him: networks of mysterious pipes, sooty tin ceilings, hissing steam radiators. Whenever his eyes fall on the frosted glass panel of his door, he can read these clumsily stencilled letters in reverse: R.M. Pooley, Licensed Electrician. People were never supposed to live here. It is a room meant for machines, cuspidors, and sweat.

He cannot call it home, but for the past nine months it is all he has had. A few dozen books, a mattress on the floor, a table, three chairs, a hot plate, and a corroded cold water sink. The toilet is down the hall, but he uses it only when he has to shit. Pissing he does in the sink. For the past three days the elevator has been out of service, and since this is the top floor, it has made him reluctant to go out. It is not so much that he dreads climbing the ten flights of stairs when he gets back, but that he finds it disheartening to exhaust himself so thoroughly only to return to such bleakness. By staying in this room for long stretches at a time, he can usually manage to fill it with his thoughts, and this in turn seems to dispel the dreariness, or at least make him unaware of it. Each time he goes out, he takes his thoughts with him, and during his absence the room gradually empties of his efforts to inhabit it. When he returns, he has to begin the process all over again, and that takes work, real spiritual work. Considering his physical condition after the climb (chest heaving like a bellows, legs as tight and heavy as tree trunks), this inner struggle takes all that much longer to get started. In the interim, in the void between the moment he opens the door and the moment he begins to reconquer the emptiness, his mind flails in a wordless panic. It is as if he were being forced to watch his own disappearance, as if, by crossing the threshold of this room, he were entering another dimension, taking up residence inside a black hole.

Above him, dim clouds float past the tar-stained skylight, drifting off into the Manhattan evening. Below him, he hears the traffic rushing toward the Holland Tunnel: streams of cars heading home to New Jersey on the night before Christmas. Next door it is quiet. The Pomponio brothers, who arrive there each morning to smoke their cigars and grind out plastic display letters—a business they keep going by working twelve or fourteen hours a day—are probably at home, getting ready to eat a holiday meal. That is all to the good. Lately, one of them has been spending the night in his shop, and his snoring invariably keeps A. awake. The man sleeps directly opposite A., on the other side of the thin wall that divides their two rooms, and hour after hour A. lies in bed, staring into the darkness, trying to pace his thoughts to the ebb and flow of the man's troubled, adenoidal dreams. The snores swell gradually, and at the peak of each cycle they become long, piercing, almost hysterical, as if, when night comes, the snorer had to imitate the noise of the machine that holds him captive during the day. For once A. can count on a calm, unbroken sleep. Not even the arrival of Santa Claus will disturb him.

Winter solstice: the darkest time of the year. No sooner has he woken up in the morning than he feels the day beginning to slip away from him. There is no light to sink his teeth into, no sense of time unfolding. Rather, a feeling of doors being shut, of locks being turned. It is a hermetic season, a long moment of inwardness. The outer world, the tangible world of materials and bodies, has come to seem no more than an emanation of his mind. He feels himself sliding through events, hovering like a ghost around his own presence, as if he were living somewhere to the side of himself—not really here, but not anywhere else either. A feeling of having been locked up, and at the same time of being able to walk through walls. He notes somewhere in the margins of a thought: a darkness in the bones; make a note of this.

By day, heat gushes from the radiators at full blast. Even now, in coldest winter, he is forced to keep the window open. At night, however, there is no heat at all. He sleeps fully clothed, with two or three sweaters, curled up tightly in a sleeping bag. During the weekends, the heat is off altogether, both day and night, and there have been times lately when he has sat at his table, trying to write, and could not feel the pen in his hand anymore. In itself, this lack of comfort does not disturb him. But it has the effect of keeping him off balance, of prodding him into a state of constant inner watchfulness. In spite of what it might seem to be, this room is not a retreat from the world. There is nothing here to welcome him, no promise of a soma holiday to woo him into oblivion. These four walls hold only the signs of his own disquiet, and in order to find some measure of peace in these surroundings, he must dig more and more deeply into himself. But the more he digs, the less there will be to go on digging into. This seems undeniable to him. Sooner or later, he is bound to use himself up.

When night comes, the electricity dims to half-strength, then goes up again, then comes down, for no apparent reason. It is as though the lights were controlled by some prankster deity. Con Edison has no record of the place, and no one has ever had to pay for power. At the same time, the phone company has refused to acknowledge A.'s existence. The phone has been here for nine months, functioning without a flaw, but he had not yet received a bill for it. When he called the other day to straighten out the problem, they insisted they had never heard of him. Somehow, he has managed to escape the clutches of the computer, and none of his calls has ever been recorded. His name is off the books. If he felt like it, he could spend his idle moments making free calls to faraway places. But the fact is, there is no one he wants to talk to. Not in California, not in Paris, not in China. The world has shrunk to the size of this room for him, and for as long as it takes him to understand it, he must stay where he is. Only one thing is certain: he cannot be anywhere until he is here. And if he does not manage to find this place, it would be absurd for him to think of looking for another.

Life inside the whale. A gloss on Jonah, and what it means to refuse to speak. Parallel text: Gepetto in the belly of the shark (whale in the Disney version), and the story of how Pinocchio rescues him. Is it true that one must dive to the depths of the sea and save one's father to become a real boy?

Initial statement of these themes. Further installments to follow.

* * *

Then shipwreck. Crusoe on his island. "That boy might be happy if he would stay at home, but if he goes abroad he will be the most miserable wretch that was ever born." Solitary consciousness. Or in George Oppen's phrase: "the shipwreck of the singular."

A vision of waves all around, water as endless as air, and the jungle heat behind. "I am divided from mankind, a solitaire, one banished from human society."

And Friday? No, not yet. There is no Friday, at least not here. Everything that happens is prior to that moment. Or else: the waves will have washed the footprints away.

First commentary on the nature of chance.

This is where it begins. A friend of his tells him a story. Several years go by, and then he finds himself thinking about the story again. It is not that it begins with the story. Rather, in the act of remembering it, he has become aware that something is happening to him. For the story would not have occurred to him unless whatever summoned its memory had not already been making itself felt. Unknown to himself, he had been burrowing down to a place of almost vanished memory, and now that something had surfaced, he could not even guess how long the excavation had taken.

During the war, M.'s father had hidden out from the Nazis for several months in a Paris *chambre de bonne*. Eventually, he managed to escape, made his way to America, and began a new life. Years passed, more than twenty years. M. had been born, had grown up, and was now going off to study in Paris. Once there, he spent several difficult weeks looking for a place to live. Just when he was about to give up in despair, he found a small *chambre de bonne*. Immediately upon moving in, he wrote a letter to his father to tell him the good news. A week or so later he received a reply: your address, wrote M.'s father, that is the same building I hid out in during the war. He then went on to describe the details of the room. It turned out to be the same room his son had rented.

It begins, therefore, with this room. And then it begins with that room. And beyond that there is the father, there is the son, and there is the war. To speak of fear, and to remember that the man who hid in that little room was a Jew. To note as well: that the city was Paris, a place A. had just returned from (December fifteenth), and that for a whole year he once lived in a Paris *chambre de bonne*—where he wrote his first book of poems, and where his own father, on his only trip to Europe, once came to see him. To remember his father's death. And beyond that, to understand—this most important of all—that M.'s story has no meaning.

Nevertheless, this is where it begins. The first word appears only at a moment when nothing can be explained anymore, at some instant of experience that defies all sense. To be reduced to saying nothing. Or else, to say to himself: this is what haunts me. And then to realize, almost in the same breath, that this is what he haunts.

He lays out a blank sheet of paper on the table before him and writes these words with his pen. Possible epigraph for The Book of Memory.

Then he opens a book by Wallace Stevens *(Opus Posthumous)* and copies out the following sentence.

"In the presence of extraordinary reality, consciousness takes the place of imagination."

Later that same day he writes steadily for three or four hours. Afterwards, when he reads over what he has written, he finds only one paragraph of any interest. Although he is not sure what to make of it, he decides to keep it for future reference and copies it into a lined notebook:

When the father dies, he writes, the son becomes his own father and his own son. He looks at his son and sees himself in the face of the boy. He imagines what the boy sees when he looks at him and finds himself becoming his own father. Inexplicably, he is moved by this. It is not just the sight of the boy that moves him, nor even the thought of standing inside his father, but what he sees in the boy of his own vanished past. It is a nostalgia for his own life that he feels, perhaps, a memory of his own boyhood as a son to his father. Inexplicably, he finds himself shaking at that moment with both happiness and sorrow, if this is possible, as if he were going both forward and backward, into the future and into the past. And there are times, often there are times, when these feelings are so strong that his life no longer seems to dwell in the present.

Memory as a place, as a building, as a sequence of columns, cornices, porticoes. The body inside the mind, as if we were moving around in there, going from one place to the next, and the sound of our footsteps as we walk, moving from one place to the next.

"One must consequently employ a large number of places," writes

Cicero, "which must be well lighted, clearly set out in order, spaced out at moderate intervals; and images which are active, sharply defined, unusual, and which have the power of speedily encountering and penetrating the psyche. . . . For the places are very much like wax tablets or papyrus, the images like the letters, the arrangement and disposition of the images like the script, and the speaking like the reading."

He returned from Paris ten days ago. He had gone there on a work visit, and it was the first time he had been abroad in more than five years. The business of traveling, of continual conversation, of too much drinking with old friends, of being away from his little son for so long, had finally worn him out. With a few days to spare at the end of his trip, he decided to go to Amsterdam, a city he had never been to before. He thought: the paintings. But once there, it was a thing he had not planned on doing that made the greatest impression on him. For no particular reason (idly looking through a guide book he found in his hotel room) he decided to go to Anne Frank's house, which has been preserved as a museum. It was a Sunday morning, gray with rain, and the streets along the canal were deserted. He climbed the steep and narrow staircase inside the house and entered the secret annex. As he stood in Anne Frank's room, the room in which the diary was written, now bare, with the faded pictures of Hollywood movie stars she had collected still pasted to the walls, he suddenly found himself crying. Not sobbing, as might happen in response to a deep inner pain, but crying without sound, the tears streaming down his cheeks, as if purely in response to the world. It was at that moment, he later realized, that The Book of Memory began. As in the phrase: "she wrote her diary in this room."

From the window of that room, facing out on the backyard, you can see the rear windows of a house in which Descartes once lived. There are children's swings in the yard now, toys scattered in the grass, pretty little flowers. As he looked out the window that day, he wondered if the children those toys belonged to had any idea of what had happened thirty-five years earlier in the spot where he was standing. And if they did, what it would be like to grow up in the shadow of Anne Frank's room.

To repeat Pascal: "All the unhappiness of man stems from one thing only: that he is incapable of staying quietly in his room." At roughly the same time these words entered the *Pensées*, Descartes wrote to a friend in France from his room in that house in Amsterdam. "Is there any country," he asked with exuberance, "in which one can enjoy freedom as enormously as one does here?" Everything, in some sense, can be read as a gloss on everything else. To imagine Anne Frank, for example, had she lived on after the war, reading Descartes' *Meditations* as a university student in Amsterdam. To imagine a solitude so crushing, so unconsolable, that one stops breathing for hundreds of years.

He notes, with a certain fascination, that Anne Frank's birthday is the same as his son's. June twelfth. Under the sign of Gemini. An image of the twins. A world in which everything is double, in which the same thing always happens twice.

Memory: the space in which a thing happens for the second time.

The Book of Memory. Book Two.

Israel Lichtenstein's Last Testament. Warsaw; July 31, 1942.

"With zeal and zest I threw myself into the work to help assemble archive materials. I was entrusted to be the custodian. I hid the material. Besides me, no one knew. I confided only in my friend Hersh Wasser, my supervisor. . . . It is well hidden. Please God that it be preserved. That will be the finest and best we achieved in the present gruesome time. . . . I know that we will not endure. To survive and remain alive after such horrible murders and massacres is impossible. Therefore I write this testament of mine. Perhaps I am not worthy of being remembered, but just for my grit in working with the Society Oneg Shabbat and for being the most endangered because I hid the entire material. It would be a small thing to give my own head. I risk the head of my dear wife Gele Seckstein and my treasure, my little daughter, Margalit. . . . I don't want any gratitude, any monument, any praise. I want only a remembrance, so that my family, brother and sister abroad, may know what has become of my remains. . . . I want my wife to be remembered. Gele Seckstein, artist, dozens of works, talented, didn't manage to exhibit, did not show in public. During the three years of war worked among children as educator, teacher, made stage sets, costumes for the children's productions, received awards. Now together with me, we are preparing to receive death. . . . I want my little daughter to be remembered. Margalit, 20 months old today. Has mastered Yiddish perfectly, speaks a pure Yiddish. At 9 months began to speak Yiddish clearly. In intelligence she is on a par with 3- or 4-year old children. I don't want to brag about her. Witnesses to this, who tell me about it, are the teaching staff of the school at Nowolipki 68. . . . I am not sorry about my life and that of my wife. But I am sorry for the gifted little girl. She deserves to be remembered also. . . . May we be the redeemers for all the rest of the Jews in the whole world. I believe in the survival of our people. Jews will not be annihilated. We, the Jews of Poland, Czechoslovakia, Lithuania, Latvia, are the scapegoat for all Israel in all the other lands."

Standing and watching. Sitting down. Lying in bed. Walking through the streets. Eating his meals at the Square Diner, alone in a booth, a newspaper spread out on the table before him. Opening his mail. Writing letters. Standing and watching. Walking through the streets. Learning from an old English friend, T., that both their families had originally come from the same town (Stanislav) in Eastern Europe. Before World War I it had been part of the Austro-Hungarian Empire; between the wars it had been part of Poland; and now, since the end of World War II, part of the Soviet Union. In the first letter from T. there is some speculation that they might, after all, be cousins. A second letter, however, offers clarification. T. has learned from an ancient aunt that in Stanislav his family was quite wealthy; A.'s family, on the other hand (and this is consistent with everything he has ever known), was poor. The story is that one of A.'s relatives (an uncle or cousin of some sort) lived in a small cottage on the property of T.'s family. He fell in love with the young lady of the household, proposed marriage, and was turned down. At that point he left Stanislav forever.

What A. finds particularly fascinating about this story is that the man's name was precisely the same as his son's.

Some weeks later he reads the following entry in the Jewish Encyclopedia:

AUSTER, DANIEL (1893–1962). Israel lawyer and mayor of Jerusalem. Auster, who was born in Stanislav (then Western Galicia), studied law in Vienna, graduated in 1914, and moved to Palestine. During World War I he served in the Austrian expeditionary force headquarters in Damascus, where he assisted Arthur Ruppin in sending financial help from Constantinople to the starving *yishuv*. After the war he established a law practice in Jerusalem that represented several Jewish-Arab interests, and served as secretary of the Legal Department of the Zionist Commission (1919, 20). In 1934 Auster was elected a Jerusalem councillor; in 1935 he was appointed deputy mayor of Jerusalem; and in 1936–38 and 1944–45 he was acting mayor. Auster represented the Jewish case against internationalization of Jerusalem brought before the United Nations in 1947–48. In 1948 Auster (who represented the Progressive Party) was elected mayor of Jerusalem, the first to hold that office in an independent Israel. Auster held that post until 1951. He also served as a member of the Provisional Council of Israel in 1948. He headed the Israel United Nations Association from its inception until his death."

All during the three days he spent in Amsterdam, he was lost. The plan of the city is circular (a series of concentric circles, bisected by canals, a cross-hatch of hundreds of tiny bridges, each one connecting to another, and then another, as though endlessly), and you cannot simply "follow" a street as you can in other cities. To get somewhere you have to know in advance where you are going. A. did not, since he was a stranger, and moreover found himself curiously reluctant to consult a map. For three days it rained, and for three days he walked around in circles. He realized that in comparison to New York (or New Amsterdam, as he was fond of saying to himself after he returned), Amsterdam was a small place, a city whose streets could probably be memorized in ten days. And yet, even if he was lost, would it not have been possible for him to ask directions of some passerby? Theoretically, yes, but in fact he was unable to bring himself to do so. It was not that he was afraid of strangers, nor that he was physically reluctant to speak. More subtly, he found himself hesitating to speak English to the Dutch. Nearly everyone speaks excellent English in Amsterdam. This ease of communication, however, was upsetting to him, as if it would somehow rob the place of its foreignness. Not in the sense that he was seeking the exotic, but in the sense that the place would no longer be itself—as if the Dutch, by speaking English, would be denied their Dutchness. If he could have been sure that no one would understand him, he would not have hesitated to rush up to a stranger and speak English, in a comical effort to make himself understood: with words, gestures, grimaces, etc. As it was, he felt himself unwilling to violate the Dutch people's Dutchness, even though they themselves had long ago allowed it to be violated. He therefore held his tongue. He wandered. He walked around in circles. He allowed himself to be lost. Sometimes, he later discovered, he would be only a few feet from his destination, but not knowing where to turn, would then go off in the wrong direction, thereby taking himself farther and farther from where he thought he was going. It occurred to him that perhaps he was wandering in the circles of hell, that the city had been designed as a model of the underworld, based on some classical representation of the place. Then he remembered that various diagrams of hell had been used as memory systems by some of the sixteenth century writers on the subject. (Cosmas Rossellius, for example, in his *Thesaurus Artificiosae Memoriae*, Venice, 1579). And if Amsterdam was hell, and if hell was memory, then he realized that perhaps there was some purpose to his being lost. Cut off from everything that was familiar to him, unable to discover even a single point of reference, he saw that his steps, by taking him nowhere, were taking him nowhere but into himself. He was wandering inside himself, and he was lost. Far from troubling him, this state of being lost became a source of happiness, of exhilaration. He breathed it into his very bones. As if on the brink of some previously hidden knowledge, he breathed it into his very bones and said to himself, almost triumphantly: I am lost.

His life no longer seemed to dwell in the present. Each time he saw a child, he would try to imagine what it would look like as a grown-up. Each time he saw an old person, he would try to imagine what that person had looked like as a child.

It was worst with women, especially if the woman was young and beautiful. He could not help looking through the skin of her face and imagining the anonymous skull behind it. And the more lovely the face, the more ardent his attempt to seek in it the encroaching signs of the future: the incipient wrinkles, the later-to-be-sagging chin, the glaze of disappointment in the eyes. He would put one face on top of another: this woman at forty; this woman at sixty; this woman at eighty; as if, even as he stood in the present, he felt compelled to hunt out the future, to track down the death that lives in each one of us.

Some time later, he came across a similar thought in one of Flaubert's letters to Louise Colet (August 1846) and was struck by the parallel: ". . . I always sense the future, the antithesis of everything is always before my eyes. I have never seen a child without thinking that it would grow old, nor a cradle without thinking of a grave. The sight of a naked woman makes me imagine her skeleton."

Walking through the hospital corridor and hearing the man whose leg had been amputated calling out at the top of his voice: it hurts, it hurts. That summer (1979), every day for more than a month, traveling across town to the hospital, the unbearable heat. Helping his grandfather put in his false teeth. Shaving the old man's face with an electric razor. Reading him the baseball scores from the *New York Post*.

Initial statement of these themes. Further installments to follow.

Second commentary on the nature of chance.

He remembers cutting school one drizzly day in April 1962 with his friend D. and going to the Polo Grounds to see one of the first games ever played by the New York Mets. The stadium was nearly empty (attendance was eight or nine thousand), and the Mets lost soundly to the Pittsburgh Pirates. The two friends sat next to a boy from Harlem, and A. remembers the pleasant ease of the conversation among the three of them during the course of the game.

He returned to the Polo Grounds only once that season, and that was for a holiday doubleheader (Memorial Day: day of memory, day of the dead) against the Dodgers: more than fifty thousand people in the stands, resplendent sun, and an afternoon of crazy events on the field: a triple play, inside-the-park homeruns, double steals. He was with the same friend that day, and they sat in a remote corner of the stadium, unlike the good seats they had managed to sneak into for the earlier game. At one point they left their places to go to the hot dog stand, and there, just several rows down the concrete steps was the same boy they had met in April, this time sitting beside his mother. They all recognized each other and gave warm greetings, each amazed at the coincidence of meeting again. And make no mistake: the odds against this meeting were astronomical. Like the two friends, A. and D., the boy now sitting with his mother had not been to another game since that wet day in April.

Memory as a room, as a body, as a skull, as a skull that encloses the room in which a body sits. As in the image: "a man sat alone in his room."

"The power of memory is prodigious," observed Saint Augustine. "It is a vast, immeasurable sanctuary. Who can plumb its depths? And yet it is a faculty of my soul. Although it is part of my nature, I cannot understand all that I am. This means, then, that the mind is too narrow to contain itself entirely. But where is that part of it which it does not itself contain? Is it somewhere outside itself and not within it? How, then, can it be part of it, if it is not contained in it?"

* * *

The Book of Memory. Book Three.

It was in Paris, in 1965, that he first experienced the infinite possibilities of a limited space. Through a chance encounter with a stranger in a café, he was introduced to S. A. was just eighteen at the time, in the summer between high school and college, and he had never been to Paris before. These are his earliest memories of that city, where so much of his life would later be spent, and they are inescapably bound up with the idea of a room.

Place Pinel in the thirteenth arrondissement, where S. lived, was a working class neighborhood, and even then one of the last vestiges of the old Paris—the Paris one still talks about but which is no longer there. S. lived in a space so small that at first it seemed to defy you, to resist being entered. The presence of one person crowded the room, two people choked it. It was impossible to move inside it without contracting your body to its smallest dimensions, without contracting your mind to some infinitely small point within itself. Only then could you begin to breathe, to feel the room expand, and to watch your mind explore the excessive, unfathomable reaches of that space. For there was an entire universe in that room, a miniature cosmology that contained all that is most vast, most distant, most unknowable. It was a shrine, hardly bigger than a body, in praise of all that exists beyond the body: the representation of one man's inner world, even to the slightest detail. S. had literally managed to surround himself with the things that were inside him. The room he lived in was a dream space, and its walls were like the skin of some second body around him, as if his own body had been transformed into a mind, a breathing instrument of pure thought. This was the womb, the belly of the whale, the original site of the imagination. By placing himself in that darkness, S. had invented a way of dreaming with open eyes.

A former student of Vincent D'Indy's, S. had once been considered a highly promising young composer. For more than twenty years, however, none of his pieces had been performed in public. Naive in all things, but most especially in politics, he had made the mistake of allowing two of his larger orchestral works to be played in Paris during the war—*Symphonie de Feu* and *Hommage à Jules Verne*, each requiring more than one hundred-thirty musicians. That was in 1943, and the Nazi occupation was still at full strength. When the war ended, people concluded that S. had been a collaborator, and although nothing could have been farther from the truth, he was blackballed by the French music world—by innuendo and silent consent, never by direct confrontation. The only sign that any of his colleagues still remembered him was the annual Christmas card he received from Nadia Boulanger.

A stammerer, a child-man with a weakness for red wine, he was so lacking in guile, so ignorant of the world's malice, that he could not even begin to defend himself against his anonymous accusers. He simply withdrew, hiding behind a mask of eccentricity. He appointed himself an Orthodox priest (he was Russian), grew a long beard, dressed in a black cassock, and changed his name to the Abbaye de la Tour du Calame, all the while continuing—fitfully, between bouts of stupor—with the work of his life: a piece for three orchestras and four choruses that would take twelve days to perform. In his misery, in the totally abject conditions of his life, he would turn to A. and observe, stuttering helplessly, his gray eyes gleaming, "Everything is miraculous. There has never been an age more wonderful than this one."

The sun did not penetrate his room on the Place Pinel. He had covered his window with heavy black cloth, and what little light there was came from a few strategically placed and faintly glowing lamps. The room was hardly bigger than a second class train compartment, and it had more or less the same shape: narrow, high-ceilinged, with a single window at the far end. S. had cluttered this tiny place with a multitude of objects, the debris of an entire lifetime: books, photographs, manuscripts, private totems—everything that was of any significance to him. Shelves, densely packed with this accumulation, climbed up to the ceiling along each wall, each one sagging, tipping slightly inward, as if the slightest disturbance would loosen the structure and send the whole mass of things falling in on him. S. lived, worked, ate, and slept in his bed. Immediately to the left of him, fit snugly into the wall, was a set of small, cubbied shelves, which seemed to hold all he needed to get through the day: pens, pencils, ink, music paper, cigarette holder, radio, penknife, bottles of wine, bread, books, magnifying glass. To his right was a metal stand with a tray fastened to the top of it, which he could swing in and out, over the bed and away from it, and which he used as both his work table and his eating table. This was life as Crusoe would have lived it: shipwreck in the heart of the city. For there was nothing S. had not thought of. In his penury, he had managed to provide for himself more efficiently than many millionaires do. The evidence notwithstanding, he was a realist, even in his eccentricity. He had examined himself thoroughly enough to know what was necessary for his own survival, and he accepted these quirks as the conditions of his life. There was nothing in his attitude that was either faint-hearted or pious, nothing to suggest a hermit's renunciation. He embraced his condition with passion and joyful enthusiasm, and as A. looks back on it now, he realizes that he has never known anyone who laughed so hard and so often.

The giant composition, on which S. had spent the last fifteen years, was nowhere near completion. S. referred to it as his "work in progress," consciously echoing Joyce, whom he greatly admired, or else as the *Dodecalogue*, which he would describe as the-work-to-be-done-that-is-done-in-the-process-of-doing-it. It was unlikely that he ever imagined he would finish the piece. He seemed to accept the inevitability of his failure almost as a theological premise, and what for another man might have led to an impasse of despair was for him a source of boundless, quixotic hope. At some anterior moment, perhaps at his very darkest moment, he had made the equation between his life and his work, and now he was no longer able to distinguish between the two. Every idea fed into his work; the idea of his work gave purpose to his life. To have conceived of something within the realm of possibility—a work that could have been finished, and therefore detached from himself—would have vitiated the enterprise. The point was to fall short, but to do so only in attempting the most outlandish thing he could conjure for himself. The end result, paradoxically, was humility, a way of gaging his own insignificance in relation to God. For only in the mind of God were such dreams as S.'s possible. But by dreaming in the way he did, S. had found a way of participating in all that was beyond him, of drawing himself several inches closer to the heart of the infinite.

For more than a month during that summer of 1965, A. paid S. two or three visits a week. He knew no one else in the city, and S. therefore had become his anchor to the place. He could always count on S. to be in, to greet him with enthusiasm (Russian style; three kisses on the cheeks: left, right, left), and to be more than willing to talk. Many years later, at a time of great personal distress, he realized that what drew him continually to these meetings with S. was that they allowed him to experience, for the first time, what it felt like to have a father.

His own father was a remote, almost absent figure with whom he had very little in common. S., for his part, had two grown sons, and both had turned away from his example and adopted an aggressive, hard-nosed attitude towards the world. Beyond the natural rapport that existed between them, S. and A. drew together out of a congruent want: the one for a son who would accept him as he was, the other for a father who would accept him as he was. This was further underscored by a parallel of births: S. had been born in the same year as A.'s father; A. had been born in the same year as S.'s younger son. For A., S. satisfied his paternal hunger through a curious combination of generosity and need. He listened to him seriously and took his ambition to be a writer as the most natural thing a young man could hope to do with himself. If A.'s father, in his strange, self-enclosed manner of being in the world, had made A. feel superfluous to his life, as if nothing he did could ever have an effect on him, S., in his vulnerability and destitution, allowed A. to become necessary to him. A. brought food to him, supplied him with wine and cigarettes, made sure he did not starve—which was a true danger. For that was the point about S.: he never asked anyone for anything. He would wait for the world to come to him, entrusting his deliverance to chance. Sooner or later, someone was bound to turn up: his ex-wife, one of his sons, a friend. Even then, he would not ask. But neither would he refuse.

Each time A. arrived with a meal (usually roast chicken, from a charcuterie on the Place d'Italie), it was turned into a mock feast, an excuse for celebration. "Ah, chicken," S. would exclaim, biting into a drumstick. And then again, chewing away at it, the juice dribbling into his beard: "Ah, chicken," with an impish, self-deprecatory burst of laughter, as if acknowledging the irony of his need and the undeniable pleasure the food gave him. Everything became absurd and luminous in that laughter. The world was turned inside out, swept away, and then immediately reborn as a kind of metaphysical jest. There was no room in that world for a man who did not have a sense of his own ridiculousness.

Further encounters with S. Letters between Paris and New York, a few photographs exchanged, all of this now lost. In 1967: another visit for several months. By then S. had given up his priest's robes and was back to using his own name. But the costumes he wore on his little excursions through the streets of his neighborhood were just as marvelous. Beret, silk shirt, scarf, heavy corduroy pants, leather riding boots, ebony walking stick with a silver handle: a vision of Paris via Hollywood, circa 1920. It was no accident, perhaps, that S.'s younger son became a film producer.

In February 1971, A. returned to Paris, where he would remain for the next three and a half years. Although he was no longer there as a visitor, which meant that more claims were made on his time, he still saw S. on a fairly regular basis, perhaps once every other month. The bond was still there, but as time went on A. began to wonder if it was not, in fact, a memory of that other bond, formed six years earlier, which sustained this bond in the present. For it turns out that after A. moved back to New York (July 1974), he no longer wrote any letters to S. It was not that he did not continue to think of him. But it was the memory of him, more than any need to carry on contact with S. into the future, that seemed to concern A. now. In this way he began to feel, as if palpably in his own skin, the passage of time. It sufficed him to remember. And this, in itself, was a startling discovery.

Even more startling to him, however, was that when he finally went back to Paris (November 1979), after an absence of more than five years, he failed to look up S. And this in spite of the fact that he had fully intended to do so. Every morning for the several weeks of his visit, he would wake up and say to himself, I must make time today to see S., and then, as the day wore on, invent an excuse for not going to see him. This reluctance, he began to realize, was a product of fear. But fear of what? Of walking back into his own past? Of discovering a present that would contradict the past, and thus alter it, which in turn would destroy the memory of the past he wanted to preserve? No, he realized, nothing so simple. Then what? Days went by, and gradually it began to come clear. He was afraid that S. was dead. Irrationally, he knew. But since A.'s father had died less than a year before, and since S. had become important to him precisely in relation to his thoughts about his father, he felt that somehow the death of one automatically entailed the death of the other. In spite of what he tried to tell himself, he actually believed this. Beyond that he thought: if I go to see S., then I will learn he is dead; but if I stay away, it will mean he is alive. By remaining absent, therefore, A. felt that he would be helping to keep S. in the world. Day after day, he walked around Paris with an image of S. in his mind. A hundred times a day, he imagined himself entering the little room on the Place Pinel. And still, he could not bring himself to go there. It was then that he realized he was living in a state of extreme duress.

Further commentary on the nature of chance.

From his last visit to S., at the end of those years in Paris (1974), a photograph has been preserved. A. and S. are standing outside, by the doorway of S.'s house. They each have an arm around the other's shoulder, and there is an unmistakeable glow of friendship and comraderie on their faces. This picture is one of the few personal tokens A. has brought with him to his room on Varick Street.

As he studies this picture now (Christmas Eve, 1979), he is reminded of another picture he used to see on the wall of S.'s room: S. as a young man, perhaps eighteen or nineteen, standing with a boy of twelve or thirteen. Same evocation of friendship, same smiles, same arms-around-the-shoulders pose. The boy, S. had told him, was the son of Marina Tsvetayeva. Marina Tsvetayeva, who stands in A.'s mind along with Mandelstam as the greatest of Russian poets. To look at this 1974 photograph for him is to imagine her impossible life, which ended when she hanged herself in 1941. For many of the years between the Civil War and her death she had lived in the Russian emigré circles in France, the same community in which S. had been raised, and he had known her and had been a friend of her son, Mur. Marina Tsvetayeva, who had written: "It may be that a better way / To conquer time and the world / Is to pass, and not to leave a trace—/ To pass, and not to leave a shadow / on the walls . . ."; who had written: "I didn't want this, not / this (but listen, quietly, / to want is what bodies do / and now we are ghosts only) . . ."; who had written: "In this most Christian of worlds / All poets are Jews."

When A. and his wife returned to New York in 1974, they moved into an apartment on Riverside Drive. Among their neighbors in the building was an old Russian doctor, Gregory Altschuller, a man well into his eighties, who still did research work at one of the city hospitals and who, along with his wife, had a great interest in literature. Dr. Altschuller's father had been Tolstoy's personal physician, and propped up on a table in the Riverside Drive apartment was an enormous photograph of the bearded writer, duly inscribed, in an equally enormous hand, to his friend and doctor. In conversations with the younger Dr. Altschuller, A. learned something that struck him as nothing less than extraordinary. In a small village outside Prague, in the dead of winter in 1925, this man had delivered Marina Tsvetayeva's son: the same son who had grown up into the boy in the photograph on S.'s wall. More than that: this was the only baby he ever delivered in his career as a doctor.

"It was night," Dr. Altschuller wrote recently, "the last day of January, 1925. . . . The snow was falling, a terrible storm which snowed-in everything. A Czech boy came running to me from the village where Tsvetayeva now lived with her family, though her husband was not with her at the time. Her daughter was also away with her father. Marina was alone.

"The boy rushed into the room and said: 'Pani Tsvetayeva wants you to come to her immediately because she's already in labor! You have to hurry, it's already on the way.' What could I say? I quickly dressed and walked through the forest, snow up to my knees, in a raging storm. I opened the door and went in. In the pale light of a lonely electric bulb I saw piles of books in one corner of the room; they nearly reached the ceiling. Days of accumulated rubbish was shoveled into another corner of the room. And there was Marina, chain-smoking in bed, baby already on the way. Greeting me gaily: 'You're almost late!' I looked around the room for something clean, for a piece of soap. Nothing, not a clean handkerchief, not a piece of anything. She was lying in bed, smoking and smiling, saying: 'I told you that you'd deliver my baby. You came—and now it's your business, not mine'. . . .

"Everything went smoothly enough. The baby, however, was born with the umbilical cord wrapped around his neck so tightly that he could hardly breathe. He was blue. . . .

"I tried desperately to restore the baby's respiration and finally he started breathing; he turned from blue to pink. All this time Marina was smoking, silent, not uttering a sound, looking steadily at the baby, at me. . . .

"I came back the next day and then saw the child every Sunday for a good many weeks. In a letter (May 10, 1925), Marina wrote: 'Altschuller directs everything concerning Mur with pride and love. Before eating, Mur gets one teaspoonful of lemon juice without sugar. He's fed according to the system of Professor Czerny, who saved thousands of newborn children in Germany during the war. Altschuller sees Mur every Sunday. Percussion, auscultation, some kind of arithmetic calculation. Then he writes down for me how to feed Mur next week, what to give him, how much butter, how much lemon, how much milk, how gradually to increase the amount. Every time he comes he remembers what was given last time, without carrying any notes. . . . Sometimes I have a crazy desire just to take his hand and kiss it'. . . .

"The boy grew quickly and became a healthy child adored by his mother and her friends. I saw him for the last time when he was not yet one year old. At that time Marina moved to France and there she lived for the next fourteen years. George (Mur's formal name) went to school and soon became an ardent student of literature, music, and art. In 1936 his sister Alia, then in her early twenties, left the family and France and returned to Soviet Russia, following her father. Marina stayed now with her very young son, alone in France . . . under extreme hardship, financial and moral. In 1939 she applied for a Soviet visa and returned to Moscow with her son. Two years later, in August 1941, her life came to a tragic end. . . .

"The war was still on. Young George Efron was at the front. 'Goodbye literature, music, school,' he wrote to his sister. He signed his letter 'Mur.' As a soldier he proved to be a courageous and fearless fighter, took part in many battles, and died in July 1944, one of hundreds of victims of a battle near the village of Druika on the Western Front. He was only twenty years old."

The Book of Memory. Book Four.

Several blank pages. To be followed by profuse illustrations. Old family photographs, for each person his own family, going back as many generations as possible. To look at these with utmost care.

Afterwards, several sequences of reproductions, beginning with the portraits Rembrandt painted of his son, Titus. To include all of them: from the view of the little boy in 1650 (golden hair, red feathered hat) to the 1655 portrait of Titus "puzzling over his lessons" (pensive, at his desk, compass dangling from his left hand, right thumb pressed against his chin) to Titus in 1658 (seventeen years old, the extraordinary red hat, and, as one commentator has written, "The artist has painted his son with the same sense of penetration usually reserved for his own features") to the last surviving canvas of Titus, from the early 1660's: "The face seems that of a weak old man ravaged with disease. Of course, we look at it with hindsight—we know that Titus will predecease his father. . . ."

To be followed by the 1602 portrait of Sir Walter Raleigh and his eight-year old son Wat (artist unknown) that hangs in the National Portrait Gallery in London. To note: the uncanny similarity of their poses. Both father and son facing forward, left hands on hips, right feet pointing out at forty-five degree angles, the left feet pointing forward, and the somber determination on the boy's face to imitate the self-confident, imperious stare of the father. To remember: that when Raleigh was released after a thirteen-year incarceration in the Tower of London (1618) and launched out on the doomed voyage to Guiana to clear his name, Wat was with him. To remember that Wat, leading a reckless military charge against the Spanish, lost his life in the jungle. Raleigh to his wife: "I never knew what sorrow meant until now." And so he went back to England, and allowed the King to chop off his head.

To be followed by more photographs, perhaps several dozen: Mallarmé's son, Anatole; Anne Frank ("This is a photo that shows me as I should always like to look. Then I would surely have a chance to go to Hollywood. But now, unfortunately, I usually look different"); Mur; the children of Cambodia; the children of Atlanta. The dead children. The children who will vanish, the children who are dead. Himmler: "I have made the decision to annihilate every Jewish child from the face of the earth." Nothing but pictures. Because, at a certain point, the words lead one to conclude that it is no longer possible to speak. Because these pictures are the unspeakable.

He has spent the greater part of his adult life walking through cities, many of them foreign. He has spent the greater part of his adult life hunched over a small rectangle of wood, concentrating on an even smaller rectangle of white paper. He has spent the greater part of his adult life standing up and sitting down and pacing back and forth. These are the limits of the known world. He listens. When he hears something, he begins to listen again. Then he waits. He watches and waits. And when he begins to see something, he watches and waits again. These are the limits of the known world.

The room. Brief mention of the room and/or the dangers lurking inside it. As in the image: Hölderlin in his room.

To revive the memory of that mysterious, three-month journey on foot, crossing the mountains of the Massif Central alone, his fingers gripped tightly around the pistol in his pocket; that journey from Bordeaux to Stuttgart (hundreds of miles) that preceded his first mental breakdown in 1802.

"Dear friend . . . I have not written to you for a long time, and meanwhile have been in France and have seen the sad, lonely earth; the shepherds and shepherdesses of southern France and individual beauties, men and women, who grew up in fear of political uncertainty and of hunger. . . . The mighty element, the fire of heaven and the silence of the people, their life in nature, their confinedness and their contentment, moved me continually, and as one says of heroes, I can well say of myself that Apollo has struck me."

Arriving in Stuttgart, "deathly pale, very thin, with hollow wild eyes, long hair and a beard, and dressed like a beggar," he stood before his friend Matthison and spoke one word only: "Hölderlin."

Six months later, his beloved Suzette was dead. By 1806, schizophrenia, and thereafter, for thirty-six years, fully half his life, he lived alone in the tower built for him by Zimmer, the carpenter from Tubingen—*zimmer*, which in German means *room*.

TO ZIMMER

The lines of life are various as roads or as
The limits of the mountains are, and what we are
Down here, in harmonies, in recompense,
In peace for ever, a god will finish there.

Toward the end of Hölderlin's life, a visitor to the tower mentioned Suzette's name. The poet replied: "Ah, my Diotima. Don't speak to me about my Diotima. Thirteen sons she bore me. One is Pope, another is the Sultan, the third is the Emperor of Russia. . . ." And then: "Do you know what happened to her? She went mad, she did, mad, mad, mad."

During those years, it is said, Hölderlin rarely went out. When he did leave his room, it was only to take aimless walks through the countryside, filling his pockets with stones and picking flowers, which he would later tear to shreds. In town, the students laughed at him, and children ran away in fear whenever he approached to greet them. Towards the end, his mind became so muddled that he began to call himself by different names—Scardinelli, Killalusimeno—and once, when a visitor was slow to leave his room, he showed him the door and said, with a finger raised in warning, "I am the Lord God."

In recent years, there has been renewed speculation about Hölderlin's life in that room. One man contends that Hölderlin's madness was feigned, and that in response to the stultifying political reaction that overwhelmed Germany following the French revolution, the poet withdrew from the world. He lived, so to speak, underground in the tower. According to this theory, all of the writings of Hölderlin's madness (1806–1843) were in fact composed in a secret, revolutionary code. There is even a play that expands upon this idea. In the final scene of that work, the young Marx pays Hölderlin a visit in his tower. We are led to presume from this encounter that it was the old and dying poet who inspired Marx to write *The Economic and Philosophical Manuscripts of 1844*. If this were so, then Hölderlin would not only have been the greatest German poet of the nineteenth century, but also a central figure in the history of political thought: the link between Hegel and Marx. For it is a documented fact that as young men Hölderlin and Hegel were friends. They were students together at the seminary in Tübingen.

Speculations of this sort, however, strike A. as tedious. He has no difficulty in accepting Hölderlin's presence in the room. He would even go so far as to say that Hölderlin could not have survived anywhere else. If not for Zimmer's generosity and kindness, it is possible that Hölderlin's life would have ended prematurely. To withdraw into a room does not mean that one has been blinded. To be mad does not mean that one has been struck dumb. More than likely, it is the room that restored Hölderlin to life, that gave him back whatever life it was left for him to live. As Jerome commented on the Book of Jonah, glossing the passage that tells of Jonah in the belly of the whale: "You will note that where you would think should be the end of Jonah, there was his safety."

"The image of man has eyes," wrote Hölderlin, during the first year of his life in that room, "whereas the moon has light. King Oedipus has an eye too many perhaps. The sufferings of this man, they seem indescribable, unspeakable, inexpressible. If the drama represents something like this, that is why. But what comes over me as I think of you now? Like brooks the end of something sweeps me away, which expands like Asia. Of course, this affliction, Oedipus has it too. Of course, that is why. Did Hercules suffer too? Indeed. . . . For to fight with God, like Hercules, that is an affliction. And immortality amidst the envy of this life, to share in that, is an affliction too. But this is also an affliction, when a man is covered with freckles, to be wholly covered with many a spot! The beautiful sun does that: for it rears up all things. It leads young men along their course with the allurements of its beams as though with roses. The afflictions that Oedipus bore seem like this, as when a poor man complains there is something he lacks. Son of Laios, poor stranger in Greece! Life is death, and death is a kind of life."

The room. Counter-argument to the above. Or: reasons for being in the room.

The Book of Memory. Book Five.

Two months after his father's death (January 1979), A.'s marriage collapsed. The problems had been brewing for some time, and at last the decision was made to separate. If it was one thing for him to accept this break-up, to be miserable about it and yet to understand that it was inevitable, it was quite another thing for him to swallow the consequences it entailed: to be separated from his son. The thought of it was intolerable to him.

He moved into his room on Varick Street in early spring. For the next few months he shuttled between that room and the house in Dutchess County where he and his wife had been living for the past three years. During the week: solitude in the city; on the weekends: visits to the country, one hundred miles away, where he slept in what was now his former work room and played with his son, not yet two years old, and read to him from the treasured books of the period: *Let's Go Trucks*, *Caps for Sale*, *Mother Goose*.

Shortly after he moved into the Varick Street room, the six-year old Etan Patz disappeared from the streets of that same neighborhood. Everywhere A. turned, there was a photograph of the boy (on lampposts, in shop windows, on blank brick walls), headlined by the words: LOST CHILD. Because the face of this child did not differ drastically from the face of his own child (and even if it had, it might not have mattered), every time he saw the photograph of this face he was made to think of his own son—and in precisely these terms: lost child. Etan Patz had been sent downstairs one morning by his mother to wait for the school bus (the first day following a long bus driver strike, and the boy had been eager to do this one little thing on his own, to make this small gesture of independence), and then was not seen again. Whatever it was that happened to him, it happened without a trace. He could have been kidnapped, he could have been murdered, or perhaps he simply wandered off and came to his death in a place where no one could see him. The only thing that can be said with any certainty is that he vanished—as if from the face of the earth. The newspapers made much of this story (interviews with the parents, interviews with the detectives assigned to the case, articles about the boy's personality: what games he liked to play, what foods he liked to eat), and A. began to realize that the presence of this disaster—superimposed on his own and admittedly much smaller disaster—was inescapable. Each thing that fell before his eyes seemed to be no more than an image of what was inside him. The days went by, and each day a little more of the pain inside him was dragged out into the open. A sense of loss took hold of him, and it would not let go. And there were times when this loss was so great, and so suffocating, that he thought it would never let go.

* * *

Some weeks later, at the beginning of summer. A radiant New York June: clarity of the light falling on the bricks; blue, transparent skies, zeroing to an azure that would have charmed even Mallarmé.

A.'s grandfather (on his mother's side) was slowly beginning to die. Only a year before he had performed magic tricks at A.'s son's first birthday party, but now, at eighty-five, he was so weak that he could no longer stand without support, could no longer move without an effort of will so intense that merely to think of moving was enough to exhaust him. There was a family conference at the doctor's office, and the decision was made to send him to Doctor's Hospital on East End Avenue and Eighty-eighth Street (the same hospital in which his wife had died of amniotropic lateral sclerosis—Lou Gehrig's disease—eleven years earlier). A. was at that conference, as were his mother and his mother's sister, his grandfather's two children. Because neither of the women could remain in New York, it was agreed that A. would be responsible for everything. A.'s mother had to return home to California to take care of her own gravely ill husband, while A.'s aunt was about to go to Paris to visit her first grandchild, the recently born daughter of her only son. Everything, it seemed, had quite literally become a matter of life and death. At which point, A. suddenly found himself thinking (perhaps because his grandfather had always reminded him of W.C. Fields) of a scene from the 1932 Fields film, *Million Dollar Legs:* Jack Oakey runs frantically to catch up with a departing stage coach and beseeches the driver to stop; "It's a matter of life and death!" he shouts. And the driver calmly and cynically replies: "What isn't?"

During this family conference A. could see the fear on his grandfather's face. At one point the old man caught his eye and gestured up to the wall beside the doctor's desk, which was covered with laminated plaques, framed certificates, awards, degrees, and testimonials, and gave a knowing nod, as if to say, "Pretty impressive, eh? This guy will take good care of me." The old man had always been taken in by pomp of this sort. "I've just received a letter from the president of the Chase Manhattan Bank," he would say, when in fact it was nothing more than a form letter. That day in the doctor's office, however, it was painful for A. to see it: the old man's refusal to recognize the thing that was looking him straight in the eyes. "I feel good about all this, doctor," his grandfather said. "I know you're going to get me better again." And yet, almost against his will, A. found himself admiring this capacity for blindness. Later that day, he helped his grandfather pack a small satchel of things to take to the hospital. The old man tossed three or four of his magic tricks into the bag. "Why are you bothering with those?" A. asked. "So I can entertain the nurses," his grandfather replied, "in case things get dull."

A. decided to stay in his grandfather's apartment for as long as the old man was in the hospital. The place could not remain empty (someone had to pay the bills, collect the mail, water the plants), and it was bound to be more comfortable than the room on Varick Street. Above all, the illusion had to be maintained that the old man was coming back. Until there was death, there was always the possibility there would not be death, and this chance, slight though it was, had to be credited.

A. remained in that apartment for the next six or seven weeks. It was the same place he had been visiting since earliest childhood: that tall, squat, oddly shaped building that stands on the corner of Central Park South and Columbus Circle. He wondered how many hours he had spent as a boy looking out at the traffic as it wove around the statue of Christopher Columbus. Through those same sixth floor windows he had watched the Thanksgiving Day parades, seen the construction of the Colosseum, spent entire afternoons counting the people as they walked by on the streets below. Now he was surrounded by this place again, with the Chinese telephone table, his grandmother's glass menagerie, and the old humidor. He had walked straight back into his childhood.

A. continued to hope for a reconciliation with his wife. When she agreed to come to the city with their son to stay at the apartment, he felt that perhaps a real change would be possible. Cut off from the objects and cares of their own life, they seemed to settle in nicely to these neutral surroundings. But neither one of them was ready at that point to admit that this was not an illusion, an act of memory coupled with an act of groundless hope.

Every afternoon A. would travel to the hospital by boarding two buses, spend an hour or two with his grandfather, and then return by the same route he had come. This arrangement worked for about ten days. Then the weather changed. An excruciating heat fell on New York, and the city became a nightmare of sweat, exhaustion, and noise. None of this did the little boy any good (cooped up in the apartment with a sputtering air conditioner, or else traipsing through the steamy streets with his mother), and when the weather refused to break (record humidity for several weeks running), A. and his wife decided that she and the boy should return to the country.

He stayed on in his grandfather's apartment alone. Each day became a repetition of the day before. Conversations with the doctor, the trip to the hospital, hiring and firing private nurses, listening to his grandfather's complaints, straightening the pillows under his head. There was a horror that went through him each time he glimpsed the old man's flesh. The emaciated limbs, the shriveled testicles, the body that had shrunk to less than a hundred pounds. This was a once corpulent man, whose proud, well-stuffed belly had preceded his every step through the world, and now he was hardly there. If A. had experienced one kind of death earlier in the year, a death so sudden that even as it gave him over to death it deprived him of the knowledge of that death, now he was experiencing death of another kind, and it was this slow, mortal exhaustion, this letting go of life in the heart of life, that finally taught him the thing he had known all along.

Nearly every day there was a phone call from his grandfather's former secretary, a woman who had worked in the office for more than twenty years. After his grandmother's death, she had become the steadiest of his grandfather's lady companions, the respectable woman he trotted out for public view on formal occasions: family gatherings, weddings, funerals. Each time she called, she would make copious inquiries about his grandfather's health, and then ask A. to arrange for her to visit the hospital. The problem was her own bad health. Although not old (late sixties at most), she suffered from Parkinson's disease, and for some time had been living in a nursing home in the Bronx. After numerous conversations (her voice so faint over the telephone that it took all of A.'s powers of concentration to hear even half of what she said), he finally agreed to meet her in front of the Metropolitan Museum, where a special bus from the nursing home deposited ambulatory patients once a week for an afternoon in Manhattan. On that particular day, for the first time in nearly a month, it rained. A. arrived in advance of the appointed time, and then, for more than an hour, stood on the museum steps, keeping his head dry with a newspaper, on the lookout for the woman. At last, deciding to give up, he made one final tour of the area. It was then that he found her: a block or two up Fifth Avenue, standing under a pathetic sapling, as if to protect herself from the rain, a clear plastic bonnet on her head, leaning on her walking stick, body bent forward, all of her rigid, afraid to take a step, staring down at the wet sidewalk. Again that feeble voice, and A. almost pressing his ear against her mouth to hear her—only to glean some paltry and insipid remark: the bus driver had forgotten to shave, the newspaper had not been delivered. A. had always been bored by this woman, and even when she had been well he had cringed at having to spend more than five minutes in her company. Now he found himself almost angry at her, resenting the way in which she seemed to expect him to pity her. He lashed out at her in his mind for being such an abject creature of self-absorption.

More than twenty minutes went by before he could get a cab. And then the endless ordeal of walking her to the curb and putting her into the taxi. Her shoes scraping on the pavement: one inch and then pause; another inch and then pause; another inch and then another inch. He held her arm and did his best to encourage her along. When they reached the hospital and he finally managed to disentangle her from the back seat of the cab, they began the slow journey toward the entrance. Just in front of the door, at the very instant A. thought they were going to make it, she froze. She had suddenly been gripped by the fear that she could not move, and therefore she could not move. No matter what A. said to her, no matter how gently he tried to coax her forward, she would not budge. People were going in and out—doctors, nurses, visitors—and there they stood, A. and the helpless woman, locked in the middle of that human traffic. A. told her to wait where she was (as if she could have done anything else), and went into the lobby, where he found an empty wheelchair, which he snatched out from under the eyes of a suspicious woman administrator. Then he eased his helpless companion into the chair and bustled her through the lobby toward the elevator, fending off the shouts of the administrator: "Is she a patient? Is that woman a patient? Wheelchairs are for patients only."

When he wheeled her into his grandfather's room, the old man was drowsing, neither asleep nor awake, lolling in a torpor at the edge of consciousness. He revived enough at the sound of their entering to perceive their presence, and then, at last understanding what had happened, smiled for the first time in weeks. Tears suddenly filled his eyes. He took hold of the woman's hand and said to A., as if addressing the entire world (but feebly, ever so feebly): "Shirley is my sweetheart. Shirley is the one I love."

In late July, A. decided to spend a weekend out of the city. He wanted to see his son, and he needed a break from the heat and the hospital. His wife came into New York, leaving the boy with her parents. What they did in the city that day he cannot remember, but by late afternoon they had made it out to the beach in Connecticut where the boy had spent the day with his grandparents. A. found his son sitting on a swing, and the first words out of the boy's mouth (having been coached all afternoon by his grandmother) were surprising in their lucidity. "I'm very happy to see you, daddy," he said.

At the same time, the voice sounded strange to A. The boy seemed to be short of breath, and he spoke each word in a staccato of separate syllables. A. had no doubt that something was wrong. He insisted that they all leave the beach at once and go back to the house. Although the boy was in good spirits, this curious, almost mechanical voice continued to speak through him, as though he were a ventriloquist's dummy. His breathing was extremely rapid: heaving torso, in and out, in and out, like the breathing of a little bird. Within an hour, A. and his wife were looking down a list of local pediatricians, trying to reach one who was in (it was dinner hour on Friday night). On the fifth or sixth try they got hold of a young woman doctor who had recently taken over a practice in town. By some fluke, she happened to be in her office at that hour, and she told them to come right over. Either because she was new at her work, or because she had an excitable nature, her examination of the little boy threw A. and his wife into a panic. She sat the boy up on the table, listened to his chest, counted his breaths per minute, observed his flared nostrils, the slightly bluish tint to the skin of his face. Then a mad rush about the office, trying to rig up a complicated breathing device: a vapor machine with a hood, reminiscent of a nineteenth century camera. But the boy would not keep his head under the hood, and the hissing of the cold steam frightened him. The doctor then tried a shot of adrenalin. "We'll try this one," she said, "and if it doesn't work we'll give him another." She waited a few minutes, went through the breath-rate calculations again, and then gave him the second shot. Still no effect. "That's it," she said. "We'll have to take him to the hospital." She made the necessary phone call, and with a furious energy that seemed to gather up everything into her small body, told A. and his wife how to follow her to the hospital, where to go, what to do, and then led them outside, where they left in separate cars. Her diagnosis was pneumonia with asthmatic complications—which, after X-rays and more sophisticated tests at the hospital, turned out to be the case.

The boy was put in a special room in the children's ward, pricked and poked by nurses, held down screaming as liquid medicine was poured into his throat, hooked up to an I.V. line, and placed in a crib that was then covered by a clear plastic tent—into which a mist of cold oxygen was pumped from a valve in the wall. The boy remained in this tent for three days and three nights. His parents were allowed to be with him continuously, and they took turns sitting beside the boy's crib, head and arms under the tent, reading him books, telling him stories, playing games, while the other sat in a small reading room reserved for adults, watching the faces of the other parents whose children were in the hospital: none of these strangers daring to talk to each other, since they were all thinking of only one thing, and to speak of it would only have made it worse.

It was exhausting for the boy's parents, since the medicine dripping into his veins was composed essentially of adrenalin. This charged him with extra doses of energy—above and beyond the normal energy of a two-year old—and much of their time was spent in trying to calm him down, restraining him from breaking out of the tent. For A. this was of little consequence. The fact of the boy's illness, the fact that had they not taken him to the doctor in time he might actually have died, (and the horror that washed over him when he thought: what if he and his wife had decided to spend the night in the city, entrusting the boy to his grandparents—who, in their old age, had ceased to be observant of details, and who, in fact, had not noticed the boy's strange breathing at the beach and had scoffed at A. when he first mentioned it), the fact of all these things made the struggle to keep the boy calm as nothing to A. Merely to have contemplated the possibility of the boy's death, to have had the thought of his death thrown in his face at the doctor's office, was enough for him to treat the boy's recovery as a sort of resurrection, a miracle dealt to him by the cards of chance.

His wife, however, began to show the strain. At one point she walked out to A., who was in the adult sitting room, and said: "I give up, I can't handle him anymore"—and there was such resentment in her voice against the boy, such an anger of exasperation, that something inside A. fell to pieces. Stupidly, cruelly, he wanted to punish his wife for such selfishness, and in that one instant all the newly won harmony that had been growing between them for the past month vanished: for the first time in all their years together, he had turned against her. He stormed out of the room and went to his son's bedside.

The modern nothingness. Interlude on the force of parallel lives.

In Paris that fall he attended a small dinner party given by a friend of his, J., a well-known French writer. There was another American among the guests, a scholar who specialized in modern French poetry, and she spoke to A. of a book she was in the process of editing: the selected writings of Mallarmé. Had A., she wondered, ever translated any Mallarmé?

The fact was that he had. More than five years earlier, shortly after moving into the apartment on Riverside Drive, he had translated a number of the fragments Mallarmé wrote at the bedside of his dying son, Anatole, in 1879. These were short works of the greatest obscurity: notes for a poem that never came to be written. They were not even discovered until the late 1950s. In 1974, A. had done rough translation drafts of thirty or forty of them and then had put the manuscript away. When he returned from Paris to his room on Varick Street (December 1979, exactly one hundred years after Mallarmé had scribbled those death notes to his son), he dug out the folder that contained the handwritten drafts and began to work up final versions of his translations. These were later published in the *Paris Review*, along with a photograph of Anatole in a sailor suit. From his prefatory note: "On October 6, 1879, Mallarmé's only son, Anatole, died at the age of eight after a long illness. The disease, diagnosed as child's rheumatism, had slowly spread from limb to limb and eventually overtaken the boy's entire body. For several months Mallarmé and his wife had sat helplessly at Anatole's bedside as doctors tried various remedies and administered unsuccessful treatments. The boy was shuttled from the city to the country and back to the city again. On August 22 Mallarmé wrote to his friend Henry Ronjon 'of the struggle between life and death our poor little darling is going through . . . But the real pain is that this little being might vanish. I confess that it is too much for me; I cannot bring myself to face this idea.' "

It was precisely this idea, A. realized, that moved him to return to these texts. The act of translating them was not a literary exercise. It was a way for him to relive his own moment of panic in the doctor's office that summer: it is too much for me, I cannot face it. For it was only at that moment, he later came to realize, that he had finally grasped the full scope of his own fatherhood: the boy's life meant more to him than his own; if dying were necessary to save his son, he would be willing to die. And it was therefore only in that moment of fear that he had become, once and for all, the father of his son. Translating those forty or so fragments by Mallarmé was perhaps an insignificant thing, but in his own mind it had become the equivalent of offering a prayer of thanks

you can, with your little
hands, drag me
into the grave—you
have the right—
—I
who follow you, I
let myself go—
—but if you
wish, the two
of us, let us make . . .

an alliance
a hymen, superb
—and the life
remaining in me
I will use for——

*

no—nothing
to do with the great
deaths—etc.
—as long as we
go on living, he
lives—in us

it will only be after our
death that he will be dead
—and the bells
of the Dead will toll for
him

*

sail—
navigates
river,
your life that
goes by, that flows

*

for the life of his son. A prayer to what? To nothing perhaps. To his sense of life. To *the modern nothingness.*

Brief commentary on the word "radiance."

He first heard this word used in connection with his son when he had shown a photograph of the boy to his good friend, R., an American poet who had lived for eight years in Amsterdam. They were drinking in a bar that night, surrounded by a press of bodies and loud music. A. pulled the snapshot out of his wallet and handed it to R., who studied the picture for a long time. Then he turned to A., a little drunk, and said with great emotion in his voice: "He has the same radiance as Titus."

About one year later, shortly after the publication of "A Tomb for Anatole" in the *Paris Review*, A. happened to be visiting R. R. (who had grown extremely fond of A.'s son) explained to A.: "An extraordinary thing happened to me today. I was in a bookstore, leafing through various magazines, and I happened to open the *Paris Review* to a photograph of Mallarmé's son. For a second I thought it was your son. The resemblance was that striking."

A. replied: "But those were my translations. I was the one who made them put in that picture. Didn't you know that?"

And then R. said: "I never got that far. I was so struck by the picture that I had to close the magazine. I put it back on the shelf and then walked out of the store."

His grandfather lasted another two or three weeks. A. returned to the apartment overlooking Columbus Circle, his son now out of danger, his marriage now at a permanent standstill. These were probably the worst days of all for him. He could not work, he could not think. He began to neglect himself, ate only noxious foods (frozen dinners, pizza, take-out Chinese noodles), and left the apartment to its own devices: dirty clothes strewn in a bedroom corner, unwashed dishes piled in the kitchen sink. Lying on the couch, smoking cigarette after cigarette, he would watch old movies on television and read second-rate mystery novels. He did not try to reach any of his friends. The one person he did call—a girl he had met in Paris when he was eighteen—had moved to Colorado.

One night, for no particular reason, he went out to wander around the lifeless neighborhood of the West Fifties and walked into a topless bar. As he sat there at his table drinking a beer, he suddenly found himself

Setting sun
and wind
now vanished, and
wind of *nothing*
that breathes
(here, the modern
? nothingness)

*

death—whispers softly
—I am no one—
I do not even know who I am
(for the dead do not
know they are
dead—, nor even that they
die
—for children
at least
—or

heroes—sudden
deaths

for otherwise
my beauty is
made *of last*
moments—
lucidity, beauty
face—of what would be

me, without myself

*

sitting next to a voluptuously naked young woman. She sidled up to him and began to describe all the lewd things she would do to him if he paid her to go to "the back room." There was something so openly humorous and matter-of-fact about her approach that he finally agreed to her proposition. The best thing, they decided, would be for her to suck his penis, since she claimed an extraordinary talent for this activity. And indeed, she threw herself into it with an enthusiasm that fairly astonished him. As he came in her mouth a few moments later, with a long and throbbing flood of semen, he had this vision, at just that second, which has continued to radiate inside him: that each ejaculation contains several billion sperm cells—or roughly the same number as there are people in the world—which means that, in himself, each man holds the potential of an entire world. And what would happen, could it happen, is the full range of possibilities: a spawn of idiots and geniuses, of the beautiful and the deformed, of saints, catatonics, thieves, stock brokers, and high-wire artists. Each man, therefore, is the entire world, bearing within his genes a memory of all mankind. Or, as Leibniz put it: "Every living substance is a perpetual living mirror of the universe." For the fact is, we are of the same stuff that came into being with the first explosion of the first spark in the infinite emptiness of space. Or so he said to himself, at that moment, as his penis exploded into the mouth of that naked woman, whose name he has now forgotten. He thought: the irreducible monad. And then, as though taking hold of it at last, he thought of the furtive, microscopic cell that had fought its way up through his wife's body, some three years earlier, to become his son.

Otherwise nothing. He languished. He sweltered in the summer heat. Like some latter-day Oblomov curled on his couch, he did not move unless he had to.

There was a cable television in his grandfather's apartment, with more channels than A. had ever known existed. Whenever he turned it on, there seemed to be a baseball game in progress. Not only was he able to follow the Yankees and Mets of New York, but the Red Sox of Boston, the Phillies of Philadelphia, and the Braves of Atlanta. Not to speak of the little bonuses occasionally provided during the afternoon: the games from the Japanese major leagues, for example (and his fascination with the constant beating of drums during the course of the game), or, even more strangely, the Little League championships from Long Island. To

Oh! you understand
that if I consent
to live—to seem
to forget you—
it is to
feed my pain
—and so that this apparent
forgetfulness
can spring forth more
horribly in tears, at

some random
moment, in
the middle of this
life, when you
appear to me

*

true mourning in
the apartment
—not cemetery—

furniture

*

to find *only*
absence—
—in presence
of little clothes
—etc—

*

no—I will not
give up
nothingness

father—I
feel nothingness
invade me

immerse himself in these games was to feel his mind striving to enter a place of pure form. Despite the agitation on the field, baseball offered itself to him as an image of that which does not move, and therefore a place where his mind could be at rest, secure in its refuge against the mutabilities of the world.

He had spent his entire childhood playing it. From the first muddy days in early March to the last frozen afternoons of late October. He had played well, with an almost obsessive devotion. Not only had it given him a feeling for his own possibilities, convinced him that he was not entirely hopeless in the eyes of others, but it had been the thing that drew him out from the solitary enclosures of his early childhood. It had initiated him into the world of the other, but at the same time it was something he could also keep within himself. Baseball was a terrain rich in potential for reverie. He fantasized about it continually, projecting himself into a New York Giants uniform and trotting out to his position at third base in the Polo Grounds, with the crowd cheering wildly at the mention of his name over the loudspeakers. Day after day, he would come home from school and throw a tennis ball against the steps of his house, pretending that each gesture was a part of the World Series game unfolding in his head. It always came down to two outs in the bottom of the ninth, a man on base, the Giants trailing by one. He was always the batter, and he always hit the game-winning homerun.

As he sat through those long summer days in his grandfather's apartment, he began to see that the power of baseball was for him the power of memory. Memory in both senses of the word: as a catalyst for remembering his own life and as an artificial structure for ordering the historical past. 1960, for example, was the year Kennedy was elected president; it was also the year of A.'s Bar Mitzvah, the year he supposedly reached manhood. But the first image that springs to his mind when 1960 is mentioned is Bill Mazeroski's homerun that beat the Yankees in the World Series. He can still see the ball soaring over the Forbes Field fence—that high, dark barrier, so densely cluttered with white numbers—and by recalling the sensations of that moment, that abrupt and stunning instant of pleasure, he is able to re-enter his own past, to stand in a world that would otherwise be lost to him.

He reads in a book: since 1893 (the year before his grandfather was born), when the pitcher's mound was moved back ten feet, the shape of the field has not changed. The diamond is a part of our consciousness.

Its pristine geometry of white lines, green grass, and brown dirt is an icon as familiar as the stars and stripes. As opposed to just about everything else in American life during this century, baseball has remained constant. Except for a few minor alterations (artificial turf, designated hitters), the game as it is played today is remarkably similar to the one played by Wee Willie Keeler and the old Baltimore Orioles: those long dead young men of the photographs, with their handlebar moustaches and heroic poses.

What happens today is merely a variation on what happened yesterday. Yesterday echoes today, and tomorrow will foreshadow what happens next year. Professional baseball's past is intact. There is a record of every game played, a statistic for every hit, error, and base on balls. One can measure performances against each other, compare players and teams, speak of the dead as if they were still alive. To play the game as a child is simultaneously to imagine playing it as an adult, and the power of this fantasy is present in even the most casual pick-up game. How many hours of his boyhood, A. wonders, were spent trying to imitate Stan Musial's batting stance (feet together, knees bent, back hunched over in a taut French curve) or the basket catches of Willie Mays? Reciprocally, for those who grow up to be professionals, there is an awareness that they are living out their childhood dreams—in effect, being paid to remain children. Nor should the depth of those dreams be minimized. In his own Jewish childhood, A. can remember confusing the last words of the Passover Seder, "Next year in Jerusalem," with the ever-hopeful refrain of disappointed fandom, "Wait till next year," as if the one were a commentary on the other: to win the pennant was to enter the promised land. Baseball had somehow become entangled in his mind with the religious experience.

It was just then, as A. was beginning to sink into this baseball quicksand, that Thurman Munson was killed. A. noted that Munson was the first Yankee captain since Lou Gehrig, that his grandmother had died of Lou Gehrig's disease, and that his grandfather's death would come quickly in the wake of Munson's.

The newspapers were filled with articles about the catcher. A. had always admired Munson's play on the field: the quick bat flicking singles to right, the stumpy body chugging around the bases, the anger that seemed to consume him as he went about his business behind the plate. Now A. was moved to learn of Munson's work with children and the troubles he had had with his own hyperactive son. Everything seemed to be repeating itself. Reality was a Chinese box, an infinite series of containers within containers. For here again, in the most unlikely of places, the theme had reappeared: the curse of the absent father. It seemed that Munson himself was the only one who had the power to calm down the little boy. Whenever he was at home, the boy's outbursts stopped, his frenzies abated. Munson was learning how to fly a plane so that he could go home more often during the baseball season to be with his son, and it was the plane that killed him.

Inevitably, A.'s memories of baseball were connected with his memories of his grandfather. It was his grandfather who had taken him to his first game, had talked to him about the old players, had shown him that baseball was as much about talk as it was about watching. As a little boy, A. would be dropped off at the office on Fifty-seventh Street, play around with the typewriters and adding machines until his grandfather was ready to leave, and then walk out with him for a leisurely stroll down Broadway. The ritual always included a few rounds of Pokerino in one of the amusement arcades, a quick lunch, and then the subway—to one of the city ball parks. Now, with his grandfather disappearing into death, they continued to talk about baseball. It was the one subject they could still come to as equals. Each time he visited the hospital, A. would buy a copy of the *New York Post*, and then sit by the old man's bed, reading to him about the games of the day before. It was his last contact with the outside world, and it was painless, a series of coded messages he could understand with his eyes closed. Anything else would have been too much.

Toward the very end, with a voice that could barely produce a sound, his grandfather told him that he had begun to remember his life. He had been dredging up the days of his Toronto boyhood, reliving events that had taken place as far back as eighty years ago: defending his younger brother against a gang of bullies, delivering bread on Friday afternoon to the Jewish families in the neighborhood, all the trivial, long-forgotten things that now, coming back to him as he lay immobilized in bed, took on the importance of spiritual illuminations. "Lying here gives me a chance to remember," he told A., as if this were a new power he had discovered in himself. A. could sense the pleasure it gave him. Little by little, it had begun to dominate the fear that had been in his grandfather's face these past weeks. Memory was the only thing keeping him alive, and it was as though he wanted to hold off death for as long as possible in order to go on remembering.

He knew, and yet he would not say he knew. Until the final week, he continued to talk about returning to his apartment, and not once was the word "death" mentioned. Even on the last day, he waited until the last possible moment to say good-bye. A. was leaving, walking through the door after a visit, when his grandfather called him back. Again, A. stood beside the bed. The old man took hold of his hand and squeezed as hard as he could. Then: a long, long moment. At last, A. bent down and kissed his grandfather's face. Neither one of them said a word.

A. remembers a schemer, a maker of deals, a man of bizarre and grandiose optimisms. Who else, after all, could have named his daughter Queenie with a straight face? But at her birth he had declared, "she'll be a queen," and could not resist the temptation. He thrived on bluff, the symbolic gesture, on being the life of the party. Lots of jokes, lots of cronies, an impeccable sense of timing. He gambled on the sly, cheated on his wife (the older he got, the younger the girls), and never lost his taste for any of it. His locutions were particularly splendid. A towel was never just a towel, but a "Turkish towel." A taker of drugs was a "dope fiend." Nor would he ever say "I saw . . .," but rather, "I've had an opportunity to observe. . . ." In so doing, he managed to inflate the world, to turn it into a more compelling and exotic place for himself. He played the bigshot and reveled in the side-effects of the pose: the headwaiters calling him Mr. B., the delivery boys smiling at his excessive tips, the whole world tipping its hat to him. He had come down to New York from Canada just after the First World War, a poor Jewish boy on the make, and in the end he had done all right for himself. New York was his passion, and in his last years he refused to move away, resisting his daughter's offer of a life in sunny California with these words, which became a popular refrain: "I can't leave New York. This is where the action is."

A. remembers a day when he was four or five. His grandparents came for a visit, and his grandfather did a magic trick for him, some little thing he had found in a novelty shop. On the next visit, when he failed to show up with a new trick, A. raised a fuss of disappointment. From then on there was always a new piece of magic: disappearing coins, silk scarves produced from thin air, a machine that turned strips of blank paper into money, a big rubber ball that became five little rubber balls when you squeezed it in your hand, a cigarette extinguished in a handkerchief that made no burn, a pitcher of milk poured into a cone of newspaper that made no spill. What had started out as a curiosity to amuse his grandson became a genuine calling for him. He turned himself into an accomplished amateur magician, a deft sleight-of-hand artist, and he took special pride in his membership card from the Magician's Guild. He appeared at each of A.'s childhood birthday parties with his magic and went on performing until the last year of his life, touring the senior citizen clubs of New York with one of his lady friends (a blowsy woman with a pile of fake red hair) who would sing a song, accompanying herself on the accordion, that introduced him as the Great Zavello. It was only natural. His life was so steeped in the hocus-pocus of illusion, he had pulled off so many business deals by making people believe in him (convincing them that something not there was actually there, and vice versa) that it was a small matter for him to step up on stage and fool them in a more formal way. He had the ability to make people pay attention to him, and it was clear to everyone who saw him how delighted he was to be the center of their attention. No one is less cynical than a magician. He knows, and everyone else knows, that everything he does is a sham. The trick is not really to deceive them, but to delight them into wanting to be deceived: so that for the space of a few minutes the grip of cause-and-effect is loosened, the laws of nature countermanded. As Pascal put it in the *Pensées:* "It is not possible to have reasonable grounds for not believing in miracles."

A.'s grandfather, however, did not content himself merely with magic. He was equally fond of jokes, which he called "stories"—all of them written down in a little notebook that he carried around in his coat pocket. At some point during every family gathering, he would take out the notebook, skim through it quickly in some corner of the room, put it back in his pocket, sit down in a chair, and then launch into an hour's worth of verbal nonsense. Here, too, the memory is of laughter. Not, as with S., a laughter bursting from the belly, but a laughter that meandered outward from the lungs, a long sing-song loop of sound that began as a wheeze and dispersed, gradually, into a fainter and fainter chromatic whistle. That, too, is how A. would like to remember him: sitting in that chair and making everyone laugh.

His grandfather's greatest stunt, though, was neither a magic trick nor a joke, but a kind of extra-sensory voodoo that kept everyone in the family baffled for years. It was a game called the Wizard. A.'s grandfather would take out a deck of cards, ask someone to pick a card, any card, and hold it up for everyone to see. The five of hearts. Then he would go to the phone, dial a number, and ask to speak to the Wizard. That's right, he would say, I want to speak to the Wizard. A moment later he would pass around the telephone, and coming out of the receiver there would be a voice, a man's voice, saying over and over: five of hearts, five of hearts, five of hearts. Then he would thank the Wizard, hang up the phone, and stand there grinning at everyone.

Years later, when it was finally explained to A., it all seemed so simple. His grandfather and a friend had each agreed to be the Wizard for the other. The question, May I speak to the Wizard, was a signal, and the man on the other end of the line would start reeling off the suits: spade, heart, diamond, club. When he hit the right one, the caller would say something, anything, meaning go no further, and then the Wizard would go through the litany of numbers: ace, two, three, four, five, etc. When he came to the right one, the caller would again say something, and the Wizard would stop, put the two elements together, and repeat them into the phone: five of hearts, five of hearts, five of hearts.

The Book of Memory. Book Six.

He finds it extraordinary, even in the ordinary actuality of his experience, to feel his feet on the ground, to feel his lungs expanding and contracting with the air he breathes, to know that if he puts one foot in front of the other he will be able to walk from where he is to where he is going. He finds it extraordinary that on some mornings, just after he has woken up, as he bends down to tie his shoes, he is flooded with a happiness so intense, a happiness so naturally and harmoniously at one with the world, that he can feel himself alive in the present, a present that surrounds him and permeates him, that breaks through him with the sudden, overwhelming knowledge that he is alive. And the happiness he discovers in himself at that moment is extraordinary. And whether or not it is extraordinary, he finds this happiness extraordinary.

Sometimes it feels as though we are wandering through a city without purpose. We walk down the street, turn at random down another street, stop to admire the cornice of a building, bend down to inspect a splotch of tar on the pavement that reminds us of certain paintings we have admired, look at the faces of the people who pass us on the street, trying to imagine the lives they carry around inside them, go into a cheap restaurant for lunch, walk back outside and continue on our way toward the river (if this city has a river), to watch the boats as they sail by, or the big ships docked in the harbor, perhaps singing to ourselves as we walk, or perhaps whistling, or perhaps trying to remember something we have forgotten. Sometimes it seems as though we are not going anywhere as we walk through the city, that we are only looking for a way to pass the time, and that it is only our fatigue that tells us where and when we should stop. But just as one step will inevitably lead to the next step, so it is that one thought inevitably follows from the previous thought, and in the event that a thought should engender more than a single thought (say two or three thoughts, equal to each other in all their consequences), it will be necessary not only to follow the first thought to its conclusion, but also to backtrack to the original position of that thought in order to follow the second thought to its conclusion, and then the third thought, and so on, and in this way, if we were to try to make an image of this process in our minds, a network of paths begins to be drawn, as in the image of the human bloodstream (heart, arteries, veins, capillaries), or as in the image of a map (of city streets, for example, preferably a large city, or even of roads, as in the gas station maps of roads that stretch, bisect, and meander across a continent), so that what we are really doing when we walk through the city is thinking, and thinking in such a way that our thoughts compose a journey, and this journey is no more or less than the steps we have taken, so that, in the end, we might safely say that we have been on a journey, and even if we do not leave our room, it has been a journey, and we might safely say that we have been somewhere, even if we don't know where it is.

He takes down from his bookshelf a brochure he bought ten years ago in Amherst, Massachusetts, a souvenir of his visit to Emily Dickinson's house, thinking now of the strange exhaustion that had afflicted him that day as he stood in the poet's room: a shortness of breath, as if he had just climbed to the top of a mountain. He had walked around that small, sun-drenched room, looking at the white bedspread, the polished furniture, thinking of the seventeen hundred poems that were written there, trying to see them as a part of those four walls, and yet failing to do so. For if words are a way of being in the world, he thought, then even if there were no world to enter, the world was already there, in that room, which meant it was the room that was present in the poems and not the reverse. He reads now, on the last page of the brochure, in the awkward prose of the anonymous writer:

"In this bedroom-workroom, Emily announced that the soul could be content with its own society. But she discovered that consciousness was captivity as well as liberty, so that even here she was prey to her own self-imprisonment in despair or fear. . . . For the sensitive visitor, then, Emily's room acquires an atmosphere encompassing the poet's several moods of superiority, anxiety, anguish, resignation or ecstasy. Perhaps more than any other concrete place in American literature, it symbolizes a native tradition, epitomized by Emily, of an assiduous study of the inner life."

Song to accompany The Book of Memory. *Solitude*, as sung by Billie Holiday. In the recording of May 9, 1941 by Billie Holiday and Her Orchestra. Performance time: three minutes and fifteen seconds. As follows: In my solitude you haunt me / With reveries of days gone by. / In my solitude you taunt me / With memories that never die . . . Etc. With credits to D. Ellington, E. De Lange, and I. Mills.

First allusions to a woman's voice. To be followed by specific reference to several.

For it is his belief that if there is a voice of truth—assuming there is such a thing as truth, and assuming this truth can speak—it comes from the mouth of a woman.

It is also true that memory sometimes comes to him as a voice. It is a voice that speaks inside him, and it is not necessarily his own. It speaks to him in the way a voice might tell stories to a child, and yet at times this voice makes fun of him, or calls him to attention, or curses him in no uncertain terms. At times it willfully distorts the story it is telling him, changing facts to suit its whims, catering to the interests of drama rather than truth. Then he must speak to it in his own voice and tell it to stop, thus returning it to the silence it came from. At other times it sings to him. At still other times it whispers. And then there are the times it merely hums, or babbles, or cries out in pain. And even when it says nothing, he knows it is still there, and in the silence of this voice that says nothing, he waits for it to speak.

Jeremiah: "Then said I, Ah, Lord God! behold, I cannot speak: for I am a child. But the Lord said unto me, say not, I am a child: for thou shalt go to all that I shall send thee, and whatsoever I command thee thou shalt speak. . . . Then the Lord put forth his hand, and touched my mouth. And the Lord said unto me, Behold, I have put my words in thy mouth."

The Book of Memory. Book Seven.

First commentary on the Book of Jonah.

One is immediately struck by its oddness in relation to the other prophetic books. This brief work, the only one to be written in the third person, is more dramatically a story of solitude than anything else in the Bible, and yet it is told as if from outside that solitude, as if, by plunging into the darkness of that solitude, the "I" has vanished from itself. It cannot speak about itself, therefore, except as another. As in Rimbaud's phrase: "Je est un autre."

Not only is Jonah reluctant to speak (as Jeremiah is, for example), but he actually refuses to speak. "Now the word of the Lord came unto Jonah. . . . But Jonah rose up to flee from the presence of the Lord."

Jonah flees. He books passage aboard a ship. A terrible storm rises up, and the sailors fear they will drown. Everyone prays for deliverance. But Jonah has "gone down into the sides of the ship; and he lay, and was fast asleep." Sleep, then, as the ultimate withdrawal from the world. Sleep as an image of solitude. Oblomov curled on his couch, dreaming himself back into his mother's womb. Jonah in the belly of the ship; Jonah in the belly of the whale.

The captain of the ship finds Jonah and tells him to pray to his God. Meanwhile, the sailors have drawn lots, to see which among them has been responsible for the storm, ". . . and the lot fell upon Jonah.

"And then he said unto them, Take me up, and cast me forth into the sea; so shall the sea be calm unto you; for I know that for my sake this great tempest is upon you.

"Nevertheless the men rowed hard to bring it to the land; but they could not; for the sea wrought, and was tempestuous against them. . . .

"So they took up Jonah, and cast him forth into the sea; and the sea ceased from her raging."

The popular mythology about the whale notwithstanding, the great fish that swallows Jonah is by no means an agent of destruction. The fish is what saves him from drowning in the sea. "The waters compassed me about, even to the soul: the depth closed me round about, the weeds were wrapped about my head." In the depth of that solitude, which is equally the depth of silence, as if in the refusal to speak there were an equal refusal to turn one's face to the other ("Jonah rose up to flee from the presence of the Lord")—which is to say: who seeks solitude seeks silence; who does not speak is alone; is alone, even unto death—Jonah encounters the darkness of death. We are told that "Jonah was in the belly of the fish three days and three nights," and elsewhere, in a chapter of the *Zohar*, we are told, " 'Three days and three nights': which means the three days that a man is in his grave before his belly bursts apart." And when the fish then vomits Jonah onto dry land, Jonah is given back to life, as if the death he had found in the belly of the fish were a preparation for new life, a life that has passed through death, and therefore a life that can at last speak. For death has frightened him into opening his mouth. "I cried by reason of mine affliction unto the Lord, and he heard me; out of the belly of hell cried I, and thou heardest my voice." In the darkness of the solitude that is death, the tongue is finally loosened, and at the moment it begins to speak, there is an answer. And even if there is no answer, the man has begun to speak.

The prophet. As in false: speaking oneself into the future, not by knowledge but by intuition. The real prophet knows. The false prophet guesses.

This was Jonah's greatest problem. If he spoke God's message, telling the Ninevites they would be destroyed in forty days for their wickedness, he was certain they would repent, and thus be spared. For he knew that God was "merciful, slow to anger, and of great kindness."

"So the people of Ninevah believed God, and proclaimed a fast, and put on sackcloth, from the greatest of them even to the least of them."

And if the Ninevites were spared, would this not make Jonah's prophecy false? Would he not, then, be a false prophet? Hence the paradox at the heart of the book: the prophecy would remain true only if he did not speak it. But then, of course, there would be no prophecy, and Jonah would no longer be a prophet. But better to be no prophet at all than to be a false prophet. "Therefore now, O lord, take, I beseech thee, my life from me; for it is better for me to die than to live."

Therefore, Jonah held his tongue. Therefore, Jonah ran away from the presence of the Lord and met the doom of shipwreck. That is to say, the shipwreck of the singular.

* * *

Remission of cause and effect.

A. remembers a moment from boyhood (twelve, thirteen years old). He was wandering aimlessly one November afternoon with his friend D. Nothing was happening. But in each of them, at that moment, a sense of infinite possibilities. Nothing was happening. Or else one could say that it was this consciousness of possibility, in fact, that was happening.

As they walked along through the cold, gray air of that afternoon, A. suddenly stopped and announced to his friend: One year from today something extraordinary will happen to us, something that will change our lives forever.

The year passed, and on the appointed day nothing extraordinary happened. A. explained to D.: No matter; the important thing will happen next year. When the second year rolled around, the same thing happened: nothing. But A. and D. were undaunted. All through the years of high school, they continued to commemorate that day. Not with ceremony, but simply with acknowledgement. For example, seeing each other in the school corridor and saying: Saturday is the day. It was not that they still expected a miracle to happen. But, more curiously, over the years they had both become attached to the memory of their prediction.

The reckless future, the mystery of what has not yet happened: this, too, he learned, can be preserved in memory. And it sometimes strikes him that the blind, adolescent prophecy he made twenty years ago, that fore-seeing of the extraordinary, was in fact the extraordinary thing itself: his mind leaping happily into the unknown. For the fact of the matter is, many years have passed. And still, at the end of each November, he finds himself remembering that day.

Prophecy. As in true. As in Cassandra, speaking from the solitude of her cell. As in a woman's voice.

The future falls from her lips in the present, each thing exactly as it will happen, and it is her fate never to be believed. Madwoman, the daughter of Priam: "the shrieks of that ill-omened bird" from whom ". . . sounds of woe / Burst dreadful, as she chewed the laurel leaf, / And ever and anon, like the black Sphinx, / Poured the full tide of enigmatic song." (Lycophron's *Cassandra;* in Royston's translation, 1806). To speak of the future is to use a language that is forever ahead of itself, consigning things that have not yet happened to the past, to an "already" that is forever behind itself, and in this space between utterance and act, word after word, a chasm begins to open, and for one to contemplate such emptiness for any length of time is to grow dizzy, to feel oneself falling into the abyss.

A. remembers the excitement he felt in Paris in 1974, when he discovered the seventeen-hundred line poem by Lycophron (circa 300 B.C.), which is a monologue of Cassandra's ravings in prison before the fall of Troy. He came to the poem through a translation into French by Q., a writer just his own age (twenty-four). Three years later, when he got together with Q. in a cafe on the rue Condé, he asked him whether he knew of any translations of the poem into English. Q. himself did not read or speak English, but yes, he had heard of one, by a certain Lord Royston at the beginning of the nineteenth century. When A. returned to New York in the summer of 1974, he went to the Columbia University library to look for the book. Much to his surprise, he found it. *Cassandra, translated from the original Greek of Lycophron and illustrated with notes;* Cambridge, 1806.

This translation was the only work of any substance to come from the pen of Lord Royston. He had completed the translation while still an undergraduate at Cambridge and had published the poem himself in a luxurious private edition. Then he had gone on the traditional continental tour following his graduation. Because of the Napoleonic tumult in France, he did not head south—which would have been the natural route for a young man of his interests—but instead went north, to the Scandinavian countries, and in 1808, while traveling through the treacherous waters of the Baltic Sea, drowned in a shipwreck off the coast of Russia. He was just twenty-four years old.

Lycophron: "the obscure." In his dense, bewildering poem, nothing is ever named, everything becomes a reference to something else. One is quickly lost in the labyrinth of its associations, and yet one continues to run through it, propelled by the force of Cassandra's voice. The poem is a verbal outpouring, breathing fire, consumed by fire, which obliterates itself at the edge of sense. "Cassandra's word," as a friend of A.'s put it (B.: in a lecture, curiously enough, about Hölderlin's poetry—a poetry which he compares in manner to Cassandra's speech), "this irreducible sign—*deutungslos*—a word beyond grasping, Cassandra's word, a word from which no lesson is to be drawn, a word, each time, and every time, spoken to say nothing. . . ."

After reading through Royston's translation, A. realized that a great talent had been lost in that shipwreck. Royston's English rolls along with such fury, such deft and acrobatic syntax, that to read the poem is to feel yourself trapped inside Cassandra's mouth.

line 240 An oath! they have an oath in heaven!
Soon shall their sail be spread, and in their hands
The strong oar quivering cleave the refluent wave;
While songs, and hymns, and carols jubilant
Shall charm the rosy God, to whom shall rise,
Rife from Apollo's Delphic shrine, the smoke
Of numerous holocausts: Well pleased shall hear
Enorches, where the high-hung taper's light
Gleams on his dread carousals, and when forth
The Savage rushes on the corny field
Mad to destroy, shall bid his vines entwist
His sinewy strength, and hurl them to the ground.

*

line 426 . . . then Greece
For this one crime, aye for this one, shall weep
Myriads of sons: no funeral urn, but rocks
Shall hearse their bones; no friends upon their dust
Shall pour the dark libations of the dead;
A name, a breath, an empty sound remains,
A fruitless marble warm with bitter tears
Of sires, and orphan babes, and widowed wives!

*

line 1686 Why pour the fruitless strain? to winds, and waves,
Deaf winds, dull waves, and senseless shades of woods
I chaunt, and sing mine unavailing song.
Such woes has Lepsieus heaped upon my head,
Steeping my words in incredulity;
The jealous God! for from my virgin couch
I drove him amorous, nor returned his love.
But fate is in my voice, truth on my lips;
What must come, will come; and when rising woes
Burst on his head, when rushing from her seat
His country falls, nor man nor God can save,
Some wretch shall groan, "From her no falsehood
flowed,
True were the shrieks of that ill-omened bird."

It intrigues A. to consider that both Royston and Q. had translated this work while still in their early twenties. In spite of the century and a half that separated them, each had given some special force to his own language through the medium of this poem. At one point, it occurred to him that perhaps Q. was a reincarnation of Royston. Every hundred years or so Royston would be reborn to translate the poem into another language, and just as Cassandra was destined never to be believed, the work of Lycophron would remain unread, generation after generation. A useless task therefore: to write a book that would stay forever closed. And still, the image rises up in his mind: shipwreck. Consciousness falling to the bottom of the sea, and the horrible noise of cracking wood, the tall masts tumbling into the waves. To imagine Royston's thoughts the moment his body smacked against the water. To imagine the havoc of that death.

The Book of Memory. Book Eight.

By the time of his third birthday, A.'s son's taste in literature had begun to expand from simple, heavily illustrated baby books to more sophisticated children's books. The illustration was still a source of great pleasure, but it was no longer crucial. The story itself had become enough to hold his attention, and when A. came to a page with no picture at all, he would be moved to see the little boy looking intently ahead, at nothing, at the emptiness of the air, at the blank wall, imagining what the words were telling him. "It's fun to imagine that we can't see," he told his father once, as they were walking down the street. Another time, the boy went into the bathroom, closed the door, and did not come out. A. asked through the closed door: "What are you doing in there?" "I'm thinking," the boy said. "I have to be alone to think."

Little by little, they both began to gravitate toward one book. The story of Pinocchio. First in the Disney version, and then, soon after, in the original version, with text by Collodi and illustrations by Mussino. The little boy never tired of hearing the chapter about the storm at sea, which tells of how Pinocchio finds Gepetto in the belly of the Terrible Shark.

"Oh, Father, dear Father! Have I found you at last? Now I shall never, never leave you again!"

Gepetto explains: "The sea was rough and the whitecaps overturned the boat. Then a Terrible Shark came up out of the sea and, as soon as he saw me in the water, swam quickly toward me, put out his tongue, and swallowed me as easily as if I had been a chocolate peppermint."

"And how long have you been shut away in here?"

"From that day to this, two long weary years—two years, my Pinocchio. . . ."

"And how have you lived? Where did you find the candle? And the matches to light it with—where did you get them?"

"In the storm which swamped my boat, a large ship also suffered the same fate. The sailors were all saved, but the ship went right down to the bottom of the sea, and the same Terrible Shark that swallowed me, swallowed most of it. . . . To my own good luck, that ship was loaded with meat, preserved foods, crackers, bread, bottles of wine, raisins, cheese, coffee, sugar, wax candles, and boxes of matches. With all these blessings, I have been able to live on for two whole years, but now I am at the very last crumbs. Today there is nothing left in the cupboard, and this candle you see here is the last one I have."

"And then?"

"And then, my dear, we'll find ourselves in darkness."

For A. and his son, so often separated from each other during the past year, there was something deeply satisfying in this passage of reunion. In effect, Pinocchio and Gepetto are separated throughout the entire book. Gepetto is given the mysterious piece of talking wood by the carpenter, Master Cherry, in the second chapter. In the third chapter the old man sculpts the Marionette. Even before Pinocchio is finished, his pranks and mischief begin. "I deserve it," says Gepetto to himself. "I should have thought of this before I made him. Now it's too late." At this point, like any newborn baby, Pinocchio is pure will, libidinous need without consciousness. Very rapidly, over the next few pages, Gepetto teaches his son to walk, the Marionette experiences hunger and accidentally burns his feet off—which his father rebuilds for him. The next day Gepetto sells his coat to buy Pinocchio an A-B-C book for school ("Pinocchio understood . . . and, unable to restrain his tears, he jumped on his father's neck and kissed him over and over"), and then, for more than two hundred pages, they do not see each other again. The rest of the book tells the story of Pinocchio's search for his father—and Gepetto's search for his son. At some point, Pinocchio realizes that he wants to become a real boy. But it also becomes clear that this will not happen until he is reunited with his father. Adventures, misadventures, detours, new resolves, struggles, happenstance, progress, setbacks, and through it all, the gradual dawning of conscience. The superiority of the Collodi original to the Disney adaptation lies in its reluctance to make the inner motivations of the story explicit. They remain intact, in a pre-conscious, dream-like form, whereas in Disney these things are expressed—which sentimentalizes them, and therefore trivializes them. In Disney, Gepetto prays for a son; in Collodi, he simply makes him. The physical act of shaping the puppet (from a piece of wood that talks, that is *alive*, which mirrors Michaelangelo's notion of sculpture: the figure is already there in the material; the artist merely hews away at the excess matter until the true form is revealed, implying that Pinocchio's being precedes his body: his task throughout the book is to find it, in other words to find himself, which means that this is a story of becoming rather than of birth), this act of shaping the puppet is enough to convey the idea of the prayer, and surely it is more powerful for remaining silent. Likewise with Pinocchio's efforts to attain real boyhood. In Disney, he is commanded by the Blue Fairy to be "brave, truthful, and unselfish," as though there were an easy formula for taking hold of the self. In Collodi, there are no directives. Pinocchio simply blunders about, simply lives, and little by little comes to an awareness of what he can become. The only improvement Disney makes on the story, and this is perhaps arguable, comes at the end, in the episode of the escape from the Terrible Shark (Monstro the Whale). In Collodi, the Shark's mouth is open (he suffers from asthma and heart disease), and to organize the escape Pinocchio needs no more than courage. "Then, my dear Father, there is no time to lose. We must escape."

"Escape! How?"

"We can run out of the Shark's mouth and dive into the sea."

"You speak well, but I cannot swim, my dear Pinocchio."

"Why should that matter? You can climb on my shoulders and I, who am a fine swimmer, will carry you safely to shore."

"Dreams, my boy!" answered Gepetto, shaking his head and smiling sadly. "Do you think it possible for a Marionette, a yard high, to have the strength to carry me on his shoulders and swim?"

"Try it and see! And in any case, if it is written that we must die, we shall at least die together." Not adding another word, Pinocchio took the candle in his hand and going ahead to light the way, he said to his father: "Follow me and have no fear."

In Disney, however, Pinocchio needs resourcefulness as well. The whale's mouth is shut, and when it opens, it is only to let water in, not out. Pinocchio cleverly decides to build a fire inside the whale—which induces Monstro to sneeze, thereby launching the puppet and his father into the sea. But more is lost with this flourish than gained. For the crucial image of the story is eliminated: Pinocchio swimming through the desolate water, nearly sinking under the weight of Gepetto's body, making his way through the gray-blue night (page 296 of the American edition), with the moon shining above them, a benign smile on its face, and the huge open mouth of the shark behind them. The father on his son's back: the image evoked here is so clearly that of Aeneas bearing Anchises on his back from the ruins of Troy that each time A. reads the story aloud to his son, he cannot help seeing (for it is not thinking, really, so quickly do these things happen in his mind) certain clusters of other images, spinning outward from the core of his preoccupations: Cassandra, for example, predicting the ruin of Troy, and thereafter loss, as in the wanderings of Aeneas that precede the founding of Rome, and in that wandering the image of another wandering: the Jews in the desert, which, in its turn, yields further clusters of images: "Next year in Jerusalem," and with it the photograph in the Jewish Encyclopedia of his relative, who bore the name of his son.

A. has watched his son's face carefully during these readings of *Pinocchio*. He has concluded that it is the image of Pinocchio saving Gepetto (swimming away with the old man on his back) that gives the story meaning for him. A boy of three is indeed very little. A wisp of puniness against the bulk of his father, he dreams of acquiring inordinate powers to conquer the paltry reality of himself. He is still too young to understand that one day he will be as big as his father, and even when it is explained to him very carefully, the facts are still open to gross misinterpretations: "And some day I'll be the same tall as you, and you'll be the same little as me." The fascination with comic book super-heroes is perhaps understandable from this point of view. It is the dream of being big, of becoming an adult. "What does Superman do?" "He saves people." For this act of saving is in effect what a father does: he saves his little boy from harm. And for the little boy to see Pinocchio, that same foolish puppet who has stumbled his way from one misfortune to the next, who has wanted to be "good" and could not help being "bad," for this same incompetent little marionette, who is not even a real boy, to become a figure of redemption, the very being who saves his father from the grip of death, is a sublime moment of revelation. The son saves the father. This must be fully imagined from the perspective of the little boy. And this, in the mind of the father who was once a little boy, a son, that is, to his own father, must be fully imagined. *Puer aeternus*. The son saves the father.

* * *

Further commentary on the nature of chance.

He does not want to neglect to mention that two years after meeting S. in Paris, he happened to meet S.'s younger son on a subsequent visit—through channels and circumstances that had nothing to do with S. himself. This young man, P., who was precisely the same age as A., was working his way to a position of considerable power with an important French film producer. A. himself would later work for this same producer, doing a variety of odd jobs for him in 1971 and 1972 (translating, ghost writing), but none of that is essential. What matters is that by the mid to late seventies, P. had managed to achieve the status of co-producer, and along with the son of the French producer put together the movie *Superman*, which had cost so many millions of dollars, A. read, that it had been described as the most expensive work of art in the history of the Western world.

Early in the summer of 1980, shortly after his son turned three, A. and the boy spent a week together in the country, in a house owned by friends who were off on vacation. A. noticed in the newspaper that *Superman* was playing in a local theater and decided to take the boy, on the off-chance that he would be able to sit through it. For the first half of the film, the boy was calm, working his way through a bin of popcorn, whispering his questions as A. had instructed him to do, and taking the business of exploding planets, rocket ships, and outer space without much fuss. But then something happened. Superman began to fly, and all at once the boy lost his composure. His mouth dropped open, he stood up in his seat, spilled his popcorn, pointed at the screen, and began to shout: "Look! Look! He's flying!" For the rest of the film, he was beside himself, his face taut with fear and fascination, rattling off questions to his father, trying to absorb what he had seen, marveling, trying to absorb it again, marveling. Toward the end, it became a little too much for him. "Too much booming," he said. His father asked him if he wanted to leave, and he said yes. A. picked him up and carried him out of the theater—into a violent hail storm. As they ran toward the car, the boy said (bouncing up and down in A.'s arms), "We're having quite an adventure tonight, aren't we?"

For the rest of the summer, Superman was his passion, his obsession, the unifying purpose of his life. He refused to wear any shirt except the blue one with the S on the front. His mother sewed a cape together for him, and each time he went outside, he insisted on wearing it, charging down the streets with his arms in front of him, as if flying, stopping only to announce to each passerby under the age of ten: "I'm Superman!" A. was amused by all this, since he could remember these same things from his own childhood. It was not this obsession that struck him; nor even, finally, the coincidence of knowing the men who had made the film that led to this obsession. Rather, it was this. Each time he saw his son pretending to be Superman, he could not help thinking of his friend S., as if even the S on his son's T-shirt were not a reference to Superman but to his friend. And he wondered at this trick his mind continued to play on him, this constant turning of one thing into another thing, as if behind each real thing there were a shadow thing, as alive in his mind as the thing before his eyes, and in the end he was at a loss to say which of these things he was actually seeing. And therefore it happened, often it happened, that his life no longer seemed to dwell in the present.

The Book of Memory. Book Nine.

For most of his adult life, he has earned his living by translating the books of other writers. He sits at his desk reading the book in French and then picks up his pen and writes the same book in English. It is both the same book and not the same book, and the strangeness of this activity has never failed to impress him. Every book is an image of solitude. It is a tangible object that one can pick up, put down, open, and close, and its words represent many months, if not many years, of one man's solitude, so that with each word one reads in a book one might say to himself that he is confronting a particle of that solitude. A man sits alone in a room and writes. Whether the book speaks of loneliness or companionship, it is necessarily a product of solitude. A. sits down in his own room to translate another man's book, and it is as though he were entering that man's solitude and making it his own. But surely that is impossible. For once a solitude has been breached, once a solitude has been taken on by another, it is no longer solitude, but a kind of companionship. Even though there is only one man in the room, there are two. A. imagines himself as a kind of ghost of that other man, who is both there and not there, and whose book is both the same and not the same as the one he is translating. Therefore, he tells himself, it is possible to be alone and not alone at the same moment.

A word becomes another word, a thing becomes another thing. In this way, he tells himself, it works in the same way that memory does. He imagines an immense Babel inside him. There is a text, and it translates itself into an infinite number of languages. Sentences spill out of him at the speed of thought, and each word comes from a different language, a thousand tongues that clamor inside him at once, the din of it echoing through a maze of rooms, corridors, and stairways, hundreds of stories high. He repeats. In the space of memory, everything is both itself and something else. And then it dawns on him that everything he is trying to record in The Book of Memory, everything he has written so far, is no more than the translation of a moment or two of his life—those moments he lived through on Christmas Eve, 1979, in his room at 6 Varick Street.

The moment of illumination that burns across the sky of solitude.

Pascal in his room on the night of November 23, 1654, sewing the Memorial into the lining of his clothes, so that at any moment, for the rest of his life, he could find beneath his hand the record of that ecstasy.

In the Year of Grace 1654
On Monday, November 23rd, Feast of Saint Clement,
Pope and Martyr,
and of others in the Martyrology.
and eve of Saint Chrysogomus and other Martyrs.
From about half past ten at night until about half past twelve.

Fire
"God of Abraham, God of Isaac, God of Jacob,"
not of the philosophers and scientists.
Certainty. Certainty. Feeling. Joy. Peace.

• • •

Greatness of the human soul.

• • •

Joy, joy, joy, tears of joy.

• • •

I will not forget thy word. Amen.

• • •

Concerning the power of memory.

In the spring of 1966, not long after meeting his future wife, A. was invited by her father (an English professor at Columbia) to the family apartment on Morningside Drive for dessert and coffee. The dinner guests were Francis Ponge and his wife, and A.'s future father-in-law thought that the young A. (just nineteen at the time), would enjoy meeting so famous a writer. Ponge, the master poet of the object, who had invented a poetry more firmly placed in the outer world perhaps than any other, was teaching a course at Columbia that semester. By then A. already spoke reasonably good French. Since Ponge and his wife spoke no English, and A.'s future in-laws spoke almost no French, A. joined in the discussion more fully than he might have, given his innate shyness and penchant for saying nothing whenever possible. He remembers Ponge as a gracious and lively man with sparkling blue eyes.

The second time A. met Ponge was in 1969 (although it could have been 1968 or 1970) at a party given in Ponge's honor by G., a Barnard professor who had been translating his work. When A. shook Ponge's hand, he introduced himself by saying that although he probably didn't remember it, they had once met in New York several years ago. On the contrary, Ponge replied, he remembered the evening quite well. And then he proceeded to talk about the apartment in which that dinner had taken place, describing it in all its details, from the view out the windows to the color of the couch and the arrangement of the furniture in each of the various rooms. For a man to remember so precisely things he had seen only once, things which could not have had any bearing on his life except for a fleeting instant, struck A. with all the force of a supernatural act. He realized that for Ponge there was no division between the work of writing and the work of seeing. For no word can be written without first having been seen, and before it finds its way to the page it must first have been part of the body, a physical presence that one has lived with in the same way one lives with one's heart, one's stomach, and one's brain. Memory, then, not so much as the past contained within us, but as proof of our life in the present. If a man is to be truly present among his surroundings, he must be thinking not of himself, but of what he sees. He must forget himself in order to be there. And from that forgetfulness arises the power of memory. It is a way of living one's life so that nothing is ever lost.

It is also true that "the man with a good memory does not remember anything because he does not forget anything," as Beckett has written about Proust. And it is true that one must make a distinction between voluntary and involuntary memory, as Proust does during the course of his long novel about the past.

What A. feels he is doing, however, as he writes the pages of his own book, is something that does not belong to either one of these two types of memory. A. has both a good memory and a bad memory. He has lost much, but he has also retained much. As he writes, he feels that he is moving inward (through himself) and at the same time moving outward (toward the world). What he experienced, perhaps, during those few moments on Christmas Eve, 1979, as he sat alone in his room on Varick Street, was this: the sudden knowledge that came over him that even alone, in the deepest solitude of his room, he was not alone, or, more precisely, that the moment he began to try to speak of that solitude, he had become more than just himself. Memory, therefore, not simply as the resurrection of one's private past, but an immersion in the past of others, which is to say: history—which one both participates in and is a witness to, is a part of and apart from. Everything, therefore, is present in his mind at once, as if each element were reflecting the light of all the others, and at the same time emitting its own unique and unquenchable radiance. If there is any reason for him to be in this room now, it is because there is something inside him hungering to see it all at once, to savor the chaos of it in all its raw and urgent simultaneity. And yet, the telling of it is necessarily slow, a delicate business of trying to remember what has already been remembered. The pen will never be able to move fast enough to write down every word discovered in the space of memory. Some things have been lost forever, other things will perhaps be remembered again, and still other things have been lost and found and lost again. There is no way to be sure of any of this.

Possible epigraph(s) for The Book of Memory.

"Thoughts come at random, and go at random. No device for holding on to them or for having them. A thought has escaped: I was trying to write it down: instead I write that it has escaped me." (Pascal)

"As I write down my thought, it sometimes escapes me; but this makes me remember my own weakness, which I am constantly forgetting. This teaches me as much as my forgotten thought, for I strive only to know my own nothingness." (Pascal)

The Book of Memory. Book Ten.

When he speaks of the room, he does not mean to neglect the windows that are sometimes present in the room. The room need not be an image of hermetic consciousness, and when a man or a woman stands or sits alone in a room there is more that happens there, he realizes, than the silence of thought, the silence of a body struggling to put its thoughts into words. Nor does he mean to imply that only suffering takes place within the four walls of consciousness, as in the allusions made to Hölderlin and Emily Dickinson previously. He thinks, for example, of Vermeer's women, alone in their rooms, with the bright light of the real world pouring through a window, either open or closed, and the utter stillness of those solitudes, an almost heartbreaking evocation of the everyday and its domestic variables. He thinks, in particular, of a painting he saw on his trip to Amsterdam, *Woman in Blue*, which nearly immobilized him with contemplation in the Rijksmuseum. As one commentator has written: "The letter, the map, the woman's pregnancy, the empty chair, the open box, the unseen window—all are reminders or natural emblems of absence, of the unseen, of other minds, wills, times, and places, of past and future, of birth and perhaps of death—in general, of a world that extends beyond the edges of the frame, and of larger, wider horizons that encompass and impinge upon the scene suspended before our eyes. And yet it is the fullness and self-sufficiency of the present moment that Vermeer insists upon—with such conviction that its capacity to orient and contain is invested with metaphysical value."

Even more than the objects mentioned in this list, it is the quality of the light coming through the unseen window to the viewer's left that so warmly beckons him to turn his attention to the outside, to the world beyond the painting. A. stares hard at the woman's face, and as time passes he almost begins to hear the voice inside the woman's head as she reads the letter in her hands. She, so very pregnant, so tranquil in the immanence of motherhood, with the letter taken out of the box, no doubt being read for the hundredth time; and there, hanging on the wall to her right, a map of the world, which is the image of everything that exists outside the room: that light, pouring gently over her face and shining on her blue smock, the belly bulging with life, and its blueness bathed in luminosity, a light so pale it verges on whiteness. To follow with more of the same: *Woman Pouring Milk, Woman Holding a Balance, Woman Putting on Pearls, Young Woman at a Window with a Pitcher, Girl Reading a Letter at an Open Window.*

"The fullness and self-sufficiency of the present moment."

* * *

If it was Rembrandt and Titus who in some sense lured A. to Amsterdam, where he then entered rooms and found himself in the presence of women (Vermeer's women, Anne Frank), his trip to that city was at the same time conceived as a pilgrimage to his own past. Again, his inner movements were expressed in the form of paintings: an emotional state finding tangible representation in a work of art, as though another's solitude were in fact the echo of his own.

In this case it was Van Gogh, and the new museum that had been built to house his work. Like some early trauma buried in the unconscious, forever linking two unrelated objects (this shoe is my father; this rose is my mother), Van Gogh's paintings stand in his mind as an image of his adolescence, a translation of his deepest feelings of that period. He can even be quite precise about it, pinpointing events and his reactions to events by place and time (exact locations, exact moments: year, month, day, even hour and minute). What matters, however, is not so much the sequence of the chronicle as its consequences, its permanence in the space of memory. To remember, therefore, a day in April when he was sixteen, and cutting school with the girl he had fallen in love with: so passionately and hopelessly that the thought of it still smarts. To remember the train, and then the ferry to New York (that ferry, which has long since vanished: industrial iron, the warm fog, rust), and then going to a large exhibition of Van Gogh paintings. To remember how he had stood there, trembling with happiness, as if the shared seeing of these works had invested them with the girl's presence, had mysteriously varnished them with the love he felt for her.

Some days later, he began writing a sequence of poems (now lost) based on the canvases he had seen, each poem bearing the title of a different Van Gogh painting. These were the first real poems he ever wrote. More than a method for entering those paintings, the poems were an attempt to recapture the memory of that day. Many years went by, however, before he realized this. It was only in Amsterdam, studying the same paintings he had seen with the girl (seeing them for the first time since then—almost half his life ago), that he remembered having written those poems. At that moment the equation became clear to him: the act of writing as an act of memory. For the fact of the matter is, other than the poems themselves, he has not forgotten any of it.

Standing in the Van Gogh Museum in Amsterdam (December 1979) in front of the painting *The Bedroom*, completed in Arles, October 1888.

Van Gogh to his brother: "This time it is just simply my bedroom . . . To look at the picture ought to rest the brain or rather the imagination . . .

"The walls are pale violet. The floor is of red tiles.

"The wood of the bed and chairs is the yellow of fresh butter, the sheet and pillows very light lemon-green.

"The coverlet scarlet. The window green.

"The toilet table orange, the basin blue.

"The doors lilac.

"And that is all—there is nothing in this room with closed shutters. . . .

"This by way of revenge for the enforced rest I have been obliged to take. . . .

"I will make you sketches of the other rooms too some day."

As A. continued to study the painting, however, he could not help feeling that Van Gogh had done something quite different from what he thought he had set out to do. A.'s first impression was indeed a sense of calm, of "rest," as the artist describes it. But gradually, as he tried to inhabit the room presented on the canvas, he began to experience it as a prison, an impossible space, an image, not so much of a place to live, but of the mind that has been forced to live there. Observe carefully. The bed blocks one door, a chair blocks the other door, the shutters are closed: you can't get in, and once you are in, you can't get out. Stifled among the furniture and everyday objects of the room, you begin to hear a cry of suffering in this painting, and once you hear it, it does not stop. "I cried by reason of mine affliction . . . ." But there is no answer to this cry. The man in this painting (and this is a self-portrait, no different from a picture of a man's face, with eyes, nose, lips, and jaw) has been alone too much, has struggled too much in the depths of solitude. The world ends at that barricaded door. For the room is not a representation of solitude, it is the substance of solitude itself. And it is a thing so heavy, so unbreathable, that it cannot be shown in any terms other than what it is. "And that is all—there is nothing in this room with closed shutters. . . ."

Further commentary on the nature of chance.

A. arrived in London and departed from London, spending a few days on either end of his trip visiting with English friends. The girl of the ferry and the Van Gogh paintings was English (she had grown up in London, had lived in America from the age of about twelve to eighteen, and had then returned to London to go to art school), and on the first leg of his trip, A. spent several hours with her. Over the years since their graduation from high school, they had kept in touch at best fitfully, had seen each other perhaps five or six times. A. was long cured of his passion, but he had not dismissed her altogether from his mind, clinging somehow to the feeling of that passion, although she herself had lost importance for him. It had been several years since their last meeting, and now he found it gloomy, almost oppressive to be with her. She was still beautiful, he thought, and yet solitude seemed to enclose her, in the same way an egg encloses an unborn bird. She lived alone, had almost no friends. For many years she had been working on sculptures in wood, but she refused to show them to anyone. Each time she finished a piece, she would destroy it, and then begin on the next one. Again, A. had come face to face with a woman's solitude. But here it had turned in on itself and dried up at its source.

A day or two later, he went to Paris, eventually to Amsterdam, and afterwards back to London. He thought to himself: there will be no time to see her again. On one of those days before returning to New York, he was to have dinner with a friend (T., the same friend who had thought they might be cousins) and decided to spend the afternoon at the Royal Academy of Art, where a large exhibition of "Post Impressionist" paintings was on view. The enormous crush of visitors at the museum, however, made him reluctant to stay for the afternoon, as he had planned, and he found himself with three or four extra hours before his dinner appointment. He went to a cheap fish and chips place in Soho for lunch, trying to decide what to do with himself during this free time. He paid up his bill, left the restaurant, turned the corner, and there, as she stood gazing into the display window of a large shoe store, he saw her.

It was not every day that he ran into someone on the London streets (in that city of millions, he knew no more than a few people), and yet this encounter seemed perfectly natural to him, as though it were a commonplace event. He had been thinking about her only a moment before, regretting his decision not to call her, and now that she was there, suddenly standing before his eyes, he could not help feeling that he had willed her to appear.

He walked toward her and spoke her name.

Paintings. Or the collapse of time in images.

In the Royal Academy exhibition he had seen in London, there were several paintings by Maurice Denis. While in Paris, A. had visited the widow of the poet Jean Follain (Follain, who had died in a traffic accident in 1971, just days before A. had moved to Paris) in connection with an anthology of French poetry that A. was preparing, which in fact was what had brought him back to Europe. Madame Follain, he soon learned, was the daughter of Maurice Denis, and many of her father's paintings hung on the walls of the apartment. She herself was now in her late seventies, perhaps eighty, and A. was impressed by her Parisian toughness, her gravel voice, her devotion to her dead husband's work.

One of the paintings in the apartment bore a title: Madelaine à 18 mois (Madelaine at 18 months), which Denis had written out across the top of the canvas. This was the same Madelaine who had grown up to become Follain's wife and who had just asked A. to enter her apartment. For a moment, without being aware of it, she stood in front of that picture, which had been painted nearly eighty years before, and A. saw, as though leaping incredibly across time, that the child's face in the painting and the old woman's face before him were exactly the same. For that one instant, he felt he had cut through the illusion of human time and had experienced it for what it was: as no more than a blink of the eyes. He had seen an entire life standing before him, and it had been collapsed into that one instant.

O. to A. in conversation, describing what it felt like to have become an old man. O., now in his seventies, his memory failing, his face as wrinkled as a half-closed palm. Looking at A. and shaking his head with deadpan wit: "What a strange thing to happen to a little boy."

Yes, it is possible that we do not grow up, that even as we grow old, we remain the children we always were. We remember ourselves as we were then, and we feel ourselves to be the same. We made ourselves into what we are now then, and we remain what we were, in spite of the years. We do not change for ourselves. Time makes us grow old, but we do not change.

The Book of Memory. Book Eleven.

He remembers returning home from his wedding party in 1974, his wife beside him in her white dress, and taking the front door key out of his pocket, inserting the key in the lock, and then, as he turned his wrist, feeling the blade of the key snap off inside the lock.

He remembers that in the spring of 1966, not long after he met his future wife, one of the keys of her piano broke: F above Middle C. That summer the two of them traveled to a remote part of Maine. One day, as they walked through a nearly abandoned town, they wandered into an old meeting hall, which had not been used for years. Remnants of some men's society were scattered about the place: Indian headdresses, lists of names, the detritus of drunken gatherings. The hall was dusty and deserted, except for an upright piano that stood in one corner. His wife began to play (she played well) and discovered that all the keys worked except one: F above Middle C.

It was at that moment, perhaps, that A. realized the world would go on eluding him forever.

If a novelist had used these little incidents of broken piano keys (or the wedding day accident of losing the key inside the door), the reader would be forced to take note, to assume the novelist was trying to make some point about his characters or the world. One could speak of symbolic meanings, of subtext, or simply of formal devices (for as soon as a thing happens more than once, even if it is arbitrary, a pattern takes shape, a form begins to emerge). In a work of fiction, one assumes there is a conscious mind behind the words on the page. In the presence of happenings in the so-called real world, one assumes nothing. The made-up story consists entirely of meanings, whereas the story of fact is devoid of any significance beyond itself. If a man says to you, "I'm going to Jerusalem," you think to yourself: how nice, he's going to Jerusalem. But if a character in a novel were to speak those same words, "I'm going to Jerusalem," your response is not at all the same. You think, to begin with, of Jerusalem itself: its history, its religious role, its function as a mythical place. You would think of the past, of the present (politics; which is also to think of the recent past), and of the future—as in the phrase: "Next year in Jerusalem." On top of that, you would integrate these thoughts into whatever it is you already know about the character who is going to Jerusalem and use this new synthesis to draw further conclusions, refine perceptions, think more cogently about the book as a whole. And then, once the work is finished, the last page read and the book closed, interpretations begin: psychological, historical, sociological, structural, philological, religious, sexual, philosophical, either singly or in various combinations, depending on your bent. Although it is possible to interpret a real life according to any of these systems (people do, after all, go to priests and psychiatrists; people do sometimes try to understand their lives in terms of historical conditions), it does not have the same effect. Something is missing: the grandeur, the grasp of the general, the illusion of metaphysical truth. One says: Don Quixote is consciousness gone haywire in a realm of the imaginary. One looks at a mad person in the world (A. at his schizophrenic sister, for example), and says nothing. This is the sadness of a wasted life, perhaps—but no more.

Now and then, A. finds himself looking at a work of art with the same eyes he uses to look at the world. To read the imaginary in this way is to destroy it. He thinks, for example, of Tolstoy's description of the opera in *War and Peace*. Nothing is taken for granted in this passage, and therefore everything is reduced to absurdity. Tolstoy makes fun of what he sees simply by describing it. "In the second act there were cardboard monuments on the stage, and a round hole in the backdrop representing a moon. Shades had been put over the footlights and deep notes were played on the horns and contrabass as a number of people appeared from both sides of the stage wearing black cloaks and flourishing what looked like daggers. Then some other men ran onto the stage and began dragging away the maiden who had been in white and was now in pale blue. They did not take her away at once, but spent a long time singing with her, until at last they dragged her off, and behind the scenes something metallic was struck three times, and everyone knelt down and sang a prayer. All these actions were repeatedly interrupted by the enthusiastic shouts of the audience."

There is also the equal and opposite temptation to look at the world as though it were an extension of the imaginary. This, too, has sometimes happened to A., but he is loathe to accept it as a valid solution. Like everyone else, he craves a meaning. Like everyone else, his life is so fragmented that each time he sees a connection between two fragments he is tempted to look for a meaning in that connection. The connection exists. But to give it a meaning, to look beyond the bare fact of its existence, would be to build an imaginary world inside the real world, and he knows it would not stand. At his bravest moments, he embraces meaninglessness as the first principle, and then he understands that his obligation is to see what is in front of him (even though it is also inside him) and to say what he sees. He is in his room on Varick Street. His life has no meaning. The book he is writing has no meaning. There is the world, and the things one encounters in the world, and to speak of them is to be in the world. A key breaks off in a lock, and something has happened. That is to say, a key has broken off in a lock. The same piano seems to exist in two different places. A young man, twenty years later, winds up living in the same room where his father faced the horror of solitude. A man encounters his old love on a street in a foreign city. It means only what it is. Nothing more, nothing less. Then he writes: to enter this room is to vanish in a place where past and present meet. And then he writes: as in the phrase: "he wrote The Book of Memory in this room."

The invention of solitude.

He wants to say. That is to say, he means. As in the French, "vouloir dire," which means, literally, to want to say, but which means, in fact, to mean. He means to say what he wants. He wants to say what he means. He says what he wants to mean. He means what he says.

Vienna, 1919.

No meaning, yes. But it would be impossible to say that we are not haunted. Freud has described such experiences as "uncanny," or *unheimlich*—the opposite of *heimlich*, which means "familiar," "native," "belonging to the home." The implication, therefore, is that we are thrust out from the protective shell of our habitual perceptions, as though we were suddenly outside ourselves, adrift in a world we do not understand. By definition, we are lost in that world. We cannot even hope to find our way in it.

Freud argues that each stage of our development co-exists with all the others. Even as adults, we have buried within us a memory of the way we perceived the world as children. And not simply a memory of it: the structure itself is intact. Freud connects the experience of the uncanny with a revival of the egocentric, animistic world-view of childhood. "It would seem as though each one of us has been through a phase of individual development corresponding to that animistic stage in primitive men, that none of us has traversed it without certain traces of it which can be re-activated, and that everything which now strikes us as 'uncanny' fulfills the condition of stirring those vestiges of animistic mental activity within us and bringing them to expression." He concludes: "An uncanny experience occurs either when repressed infantile complexes have been revived by some impression, or when the primitive beliefs we have surmounted seem once more to be confirmed."

None of this, of course, is an explanation. At best it serves to describe the process, to point out the terrain on which it takes place. As such, A. is more than willing to accept it as true. Unhomeness, therefore, as a memory of another, much earlier home of the mind. In the same way a dream will sometimes resist interpretation until a friend suggests a simple, almost obvious meaning, A. cannot prove Freud's argument true or false, but it feels right to him, and he is more than willing to accept it. All the coincidences that seem to have been multiplying around him, then, are somehow connected with a memory of his childhood, as if by beginning to remember his childhood, the world were returning to a prior state of its being. This feels right to him. He is remembering his childhood, and it has appeared to him in the present in the form of these experiences. He is remembering his childhood, and it is writing itself out for him in the present. Perhaps that is what he means when he writes: "meaninglessness is the first principle." Perhaps that is what he means when he writes: "He means what he says." Perhaps that is what he means. And perhaps it is not. There is no way to be sure of any of this.

The invention of solitude. Or stories of life and death.

The story begins with the end. Speak or die. And for as long as you go on speaking, you will not die. The story begins with death. King Shehriyar has been cuckolded: "and they ceased not from kissing and clipping and clicketing and carousing." He retreats from the world, vowing never to succumb to feminine trickery again. Later, returning to his throne, he gratifies his physical desires by taking in women of the kingdom. Once satisfied, he orders their execution. "And he ceased not to do this for three years, till the land was stripped of marriageable girls, and all the women and mothers and fathers wept and cried out against the King, cursing him and complaining to the Creator of heaven and earth and calling for succor upon Him who heareth prayer and answereth those that cry to Him; and those that had daughters left fled with them, till at last there remained not a single girl in the city apt for marriage."

At this point, Shehrzad, the vizier's daughter, volunteers to go to the King. ("Her memory was stored with verses and stories and folklore and the sayings of Kings and sages, and she was wise, witty, prudent, and well-bred.") Her desperate father tries to dissuade her from going to this sure death, but she is unperturbed. "Marry me to this king, for either I will be the means of the deliverance of the daughters of the

Muslims from slaughter, or I will die and perish as others have perished." She goes off to sleep with the king and puts her plan into action: "to tell . . . delightful stories to pass away the watches of our night . . . ; it shall be the means of my deliverance and the ridding of the folk of this calamity, and by it I will turn the king from his custom."

The king agrees to listen to her. She begins her story, and what she tells is a story about story-telling, a story within which are several stories, each one, in itself, about story-telling—by means of which a man is saved from death.

Day begins to dawn, and mid-way through the first story-within-the-story, Shehrzad falls silent. "This is nothing to what I will tell tomorrow night," she says, "if the king let me live." And the king says to himself, "By Allah, I will not kill her, till I hear the rest of the story." So it goes for three nights, each night's story stopping before the end and spilling over into the beginning of the next night's story, by which time the first cycle of stories has ended and a new one begun. Truly, it is a matter of life and death. On the first night, Shehrzad begins with The Merchant and the Genie. A man stops to eat his lunch in a garden (an oasis in the desert), throws away a date stone, and behold "there started up before him a gigantic spirit, with a naked sword in his hand, who came up to him and said, 'Arise, that I may slay thee, even as thou hast slain my son.' 'How did I slay thy son?' asked the merchant, and the genie replied, 'When thou threwest away the date stone, it smote my son, who was passing at the time, on the breast, and he died forthright.' "

This is guilt out of innocence (echoing the fate of the marriageable girls in the kingdom), and at the same time the birth of enchantment—turning a thought into a thing, bringing the invisible to life. The merchant pleads his case, and the genie agrees to stay his execution. But in exactly one year the merchant must return to the same spot, where the genie will mete out the sentence. Already, a parallel is being drawn with Sherhzad's situation. She wishes to delay her execution, and by planting this idea in the king's mind she is pleading her case—but doing it in such a way that the king cannot recognize it. For this is the function of the story: to make a man see the thing before his eyes by holding up another thing to view.

The year passes, and the merchant, good to his word, returns to the garden. He sits down and begins to weep. An old man wanders by, leading a gazelle by a chain, and asks the merchant what is wrong. The old man is fascinated by what the merchant tells him (as if the merchant's life were a story, with a beginning, middle, and end, a fiction concocted by some other mind—which in fact it is), and decides to wait and see how it will turn out. Then another old man wanders by, leading two black dogs. The conversation is repeated, and then he, too, sits down and waits. Then a third old man wanders by, leading a dappled she-mule, and once again the same thing happens. Finally, the genie appears, in a "cloud of dust and a great whirling column from the heart of the desert." Just as he is about to drag off the merchant and slay him with his sword, "as thou slewest my son, the darling of my heart!," the first old man steps forward and says to the genie: "If I relate to thee my history with this gazelle and it seem to thee wonderful, wilt thou grant me a third of this merchant's blood?" Astonishingly, the genie agrees, just as the king has agreed to listen to Sherhzad's story: readily, without a struggle.

Note: the old man does not propose to defend the merchant as one would in a court of law, with arguments, counter-arguments, the presentation of evidence. This would be to make the genie look at the thing he already sees: and about this his mind has been made up. Rather, the old man wishes to turn him away from the facts, turn him away from thoughts of death, and in so doing delight him (literally, "to entice away," from the Latin *delectare*) into a new feeling for life, which in turn will make him renounce his obsession with killing the merchant. An obsession of this sort walls one up in solitude. One sees nothing but one's own thoughts. A story, however, in that it is not a logical argument, breaks down those walls. For it posits the existence of others and allows the listener to come into contact with them—if only in his thoughts.

The old man launches into a preposterous story. This gazelle you see before you, he says, is actually my wife. For thirty years she lived with me and in all that time she could not produce a son. (Again: an allusion to the absent child—the dead child, the child not yet born—referring the genie back to his own sorrow, but obliquely, as part of a world in which life stands equal to death.) "So I took me a concubine and had by her a son like the rising full moon with eyes and eyebrows of perfect beauty. . . ." When the boy was fifteen, the old man went off to another city (he, too, is a merchant), and in his absence the jealous wife used magic to transform the boy and his mother into a calf and a cow. "Thy slave died and her son ran away," the wife told him on his return. After a year of mourning, the cow was slaughtered as a sacrifice—through the machinations of the jealous wife. When the man was about to slaughter the calf a moment later, his heart failed him. "And when the calf saw me, he broke his halter and came up to me and fawned on me and moaned and wept, till I took pity on him and said . . . 'Bring me a cow and let this calf go.' " The herdsman's daughter, also learned in the art of magic, later discovered the true identity of the calf. After the merchant granted her the two things she asked for (to marry the son and to bewitch the jealous wife, by imprisoning her in the shape of a beast—"else I shall not be safe from her craft"), she returned the son to his original form. Nor does the story quite end there. The son's bride, the old man goes on to explain, "dwelt with us days and nights and nights and days, till God took her to Himself; and after her death, my son set out on a journey to the land of Ind, which is this merchant's native country; and after a while I took the gazelle and travelled with her from place to place, seeking news of my son, till chance led me to this garden, where I found this merchant sitting weeping; and this is my story." The genie agrees that this is a marvelous story and remits to the old man a third part of the merchant's blood.

One after the other, the two remaining old men propose the same bargain to the genie and begin their stories in the same way. "These two dogs are my elder brothers," says the second old man. "This mule was my wife," says the third. These opening sentences contain the essence of the entire project. For what does it mean to look at something, a real object in the real world, an animal, for example, and say that it is something other than what it is? It is to say that each thing leads a double life, at once in the world and in our minds, and that to deny either one of these lives is to kill the thing in both its lives at once. In the stories of the three old men, two mirrors face each other, each one reflecting the light of the other. Both are enchantments, both the real and the imaginary, and each exists by virtue of the other. And it is, truly, a matter of life and death. The first old man has come to the garden in search of his son; the genie has come to the garden to slay his son's unwitting killer. What the old man is telling him is that our sons are always invisible. It is the simplest of truths: a life belongs only to the person who lives it; life itself will claim the living; to live is to let live. And in the end, by means of these three stories, the merchant's life is spared.

This is how *The Thousand and One Nights* begins. At the end of the entire chronicle, after story after story after story, there is a specific result, and it carries with it all the unalterable gravity of a miracle.

Sherhzad has borne the king three sons. Again, the lesson is made clear. A voice that speaks, a woman's voice that speaks, a voice that speaks stories of life and death, has the power to give life.

" 'May I then make bold to crave a boon of thy Majesty?'

" 'Ask, O Sherhzad,' answered he, 'and it shall be given unto thee.'

"Whereupon she cried to the nurses and the eunuchs, saying, 'Bring me my children.'

"So they brought them to her in haste, and they were three male children, one walking, one crawling, and one sucking at the breast. She took them and, setting them before the king, kissed the ground and said, 'O King of the age, these are thy children and I crave that thou release me from the doom of death, for the sake of these infants.' "

When the king hears these words, he begins to weep. He gathers the little children up into his arms and declares his love for Sherhzad.

"So they decorated the city in splendid fashion, never before was seen the like thereof, and the drums beat and the pipes sounded, whilst all the mimes and mountebanks and players plied their various arts and the King lavished on them gifts and largesse. Moreover he gave alms to the poor and needy and extended his bounty to all his subjects and the people of his realm."

Mirror text.

If the voice of a woman telling stories has the power to bring children into the world, it is also true that a child has the power to bring stories to life. It is said that a man would go mad if he could not dream at night. In the same way, if a child is not allowed to enter the imaginary, he will never come to grips with the real. A child's need for stories is as fundamental as his need for food, and it manifests itself in the same way hunger does. Tell me a story, the child says. Tell me a story. Tell me a story, daddy, please. The father then sits down and tells a story to his son. Or else he lies down in the dark beside him, the two of them in the child's bed, and begins to speak, as if there were nothing left in the world but his voice, telling a story in the dark to his son. Often it is a fairy tale, or a tale of adventure. Yet often it is no more than a simple leap into the imaginary. Once upon a time there was a little boy named Daniel, A. says to his son named Daniel, and these stories in which the boy himself is the hero are perhaps the most satisfying to him of all. In the same way, A. realizes, as he sits in his room writing The Book of Memory, he speaks of himself as another in order to tell the story of himself. He must make himself absent in order to find himself there. And so he says A., even as he means to say I. For the story of memory is the story of seeing. And even if the things to be seen are no longer there, it is a story of seeing. The voice, therefore, goes on. And even as the boy closes his eyes and goes to sleep, his father's voice goes on speaking in the dark.

The Book of Memory. Book Twelve.

He can go no farther than this. Children have suffered at the hands of adults, for no reason whatsoever. Children have been abandoned, have been left to starve, have been murdered, for no reason whatsoever. It is not possible, he realizes, to go any farther than this.

"But then there are the children," says Ivan Karamazov, "and what am I to do with them?" And again: "I want to forgive. I want to embrace. I don't want any more suffering. And if the sufferings of children go to make up the sum of sufferings which is necessary for the purchase of truth, then I say beforehand that the entire truth is not worth such a price."

Every day, without the least effort, he finds it staring him in the face. These are the days of Cambodia's collapse, and everyday it is there, looking out at him from the newspaper, with the inevitable photographs of death: the emaciated children, the grownups with nothing left in their eyes. Jim Harrison, for example, an Oxfam engineer, noting in his diary: "Visited small clinic at kilometer 7. Absolutely no drugs or medicines—serious cases of starvation—clearly just dying for lack of food. . . . The hundreds of children were all marasmic—much skin disease, baldness, discolored hair and great fear in the whole population." Or later, describing what he saw on a visit to the 7th of January Hospital in Phnom Penh: ". . . terrible conditions—children in bed in filthy rags dying with starvation–no drugs—no food. . . . The TB allied to starvation gives the people a Belsen-like appearance. In one ward a boy of thirteen tied down to the bed because he was going insane—many children now orphans—or can't find families—and a lot of nervous twitches and spasms to be seen among the people. The face of one small boy of eighteen months was in a state of destruction by what appeared to be infected skin and flesh which had broken down under severe kwashiorkor—his eyes full of pus, held in the arms of his five-year-old sister . . . I find this sort of thing very tough to take—and this situation must be applicable to hundreds of thousands of Kampuchean people today."

Two weeks before reading these words, A. went out to dinner with a friend of his, P., a writer and editor for a large weekly news magazine. It so happens that she was handling the "Cambodia story" for her publication. Nearly everything written in the American and foreign press about the conditions there had passed before her eyes, and she told A. about a story written for a North Carolina newspaper—by a volunteer American doctor in one of the refugee camps across the Thai border. It concerned the visit of the American President's wife, Rosalynn Carter, to those camps. A. could remember the photographs that had been published in the newspapers and magazines (the First Lady embracing a Cambodian child, the First Lady talking to doctors), and in spite of everything he knew about America's responsibility for creating the conditions Mrs. Carter had come to protest, he had been moved by those pictures. It turned out that Mrs. Carter visited the camp where the American doctor was working. The camp hospital was a make-shift affair: a thatched roof, a few support beams, the patients lying on mats on the ground. The President's wife arrived, followed by a swarm of officials, reporters, and cameramen. There were too many of them, and as they trooped through the hospital, patients' hands were stepped on by heavy Western shoes, I.V. lines were disconnected by passing legs, bodies were inadvertently kicked. Perhaps this confusion was avoidable, perhaps not. In any case, after the visitors had completed their inspection, the American doctor made an appeal. Please, he said, would some of you spare a bit of your time to donate blood to the hospital; even the blood of the healthiest Cambodian is too thin to be of use; our supply has run out. But the First Lady's tour was behind schedule. There were other places to go that day, other suffering people to see. There was just no time, they said. Sorry. So very sorry. And then, as abruptly as they had come, the visitors left.

In that the world is monstrous. In that the world can lead a man to nothing but despair, and a despair so complete, so resolute, that nothing can open the door of this prison, which is hopelessness, A. peers through the bars of his cell and finds only one thought that brings him any consolation: the image of his son. And not just his son, but any son, any daughter, any child of any man or woman.

In that the world is monstrous. In that it seems to offer no hope of a future, A. looks at his son and realizes that he must not allow himself to despair. There is this responsibility for a young life, and in that he has brought this life into being, he must not despair. Minute by minute, hour by hour, as he remains in the presence of his son, attending to his needs, giving himself up to this young life, which is a continual injunction to remain in the present, he feels his despair evaporate. And even though he continues to despair, he does not allow himself to despair.

The thought of a child's suffering, therefore, is monstrous to him. It is even more monstrous than the monstrosity of the world itself. For it robs the world of its one consolation, and in that a world can be imagined without consolation, it is monstrous.

He can go no farther than this.

This is where it begins. He stands alone in an empty room and begins to cry. "It is too much for me, I cannot face it" (Mallarmé). "A Belsen-like appearance," as the engineer in Cambodia noted. And yes, that is the place where Anne Frank died.

"It's really a wonder," she wrote, just three weeks before her arrest, "that I haven't dropped all my ideals, because they seem so absurd and impossible to carry out. . . . I see the world gradually being turned into a wilderness, I hear the ever-approaching thunder, which will destroy us too, I can feel the sufferings of millions and yet, if I look up into the heavens, I think that it will all come right, that this cruelty too will end. . . ."

No, he does not mean to say that this is the only thing. He does not even pretend to say that it can be understood, that by talking about it and talking about it a meaning can be discovered for it. No, it is not the only thing, and life nevertheless continues, for some, if not for most. And yet, in that it is a thing that will forever escape understanding, he wants it to stand for him as the thing that will always come before the beginning. As in the sentences: "This is where it begins. He stands alone in an empty room and begins to cry."

Return to the belly of the whale.

"The word of the Lord came unto Jonah . . . saying, Arise, go to Ninevah, that great city, and cry against it. . . ."

In this command as well, Jonah's story differs from that of all the other prophets. For the Ninevites are not Jews. Unlike the other carriers of God's word, Jonah is not asked to address his own people, but foreigners. Even worse, they are the enemies of his people. Nineveh was the capital of Assyria, the most powerful empire in the world at that time. In the words of Nahum (whose prophecies have been preserved on the same scroll as the story of Jonah): "the bloody city . . . full of lies and rapine."

"Arise, go to Nineveh," God tells Jonah. Nineveh is to the east. Jonah promptly goes west, to Tarshish (Tartessus, on the farthest tip of Spain). Not only does he run away, he goes to the limit of the known world. This flight is not difficult to understand. Imagine an analogous case: a Jew being told to enter Germany during the Second World War and preach against the National Socialists. It is a thought that begs the impossible.

As early as the second century, one of the rabbinical commentators argued that Jonah boarded the ship to drown himself in the sea for the sake of Israel, not to flee from the presence of God. This is the political reading of the book, and Christian interpreters quickly turned it against the Jews. Theodore of Mopsuestia, for example, says that Jonah was sent to Nineveh because the Jews refused to listen to the prophets, and the book about Jonah was written to teach a lesson to the "stiff-necked people." Rupert of Deutz, however, another Christian interpreter (twelfth century), contends that the prophet refused God's command out of piety to his people, and for this reason God did not become very angry with Jonah. This echoes the opinion of Rabbi Akiba himself, who stated that "Jonah was jealous for the glory of the son (Israel) but not for the glory of the father (God)."

Nevertheless, Jonah finally agrees to go to Nineveh. But even after he delivers his message, even after the Ninevites repent and change their ways, even after God spares them, we learn that "it displeased Jonah exceedingly, and he was very angry." This is a patriotic anger. Why should the enemies of Israel be spared? It is at this point that God teaches Jonah the lesson of the book—in the parable of the gourd that follows.

"Doest thou well to be angry?" he asks. Jonah then removes himself to the outskirts of Nineveh, "till he might see what would become of the city"—implying that he still felt there was a chance Nineveh would be destroyed, or that he hoped the Ninevites would revert to their sinful ways and bring down punishment on themselves. God prepares a gourd (a castor plant) to protect Jonah from the sun, and "Jonah was exceedingly glad of the gourd." But by the next morning God has made the plant wither away. A vehement east wind blows, a fierce sun beats down on Jonah, and "he fainted, and wished himself to die, and said, it is better for me to die than to live"—the same words he had used earlier, indicating that the message of this parable is the same as in the first part of the book. "And God said to Jonah, Doest thou well to be angry for the gourd? And he said, I do well to be angry, even unto death. Then said the Lord, Thou hast had pity on the gourd, for which thou has not labored, neither madest it grow; which came up in a night and perished in a night; And should I not spare Ninevah, that great city, wherein are more than sixscore thousand persons that cannot discern between their right hand and their left hand; and also much cattle?"

These sinners, these heathen—and even the beasts that belong to them—are as much God's creatures as the Hebrews. This is a startling and original notion, especially considering the date of the story—eighth century B.C. (the time of Heraclitus). But this, finally, is the essence of what the rabbis have to teach. If there is to be any justice at all, it must be a justice for everyone. No one can be excluded, or else there is no such thing as justice. The conclusion is inescapable. This tiniest of books, which tells the curious and even comical story of Jonah, occupies a central place in the liturgy: it is read each year in the synagogue on Yom Kippur, the Day of Atonement, which is the most solemn day on the Jewish calendar. For everything, as has been noted before, is connected to everything else. And if there is everything, then it follows there is everyone. He does not forget Jonah's last words: "I do well to be angry, even unto death." And still, he finds himself writing these words on the page before him. If there is everything, then it follows there is everyone.

The words rhyme, and even if there is no real connection between them, he cannot help thinking of them together. Room and tomb, tomb and womb, womb and room. Breath and death. Or the fact that the letters of the word "live" can be rearranged to spell out the word "evil." He knows this is no more than a schoolboy's game. Surprisingly, however, as he writes the word "schoolboy," he can remember himself at eight or nine years old, and the sudden sense of power he felt in himself when he discovered he could play with words in this way—as if he had accidentally found a secret path to the truth: the absolute, universal, and unshakeable truth that lies hidden at the center of the world. In his schoolboy enthusiasm, of course, he had neglected to consider the existence of languages other than English, the great Babel of tongues buzzing and battling in the world outside his schoolboy life. And how can the absolute and unshakeable truth change from language to language?

Still, the power of rhyming words, of word transformations, cannot altogether be dismissed. The feeling of magic remains, even if it cannot be connected with a search for the truth, and this same magic, these same correspondences between words, are present in every language, even though the particular combinations are different. At the heart of each language there is a network of rhymes, assonances, and overlapping meanings, and each of these occurrences functions as a kind of bridge that joins opposite and contrasting aspects of the world with one another. Language, then, not simply as a list of separate things to be added up and whose sum total is equal to the world. Rather, language as it is laid out in the dictionary: an infinitely complex organism, all of whose elements—cells and sinews, corpuscles and bones, digits and fluids—are present in the world simultaneously, none of which can exist on its own. For each word is defined by other words, which means that to enter any part of language is to enter the whole of it. Language, then, as a monadology, to echo the term used by Leibniz. ("Since all is a plenum, all matter is connected and all movement in the plenum produces some effect on the distant bodies, in proportion to the distance. Hence every body is affected not only by those with which it is in contact, and thus feels in some way everything that happens to them; but through them it also feels those that touch the ones with which it is in immediate contact. Hence it follows that this communication extends over any distance whatever. Consequently, every body experiences everything that goes on in the universe, so much so that he who sees everything might read in any body what is happening anywhere, and even what has happened or will happen. He would be able to observe in the present what is remote in both time and space. . . . A soul, however, can read in itself only what is directly represented in it; it is unable to unfold all at once all its folds; for these go on into infinity.")

Playing with words in the way A. did as a schoolboy, then, was not so much a search for the truth as a search for the world as it appears in language. Language is not truth. It is the way we exist in the world. Playing with words is merely to examine the way the mind functions, to mirror a particle of the world as the mind perceives it. In the same way, the world is not just the sum of the things that are in it. It is the infinitely complex network of connections among them. As in the meanings of words, things take on meaning only in relationship to each other. "Two faces are alike," writes Pascal. "Neither is funny by itself, but side by side their likeness makes us laugh." The faces rhyme for the eye, just as two words can rhyme for the ear. To carry the proposition one step further, A. would contend that it is possible for events in one's life to rhyme as well. A young man rents a room in Paris and then discovers that his father had hid out in this same room during the war. If these two events were to be considered separately, there would be little to say about either one of them. The rhyme they create when looked at together alters the reality of each. Just as two physical objects, when brought into proximity of each other, give off electromagnetic forces that not only effect the molecular structure of each but the space between them as well, altering, as it were, the very environment, so it is that two (or more) rhyming events set up a connection in the world, adding one more synapse to be routed through the vast plenum of experience.

These connections are commonplace in literary works (to return to that argument), but one tends not to see them in the world—for the world is too big and one's life is too small. It is only at those rare moments when one happens to glimpse a rhyme in the world that the mind can leap out of itself and serve as a bridge for things across time and space, across seeing and memory. But there is more to it than just rhyme. The grammar of existence includes all the figures of language itself: simile, metaphor, metonymy, synecdoche—so that each thing encountered in the world is actually many things, which in turn give way to many other things, depending on what these things are next to, contained by, or removed from. Often, too, the second term of a comparison is missing. It can be forgotten, or buried in the unconscious, or somehow made unavailable. "The past is hidden," Proust writes in an important passage of his novel, "beyond the reach of intellect, in some material object (in the sensation which that material object will give us) which we do not suspect. And as for that object, it depends on chance whether we come upon it or not before we ourselves must die." Everyone has experienced in one way or another the strange sensations of forgetfulness, the mystifying force of the missing term. I walked into that room, a man will say, and the oddest feeling came over me, as if I had been there before, although I cannot remember it at all. As in Pavlov's experiments with dogs (which, at the simplest possible level, demonstrate the way in which the mind can make a connection between two dissimilar things, eventually forget the first thing, and thereby turn one thing into another thing), something has happened, although we are at a loss to say what it is. What A. is struggling to express, perhaps, is that for some time now none of the terms has been missing for him. Wherever his eye or mind seems to stop, he discovers another connection, another bridge to carry him to yet another place, and even in the solitude of his room, the world has been rushing in on him at a dizzying speed, as if it were all suddenly converging in him and happening to him at once. Coincidence: to fall on with; to occupy the same place in time or space. The mind, therefore, as that which contains more than itself. As in the phrase from Augustine: "But where is the part of it which it does not itself contain?"

Second return to the belly of the whale.

"When he recovered his senses the Marionette could not remember where he was. Around him all was darkness, a darkness so deep and so black that for a moment he thought he had been dipped head first into an inkwell."

This is Collodi's description of Pinocchio's arrival in the belly of the shark. It would have been one thing to write it in the ordinary way: "a darkness as black as ink"—as a trite literary flourish to be forgotten the moment it is read. But something different is happening here, something that transcends the question of good or bad writing (and this is manifestly not bad writing). Take careful note: Collodi makes no comparisons in this passage; there is no "as if," no "like," nothing to equate or contrast one thing with another. The image of absolute darkness immediately gives way to an image of an inkwell. Pinocchio has just entered the belly of the shark. He does not know yet that Gepetto is also there. Everything, at least for this brief moment, has been lost. Pinocchio is surrounded by the darkness of solitude. And it is in this darkness, where the puppet will eventually find the courage to save his father and thereby bring about his transformation into a real boy, that the essential creative act of the book takes place.

By plunging his marionette into the darkness of the shark, Collodi is telling us, he is dipping his pen into the darkness of his inkwell. Pinocchio, after all, is only made of wood. Collodi is using him as the instrument (literally, the pen) to write the story of himself. This is not to indulge in primitive psychologizing. Collodi could not have achieved what he does in *Pinocchio* unless the book was for him a book of memory. He was over fifty years old when he sat down to write it, recently retired from an undistinguished career in government service, which had been marked, according to his nephew, "neither by zeal nor by punctuality nor by subordination." No less than Proust's novel in search of lost time, his story is a search for his lost childhood. Even the name he chose to write under was an evocation of the past. His real name was Carlo Lorenzini. Collodi was the name of the small town where his mother had been born and where he spent his holidays as a young child. About this childhood, a few facts are available. He was a teller of tall tales, admired by his friends for his ability to fascinate them with stories. According to his brother Ippolito, "He did it so well and with such mimickry that half the world took delight and the children listened to him with their mouths agape." In an autobiographical sketch written late in life, long after the completion of *Pinocchio*, Collodi leaves little doubt that he conceived of himself as the puppet's double. He portrays himself as a prankster and a clown—eating cherries in class and stuffing the pits into a schoolmate's pockets, catching flies and putting them into someone else's ears, painting figures on the clothes of the boy in front of him: in general, creating havoc for everyone. Whether or not this is true is beside the point. Pinocchio was Collodi's surrogate, and after the puppet had been created, Collodi saw himself as Pinocchio. The puppet had become the image of himself as a child. To dip the puppet into the inkwell, therefore, was to use his creation to write the story of himself. For it is only in the darkness of solitude that the work of memory begins.

Possible epigraph(s) for The Book of Memory.

"We ought surely to look in the child for the first traces of imaginative activity. The child's best loved and most absorbing occupation is play. Perhaps we may say that every child at play behaves like an imaginative writer, in that he creates a world of his own or, more truly, he rearranges the things of his world and orders it in a new way. . . . It would be incorrect to think that he does not take this world seriously; on the contrary, he takes his play very seriously and expends a great deal of emotion on it." (Freud)

"You will not forget that the stress laid on the writer's memories of his childhood, which perhaps seem so strange, is ultimately derived from the hypothesis that imaginative creation, like day dreaming, is a continuation of and substitute for the play of childhood." (Freud)

He watches his son. He watches the little boy move around the room and listens to what he says. He sees him playing with his toys and hears him talking to himself. Each time the boy picks up an object, or pushes a truck across the floor, or adds another block to the tower of blocks growing before him, he speaks of what he is doing, in the same way a narrator in a film would speak, or else he makes up a story to accompany the actions he has set in motion. Each movement engenders a word, or a series of words; each word triggers off another movement: a reversal, a continuation, a new set of movements and words. There is no fixed center to any of this ("a universe in which the center is everywhere, the circumference nowhere") except perhaps the child's consciousness, which is itself a constantly shifting field of perceptions, memories, and utterances. There is no law of nature that cannot be broken: trucks fly, a block becomes a person, the dead are resurrected at will. From one thing, the child's mind careens without hesitation to another thing. Look, he says, my broccoli is a tree. Look, my potatoes are a cloud. Look at the cloud, it's a man. Or else, feeling the food as it touches his tongue, and looking up, with a sly glint in his eyes: "Do you know how Pinocchio and his father escape from the shark?" Pause, letting the question sink in. Then, in a whisper: "They tiptoe quietly over his tongue."

It sometimes seems to A. that his son's mental perambulations while at play are an exact image of his own progress through the labyrinth of his book. He has even thought that if he could somehow make a diagram of his son at play (an exhaustive description, containing every shift, association, and gesture) and then make a similar diagram of his book (elaborating what takes place in the gaps between words, the interstices of the syntax, the blanks between sections—in other words, unraveling the spool of connections), the two diagrams would be the same: the one would fit perfectly over the other.

During the time he has worked on The Book of Memory, it has given him special pleasure to watch the boy remember. Like all preliterate beings, the boy's memory is astonishing. The capacity for detailed observation, for seeing an object in its singularity, is almost boundless.

Written language absolves one of the need to remember much of the world, for the memories are stored in the words. The child, however, standing in a place before the advent of the written word, remembers in the same way Cicero would recommend, in the same way devised by any number of classical writers on the subject: image wed to place. One day, for example (and this is only one example, plucked from a myriad of possibilities), A. and his son were walking down the street. They ran into a nursery school playmate of the boy's standing outside a pizza parlor with his father. A.'s son was delighted to see his friend, but the other boy seemed to shy away from the encounter. Say hello, Kenny, his father urged him, and the boy managed to summon forth a feeble greeting. Then A. and his son continued on their walk. Three or four months later, they happened to be walking past the same spot together. A. suddenly heard his son muttering to himself, in a barely audible voice: Say hello, Kenny, say hello. It occurred to A. that if in some sense the world imprints itself on our minds, it is equally true that our experiences are imprinted on the world. For that brief moment, as they walked by the pizza parlor, the boy was literally seeing his own past. The past, to repeat the words of Proust, is hidden in some material object. To wander about in the world, then, is also to wander about in ourselves. That is to say, the moment we step into the space of memory, we walk into the world.

It is a lost world. And it strikes him to realize that it will be lost forever. The boy will forget everything that has happened to him so far. There will be nothing left but a kind of after-glow, and perhaps not even that. All the thousands of hours that A. has spent with him during the first three years of his life, all the millions of words he has spoken to him, the books he has read to him, the meals he has made for him, the tears he has wiped for him—all these things will vanish from the boy's memory forever.

The Book of Memory. Book Thirteen.

He remembers that he gave himself a new name, John, because all cowboys were named John, and that each time his mother addressed him by his real name he would refuse to answer her. He remembers running out of the house and lying in the middle of the road with his eyes shut, waiting for a car to run him over. He remembers that his grandfather gave him a large photograph of Gabby Hayes and that it sat in a place of honor on the top of his bureau. He remembers thinking the world was flat. He remembers learning how to tie his shoes. He remembers that his father's clothes were kept in the closet in his room and that it was the noise of hangers clicking together in the morning that would wake him up. He remembers the sight of his father knotting his tie and saying to him, Rise and shine little boy. He remembers wanting to be a squirrel, because he wanted to be light like a squirrel and have a bushy tail and be able to jump from tree to tree as though he were flying. He remembers looking through the venetian blinds and seeing his newborn sister coming home from the hospital in his mother's arms. He remembers the nurse in a white dress who sat beside his baby sister and gave him little squares of Swiss chocolate. He remembers that she called them Swiss although he did not know what that meant. He remembers lying in his bed at dusk in midsummer and looking at the tree through his window and seeing different faces in the configuration of the branches. He remembers sitting in the bathtub and pretending that his knees were mountains and that the white soap was an ocean liner. He remembers the day his father gave him a plum and told him to go outside and ride his tricycle. He remembers that he did not like the taste of the plum and that he threw it into the gutter and was overcome by a feeling of guilt. He remembers the day his mother took him and his friend B. to the television studio in Newark to see a showing of Junior Frolics. He remembers that Uncle Fred had makeup on his face, just like his mother wore, and that he was surprised by this. He remembers that the cartoons were shown on a little television set, no bigger than the one at home, and the disappointment he felt was so crushing that he wanted to stand up and shout his protests to Uncle Fred. He remembers that he had been expecting to see Farmer Gray and Felix the Cat run around on a stage, as large as life, going at each other with real pitchforks and rakes. He remembers that B.'s favorite color was green and that he claimed his teddy bear had green blood running through its veins. He remembers that B. lived with both his grandmothers and that to get to B.'s room you had to go through an upstairs sitting room where the two white-haired women spent all their time watching television. He remembers that he and B. would go scavenging through the bushes and backyards of the neighborhood looking for dead animals. He remembers burying them by the side of his house, deep in the darkness of the ivy, and that mostly they were birds, little birds like sparrows and robins and wrens. He remembers building crosses for them out of twigs and saying a prayer over their bodies as he and B. laid them in the hole they had dug in the ground, the dead eyes touching the loose damp earth. He remembers taking apart the family radio one afternoon with a hammer and screwdriver and explaining to his mother that he had done it as a scientific experiment. He remembers these were the words he used and that his mother spanked him. He remembers trying to chop down a small fruit tree in the back yard with a dull axe he had found in the garage and managing to make no more than a few dents in it. He remembers seeing the green on the underside of the bark and getting spanked for that too. He remembers sitting at his desk in the first grade away from the other children because he had been punished for talking in class. He remembers sitting at that desk and reading a book with a red cover and red illustrations with green-blue backgrounds. He remembers the teacher coming up to him from behind and very gently putting her hand on his shoulder and whispering a question into his ear. He remembers that she was wearing a white sleeveless blouse and that her arms were thick and covered with freckles. He remembers colliding with another boy during a softball game in the schoolyard and being thrown to the ground so violently that for the next five or ten minutes he saw everything as in a photographic negative. He remembers getting to his feet and walking toward the school building and thinking to himself, I'm going blind. He remembers how his panic gradually turned to acceptance and even fascination in the space of those few minutes and how, when his normal sight returned to him, he had the feeling that some extraordinary thing had taken place inside him. He remembers wetting his bed long after it was an acceptable thing to do and the icy sheets when he woke up in the morning. He remembers being invited for the first time to sleep over at a friend's house and how he stayed awake all night for fear of wetting the bed and humiliating himself, staring at the luminescent green hands of the watch he had been given for his sixth birthday. He remembers studying the illustrations in a children's Bible and accepting the fact that God had a long white beard. He remembers thinking that the voice he heard inside himself was the voice of God. He remembers going to the circus at Madison Square Garden with his grandfather and taking a ring off the finger of an eight and a half foot giant at the sideshow for fifty cents. He remembers keeping the ring on the top of his bureau beside the photograph of Gabby Hayes and that he could put four of his fingers through it. He remembers speculating that perhaps the entire world was enclosed in a glass jar and that it sat on a shelf next to dozens of other jar-worlds in the pantry of a giant's house. He remembers refusing to sing Christmas carols at school because he was Jewish and staying behind in the classroom while the other children went to rehearse in the auditorium. He remembers coming home from the first day of Hebrew school wearing a new suit and being pushed into a creek by older boys in leather jackets who called him a Jew shit. He remembers writing his first book, a detective story he composed with green ink. He remembers thinking that if Adam and Eve were the first people in the world, then everyone was related to everyone else. He remembers wanting to throw a penny out the window of his grandparents' apartment on Columbus Circle and his grandmother telling him that it would go straight through someone's head. He remembers looking down from the top of the Empire State Building and being surprised that the taxicabs were still yellow. He remembers visiting the Statue of Liberty with his mother and remembers that she got very nervous inside the torch and made him go back down the stairs sitting, one step at a time. He remembers the boy who was killed by lightning on a hike at summer camp. He remembers lying there in the rain next to him and seeing the boy's lips turn blue. He remembers his grandmother telling him how she remembered coming to America from Russia when she was five years old. He remembers that she told him she remembered waking up from a deep sleep and finding herself in the arms of a soldier who was carrying her onto a ship. He remembers that she told him this was the only thing she could remember.

The Book of Memory. Later that evening.

Not long after writing the words, "this was the only thing she could remember," A. stood up from his table and left his room. Walking along the street, feeling drained by his efforts that day, he decided to go on walking for a while. Darkness came. He stopped for supper, spread out a newspaper on the table before him, and then, after paying his bill, decided to spend the rest of the evening at the movies. It took him nearly an hour to walk to the theater. As he was about to buy his ticket, he changed his mind, put the money back in his pocket, and walked away. He retraced his steps, following the same route that had taken him there in reverse. At some point along the way he stopped to drink a glass of beer. Then he continued on his walk. It was nearly twelve when he opened the door of his room.

That night, for the first time in his life, he dreamed that he was dead.

Twice he woke up during the dream, trembling with panic. Each time, he tried to calm himself down, told himself that by changing position in bed the dream would end, and each time, upon falling back to sleep, the dream started up again at precisely the spot it had left off.

It was not exactly that he was dead, but that he was going to die. This was certain, an absolute and immanent fact. He was lying in a hospital bed, suffering from a fatal disease. His hair had fallen out in patches, and his head was half bald. Two nurses dressed in white walked into the room and told him: "Today you are going to die. It's too late to help you." They were almost mechanical in their indifference to him. He cried and pleaded with them, "I'm too young to die, I don't want to die now." "It's too late," the nurses answered. "We have to shave your head now." With tears pouring from his eyes, he allowed them to shave his head. Then they said: "The coffin is over there. Just go and lie down in it, close your eyes, and soon you'll be dead." He wanted to run away. But he knew that it was not permitted to disobey their orders. He went over to the coffin and climbed into it. The lid was closed over him, but once inside he kept his eyes open.

Then he woke up for the first time.

After he went back to sleep, he was climbing out of the coffin. He was dressed in a white patient's gown and had no shoes on. He left the room, wandered for a long time through many corridors, and then walked out of the hospital. Soon afterwards, he was knocking on the door of his ex-wife's house. "I have to die today," he told her, "there's nothing I can do about it." She took this news calmly, acting much as the nurses had. But he was not there for her sympathy. He wanted to give her instructions about what to do with his manuscripts. He went through a long list of his writings and told her how and where to have each of them published. Then he said: "The Book of Memory isn't finished yet. There's nothing I can do about it. There won't be time to finish. You finish it for me and then give it to Daniel. I trust you. You finish it for me." She agreed to do this, but without much enthusiasm. And then he began to cry, just as he had before: "I'm too young to die. I don't want to die now." But she patiently explained to him that if it had to be, then he should accept it. Then he left her house and returned to the hospital. When he reached the parking lot, he woke up for the second time.

After he went back to sleep, he was inside the hospital again, in a basement room next to the morgue. The room was large, bare, and white, a kind of old-fashioned kitchen. A group of his childhood friends, now grownups, were sitting around a table eating a large and sumptuous meal. They all turned and stared at him when he entered the room. He explained to them: "Look, they've shaved my head. I have to die today, and I don't want to die." His friends were moved by this. They invited him to sit down and eat with them. "No," he said, "I can't eat with you. I have to go into the next room and die." He pointed to a white swinging door with a circular window in it. His friends stood up from their chairs and joined him by the door. For a little while they all reminisced about their childhood together. It soothed him to talk to them, but at the same time he found it all the more difficult to summon the courage to walk through the door. Finally, he announced: "I have to go now. I have to die now." One by one, with tears pouring down his cheeks, he embraced his friends, squeezing them with all his strength, and said good-bye.

Then he woke up for the last time.

Concluding sentences for The Book of Memory.

From a letter by Nadezhda Mandelstam to Osip Mandelstam, dated 10/22/38, and never sent.

"I have no words, my darling, to write this letter . . . I am writing it into empty space. Perhaps you will come back and not find me here. Then this will be all you have left to remember me by. . . . Life can last so long. How hard and long for each of us to die alone. Can this fate be for us who are inseparable? Puppies and children, did we deserve this? Did you deserve this, my angel? Everything goes on as before. I know nothing. Yet I know everything—each day and hour of your life are plain and clear to me as in a delirium—In my last dream I was buying food for you in a filthy hotel restaurant. The people with me were total strangers. When I had bought it, I realized I did not know where to take it, because I do not know where you are. . . . When I woke up, I said to Shura: 'Osia is dead.' I do not know whether you are still alive, but from the time of that dream, I have lost track of you. I do not know where you are. Will you hear me? Do you know how much I love you? I could never tell you how much I love you. I cannot tell you even now. I speak to you, only to you. You are with me always, and I who was such a wild and angry one and never learned to weep simple tears—now I weep and weep and weep . . . It's me: Nadia. Where are you?"

* * *

He lays out a piece of blank paper on the table before him and writes these words with his pen.

The sky is blue and black and gray and yellow. The sky is not there, and it is red. All this was yesterday. All this was a hundred years ago. The sky is white. It smells of the earth, and it is not there. The sky is white like the earth, and it smells of yesterday. All this was tomorrow. All this was a hundred years from now. The sky is lemon and rose and lavender. The sky is the earth. The sky is white, and it is not there.

He wakes up. He walks back and forth between the table and the window. He sits down. He stands up. He walks back and forth between the bed and the chair. He lies down. He stares at the ceiling. He closes his eyes. He opens his eyes. He walks back and forth between the table and the window.

He finds a fresh sheet of paper. He lays it out on the table before him and writes these words with his pen.

It was. It will never be again. Remember.

1980–1981

REFERENCES

(Sources of quotations not mentioned in text)

page 68 "Israel Lichtenstein's Last Testament." In *A Holocaust Reader*, edited by Lucy S. Dawidowicz. Behrman House. New York, 1976.

page 71 Flaubert. *The Letters of Gustave Flaubert*, selected, edited, and translated by Francis Steegmuller. Harvard University Press. Cambridge, 1979.

page 78 Marina Tsvetayeva. Quotations of translations by Elaine Feinstein. In *Marina Tsvetayeva: Selected Poems*. Oxford University Press, 1971.

page 78 Gregory I. Altschuller, M.D. *Marina Tsvetayeva: A Physician's Memoir*. In SUN. Volume IV, Number 3: Winter, 1980. New York.

page 80 Christopher Wright. In *Rembrandt and His Art*. Galahad Books. New York, 1975.

page 81 Hölderlin. Prose quotations translated by Michael Hamburger. In *Friedrich Hölderlin: Poems and Fragments*. University of Michigan Press. Ann Arbor, 1966.

page 82 Hölderlin. *To Zimmer*. Translated by John Riley and Tim Longville. In *What I Own: Versions of Hölderlin*. Grosseteste Review Press, 1973.

page 108 B. = André du Bouchet. In *Hölderlin Aujourd'hui*, a lecture delivered in Stuttgart, 1970.

page 110 Collodi. *The Adventures of Pinocchio*. Translated by Carol Della Chiesa. Macmillan. New York, 1925. All further quotations from this edition. Translations sometimes slightly adapted.

page 119 Edward A. Snow. *A Study of Vermeer*. University of California Press. Berkeley, 1979.

page 121 Van Gogh. *The Letters of Vincent Van Gogh*. Edited by Mark Roskill. Atheneum. New York, 1972.

page 125 Tolstoy. Ann Dunnigan's translation of *War and Peace*. New American Library. New York, 1968.

page 126 Freud. "The 'Uncanny." In *On Creativity and the Unconscious*. Harper and Row. New York, 1958.

page 127 *The Thousand and One Nights*. All quotations from *The Portable Arabian Nights*. Translated by John Payne. Edited by Joseph Campbell. Viking. New York, 1952.

page 132 Dostoyevsky. *The Brothers Karamazov*. Translated by David Magarshack. Penguin. Baltimore, 1958.

page 132 Jim Harrison. Quoted in "The End of Cambodia?" by William Shawcross. *The New York Review of Books*. January 24, 1980.

page 134 Anne Frank. *The Diary of a Young Girl*. Doubleday. New York, 1952.

page 135 Quotations of commentaries on the Book of Jonah from "Jonah, or the Unfulfilled Prophecy" in *Four Strange Books of the Bible*, by Elias Bickerman. Schocken. New York, 1967.

page 137 Leibniz. In *Monadology and Other Philosophical Essays*. Translated by Paul Schrecker and Anne Martin Schrecker. Bobbs-Merrill. Indianapolis, 1965.

page 138 Proust. *Swann's Way*. Translated by C.K. Scott Moncrieff. Random House. New York, 1928.

page 140 Freud. "The Relation of the Poet to Day-Dreaming." In *On Creativity and the Unconscious*.

page 147 Nadezhda Mandelstam. *Hope Abandoned*. Translated by Max Hayward. Collins & Harvill. London, 1974.

HAND TO MOUTH

A Chronicle of Early Failure

In my late twenties and early thirties, I went through a period of several years when everything I touched turned to failure. My marriage ended in divorce, my work as a writer foundered, and I was overwhelmed by money problems. I'm not just talking about an occasional shortfall or some periodic belt tightenings—but a constant, grinding, almost suffocating lack of money that poisoned my soul and kept me in a state of never-ending panic.

There was no one to blame but myself. My relationship to money had always been flawed, enigmatic, full of contradictory impulses, and now I was paying the price for refusing to take a clear-cut stand on the matter. All along, my only ambition had been to write. I had known that as early as sixteen or seventeen years old, and I had never deluded myself into thinking I could make a living at it. Becoming a writer is not a "career decision" like becoming a doctor or a policeman. You don't choose it so much as get chosen, and once you accept the fact that you're not fit for anything else, you have to be prepared to walk a long, hard road for the rest of your days. Unless you turn out to be a favorite of the gods (and woe to the man who banks on that), your work will never bring in enough to support you, and if you mean to have a roof over your head and not starve to death, you must resign yourself to doing other work to pay the bills. I understood all that, I was prepared for it, I had no complaints. In that respect, I was immensely lucky. I didn't particularly want anything in the way of material goods, and the prospect of being poor didn't frighten me. All I wanted was a chance to do the work I felt I had it in me to do.

Most writers lead double lives. They earn good money at legitimate professions and carve out time for their writing as best they can: early in the morning, late at night, weekends, vacations. William Carlos Williams and Louis-Ferdinand Céline were doctors. Wallace Stevens worked for an insurance company. T. S. Eliot was a banker, then a publisher. Among my own acquaintances, the French poet Jacques Dupin is codirector of an art gallery in Paris. William Bronk, the American poet, managed his family's coal and lumber business in upstate New York for over forty years. Don DeLillo, Peter Carey, Salman Rushdie, and Elmore Leonard all worked for long stretches in advertising. Other writers teach. That is probably the most common solution today, and with every major university and Podunk college offering so-called creative writing courses, novelists and poets are continually scratching and scrambling to land themselves a spot. Who can blame them? The salaries might not be big, but the work is steady and the hours are good.

My problem was that I had no interest in leading a double life. It's not that I wasn't willing to work, but the idea of punching a clock at some nine-to-five job left me cold, utterly devoid of enthusiasm. I was in my early twenties, and I felt too young to settle down, too full of other plans to waste my time earning more money than I either wanted or needed. As far as finances went, I just wanted to get by. Life was cheap in those days, and with no responsibility for anyone but myself, I figured I could scrape along on an annual income of roughly three thousand dollars.

I tried graduate school for a year, but that was only because Columbia offered me a tuition-free fellowship with a two-thousand-dollar stipend—which meant that I was actually paid to study. Even under those ideal conditions, I quickly understood that I wanted no part of it. I had had enough of school, and the prospect of spending another five or six years as a student struck me as a fate worse than death. I didn't want to talk about books anymore, I wanted to write them. Just on principle, it felt wrong to me for a writer to hide out in a university, to surround himself with too many like-minded people, to get too comfortable. The risk was complacency, and once that happens to a writer, he's as good as lost.

I'm not going to defend the choices I made. If they weren't practical, the truth was that I didn't want to be practical. What I wanted were new experiences. I wanted to go out into the world and test myself, to move from this to that, to explore as much as I could. As long as I kept my eyes open, I figured that whatever happened to me would be useful, would teach me things I had never known before. If this sounds like a rather old-fashioned approach, perhaps it was. Young writer bids farewell to family and friends and sets out for points unknown to discover what he's made of. For better or worse, I doubt that any other approach would have suited me. I had energy, a head crammed full of ideas, and itchy feet. Given how big the world was, the last thing I wanted was to play it safe.

* * *

It's not difficult for me to describe these things and to remember how I felt about them. The trouble begins only when I question why I did them and why I felt what I felt. All the other young poets and writers in my class were making sensible decisions about their futures. We weren't rich kids who could depend on handouts from our parents, and once we left college, we would be out on our own for good. We were all facing the same situation, we all knew the score, and yet they acted in one way and I acted in another. That's what I'm still at a loss to explain. Why did my friends act so prudently, and why was I so reckless?

I came from a middle-class family. My childhood was comfortable, and I never suffered from any of the wants and deprivations that plague most of the human beings who live on this earth. I never went hungry, I never was cold, I never felt in danger of losing any of the things I had. Security was a given, and yet for all the ease and good fortune in the household, money was a subject of continual conversation and worry. Both of my parents had lived through the Depression, and neither one had fully recovered from those hard times. Each had been marked by the experience of not having enough, and each bore the wound in a different way.

My father was tight; my mother was extravagant. She spent; he didn't. The memory of poverty had not loosened its hold on his spirit, and even though his circumstances had changed, he could never quite bring himself to believe it. She, on the other hand, took great pleasure in those altered circumstances. She enjoyed the rituals of consumerism, and like so many Americans before her and since, she cultivated shopping as a means of self-expression, at times raising it to the level of an art form. To enter a store was to engage in an alchemical process that imbued the cash register with magical, transformative properties. Inexpressible desires, intangible needs, and unarticulated longings all passed through the money box and came out as real things, palpable objects you could hold in your hand. My mother never tired of reenacting this miracle, and the bills that resulted became a bone of contention between her and my father. She felt that we could afford them; he didn't. Two styles, two worldviews, two moral philosophies were in eternal conflict with each other, and in the end it broke their marriage apart. Money was the fault line, and it became the single, overpowering source of dispute between them. The tragedy was that they were both good people—attentive, honest, hardworking—and aside from that one ferocious battleground, they seemed to get along rather well. For the life of me I could never understand how such a relatively unimportant issue could cause so much trouble between them. But money, of course, is never just money. It's always something else, and it's always something more, and it always has the last word.

As a small boy, I was caught in the middle of this ideological war. My mother would take me shopping for clothes, sweeping me up in the whirlwind of her enthusiasm and generosity, and again and again I would allow myself to be talked into wanting the things she offered me—always more than I was expecting, always more than I thought I needed. It was impossible to resist, impossible not to enjoy how the clerks doted on her and hopped to her commands, impossible not to be carried away by the power of her performance. My happiness was always mixed with a large dose of anxiety, however, since I knew exactly what my father was going to say when he got the bill. And the fact was that he always said it. The inevitable outburst would come, and almost inevitably the matter would be resolved with my father declaring that the next time I needed something, he was the one who would take me shopping. So the moment would roll around to buy me a new winter jacket, say, or a new pair of shoes, and one night after dinner my father and I would drive off to a discount store located on a highway somewhere in the New Jersey darkness. I remember the glare of fluorescent lights in those places, the cinder-block walls, the endless racks of cheap men's clothing. As the jingle on the radio put it: "Robert Hall this season / Will tell you the reason— / Low overhead / Bum, bum, bum / Low overhead!" When all is said and done, that song is as much a part of my childhood as the Pledge of Allegiance or the Lord's Prayer.

The truth was that I enjoyed this bargain hunting with my father as much as I enjoyed the buying sprees orchestrated by my mother. My loyalties were equally divided between my two parents, and there was never any question of pitching my tent in one camp or the other. My mother's approach was more appealing, perhaps, at least in terms of the fun and excitement it generated, but there was something about my father's stubbornness that gripped me as well, a sense of hard-won experience and knowledge at the core of his beliefs, an integrity of purpose that made him someone who never backed down, not even at the risk of looking bad in the eyes of the world. I found that admirable, and much as I adored my beautiful, endlessly charming mother for dazzling the world as she did, I also adored my father for resisting that same world. It could be maddening to watch him in action—a man who never seemed to care what others thought of him—but it was also instructive, and in the long run I think I paid more attention to those lessons than I ever realized.

As a young boy I fell into the mold of your classic go-getter. At the first sign of snow, I would run out with my shovel and start ringing doorbells, asking people if they would hire me to clear their driveways and front walks. When the leaves fell in October, I would be out there with my rake, ringing those same doorbells and asking about the lawns. At other times, when there was nothing to remove from the ground, I would inquire about "odd jobs." Straightening up the garage, cleaning out the cellar, pruning the hedges—whatever needed to be done, I was the man to do it. In the summer, I sold lemonade for ten cents a glass on the sidewalk in front of my house. I gathered up empty bottles from the kitchen pantry, loaded them in my little red wagon, and lugged them to the store to turn in for cash. Two cents for the small ones; five cents for the big. I mostly used my earnings to buy baseball cards, sports magazines, and comic books, and whatever was left over I would diligently put in my piggy bank, which was built in the shape of a cash register. I was truly the child of my parents, and I never questioned the principles that animated their world. Money talked, and to the degree that you listened to it and followed its arguments, you would learn to speak the language of life.

Once, I remember, I was in possession of a fifty-cent piece. I can't recall how I came to have that coin—which was just as rare then as it is now—but whether it had been given to me or whether I had earned it myself, I have a keen sense of how much it meant to me and what a large sum it represented. For fifty cents in those days you could buy ten packs of baseball cards, five comic books, ten candy bars, fifty jawbreakers—or, if you preferred, various combinations of all of them. I put the half-dollar in my back pocket and marched off to the store, feverishly calculating how I was going to spend my little fortune. Somewhere along the way, however, for reasons that still confound me, the coin disappeared. I reached into my back pocket to check on it—knowing it was there, just wanting to make sure—and the money was gone. Was there a hole in my pocket? Had I accidentally slid the coin out of my pants the last time I'd touched it? I have no idea. I was six or seven years old, and I still remember how wretched I felt. I had tried to be so careful, and yet for all my precautions, I had wound up losing the money. How could I have allowed such a thing to happen? For want of any logical explanation, I decided that God had punished me. I didn't know why, but I was certain that the All-Powerful One had reached into my pocket and plucked out the coin Himself.

Little by little, I started turning my back on my parents. It's not that I began to love them less, but the world they came from no longer struck me as such an inviting place to live. I was ten, eleven, twelve years old, and already I was becoming an internal émigré, an exile in my own house. Many of these changes can be attributed to adolescence, to the simple fact that I was growing up and beginning to think for myself—but not all of them. Other forces were at work on me at the same time, and each one had a hand in pushing me onto the road I later followed. It wasn't just the pain of having to witness my parents' crumbling marriage, and it wasn't just the frustration of being trapped in a small suburban town, and it wasn't just the American climate of the late 1950s—but put them all together, and suddenly you had a powerful case against materialism, an indictment of the orthodox view that money was a good to be valued above all others. My parents valued money, and where had it gotten them? They had struggled so hard for it, had invested so much belief in it, and yet for every problem it had solved, another one had taken its place. American capitalism had created one of the most prosperous moments in human history. It had produced untold numbers of cars, frozen vegetables, and miracle shampoos, and yet Eisenhower was President, and the entire country had been turned into a gigantic television commercial, an incessant harangue to buy more, make more, spend more, to dance around the dollar-tree until you dropped dead from the sheer frenzy of trying to keep up with everyone else.

It wasn't long before I discovered that I wasn't the only person who felt this way. At ten, I stumbled across an issue of *Mad* magazine in a candy store in Irvington, New Jersey, and I remember the intense, almost stupefying pleasure I felt at reading those pages. They taught me that I had kindred spirits in this world, that others had already unlocked the doors I was trying to open myself. Fire hoses were being turned on black people in the American South, the Russians had launched the first Sputnik, and I was starting to pay attention. No, you didn't have to swallow the dogma they were trying to sell you. You could resist them, poke fun at them, call their bluff. The wholesomeness and dreary rectitude of American life were no more than a sham, a halfhearted publicity stunt. The moment you began to study the facts, contradictions bubbled to the surface, rampant hypocrisies were exposed, a whole new way of looking at things suddenly became possible. We had been taught to believe in "liberty and justice for all," but the fact was that liberty and justice were often at odds with one another. The pursuit of money had nothing to do with fairness; its driving engine was the social principle of "every man for himself." As if to prove the essential inhumanity of the marketplace, nearly all of its metaphors had been taken from the animal kingdom: dog eat dog, bulls and bears, the rat race, survival of the fittest. Money divided the world into winners and losers, haves and have-nots. That was an excellent arrangement for the winners, but what about the people who lost? Based on the evidence available to me, I gathered that they were to be cast aside and forgotten. Too bad, of course, but those were the breaks. If you construct a world so primitive as to make Darwin your leading philosopher and Aesop your leading poet, what else can you expect? It's a jungle out there, isn't it? Just look at that Dreyfus lion strolling down the middle of Wall Street. Could the message be any clearer? Either eat or be eaten. That's the law of the jungle, my friend, and if you don't have the stomach for it, then get out while you still can.

I was out before I was ever in. By the time I entered my teens, I had already concluded that the world of business would have to get along without me. I was probably at my worst then, my most insufferable, my most confused. I burned with the ardor of a newfound idealism, and the stringencies of the perfection I sought for myself turned me into a pint-sized puritan-in-training. I was repulsed by the outward trappings of wealth, and every sign of ostentation my parents brought into the house I treated with scorn. Life was unfair. I had finally figured this out, and because it was my own discovery, it hit me with all the force of a revelation. As the months went by, I found it increasingly difficult to reconcile my good luck with the bad luck of so many others. What had I done to deserve the comforts and advantages that had been showered on me? My father could afford them—that was all—and whether or not he and my mother fought over money was a small point in comparison to the fact that they had money to fight over in the first place. I squirmed every time I had to get into the family car—so bright and new and expensive, so clearly an invitation to the world to admire how well off we were. All my sympathies were for the downtrodden, the dispossessed, the underdogs of the social order, and a car like that filled me with shame—not just for myself, but for living in a world that allowed such things to be in it.

My first jobs don't count. My parents were still supporting me, and I was under no obligation to fend for myself or contribute to the family budget. The pressure was therefore off, and without any pressure, nothing important can ever be at stake. I was glad to have the money I earned, but I never had to use it on nuts-and-bolts necessities, I never had to worry about putting food on the table or not falling behind with the rent. Those problems would come later. For now I was just a high school kid looking for a pair of wings to carry me away from where I was.

At sixteen, I spent two months working as a waiter at a summer camp in upstate New York. The next summer, I worked at my uncle Moe's appliance store in Westfield, New Jersey. The jobs were similar in that most of the tasks were physical and didn't require much thought. If carrying trays and scraping dishes was somewhat less interesting than installing air conditioners and unloading refrigerators from forty-foot trailer trucks, I wouldn't want to make too big a point of it. This isn't a question of apples and oranges—but of two kinds of apples, both the same shade of green. Dull as the work might have been, however, I found both jobs immensely satisfying. There were too many colorful characters around, too many surprises, too many new thoughts to absorb for me to resent the drudgery, and I never felt that I was wasting my time just to earn a paycheck. The money was an important part of it, but the work wasn't just about money. It was about learning who I was and how I fit into the world.

Even at the camp, where my coworkers were all sixteen- and seventeen-year-old high school boys, the kitchen help came from a starkly different universe. Down-and-outs, Bowery bums, men with dubious histories, they had been rounded up from the New York streets by the owner of the camp and talked into accepting their low-paying jobs—which included two months of fresh air and free room and board. Most of them didn't last long. One day they would just disappear, wandering back to the city without bothering to say good-bye. A day or two later, the missing man would be replaced by a similar lost soul, who rarely lasted very long himself. One of the dishwashers, I remember, was named Frank, a grim, surly guy with a serious drinking problem. Somehow or other, we managed to become friends, and in the evening after work was done we would sometimes sit on the steps behind the kitchen and talk. Frank turned out to be a highly intelligent, well-read man. He had worked as an insurance agent in Springfield, Massachusetts, and until the bottle got the better of him, he had lived the life of a productive, tax-paying citizen. I distinctly remember not daring to ask him what had happened, but one evening he told me anyway, turning what must have been a complicated story into a short, dry account of the events that had done him in. In the space of sixteen months, he said, every person who had ever meant anything to him died. He sounded philosophical about it, almost as if he were talking about someone else, and yet there was an undertow of bitterness in his voice. First his parents, he said, then his wife, and then his two children. Diseases, accidents, and burials, and by the time they were all gone, it was as if his insides had shattered. "I just gave up," he said. "I didn't care what happened to me anymore, so I became a bum."

The following year, in Westfield, I made the acquaintance of several more indelible figures. Carmen, for example, the voluminously padded, wisecracking bookkeeper, who to this day is still the only woman I've known with a beard (she actually had to shave), and Joe Mansfield, the assistant repairman with two hernias and a ravaged Chrysler that had wiped out the odometer three times and was now up to 360,000 miles. Joe was sending two daughters through college, and in addition to his day job at the appliance store, he worked eight hours every night as a foreman in a commercial bakery, reading comic books beside the huge vats of dough so as not to fall asleep. He was the single most exhausted man I have ever met—and also one of the most energetic. He kept himself going by smoking menthol cigarettes and downing twelve to sixteen bottles of orange soda a day, but not once did I ever see him put a morsel of food in his mouth. If he ate lunch, he said, it would make him too tired and he would collapse. The hernias had come a few years earlier, when he and two other men were carrying a jumbo refrigerator up a narrow flight of stairs. The other men had lost their grip, leaving Joe to bear the entire weight of the thing himself, and it was exactly then, as he struggled not to be crushed by the several hundred pounds he was holding, that his testicles had shot up out of his scrotum. First one ball, he said, and then the other. Pop ... pop. He wasn't supposed to lift heavy objects anymore, but every time there was an especially large appliance to deliver, he would come along and help us—just to make sure we didn't kill ourselves.

The *us* included a nineteen-year-old redhead named Mike, a tense, wiry shrimp with a missing index finger and one of the fastest tongues I had yet encountered. Mike and I were the air conditioner installation team, and we spent a lot of time together in the store van, driving to and from jobs. I never tired of listening to the onslaught of loopy, unexpected metaphors and outrageous opinions that came pouring out of him whenever he opened his mouth. If he found one of the customers too snotty, for example, he wouldn't say "that person's an asshole" (as most would) or "that person's stuck-up" (as some would), but "that person acts as if his shit doesn't smell." Young Mike had a special gift, and on several occasions that summer I was able to see how well it served him. Again and again we would enter a house to install an air conditioner, and again and again, just as we were in the middle of the job (screwing in the screws, measuring strips of caulking to seal up the window), a girl would walk into the room. It never seemed to fail. She was always seventeen, always pretty, always bored, always "just hanging around the house." The instant she appeared, Mike would turn on the charm. It was as if he knew she was going to come in, as if he had already rehearsed his lines and was fully prepared. I, on the other hand, was always caught with my guard down, and as Mike launched into his song and dance (a combination of bullshit, razzle-dazzle, and raw nerve), I would dumbly plod on with the work. Mike would talk, and the girl would smile. Mike would talk a little more, and the girl would laugh. Within two minutes they were old friends, and by the time I'd put the finishing touches on the job, they were swapping phone numbers and arranging where to meet on Saturday night. It was preposterous; it was sublime; it made my jaw drop. If it had happened only once or twice, I would have dismissed it as a fluke, but this scene was played out repeatedly, no less than five or six times over the course of the summer. In the end, I grudgingly had to admit that Mike was more than just lucky. He was someone who created his own luck.

In September, I started my senior year of high school. It was the last year I spent at home, and it was also the last year of my parents' marriage. Their breakup had been so long in coming that when the news was announced to me at the end of Christmas vacation, I wasn't upset so much as relieved.

It had been a mismatch from the start. If they hung in together as long as they did, it was more for "the children's sake" than for their own. I don't presume to have any answers, but I suspect that a decisive moment occurred two or three years before the end, when my father took over the grocery-shopping duties for the household. That was the last great money battle my parents fought, and it stands in my mind as the symbolic last straw, the thing that finally knocked the stuffing out of both of them. It was true that my mother enjoyed filling her cart at the local Shop-Rite until it was almost too heavy to push; it was true that she took pleasure in providing the treats my sister and I asked her for; it was true that we ate well at home and that the pantry was abundantly stocked. But it was also true that we could afford these things and that the family finances were in no way threatened by the sums my mother forked over at the checkout counter. In my father's eyes, however, her spending was out of control. When he finally put his foot down, it landed in the wrong place, and he wound up doing what no man should ever do to his wife. In effect, he relieved her of her job. From then on, he was the one who took responsibility for bringing food into the house. Once, twice, even three times a week, he would stop off somewhere on the way home from work (as if he didn't have enough to do already) and load up the back of his station wagon with groceries. The choice cuts of meat my mother had brought home were replaced by chuck and shoulder. Name-brand products became generic products. After-school snacks vanished. I don't remember hearing my mother complain, but it must have been a colossal defeat for her. She was no longer in charge of her own house, and the fact that she didn't protest, that she didn't fight back, must have meant that she had already given up on the marriage. When the end came, there were no dramas, no noisy showdowns, no last-minute regrets. The family quietly dispersed. My mother moved to an apartment in the Weequahic section of Newark (taking my sister and me along with her), and my father stayed on alone in the big house, living there until the day he died.

In some perverse way, these events made me extremely happy. I was glad that the truth was finally out in the open, and I welcomed the upheavals and changes that followed as a consequence of that truth. There was something liberating about it, an exhilaration in knowing that the slate had been wiped clean. An entire period of my life had ended, and even as my body continued to go through the motions of finishing up high school and helping my mother move to her new place, my mind had already decamped. Not only was I about to leave home, but home itself had disappeared. There was nothing to return to anymore, nowhere to go but out and away.

I didn't even bother to attend my high school graduation. I offer that as proof, evidence of how little it meant to me. By the time my classmates were donning their caps and gowns and receiving their diplomas, I was already on the other side of the Atlantic. The school had granted me a special dispensation to leave early, and I had booked passage on a student boat that sailed out of New York at the beginning of June. All my savings went into that trip. Birthday money, graduation money, bar mitzvah money, the little bits I'd hoarded from summer jobs—fifteen hundred dollars or so, I can't remember the exact amount. That was the era of Europe on Five Dollars a Day, and if you watched your funds carefully, it was actually possible to do it. I spent over a month in Paris, living in a hotel that cost seven francs a night ($1.40); I traveled to Italy, to Spain, to Ireland. In two and a half months, I lost more than twenty pounds. Everywhere I went, I worked on the novel I had started writing that spring. Mercifully, the manuscript has disappeared, but the story I carried around in my head that summer was no less real to me than the places I went to and the people I crossed paths with. I had some extraordinary encounters, especially in Paris, but more often than not I was alone, at times excessively alone, alone to the point of hearing voices in my head. God knows what to make of that eighteen-year-old boy now. I see myself as a conundrum, the site of inexplicable turmoils, a weightless, wild-eyed sort of creature, slightly touched, perhaps, prone to desperate inner surges, sudden about-faces, swoons, soaring thoughts. If someone approached me in the right way, I could be open, charming, positively gregarious. Otherwise, I was walled off and taciturn, barely present. I believed in myself and yet had no confidence in myself. I was bold and timid, light-footed and clumsy, single-minded and impulsive—a walking, breathing monument to the spirit of contradiction. My life had only just begun, and already I was moving in two directions at once. I didn't know it yet, but in order for me to get anywhere, I was going to have to work twice as hard as anyone else.

The last two weeks of the trip were the strangest. For reasons that had everything to do with James Joyce and *Ulysses*, I went to Dublin. I had no plans. My only purpose in going was to be there, and I figured the rest would take care of itself. The tourist office steered me to a bed-and-breakfast in Donnybrook, a fifteen-minute bus ride from the center of town. Besides the elderly couple who ran the place and two or three of the guests, I scarcely talked to anyone in all that time. I never even found the courage to set foot in a pub. Somewhere during the course of my travels, I had developed an ingrown toenail, and while it sounds like a comical condition, it wasn't the least bit funny to me. It felt as if the tip of a knife had been lodged in my big toe. Walking was turned into a trial, and yet from early in the morning to late in the afternoon, I did little else but walk, hobbling around Dublin in my too-tight, disintegrating shoes. I could live with the pain, I found, but the effort it called for seemed to drive me ever further into myself, to erase me as a social being. There was a crotchety American geezer in full-time residence at the boardinghouse—a seventy-year-old retiree from Illinois or Indiana—and once he got wind of my condition, he started filling my head with stories about how his mother had left an ingrown toenail untended for years, treating it with patchwork home remedies—dabs of disinfectant, little balls of cotton—but never *taking the bull by the horns*, and wouldn't you know it, she came down with *cancer of the toe*, which worked its way into her foot, and then into her leg, and then spread through her whole body and eventually did her in. He loved elaborating on the small, gruesome details of his mother's demise (for my own good, of course), and seeing how susceptible I was to what he told me, he never tired of telling the story again. I'm not going to deny that I was affected. A cumbersome annoyance had been turned into a life-threatening scourge, and the longer I delayed taking action, the more dismal my prospects would become. Every time I rode past the Hospital for Incurables on my way into town, I turned my eyes away. I couldn't get the old man's words out of my head. Doom was stalking me, and signs of impending death were everywhere.

Once or twice, I was accompanied on my rambles by a twenty-six-year-old nurse from Toronto. Her name was Pat Gray, and she had checked into the bed-and-breakfast the same evening I had. I fell desperately in love with her, but it was a hopeless infatuation, a lost cause from the start. Not only was I too young for her, and not only was I too shy to declare my feelings, but she was in love with someone else—an Irishman, of course, which explained why she'd come to Dublin in the first place. One night, I recall, she came home from a date with her beloved at around half-past twelve. I was still up at that hour, scribbling away at my novel, and when she saw light coming through the crack under my door, she knocked and asked to come in. I was already in bed, working with a notebook propped against my knees, and she burst in laughing, her cheeks flushed with drink, bubbling over with excitement. Before I could say anything, she threw her arms around my neck and kissed me, and I thought: Miracle of miracles, my dream has come true. But alas, it was only a false alarm. I didn't even have a chance to kiss her back before she was drawing away from me and explaining that her Irishman had proposed to her that night and that she was the happiest girl in the world. It was impossible not to feel glad for her. This straightforward, pretty young woman, with her short hair and innocent eyes and earnest Canadian voice, had chosen me as the person to share the news with. I did my best to congratulate her, to hide my disappointment after that brief, wholly implausible rush of expectation, but the kiss had undone me, had absolutely melted my bones, and it was all I could do not to commit a serious blunder. If I managed to control myself, it was only by turning myself into a block of wood. No doubt a block of wood has good manners, but it's hardly a fitting companion for a celebration.

Everything else was solitude, silence, walking. I read books in Phoenix Park, journeyed out to Joyce's Martello Tower along the strand, crossed and recrossed the Liffey more times than I could count. The Watts riots took place then, and I remember reading the headlines at a kiosk on O'Connell Street, but I also remember a small girl singing with a Salvation Army band early one evening as people shuffled home from work—some sad, plaintive song about human misery and the wonders of God—and that voice is still inside me, a voice so crystalline as to make the toughest person fall down and weep, and the remarkable thing about it was that no one paid the slightest attention to her. The rush-hour crowd rushed past her, and she just stood on the corner singing her song in the eerie, dusky, northern light, as oblivious of them as they were of her, a tiny bird in tattered clothes chanting her psalm to the broken heart.

Dublin is not a big city, and it didn't take me long to learn my way around. There was something compulsive about the walks I took, an insatiable urge to prowl, to drift like a ghost among strangers, and after two weeks the streets were transformed into something wholly personal for me, a map of my inner terrain. For years afterward, every time I closed my eyes before going to sleep, I was back in Dublin. As wakefulness dribbled out of me and I descended into semiconsciousness, I would find myself there again, walking through those same streets. I have no explanation for it. Something important had happened to me there, but I have never been able to pinpoint exactly what it was. Something terrible, I think, some mesmerizing encounter with my own depths, as if in the loneliness of those days I had looked into the darkness and seen myself for the first time.

I started Columbia College in September, and for the next four years the last thing on my mind was money. I worked intermittently at various jobs, but those years were not about making plans, not about preparing for my financial future. They were about books, the war in Vietnam, the struggle to figure out how to do the thing I was proposing to do. If I thought about earning a living at all, it was only in a fitful, haphazard sort of way. At most I imagined some kind of marginal existence for myself—scrounging for crumbs at the far edges of the workaday world, the life of a starving poet.

The jobs I had as an undergraduate were nevertheless instructive. If nothing else, they taught me that my preference for blue-collar work over white-collar work was well founded. At one point in my sophomore year, for example, I was hired by the subdivision of a publishing company to write material for educational filmstrips. I had been subjected to a barrage of "audiovisual aids" during my childhood, and I remembered the intense boredom they invariably produced in me and my friends. It was always a pleasure to leave the classroom and sit in the dark for twenty or thirty minutes (just like going to the movies!), but the clunky images on screen, the monotone voice of the narrator, and the intermittent *ping* that told the teacher when to push the button and move on to the next picture soon took their toll on us. Before long, the room was abuzz with whispered conversations and frantic, half-suppressed giggles. A minute or two later, the spitballs would begin to fly.

I was reluctant to impose this tedium on another generation of kids, but I figured I'd do my best and see if I couldn't put some spark into it. My first day on the job, the supervisor told me to take a look at some of the company's past filmstrips and acquaint myself with the form. I picked out one at random. It was called "Government" or "Introduction to Government," something like that. He set up the spool on a machine and then left me alone to watch the film. About two or three frames into it, I came across a statement that alarmed me. The ancient Greeks had invented the idea of democracy, the text said, accompanied by a painting of bearded men standing around in togas. That was fine, but then it went on to say (*ping:* cut to a painting of the Capitol) that America was a democracy. I turned off the machine, walked down the hall, and knocked on the door of the supervisor's office. "There's a mistake in the filmstrip," I said. "America isn't a democracy. It's a republic. There's a big difference."

He looked at me as if I had just informed him that I was Stalin's grandson. "It's for little children," he said, "not college students. There's no room to go into detail."

"It's not a detail," I answered, "it's an important distinction. In a pure democracy, everyone votes on every issue. We elect representatives to do that for us. I'm not saying that's bad. Pure democracy can be dangerous. The rights of minorities need to be protected, and that's what a republic does for us. It's all spelled out in *The Federalist Papers*. The government has to guard against the tyranny of the majority. Kids should know that."

The conversation became quite heated. I was determined to make my point, to prove that the statement in the filmstrip was wrong, but he refused to swallow it. He pegged me as a troublemaker the instant I opened my mouth, and that was that. Twenty minutes after starting the job, I was given the boot.

Much better was the job I had in the summer after my freshman year—as groundskeeper at the Commodore Hotel in the Catskills. I was hired through the New York State Employment Agency in midtown Manhattan, a vast government office that found work for the unskilled and the unfortunate, the bottom dogs of society. Humble and badly paid as the position was, at least it offered a chance to get out of the city and escape the heat. My friend Bob Perelman and I signed on together, and the next morning we were dispatched to Monticello, New York, via the Short Line Bus Company. It was the same setup I'd seen three years before, and our fellow passengers were the same bums and down-and-outs I'd rubbed shoulders with during my stint as a summer camp waiter. The only difference was that now I was one of them. The bus fare was deducted from the first paycheck, as was the employment agency's fee, and unless you hung in with the job for some little time, you weren't going to make any money. There were those who didn't like the work and quit after a couple of days. They wound up with nothing—dead broke and a hundred miles from home, feeling they'd been had.

The Commodore was a small, down-at-the-heels Borscht Belt establishment. It was no match for the local competition, the Concord and Grossinger's, and a certain wistfulness and nostalgia hung about the place, a memory of rosier days. Bob and I arrived several weeks in advance of the summer season, and we were responsible for getting the grounds into shape to welcome an influx of visitors in July and August. We mowed lawns, clipped bushes, collected trash, painted walls, repaired screen doors. They gave us a little hut to live in, a ramshackle box with less square footage than a beach cabana, and bit by bit we covered the walls of our room with poems—crazy doggerel, filthy limericks, flowery quatrains—laughing our heads off as we downed endless bottles of Budweiser chug-a-lug beer. We drank the beer because there was nothing better to do, but given the food we had to eat, the hops became a necessary component of our diet as well. There were only a dozen or so workers on the premises at the time, and they gave us the low-budget treatment where culinary matters were concerned. The menu for every lunch and dinner was the same: Chun King chicken chow mein, straight out of the can. Thirty years have gone by since then, and I would still rather go hungry than put another morsel of that stuff in my mouth.

None of this would be worth mentioning if not for Casey and Teddy, the two indoor maintenance men I worked with that summer. Casey and Teddy had been palling around together for more than ten years, and by now they were a pair, an indissoluble team, a dialectical unit. Everything they did, they did in tandem, traveling from place to place and job to job as if they were one. They were chums for life, two peas in a pod, buddies. Not gay, not the least bit interested in each other sexually—but buddies. Casey and Teddy were classic American drifters, latter-day hoboes who seemed to have stepped forth from the pages of a Steinbeck novel, and yet they were so funny together, so full of wisecracks and drunkenness and good cheer, that their company was irresistible. At times they made me think of some forgotten comedy duo, a couple of clowns from the days of vaudeville and silent films. The spirit of Laurel and Hardy had survived in them, but these two weren't bound by the constraints of show business. They were part of the real world, and they performed their act on the stage of life.

Casey was the straight man, Teddy was the card. Casey was thin, Teddy was round. Casey was white, Teddy was black. On their days off they would tramp into town together, drink themselves silly, and then return for their chow mein dinner sporting identical haircuts or dressed in identical shirts. The idea was always to spend all their money in one big binge—and to spend it in exactly the same way, even-steven, penny for penny. The shirts stand out in my mind as a particularly raucous event. They couldn't stop laughing when they showed up in those twin outfits, holding their sides and pointing at each other as if they'd just played an enormous joke on the world. They were the loudest, ugliest shirts imaginable, a double insult to good taste, and Casey and Teddy were positively seized with mirth as they modeled them for me and Bob. Teddy then shuffled off to the empty ballroom on the ground floor of the main building, sat down at the piano, and launched into what he called his Port Wine Concerto. For the next hour and a half, he clanged forth tuneless improvisations, filling the hall with a tempest of inebriation and noise. Teddy was a man of many gifts, but music was not one of them. Yet there he sat, happy as a clam in the fading light, a Dada maestro at peace with himself and the world.

Teddy had been born in Jamaica, he told me, and had joined the British Navy during World War II. Somewhere along the line, his ship was torpedoed. I don't know how much time elapsed before he was rescued (minutes? hours? days?), but whenever he was found, it was an American ship that found him. From then on he was in the American Navy, he said, and by the end of the war he was an American citizen. It sounded a little fishy to me, but that's the story he told, and who was I to doubt him? In the past twenty years, he seemed to have done everything a man can possibly do, to have run the entire gamut of occupations. Salesman, sidewalk artist in Greenwich Village, bartender, skid row drunk. None of it mattered to him. A great, rumbling basso laugh accompanied every story he told, and that laugh was like an unending bow to his own ridiculousness, a sign that his only purpose in talking was to poke fun at himself. He made scenes in public places, misbehaved like a willful child, was forever calling people's bluff. It could be exhausting to be with him, but there was also something admirable about the way he caused trouble. It had an almost scientific quality to it, as if he were conducting an experiment, shaking things up for the pure pleasure of seeing where they would land once the dust had settled. Teddy was an anarchist, and because he was also without ambition, because he didn't want the things that other people wanted, he never had to play by anybody's rules but his own.

I have no idea how or where he met Casey. His sidekick was a less flamboyant character than he was, and what I remember best about him was that he had no sense of taste or smell. Casey had been in a barroom fight some years back, had received a knock on the head, and had thenceforth lost all of his olfactory functions. As a result, everything tasted like cardboard to him. Cover his eyes, and he couldn't tell you what he was eating. Chow mein or caviar, potatoes or pudding—there was no difference. Aside from this affliction, Casey was in excellent trim, a feisty welterweight with a New York Irish voice that made him sound like a Dead End Kid. His job was to laugh at Teddy's jokes and make sure his friend didn't take things too far and get himself hauled off to jail. Teddy got close to it one night that summer—standing up in a Monticello restaurant and waving around the menu as he shouted, "I ain't gonna eat this Japanese dog food!"—but Casey calmed him down, and we all managed to finish our meal. I don't suppose it's necessary to add that we weren't in a Japanese restaurant.

By any objective standard, Casey and Teddy were nobodies, a pair of eccentric fools, but they made an unforgettable impression on me, and I have never run across their likes since. That was the reason for going off to work at places like the Commodore Hotel, I think. It's not that I wanted to make a career of it, but those little excursions into the backwaters and shit holes of the world never failed to produce an interesting discovery, to further my education in ways I hadn't expected. Casey and Teddy are a perfect example. I was nineteen years old when I met them, and the things they did that summer are still feeding my imagination today.

In 1967, I signed up for Columbia's Junior Year Abroad Program in Paris. The weeks I'd spent there after finishing high school had whetted my appetite for the place, and I jumped at the chance to go back.

Paris was still Paris, but I was no longer the same person I'd been during my first visit. I had spent the past two years living in a delirium of books, and whole new worlds had been poured into my head, life-altering transfusions had reconstituted my blood. Nearly everything that is still important to me in the way of literature and philosophy I first encountered during those two years. Looking back on that time now, I find it almost impossible to absorb how many books I read. I drank them up in staggering numbers, consumed entire countries and continents of books, could never even begin to get enough of them. Elizabethan playwrights, pre-Socratic philosophers, Russian novelists, Surrealist poets. I read books as if my brain had caught fire, as if my very survival were at stake. One work led to another work, one thought led to another thought, and from one month to the next, I changed my ideas about everything.

The program turned out to be a bitter disappointment. I went to Paris with all sorts of grandiose plans, assuming I would be able to attend any lectures and courses I wanted to (Roland Barthes at the Collège de France, for example), but when I sat down to discuss these possibilities with the director of the program, he flat out told me to forget them. Out of the question, he said. You're required to study French language and grammar, to pass certain tests, to earn so many credits and half-credits, to put in so many class hours here and so many hours there. I found it absurd, a curriculum designed for babies. I'm past all that, I told him. I already know how to speak French. Why go backward? Because, he said, those are the rules, and that's the way it is.

He was so unbending, so contemptuous of me, so ready to interpret my enthusiasm as arrogance and to think I was out to insult him, that we immediately locked horns. I had nothing against the man personally, but he seemed bent on turning our disagreement into a personal conflict. He wanted to belittle me, to crush me with his power, and the longer the conversation went on, the more I felt myself resisting him. At last, a moment came when I'd had enough. All right, I said, if that's the way it is, then I quit. I quit the program, I quit the college, I quit the whole damn thing. And then I got up from my chair, shook his hand, and walked out of the office.

It was a crazy thing to do. The prospect of not getting a B.A. didn't worry me, but turning my back on college meant that I would automatically lose my student deferment. With the troop buildup in Vietnam growing at an alarming rate, I had suddenly put myself in a good position to be drafted into the army. That would have been fine if I supported the war, but I didn't. I was against it, and nothing was ever going to make me fight in it. If they tried to induct me into the army, I would refuse to serve. If they arrested me, I would go to jail. That was a categorical decision—an absolute, unbudgeable stance. I wasn't going to take part in the war, even if it meant ruining my life.

Still, I went ahead and quit college. I was utterly fearless about it, felt not the slightest tremor of hesitation or doubt, and took the plunge with my eyes wide open. I was expecting to fall hard, but I didn't. Instead, I found myself floating through the air like a feather, and for the next few months I felt as free and happy as I had ever been.

I lived in a small hotel on the rue Clément, directly across from the Marché Saint-Germain, an enclosed market that has long since been torn down. It was an inexpensive but tidy place, several notches up from the fleabag I'd stayed in two years before, and the young couple who ran it were exceedingly kind to me. The man's name was Gaston (stout, small mustache, white shirt, ever-present black apron), and he spent the bulk of his time serving customers in the café on the ground floor, a minuscule hole-in-the-wall that doubled as neighborhood hangout and hotel reception desk. That's where I drank my coffee in the morning, read the newspaper, and became addicted to pinball. I walked a lot during those months, just as I had in Dublin, but I also spent countless hours upstairs in my room, reading and writing. Most of the work I did then has been lost, but I remember writing poems and translating poems, as well as composing a long, exhaustingly complex screenplay for a silent film (part Buster Keaton movie, part philosophical tap dance). On top of all the reading I'd done in the past two years, I had also been going to the movies, primarily at the Thalia and New Yorker theaters, which were no more than a short walk down Broadway from Morningside Heights. The Thalia ran a different double feature every day, and with the price of admission just fifty cents for students, I wound up spending as much time there as I did in the Columbia classrooms. Paris turned out to be an even better town for movies than New York. I became a regular at the Cinémathèque and the Left Bank revival houses, and after a while I got so caught up in this passion that I started toying with the idea of becoming a director. I even went so far as to make some inquiries about attending IDHEC, the Paris film institute, but the application forms proved to be so massive and daunting that I never bothered to fill them out.

When I wasn't in my room or sitting in a movie theater, I was browsing in bookstores, eating in cheap restaurants, getting to know various people, catching a dose of the clap (very painful), and generally exulting in the choice I had made. It would be hard to exaggerate how good I felt during those months. I was at once stimulated and at peace with myself, and though I knew my little paradise would have to end, I did everything I could to prolong it, to put off the hour of reckoning until the last possible moment.

I managed to hold out until mid-November. By the time I returned to New York, the fall semester at Columbia was half over. I assumed there was no chance of being reinstated as a student, but I had promised my family to come back and discuss the matter with the university. They were worried about me, after all, and I figured I owed them that much. Once I had taken care of that chore, I intended to go back to Paris and start looking for a job. Let the draft be damned, I said to myself. If I wound up as a "fugitive from justice," so be it.

None of it worked out as I thought it would. I made an appointment to see one of the deans at Columbia, and this man turned out to be so sympathetic, so fully on my side, that he broke down my defenses within a matter of minutes. No, he said, he didn't think I was being foolish. He understood what I was doing, and he admired the spirit of the enterprise. On the other hand, there was the question of the war, he said. Columbia didn't want to see me go into the army if I didn't want to go, much less wind up in jail for refusing to serve in the army. If I wanted to come back to college, the door was open. I could start attending classes tomorrow, and officially it would be as if I had never missed a day.

How to argue with a man like that? He wasn't some functionary who was just doing his job. He spoke too calmly for that and listened too carefully to what I said, and before long I understood that the only thing in it for him was an honest desire to prevent a twenty-year-old kid from making a mistake, to talk someone out of fucking up his life when he didn't have to. There would be time for that later, n'est-ce pas? He wasn't very old himself—thirty, thirty-five, perhaps—and I still remember his name, even though I never saw him again. Dean Platt. When the university shut down that spring because of the student strike, he quit his job in protest over the administration's handling of the affair. The next thing I heard, he had gone to work for the UN.

The troubles at Columbia lasted from early 1968 until my class graduated the following June. Normal activity all but stopped during that time. The campus became a war zone of demonstrations, sit-ins, and moratoriums. There were riots, police raids, slugfests, and factional splits. Rhetorical excesses abounded, ideological lines were drawn, passions flowed from all sides. Whenever there was a lull, another issue would come up, and the outbursts would begin all over again. In the long run, nothing of any great importance was accomplished. The proposed site for a university gymnasium was changed, a number of academic requirements were dropped, the president resigned and was replaced by another president. That was all. In spite of the efforts of thousands, the ivory tower did not collapse. But still, it tottered for a time, and more than a few of its stones crumbled and fell to the ground.

I took part in some things and kept my distance from others. I helped occupy one of the campus buildings, was roughed up by the cops and spent a night in jail, but mostly I was a bystander, a sympathetic fellow traveler. Much as I would have liked to join in, I found myself temperamentally unfit for group activities. My loner instincts were far too ingrained, and I could never quite bring myself to climb aboard the great ship *Solidarity*. For better or worse, I went on paddling my little canoe—a bit more desperately, perhaps, a bit less sure of where I was going now, but much too stubborn to get out. There probably wouldn't have been time for that anyway. I was steering through rapids, and it took every ounce of my strength just to hold on to the paddle. If I had flinched, there's a good chance I would have drowned.

Some did. Some became casualties of their own righteousness and noble intentions, and the human loss was catastrophic. Ted Gold, one class ahead of me, blew himself to smithereens in a West Village brownstone when the bomb he was building accidentally went off. Mark Rudd, a childhood friend and Columbia dorm neighbor, joined the Weather Underground and lived in hiding for more than a decade. Dave Gilbert, an SDS spokesman whose speeches had impressed me as models of insight and intelligence, is now serving a seventy-five-year prison sentence for his involvement in the Brinks robbery. In the summer of 1969, I walked into a post office in western Massachusetts with a friend who had to mail a letter. As she waited in line, I studied the posters of the FBI's ten most wanted men pinned to the wall. It turned out that I knew seven of them.

That was the climate of my last two years of college. In spite of the distractions and constant turmoil, I managed to do a fair amount of writing, but none of my efforts ever added up to much. I started two novels and abandoned them, wrote several plays I didn't like, worked on poem after poem with largely disappointing results. My ambitions were much greater than my abilities at that point, and I often felt frustrated, dogged by a sense of failure. The only accomplishment I felt proud of was the French poetry I had translated, but that was a secondary pursuit and not even close to what I had in mind. Still, I must not have been totally discouraged. I kept on writing, after all, and when I began publishing articles on books and films in the *Columbia Daily Spectator*, I actually got to see my work in print fairly often. You have to start somewhere, I suppose. I might not have been moving as fast as I wanted to, but at least I was moving. I was up on my feet and walking forward, step by wobbly step, but I still didn't know how to run.

When I look back on those days now, I see myself in fragments. Numerous battles were being fought at the same time, and parts of myself were scattered over a broad field, each one wrestling with a different angel, a different impulse, a different idea of who I was. It sometimes led me to act in ways that were fundamentally out of character. I would turn myself into someone I was not, try wearing another skin for a while, imagine I had reinvented myself. The morose and contemplative stuffed shirt would dematerialize into a fast-talking cynic. The bookish, overly zealous intellectual would suddenly turn around and embrace Harpo Marx as his spiritual father. I can think of several examples of this antic bumbling, but the one that best captures the spirit of the time was a little piece of jabberwocky I contributed to the *Columbia Review*, the undergraduate literary magazine. For reasons that utterly escape me now, I took it upon myself to launch the First Annual Christopher Smart Award. I was a senior then, and the contest rules were published on the last page of the fall issue. I pluck these sentences from the text at random: "The purpose of the award is to give recognition to the great anti-men of our time . . . men of talent who have renounced all worldly ambition, who have turned their backs on the banquet tables of the rich. . . . We have taken Christopher Smart as our model . . . the eighteenth-century Englishman who spurned the easy glory that awaited him as an inventor of rhymed couplets . . . for a life of drunkenness, insanity, religious fanaticism, and prophetic writings. In excess he found his true path, in rejecting the early promise he showed to the academic poets of England, he realized his true greatness. Defamed and ridiculed over the past two centuries, his reputation run through the mud . . . Christopher Smart has been relegated to the sphere of the unknowns. We attempt now, in an age without heroes, to resurrect his name."

The object of the competition was to reward failure. Not common, everyday setbacks and stumbles, but monumental falls, gargantuan acts of self-sabotage. In other words, I wanted to single out the person who had done the least with the most, who had begun with every advantage, every talent, every expectation of worldly success, and had come to nothing. Contestants were asked to write an essay of fifty words or more describing their failure or the failure of someone they knew. The winner would receive a two-volume boxed set of Christopher Smart's *Collected Works*. To no one's surprise but my own, not one entry was submitted.

It was a joke, of course, an exercise in literary leg pulling, but underneath my humorous intentions there was something disturbing, something that was not funny at all. Why the compulsion to sanctify failure? Why the mocking, arrogant tone, the know-it-all posturing? I could be wrong, but it strikes me now that they were an expression of fear—dread of the uncertain future I had prepared for myself—and that my true motive in setting up the contest was to declare myself the winner. The cockeyed, Bedlamite rules were a way of hedging my bets, of ducking the blows that life had in store for me. To lose was to win, to win was to lose, and therefore even if the worst came to pass, I would be able to claim a moral victory. Small comfort, perhaps, but no doubt I was already clutching at straws. Rather than bring my fear out into the open, I buried it under an avalanche of wisecracks and sarcasm. None of it was conscious. I was trying to come to terms with anticipated defeats, hardening myself for the struggles that lay ahead. For the next several years, my favorite sentence in the English language was from the Elizabethan poet Fulke Greville: "I write for those on whom the black ox hath trod."

As it happened, I wound up meeting Christopher Smart. Not the real Christopher Smart, perhaps, but one of his reincarnations, a living example of failed promise and blighted literary fortune. It was the spring of my senior year, just weeks before I was supposed to graduate. Out of nowhere, a man turned up on the Columbia campus and started causing a stir. At first I was only dimly aware of his presence, but little fragments of the stories circulating about him occasionally fell within my earshot. I'd heard that he called himself "Doc," for example, and that for obscure reasons that had something to do with the American economic system and the future of mankind, he was handing out money to strangers, no strings attached. With so many oddball doings in the air back then, I didn't pay much attention.

One night, a couple of my friends talked me into going down to Times Square with them to see the latest Sergio Leone spaghetti western. After the movie let out, we decided to cap off the evening with a little lark and repaired to the Metropole Café at Broadway and Forty-eighth Street. The Metropole had once been a quality jazz club, but now it was a topless go-go bar, complete with wall-to-wall mirrors, strobe lights, and half a dozen girls in glittering G-strings dancing on an elevated platform. We took a table in one of the back corners and started drinking our drinks. Once our eyes had adjusted to the darkness, one of my friends spotted "Doc" sitting alone in the opposite corner of the room. My friend went over and asked him to join us, and when the bearded, somewhat disheveled mystery man sat down beside me, mumbling something about Gene Krupa and what the hell had happened to this place, I turned my eyes away from the dancers for a moment and shook hands with the legendary, forgotten novelist, H.L. Humes.

He had been one of the founders of the *Paris Review* back in the fifties, had published two successful early books (*The Underground City* and *Men Die*), and then, just as he was beginning to make a name for himself, had vanished from sight. He just dropped off the literary map and was never heard from again.

I don't know the full story, but the bits and pieces I heard from him suggested that he'd had a rough time of it, had endured a long run of reversals and miseries. Shock treatments were mentioned, a ruined marriage, several stays in mental hospitals. By his own account, he'd been forced to stop writing for physical reasons—not by choice. The electroshock therapy had damaged his system, he said, and every time he picked up a pen, his legs would start to swell up, causing him unbearable pain. With the written word no longer available to him, he now had to rely on talk to get his "message" across to the world. That night, he gave a full-scale demonstration of how thoroughly he had mastered this new medium. First in the topless bar, and then on a nearly seventy-block walk up Broadway to Morningside Heights, the man talked a blue streak, rattling and rambling and chewing our ears off with a monologue that resembled nothing I had ever heard before. It was the rant of a hipster-visionary-neoprophet, a relentless, impassioned outflow of paranoia and brilliance, a careening mental journey that bounced from fact to metaphor to speculation with such speed and unpredictability that one was left dumbfounded, unable to say a word. He had come to New York on a mission, he told us. There were fifteen thousand dollars in his pocket, and if his theories about finance and the structures of capitalism were correct, he would be able to use that money to bring down the American government.

It was all quite simple, really. His father had just died, leaving Doc the aforementioned sum as an inheritance, and rather than squander the money on himself, our friend was proposing to give it away. Not in a lump, and not to any particular charity or person, but to everyone, to the whole world all at once. To that end he had gone to the bank, cashed the check, and converted it into a stack of fifty-dollar bills. With those three hundred portraits of Ulysses S. Grant as his calling cards, he was going to introduce himself to his coconspirators and unleash the greatest economic revolution in history. Money is a fiction, after all, worthless paper that acquires value only because large numbers of people choose to give it value. The system runs on faith. Not truth or reality, but collective belief. And what would happen if that faith were undermined, if large numbers of people suddenly began to doubt the system? Theoretically, the system would collapse. That, in a nutshell, was the object of Doc's experiment. The fifty-dollar bills he handed out to strangers weren't just gifts; they were weapons in the fight to make a better world. He wanted to set an example with his profligacy, to prove that one could disenchant oneself and break the spell that money held over our minds. Each time he disbursed another chunk of cash, he would instruct the recipient to spend it as fast as he could. Spend it, give it away, get it circulating, he would say, and tell the next person to do the same. Overnight, a chain reaction would be set in motion, and before you knew it, so many fifties would be flying through the air that the system would start to go haywire. Waves would be emitted, neutron charges from thousands, even millions of different sources would bounce around the room like little rubber balls. Once they built up enough speed and momentum, they would take on the strength of bullets, and the walls would begin to crack.

I can't say to what degree he actually believed this. Deranged as he might have been, a man of his intelligence surely would have known a stupid idea when he heard it. He never came out and said so, but deep down I think he understood what drivel it was. That didn't stop him from enjoying it, of course, and from spouting off about his plan at every opportunity, but it was more in the spirit of a wacko performance piece than a genuine political act. H. L. Humes wasn't some crackpot schizo taking orders from Martian command center. He was a ravaged, burnt-out writer who had run aground on the shoals of his own consciousness, and rather than give up and renounce life altogether, he had manufactured this little farce to boost his morale. The money gave him an audience again, and as long as people were watching, he was inspired, manic, the original one-man band. He pranced about like a buffoon, turning cartwheels and jumping through flames and shooting himself out of cannons, and from all I could gather, he loved every minute of it.

As he marched up Broadway that night with me and my friends, he put on a spectacular show. Between the cascading words and the barks of laughter and the jags of cosmological music, he would wheel around and start addressing strangers, breaking off in midsentence to slap another fifty-dollar bill in someone's hand and urge him to spend it like there was no tomorrow. Rambunctiousness took control of the street that night, and Doc was the prime attraction, the pied piper of mayhem. It was impossible not to get caught up in it, and I must admit that I found his performance highly entertaining. However, just as we neared the end of our journey and I was about to go home, I made a serious blunder. It must have been one or two in the morning by then. Somewhere off to my right, I heard Doc muttering to himself. "Any of you cats got a place to crash?" he said, and because he sounded so cool and nonchalant, so profoundly indifferent to the matters of this world, I didn't think twice about it. "Sure," I said, "you can sleep on my couch if you want to." Needless to say, he accepted my invitation. Needless to say, I had no idea what I had gotten myself into.

It's not that I didn't like him, and it's not that we didn't get along. For the first couple of days, in fact, things went rather smoothly. Doc planted himself on the couch and rarely stirred, rarely even brought the soles of his feet into contact with the floor. Aside from an occasional trip to the bathroom, he did nothing but sit, eat pizza, smoke marijuana, and talk. I bought the pizza for him (with his money), and after telling him five or six times that I wasn't interested in dope, he finally got the message and stopped offering it to me. The talk was incessant, however, the same repertoire of addled riffs he'd unfurled on the first night, but his arguments were more ample now, more fleshed out, more focused. Hours would go by, and his mouth never stopped moving. Even when I got up and left the room, he would go on talking, delivering his ideas to the wall, the ceiling, the light fixtures, and scarcely even notice that I was gone.

There wouldn't have been a problem if the place had been a little larger. The apartment had just two rooms and a kitchen, and since my bedroom was too small to hold anything but a bed, my work table was set up in the living room—which also happened to be where the couch was. With Doc permanently installed on the couch, it was all but impossible for me to get any work done. The spring semester was drawing to a close, and I had a number of term papers to write in order to complete my courses and graduate, but for the first two days I didn't even bother to try. I figured that I had a little margin and therefore didn't panic. Doc would be leaving soon, and once I had my desk back, I would be able to get down to work. By the morning of the third day, however, I realized that my houseguest had no intention of leaving. It wasn't that he was overstaying his welcome on purpose; the thought of leaving simply hadn't entered his head. What was I supposed to do? I didn't have the heart to kick him out. I already felt too sorry for him, and I couldn't find the courage to take such a drastic step.

The next few days were exceedingly difficult. I did what I could to cope, to see if some minor adjustments could improve the situation. In the end, things might have panned out—I don't know—but three or four days after I put Doc in the bedroom and took over the living room for myself, disaster struck. It happened on one of the most beautiful Sundays I can remember, and it was no one's fault but my own. A friend called to invite me to play in an outdoor basketball game, and rather than leave Doc alone in the apartment, I took him along with me. Everything went well. I played in the game and he sat by the side of the court, listening to the radio and yakking to himself or my friends, depending on whether anyone was within range. As we were returning home that evening, however, someone spotted us on the street. "Aha," this person said to me, "so that's where he's been hiding." I had never particularly liked this person, and when I told him to keep Doc's whereabouts under his hat, I realized that I might just as well have been talking to a lamppost. Sure enough, the buzzer of my apartment started ringing early the next morning. The campus celebrity had been found, and after his mysterious weeklong absence, H. L. Humes was more than happy to indulge his followers. All day long, groups of nineteen- and twenty-year-olds tramped into my apartment to sit on the floor and listen to Doc impart his skewed wisdom to them. He was the philosopher king, the metaphysical pasha, the bohemian holy man who saw through the lies their professors had taught them, and they couldn't get enough of it.

I was deeply pissed off. My apartment had been turned into a twenty-four-hour meeting hall, and much as I would have liked to hold Doc responsible for it, I knew that he wasn't to blame. His acolytes had come of their own accord, without invitations or appointments, and once the crowds began to gather, I could no more ask him to turn them away than I could ask the sun to stop shining. Talk was what he lived for. It was his final barrier against oblivion, and because those kids were there with him now, because they sat at his feet and hung on his every word, he could temporarily delude himself into thinking that all was not lost for him. I had no problem with that. For all I cared, he could go on talking until the next century. I just didn't want him doing it in my apartment.

Torn between compassion and disgust, I came up with a coward's compromise. It happened during one of the rare lulls of that period, at a moment when no unannounced visitors were in the apartment. I told Doc that he could stay—and that I would clear out instead. I had piles of work to do, I explained, and rather than dump him on the street before he'd found another place to live, I would go to my mother's apartment in Newark and write my school papers. In exactly one week I would return, and when I came back I expected him to be gone. Doc listened carefully as I outlined this plan to him. When I had finished, I asked him if he understood. "I dig, man," he said, speaking in his calmest, most gravelly jazzman's voice, "it's cool," and that was all there was to it. We went on to talk about other things, and somewhere in the course of our conversation that night he mentioned that many years back, as a young man in Paris, he had occasionally played chess with Tristan Tzara. This is one of the few concrete facts that has stayed with me. Over time, nearly everything else I heard from the mouth of H. L. Humes has disappeared. I can remember what his voice sounded like, but very little of what he said. All those great verbal marathons, those forced marches to the hinterlands of reason, those countless hours of listening to him unravel his plots and conspiracies and secret correspondences—all that has been reduced to a blur. The words are no more than a buzzing in my brain now, an unintelligible swarm of nothingness.

The next morning, as I was packing my bag and getting ready to leave, he tried to give me money. I turned him down, but he kept insisting, peeling off fifties from his wad like some racetrack gambler, telling me to take it, that I was a good kid, that we had to "share the wealth," and in the end I caved in to the pressure and accepted three hundred dollars from him. I felt terrible about it then and still feel terrible about it now. I had wanted to stay above that business, to resist taking part in the pathetic game he was playing, and yet when my principles were finally put on the line, I succumbed to temptation and allowed greed to get the better of me. Three hundred dollars was a large sum in 1969, and the lure of that money turned out to be stronger than I was. I put the bills in my pocket, shook Doc's hand good-bye, and hurried out of the apartment. When I returned a week later, the place was neat as a pin, and there was no sign of him anywhere. Doc had left, just as he had promised he would.

I saw him only once more after that. It was about a year later, and I was riding uptown on the number 4 bus. Just as we made the turn onto 110th Street, I spotted him through the window—standing on the corner of Fifth Avenue and the northern edge of Central Park. He appeared to be in bad shape. His clothes were rumpled, he looked dirty, and his eyes had a lost, vacant expression that had not been there before. He's slipped into hard drugs, I said to myself. Then the bus moved on, and I lost sight of him. Over the next days and weeks, I kept expecting to see him again, but I never did. Twenty-five years went by, and then, just five or six months ago, I opened *The New York Times* and stumbled across a small article on the obituary page announcing that he was dead.

Little by little, I learned how to improvise, trained myself to roll with the punches. During my last two years at Columbia, I took any number of odd freelance jobs, gradually developing a taste for the kind of literary hackwork that would keep me going until I was thirty—and which ultimately led to my downfall. There was a certain romance in it, I suppose, a need to affirm myself as an outsider and prove that I could make it on my own without kowtowing to anyone else's idea of what constituted the good life. My life would be good if and only if I stuck to my guns and refused to give in. Art was holy, and to follow its call meant making any sacrifice that was demanded of you, maintaining your purity of purpose to the bitter end.

Knowing French helped. It was hardly a rarefied skill, but I was good enough at it to have some translation jobs tossed my way. Art writings, for example, and an exceptionally tedious document from the French Embassy about the reorganization of its staff that droned on for more than a hundred pages. I also tutored a high school girl one spring, traveling across town every Saturday morning to talk to her about poetry, and another time I was collared by a friend (for no pay) to stand on an outdoor podium with Jean Genet and translate his speech in defense of the Black Panthers. Genet walked around with a red flower tucked behind his ear and rarely stopped smiling the whole time he was on the Columbia campus. New York seemed to make him happy, and he handled the attention he received that day with great poise. One night not long after that, I bumped into an acquaintance in the West End, the old student watering hole at Broadway and 114th Street. He told me that he had just started working for a pornography publisher, and if I wanted to try my hand at writing a dirty book, the price was fifteen hundred dollars per novel. I was more than willing to have a go at it, but my inspiration petered out after twenty or thirty pages. There were just so many ways to describe that one thing, I discovered, and my stock of synonyms soon dried up. I started writing book reviews instead—for a shoddily put together publication aimed at students. Sensing that the magazine wasn't going to add up to much, I signed my articles with a pseudonym, just to keep things interesting. Quinn was the name I chose for myself, Paul Quinn. The pay, I remember, was twenty-five dollars per review.

When the results of the draft lottery were announced at the end of 1969, I lucked out with number 297. A blind draw of the cards saved my skin, and the nightmare I had been girding myself against for several years suddenly evaporated. Who to thank for that unexpected mercy? I had been spared immense amounts of pain and trouble, had literally been given back control of my life, and the sense of relief was incalculable. Jail was no longer in the picture for me. The horizon was clear on all sides, and I was free to walk off in any direction I chose. As long as I traveled light, there was nothing to stop me from going as far as my legs would take me.

That I wound up working on an oil tanker for several months was largely a matter of chance. You can't work on a ship without a Merchant Seaman's card, and you can't obtain a Merchant Seaman's card without a job on a ship. Unless you know someone who can break through the circle for you, it's impossible to get in. The someone who did it for me was my mother's second husband, Norman Schiff. My mother had remarried about a year after her divorce from my father, and by 1970 my stepfather and I had been fast friends for nearly five years. An excellent man with a generous heart, he had consistently stood behind me and supported my vague, impractical ambitions. His early death in 1982 (at age fifty-five) remains one of the great sorrows of my life, but back then as I was finishing up my year of graduate work and preparing to leave school, his health was still reasonably good. He practiced law, mostly as a labor negotiator, and among his many clients at the time was the Esso Seaman's Union, for which he worked as legal counsel. That was how the idea got planted in my head. I asked him if he could swing me a job on one of the Esso tankers, and he said he would handle it. And without further ado, that was precisely what he did.

There was a lot of paperwork to take care of, trips to the union hall in Belleville, New Jersey, physical exams in Manhattan, and then an indefinite period of waiting until a slot opened up on one of the ships coming into the New York area. In the meantime, I took a temporary job with the United States Census Bureau, collecting data for the 1970 census in Harlem. The work consisted of climbing up and down staircases in dimly lit tenement buildings, knocking on apartment doors, and helping people fill out the government forms. Not everyone wanted to be helped, of course, and more than a few were suspicious of the white college boy prowling around their hallways, but enough people welcomed me in to make me feel that I wasn't completely wasting my time. I stayed with it for approximately a month, and then—sooner than I was expecting—the ship called.

I happened to be sitting in a dentist's chair at that moment, about to have a wisdom tooth pulled. Every morning since my name had gone on the list, I had checked in with my stepfather to let him know where I could be reached that day, and he was the one who tracked me down at the dentist's office. The timing couldn't have been more comical. The Novocain had already been injected into my gums, and the dentist had just picked up the pliers and was about to attack my rotten tooth when the receptionist walked in and announced that I was wanted on the phone. Extremely urgent. I climbed out of the chair with the bib still tied around my neck, and the next thing I knew, Norman was telling me that I had three hours to pack and get myself aboard the S.S. *Esso Florence* in Elizabeth, New Jersey. I stammered my apologies to the dentist and hightailed it out of there.

The tooth stayed in my mouth for another week. When it finally came out, I was in Baytown, Texas.

The *Esso Florence* was one of the oldest tankers in the fleet, a pip-squeak relic from a bygone age. Put a two-door Chevy next to a stretch limousine, and you'll have some idea of how it compared to the supertankers they build today. Already in service during World War II, my ship had logged untold thousands of watery miles by the time I set foot on it. There were enough beds on board to accommodate a hundred men, but only thirty-three of us were needed to take care of the work that had to be done. That meant that each person had his own room—an enormous benefit when you considered how much time we had to spend together. With other jobs you get to go home at night, but we were boxed in with each other twenty-four hours a day. Every time you looked up, the same faces were there. We worked together, lived together, and ate together, and without the chance for some genuine privacy, the routine would have been intolerable.

We shuttled between the Atlantic coast and the Gulf of Mexico, loading and unloading airplane fuel at various refineries along the way: Charleston, South Carolina; Tampa, Florida; Galveston, Texas. My initial responsibilities were mopping floors and making beds, first for the crew and then for the officers. The technical term for the position was "utilityman," but in plain language the job was a combination of janitor, garbage collector, and chambermaid. I can't say that I was thrilled to be scrubbing toilets and picking up dirty socks, but once I got the hang of it, the work turned out to be incredibly easy. In less than a week, I had polished my custodial skills to such a point that it took me only two or two and a half hours to finish my chores for the day. That left me with abundant quantities of free time, most of which I spent alone in my room. I read books, I wrote, I did everything I had done before—but more productively, somehow, with better powers of concentration now that there was so little to distract me. In many ways, it felt like an almost ideal existence, a perfect life.

Then, after a month or two of this blissful regimen, I was "bumped." The ship rarely traveled more than five days between ports, and nearly everywhere we docked some crew members would get off and others would get on. The jobs for the fresh arrivals were doled out according to seniority. It was a strict pecking order, and the longer you had worked for the company, the more say you had in what you were given. As low man on the totem pole, I had no say at all. If an old-timer wanted my job, he had only to ask for it, and it was his. After my long run of good luck, the boom finally fell on me somewhere in Texas. My replacement was a man named Elmer, a bovine Fundamentalist bachelor who happened to be the longest-serving, most famous utilityman of them all. What I had been able to do in two hours, Elmer now did in six. He was the slowest of the slow, a smug and untalkative mental lightweight who waddled about the ship in a world of his own, utterly ignored by the other crew members, and in all my experience I have never met a person who ate as much as he did. Elmer could pack away mountains of food—two, three, and four helpings at every meal—but what made it fascinating to watch him was not so much the scope of his appetite as the way he went about satisfying it: daintily, fastidiously, with a compulsive sense of decorum. The best part was the cleanup operation at the end. Once Elmer had eaten his fill, he would spread his napkin on the table before him and begin patting and smoothing the flimsy paper with his hands, slowly transforming it into a flat square. Then he would fold the napkin into precise longitudinal sections, methodically halving the area until it had been divided into eighths. In the end, the square would be turned into a long, rectilinear strip with all four edges exactly aligned. At that point, Elmer would carefully take hold of the edges, raise the napkin to his lips, and begin to rub. The action was all in the head: a slow back-and-forth swiveling that went on for twenty or thirty seconds. From start to finish, Elmer's hands never stirred. They would be fixed in the air as his large head turned left, right, and left again, and through it all his eyes never betrayed the slightest thought or emotion. The Cleaning of the Lips was a dogged, mechanical procedure, an act of ritual purification. Cleanliness is next to godliness, Elmer once told me. To see him with that napkin, you understood that he was doing God's work.

I was able to observe Elmer's eating habits at such close range because I had been bumped into the galley. The job of messman quadrupled my hours and made my life altogether more eventful. My responsibilities now included serving three meals a day to the crew (about twenty men), washing dishes by hand, cleaning the mess hall, and writing out the menus for the steward, who was generally too drunk to bother with them himself. My breaks were short—no more than an hour or two between meals—and yet in spite of having to work much harder than before, my income actually shrank. On the old job, there had been plenty of time for me to put in an extra hour or two in the evenings, scraping and painting in the boiler room, for example, or refurbishing rusty spots on deck, and those volunteer jobs had padded my paycheck quite nicely. Still, in spite of the disadvantages, I found working in the mess hall more of a challenge than mopping floors had been. It was a public job, so to speak, and in addition to all the hustling around that was now required of me, I had to stay on my toes as far as the men were concerned. That, finally, was my most important task: to learn how to handle the griping and rough-tempered complaints, to fend off insults, to give as good as I got.

Elmer aside, the crew was a fairly grimy, ill-mannered bunch. Most of the men lived in Texas and Louisiana, and apart from a handful of Chicanos, one or two blacks, and the odd foreigner who cropped up now and then, the dominant tone on board was white, redneck, and blue collar. A jocular atmosphere prevailed, replete with funny stories and dirty jokes and much talk about guns and cars, but there were deep, smoldering currents of racism in many of those men, and I made a point of choosing my friends carefully. To hear one of your coworkers defend South African apartheid as you sat with him over a cup of coffee ("they know how to treat niggers down there") doesn't bring much joy to the soul, and if I found myself hanging out mostly with the dark-skinned and Spanish-speaking men around me, there was a good reason for it. As a New York Jew with a college degree, I was an entirely alien specimen on that ship, a man from Mars. It would have been easy to make up stories about myself, but I had no interest in doing that. If someone asked me what my religion was or where I came from, I told him. If he didn't like it, I figured that was his problem. I wasn't going to hide who I was or pretend to be someone else just to avoid trouble. As it happened, I had only one awkward run-in the whole time I was there. One of the men started calling me Sammy whenever I walked by. He seemed to think it was funny, but as I failed to see any humor in the epithet, I told him to stop it. He did it again the next day, and once again I told him to stop it. When he did it again the day after that, I understood that polite words were not going to be enough. I grabbed hold of his shirt, slammed him against the wall, and very calmly told him that if he ever called me that again, I would kill him. It shocked me to hear myself talk like that. I was not someone who trafficked in violence, and I had never made that kind of threat to anyone, but for that one brief instant, a demon took possession of my soul. Luckily, my willingness to fight was enough to defuse the fight before it began. My tormentor threw up his hands in a gesture of peace. "It was just a joke," he said, "just a joke," and that was the end of it. As time went on, we actually became friends.

I loved being out on the water, surrounded by nothing but sky and light, the immensity of the vacant air. Seagulls accompanied us wherever we went, circling overhead as they waited for buckets of garbage to be dumped overboard. Hour after hour, they would hover patiently just above the ship, scarcely beating their wings until the scraps went flying, at which point they would plunge frantically into the foam, calling out to each other like drunks at a football game. Few pleasures can match the spectacle of that foam, of sitting at the stern of a large ship and staring into the white, churning tumult of the wake below. There is something hypnotic about it, and on still days the sense of well-being that washes through you can be overpowering. On the other hand, rough weather also holds its charms. As summer melted away and we headed into autumn, the inclemencies multiplied, bringing down some wild winds and pelting rains, and at those moments the ship felt no more safe or solid than a child's paper boat. Tankers have been known to crack in half, and all it takes is one wrong wave to do the job. The worst stretch, I remember, occurred when we were off Cape Hatteras in late September or early October, a twelve-or fifteen-hour period of flipping and flopping through a tropical storm. The captain stayed at the wheel all night, and even after the worst of it was over and the steward instructed me to carry the captain his breakfast the next morning, I was nearly blown overboard when I stepped onto the bridge with my tray. The rain might have stopped, but the wind speed was still at gale force.

For all that, working on the *Esso Florence* had little to do with high-seas adventure. The tanker was essentially a floating factory, and rather than introduce me to some exotic, swashbuckling life, it taught me to think of myself as an industrial laborer. I was one of millions now, an insect toiling beside countless other insects, and every task I performed was part of the great, grinding enterprise of American capitalism. Petroleum was the primary source of wealth, the raw material that fueled the profit machine and kept it running, and I was glad to be where I was, grateful to have landed in the belly of the beast. The refineries where we loaded and unloaded our cargo were enormous, hellish structures, labyrinthine networks of hissing pipes and towers of flame, and to walk through one of them at night was to feel that you were living in your own worst dream. Most of all, I will never forget the fish, the hundreds of dead, iridescent fish floating on the rank, oil-saturated water around the refinery docks. That was the standard welcoming committee, the sight that greeted us every time the tugboats pulled us into another port. The ugliness was so universal, so deeply connected to the business of making money and the power that money bestowed on the ones who made it—even to the point of disfiguring the landscape, of turning the natural world inside out—that I began to develop a grudging respect for it. Get to the bottom of things, I told myself, and this was how the world looked. Whatever you might think of it, this ugliness was the truth.

Whenever we docked somewhere, I made it my business to leave the ship and spend some time ashore. I had never been south of the Mason-Dixon line, and those brief jaunts onto solid ground took me to places that felt a lot less familiar or understandable than anything I'd met up with in Paris or Dublin. The South was a different country, a separate

American universe from the one I'd known in the North. Most of the time, I tagged along with one or two of my shipmates, going the rounds with them as they visited their customary haunts. If Baytown, Texas, stands out with particular clarity, that is because we spent more time there than anywhere else. I found it a sad, crumbling little place. Along the main drag, a row of once elegant movie theaters had been turned into Baptist churches, and instead of announcing the titles of the latest Hollywood films, the marquees now sported fiery quotations from the Bible. More often than not, we wound up in sailors' bars on the back streets of broken-down neighborhoods. All of them were essentially the same: squalid, low-life joints; dim drinking holes; dank corners of oblivion. Everything was always bare inside. Not a single picture on the walls, not one touch of publican warmth. At most there was a quarter-a-rack pool table, a jukebox stuffed with country-and-western songs, and a drink menu that consisted of just one drink: beer.

Once, when the ship was in a Houston dry dock for some minor repairs, I spent the afternoon in a skid row bar with a Danish oiler named Freddy, a wild man who laughed at the slightest provocation and spoke English with an accent so thick that I scarcely understood a word he said. Walking down the street in the blinding Texas sun, we crossed paths with a drunken couple. It was still early in the day, but this man and woman were already so soused, so entrenched in their inebriation, they must have been going at the booze since dawn. They wobbled along the sidewalk with their arms around each other, listing this way and that, their heads lolling, their knees buckling, and yet both with enough energy left to be engaged in a nasty, foul-mouthed quarrel. From the sound of their voices, I gathered they'd been at it for years—a pair of bickering stumblebums in search of their next drink, forever repeating the same lines to each other, forever shuffling through the same old song and dance. As it turned out, they wound up in the same bar where Freddy and I chose to while away the afternoon, and because I was not more than ten feet away from them, I was in a perfect position to observe the following little drama:

The man leaned forward and barked out at the woman across the table. "Darlene," he said, in a drawling, besotted voice, "get me another beer."

Darlene had been nodding off just then, and it took her a good long moment to open her eyes and bring the man into focus. Another long moment ticked by, and then she finally said, "What?"

"Get me a beer," the man repeated. "On the double."

Darlene was waking up now, and a lovely, fuck-you sassiness suddenly brightened her face. She was clearly in no mood to be pushed around. "Get it yourself, Charlie," she snapped back at him. "I ain't your slave, you know."

"Damn it, woman," Charlie said. "You're my wife, ain't you? What the hell did I marry you for? Get me the goddamn beer!"

Darlene let out a loud, histrionic sigh. You could tell she was up to something, but her intentions were still obscure. "Okay, darling," she said, putting on the voice of a meek, simpering wife, "I'll get it for you," and then stood up from the table and staggered over to the bar.

Charlie sat there with a grin on his face, gloating over his small, manly victory. He was the boss, all right, and no one was going to tell him different. If you wanted to know who wore the pants in that family, just talk to him.

A minute later, Darlene returned to the table with a fresh bottle of Bud. "Here's your beer, Charlie," she said, and then, with one quick flick of the wrist, proceeded to dump the contents of the bottle onto her husband's head. Bubbles foamed up in his hair and eyebrows; rivulets of amber liquid streamed down his face. Charlie made a lunge for her, but he was too drunk to get very close. Darlene threw her head back and burst out laughing. "How do you like your beer, Charlie?" she said. "How do you like your fucking beer?"

Of all the scenes I witnessed in those bars, nothing quite matched the bleak comedy of Charlie's baptism, but for overall oddness, a plunge into the deepest heart of the grotesque, I would have to single out Big Mary's Place in Tampa, Florida. This was a large, brightly lit emporium that catered to the whims of dockhands and sailors, and it had been in business for many years. Among its features were half a dozen pool tables, a long mahogany bar, inordinately high ceilings, and live entertainment in the form of quasi-naked go-go dancers. These girls were the cornerstone of the operation, the element that set Big Mary's Place apart from other establishments of its kind—and one look told you that they weren't hired for their beauty, nor for their ability to dance. The sole criterion was size. The bigger the better was how Big Mary put it, and the bigger you got, the more money you were paid. The effect was quite disturbing. It was a freak show of flesh, a cavalcade of bouncing white blubber, and with four girls dancing on the platform behind the bar at once, the act resembled a casting call for the lead role in *Moby-Dick*. Each girl was a continent unto herself, a mass of quivering lard decked out in a string bikini, and as one shift replaced another, the assault on the eyes was unrelenting. I have no memory of how I got there, but I distinctly recall that my companions that night were two of the gentler souls from the ship (Martinez, a family man from Texas, and Donnie, a seventeen-year-old boy from Baton Rouge) and that they were both just as flummoxed as I was. I can still see them sitting across from me with their mouths hanging open, doing everything they could not to laugh from embarrassment. At one point, Big Mary herself came over and sat down with us at our table. A splendid dirigible of a woman dressed in an orange pants suit and wearing a ring on every finger, she wanted to know if we were having a good time. When we assured her that we were, she waved to one of the girls at the bar. "Barbara," she yelled, belting out the word in a brassy, three-pack-a-day voice, "get your fat butt over here!" Barbara came, all smiles and good humor, laughing as Big Mary poked her in the stomach and pinched the ample rolls bulging from her hips. "She was a scrawny one at first," Mary explained, "but I've fattened her up pretty good. Ain't that so, Barbara?" she said, cackling like some mad scientist who's just pulled off a successful experiment, and Barbara couldn't have agreed with her more. As I listened to them talk, it suddenly occurred to me that I had it all wrong. I hadn't gone to sea. I'd run off and joined the circus.

Another friend was Jeffrey, the second cook (a.k.a. breakfast chef), from Bogalusa, Louisiana. We happened to have been born on the same day, and apart from the near-infant Donnie, we were the youngest members of the crew. It was the first time out for both of us, and since we worked together in the galley, we got to know each other reasonably well. Jeffrey was one of life's winners—a bright, handsome, fun-loving ladies' man with a taste for flashy clothes—and yet very practical and ambitious, a down-to-earth schemer who was quite consciously using his job on the ship to learn the ins and outs of cooking. He had no intention of making a career out of oil tankers, no desire to turn himself into an old salt. His dream was to become a chef in a high-class restaurant, maybe even to own that restaurant himself, and if nothing unexpected rose up to stop him, I don't doubt that that's exactly what he's doing today. We couldn't have been more unlike, Jeffrey and I, but we got along comfortably with each other. It was only natural that we should sometimes go ashore together when the ship was in port, but because Jeffrey was black, and because he had spent his whole life in the South, he knew that many of the places I went to with white crew members were off-limits to him. He made that perfectly clear to me the first time we planned an outing. "If you want me to go with you," he said, "you'll have to go where I can go." I tried to convince him that he could go anywhere he pleased, but Jeffrey wasn't buying the argument. "Maybe up North," he said. "Down here it's different." I didn't force the issue. When I went out for beers with Jeffrey, we drank them in black bars instead of white bars. Except for the skin color of the clientele, the atmosphere was the same.

One night in Houston, Jeffrey talked me into going to a dance club with him. I never danced and never went to clubs, but the thought of spending a few hours in a place that wasn't a low-rent dive tempted me, and I decided to take my chances. The club turned out to be a splashy disco hall thronged with hundreds of young people, the hottest black nightspot in town. There was a live band onstage, psychedelic strobe lights bouncing off the walls, hard liquor available at the bar. Everything pulsed with sex and chaos and loud music. It was Saturday night fever, Texas style.

Jeffrey was dressed to the teeth, and within four minutes he struck up a conversation with one of the many stunning girls floating around the bar, and four minutes after that they were out on the dance floor together, lost in an ocean of bodies. I sat down at a table and sipped my drink, the only white person in the building. No one gave me any trouble, but I got some odd, penetrating looks from a number of people, and by the time I finished my bourbon, I understood that I should be shoving off. I phoned for a cab and then went outside to wait in the parking lot. When the driver showed up a few minutes later, he started cursing. "Goddammit," he said. "Goddammit to hell. If I'd known you were calling from here, I wouldn't have come." "Why not?" I asked. "Because this is the worst fucking place in Houston," he said. "They've had six murders here in the past month. Every damn weekend, somebody else gets shot."

In the end, the months I spent on that ship felt like years. Time passes in a different way when you're out on the water, and given that the bulk of what I experienced was utterly new to me, and given that I was constantly on my guard because of that, I managed to crowd an astonishing number of impressions and memories into a relatively small sliver of my life. Even now, I don't fully understand what I was hoping to prove by shipping out like that. To keep myself off balance, I suppose.

Or, very simply, just to see if I could do it, to see if I could hold my own in a world I didn't belong to. In that respect, I don't think I failed. I can't say what I accomplished during those months, but at the same time I'm certain I didn't fail.

I received my discharge papers in Charleston. The company provided airfare home, but you could pocket the money if you wanted to and make your own travel arrangements. I chose to keep the money. The trip by milk train took twenty-four hours, and I rode back with a fellow crew member from New York, Juan Castillo. Juan was in his late forties or early fifties, a squat, lumpy man with a big head and a face that looked like something pieced together with the skins and pulps of nineteen mashed potatoes. He had just walked off an oil tanker for the last time, and in appreciation of his twenty-five years of service to the company, Esso had given him a gold watch. I don't know how many times Juan pulled that watch out of his pocket and looked at it during the long ride home, but every time he did, he would shake his head for a few seconds and then burst out laughing. At one point, the ticket collector stopped to talk to us during one of his strolls down the aisle of the car. He looked very natty in his uniform, I remember, a black Southern gentleman of the old school. In a haughty, somewhat condescending manner, he opened the conversation by asking: "You boys going up North to work in the steel mills?"

We must have been a curious pair, Juan and I. I recall that I was wearing a beat-up leather jacket at the time, but other than that I can't see myself, have no sense of what I looked like or what other people saw when they looked at me. The ticket collector's question is the only clue I have. Juan had taken pictures of his shipmates to put in the family album at home, and I remember standing on the deck and looking into the camera for him as he clicked the shutter. He promised to send me a copy of the photo, but he never did.

I toyed with the idea of going out for another run on an Esso tanker, but in the end I decided against it. My salary was still being sent to me through the mail (for every two days I'd been on the ship, I received one day's pay on land), and my bank account was beginning to look fairly robust. For the past few months, I had been slowly coming to the conclusion that my next step should be to leave the country and live abroad for a while. I was willing to ship out again if necessary, but I wondered if I hadn't built up a large enough stake already. The three or four thousand dollars I'd earned from the tanker struck me as a sufficient sum to get started with, and so rather than continue in the merchant marine, I abruptly shifted course and began plotting a move to Paris.

France was a logical choice, but I don't think I went there for logical reasons. That I spoke French, that I had been translating French poetry, that I knew and cared about a number of people who lived in France—surely those things entered into my decision, but they were not determining factors. What made me want to go, I think, was the memory of what had happened to me in Paris three years earlier. I still hadn't gotten it out of my system, and because that visit had been cut short, because I had left on the assumption that I would soon be returning, I had walked around with a feeling of unfinished business, of not having had my fill. The only thing I wanted just then was to hunker down and write. By recapturing the inwardness and freedom of that earlier time, I felt that I would be putting myself in the best possible position to do that. I had no intention of becoming an expatriate. Giving up America was not part of the plan, and at no time did I think I wouldn't return. I just needed a little breathing room, a chance to figure out, once and for all, if I was truly the person I thought I was.

What comes back to me most vividly from my last weeks in New York is the farewell conversation I had with Joe Reilly, a homeless man who used to hang around the lobby of my apartment building on West 107th Street. The building was a run-down, nine-story affair, and like most places on the Upper West Side, it housed a motley collection of people. With no effort at all, I can summon forth a fair number of them, even after a quarter of a century. The Puerto Rican mailman, for example, and the Chinese waiter, and the fat blonde opera singer with the Lhasa apso. Not to mention the black homosexual fashion designer with his black fur coat and the quarreling clarinetists whose vicious spats would seep through the walls of my apartment and poison my nights. On the ground floor of this gray brick building, one of the apartments had been divided down the middle, and each half was occupied by a man confined to a wheelchair. One of them worked at the news kiosk on the corner of Broadway and 110th Street; the other was a retired rabbi. The rabbi was a particularly charming fellow, with a pointy artist's goatee and an ever-present black beret, which he wore at a rakish, debonair angle. On most days, he would wheel himself out of his apartment and spend some time in the lobby, chatting with Arthur, the superintendent, or with various tenants getting in and out of the elevator. Once, as I entered the building, I caught sight of him through the glass door in his usual spot, talking to a bum in a long, dark overcoat. It struck me as an odd conjunction, but from the way the bum stood there and from the tilt of the rabbi's head, it was clear that they knew each other well. The bum was an authentic down-and-outer, a scab-faced wino with filthy clothes and cuts dotting his half-bald scalp, a scrofulous wreck of a man who appeared to have just crawled out of a storm drain. Then, as I pushed open the door and stepped into the lobby, I heard him speak. Accompanied by wild, theatrical gestures—a sweep of the left arm, a finger darting from his right hand and pointing to the sky—a sentence came booming out of him, a string of words so unlikely and unexpected that at first I didn't believe my ears. "It was no mere fly-by-night acquaintance!" he said, rolling each syllable of that florid, literary phrase off his tongue with such relish, such blowhard bravura, such magnificent pomposity, that he sounded like some tragic ham delivering a line from a Victorian melodrama. It was pure W. C. Fields—but several octaves lower, with the voice more firmly in control of the effects it was striving to create. W. C. Fields mixed with Ralph Richardson, perhaps, with a touch of barroom bombast thrown in for good measure. However you wanted to define it, I had never heard a voice do what that voice did.

When I walked over to say hello to the rabbi, he introduced me to his friend, and that was how I learned the name of that singular gentleman, that mightiest of fallen characters, the one and only Joe Reilly.

According to the rabbi, who filled me in on the story later, Joe had started out in life as the privileged son of a wealthy New York family, and in his prime he had owned an art gallery on Madison Avenue. That was when the rabbi had met him—back in the old days, before Joe's disintegration and collapse. The rabbi had already left the pulpit by then and was running a music publishing company. Joe's male lover was a composer, and as the rabbi happened to publish that man's work, in the natural course of things he and Joe crossed paths. Then, very suddenly, the lover died. Joe had always had a drinking problem, the rabbi said, but now he hit the bottle in earnest, and his life began to fall apart. He lost his gallery; his family turned its back on him; his friends walked away. Little by little, he sank into the gutter, the last hole at the bottom of the world, and in the rabbi's opinion he would never climb out again. As far as he was concerned, Joe was a hopeless case.

Whenever Joe came around after that, I would dig into my pocket and hand him a few coins. What moved me about these encounters was that he never let his mask drop. Blustering forth his thanks in the highly embroidered, Dickensian language that came so effortlessly to him, he would assure me that I would be paid back promptly, just as soon as circumstances allowed. "I am most grateful to you for this bounty, young man," he would say, "most grateful indeed. It's just a loan, of course, so you needn't fret about being reimbursed. As you might or might not know, I've suffered some small setbacks lately, and this generosity of yours will go a long way towards helping me back to my feet." The sums in question were never more than a pittance—forty cents here, twenty-five cents there, whatever I happened to be carrying around with me—but Joe never flagged in his enthusiasm, never once let on that he realized what an abject figure he was. There he stood, dressed in a circus clown's rags, his unwashed body emitting the foulest of stinks, and still he persisted in keeping up his pose as a man of the world, a dandy temporarily down on his luck. The pride and self-deception that went into this act were both comical and heartbreaking, and every time I went through the ritual of giving him another handout, I had trouble keeping my balance. I never knew whether to laugh or cry, whether to admire him or shower him with pity. "Let me see, young man," he would continue, studying the coins I had just put in his palm. "I have, let's see, I have here in my hand, hmmm, fifty-five cents. Add that to the eighty cents you gave me the last time, and then add that, hmmm, add that to the forty cents you gave me the time before that, and it turns out that I owe you a grand total of, hmmm, let's see, a grand total of . . . one dollar and fifteen cents." Such was Joe's arithmetic. He just plucked figures out of thin air and hoped they sounded good. "No problem, Joe," I would say. "A dollar and fifteen cents. You'll give it to me the next time."

When I came back to New York from the Esso ship, he seemed to be floundering, to have lost some ground. He looked more bruised to me, and the old panache had given way to a new heaviness of spirit, a whining, tearful sort of despair. One afternoon, he broke down in front of me as he recounted how he had been beaten up in some alleyway the night before. "They stole my books," he said. "Can you imagine that? The animals stole my books!" Another time, in the middle of a snowstorm, as I left my ninth-floor apartment and walked to the elevator down the hall, I found him sitting alone on the staircase, his head buried in his hands.

"Joe," I said, "are you all right?"

He lifted his head. His eyes were infused with sorrow, misery, and defeat. "No, young man," he said. "I'm not all right, not the least bit all right."

"Is there anything I can do for you?" I asked. "You look terrible, just terrible."

"Yes," he said, "now that you mention it, there is one thing you can do for me," and at that point he suddenly reached out and took hold of my hand. Then, looking me straight in the eye, he gathered up his strength and said, in a voice trembling with emotion, "You can take me back into your apartment, lie down on the bed, and let me make love to you."

The bluntness of his request took me completely by surprise. I had been thinking more along the lines of a cup of coffee or a bowl of soup. "I can't do that," I said. "I like women, Joe, not men. Sorry, but I don't do that kind of thing."

What he said next lingers in my mind as one of the best and most pungent statements I have ever heard. Without wasting a second, and without the slightest trace of disappointment or regret, he dismissed my answer with a shrug of the shoulders and said, in a buoyant, ringing tone of voice, "Well, you asked me—and I told you."

I left for Paris some time in the middle of February 1971. After that encounter on the staircase, I didn't see Joe again for several weeks. Then, just days before my departure, I bumped into him on Broadway. He was looking much better, and the hangdog look had disappeared from his face. When I told him I was about to move to Paris, he was off and running again, as effusive and full of himself as ever. "It's odd that you should mention Paris," he said. "Indeed, it's a most timely coincidence. Not two or three days ago, I happened to be walking down Fifth Avenue, and who should I bump into but my old friend Antoine, director of the Cunard Lines. 'Joe,' he said to me, 'Joe, you're not looking too well,' and I said, 'No, Antoine, it's true, I haven't been at my best lately,' and Antoine said that he wanted to do something for me, lend a helping hand, so to speak, and put me back on track. What he proposed, right there on Fifth Avenue the other day, was to sail me over to Paris on one of his ships and put me up at the Hôtel Georges V. All expenses paid, of course, with a new wardrobe thrown into the bargain. He said I could stay there as long as I liked. Two weeks, two months, even two years if I wanted. If I decide to go, which I think I will, I'll be leaving before the end of the month. Which means, young man, that we'll be in

Paris at the same time. A pleasant prospect, no? Expect to see me there. We'll have tea, dinner. Just leave a message for me at the hotel. On the Champs-Elysées. That's where we'll meet next, my friend. In Paris, on the Champs-Elysées." And then, bidding me farewell, he shook my hand and wished me a safe and happy voyage.

I never saw Joe Reilly again. Even before we said good-bye that day, I knew that I was talking to him for the last time, and when he finally disappeared into the crowd a few minutes later, it was as if he had already turned into a ghost. All during the years I lived in Paris, I thought of him every time I set foot on the Champs-Elysées. Even now, whenever I go back there, I still do.

My money didn't last as long as I thought it would. I found an apartment within a week of my arrival, and once I had shelled out for the agency commission, the security deposit, the gas and electric service, the first month's rent, the last month's rent, and the state-mandated insurance policy, I didn't have much left. Right from the start, therefore, I had to scramble to keep my head above water. In the three and a half years I lived in France, I had any number of jobs, bounced from one part-time gig to another, freelanced until I was blue in the face. When I didn't have work, I was looking for work. When I had work, I was thinking about how to find more. Even at the best of times, I rarely earned enough to feel secure, and yet in spite of one or two close calls, I managed to avoid total ruin. It was, as they say, a hand-to-mouth existence. Through it all, I wrote steadily, and if much of what I wrote was discarded (mostly prose), a fair chunk of it (mostly poems and translations) was not. For better or worse, by the time I returned to New York in July 1974, the idea of not writing was inconceivable to me.

Most of the work I landed came through friends or the friends of friends or the friends of friends of friends. Living in a foreign country restricts your opportunities, and unless you know some people who are willing to help you, it is next to impossible to get started. Not only will doors not open when you knock on them, but you won't even know where to look for those doors in the first place. I was lucky enough to have some allies, and at one time or another they all moved small mountains on my behalf. Jacques Dupin, for example, a poet whose work I had been translating for several years, turned out to be director of publications at the Galerie Maeght, one of the leading art galleries in Europe. Among the painters and sculptors shown there were Miró,

Giacometti, Chagall, and Calder, to mention just a few. Through Jacques's intervention, I was hired to translate several art books and catalogues, and by my second year in Paris, when my funds were perilously close to bottoming out, he saved the situation by giving me a room to live in—free of charge. These acts of kindness were essential, and I can't imagine how I would have survived without them.

At one point, I was steered to the Paris bureau of *The New York Times*. I can't remember who was responsible for the connection, but an editor named Josette Lazar began throwing translations my way whenever she could: articles for the Sunday *Book Review*, op-ed pieces by Sartre and Foucault, this and that. One summer, when my money was at low ebb again, she finagled a position for me as the nighttime switchboard operator at the *Times* office. The phone didn't ring very often, and mostly I just sat at a desk, working on poems or reading books. One night, however, there was a frantic call from a reporter stationed somewhere in Europe. "Sinyavsky's defected," she said. "What should I do?" I had no idea what she should do, but since none of the editors was around at that hour, I figured I had to tell her something. "Follow the story," I said. "Go where you have to go, do what you have to do, but stick with the story, come hell or high water." She thanked me profusely for the advice and then hung up.

Some jobs started out as one thing and ended up as another, like a botched stew you can't stop tinkering with. Just stir in some additional ingredients and see if it doesn't taste better. A good example would be my little adventure among the North Vietnamese in Paris, which began with an innocent phone call from Mary McCarthy to my friend André du Bouchet. She asked him if he knew of anyone who could translate poetry from French into English, and when he gave her my name, she called and invited me to her apartment to discuss the project. It was early 1973, and the war in Vietnam was still dragging on. Mary McCarthy had been writing about the war for several years, and I had read most of her articles, which I found to be among the best pieces of journalism published at the time. In the course of her work, she had come in contact with many Vietnamese from both the northern and southern halves of the country. One of them, a professor of literature, was putting together an anthology of Vietnamese poetry, and she had offered to help arrange for an English-language version to be published in America. The poems had already been translated into French, and the idea was to translate those translations into English. That was how my name had come up, and that was why she wanted to talk to me.

In her private life, Mary McCarthy was Mrs. West. Her husband was a well-to-do American businessman, and their Paris apartment was a large, richly appointed place filled with art objects, antiques, and fine furniture. Lunch was served to us by a maid in a black and white uniform. A china bell sat on the table next to my hostess's right hand, and every time she picked it up and gave it a little shake, the maid would return to the dining room to receive further instructions. There was an impressive, *grande dame* quality to the way Mary McCarthy handled these domestic protocols, but the truth was that she turned out to be everything I had hoped she would be: sharp-witted, friendly, unpretentious. We talked about many things that afternoon, and by the time I left her apartment several hours later, I was loaded down with six or seven books of Vietnamese poetry. The first step was for me to familiarize myself with their contents. After that, the professor and I would meet and get down to work on the anthology.

I read the books and enjoyed them, particularly *The Book of Kieu*, the national epic poem. The details escape me now, but I remember becoming interested in some of the formal problems presented by traditional Vietnamese verse structures, which have no equivalents in Western poetry. I was happy to have been offered the job. Not only was I going to be paid well, but it looked as if I might learn something into the bargain. A week or so after our lunch, however, Mary McCarthy called to tell me that there had been an emergency, and her professor friend had gone back to Hanoi. She wasn't sure when he would be returning to Paris, but for the time being at least, the project had been put on hold.

Such were the breaks. I pushed the books aside and hoped the job wasn't dead, even though I knew it was. Several days went by, and then, out of the blue, I received a telephone call from a Vietnamese woman living in Paris. "Professor So-and-so gave us your name," she said. "He told us you can translate into English. Is that true?" "Yes," I said, "it's true." "Good," she said. "We have a job for you."

The job turned out to be a translation of the new North Vietnamese constitution. I had no qualms about doing the work, but I found it strange that they should have come to me. You would think that a document of that sort would be translated by someone in the government—directly from Vietnamese into English, and not from French, and if from French, not by an enemy American living in Paris. I didn't ask any questions, however. I still had my fingers crossed about the anthology and didn't want to ruin my chances, so I accepted the job. The following evening, the woman came to my apartment to drop off the manuscript. She was a biologist in her mid-thirties—thin, unadorned, exceptionally reserved in her manner. She didn't say anything about a fee for the work, and from her silence I gathered that there wasn't going to be one. Given the tangled political nuances of the situation (the war between our two countries, my feelings about that war, and so on), I was hardly disposed to press her about money. Instead, I began asking her questions about the Vietnamese poems I had been reading. At one point, I got her to sit down at my desk with me and draw a diagram that explained the traditional verse forms that had piqued my curiosity. Her sketch proved to be very helpful, but when I asked her if I could keep it for future reference, she shook her head, crumpled up the paper, and put it in her pocket. I was so startled, I didn't say a word. In that one small gesture, an entire world had been revealed to me, an underground universe of fear and betrayal in which even a scrap of paper was suspect. Trust no one; cover your tracks; destroy the evidence. It wasn't that she was afraid of what I might do with the diagram. She was simply acting out of habit, and I couldn't help feeling sorry for her, sorry for both of us. It meant that the war was everywhere, that the war had tainted everything.

The constitution was eight or ten pages long, and apart from some standard Marxist-Leninist phrases ("running dogs of imperialism," "bourgeois lackeys"), it was pretty dry stuff. I did the translation the next day, and when I called my biologist friend to tell her that the work was finished, she sounded inordinately pleased and grateful. It was only then that she told me about my payment: an invitation to dinner. "By way of thanks," as she put it. The restaurant happened to be in the Fifth Arrondissement, not far from where I lived, and I had eaten there several times before. It was the simplest and cheapest Vietnamese restaurant in Paris, but also the best. The only ornament in the place was a black-and-white photograph of Ho Chi Minh hanging on the wall.

Other jobs were entirely straightforward, the essence of simplicity: tutoring a high school boy in English, serving as simultaneous translator at a small international conference of Jewish scholars (dinner included), translating material by and about Giacometti for the art critic David Sylvester. Few of these jobs paid well, but they all brought in something, and if I didn't always have great stocks of food in my refrigerator, I was rarely without a pack of cigarettes in my pocket. Still, I couldn't have sustained myself on odds and ends alone. They helped to keep me going, but add them all together, and they wouldn't have been enough to live on for more than a few weeks, a few months at most. I needed another source of income to pay the bills, and as luck would have it, I found one. To put it more accurately, it found me. For the first two years I spent in Paris, it was the difference between eating and not eating.

The story goes back to 1967. During my earlier stay as a student, an American friend had introduced me to a woman I will call Madame X. Her husband, Monsieur X, was a well-known film producer of the old style (epics, extravaganzas, a maker of deals), and it was through her that I started working for him. The first opportunity arose just a few months after I arrived. There was no telephone in the apartment I had rented, which was still the case with many Paris apartments in 1971, and there were only two ways of contacting me: by *pneumatique*, a rapid intracity telegram sent through the post office, or by coming to the apartment and knocking on the door. One morning, not long after I had woken up, Madame X knocked on the door. "How would you like to earn a hundred dollars today?" she said. The job seemed simple enough: read a movie script, then write out a six- or seven-page summary. The only constraint was time. A potential backer of the film was waiting on a yacht somewhere in the Mediterranean, and the outline had to be delivered to him within forty-eight hours.

Madame X was a flamboyant, stormy character, the first larger-than-life woman I had ever met. Mexican by birth, married since the age of eighteen or nineteen, the mother of a boy just a few years younger than I was, she lived her own independent life, drifting in and out of her husband's orbit in ways I was still too unsophisticated to understand. Artistic by temperament, she dabbled by turns at painting and writing, showing talent in both fields but with too little discipline or concentration to take those talents very far. Her true gift was encouraging others, and she surrounded herself with artists and would-be artists of all ages, hobnobbing with the known and the unknown as both a colleague and a patroness. Wherever she went, she was the center of attention, the gorgeous, soulful woman with the long black hair and the hooded cloaks and the clattering Mexican jewelry—moody, generous, loyal, her head full of dreams. Somehow or other, I had made it onto her list, and because I was young and just starting out, she counted me among those friends who needed looking after, the poor and struggling ones who required an occasional helping hand.

There were others too, of course, and a couple of them were invited along with me that morning to earn the same round figure that I had been promised. A hundred dollars sounds like pocket change today, but back then it represented more than half a month's rent, and I was in no position to turn down a sum of that magnitude. The work was to be done at the X's' apartment, an immense, palatial establishment in the Sixteenth Arrondissement with untold numbers of high-ceilinged rooms. The starting time was set for eleven o'clock, and I showed up with half an hour to spare.

I had met each of my coworkers before. One of them was an American in his mid-twenties, a fey unemployed pianist who walked around in women's high heels and had recently spent time in a hospital with a collapsed lung. The other was a Frenchman with decades of film experience, mostly as a second-unit director. Among his credits were the chariot scenes in *Ben-Hur* and the desert scenes in *Lawrence of Arabia*, but since those days of wealth and success, he had fallen on hard times: nervous breakdowns, periods of confinement in mental wards, no work. He and the pianist were major reclamation projects for Madame X, and throwing me together with them was just one example of how she operated. No matter how good her intentions were, they were invariably undermined by complex, impractical schemes, a desire to kill too many birds with a single stone. Rescuing one person is hard enough, but to think you can save the whole world at once is to ask for disappointment.

So there we were, the most mismatched trio ever assembled, gathered around the gigantic table in the dining room of the X's' gigantic apartment. The script in question was also gigantic. A work of nearly three hundred pages (three times the length of the normal script), it looked like the telephone book of a large city. Because the Frenchman was the only one with any professional knowledge of the movies, the pianist and I deferred to him and allowed him to take charge of the discussion. The first thing he did was pull out a sheet of blank paper and begin jotting down the names of actors. Frank Sinatra, Dean Martin, Sammy Davis, Jr., followed by six or seven others. When he was finished, he slapped his hands on the table with great satisfaction. "You see this piece of paper?" he asked. The pianist and I nodded our heads. "Believe it or not, this little piece of paper is worth ten million dollars." He patted the list once or twice and then pushed it aside. "Ten, maybe twelve million dollars." He spoke with the utmost conviction, betraying not the slightest hint of humor or irony. After a brief pause, he opened the manuscript to the first page. "Well," he said, "are we ready to begin?"

Almost immediately, he became excited. On the second or third line of the first page, he noticed that the name of one of the characters began with the letter Z. "Aha!" he said. "Z. This is very important. Pay close attention, my friends. This is going to be a political film. Mark my words."

Z was the title of a film by Costa-Gavras, a popular hit two years earlier. That film had most assuredly been about politics, but the screenplay we had been asked to summarize was not. It was an action thriller about smuggling. Largely set in the Sahara Desert, it featured trucks, motorcycles, several gangs of warring bad guys, and a number of spectacular explosions. The only thing that set it apart from a thousand other movies was its length.

We had been at work for approximately a minute and a half, and already the pianist had lost interest. He stared down at the table and snickered to himself as the Frenchman rambled on, lurching from one bit of nonsense to another. Suddenly, without any transition or preamble, the poor man started talking about David Lean, recalling several philosophical discussions he'd had with the director fifteen years earlier. Then, just as abruptly, he broke off from his reminiscences, stood up from the table, and walked around the room, straightening the pictures on the walls. When he was finished with that task, he announced that he was going to the kitchen to look for a cup of coffee. The pianist shrugged. "I think I'll go play the piano," he said, and just like that, he was gone as well.

As I waited for them to return, I started reading the script. I couldn't think of anything else to do, and by the time it dawned on me that neither one of them would be coming back, I had worked my way through most of it. Eventually, one of Monsieur X's associates drifted into the room. He was a youngish, good-natured American who also happened to be Madame X's special friend (the complexities of the household were fathomless), and he instructed me to finish the job on my own, guaranteeing that if I managed to produce an acceptable piece of work by seven o'clock, all three of the hundred-dollar payments would be mine. I told him I would do my best. Before I hustled out of there and went home to my typewriter, he gave me an excellent bit of advice. "Just remember," he said. "This is the movies, not Shakespeare. Make it as vulgar as you can."

I wound up writing the synopsis in the extravagant, over-heated language of Hollywood coming attractions. If they wanted vulgar, I would give them vulgar. I had sat through enough movie trailers to know what they sounded like, and by dredging up every hackneyed phrase I could think of, by piling one excess on top of another, I boiled the story down to seven pages of frantic, nonstop action, a bloodbath wrought in pulsing, Technicolor prose. I finished typing at six-thirty. An hour later, a chauffeur-driven car arrived downstairs to take me and my girlfriend to the restaurant where Madame and Monsieur X had invited us for dinner. The moment we got there, I was supposed to deliver the pages to him in person.

Monsieur X was a small, enigmatic man in his mid to late fifties. Of Russian-Jewish origin, he spoke several languages with equal fluency, often shifting from French to English to Spanish in the course of a single conversation, but always with the same cumbersome accent, as if in the end he didn't feel at home in any of them. He had been producing movies for over thirty years, and in a career of countless ups and downs, he had backed good films and bad films, big films and small films, art films and trash films. Some had made piles of money for him, others had put him miserably in debt. I had crossed paths with him only a few times before that night, but he had always struck me as a lugubrious person, a man who played things close to the vest—shrewd, hidden, unknowable. Even as he talked to you, you sensed that he was thinking about something else, working out some mysterious calculations that might or might not have had anything to do with what he was saying. It's not that they didn't, but at the same time it would have been wrong to assume that they did.

That night in the restaurant, he was noticeably edgy when I arrived. A potentially lucrative deal hinged on the work of one of his wife's arty friends, and he was anything but optimistic. I had barely settled into my seat when he asked to see the pages I had written. As the rest of us made small talk around the table, Monsieur X sat hunched in silence, reading through my florid, slam-bang paragraphs. Little by little, a smile began to form on his lips. He started nodding to himself as he turned the pages, and once or twice he was even heard to mutter the word "good" under his breath. He didn't look up, however. Not until he'd come to the last sentence did he finally raise his head and give me the verdict.

"Excellent," he said. "This is just what I wanted." The relief in his voice was almost palpable.

Madame X said something about how she'd told him so, and he confessed that he'd had his doubts. "I thought it would be too literary," he said. "But this is good. This is just right."

He became very effusive after that. We were in a large, gaudy restaurant in Montmartre, and he immediately started snapping his fingers for the flower girl. She came scurrying over to our table, and Monsieur X bought a dozen roses, which he handed to my girlfriend as an impromptu gift. Then he reached into his breast pocket, pulled out his checkbook, and wrote me a check for three hundred dollars. It was the first check I had ever seen from a Swiss bank.

I was glad to have delivered the goods under pressure, glad to have earned my three hundred bucks, glad to have been roped into the absurd events of that day, but once we left the restaurant and I returned to my apartment on the rue Jacques Mawas, I assumed that the story was over. It never once crossed my mind that Monsieur X might have further plans for me. One afternoon the following week, however, as I sat at my table working on a poem, I was interrupted by a loud knock on the door. It was one of Monsieur X's gofers, an elderly gentleman I'd seen lurking about the house on my visits there but had never had the pleasure of talking to. He wasted no time in getting to the point. Are you Paul Auster? he asked. When I told him I was, he informed me that Monsieur X wanted to see me. When? I asked. Right now, he said. There's a taxi waiting downstairs.

It was a little like being arrested by the secret police. I suppose I could have refused the invitation, but the cloak-and-dagger atmosphere made me curious, and I decided to go along to see what was up. In the cab, I asked my chaperon why I had been summoned like this, but the old man merely shrugged. Monsieur X had told him to bring me back to the house, and that was what he was doing. His job was to follow orders, not ask questions. I therefore remained in the dark, and as I mulled over the question myself, the only answer I could think of was that Monsieur X was no longer satisfied with the work I had done for him. By the time I walked into his apartment, I was fully expecting him to ask me for the money back.

He was dressed in a paisley smoking jacket with satin lapels, and as he entered the room where I'd been told to wait for him, I noticed that he was rubbing his hands together. I had no idea what that gesture meant.

"Last week," he said, "you do good works for me. Now I want to make package deal."

That explained the hands. It was the gesture of a man ready to do business, and all of a sudden, on the strength of that dashed-off, tongue-in-cheek manuscript I'd concocted for him the other day, it looked as though I was about to be in business with Monsieur X. He had at least two jobs for me right away, and if all went well with those, the implication was that others would follow. I needed the money and accepted, but not without a certain wariness. I was stepping into a realm I didn't understand, and unless I kept my wits about me, I realized that strange things could be in store for me. I don't know how or why I knew that, but I did. When Monsieur X started talking about giving me a role in one of his upcoming movies, a swashbuckling adventure story for which I would need fencing and riding lessons, I held my ground. "We'll see," I said. "The fact is, I'm not much interested in acting."

Apparently, the man on the yacht had liked my synopsis just as much as Monsieur X had. Now he wanted to take things to the next level and was commissioning a translation of the screenplay from French into English. That was the first job. The second job was somewhat less cut-and-dried. Madame X was at work on a play, Monsieur X told me, and he had agreed to finance a production at the Round House Theatre in London next season. The piece was about Quetzalcoatl, the mythical plumed serpent, and since much of it was written in verse, and since much of that verse was written in Spanish, he wanted me to turn it into English and make sure that the drama was in playable shape. Fine, I said, and that was how we left it. I did both jobs, everyone was satisfied, and two or three months later, Madame X's play was performed in London. It was a vanity production, of course, but the reviews were good, and all in all the play was quite well received. A British publisher happened to attend one of the performances, and he was so impressed by what he'd seen that he proposed to Madame X that she turn the play into a prose narrative, which he would then publish as a book.

That was where things started getting sticky between me and Monsieur X. Madame X didn't have it in her to write the book on her own, and he believed that I was the one person on earth capable of helping her. I might have accepted the job under different circumstances, but since he also wanted me to go to Mexico to do the work, I told him I wasn't interested. Why the book had to be written in Mexico was never made clear to me. Research, local color, something along those lines, I'm not sure. I was fond of Madame X, but being thrown together with her for an unspecified length of time struck me as less than a good idea. I didn't even have to think about Monsieur X's offer. I turned him down on the spot, figuring that would close the matter once and for all. Events proved me wrong. True indifference has power, I learned, and my refusal to take the job irritated Monsieur X and got under his skin. He wasn't in the habit of having people say no to him, and he became hell-bent on changing my mind. Over the next several months, he launched an all-out campaign to wear down my resistance, besieging me with letters, telegrams, and promises of ever greater sums of money. In the end, I reluctantly gave in. As with every other bad decision I've made in my life, I acted against my better judgment, allowing secondary considerations to interfere with the clarity of my instincts. In this case, what tipped the balance was money. I was having a hard time of it just then, desperately falling behind in my struggle to remain solvent, and Monsieur X's offer had grown so large, would eliminate so many of my problems at once, that I talked myself into accepting the wisdom of compromise. I thought I was being clever. Once I had climbed down from my high horse, I laid out my conditions in the toughest terms I could think of. I would go to Mexico for exactly one month, I told him—no more, no less—and I wanted full payment in cash before I left Paris. It was the first time I had ever negotiated for anything, but I was determined to protect myself, and I refused to yield on any of these points. Monsieur X was less than thrilled with my intractability, but he understood that I'd gone as far as I would go and gave in to my demands. The same day I left for Mexico, I deposited twenty-five one-hundred-dollar bills in my bank account. Whatever happened in the next month, at least I wouldn't be broke when I returned.

I was expecting things to go wrong, but not quite to the degree that they did. Without rehashing the whole complicated business (the man who threatened to kill me, the schizophrenic girl who thought I was a Hindu god, the drunken, suicidal misery that permeated every household I entered), the thirty days I spent in Mexico were among the grimmest, most unsettling days of my life. Madame X had already been there for a couple of weeks when I arrived, and I quickly learned that she was in no shape to work on the book. Her boyfriend had just left her, and this love drama had plunged her into the throes of an acute despair. It's not that I blamed her for her feelings, but she was so distraught, so distracted by her suffering, that the book was the last thing she wanted to think about. What was I supposed to do? I tried to get her started, tried to make her sit down with me and discuss the project, but she simply wasn't interested. Every time we took a stab at it, the conversation would quickly veer off onto other subjects. Again and again, she broke down and cried. Again and again, we got nowhere. After several of these attempts, I understood that the only reason she was bothering to make an effort was because of me. She knew that I was being paid to help her, and she didn't want to let me down, didn't want to admit that I had come all this way for nothing.

That was the essential flaw in the arrangement. To assume that a book can be written by a person who is not a writer is already a murky proposition, but granting that such a thing is possible, and granting that the person who wants to write the book has someone else to help with the writing of it, perhaps the two of them, with much hard work and dedication, can arrive at an acceptable result. On the other hand, if the person who is not a writer does not want to write a book, of what use is the someone else? Such was the quandary I found myself in. I was willing to help Madame X write her book, but I couldn't help her unless she wanted to write it, and if she didn't want to, there was nothing I could do but sit around and wait until she did.

So there I sat, biding my time in the little village of Tepotzolán, hoping that Madame X would wake up one morning and discover that she had a new outlook on life. I was staying with Madame X's brother (whose unhappy marriage to an American woman was on its last legs), and I filled my days with aimless walks around the dusty town, stepping over mangy dogs, batting flies out of my face, and accepting invitations to drink beers with the local drunks. My room was in a stucco outbuilding on the brother's property, and I slept under muslin netting to guard against the tarantulas and mosquitoes. The crazy girl kept showing up with one of her friends, a Central American Hare Krishna with a shaved head and orange robes, and boredom ate away at me like some tropical disease. I wrote one or two short poems, but otherwise I languished, unable to think, bogged down by a persistent, nameless anxiety. Even the news from the outside world was bad. An earthquake killed thousands of people in Nicaragua, and my favorite baseball player, Roberto Clemente, the most elegant and electrifying performer of his generation, went down in a small plane that was trying to deliver emergency relief to the victims. If anything pleasant stands out from the miasma and stupor of that month, it would be the hours I spent in Cuernavaca, the radiant little city that Malcolm Lowry wrote about in *Under the Volcano*. There, quite by chance, I was introduced to a man who was described to me as the last living descendant of Montezuma. A tall, stately gent of around sixty, he had impeccable manners and wore a silk ascot around his neck.

When I finally returned to Paris, Monsieur X arranged to meet me in the lobby of a hotel on the Champs-Elysées. Not the Hôtel Georges V, but another one directly across the street. I can't remember why he chose that place, but I think it had something to do with an appointment he'd scheduled there before mine, strictly a matter of convenience. In any case, we didn't talk in the hotel. The instant I showed up, he led me outside again and pointed to his car, which was waiting for us just in front of the entrance. It was a tan Jaguar with leather upholstery, and the man behind the wheel was dressed in a white shirt. "We'll talk in there," Monsieur X said. "It's more private." We climbed into the back seat, the driver started up the engine, and the car pulled away from the curb. "Just drive around," Monsieur X said to the chauffeur. I suddenly felt as if I had landed in a gangster movie.

Most of the story was known by then, but he wanted me to give him a full report, an autopsy of the failure. I did my best to describe what had happened, expressing more than once how sorry I was that things hadn't worked out, but with Madame X's heart no longer in the book, I said, there wasn't much I could do to motivate her. Monsieur X seemed to accept all this with great calm. As far as I could tell, he wasn't angry, not even especially disappointed. Just when I thought the interview was about to end, however, he brought up the subject of my payment. Since nothing had been accomplished, he said, it seemed only right that I should give him back the money, didn't it? No, I said, it didn't seem right at all. A deal is a deal, and I had gone to Mexico in good faith and had kept up my end of the bargain. No one had ever suggested that I write the book *for* Madame X. I was supposed to write it *with* her, and if she didn't want to do the work, it wasn't my job to force her to do it. That was precisely why I'd asked for the money in advance. I was afraid that something like this would happen, and I needed to know that I would be paid for my time—no matter how things turned out.

He saw the logic of my argument, but that didn't mean he was willing to back down. All right, he said, keep the money, but if you want to go on working for me, you'll have to do some more jobs to square the account. In other words, instead of asking me to return the money in cash, he wanted me to give it back in labor. I told him that was unacceptable. Our account was square, I said, I wasn't in debt to him, and if he wanted to hire me for other jobs, he would have to pay me what those jobs were worth. Needless to say, that was unacceptable to him. I thought you wanted a part in the movie, he said. I never said that, I answered. Because if you do, he continued, we'll have to clear up this business first. Once again, I told him there was nothing to clear up. All right, he said, if that's how you feel about it, then we have nothing to say to each other anymore. And with that remark he turned away from me and told the driver to stop the car.

We had been riding around for about half an hour by then, slowly drifting toward the outer fringes of Paris, and the neighborhood where the car had stopped was unfamiliar to me. It was a cold January night, and I had no idea where I was, but the conversation was over, and there was nothing for me to do but say good-bye to him and get out of the car. If I remember correctly, we didn't even shake hands. I stepped out onto the sidewalk, shut the door, and the car drove off. And that was the end of my career in the movies.

I stayed on in France for another eighteen months—half of them in Paris and half of them in Provence, where my girlfriend and I worked as caretakers of a farmhouse in the northern Var. By the time I returned to New York, I had under ten dollars in my pocket and not a single concrete plan for the future. I was twenty-seven years old, and with nothing to show for myself but a book of poems and a handful of obscure literary essays, I was no closer to having solved the problem of money than I'd been before I left America. To further complicate the situation, my girlfriend and I decided to get married. It was an impulsive move, but with so many things about to change, we figured why not go ahead and change everything at once?

I immediately began casting about for work. I made telephone calls, followed up on leads, went in for interviews, explored as many possibilities as I could. I was trying to act sensibly, and after all the ups and downs I'd been through, all the tight corners and desperate squeezes that had trapped me over the years, I was determined not to repeat my old mistakes. I had learned my lesson, I told myself, and this time I was going to take care of business.

But I hadn't, and I didn't. For all my high-minded intentions, it turned out that I was incorrigible. It's not that I didn't find a job, but rather than accept the full-time position I had been offered (as junior editor in a large publishing house), I opted for a half-time job at half the pay. I had vowed to swallow my medicine, but just when the spoon was coming toward me, I shut my mouth. Until it happened, I had no idea that I was going to balk like that, no idea how stubbornly I was going to resist. Against all the odds, it seemed that I still hadn't given up the vain and stupid hope of surviving on my own terms. A part-time job looked like a good solution, but not even that was enough. I wanted total independence, and when some freelance translation work finally came my way, I quit the job and went off on my own again. From start to finish, the experiment lasted just seven months. Short as that time might have been, it was the only period of my adult life when I earned a regular paycheck.

By every standard, the job I had found was an excellent one. My boss was Arthur Cohen, a man of many interests, much money, and a first-rate mind. A writer of both novels and essays, a former publishing executive, and a passionate collector of art, he had recently set up a little business as an outlet for his excess energies. Part hobbyhorse, part serious commercial venture, Ex Libris was a rare-book concern that specialized in publications connected with twentieth-century art. Not books *about* art, but manifestations of the art itself. Magazines from the Dada movement, for example, or books designed by members of the Bauhaus, or photographs by Stieglitz, or an edition of Ovid's *Metamorphoses* illustrated by Picasso. As the back cover of each Ex Libris catalogue announced: "Books and Periodicals in Original Editions for the Documentation of the Art of the 20th Century: Futurism, Cubism, Dada, Bauhaus and Constructivism, De Stijl, Surrealism, Expressionism, Post War Art, as well as Architecture, Typography, Photography and Design."

Arthur was just getting the operation off the ground when he hired me as his sole employee. My chief task was to help him write the Ex Libris catalogues, which were issued twice a year and ran to a little over a hundred pages. Other duties included writing letters, preparing the catalogues for bulk mailings, fulfilling orders, and making tuna fish sandwiches for lunch. Mornings I spent at home, working for myself, and at twelve o'clock I would go downstairs to Riverside Drive and take the number 4 bus to the office. An apartment had been rented in a brownstone building on East Sixty-ninth Street to store Ex Libris's holdings, and the two rooms were crammed with thousands of books, magazines, and prints. Stacked on tables, wedged onto shelves, piled high in closets, these precious objects had overwhelmed the entire space. I spent four or five hours there every afternoon, and it was a bit like working in a museum, a small shrine to the avant-garde.

Arthur worked in one room and I worked in the other, each of us planted at a desk as we combed through the items for sale and prepared our meticulous catalogue entries on five-by-seven index cards. Anything having to do with French and English was given to me; Arthur handled the German and Russian materials. Typography, design, and architecture were his domain; I was in charge of all things literary. There was a certain fusty precision to the work (measuring the books, examining them for imperfections, detailing provenances when necessary), but many of the items were quite thrilling to hold, and Arthur gave me free rein to express my opinions about them, even to inject an occasional dose of humor if I felt like it. A few examples from the second catalogue will give some idea of what the job entailed:

233. DUCHAMP, M. & HALBERSTADT, V. L'Opposition et les cases conjuguées sont réconciliées par M. Duchamp et V. Halberstadt. Editions de L'Echiquier. St. Germain-en-Laye and Brussels, 1932. Parallel text in German and English on left-hand pages. 112 double-numbered pp., with 2-color illustrations. 9 5/8 × 11". Printed paper covers.

The famous book on chess written and designed by Duchamp. (Schwarz, p. 589). Although it is a serious text, devoted to a real chess problem, it is nevertheless so obscure as to be virtually worthless. Schwarz quotes Duchamp as having said: "The endgames on which this fact turns are of no interest to any chess player; and that's the funniest thing about it. Only three or four people in the world are interested in it, and they're the ones who've tried the same lines of research as Halberstadt and myself, since we wrote the book together. Chess champions never read this book, because the problem it poses never really turns up more than once in a lifetime. These are possible endgame problems, but they're so rare that they're almost utopian." (p. 63). $1000.00

394. (STEIN, GERTRUDE). Testimony: Against Gertrude Stein. Texts by Georges Braque, Eugene Jolas, Maria Jolas, Henri Matisse, André

Salmon, Tristan Tzara. Servire Press. The Hague, February, 1935. (Transition Pamphlet no. 1; supplement to Transition 1934–1935; no. 23). 16 pp. 5 11/16 × 8 7/8". Printed paper covers. Stapled.

In light of the great Stein revival of the Seventies, the continuing value of this pamphlet cannot be denied. It serves as an antidote to literary self-serving and, in its own right, is an important document of literary and artistic history. Occasioned by the inaccuracies and distortions of fact in The Autobiography of Alice B. Toklas, Transition produced this forum in order to allow some of the figures treated in Miss Stein's book to rebut her portrayal of them. The verdict seems to be unanimous. Matisse: "In short, it is more like a harlequin's costume the different pieces of which, having been more or less invented by herself, have been sewn together without taste and without relation to reality." Eugene Jolas: "The Autobiography of Alice B. Toklas, in its hollow, tinsel bohemianism and egocentric deformations, may very well become one day the symbol of the decadence that hovers over contemporary literature." Braque: "Miss Stein understood nothing of what went on around her." Tzara: "Underneath the 'baby' style, which is pleasant enough when it is a question of simpering at the interstices of envy, it is easy to discern such a really coarse spirit, accustomed to the artifices of the lowest literary prostitution, that I cannot believe it necessary for me to insist on the presence of a clinical case of megalomania." Salmon: "And what confusion! What incomprehension of an epoch! Fortunately there are others who have described it better." Finally, the piece by Maria Jolas is particularly noteworthy for its detailed description of the early days of Transition. This pamphlet was originally not for sale separately. $95.00

437. GAUGUIN, PAUL. Noa Noa. Voyage de Tahiti. Les Editions G. Crès & Cie. Paris, 1924. 154 pp., illustrated with 22 woodcuts after Paul Gauguin by Daniel de Monfreid. 5 3/4 × 7 15/16". Illustrated paper wrappers over paper.

This is the first definitive edition, including introductory material and poems by Charles Morice. The record of Gauguin's first two years in Tahiti, remarkable not only for its significant biographical revelations, but for its insightful anthropological approach to a strange culture. Gauguin follows Baudelaire's persuasive dictum: "Dites, qu'avez vous vu?" and the result is this miracle of vision: a Frenchman, at the height of European colonialism, travelling to an "underdeveloped country" neither to conquer nor convert, but to learn. This experience is the central event of Gauguin's life, both as an artist and as a man. Also: Noa Noa, translated into English by O.F. Theis. Nicholas L. Brown. New York, 1920. (Fifth printing; first printing in 1919). 148 pp. + 10 Gauguin reproductions. 5 5/16 × 7 13/16". Paper and cloth over boards. (Some minor foxing in French edition; slight fraying of spine in both French and English editions.) $65.00

509. RAY, MAN. Mr. and Mrs. Woodman. Edition Unida. No place, 1970. Pages unnumbered; with 27 original photographs and 1 signed and numbered engraving by Man Ray. 10 1/2 × 11 7/8″. Leather bound, gilt-edged cardboard pages; leather and marbleized fitted box.

One of the very strangest of Man Ray's many strange works. Mr. and Mrs. Woodman are two puppet-like wood figures constructed by Man Ray in Hollywood in 1947, and the book, composed in 1970, is a series of mounted photographs of these witty, amazingly life-like characters in some of the most contorted erotic postures imaginable. In some sense, this book can best be described as a wood-people's guide to sex. Of an edition of only 50 copies, this is number 31, signed by Man Ray. All photographs are originals of the artist and carry his mark. Inserted is an original, numbered and signed engraving, specially made by Man Ray for this edition. $2100.00

Arthur and I got along well, with no strain or conflict, and we worked together in a friendly, unruffled atmosphere. Had I been a somewhat different person, I might have held on to that job for years, but seeing that I wasn't, I began to grow bored and restless after a few months. I enjoyed looking through the material I had to write about, but I didn't have the mind of a collector, and I could never bring myself to feel the proper awe or reverence for the things we sold. When you sit down to write about the catalogue that Marcel Duchamp designed for the 1947 Surrealist exhibition in Paris, for example—the one with the rubber breast on the cover, the celebrated bare falsie that came with the admonition "*Prière de Toucher*" ("Please Touch")—and you find that catalogue protected by several layers of bubble wrap, which in turn have been swathed in thick brown paper, which in turn has been slipped into a plastic bag, you can't help but pause for a moment and wonder if you aren't wasting your time. *Prière de toucher*. Duchamp's imperative is an obvious play on the signs you see posted all over France: *Prière de ne pas toucher* (Do Not Touch). He turns the warning on its head and asks us to fondle the thing he has made. And what better thing than this spongy, perfectly formed breast? Don't venerate it, he says, don't take it seriously, don't worship this frivolous activity we call art. Twenty-seven years later, the warning is turned upside down again. The naked breast has been covered. The thing to be touched has been made untouchable. The joke has been turned into a deadly serious transaction, and once again money has the last word.

This is not to criticize Arthur. No one loved these things more than he did, and if the catalogues we mailed out to potential customers were vehicles of commerce, they were also works of scholarship, rigorous documents in their own right. The difference between us was not that I understood the issues any better than he did (if anything, it was just the opposite), but that he was a businessman and I wasn't, which explained why he was the boss and I made just a few measly dollars per hour. Arthur took pleasure in turning a profit, enjoyed the push and pull of running the enterprise and making it succeed, and while he was also a man of great sophistication and refinement, a genuine intellectual who lived in and for the world of ideas, there was no getting around the fact that he was a crafty entrepreneur. Apparently, a life of the mind was not incompatible with the pursuit of money. I understood myself well enough to know that such a thing wasn't possible for me, but I saw now that it was possible for others. Some people didn't have to choose. They didn't have to divide the world into two separate camps. They could actually live in both places at the same time.

A few weeks after I started working for him, Arthur recommended me to a friend who was looking to hire someone for a short-term job. Arthur knew that I could use the extra money, and I mention this small favor as an example of how well he treated me. That the friend turned out to be Jerzy Kosinski, and that the job involved me in editing the manuscript of Kosinski's latest book, makes the episode worth talking about a little more. Intense controversy has surrounded Kosinksi in recent years, and since a large share of it emanated from the novel I worked on (*Cockpit*), I feel that I should add my testimony to the record. As Arthur explained it to me, the job was a simple matter of looking through the manuscript and making sure that the English was in good order. Since English wasn't Kosinski's first language, it seemed perfectly reasonable to me that he should want to have the prose checked before he handed the book to his publisher. What I didn't know was that other people had worked on the manuscript before me—three or four others, depending on which account you read. Kosinski never mentioned this earlier help to me, but whatever problems the book still had were not because the English didn't sound like English. The flaws were more fundamental than that, more about the book itself than how the story was told. I corrected a few sentences here, changed a few words there, but the novel was essentially finished by the time the manuscript was given to me. If left to my own devices, I could have completed the work in one or two days, but because Kosinski wouldn't let the manuscript out of his house, I had to go to his apartment on West Fifty-seventh Street to do the work, and because he hovered around me constantly, interrupting me every twenty minutes with stories, anecdotes, and nervous chatter, the job dragged on for seven days. I don't know why, but Kosinski seemed terribly eager to impress me, and the truth was that he did. He was so thoroughly high-strung, so odd and manic in his behavior, that I couldn't help but be impressed. What made these interruptions doubly odd and intriguing was that nearly every story he told me also appeared in the book he had written—the very novel spread out before me when he came into the room to talk. How he had masterminded his escape from Poland, for example. Or how he would prowl around Times Square at two in the morning disguised as a Puerto Rican undercover cop. Or how, occasionally, he would turn up at expensive restaurants dressed in a sham military uniform (made for him by his tailor and representing no identifiable rank, country, or branch of service), but because that uniform looked good, and because it was covered with countless medals and stars, he would be given the best table in the house by the awestruck maître d'—without a reservation, without a tip, without so much as a glance. The book was supposedly a work of fiction, but when Kosinski told me these stories, he presented them as facts, real events from his life. Did he know the difference? I can't be sure, can't even begin to guess, but if I had to give an answer, I would say that he did. He struck me as too clever, too cunningly aware of himself and his effect on others not to enjoy the confusion he created. The common theme in the stories was deception, after all, playing people for fools, and from the way he laughed when he told them—as if gloating, as if reveling in his own cynicism—I felt that perhaps he was only toying with me, buttering me up with compliments in order to test the limits of my credulity. Perhaps. And then again, perhaps not. The only thing I know for certain is that Kosinski was a man of labyrinthine complexity. When the rumors started circulating about him in the mid-eighties and magazine articles began to appear with accusations of plagiarism and the use of ghost writers and false claims concerning his past, I wasn't surprised. Years later, when he took his own life by suffocating himself with a plastic bag, I was. He died in the same apartment where I had worked for him in 1974, in the same bathroom where I had washed my hands and used the toilet. I have only to think about it for a moment, and I can see it all.

Otherwise, my months at Ex Libris passed quietly. Nothing much happened, and since most of the business was conducted through the mail, it was a rare day when anyone came to the apartment and disturbed us at our work. Late one afternoon, however, when Arthur was out on an errand, John Lennon knocked on the door, wanting to look at Man Ray photographs.

"Hi," he said, thrusting out his hand at me, "I'm John."

"Hi," I said, taking hold of the hand and giving it a good shake, "I'm Paul."

As I searched for the photographs in one of the closets, Lennon stopped in front of the Robert Motherwell canvas that hung on the wall beside Arthur's desk. There wasn't much to the painting—a pair of straight black lines against a broad orange background—and after studying it for a few moments, he turned to me and said, "Looks like that one took a lot of work, huh?" With all the pieties floating around the art world, I found it refreshing to hear him say that.

Arthur and I parted on good terms, with no hard feelings on either side. I made it my business to find a replacement for myself before I quit, and that made my departure relatively simple and painless. We stayed in touch for a little while, occasionally calling each other to catch up on the news, but eventually we lost contact, and when Arthur died of leukemia several years ago, I couldn't even remember the last time I had talked to him. Then came Kosinski's suicide. Add that to John Lennon's murder more than a decade earlier, and nearly everyone associated with the months I spent in that office has disappeared. Even Arthur's friend Robert Motherwell, the good artist responsible for the bad painting that provoked Lennon's comment, is no longer with us. Reach a certain moment in your life, and you discover that your days are spent as much with the dead as they are with the living.

The next two years were an intensely busy time. Between March 1975, when I stopped working for Ex Libris, and June 1977, when my son was born, I came out with two more books of poetry, wrote several one-act plays, published fifteen or twenty critical pieces, and translated half a dozen books with my wife, Lydia Davis. These translations were our primary source of income, and we worked together as a team, earning so many dollars per thousand words and taking whatever jobs we were offered. Except for one book by Sartre (*Life/Situations*, a collection of essays and interviews), the books the publishers gave us were dull, undistinguished works that ranged in quality from not very good to downright bad. The money was bad as well, and even though our rate kept increasing from book to book, if you broke down what we did on an hourly basis, we were scarcely a penny or two ahead of the minimum wage. The key was to work fast, to crank out the translations as quickly as we could and never stop for breath. There are surely more inspiring ways to make a living, but Lydia and I tackled these jobs with great discipline. A publisher would hand us a book, we would split the work in two (literally tearing the book in half if we had only one copy), and set a daily quota for ourselves. Nothing was allowed to interfere with that number. So many pages had to be done every day, and every day, whether we felt in the mood or not, we sat down and did them. Flipping hamburgers would have been just as lucrative, but at least we were free, or at least we thought we were free, and I never felt any regrets about having left my job. For better or worse, this was how I had chosen to live. Between translating for money and writing for myself, there was rarely a moment during those years when I wasn't sitting at my desk, putting words on a piece of paper.

I didn't write criticism for money, but I was paid for most of the articles I published, and that helped pad my income to a certain degree. Still, getting by was a struggle, and from month to month we were no more than a short dry spell away from real poverty. Then, in the fall of 1975, just half a year into this tightrope walk *à deux*, my luck turned. I was given a five-thousand-dollar grant from the Ingram Merrill Foundation, and for the next little while the worst of the pressure was off. The money was so unexpected, so enormous in its ramifications, that I felt as if an angel had dropped down from the sky and kissed me on the forehead.

The man most responsible for this stroke of good fortune was John Bernard Myers. John didn't give me the money out of his own pocket, but he was the person who told me about the foundation and encouraged me to apply for the grant. The real benefactor, of course, was the poet James Merrill. In the quietest, most discreet manner possible, he had been sharing his family's wealth with other writers and artists for many years, hiding behind his middle name so as not to call attention to his astounding generosity. A committee met every six months to consider new applications and to dole out the awards. John was secretary of the committee, and although he didn't take part in choosing the recipients, he sat in on the meetings and knew how the members thought.

Nothing was sure, he said, but he suspected that they would be inclined to support my work. So I put together a sampling of my poems and sent them in. At the next semiannual meeting, John's hunch proved to be correct.

I don't think I've ever known a funnier or more effusive person than John. When I first met him, in late 1974, he had been an integral part of the New York scene for the past thirty years, most famously as director of the Tibor de Nagy Gallery in the fifties, but also as cofounder of the Artists Theatre, editor of various short-lived literary magazines, and all-around champion and impresario of young talent. John was the first to give major shows to such artists as Red Grooms, Larry Rivers, Helen Frankenthaler, and Fairfield Porter, and he published the first books of Frank O'Hara, John Ashbery, and other poets of the New York School. The plays he produced were collaborations between many of these same poets and painters—O'Hara and Rivers, for example, or James Schuyler and Elaine de Kooning, the one writing the words and the other designing the sets. The Artists Theatre didn't bring in much at the box office, but John and his partner kept it running for years, and at a time when Off Broadway had yet to come into being, it was about the only experimental theater available in New York. What set John apart from all the other dealers, publishers, and producers I've known is that he wasn't in it for the money. Truth be told, he probably wasn't much of a businessman, but he had a genuine passion for art in all its forms, rigorous standards, openness of spirit, and an immense hunger for work that was different, challenging, new. A large man of six three or six four, he often made me think of John Wayne in his physical appearance. This John, however, in that he was proudly and flagrantly homosexual, in that he gleefully mocked himself with all manner of mincing gestures and extravagant poses, in that he took delight in silly jokes and ridiculous songs and a whole repertoire of childish humor, had nothing to do with that other John. No tough guy stuff for him. This John was all enthusiasm and goodwill, a man who had dedicated his life to beautiful things, and he wore his heart on his sleeve.*

When I met him, he was just starting up a new magazine—"of words and pictures"—called *Parenthèse*. I can't remember who suggested that I send him my work, but I did, and from then on John made a point of

* For a vivid account of his adventures, see John's *Tracking the Marvelous: A Life in the New York Art World*, published by Random House in 1983.

putting something of mine in nearly every issue. Later, when he discontinued the magazine and began publishing books instead, the first title on the list was a collection of my poems. John's belief in my work was absolute, and he backed me at a time when few people even knew that I was alive. In the endnotes to *Parenthèse* 4, for example, buried among the dry accounts of contributors' past achievements, he took it upon himself to declare that "Paul Auster has created a stir in the literary world by his brilliant analysis of the work of Laura Riding Jackson, by his essays on French paintings, and his poetry." It didn't matter that this statement wasn't true, that John was the only one paying attention. *Someone* was behind me, and in those early days of struggle and uncertainty, of not stirring up much of anything, that encouragement made all the difference. John was the first person who took a stand for me, and I have never stopped feeling grateful to him for that.

When the grant money came, Lydia and I hit the road again. We sublet our apartment and went to the Laurentian Mountains in Quebec, holing up in the house of a painter friend for a couple of months while he was away, then returned to New York for a week or two, and then promptly packed our bags again and took a cross-country train to San Francisco. We eventually settled in Berkeley, renting a small efficiency apartment not far from the university, and lived there for six months. We weren't flush enough to stop translating, but the pace was less frantic now, and that allowed me to spend more time with my own work. I went on writing poems, but new impulses and ideas started coming as well, and before long I found myself writing a play. That led to another play, which in turn led to another play, and when I returned to New York in the fall, I showed them to John. I didn't know what to make of what I had written. The pieces had surged up unexpectedly, and the results were quite different from anything I had done before. When John told me he liked them, I felt that perhaps I had taken a step in the right direction. The farthest thing from my mind was to do anything with them in a practical sense. I had given no thought to having them performed, no thought to publishing them. As far as I was concerned, they were hardly more than spare, minimalist exercises, an initial stab at something that might or might not turn out to be real. When John said that he wanted to take the longest of the plays and mount a production of it, I was caught totally by surprise.

No one was to blame for what happened. John jumped in with his customary excitement and energy, but things kept going wrong, and after a while it began to seem that we weren't putting on a play so much as trying to prove the indestructible power of Murphy's Law. A director and three actors were found, and shortly after that a reading was scheduled to drum up financial support for the production. That was the plan, in any case. It didn't help that the actors were young and inexperienced, not up to the task of delivering their lines with conviction or true feeling, but even worse was the audience who came to hear them deliver those lines. John had invited a dozen of his richest art collector friends, and not one of these potential backers was under sixty or had the slightest interest in the theater. He was counting on the play to seduce them, to overwhelm their hearts and minds with such stunning finality that they would feel no choice but to reach into their pockets and start pulling out their checkbooks. The event was held at a posh Upper East Side apartment, and my job was to charm these wealthy patrons, to smile and chat and reassure them that they were putting their money on the right horse. The problem was that I had no talent for smiling and chatting. I arrived in a state of extreme tension, nervous to the point of being ill, and quickly downed two bourbons to undo the knot in my stomach. The alcohol had precisely the opposite effect, and by the time the reading started, I had come down with a massive headache, a blistering, brain-bending assault that grew ever more unbearable as the evening wore on. The play thudded forward, and from start to finish the rich people sat in silence, utterly unmoved. Lines that I had imagined were funny did not produce the faintest titter. They were bored by the gags, indifferent to the pathos, perplexed by the whole thing. At the end, after some grim, perfunctory applause, I could only think about how to get out of there and hide. My head was cracking with pain. I felt stabbed and humiliated, unable to speak, but I couldn't abandon John, and so for the next half hour I listened to him talk about the play to his befuddled friends, doing everything I could not to pass out on the carpet. John put up a brave front, but every time he turned to me for help, I could do no more than stare down at my shoes and mumble a brief, unintelligible comment. Finally, apropos of nothing, I blurted out some lame excuse and left.

A lesser man would have given up after such a defeat, but John was undaunted. Not a penny of aid emerged from that gruesome evening, but he went ahead and started improvising a new plan, scuttling his dream of theatrical glory for a more modest, workable approach. If we couldn't afford a real theater, he said, we would make do with something else. The play was the only thing that mattered, and even if the run was limited to just a single, invitation-only performance, there was going to be a production of my play. If not for me, he said, and if not for him, then at least for his friend Herbert Machiz, who had died that summer. Herbert had directed the plays at the old Artists Theatre, and because he had been John's companion for twenty-five years, John was determined to revive the Theatre in Herbert's memory—if only for just one night.

A man who owned a restoration studio on East Sixty-ninth Street offered John the use of his space. It happened to be just down the block from the Ex Libris office—an interesting, if minor, coincidence—but more to the point was that in its previous incarnation the carriage house where John's friend now worked had been the studio of Mark Rothko. Rothko had killed himself there in 1970, and now, less than seven years later, my play was going to be presented in that same room. I don't want to sound overly superstitious about it, but given how things turned out, it feels that we were cursed, that no matter what any of us did or didn't do, the project was bound to fail.

Preparations began. The director and the three actors worked hard, and little by little the performances improved. I wouldn't go so far as to call them good, but at least they were no longer an embarrassment. One of the actors stood out from the others, and as the rehearsals went on, I began to pin my hopes on him, praying that his inventiveness and daring might pull the production up to a reasonably competent level. A date in early March was chosen for the performance, invitations were sent out, and arrangements were made for a hundred and fifty folding chairs to be delivered to the carriage house. I should have known better, but I actually began to feel optimistic. Then, just days before the big night, the good actor came down with pneumonia, and because there were no understudies (how could there have been?), it looked as if the performance would have to be canceled. The actor, however, who had put weeks of time and effort into the rehearsals, was not about to give up. In spite of a high temperature, in spite of the fact that he was coughing up blood just hours before the play was supposed to start, he crawled out of bed, pumped his system full of antibiotics, and staggered on at the appointed time. It was the noblest of noble gestures, the gutsy act of a born trouper, and I was impressed by his courage—no, more than impressed: filled with admiration—but the sad truth was that he was in no shape to do what he did. Everything that had sparkled in the rehearsals suddenly lost its shine. The performance was flat, the timing was off, scene after scene was blown. I stood at the back of the room and watched, powerless to do a thing. I saw my little play die in front of a hundred and fifty people, and I couldn't lift a finger to stop it.

Before putting the whole miserable experience behind me, I sat down and reworked the play. The performances had been only part of the problem, and I wasn't about to palm off responsibility for what had happened on the director or the actors. The play was too long, I realized, too rambling and diffuse, and radical surgery was needed to mend it. I began chopping and trimming, hacking away at everything that felt weak or superfluous, and by the time I was finished, half of the play was gone, one of the characters had been eliminated, and the title had been changed. I typed up this new version, now called *Laurel and Hardy Go to Heaven*, put it in a folder along with the other two plays I had written (*Blackouts* and *Hide and Seek*), and stuck the folder in a drawer of my desk. My plan was to keep it there and never look inside the drawer again.

Three months after the flop of the play, my son was born. Watching Daniel come into the world was a moment of supreme happiness for me, an event of such magnitude that even as I broke down and wept at the sight of his small body and held him in my arms for the first time, I understood that the world had changed, that I had passed from one state of being into another. Fatherhood was the dividing line, the great wall that stood between youth and adulthood, and I was on the other side now forever.

I was glad to be there. Emotionally, spiritually, and even physically, there was nowhere else I wanted to be, and I was fully prepared to take on the demands of living in this new place. Financially, however, I wasn't the least bit prepared for anything. You pay a toll when you climb over that wall, and by the time I landed on the other side, my pockets were nearly empty. Lydia and I had left New York by then, moving to a house about two hours up the Hudson, and it was there that the hard times finally hit. The storm lasted for eighteen months, and when the wind died down enough for me to crawl out of my hole and inspect the damage, I saw that everything was gone. The entire landscape had been leveled.

Moving out of the city was the first step in a long series of miscalculations. We figured we could live on less money in the country, but the plain fact was that we couldn't. Car expenses, heating expenses, house repairs, and pediatrician's bills ate up whatever advantage we thought we had gained, and before long we were working so hard just to make ends meet that there was no time left for anything else. In the past, I had always managed to keep a few hours to myself every day, to push on with my poems and writing projects after spending the first part of the day working for money. Now, as our need for money rose, there was less time available to me for my own work. I started missing a day, then two days, then a week, and after a while I lost my rhythm as a writer. When I did manage to find some time for myself, I was too tense to write very well. Months went by, and every piece of paper I touched with my pen wound up in the garbage.

By the end of 1977, I was feeling trapped, desperate to find a solution. I had spent my whole life avoiding the subject of money, and now, suddenly, I could think of nothing else. I dreamed of miraculous reversals, lottery millions falling down from the sky, outrageous get-rich-quick schemes. Even the ads on matchbook covers began to hold a certain fascination. "Make Money Growing Worms in Your Basement." Now that I lived in a house with a basement, don't think I wasn't tempted. My old way of doing things had led to disaster, and I was ripe for new ideas, a new way of tackling the dilemma that had dogged me from the start: how to reconcile the needs of the body with the needs of the soul. The terms of the equation were still the same: time on the one hand, money on the other. I had gambled on being able to manage both, but after years of trying to feed first one mouth, then two mouths, and then three mouths, I had finally lost. It wasn't difficult to understand why. I had put too much of myself into working for time and not enough into working for money, and the result was that now I didn't have either one.

In early December, a friend came up from the city to visit for a few days. We had known each other since college, and he, too, had turned into a struggling writer—yet one more Columbia graduate without a pot to piss in. If anything, he was having an even rougher time of it than I was. Most of his work was unpublished, and he supported himself by bouncing from one pathetic temporary job to another, aimlessly traveling around the country in search of strange, down-and-out adventures. He had recently landed in New York again and was working in a toy store somewhere in Manhattan, part of the brigade of surplus help who stand behind the counters during the Christmas shopping season. I picked him up at the train station, and during the half-hour ride back to the house, we talked mostly about toys and games, the things he sold in the store. For reasons that still mystify me, this conversation dislodged a small pebble that had been stuck somewhere in my unconscious, an obstruction that had been sitting over a tiny pinprick hole of memory, and now that I was able to look down that hole again, I found something that had been lost for nearly twenty years. Back when I was ten or twelve, I had invented a game. Using an ordinary deck of fifty-two playing cards, I had sat down on my bed one afternoon and figured out a way to play baseball with them. Now, as I went on talking to my friend in the car, the game came rushing back to me. I remembered everything about it: the basic principles, the rules, the whole setup down to the last detail.

Under normal circumstances, I probably would have forgotten all about it again. But I was a desperate man, a man with my back against the wall, and I knew that if I didn't think of something fast, the firing squad was about to fill my body with bullets. A windfall was the only way out of my predicament. If I could rustle up a nice large chunk of cash, the nightmare would suddenly stop. I could bribe off the soldiers, walk out of the prison yard, and go home to become a writer again. If translating books and writing magazine articles could no longer do the job, then I owed it to myself and my family to try something else. Well, people bought games, didn't they? What if I worked up my old baseball game into something good, something really good, and managed to sell it? Maybe I'd get lucky and find my bag of gold, after all.

It almost sounds like a joke now, but I was in dead earnest. I knew that my chances were next to nil, but once the idea grabbed hold of me, I couldn't shake free of it. Nuttier things had happened, I told myself, and if I wasn't willing to put a little time and effort into having a go at it, then what kind of spineless shit was I?

The game from my childhood had been organized around a few simple operations. The pitcher turned over cards: each red card from ace to 10 was a strike; each black card from ace to 10 was a ball. If a face card was turned over, that meant the batter swung. The batter then turned over a card. Anything from ace to 9 was an out, with each out corresponding to the position numbers of the defensive players: Pitcher = ace (1); Catcher = 2; First Baseman = 3; Second Baseman = 4; Third Baseman = 5; Shortstop = 6; Left Fielder = 7; Center Fielder = 8; Right

Fielder = 9. If the batter turned over a 5, for example, that meant the out was made by the Third Baseman. A black 5 indicated a ground ball; a red 5 indicated a ball hit in the air (diamond = pop-up; heart = line drive). On balls hit to the outfield (7, 8, 9), black indicated a shallow fly ball, red a deep fly ball. Turn over a 10, and you had yourself a single. A jack was a double, a queen was a triple, and a king was a home run.

It was crude but reasonably effective, and while the distribution of hits was mathematically off (there should have been more singles than doubles, more doubles than home runs, and more home runs than triples), the games were often close and exciting. More important, the final scores looked like the scores of real baseball games—3 to 2, 7 to 4, 8 to 0—and not football or basketball games. The fundamental principles were sound. All I had to do was get rid of the standard deck and design a new set of cards. That would allow me to make the game statistically accurate, add new elements of strategy and decision making (bunts, stolen bases, sacrifice flies), and lift the whole thing to a higher level of subtlety and sophistication. The work was largely a matter of getting the numbers right and fiddling with the math, but I was well versed in the intricacies of baseball, and it didn't take me long to arrive at the correct formulas. I played out game after game after game, and at the end of a couple of weeks there were no more adjustments to be made. Then came the tedious part. Once I had designed the cards (two decks of ninety-six cards each), I had to sit down with four fine-tipped pens (one red, one green, one black, one blue) and draw the cards by hand. I can't remember how many days it took me to complete this task, but by the time I came to the end, I felt as if I had never done anything else. The design was nothing to brag about, but since I had no experience or talent as a designer, that was to be expected. I was striving for a clear, serviceable presentation, something that could be read at a glance and not confuse anyone, and given that so much information had to be crammed onto every card, I think I accomplished at least that. Beauty and elegance could come later. If anyone showed enough interest to want to manufacture the game, the problem could be turned over to a professional designer. For the time being, after much dithering back and forth, I dubbed my little brainchild Action Baseball.

Once again, my stepfather came to the rescue. He happened to have a friend who worked for one of the largest, most successful American toy companies, and when I showed the game to this man, he was

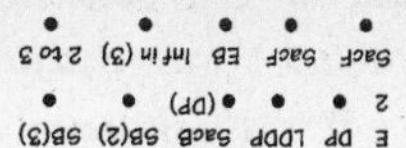

E DP LDDP SacB SB(2) SB(3)
2 • • •(DP) • •
SacF SacF EB Inf in (3) 2 to 3
FOUL OUT TO C
2

2

FOUL OUT TO C

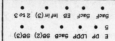

E DP LDDP SacB SB(2) SB(3)
2 • • •(DP) • •
SacF SacF EB Inf in (3) 2 to 3
• • • • •

E DP LDDP SacB SB(2) SB(3)
5 • • • • •
SacF SacF EB Inf in (3) 2 to 3
GROUND OUT TO 3B
5

5

GROUND OUT TO 3B

E DP LDDP SacB SB(2) SB(3)
5 • • • • •
SacF SacF EB Inf in (3) 2 to 3
• • • • •

E DP LDDP SacB SB(2) SB(3)
4 • • • • •
SacF SacF EB Inf in (3) 2 to 3
GROUND OUT TO 2B
4

4

GROUND OUT TO 2B

E DP LDDP SacB SB(2) SB(3)
4 • • • • •
SacF SacF EB Inf in (3) 2 to 3
• • • • •

E DP LDDP SacB SB(2) SB(3)
6 • • • • •
SacF SacF EB Inf in (3) 2 to 3
FOUL BALL

FOUL BALL

E DP LDDP SacB SB(2) SB(3)
6 • • • • •
SacF SacF EB Inf in (3) 2 to 3
• • • • •

E DP LDDP SacB SB(2) SB(3)
6 • • • • •
SacF SacF EB Inf in (3) 2 to 3
SINGLE
Runners advance 2 bases

SINGLE

Runners advance 2 bases

E DP LDDP SacB SB(2) SB(3)
6 • • • • •
SacF SacF EB Inf in (3) 2 to 3
• • • • •

E DP LDDP SacB SB(2) SB(3)
4 • • • • •
SacF SacF EB Inf in (3) 2 to 3
SINGLE
Runners advance 1 base

SINGLE

Runners advance 1 base

E DP LDDP SacB SB(2) SB(3)
4 • • • • •
SacF SacF EB Inf in (3) 2 to 3
• • • • •

E DP LDDP SacB SB(2) SB(3)
6 • • • • •
SacF SacF EB Inf in (3) 2 to 3
GROUND OUT TO SS
6

6

GROUND OUT TO SS

E DP LDDP SacB SB(2) SB(3)
6 • • • • •
SacF SacF EB Inf in (3) 2 to 3
• • • • •

E DP LDDP SacB SB(2) SB(3)
1 • • • • •
SacF SacF EB Inf in (3) 2 to 3
GROUND OUT TO P
1

1

GROUND OUT TO P

E DP LDDP SacB SB(2) SB(3)
1 • • • • •
SacF SacF EB Inf in (3) 2 to 3
• • • • •

impressed by it, thought it had a real chance of appealing to someone. I was still working on the cards at that point, but he encouraged me to get the game in order as quickly as I could and take it to the New York Toy Fair, which was just five or six weeks down the road. I had never heard of it, but by all accounts it was the most important annual event in the business. Every February, companies from around the world gathered at the Toy Center at Twenty-third Street and Fifth Avenue to display their products for the upcoming season, take note of what the competition was up to, and make plans for the future. What the Frankfurt Book Fair is for books and the Cannes Film Festival is for films, the New York Toy Fair is for toys. My stepfather's friend took charge of everything for me. He arranged to have my name put on the list of "inventors," which qualified me for a badge and an open pass to the fair, and then, as if that weren't enough, set up an appointment for me to meet with the president of his company—at nine o'clock in the morning on the first day of the fair.

I was grateful for the help, but at the same time I felt like someone who had just been booked on a flight to an unknown planet. I had no idea what to expect, no map of the terrain, no guidebook to help me understand the habits and customs of the creatures I would be talking to. The only solution I could think of was to wear a jacket and tie. The tie was the only one I owned, and it hung in my closet for emergency use at weddings and funerals. Now business meetings could be added to the list. I must have cut a ridiculous figure as I strode into the Toy Center that morning to collect my badge. I was carrying a briefcase, but the only thing inside it was the game, which was stowed inside a cigar box. That was all I had: the game itself, along with several Xeroxed copies of the rules. I was about to go in and talk to the president of a multimillion-dollar business, and I didn't even have a business card.

Even at that early hour, the place was swarming with people. Everywhere you turned, there were endless rows of corporate stands, display booths decked out with dolls and puppets and fire engines and dinosaurs and extraterrestrials. Every kiddie amusement and gadget ever dreamed of was packed into that hall, and there wasn't one of them that didn't whistle or clang or toot or beep or roar. As I made my way through the din, it occurred to me that the briefcase under my arm was the only silent object in the building. Computer games were all the rage that year, the biggest thing to hit the toy world since the invention of the wind-up jack-in-the-box, and I was hoping to strike it rich with an old-fashioned deck of cards. Maybe I would, but until I walked into that noisy fun house, I hadn't realized how likely it was that I wouldn't.

My talk with the company president turned out to be one of the shortest meetings in the annals of American business. It didn't bother me that the man rejected my game (I was prepared for that, was fully expecting bad news), but he did it in such a chilling way, with so little regard for human decency, that it still causes me pain to think about it. He wasn't much older than I was, this corporate executive, and with his sleek, superbly tailored suit, his blue eyes and blond hair and hard, expressionless face, he looked and acted like the leader of a Nazi spy ring. He barely shook my hand, barely said hello, barely acknowledged that I was in the room. No small talk, no pleasantries, no questions. "Let's see what you have," he said curtly, and so I reached into my briefcase and pulled out the cigar box. Contempt flickered in his eyes. It was as if I had just handed him a dog turd and asked him to smell it. I opened the box and took out the cards. By then, I could see that all hope was gone, that he had already lost interest, but there was nothing to do but forge ahead and start playing the game. I shuffled the decks, said something about how to read the three levels of information on the cards, and then got down to it. One or two batters into the top half of the first inning, he stood up from his chair and extended his hand to me. Since he hadn't spoken a word, I had no idea why he wanted to shake my hand. I continued to turn over cards, describing the action as it unfolded: ball, strike, swing. "Thank you," the Nazi said, finally taking hold of my hand. I still couldn't figure out what was going on. "Are you saying you don't want to see any more?" I said. "I haven't even had a chance to show you how it works." "Thank you," he said again. "You can leave now." Without another word, he turned and left me with my cards, which were still spread out on the table. It took me a minute or two to put everything back in the cigar box, and it was precisely then, during those sixty or ninety seconds, that I hit bottom, that I reached what I still consider to be the low point of my life.

Somehow or other, I managed to regroup. I went out for breakfast, pulled myself together, and returned to the fair for the rest of the day. One by one, I visited every game company I could find, shook hands, smiled, knocked on doors, demonstrated the wonders of Action Baseball to anyone willing to spare me ten or fifteen minutes. The results were uniformly discouraging. Most of the big companies had stopped working with independent inventors (too many lawsuits), and the small ones either wanted pocket-sized computer games (beep-beep) or else refused to look at anything connected with sports (low sales). At least these people were polite. After the sadistic treatment I'd been given that morning, I found some consolation in that.

Some time in the late afternoon, exhausted from hours of fruitless effort, I stumbled onto a company that specialized in card games. They had produced only one game so far, but that one had been wildly successful, and now they were in the market for a second. It was a small, low-budget operation run by two guys from Joliet, Illinois, a back-porch business with none of the corporate trappings and slick promotional methods of the other companies at the fair. That was a promising sign, but best of all, both partners admitted to being avid baseball fans. They weren't doing much at that hour, just sitting around their little booth and chewing the fat, and when I told them about my game, they seemed more than happy to have a look at it. Not just a peek, but a thorough viewing—to sit down and play a full nine-inning contest to the end.

If I had rigged the cards, the results of the game I played with them could not have been more exciting, more true to life. It was nip and tuck the whole way, tension riding on every pitch, and after eight and a half innings of threats, rallies, and two-out strikeouts with the bases loaded, the score stood at two to one. The Joliet boys were the home team, and when they came up for their last turn at bat, they needed a run to tie and two to win. The first two batters did nothing, and quickly they were down to their last out, with no runners on base. The following batter singled, however, to keep them alive. Then, to everyone's astonishment, with the count at two balls and two strikes, the next batter hit a home run to win the game. I couldn't have asked for more than that. A two-out, two-run homer in the bottom of the ninth inning to steal a victory on the last pitch. It was a classic baseball thriller, and when the man from Joliet turned over that final card, his face lit up with an expression of pure, undisguisable joy.

They wanted to think about it, they said, to mull it over for a while before giving me an answer. They would need a deck to study on their own, of course, and I told them I would send a color Xerox copy to Joliet as soon as possible. That was how we left it: shaking hands and exchanging addresses, promising each other to be in touch. After all the dismal, demoralizing events of that day, there was suddenly cause for hope, and I walked out of the Toy Fair thinking that I might actually get somewhere with my crazy scheme.

Color Xeroxing was a new process then, and it cost me a small fortune to have the copies made. I can't remember the exact amount, but it was more than a hundred dollars, I think, perhaps even two hundred. I shipped the package off to them and prayed they would write back soon. Weeks passed, and as I struggled to concentrate on the other work I had to do, it gradually dawned on me that I was in for a disappointment. Enthusiasm meant speed, indecision meant delay, and the longer they delayed, the worse the odds would be. It took almost two months for them to answer, and by then I didn't even have to read the letter to know what was in it. What surprised me was its brevity, its utter lack of personal warmth. I had spent close to an hour with them, had felt I'd entertained them and aroused their interest, but their rejection consisted of just one dry, clumsily written paragraph. Half the words were misspelled, and nearly every sentence had a grammatical error in it. It was an embarrassing document, a letter written by dunces, and once my hurt began to wear off a little, I felt ashamed of myself for having misjudged them so thoroughly. Put your faith in fools, and you end up fooling only yourself.

Still, I wasn't quite ready to give up. I had gone too far to allow one setback to throw me off course, and so I put my head down and plunged ahead. Until I had exhausted all the possibilities, I felt duty bound to continue, to see the whole misbegotten business through to the end. My in-laws put me in touch with a man who worked for Ruder and Finn, a prominent New York public relations firm. He loved the game, seemed genuinely enthused when I showed it to him, and made an all-out effort to help. That was part of the problem. Everyone liked Action Baseball, enough people at any rate to keep me from abandoning it, and with a kind, friendly, well-connected man like this one pushing on my behalf, it wouldn't have made sense to give up. My new ally's name was George, and he happened to be in charge of the General Foods account, one of Ruder and Finn's most important clients. His plan, which struck me as ingenious, was to get General Foods to put Action Baseball on the Wheaties box as a special coupon offer. ("Hey, kids! Just mail in two Wheaties box tops and a check or money order for $3.98, and this incredible game can be yours!") George proposed it to them, and for a time it looked as if it might happen. Wheaties was considering ideas for a new promotional campaign, and he thought this one might just do the trick. It didn't. They went with the Olympic decathlon champion instead, and for the next umpteen years, every box of

Wheaties was adorned with a picture of Bruce Jenner's smiling face. You can't really fault them. It was the Breakfast of Champions, after all, and they had a certain tradition to uphold. I never found out how close George came to getting his idea through, but I must confess (somewhat reluctantly) that I still find it hard to look at a box of Wheaties without feeling a little twinge.

George was almost as disappointed as I was, but now that he'd caught the bug, he wasn't about to quit trying. He knew someone in Indianapolis who was involved with the Babe Ruth League (in what capacity I forget) and thought something good might happen if he put me in contact with this man. The game was duly shipped to the Midwest again, and then followed another inordinately long silence. As the man hastened to explain to me when he finally wrote, he wasn't entirely responsible for the delay: "I am sorry to be so late in acknowledging receipt of your June 22 letter and your game, Action Baseball. They were late reaching me because of a tornado that wiped out our offices. I've been working at home since and did not get my mail until ten days or so ago." My bad luck was taking on an almost biblical dimension, and when the man wrote again several weeks later to tell me that he was passing on my game (sadly, with much regret, in the most courtly terms possible), I barely even flinched. "There is no question that your game is unique, innovative and interesting. There may well be a market for it since it is the only table-top baseball game without a lot of trappings, which makes it faster-moving, but the consensus here is that without big league players and their statistics, the established competition is insurmountable." I called George to give him the news and thank him for his help, but enough was enough, I said, and he shouldn't waste any more time on me.

Things stalled for a couple of months after that, but then another lead materialized, and I picked up my lance and sallied forth again. As long as there was a windmill somewhere in sight, I was prepared to do battle with it. I had not the least shred of hope anymore, but I couldn't quite let go of the stupid thing I had started. My stepfather's younger brother knew a man who had invented a game, and since that game had earned him a pile of money, it seemed reasonable for me to contact him and ask for advice. We met in the lobby of the Roosevelt Hotel, not far from Grand Central Station. He was a fast-talking wheeler-dealer of around forty, a wholly antipathetical man with every kind of bluff and angle up his sleeve, but I must admit that his patter had some verve to it.

"Mail order," he said, "that's the ticket. Approach a major-league star, get him to endorse the game for a share of the profits, and then take out ads in all the baseball magazines. If enough orders come in, use the money to produce the game. If not, send the money back and call it quits."

"How much would a thing like that cost?" I asked.

"Twenty, twenty-five thousand dollars. Minimum."

"I couldn't come up with that much," I said. "Not even if my life depended on it."

"Then you can't do it, can you?"

"No, I can't do it. I just want to sell the game to a company. That's all I've ever had in mind—to make some royalties from the copies they sold. I wouldn't be capable of going into business for myself."

"In other words," the man said, finally realizing what a numskull he was talking to, "you've taken a shit, and now you want someone to flush the toilet for you."

That wasn't quite how I would have expressed it myself, but I didn't argue with him. He clearly knew more than I did, and when he went on to recommend that I find a "game broker" to talk to the companies for me, I didn't doubt that he was pointing me in the right direction. Until then, I hadn't even known of the existence of such people. He gave me the name of someone who was supposed to be particularly good, and I called her the next day. That turned out to be my last move, the final chapter of the whole muddled saga. She talked a mile a minute to me, outlining terms, conditions, and percentages, what to do and what not to do, what to expect and what to avoid. It sounded like her standard spiel, a furious condensation of years of hard knocks and cutthroat maneuvers, and for the first several minutes I couldn't get a word in edgewise. Then, finally, she paused to catch her breath, and that was when she asked me about my game.

"It's called Action Baseball," I said.

"Did you say *baseball?*" she said.

"Yes, baseball. You turn over cards. It's very realistic, and you can get through a full nine-inning game in about fifteen minutes."

"Sorry," she said. "No sports games."

"What do you mean?"

"They're losers. They don't sell, and nobody wants them. I wouldn't touch your game with a ten-foot pole."

That did it for me. With the woman's blunt pronouncement still ringing in my ears, I hung up the phone, put the cards away, and stopped thinking about them forever.

Little by little, I was coming to the end of my rope. After the grim, garbled letter from Joliet, I understood that Action Baseball was no more than a long shot. To count on it as a source of money would have been an act of pure self-deception, a ludicrous error. I plugged away at it for several more months, but those final efforts took up only a small fraction of my time. Deep down, I had already accepted defeat—not just of the game, not just of my half-assed foray into the business world, but of all my principles, my lifelong stand toward work, money, and the pursuit of time. Time didn't count anymore. I had needed it in order to write, but now that I was an ex-writer, a writer who wrote only for the satisfaction of crumpling up paper and throwing it in the garbage, I was ready to abandon the struggle and live like everyone else. Nine years of freelance penury had burned me out. I had tried to rescue myself by inventing the game, but no one had wanted the game, and now I was right back where I had been—only worse, only more burned out than ever. At least the game had represented an idea, a temporary surge of hope, but now I had run out of ideas as well. The truth was that I had dug myself into a deep, dark hole, and the only way to crawl out of it was to find a job.

I made calls, wrote letters, traveled down to the city for interviews. Teaching jobs, journalism jobs, editorial jobs—it didn't matter what it was. As long as the job came with a weekly paycheck, I was interested. Two or three things almost panned out, but in the end they didn't. I won't go into the depressing details now, but several months went by without any tangible results. I sank further into confusion, my mind almost paralyzed with worry. I had made a total surrender, had capitulated on every point I had defended over the years, and still I was getting nowhere, was losing ground with every step I took. Then, out of the blue, a grant of thirty-five hundred dollars came in from the New York State Council on the Arts, and I was given an unexpected breather. It wouldn't last long, but it was something—enough to ward off the hour of doom for another minute or two.

One night not long after that, as I lay in bed battling against insomnia, a new idea occurred to me. Not an idea, perhaps, but a thought, a little notion. I had been reading a lot of detective novels that year, mostly of the hard-boiled American school, and beyond finding them to be good medicine, a balm against stress and chronic anxiety, I had developed an admiration for some of the practitioners of the genre. The best ones were humble, no-nonsense writers who not only had more to say about American life than most so-called serious writers, but often seemed to write smarter, crisper sentences as well. One of the conventional plot gimmicks of these stories was the apparent suicide that turns out to have been a murder. Again and again, a character would ostensibly die by his or her own hand, and by the end of the story, after all the tangled strands of the intrigue had finally been unraveled, it would be discovered that the villain was in fact responsible for the character's death. I thought: why not reverse the trick and stand it on its head? Why not have a story in which an apparent murder turns out to be a suicide? As far as I could tell, no one had ever done it.

It was no more than idle speculation, a two-in-the-morning brain wave, but I couldn't fall asleep, and with my heart beginning to race and flutter in my chest, I pursued the thought a little further, trying to calm myself by cooking up a story to go with my curveball premise. I had no stake in the results, was simply groping for a sedative to tranquilize my nerves, but one piece of the puzzle kept fitting beside another, and by the time I drifted off to sleep, I had worked out the bare-bones plot of a mystery novel.

The next morning, it occurred to me that it might not be such a bad idea to sit down and write the damn thing. It wasn't that I had anything better to do. I hadn't written a decent syllable in months, I couldn't find a job, and my bank account was down to almost nothing. If I could crank out a reasonably good detective novel, then surely there would be a few dollars in it. I wasn't dreaming of bags of gold anymore. Just an honest wage for an honest day's work, a chance to survive.

I started in early June, and by the end of August I had completed a manuscript of just over three hundred pages. The book was an exercise in pure imitation, a conscious attempt to write a book that sounded like other books, but just because I wrote it for money doesn't mean that I didn't enjoy myself. As an example of the genre, it seemed no worse than many others I had read, much better than some. It was good enough to be published, in any case, and that was all I was after. My sole ambition for the novel was to turn it into cash and pay off as many bills as I could.

Once again, I ran straight into problems. I was doing everything in my power to prostitute myself, offering up my wares for rock-bottom prices, and still no one would have me. In this case, the problem wasn't so much what I was trying to sell (as with the game), but my own astonishing ineptitude as a salesman. The only editors I knew were the ones who hired me to translate books, and they were ill qualified to pass judgment on popular fiction. They had no experience with it, had never read or published books like mine, and were scarcely even aware that such a thing as mystery novels existed, let alone the assorted subgenres within the field: private-eye novels, police procedurals, and so on. I sent off my manuscript to one of these editors, and when he finally got around to reading it, his response was surprisingly enthusiastic. "It's good," he said, "very good. Just get rid of the detective stuff, and you'll have yourself an excellent psychological thriller."

"But that's the whole point," I said. "It's a detective novel."

"Maybe so," he said, "but we don't publish detective novels. Rework it, though, and I guarantee that we'll be interested."

Altering the book might have interested him, but it didn't interest me. I had written it in a specific way for a specific purpose, and to begin dismantling it now would have been absurd. I realized that I needed an agent, someone to shop the novel around for me while I took care of more pressing matters. The rub was that I didn't have the first idea how to find one. Poets don't have agents, after all. Translators don't have agents. Book reviewers who make two or three hundred dollars per article don't have agents. I had lived my life in the remote provinces of the literary world, far removed from the commercial center where books and money have something to say to each other, and the only people I knew were young poets whose work appeared in little magazines, publishers of small, not-for-profit presses, and various other cranks, misfits, and exiles. There was no one to turn to for help, not one scrap of knowledge or information available to me. If there was, I was too dumb to know where to find it. Quite by chance, an old high school friend mentioned that his ex-wife happened to run a literary agency, and when I told him about my manuscript, he urged me to send it to her. I did, and after waiting nearly a month for an answer, I was turned down. There wasn't enough money in this kind of thing, she said, and it wasn't worth her trouble. No one read private-eye novels anymore. They were passé, old hat, a losing proposition all around. Word for word, it was identical to the speech the game broker had given me not ten days before.

Eventually, the book was published, but that didn't happen until four years later. In the meantime, all sorts of catastrophes occurred, one upheaval followed another, and the last thing on my mind was the fate of my pseudonymous potboiler. My marriage broke up in November 1978, and the typescript of the money novel was shoved into a plastic bag, all but lost and forgotten through several changes of address. My father died just two months after that—suddenly, unexpectedly, without ever having been sick a day in his life—and for many weeks the bulk of my time was spent taking care of estate business, settling his affairs, tying up loose ends. His death hit me hard, caused immense sorrow inside me, and whatever energy I had for writing I used to write about him. The terrible irony was that he had left me something in his will. It wasn't a great amount as far as inheritances go, but it was more money than I had ever had before, and it helped see me through the transition from one life into another. I moved back to New York and kept on writing. Eventually, I fell in love and married again. In the course of those four years, everything changed for me.

Sometime in the middle of that period, in late 1980 or early 1981, I received a call from a man I had met once before. He was the friend of a friend, and since the meeting had taken place a good eight or nine years earlier, I could scarcely remember who he was. He announced that he was planning to start a publishing company and wondered if I happened to have a manuscript he could look at. It wasn't going to be just another small press, he explained, but a real business, a *commercial operation*. Hmmm, I said, remembering the plastic bag at the bottom of my bedroom closet, if that's the case, then I just might have something for you. I told him about the detective novel, and when he said that he would be interested in reading it, I made a copy and sent it to him that week. Unexpectedly, he liked it. Even more unexpectedly, he said that he wanted to go ahead and publish it.

I was happy, of course—happy and amused, but also a trifle apprehensive. It seemed almost too good to be true. Publishing books wasn't supposed to be so easy, and I wondered if there wasn't a catch to it somewhere. He was running the company out of his Upper West Side apartment, I noticed, but the contract I received in the mail was a real contract, and after looking it over and deciding that the terms were acceptable, I couldn't think of a reason not to sign it. There was no advance, of course, no money up front, but royalties would begin with the first copy sold. I figured that was normal for a new publisher just getting off the ground, and since he had no investors or serious financial support, he couldn't very well cough up money he didn't have. Needless to say, his business didn't quite qualify as a *commercial operation*, but he was hoping it would become one, and who was I to throw a wet blanket on his hopes?

He managed to bring out one book nine months later (a paperback reprint), but production of my novel dragged on for close to two years. By the time it was printed, he had lost his distributor, had no money left, and to all intents and purposes was dead as a publisher. A few copies made it into a couple of New York bookstores, hand-delivered by the publisher himself, but the rest of the edition remained in cardboard boxes, gathering dust on the floor of a warehouse somewhere in Brooklyn. For all I know, the books are still there.

Having gone that far with the business, I felt I should make one last effort and see if I couldn't conclude it once and for all. Since the novel had been "published," a hardcover edition was no longer possible, but there were still the paperback houses to consider, and I didn't want to walk away from the book until they'd had a chance to turn it down. I started looking for an agent again, and this time I found the right one. She sent the novel to an editor at Avon Books, and three days later it was accepted. Just like that, in no time at all. They offered an advance of two thousand dollars, and I agreed to it. No haggling, no counteroffer, no tricky negotiations. I felt vindicated, and I didn't care about the details anymore. After splitting the advance with the original publisher (as per contract), I was left with a thousand dollars. Deduct the ten percent agent's commission, and I wound up making a grand total of nine hundred dollars.

So much for writing books to make money. So much for selling out.

1996

TRUE STORIES

The Red Notebook

1

In 1972, a close friend of mine ran into trouble with the law. She was in Ireland that year, living in a small village not far from the town of Sligo. As it happened, I was visiting on the day a plainclothes detective drove up to her cottage and presented her with a summons to appear in court. The charges were serious enough to require a lawyer. My friend asked around and was given a name, and the next morning we bicycled into town to meet with this person and discuss the case. To my astonishment, he worked for a firm called Argue and Phibbs.

This is a true story. If there are those who doubt me, I challenge them to visit Sligo and see for themselves if I have made it up or not. I have reveled in these names for the past twenty years, but even though I can prove that Argue and Phibbs were real men, the fact that the one name should have been coupled with the other (to form an even more delicious joke, an out-and-out sendup of the legal profession) is something I still find hard to believe.

According to my latest information (three or four years ago), the firm continues to do a thriving business.

2

The following year (1973), I was offered a job as caretaker of a farmhouse in the south of France. My friend's legal troubles were well behind her, and since our on-again off-again romance seemed to be on again, we decided to join forces and take the job together. We had both run out of money by then, and without this offer we would have been compelled to return to America—which neither one of us was prepared to do just yet.

It turned out to be a curious year. On the one hand, the place was beautiful: a large, eighteenth-century stone house bordered by vineyards on one side and a national forest on the other. The nearest village was two kilometers away, but it was inhabited by no more than forty people, none of whom was under sixty or seventy years old. It was an ideal spot for two young writers to spend a year, and L. and I both worked hard there, accomplishing more in that house than either one of us would have thought possible.

On the other hand, we lived on the brink of permanent catastrophe. Our employers, an American couple who lived in Paris, sent us a small monthly salary (fifty dollars), a gas allowance for the car, and money to feed the two Labrador retrievers who were part of the household. All in all, it was a generous arrangement. There was no rent to pay, and even if our salary fell short of what we needed to live on, it gave us a head start on each month's expenses. Our plan was to earn the rest by doing translations. Before leaving Paris and settling in the country, we had set up a number of jobs to see us through the year. What we had neglected to take into account was that publishers are often slow to pay their bills. We had also forgotten to consider that checks sent from one country to another can take weeks to clear, and that once they do, bank charges and exchange fees cut into the amounts of those checks. Since L. and I had left no margin for error or miscalculation, we often found ourselves in quite desperate straits.

I remember savage nicotine fits, my body numb with need as I scrounged among sofa cushions and crawled behind cupboards in search of loose coins. For eighteen centimes (about three and a half cents), you could buy a brand of cigarettes called Parisiennes, which were sold in packs of four. I remember feeding the dogs and thinking that they ate better than I did. I remember conversations with L. in which we seriously considered opening a can of dog food and eating it for dinner.

Our only other source of income that year came from a man named James Sugar. (I don't mean to insist on metaphorical names, but facts are facts, and there's nothing I can do about it.) Sugar worked as a staff photographer for *National Geographic*, and he entered our lives because he was collaborating with one of our employers on an article about the region. He took pictures for several months, crisscrossing Provence in a rented car provided by his magazine, and whenever he was in our neck of the woods he would spend the night with us. Since the magazine also provided him with an expense account, he would very graciously slip us the money that had been allotted for his hotel costs. If I remember correctly, the sum came to fifty francs a night. In effect, L. and I became his private innkeepers, and since Sugar was an amiable man into the bargain, we were always glad to see him. The only problem was that we never knew when he was going to turn up. He never called in advance, and more often than not weeks would go by between his visits. We therefore learned not to count on Mr. Sugar. He would arrive out of nowhere, pulling up in front of the house in his shiny blue car, stay for a night or two, and then disappear again. Each time he left, we assumed that was the last time we would ever see him.

The worst moments came for us in the late winter and early spring. Checks failed to arrive, one of the dogs was stolen, and little by little we ate our way through the stockpile of food in the kitchen. In the end, we had nothing left but a bag of onions, a bottle of cooking oil, and a packaged pie crust that someone had bought before we ever moved into the house—a stale remnant from the previous summer. L. and I held out all morning and into the afternoon, but by two-thirty hunger had gotten the better of us, and so we went into the kitchen to prepare our last meal. Given the paucity of elements we had to work with, an onion pie was the only dish that made sense.

After our concoction had been in the oven for what seemed a sufficient length of time, we took it out, set it on the table, and dug in. Against all our expectations, we both found it delicious. I think we even went so far as to say that it was the best food we had ever tasted, but no doubt that was a ruse, a feeble attempt to keep our spirits up. Once we had chewed a little more, however, disappointment set in. Reluctantly—ever so reluctantly—we were forced to admit that the pie had not yet cooked through, that the center was still too cold to eat. There was nothing to be done but put it back in the oven for another ten or fifteen minutes. Considering how hungry we were, and considering that our salivary glands had just been activated, relinquishing the pie was not easy.

To stifle our impatience, we went outside for a brief stroll, thinking the time would pass more quickly if we removed ourselves from the good smells in the kitchen. As I remember it, we circled the house once, perhaps twice. Perhaps we drifted into a deep conversation about something (I can't remember), but however it happened, and however long we were gone, by the time we entered the house again the kitchen was filled with smoke. We rushed to the oven and pulled out the pie, but it was too late. Our meal was dead. It had been incinerated, burned to a charred and blackened mass, and not one morsel could be salvaged.

It sounds like a funny story now, but at the time it was anything but funny. We had fallen into a dark hole, and neither one of us could think of a way to get out. In all my years of struggling to be a man, I doubt there has ever been a moment when I felt less inclined to laugh or crack jokes. This was really the end, and it was a terrible and frightening place to be.

That was at four o'clock in the afternoon. Less than an hour later, the errant Mr. Sugar suddenly appeared, driving up to the house in a cloud of dust, gravel and dirt crunching all around him. If I think about it hard enough, I can still see the naive and goofy smile on his face as he bounced out of the car and said hello. It was a miracle. It was a genuine miracle, and I was there to witness it with my own eyes, to live it in my own flesh. Until that moment, I had thought those things happened only in books.

Sugar treated us to dinner that night in a two-star restaurant. We ate copiously and well, we emptied several bottles of wine, we laughed our heads off. And yet, delicious as that food must have been, I can't remember a thing about it. But I have never forgotten the taste of the onion pie.

3

Not long after I returned to New York (July 1974), a friend told me the following story. It is set in Yugoslavia, during what must have been the last months of the Second World War.

S.'s uncle was a member of a Serbian partisan group that fought against the Nazi occupation. One morning, he and his comrades woke up to find themselves surrounded by German troops. They were holed up in a farmhouse somewhere in the country, a foot of snow lay on the ground, and there was no escape. Not knowing what else to do, the men decided to draw lots. Their plan was to burst out of the farmhouse one by one, dash through the snow, and see if they couldn't make it to safety. According to the results of the draw, S.'s uncle was supposed to go third.

He watched through the window as the first man ran out into the snow-covered field. There was a barrage of machine-gun fire from across the woods, and the man was cut down. A moment later, the second man ran out, and the same thing happened. The machine guns blasted, and he fell down dead in the snow.

Then it was my friend's uncle's turn. I don't know if he hesitated at the doorway, I don't know what thoughts were pounding through his head at that moment. The only thing I was told was that he started to run, charging through the snow for all he was worth. It seemed as if he ran forever. Then, suddenly, he felt pain in his leg. A second after that, an overpowering warmth spread through his body, and a second after that he lost consciousness.

When he woke up, he found himself lying on his back in a peasant's cart. He had no idea how much time had elapsed, no idea of how he had been rescued. He had simply opened his eyes—and there he was, lying in a cart that some horse or mule was pulling down a country road, staring up at the back of a peasant's head. He studied the back of that head for several seconds, and then loud explosions began to erupt from the woods. Too weak to move, he kept looking at the back of the head, and suddenly it was gone. It just flew off the peasant's body, and where a moment before there had been a whole man, there was now a man without a head.

More noise, more confusion. Whether the horse went on pulling the cart or not I can't say, but within minutes, perhaps even seconds, a large contingent of Russian troops came rolling down the road. Jeeps, tanks, scores of soldiers. When the commanding officer took a look at S.'s uncle's leg, he quickly dispatched him to an infirmary that had been set up in the neighborhood. It was no more than a rickety wooden shack—a henhouse, maybe, or an outbuilding on some farm. There the Russian army doctor pronounced the leg past saving. It was too severely damaged, he said, and he was going to have to cut it off.

My friend's uncle began to scream. "Don't cut off my leg," he cried. "Please, I beg of you, don't cut off my leg!" But no one listened to him. The medics strapped him to the operating table, and the doctor picked up the saw. Just as he was about to pierce the skin of the leg, there was another explosion. The roof of the infirmary collapsed, the walls fell down, the entire place was obliterated. And once again, S.'s uncle lost consciousness.

When he woke up this time, he found himself lying in a bed. The sheets were clean and soft, there were pleasant smells in the room, and his leg was still attached to his body. A moment later, he was looking into the face of a beautiful young woman. She was smiling at him and feeding him broth with a spoon. With no knowledge of how it had happened, he had been rescued again and carried to another farmhouse. For several minutes after coming to, S.'s uncle wasn't sure if he was alive or dead. It seemed possible to him that he had woken up in heaven.

He stayed on in the house during his recovery and fell in love with the beautiful young woman, but nothing ever came of that romance. I wish I could say why, but S. never filled me in on the details. What I do know is that his uncle kept his leg—and that once the war was over, he moved to America to begin a new life. Somehow or other (the circumstances are obscure to me), he wound up as an insurance salesman in Chicago.

4

L. and I were married in 1974. Our son was born in 1977, but by the following year our marriage had ended. None of that is relevant now—except to set the scene for an incident that took place in the spring of 1980.

We were both living in Brooklyn then, about three or four blocks from each other, and our son divided his time between the two apartments. One morning, I had to stop by L.'s house to pick up Daniel and walk him to nursery school. I can't remember if I went inside the building or if Daniel came down the stairs himself, but I vividly recall that just as we were about to walk off together, L. opened the window of her third-floor apartment to throw me some money. Why she did that is also forgotten. Perhaps she wanted me to replenish a parking meter for her, perhaps I was supposed to do an errand, I don't know. All that remains is the open window and the image of a dime flying through the air. I see it with such clarity, it's almost as if I have studied photographs of that instant, as if it's part of a recurring dream I've had ever since.

But the dime hit the branch of a tree, and its downward arc into my hand was disrupted. It bounced off the tree, landed soundlessly somewhere nearby, and then it was gone. I remember bending down and searching the pavement, digging among the leaves and twigs at the base of the tree, but the dime was nowhere to be found.

I can place that event in early spring because I know that later the same day I attended a baseball game at Shea Stadium—the opening game of the season. A friend of mine had been offered tickets, and he had generously invited me to go along with him. I had never been to an opening game before, and I remember the occasion well.

We arrived early (something about collecting the tickets at a certain window), and as my friend went off to complete the transaction, I waited for him outside one of the entrances to the stadium. Not a single soul was around. I ducked into a little alcove to light a cigarette (a strong wind was blowing that day), and there, sitting on the ground not two inches from my feet, was a dime. I bent down, picked it up, and put it in my pocket. Ridiculous as it might sound, I felt certain that it was the same dime I had lost in Brooklyn that morning.

5

In my son's nursery school, there was a little girl whose parents were going through a divorce. I particularly liked her father, a struggling painter who earned his living by doing architectural renderings. His paintings were quite beautiful, I thought, but he never had much luck in convincing dealers to support his work. The one time he did have a show, the gallery promptly went out of business.

B. was not an intimate friend, but we enjoyed each other's company, and whenever I saw him I would return home with renewed admiration for his steadfastness and inner calm. He was not a man who grumbled or felt sorry for himself. However gloomy things had become for him in recent years (endless money problems, lack of artistic success, threats of eviction from his landlord, difficulties with his ex-wife), none of it seemed to throw him off course. He continued to paint with the same passion as ever, and unlike so many others, he never expressed any bitterness or envy toward less talented artists who were doing better than he was.

When he wasn't working on his own canvases, he would sometimes go to the Metropolitan Museum and make copies of the old masters. I remember a Caravaggio he once did that struck me as utterly remarkable. It wasn't a copy so much as a replica, an exact duplication of the original. On one of those visits to the museum, a Texas millionaire spotted B. at work and was so impressed that he commissioned him to do a copy of a Renoir painting—which he then presented to his fiancée as a gift.

B. was exceedingly tall (six-five or six-six), good-looking, and gentle in his manner—qualities that made him especially attractive to women. Once his divorce was behind him and he began to circulate again, he had no trouble finding female companions. I only saw him about two or three times a year, but each time I did, there was another woman in his life. All of them were obviously mad for him. You had only to watch them looking at B. to know how they felt, but for one reason or another, none of these affairs lasted very long.

After two or three years, B.'s landlord finally made good on his threats and evicted him from his loft. B. moved out of the city, and I lost touch with him.

Several more years went by, and then one night B. came back to town to attend a dinner party. My wife and I were also there, and since we knew that B. was about to get married, we asked him to tell us the story of how he had met his future wife.

About six months earlier, he said, he had been talking to a friend on the phone. This friend was worried about him, and after a while he began to scold B. for not having married again. You've been divorced for seven years now, he said, and in that time you could have settled down with any one of a dozen attractive and remarkable women. But no one is ever good enough for you, and you've turned them all away. What's wrong with you, B.? What in the world do you want?

There's nothing wrong with me, B. said. I just haven't found the right person, that's all.

At the rate you're going, you never will, the friend answered. I mean, have you ever met one woman who comes close to what you're looking for? Name one. I dare you to name just one.

Startled by his friend's vehemence, B. paused to consider the question carefully. Yes, he finally said, there was one. A woman by the name of E., whom he had known as a student at Harvard more than twenty years ago. But she had been involved with another man at the time, and he had been involved with another woman (his future ex-wife), and nothing had developed between them. He had no idea where E. was now, he said, but if he could meet someone like her, he knew he wouldn't hesitate to get married again.

That was the end of the conversation. Until mentioning her to his friend, B. hadn't thought about this woman in over ten years, but now that she had resurfaced in his mind, he had trouble thinking about anything else. For the next three or four days, he thought about her constantly, unable to shake the feeling that his one chance for happiness had been lost many years ago. Then, almost as if the intensity of these thoughts had sent a signal out into the world, the phone rang one night, and there was E. on the other end of the line.

B. kept her on the phone for more than three hours. He scarcely knew what he said to her, but he went on talking until past midnight, understanding that something momentous had happened and that he mustn't let her escape again.

After graduating from college, E. had joined a dance company, and for the past twenty years she had devoted herself exclusively to her career. She had never married, and now that she was about to retire as a performer, she was calling old friends from her past, trying to make contact with the world again. She had no family (her parents had been killed in a car crash when she was a small girl) and had been raised by two aunts, both of whom were now dead.

B. arranged to see her the next night. Once they were together, it didn't take long for him to discover that his feelings for her were just as strong as he had imagined. He fell in love with her all over again, and several weeks later they were engaged to be married.

To make the story even more perfect, it turned out that E. was independently wealthy. Her aunts had been rich, and after they died she had inherited all their money—which meant that not only had B. found true love, but the crushing money problems that had plagued him for so many years had suddenly vanished. All in one fell swoop.

A year or two after the wedding, they had a child. At last report, mother, father, and baby were doing just fine.

6

In much the same spirit, although spanning a shorter period of time (several months as opposed to twenty years), another friend, R., told me of a certain out-of-the-way book that he had been trying to locate without success, scouring bookstores and catalogues for what was supposed to be a remarkable work that he very much wanted to read, and how, one afternoon as he made his way through the city, he took a shortcut through Grand Central Station, walked up the staircase that leads to Vanderbilt Avenue, and caught sight of a young woman standing by the marble railing with a book in front of her: the same book he had been trying so desperately to track down.

Although he is not someone who normally speaks to strangers, R. was too stunned by the coincidence to remain silent. "Believe it or not," he said to the young woman, "I've been looking everywhere for that book."

"It's wonderful," the young woman answered. "I just finished reading it."

"Do you know where I could find another copy?" R. asked. "I can't tell you how much it would mean to me."

"This one is for you," the woman answered.

"But it's yours," R. said.

"It *was* mine," the woman said, "but now I'm finished with it. I came here today to give it to you."

7

Twelve years ago, my wife's sister went off to live in Taiwan. Her intention was to study Chinese (which she now speaks with breathtaking fluency) and to support herself by giving English lessons to native Chinese speakers in Taipei. That was approximately one year before I met my wife, who was then a graduate student at Columbia University.

One day, my future sister-in-law was talking to an American friend, a young woman who had also gone to Taipei to study Chinese. The conversation came around to the subject of their families back home, which in turn led to the following exchange:

"I have a sister who lives in New York," my future sister-in-law said.

"So do I," her friend answered.

"My sister lives on the Upper West Side."

"So does mine."

"My sister lives on West 109th Street."

"Believe it or not, so does mine."

"My sister lives at 309 West 109th Street."

"So does mine!"

"My sister lives on the second floor of 309 West 109th Street."

The friend took a deep breath and said, "I know this sounds crazy, but so does mine."

It is scarcely possible for two cities to be farther apart than Taipei and New York. They are at opposite ends of the earth, separated by a distance of more than ten thousand miles, and when it is day in one it is night in the other. As the two young women in Taipei marveled over the astounding connection they had just uncovered, they realized that their two sisters were probably asleep at that moment. On the same floor of the same building in northern Manhattan, each one was sleeping in her own apartment, unaware of the conversation that was taking place about them on the other side of the world.

Although they were neighbors, it turned out that the two sisters in New York did not know each other. When they finally met (two years later), neither one of them was living in that building anymore.

Siri and I were married then. One evening, on our way to an appointment somewhere, we happened to stop in at a bookstore on Broadway to browse for a few minutes. We must have wandered into different aisles, and because Siri wanted to show me something, or because I wanted to show her something (I can't remember), one of us spoke the other's name out loud. A second later, a woman came rushing up to us. "You're Paul Auster and Siri Hustvedt, aren't you?" she said. "Yes," we said, "that's exactly who we are. How did you know that?" The woman then explained that her sister and Siri's sister had been students together in Taiwan.

The circle had been closed at last. Since that evening in the bookstore ten years ago, this woman has been one of our best and most loyal friends.

8

Three summers ago, a letter turned up in my mailbox. It came in a white oblong envelope and was addressed to someone whose name was unfamiliar to me: Robert M. Morgan of Seattle, Washington. Various post office markings were stamped across the front: *Not Deliverable, Unable to Forward, Return to Writer*. Mr. Morgan's name had been crossed out with a pen, and beside it someone had written *Not at this address*. Drawn in the same blue ink, an arrow pointed to the upper-left-hand corner of the envelope, accompanied by the words *Return to sender*. Assuming that the post office had made a mistake, I checked the upper-left-hand corner to see who the sender was. There, to my absolute bewilderment, I discovered my own name and my own address. Not only that, but this information was printed on a custom-made address label (one of those labels you can order in packs of two hundred from advertisements on matchbook covers). The spelling of my name was correct, the address was my address—and yet the fact was (and still is) that I have never owned or ordered a set of printed address labels in my life.

Inside, there was a single-spaced typewritten letter that began: "Dear Robert, In response to your letter dated July 15, 1989, I can only say that, like other authors, I often receive letters concerning my work." Then, in a bombastic, pretentious style, riddled with quotations from French philosophers and oozing with a tone of conceit and self-satisfaction, the letter-writer went on to praise "Robert" for the ideas he had developed about one of my novels in a college course on the contemporary novel.

It was a contemptible letter, the kind of letter I would never dream of writing to anyone, and yet it was signed with my name. The handwriting did not resemble mine, but that was small comfort. Someone was out there trying to impersonate me, and as far as I know he still is.

One friend suggested that this was an example of "mail art." Knowing that the letter could not be delivered to Robert Morgan (since there was no such person), the author of the letter was actually addressing his remarks to me. But that would imply an unwarranted faith in the U.S. Postal Service, and I doubt that someone who would go to the trouble of ordering address labels in my name and then sitting down to write such an arrogant, high-flown letter would leave anything to chance. Or would he? Perhaps the smart alecks of this world believe that everything will always go their way.

I have scant hope of ever getting to the bottom of this little mystery. The prankster did a good job of covering his tracks, and he has not been heard from since. What puzzles me about my own behavior is that I have not thrown away the letter, even though it continues to give me chills every time I look at it. A sensible man would have tossed the thing in the garbage. Instead, for reasons I do not understand, I have kept it on my work table for the past three years, allowing it to become a permanent fixture among my pens and notebooks and erasers. Perhaps I keep it there as a monument to my own folly. Perhaps it is a way to remind myself that I know nothing, that the world I live in will go on escaping me forever.

9

One of my closest friends is a French poet by the name of C. We have known each other for more than twenty years now, and while we don't see each other often (he lives in Paris and I live in New York), the bond between us remains strong. It is a fraternal bond, somehow, as if in some former life we had actually been brothers.

C. is a man of manifold contradictions. He is both open to the world and shut off from it, a charismatic figure with scores of friends everywhere (legendary for his kindness, his humor, his sparkling conversation) and yet someone who has been wounded by life, who struggles to perform the simple tasks that most other people take for granted. An exceptionally gifted poet and thinker about poetry, C. is nevertheless hampered by frequent writing blocks, streaks of morbid self-doubt, and surprisingly (for someone who is so generous, so profoundly lacking in mean-spiritedness), a capacity for long-standing grudges and quarrels, usually over some trifle or abstract principle. No one is more universally admired than C., no one has more talent, no one so readily commands the center of attention, and yet he has always done everything in his power to marginalize himself. Since his separation from his wife many years ago, he has lived alone in a number of small, one-room apartments, subsisting on almost no money and only fitful bouts of employment, publishing little, and refusing to write a single word of criticism, even though he reads everything and knows more about contemporary poetry than anyone in France. To those of us who love him (and we are many), C. is often a cause of concern. To the degree that we respect him and care about his well-being, we also worry about him.

He had a rough childhood. I can't say to what extent that explains anything, but the facts should not be overlooked. His father apparently ran off with another woman when C. was a little boy, and after that my friend grew up with his mother, an only child with no family life to speak of. I have never met C.'s mother, but by all accounts she is a bizarre character. She went through a series of love affairs during C.'s childhood and adolescence, each with a man younger than the man before him. By the time C. left home to enter the army at the age of twenty-one, his mother's boyfriend was scarcely older than he was. In more recent years, the central purpose of her life has been a campaign to promote the canonization of a certain Italian priest (whose name eludes me now). She has besieged the Catholic authorities with countless letters defending the holiness of this man, and at one point she even commissioned an artist to create a life-size statue of the priest—which now stands in her front yard as an enduring testament to her cause.

Although not a father himself, C. became a kind of pseudo-father seven or eight years ago. After a falling out with his girlfriend (during which they temporarily broke up), his girlfriend had a brief affair with another man and became pregnant. The affair ended almost at once, but she decided to have the baby on her own. A little girl was born, and even though C. is not her real father, he has devoted himself to her since the day of her birth and adores her as if she were his own flesh and blood.

One day about four years ago, C. happened to be visiting a friend. In the apartment there was a *Minitel*, a small computer given out for free by the French telephone company. Among other things, the *Minitel* contains the address and phone number of every person in France. As C. sat there playing with his friend's new machine, it suddenly occurred to him to look up his father's address. He found it in Lyon. When he returned home later that day, he stuffed one of his books into an envelope and sent it off to the address in Lyon—initiating the first contact with his father in over forty years. None of it made any sense to him. Until he found himself doing these things, it had never even crossed his mind that he wanted to do them.

That same night, he ran into another friend in a café—a woman psychoanalyst—and told her about these strange, unpremeditated acts. It was as if he had felt his father calling out to him, he said, as if some uncanny force had unleashed itself inside him. Considering that he had absolutely no memories of the man, he couldn't even begin to guess when they had last seen each other.

The woman thought for a moment and said, "How old is L.?," referring to C.'s girlfriend's daughter.

"Three and a half," C. answered.

"I can't be sure," the woman said, "but I'd be willing to bet that you were three and a half the last time you saw your father. I say that because you love L. so much. Your identification with her is very strong, and you're reliving your life through her."

Several days after that, there was a reply from Lyon—a warm and perfectly gracious letter from C.'s father. After thanking C. for the book, he went on to tell him how proud he was to learn that his son had grown up to become a writer. By pure coincidence, he added, the package had been mailed on his birthday, and he was moved by the symbolism of the gesture.

None of this tallied with the stories C. had heard throughout his childhood. According to his mother, his father was a monster of selfishness who had walked out on her for a "slut" and had never wanted anything to do with his son. C. had believed these stories, and therefore he had shied away from any contact with his father. Now, on the strength of this letter, he no longer knew what to believe.

He decided to write back. The tone of his response was guarded, but nevertheless it was a response. Within days he received another reply, and this second letter was just as warm and gracious as the first had been. C. and his father began a correspondence. It went on for a month or two, and eventually C. began to consider traveling down to Lyon to meet his father face to face.

Before he could make any definite plans, he received a letter from his father's wife informing him that his father was dead. He had been in ill health for the past several years, she wrote, but the recent exchange of letters with C. had given him great happiness, and his last days had been filled with optimism and joy.

It was at this moment that I first heard about the incredible reversals that had taken place in C.'s life. Sitting on the train from Paris to Lyon (on his way to visit his "stepmother" for the first time), he wrote me a letter that sketched out the story of the past month. His handwriting reflected each jolt of the tracks, as if the speed of the train were an exact image of the thoughts racing through his head. As he put it somewhere in that letter: "I feel as if I've become a character in one of your novels."

His father's wife could not have been friendlier to him during that visit. Among other things, C. learned that his father had suffered a heart attack on the morning of his last birthday (the same day that C. had looked up his address on the *Minitel*) and that, yes, C. had been precisely three and a half years old at the time of his parents' divorce. His stepmother then went on to tell him the story of his life from his father's point of view—which contradicted everything his mother had ever told him. In this version, it was his mother who had walked out on his father; it was his mother who had forbidden his father from seeing him; it was his mother who had broken his father's heart. She told C. how his father would come around to the schoolyard when he was a little boy to look at him through the fence. C. remembered that man, but not knowing who he was, he had been afraid.

C.'s life had now become two lives. There was Version A and Version B, and both of them were his story. He had lived them both in equal measure, two truths that canceled each other out, and all along, without even knowing it, he had been stranded in the middle.

His father had owned a small stationery store (the usual stock of paper and writing materials, along with a rental library of popular books). The business had earned him a living, but not much more than that, and the estate he left behind was quite modest. The numbers are unimportant, however. What counts is that C.'s stepmother (by then an old woman) insisted on splitting the money with him half and half. There was nothing in the will that required her to do that, and morally speaking she needn't have parted with a single penny of her husband's savings. She did it because she wanted to, because it made her happier to share the money than to keep it for herself.

10

In thinking about friendship, particularly about how some friendships endure and others don't, I am reminded of the fact that in all my years of driving I have had just four flat tires, and that on each of these occasions the same person was in the car with me (in three different countries, spread out over a period of eight or nine years). J. was a college friend, and though there was always an edge of unease and conflict in our relations, for a time we were close. One spring while we were still undergraduates, we borrowed my father's ancient station wagon and drove up into the wilderness of Quebec. The seasons change more slowly in that part of the world, and winter was not yet over. The first flat tire did not present a problem (we were equipped with a spare), but when a second tire blew out less than an hour later, we were stranded in the bleak and frigid countryside for most of the day. At the time, I shrugged off the incident as a piece of bad luck, but four or five years later, when J. came to France to visit the house where L. and I were working as caretakers (in miserable condition, inert with depression and self-pity, unaware that he was overstaying his welcome with us), the same thing happened. We went to Aix-en-Provence for the day (a drive of about two hours), and coming back later that night on a dark, back-country road, we had another flat. Just a coincidence, I thought, and then pushed the event out of my mind. But then, four years after that, in the waning months of my marriage to L., J. came to visit us again—this time in New York State, where L. and I were living with the infant Daniel. At one point, J. and I climbed into the car to go to the store and shop for dinner. I pulled the car out of the garage, turned it around in the rutted dirt driveway, and advanced to the edge of the road to look left, right, and left before going on. Just then, as I waited for a car to pass by, I heard the unmistakable hiss of escaping air. Another tire had gone flat, and this time we hadn't even left the house. J. and I both laughed, of course, but the truth is that our friendship never really recovered from that fourth flat tire. I'm not saying that the flat tires were responsible for our drifting apart, but in some perverse way they were an emblem of how things had always stood between us, the sign of some impalpable curse. I don't want to exaggerate, but even now I can't quite bring myself to reject those flat tires as meaningless. For the fact is that J. and I have lost contact, and we have not spoken to each other in more than ten years.

11

In 1990, I found myself in Paris again for a few days. One afternoon, I stopped by the office of a friend to say hello and was introduced to a Czech woman in her late forties or early fifties—an art historian who happened to be a friend of my friend. She was an attractive and vivacious person, I remember, but since she was on the point of leaving when I walked in, I spent no more than five or ten minutes in her company. As usually happens in such situations, we talked about nothing of any importance: a town we both knew in America, the subject of a book she was reading, the weather. Then we shook hands, she walked out the door, and I have never seen her again.

After she was gone, the friend I had come to visit leaned back in her chair and said, "Do you want to hear a good story?"

"Of course," I said, "I'm always interested in good stories."

"I like my friend very much," she continued, "so don't get the wrong idea. I'm not trying to spread gossip about her. It's just that I feel you have a right to know this."

"Are you sure?"

"Yes, I'm sure. But you have to promise me one thing. If you ever write the story, you mustn't use anyone's name."

"I promise," I said.

And so my friend let me in on the secret. From start to finish, it couldn't have taken her more than three minutes to tell the story I am about to tell now.

The woman I had just met was born in Prague during the war. When she was still a baby, her father was captured, impressed into the German army, and shipped off to the Russian front. She and her mother never heard from him again. They received no letters, no news to tell them if he was alive or dead, nothing. The war just swallowed him up, and he vanished without a trace.

Years passed. The girl grew up. She completed her studies at the university and became a professor of art history. According to my friend, she ran into trouble with the government during the Soviet crackdown in the late sixties, but exactly what kind of trouble was never made clear to me. Given the stories I know about what happened to other people during that time, it is not very difficult to guess.

At some point, she was allowed to begin teaching again. In one of her classes, there was an exchange student from East Germany. She and this young man fell in love, and eventually they were married.

Not long after the wedding, a telegram arrived announcing the death of her husband's father. The next day, she and her husband traveled to East Germany to attend the funeral. Once there, in whatever town or city it was, she learned that her now dead father-in-law had been born in Czechoslovakia. During the war he had been captured by the Nazis, impressed into the German army, and shipped off to the Russian front. By some miracle, he had managed to survive. Instead of returning to Czechoslovakia after the war, however, he had settled in Germany under a new name, had married a German woman, and had lived there with his new family until the day of his death. The war had given him a chance to start all over again, and it seems that he had never looked back.

When my friend's friend asked what this man's name had been in Czechoslovakia, she understood that he was her father.

Which meant, of course, that insofar as her husband's father was the same man, the man she had married was also her brother.

12

One afternoon many years ago, my father's car stalled at a red light. A terrible storm was raging, and at the exact moment his engine went dead, lightning struck a large tree by the side of the road. The trunk of the tree split in two, and as my father struggled to get the car started again (unaware that the upper half of the tree was about to fall), the driver of the car behind him, seeing what was about to happen, put his foot on the accelerator and pushed my father's car through the intersection. An instant later, the tree came crashing to the ground, landing in the very spot where my father's car had just been. What was very nearly the end of him proved to be no more than a close call, a brief episode in the ongoing story of his life.

A year or two after that, my father was working on the roof of a building in Jersey City. Somehow or other (I wasn't there to witness it), he slipped off the edge and started falling to the ground. Once again he was headed for certain disaster, and once again he was saved. A clothesline broke his fall, and he walked away from the accident with only a few bumps and bruises. Not even a concussion. Not a single broken bone.

That same year, our neighbors across the street hired two men to paint their house. One of the workers fell off the roof and was killed.

The little girl who lived in that house happened to be my sister's best friend. One winter night, the two of them went to a costume party (they were six or seven years old, and I was nine or ten). It had been arranged that my father would pick them up after the party, and when the time came I went along to keep him company in the car. It was bitter cold that night, and the roads were covered with treacherous sheets of ice. My father drove carefully, and we made the journey back and forth without incident. As we pulled up in front of the girl's house, however, a number of unlikely events occurred all at once.

My sister's friend was dressed as a fairy princess. To complete the outfit, she had borrowed a pair of her mother's high heels, and because her feet swam in those shoes, every step she took was turned into an adventure. My father stopped the car and climbed out to accompany her to the front door. I was in the back with the girls, and in order to let my sister's friend out, I had to get out first. I remember standing on the curb as she disentangled herself from the seat, and just as she stepped into the open air, I noticed that the car was rolling slowly in reverse—either because of the ice or because my father had forgotten to engage the emergency brake (I don't know)—but before I could tell my father what was happening, my sister's friend touched the curb with her mother's high heels and slipped. She went skidding under the car—which was still moving—and there she was, about to be crushed to death by the wheels of my father's Chevy. As I remember it, she didn't make a sound. Without pausing to think, I bent down from the curb, grabbed hold of her right hand, and in one quick gesture yanked her to the sidewalk. An instant later, my father finally noticed that the car was moving. He jumped back into the driver's seat, stepped on the brake, and brought the machine to a halt. From start to finish, the whole chain of misadventures couldn't have taken more than eight or ten seconds.

For years afterward, I walked around feeling that this had been my finest moment. I had actually saved someone's life, and in retrospect I was always astonished by how quickly I had acted, by how sure my movements had been at the critical juncture. I saw the rescue in my mind again and again; again and again I relived the sensation of pulling that little girl out from under the car.

About two years after that night, our family moved to another house.

My sister fell out of touch with her friend, and I myself did not see her for another fifteen years.

It was June, and my sister and I had both come back to town for a short visit. Just by chance, her old friend dropped by to say hello. She was all grown up now, a young woman of twenty-two who had graduated from college earlier that month, and I must say that I felt some pride in seeing that she had made it to adulthood in one piece. In a casual sort of way, I mentioned the night I had pulled her out from under the car. I was curious to know how well she remembered her brush with death, but from the look on her face when I asked the question, it was clear that she remembered nothing. A blank stare. A slight frown. A shrug. She remembered nothing!

I realized then that she hadn't known the car was moving. She hadn't even known that she was in danger. The whole incident had taken place in a flash: ten seconds of her life, an interval of no account, and none of it had left the slightest mark on her. For me, on the other hand, those seconds had been a defining experience, a singular event in my internal history.

Most of all, it stuns me to acknowledge that I am talking about something that happened in 1956 or 1957—and that the little girl of that night is now over forty years old.

13

My first novel was inspired by a wrong number. I was alone in my apartment in Brooklyn one afternoon, sitting at my desk and trying to work when the telephone rang. If I am not mistaken, it was the spring of 1980, not many days after I found the dime outside Shea Stadium.

I picked up the receiver, and the man on the other end asked if he was talking to the Pinkerton Agency. I told him no, he had dialed the wrong number, and hung up. Then I went back to work and promptly forgot about the call.

The next afternoon, the telephone rang again. It turned out to be the same person asking the same question I had been asked the day before: "Is this the Pinkerton Agency?" Again I said no, and again I hung up. This time, however, I started thinking about what would have happened if I had said yes. What if I had pretended to be a detective from the Pinkerton Agency? I wondered. What if I had actually taken on the case?

To tell the truth, I felt that I had squandered a rare opportunity. If the man ever called again, I told myself, I would at least talk to him a little bit and try to find out what was going on. I waited for the telephone to ring again, but the third call never came.

After that, wheels started turning in my head, and little by little an entire world of possibilities opened up to me. When I sat down to write *City of Glass* a year later, the wrong number had been transformed into the crucial event of the book, the mistake that sets the whole story in motion. A man named Quinn receives a phone call from someone who wants to talk to Paul Auster, the private detective. Just as I did, Quinn tells the caller he has dialed the wrong number. It happens again on the next night, and again Quinn hangs up. Unlike me, however, Quinn is given another chance. When the phone rings again on the third night, he plays along with the caller and takes on the case. Yes, he says, I'm Paul Auster—and at that moment the madness begins.

Most of all, I wanted to remain faithful to my original impulse. Unless I stuck to the spirit of what had really happened, I felt there wouldn't have been any purpose to writing the book. That meant implicating myself in the action of the story (or at least someone who resembled me, who bore my name), and it also meant writing about detectives who were not detectives, about impersonation, about mysteries that cannot be solved. For better or worse, I felt I had no choice.

All well and good. I finished the book ten years ago, and since then I have gone on to occupy myself with other projects, other ideas, other books. Less than two months ago, however, I learned that books are never finished, that it is possible for stories to go on writing themselves without an author.

I was alone in my apartment in Brooklyn that afternoon, sitting at my desk and trying to work when the telephone rang. This was a different apartment from the one I had in 1980—a different apartment with a different telephone number. I picked up the receiver, and the man on the other end asked if he could speak to Mr. Quinn. He had a Spanish accent and I did not recognize the voice. For a moment I thought it might be one of my friends trying to pull my leg. "Mr. Quinn?" I said. "Is this some kind of joke or what?"

No, it wasn't a joke. The man was in dead earnest. He had to talk to Mr. Quinn, and would I please put him on the line. Just to make sure, I asked him to spell out the name. The caller's accent was quite thick, and I was hoping that he wanted to talk to Mr. Queen. But no such luck.

"Q-U-I-N-N," the man answered. I suddenly grew scared, and for a moment or two I couldn't get any words out of my mouth. "I'm sorry," I said at last, "there's no Mr. Quinn here. You've dialed the wrong number." The man apologized for disturbing me, and then we both hung up.

This really happened. Like everything else I have set down in this red notebook, it is a true story.

1992

Why Write?

1

A German friend tells of the circumstances that preceded the births of her two daughters.

Nineteen years ago, hugely pregnant and already several weeks past due, A. sat down on the sofa in her living room and turned on the television set. As luck would have it, the opening credits of a film were just coming on screen. It was *The Nun's Story*, a 1950s Hollywood drama starring Audrey Hepburn. Glad for the distraction, A. settled in to watch the movie and immediately got caught up in it. Halfway through, she went into labor. Her husband drove her to the hospital, and she never learned how the film turned out.

Three years later, pregnant with her second child, A. sat down on the sofa and turned on the television set once again. Once again a film was playing, and once again it was *The Nun's Story* with Audrey Hepburn. Even more remarkable (and A. was very emphatic about this point), she had tuned in to the film at the precise moment where she had left off three years earlier. This time she was able to see the film through to the end. Less than fifteen minutes later, her water broke, and she went off to the hospital to give birth for the second time.

These two daughters are A.'s only children. The first labor was extremely difficult (my friend nearly didn't make it and was ill for many months afterward), but the second delivery went smoothly, with no complications of any kind.

2

Five years ago, I spent the summer with my wife and children in Vermont, renting an old, isolated farmhouse on the top of a mountain. One day, a woman from the next town stopped by to visit with her two children, a girl of four and a boy of eighteen months. My daughter Sophie had just turned three, and she and the girl enjoyed playing with each other. My wife and I sat down in the kitchen with our guest, and the children ran off to amuse themselves.

Five minutes later, there was a loud crash. The little boy had wandered into the front hall at the other end of the house, and since my wife had put a vase of flowers in that hall just two hours earlier, it wasn't difficult to guess what had happened. I didn't even have to look to know that the floor was covered with broken glass and pools of water—along with the stems and petals of a dozen scattered flowers.

I was annoyed. Goddamn kids, I said to myself. Goddamn people with their goddamn clumsy kids. Who gave them the right to drop by without calling first?

I told my wife that I'd clean up the mess, and so while she and our visitor continued their conversation, I gathered up a broom, a dustpan, and some towels and marched off to the front of the house.

My wife had put the flowers on a wooden trunk that sat just below the staircase railing. This staircase was especially steep and narrow, and there was a large window not more than a yard from the bottom step. I mention this geography because it's important. Where things were has everything to do with what happened next.

I was about half finished with the clean-up job when my daughter rushed out from her room onto the second-floor landing. I was close enough to the foot of the stairs to catch a glimpse of her (a couple of steps back and she would have been blocked from view), and in that brief moment I saw that she had that high-spirited, utterly happy expression on her face that has filled my middle age with such overpowering gladness. Then, an instant later, before I could even say hello, she tripped. The toe of her sneaker had caught on the landing, and just like that, without any cry or warning, she was sailing through the air. I don't mean to suggest that she was falling or tumbling or bouncing down the steps. I mean to say that she was flying. The impact of the stumble had literally launched her into space, and from the trajectory of her flight I could see that she was heading straight for the window.

What did I do? I don't know what I did. I was on the wrong side of the banister when I saw her trip, but by the time she was midway between the landing and the window, I was standing on the bottom step of the staircase. How did I get there? It was no more than a question of several feet, but it hardly seems possible to cover that distance in that amount of time—which is next to no time at all. Nevertheless, I was there, and the moment I got there I looked up, opened my arms, and caught her.

3

I was fourteen. For the third year in a row, my parents had sent me to a summer camp in New York State. I spent the bulk of my time playing basketball and baseball, but as it was a co-ed camp, there were other activities as well: evening "socials," the first awkward grapplings with girls, panty raids, the usual adolescent shenanigans. I also remember smoking cheap cigars on the sly, "frenching" beds, and massive water-balloon fights.

None of this is important. I simply want to underscore what a vulnerable age fourteen can be. No longer a child, not yet an adult, you bounce back and forth between who you were and who you are about to become. In my own case, I was still young enough to think that I had a legitimate shot at playing in the Major Leagues, but old enough to be questioning the existence of God. I had read the Communist Manifesto, and yet I still enjoyed watching Saturday morning cartoons. Every time I saw my face in the mirror, I seemed to be looking at someone else.

There were sixteen or eighteen boys in my group. Most of us had been together for several years, but a couple of newcomers had also joined us that summer. One was named Ralph. He was a quiet kid without much enthusiasm for dribbling basketballs or hitting the cut-off man, and while no one gave him a particularly hard time, he had trouble blending in. He had flunked a couple of subjects that year, and most of his free periods were spent being tutored by one of the counselors. It was a little sad, and I felt sorry for him—but not too sorry, not sorry enough to lose any sleep over it.

Our counselors were all New York college students from Brooklyn and Queens. Wise-cracking basketball players, future dentists, accountants, and teachers, city kids to their very bones. Like most true New Yorkers, they persisted in calling the ground the "floor," even when all that was under their feet was grass, pebbles, and dirt. The trappings of traditional summer camp life were as alien to them as the I.R.T. is to an Iowa farmer. Canoes, lanyards, mountain climbing, pitching tents, singing around the campfire were nowhere to be found in the inventory of their concerns. They could drill us on the finer points of setting picks and boxing out for rebounds, but otherwise they mostly horsed around and told jokes.

Imagine our surprise, then, when one afternoon our counselor announced that we were going for a hike in the woods. He had been seized by an inspiration and wasn't going to let anyone talk him out of it. Enough basketball, he said. We're surrounded by nature, and it's time we took advantage of it and started acting like real campers—or words to that effect. And so, after the rest period that followed lunch, the whole gang of sixteen or eighteen boys along with two or three counselors set off into the woods.

It was late July, 1961. Everyone was in a fairly buoyant mood, I remember, and half an hour or so into the trek most people agreed that the outing had been a good idea. No one had a compass, of course, or the slightest clue as to where we were going, but we were all enjoying ourselves, and if we happened to get lost, what difference would that make? Sooner or later, we'd find our way back.

Then it began to rain. At first it was barely noticeable, a few light drops falling between the leaves and branches, nothing to worry about. We walked on, unwilling to let a little water spoil our fun, but a couple of minutes later it started coming down in earnest. Everyone got soaked, and the counselors decided we should turn around and head back. The only problem was that no one knew where the camp was. The woods were thick, dense with clusters of trees and thorn-studded bushes, and we had woven our way this way and that, abruptly shifting directions in order to move on. To add to the confusion, it was becoming hard to see. The woods were dark to begin with, but with the rain falling and the sky turning black, it felt more like night than three or four in the afternoon.

Then the thunder started. And after the thunder, the lightning started. The storm was directly on top of us, and it turned out to be the summer storm to end all summer storms. I have never seen weather like that before or since. The rain poured down on us so hard that it actually hurt; each time the thunder exploded, you could feel the noise vibrating inside your body. Immediately after that, the lightning would come, dancing around us like spears. It was as if weapons had materialized out of thin air: a sudden flash that turned everything a bright, ghostly white. Trees were struck, and the branches would begin to smolder. Then it would go dark again for a moment, there would be another crash in the sky, and the lightning would return in a different spot.

The lightning was what scared us, of course. It would have been stupid not to be scared, and in our panic we tried to run away from it. But the storm was too big, and everywhere we went we were met by more lightning. It was a helter-skelter stampede, a headlong rush in circles.

Then, suddenly, someone spotted a clearing in the woods. A brief dispute broke out over whether it was safer to go into the open or continue to stand under the trees. The voice arguing for the open won, and we all ran in the direction of the clearing.

It was a small meadow, most likely a pasture that belonged to a local farm, and to get to it we had to crawl under a barbed-wire fence. One by one, we got down on our bellies and inched our way through. I was in the middle of the line, directly behind Ralph. Just as he went under the barbed wire, there was another flash of lightning. I was two or three feet away, but because of the rain pounding against my eyelids, I had trouble making out what happened. All I knew was that Ralph had stopped moving. I figured that he had been stunned, so I crawled past him under the fence. Once I was on the other side, I took hold of his arm and dragged him through.

I don't know how long we stayed in that field. An hour, I would guess, and the whole time we were there the rain and thunder and lightning continued to crash down upon us. It was a storm ripped from the pages of the Bible, and it went on and on and on, as if it would never end.

Two or three boys were hit by something—perhaps by lightning, perhaps by the shock of lightning as it struck the ground near them—and the meadow began to fill with their moans. Other boys wept and prayed. Still others, fear in their voices, tried to give sensible advice. Get rid of everything metal, they said, metal attracts the lightning. We all took off our belts and threw them away from us.

I don't remember saying anything. I don't remember crying. Another boy and I kept ourselves busy trying to take care of Ralph. He was still unconscious. We rubbed his hands and arms, we held down his tongue so he wouldn't swallow it, we told him to hang in there. After a while, his skin began to take on a bluish tinge. His body seemed colder to my touch, but in spite of the mounting evidence, it never once occurred to me that he wasn't going to come around. I was only fourteen years old, after all, and what did I know? I had never seen a dead person before.

It was the barbed wire that did it, I suppose. The other boys hit by the lightning went numb, felt pain in their limbs for an hour or so, and then recovered. But Ralph had been under the fence when the lightning struck, and he had been electrocuted on the spot.

Later on, when they told me he was dead, I learned that there was an eight-inch burn across his back. I remember trying to absorb this news and telling myself that life would never feel the same to me again.

Strangely enough, I didn't think about how I had been right next to him when it happened. I didn't think, One or two seconds later, and it would have been me. What I thought about was holding his tongue and looking down at his teeth. His mouth had been set in a slight grimace, and with his lips partly open, I had spent an hour looking down at the tips of his teeth. Thirty-four years later, I still remember them. And his half-closed, half-open eyes. I remember those, too.

4

Not many years ago, I received a letter from a woman who lives in Brussels. In it, she told me the story of a friend of hers, a man she has known since childhood.

In 1940, this man joined the Belgian army. When the country fell to the Germans later that year, he was captured and put in a prisoner-of-war camp. He remained there until the war ended in 1945.

Prisoners were allowed to correspond with Red Cross workers back in Belgium. The man was arbitrarily assigned a pen pal—a Red Cross nurse from Brussels—and for the next five years he and this woman exchanged letters every month. Over the course of time they became fast friends. At a certain point (I'm not exactly sure how long this took), they understood that something more than friendship had developed between them. The correspondence went on, growing more intimate with each exchange, and at last they declared their love for each other. Was such a thing possible? They had never seen each other, had never spent a minute in each other's company.

After the war was over, the man was released from prison and returned to Brussels. He met the nurse, the nurse met him, and neither was disappointed. A short time later, they were married.

Years went by. They had children, they grew older, the world became a slightly different world. Their son completed his studies in Belgium and went off to do graduate work in Germany. At the university there, he fell in love with a young German woman. He wrote his parents and told them that he intended to marry her.

The parents on both sides couldn't have been happier for their children. The two families arranged to meet, and on the appointed day the German family showed up at the house of the Belgian family in Brussels. As the German father walked into the living room and the Belgian father rose to welcome him, the two men looked into each other's eyes and recognized each other. Many years had passed, but neither one was in any doubt as to who the other was. At one time in their lives, they had seen each other every day. The German father had been a guard in the prison camp where the Belgian father had spent the war.

As the woman who wrote me the letter hastened to add, there was no bad blood between them. However monstrous the German regime might have been, the German father had done nothing during those five years to turn the Belgian father against him.

Be that as it may, these two men are now the best of friends. The greatest joy in their lives is the grandchildren they have in common.

5

I was eight years old. At that moment in my life, nothing was more important to me than baseball. My team was the New York Giants, and I followed the doings of those men in the black-and-orange caps with all the devotion of a true believer. Even now, remembering that team which no longer exists, that played in a ballpark which no longer exists, I can reel off the names of nearly every player on the roster. Alvin Dark, Whitey Lockman, Don Mueller, Johnny Antonelli, Monte Irvin, Hoyt Wilhelm. But none was greater, none more perfect nor more deserving of worship than Willie Mays, the incandescent Say-Hey Kid.

That spring, I was taken to my first big-league game. Friends of my parents had box seats at the Polo Grounds, and one April night a group of us went to watch the Giants play the Milwaukee Braves. I don't know who won, I can't recall a single detail of the game, but I do remember that after the game was over my parents and their friends sat talking in their seats until all the other spectators had left. It got so late that we had to walk across the diamond and leave by the center-field exit, which was the only one still open. As it happened, that exit was right below the players' locker rooms.

Just as we approached the wall, I caught sight of Willie Mays. There was no question about who it was. It was Willie Mays, already out of uniform and standing there in his street clothes not ten feet away from me. I managed to keep my legs moving in his direction and then, mustering every ounce of my courage, I forced some words out of my mouth. "Mr. Mays," I said, "could I please have your autograph?"

He had to have been all of twenty-four years old, but I couldn't bring myself to pronounce his first name.

His response to my question was brusque but amiable. "Sure, kid, sure," he said. "You got a pencil?" He was so full of life, I remember, so full of youthful energy, that he kept bouncing up and down as he spoke.

I didn't have a pencil, so I asked my father if I could borrow his. He didn't have one either. Nor did my mother. Nor, as it turned out, did any of the other grown-ups.

The great Willie Mays stood there watching in silence. When it became clear that no one in the group had anything to write with, he turned to me and shrugged. "Sorry, kid," he said. "Ain't got no pencil, can't give no autograph." And then he walked out of the ballpark into the night.

I didn't want to cry, but tears started falling down my cheeks, and there was nothing I could do to stop them. Even worse, I cried all the way home in the car. Yes, I was crushed with disappointment, but I was also revolted at myself for not being able to control those tears. I wasn't a baby. I was eight years old, and big kids weren't supposed to cry over things like that. Not only did I not have Willie Mays's autograph, I didn't have anything else either. Life had put me to the test, and in all respects I had found myself wanting.

After that night, I started carrying a pencil with me wherever I went. It became a habit of mine never to leave the house without making sure I had a pencil in my pocket. It's not that I had any particular plans for that pencil, but I didn't want to be unprepared. I had been caught empty-handed once, and I wasn't about to let it happen again.

If nothing else, the years have taught me this: if there's a pencil in your pocket, there's a good chance that one day you'll feel tempted to start using it.

As I like to tell my children, that's how I became a writer.

1995

Accident Report

1

When A. was a young woman in San Francisco and just starting out in life, she went through a desperate period in which she almost lost her mind. In the space of just a few weeks, she was fired from her job, one of her best friends was murdered when thieves broke into her apartment at night, and A.'s beloved cat became seriously ill. I don't know the exact nature of the illness, but it was apparently life-threatening, and when A. took the cat to the vet, he told her that the cat would die within a month unless a certain operation was performed. She asked him how much the operation would cost. He toted up the various charges for her, and the amount came to three hundred twenty-seven dollars. A. didn't have that kind of money. Her bank account was down to almost zero, and for the next several days she walked around in a state of extreme distress, alternately thinking about her dead friend and the impossible sum needed to prevent her cat from dying: three hundred twenty-seven dollars.

One day, she was driving through the Mission and came to a stop at a red light. Her body was there, but her thoughts were somewhere else, and in the gap between them, in that small space that no one has fully explored but where we all sometimes live, she heard the voice of her murdered friend. *Don't worry*, the voice said. *Don't worry. Things will get better soon*. The light turned green, but A. was still under the spell of this auditory hallucination, and she did not move. A moment later, a car rammed into her from behind, breaking one of the taillights and crumpling the fender. The man who was driving that car shut off his engine, climbed out of the car, and walked over to A. He apologized for doing such a stupid thing. No, A. said, it was my fault. The light turned green and I didn't go. But the man insisted that he was the one to blame. When he learned that A. didn't have collision insurance (she was too poor for luxuries like that), he offered to pay for any damages that had been done to her car. Get an estimate on what it will cost, he said, and send me the bill. My insurance company will take care of it. A. continued to protest, telling the man that he wasn't responsible for the accident, but he wouldn't take no for an answer, and finally she gave in. She took the car to a garage and asked the mechanic to assess the costs of repairing the fender and the taillight. When she returned several hours later, he handed her a written estimate. Give or take a penny or two, the amount came to exactly three hundred twenty-seven dollars.

2

W., the friend from San Francisco who told me that story, has been directing films for twenty years. His latest project is based on a novel that recounts the adventures of a mother and her teenage daughter. It is a work of fiction, but most of the events in the book are taken directly from the author's life. The author, now a grown woman, was once the teenage daughter, and the mother in the story—who is still alive—was her real mother.

W.'s film was shot in Los Angeles. A famous actress was hired to play the role of the mother, and according to what W. told me on a recent visit to New York, the filming went smoothly and the production was completed on schedule. Once he began to edit the movie, however, he decided that he wanted to add a few more scenes, which he felt would greatly enhance the story. One of them included a shot of the mother parking her car on a street in a residential neighborhood. The location manager went out scouting for an appropriate street, and eventually one was chosen—arbitrarily, it would seem, since one Los Angeles street looks more or less like any other. On the appointed morning, W., the actress, and the film crew gathered on the street to shoot the scene. The car that the actress was supposed to drive was parked in front of a house—no particular house, just one of the houses on that street—and as my friend and his leading lady stood on the sidewalk discussing the scene and the possible ways to approach it, the door of that house burst open and a woman came running out. She appeared to be laughing and screaming at the same time. Distracted by the commotion, W. and the actress stopped talking. A screaming and laughing woman was running across the front lawn, and she was headed straight for them. I don't know how big the lawn was. W. neglected to mention that detail when he told the story, but in my mind I see it as large, which would have given the woman a considerable distance to cover before she reached the sidewalk and announced who she was. A moment like that deserves to be prolonged, it seems to me—if only by a few seconds—for the thing that was about to happen was so improbable, so outlandish in its defiance of the odds, that one wants to savor it for a few extra seconds before letting go of it. The woman running across the lawn was the novelist's mother. A fictional character in her daughter's book, she was also her real mother, and now, by pure accident, she was about to meet the woman who was playing that fictional character in a film based on the book in which her character had in fact been herself. She was real, but she was also imaginary. And the actress who was playing her was both real and imaginary as well. There were two of them standing on the sidewalk that morning, but there was also just one. Or perhaps it was the same one twice. According to what my friend told me, when the women finally understood what had happened, they threw their arms around each other and embraced.

3

Last September, I had to go to Paris for a few days, and my publisher booked a room for me in a small hotel on the Left Bank. It's the same hotel they use for all their authors, and I had already stayed there several times in the past. Other than its convenient location—midway down a narrow street just off the Boulevard Saint-Germain—there is nothing even remotely interesting about this hotel. Its rates are modest, its rooms are cramped, and it is not mentioned in any guidebook. The people who run it are pleasant enough, but it is no more than a drab and inconspicuous hole-in-the-wall, and except for a couple of American writers who have the same French publisher I do, I have never met anyone who has stayed there. I mention this fact because the obscurity of the hotel plays a part in the story. Unless one stops for a moment to consider how many hotels there are in Paris (which attracts more visitors than any other city in the world) and then further considers how many rooms there are in those hotels (thousands, no doubt tens of thousands), the full import of what happened to me last year will not be understood.

I arrived at the hotel late—more than an hour behind schedule—and checked in at the front desk. I went upstairs immediately after that. Just as I was putting my key into the door of my room, the telephone started to ring. I went in, tossed my bag on the floor, and picked up the phone, which was set into a nook in the wall just beside the bed, more or less at pillow level. Because the phone was turned in toward the bed, and because the cord was short, and because the one chair in the room was out of reach, it was necessary to sit down on the bed in order to use the phone. That's what I did, and as I talked to the person on the other end of the line, I noticed a piece of paper lying under the desk on the opposite side of the room. If I had been anywhere else, I wouldn't have been in a position to see it. The dimensions of the room were so tight that the space between the desk and the foot of the bed was no more than four or five feet. From my vantage point at the head of the bed, I was in the only place that provided a low enough angle of the floor to see what was under the desk. After the conversation was over, I got off the bed, crouched down under the desk, and picked up the piece of paper. Curious, of course, always curious, but not at all expecting to find anything out of the ordinary. The paper turned out to be one of those little message forms they slip under your door in European hotels. To—— and From——, the date and the time, and then a blank square below for the message. The form had been folded in three, and printed out in block letters on the outer fold was the name of one of my closest friends. We don't see each other often (O. lives in Canada), but we have been through a number of memorable experiences together, and there has never been anything but the greatest affection between us. Seeing his name on the message form made me very happy. We hadn't spoken in a while, and I had had no inkling that he would be in Paris when I was there. In those first moments of discovery and incomprehension, I assumed that O. had somehow gotten wind of the fact that I was coming and had called the hotel to leave a message for me. The message had been delivered to my room, but whoever had brought it up had placed it carelessly on the edge of the desk, and it had blown onto the floor. Or else that person had accidentally dropped it (the chambermaid?) while preparing the room for my arrival. One way or the other, neither explanation was very plausible. The angle was wrong, and unless someone had kicked the message after it had fallen to the floor, the paper couldn't have been lying so far under the desk. I was already beginning to reconsider my hypothesis when something more important occurred to me. O.'s name was on the outside of the message form. If the message had been meant for me, my name would have been there. The recipient was the one whose name belonged on the outside, not the sender, and if my name wasn't there, it surely wasn't going to be anywhere else. I opened the message and read it. The sender was someone I had never heard of—but the recipient was indeed O. I rushed downstairs and asked the clerk at the front desk if O. was still there. It was a stupid question, of course, but I asked it anyway. How could O. be there if he was no longer in his room? I was there now, and O.'s room was no longer his room but mine. I asked the clerk when he had checked out. An hour ago, the clerk said. An hour ago I had been sitting in a taxi at the edge of Paris, stuck in a traffic jam. If I had made it to the hotel at the expected time, I would have run into O. just as he was walking out the door.

1999

It Don't Mean a Thing

1

We used to see him occasionally at the Carlyle Hotel. It would be an exaggeration to call him a friend, but F. was a good acquaintance, and my wife and I always looked forward to his arrival when he called to say that he was coming to town. A daring and prolific French poet, F. was also one of the world's leading authorities on Henri Matisse. So great was his reputation, in fact, that an important French museum asked him to organize a large exhibition of Matisse's work. F. wasn't a professional curator, but he threw himself into the job with enormous energy and skill. The idea was to gather together all of Matisse's paintings from a particular five-year period in the middle of his career. Dozens of canvases were involved, and since they were scattered around in private collections and museums all over the world, it took F. several years to prepare the show. In the end, there was only one work that could not be found—but it was a crucial one, the centerpiece of the entire exhibition. F. had not been able to track down the owner, had no idea where it was, and without that canvas years of travel and meticulous labor would go for naught. For the next six months, he devoted himself exclusively to the search for that one painting, and when he found it, he realized that it had been no more than a few feet away from him the whole time. The owner was a woman who lived in an apartment at the Carlyle Hotel. The Carlyle was F.'s hotel of choice, and he stayed there whenever he was in New York. More than that, the woman's apartment was located directly above the room that F. always reserved for himself—just one floor up. Which meant that every time F. had gone to sleep at the Carlyle Hotel, wondering where the missing painting could have been, it had been hanging on a wall directly above his head. Like an image from a dream.

2

I wrote that paragraph last October. A few days later, a friend from Boston called to tell me that a poet acquaintance of his was in bad shape. In his mid-sixties now, this man has spent his life in the far reaches of the literary solar system—the single inhabitant of an asteroid that orbits around a tertiary moon of Pluto, visible only through the strongest telescope. I have never met him, but I have read his work, and I have always imagined him living on his small planet like some latter-day Little Prince.

My friend told me that the poet's health was in decline. He was undergoing treatments for his illness, his money was at a low ebb, and he was being threatened with eviction from his apartment. As a way to raise some quick and necessary cash to rescue the poet from his troubles, my friend had come up with the idea of producing a book in his honor. He would solicit contributions from several dozen poets and writers, gather them into an attractive, limited-edition volume, and sell the copies by subscription only. He figured there were enough book collectors in the country to guarantee a handsome profit. Once the money came in, it would all be turned over to the sick and struggling poet.

He asked me if I had a page or two lying around somewhere that I might give him, and I mentioned the little story I had just written about my French friend and the missing painting. I faxed it to him that same morning, and a few hours later he called back to say that he liked the piece and wanted to include it in the book. I was glad to have done my little bit, and then, once the matter had been settled, I promptly forgot all about it.

Two nights ago (January 31, 2000), I was sitting with my twelve-year-old daughter at the dining room table in our house in Brooklyn, helping her with her math homework—a massive list of problems involving negative and positive numbers. My daughter is not terribly interested in math, and once we finished converting the subtractions into additions and the negatives into positives, we started talking about the music recital that had been held at her school several nights before. She had sung "The First Time Ever I Saw Your Face," the old Roberta Flack number, and now she was looking for another song to begin preparing for the spring recital. After tossing some ideas back and forth, we both decided that she should do something bouncy and up-tempo this time, in contrast to the slow and aching ballad she had just performed. Without any warning, she sprang from her chair and began belting out the lyrics of "It Don't Mean a Thing if it Ain't Got that Swing." I know that parents tend to exaggerate the talents of their children, but there was no question in my mind that her rendition of that song was remarkable. Dancing and shimmying as the music poured out of her, she took her voice to places it had rarely been before, and because she sensed that herself, could feel the power of her own performance, she immediately launched into it again after she had finished. Then she sang it again. And then again. For fifteen or twenty minutes, the house was filled with increasingly beautiful and ecstatic variations of a single unforgettable phrase: *It don't mean a thing if it ain't got that swing*.

The following afternoon (yesterday), I brought in the mail at around two o'clock. There was a considerable pile of it, the usual mixture of junk and important business. One letter had been sent by a small New York poetry publisher, and I opened that one first. Unexpectedly, it contained the proofs of my contribution to my friend's book. I read through the piece again, making one or two corrections, and then called the copy editor responsible for the production of the book. Her name and number had been provided in a cover letter sent by the publisher, and once we had had our brief chat, I hung up the phone and turned to the rest of my mail. Wedged inside the pages of my daughter's new issue of *Seventeen Magazine*, there was a slim white package that had been sent from France. When I turned it over to look at the return address, I saw that it was from F., the same poet whose experience with the missing painting had inspired me to write the short piece I had just read over for the first time since composing it in October. What a coincidence, I thought. My life has been filled with dozens of curious events like this one, and no matter how hard I try, I can't seem to shake free of them. What is it about the world that continues to involve me in such nonsense?

Then I opened the package. There was a thin book of poetry inside—what we would refer to as a chapbook; what the French call a *plaquette*. It was just thirty-two pages long, and it had been printed on fine, elegant paper. As I flipped through it, scanning a phrase here and a phrase there, immediately recognizing the exuberant and frenetic style that characterizes all of F.'s work, a tiny slip of paper fell out of the book and fluttered onto my desk. It was no more than two inches long and half an inch high. I had no idea what it was. I had never encountered a stray slip of paper in a new book before, and unless it was supposed to serve as some kind of rarefied, microscopic bookmark to match the refinement of the book itself, it seemed to have been put in there by mistake. I picked up the errant rectangle from my desk, turned it over, and saw that there was writing on the other side—eleven short words arranged in a single row of type. The poems had been written in French, the book had been printed in France, but the words on the slip of paper that had fallen out of the book were in English. They formed a sentence, and that sentence read: *It don't mean a thing if it ain't got that swing.*

3

Having come this far, I can't resist the temptation to add one more link to this chain of anecdotes. As I was writing the last words of the first paragraph in the second section printed above ("living on his small planet like some latter-day Little Prince"), I was reminded of the fact that *The Little Prince* was written in New York. Few people know this, but after Saint-Exupéry was demobilized following the French defeat in 1940, he came to America, and for a time he lived at 240 Central Park South in Manhattan. It was there that he wrote his celebrated book, the most French of all French children's books. *Le Petit Prince* is required reading for nearly every American high school student of French, and as was the case with so many others before me, it was the first book I happened to read in a language that wasn't English. I went on to read more books in French. Eventually, I translated French books as a way of earning my living as a young man, and at a certain point I lived in France for four years. That was where I first met F. and became familiar with his work. It might be an outlandish statement, but I believe it is safe to say that if I hadn't read *Le Petit Prince* as an adolescent in 1963, I never would have been in a position to receive F.'s book in the mail thirty-seven years later. In saying that, I am also saying that I never would have discovered the mysterious slip of paper bearing the words *It don't mean a thing if it ain't got that swing.*

240 Central Park South is an odd, misshapen building that stands on the corner overlooking Columbus Circle. Construction was completed in 1941, and the first tenants moved in just before Pearl Harbor and America's entrance into the war. I don't know the exact date when Saint-Exupéry took up residence there, but he had to have been among the first people to live in that building. By one of those curious anomalies that mean absolutely nothing, so was my mother. She moved there from Brooklyn with her parents and sister at the age of sixteen, and she did not move out until she married my father five years later. It was an extraordinary step for the family to take—from Crown Heights to one of the most elegant addresses in Manhattan—and it moves me to think that my mother lived in the same building where Saint-Exupéry wrote *The Little Prince*. If nothing else, I am moved by the fact that she had no

idea that the book was being written, no idea who the author was. Nor did she have any knowledge of his death some time later when his plane went down in the last year of the war. Around that same time, my mother fell in love with an aviator. As it happened, he, too, died in that same war.

My grandparents went on living at 240 Central Park South until their deaths (my grandmother in 1968; my grandfather in 1979), and many of my most important childhood memories are situated in their apartment. My mother moved to New Jersey after she married my father, and we changed houses several times during my early years, but the New York apartment was always there, a fixed point in an otherwise unstable universe. It was there that I stood at the window and watched the traffic swirling around the statue of Christopher Columbus. It was there that my grandfather performed his magic tricks for me. It was there that I came to understand that New York was my city.

Just as my mother had done, her sister moved out of the apartment when she married. Not long after that (in the early fifties), she and her husband moved to Europe, where they lived for the next twelve years. In thinking about the various decisions I have made in my own life, I have no doubt that their example inspired me to move to France when I was in my early twenties. When my aunt and uncle returned to New York, my young cousin was eleven years old. I had met him only once. His parents sent him to school at the French lycée, and because of the incongruities in our respective educations, we wound up reading *Le Petit Prince* at the same time, even though there was a six-year difference in our ages. Back then, neither one of us knew that the book had been written in the same building where our mothers had lived.

After their return from Europe, my cousin and his parents settled into an apartment on the Upper East Side. For the next several years, he had his hair cut every month at the barbershop in the Carlyle Hotel.

2000

GOTHAM HANDBOOK

From Double Game by Sophie Calle

THE RULES OF THE GAME

In his novel *Leviathan*, Paul Auster thanks me for having authorized him to mingle fact with fiction. And indeed, on pages 60 to 67 of his book, he uses a number of episodes from my life to create a fictive character named Maria. Intrigued by this double, I decided to turn Paul Auster's novel into a game and to make my own particular mixture of reality and fiction.

I

The life of Maria and how it influenced the life of Sophie.

In *Leviathan*, Maria puts herself through the same rituals as I did. But Paul Auster has slipped some rules of his own inventing into his portrait of Maria. In order to bring Maria and myself closer together, I decided to go by the book.

II

The life of Sophie and how it influenced the life of Maria.

The rituals that Auster "borrowed" from me to shape Maria are: *The Wardrobe, The Striptease, To Follow . . ., Suite vénitienne, The Detective, The Hotel, The Address Book,* and *The Birthday Ceremony. Leviathan* gives me the opportunity to present these artistic projects that inspired the author and which Maria and I now share.

III

One of the many ways of mingling fact with fiction, or how to try to become a character out of a novel.

Since, in *Leviathan*, Auster has taken me as a subject, I imagined swapping roles and taking him as the author of my actions. I asked him to invent a fictive character which I would attempt to resemble. Instead, Auster preferred to send me "Personal Instructions for SC on How to Improve Life in New York City (Because she asked . . .)". I followed his directives. This project is entitled *Gotham Handbook.*

Gotham Handbook

Personal Instructions for S.C. On How to Improve Life in New York City (Because she asked . . .)

SMILING

Smile when the situation doesn't call for it. Smile when you're feeling angry, when you're feeling miserable, when you're feeling most crushed by the world—and see if it makes any difference.

Smile at strangers in the street. New York can be dangerous, so you must be careful. If you prefer, smile only at female strangers. (Men are beasts, and they must not be given the wrong idea.)

Nevertheless, smile as often as possible at people you don't know. Smile at the bank teller who gives you your money, at the waitress who gives you your food, at the person sitting across from you on the IRT.

See if anyone smiles back at you.

Keep track of the number of smiles you are given each day.

Don't be disappointed when people don't smile back at you.

Consider each smile you receive a precious gift.

TALKING TO STRANGERS

There will be people who talk to you after you smile at them. You must be prepared with flattering comments.

Some of these people will talk to you because they feel confused or threatened or insulted by your show of friendliness. ("You got a problem, lady?") Plunge in immediately with a disarming compliment. "No, I was just admiring your beautiful tie." Or: "I love your dress."

Others will talk to you because they are friendly souls, happy to respond to the human overtures that come their way. Try to keep these conversations going as long as you can. It doesn't matter what you talk about. The important thing is to give of yourself and see to it that some form of genuine contact is made.

If you find yourself running out of things to say, bring up the subject of the weather. Cynics regard this as a banal topic, but the fact is that no subject gets people talking faster. Stop and think about it for a moment, and you'll begin to see a metaphysical, even religious quality to this preoccupation with wind-chill factors and Central Park snowfall accumulations. Weather is the great equalizer. There is nothing anyone can do about it, and it affects us all in the same way—rich and poor, black and white, healthy and sick. The weather makes no distinctions. When it rains on me, it also rains on you. Unlike most of the problems we face, it is not a condition created by man. It comes from nature, or God, or whatever else you want to call the forces in the universe we cannot control. To discuss the weather with a stranger is to shake hands and put aside your weapons. It is a sign of goodwill, an acknowledgement of your common humanity with the person you are talking to.

With so many things driving us apart, with so much hatred and discord in the air, it is good to remember the things that bring us together. The more we insist on them in our dealings with strangers, the better morale in the city will be.

BEGGARS AND HOMELESS PEOPLE

I'm not asking you to reinvent the world. I just want you to pay attention to it, to think about the things around you more than you think about yourself. At least while you're outside, walking down the street on your way from here to there.

Don't ignore the miserable ones. They are everywhere, and a person can grow so accustomed to seeing them that he begins to forget they are there. Don't forget.

I'm not asking you to give all your money to the poor. Even if you did, poverty would still exist (and have one more member among its ranks).

At the same time, it's our responsibility as human beings not to harden our hearts. Action is necessary, no matter how small or hopeless our gestures might seem to be.

Stock up on bread and cheese. Every time you leave the house, make three or four sandwiches and put them in your pocket. Every time you see a hungry person, give him a sandwich.

Stock up on cigarettes as well. Common wisdom says that cigarettes are bad for your health, but what common wisdom neglects to say is that they also give great comfort to the people who smoke them.

Don't just give one or two. Give away whole packs.

If you find your pockets can't hold enough sandwiches, go to the nearest McDonald's and buy as many meal coupons as you can afford. Give these coupons away when you're out of cheese sandwiches. You might not like the food at McDonald's, but most people do. Considering the alternatives, they give pretty good value for the money.

These coupons will be especially helpful on cold days. Not only will the hungry person be able to fill his stomach, he'll be able to go inside somewhere and get warm.

If you can't think of anything to say when you give the coupon to the hungry person, talk about the weather.

CULTIVATING A SPOT

People are not the only ones neglected in New York. Things are neglected as well. I don't just mean big things like bridges and subway tracks, I mean the small, barely noticeable things standing right in front of our eyes: patches of sidewalk, walls, park benches. Look closely at the things around you and you'll see that nearly everything is falling apart.

Pick one spot in the city and begin to think of it as yours. It doesn't matter where, and it doesn't matter what. A street corner, a subway entrance, a tree in the park. Take on this place as your responsibility. Keep it clean. Beautify it. Think of it as an extension of who you are, as a part of your identity. Take as much pride in it as you would in your own home.

Go to your spot every day at the same time. Spend an hour watching everything that happens to it, keeping track of everyone who passes by or stops or does anything there. Take notes, take photographs. Make a record of these daily observations and see if you learn anything about the people or the place or yourself.

Smile at the people who come there. Whenever possible, talk to them. If you can't think of anything to say, begin by talking about the weather.

March 5, 1994

THE STORY OF MY TYPEWRITER

(*with Sam Messer*)

Three and a half years later, I came home to America. It was July 1974, and when I unpacked my bags that first afternoon in New York, I discovered that my little Hermes typewriter had been destroyed. The cover was smashed in, the keys were mangled and twisted out of shape, and there was no hope of ever having it repaired.

I couldn't afford to buy a new typewriter. I rarely had much money in those days, but at that particular moment I was dead broke.

A couple of nights later, an old college friend invited me to his apartment for dinner. At some point during our conversation, I mentioned what had happened to my typewriter, and he told me that he had one in the closet that he didn't use anymore. It had been given to him as a graduation present from junior high school in 1962. If I wanted to buy it from him, he said, he would be glad to sell it to me.

We agreed on a price of forty dollars. It was an Olympia portable, manufactured in West Germany. That country no longer exists, but since that day in 1974, every word I have written has been typed out on that machine.

In the beginning, I didn't think about it much. A year went by, ten years went by, and not once did I consider it odd or even vaguely unusual to be working with a manual typewriter. The only alternative was an electric typewriter, but I didn't like the noise those contraptions made: the constant hum of the motor, the buzzing and rattling of loose parts, the jitterbug pulse of alternating current vibrating in my fingers. I preferred the stillness of my Olympia. It was comfortable to the touch, it worked smoothly, it was dependable. And when I wasn't pounding on the keyboard, it was silent.

Best of all, it seemed to be indestructible. Except for changing ribbons and occasionally having to brush out the ink buildup from the keys, I was absolved of all maintenance duties. Since 1974, I have changed the roller twice, perhaps three times. I have taken it into the shop for cleaning no more than I have voted in Presidential elections. I have never had to replace any parts. The only serious trauma it has suffered occurred in

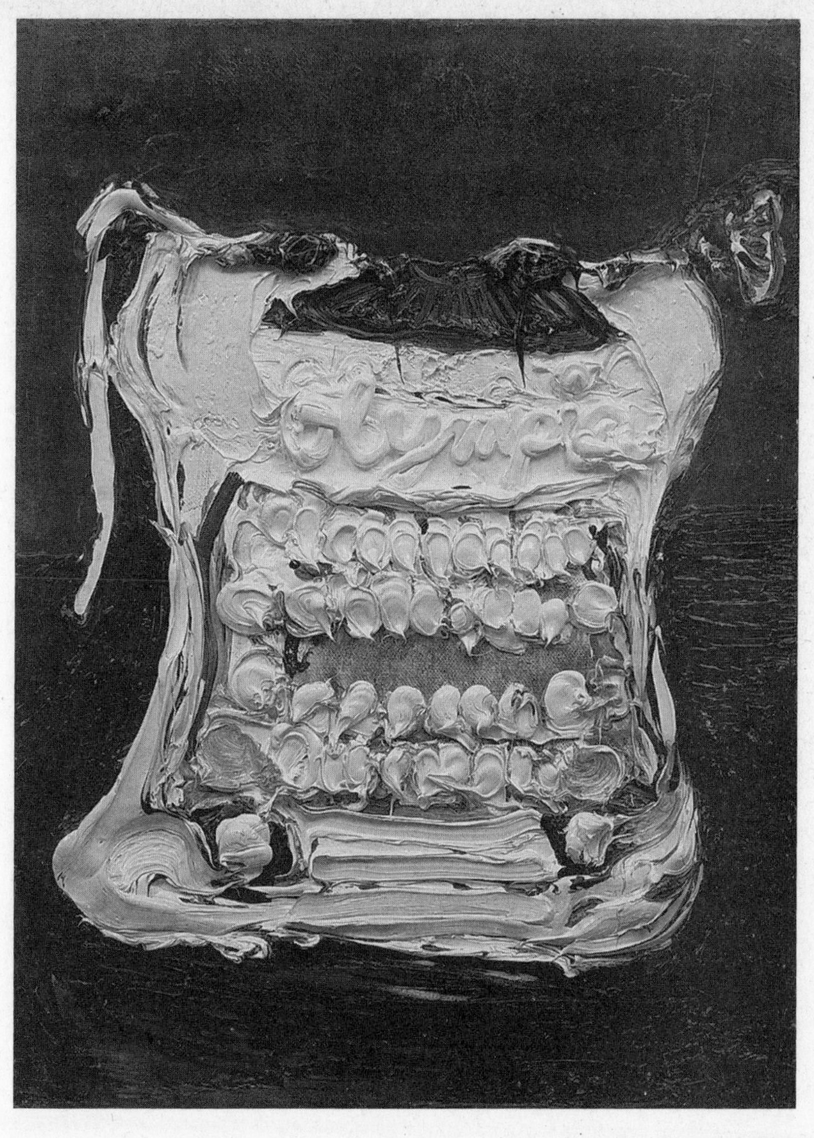

1979 when my two-year-old son snapped off the carriage return arm. But that wasn't the typewriter's fault. I was in despair for the rest of the day, but the next morning I carried it to a shop on Court Street and had the arm soldered back in place. There is a small scar on that spot now, but the operation was a success, and the arm has held ever since.

There is no point in talking about computers and word processors. Early on, I was tempted to buy one of those marvels for myself, but too many friends told me horror stories about pushing the wrong button and wiping out a day's work—or a month's work—and I heard one too many warnings about sudden power failures that could erase an entire manuscript in less than half a second. I have never been good with machines, and I knew that if there was a wrong button to be pushed, I would eventually push it.

So I held on to my old typewriter, and the 1980s became the 1990s. One by one, all my friends switched over to Macs and IBMs. I began to look like an enemy of progress, the last pagan holdout in a world of digital converts. My friends made fun of me for resisting the new ways. When they weren't calling me a curmudgeon, they called me a reactionary and a stubborn old goat. I didn't care. What was good for them wasn't necessarily good for me, I said. Why should I change when I was perfectly happy as I was?

Until then, I hadn't felt particularily attached to my typewriter. It was simply a tool that allowed me to do my work, but now that it had become an endangered species, one of the last surviving artifacts of twentieth-century *homo scriptorus*, I began to develop a certain affection for it. Like it or not, I realized, we had the same past. As time went on, I came to understand that we also had the same future.

Two or three years ago, sensing that the end was near, I went to Leon, my local stationer in Brooklyn, and asked him to order fifty typewriter ribbons for me. He had to call around for several days to scare up an order of that size. Some of them, he later told me, were shipped in from as far away as Kansas City.

I use these ribbons as cautiously as I can, typing on them until the ink is all but invisible on the page. When the supply is gone, I have little hope that there will be any ribbons left.

It was never my intention to turn my typewriter into a heroic figure. That is the work of Sam Messer, a man who stepped into my house one

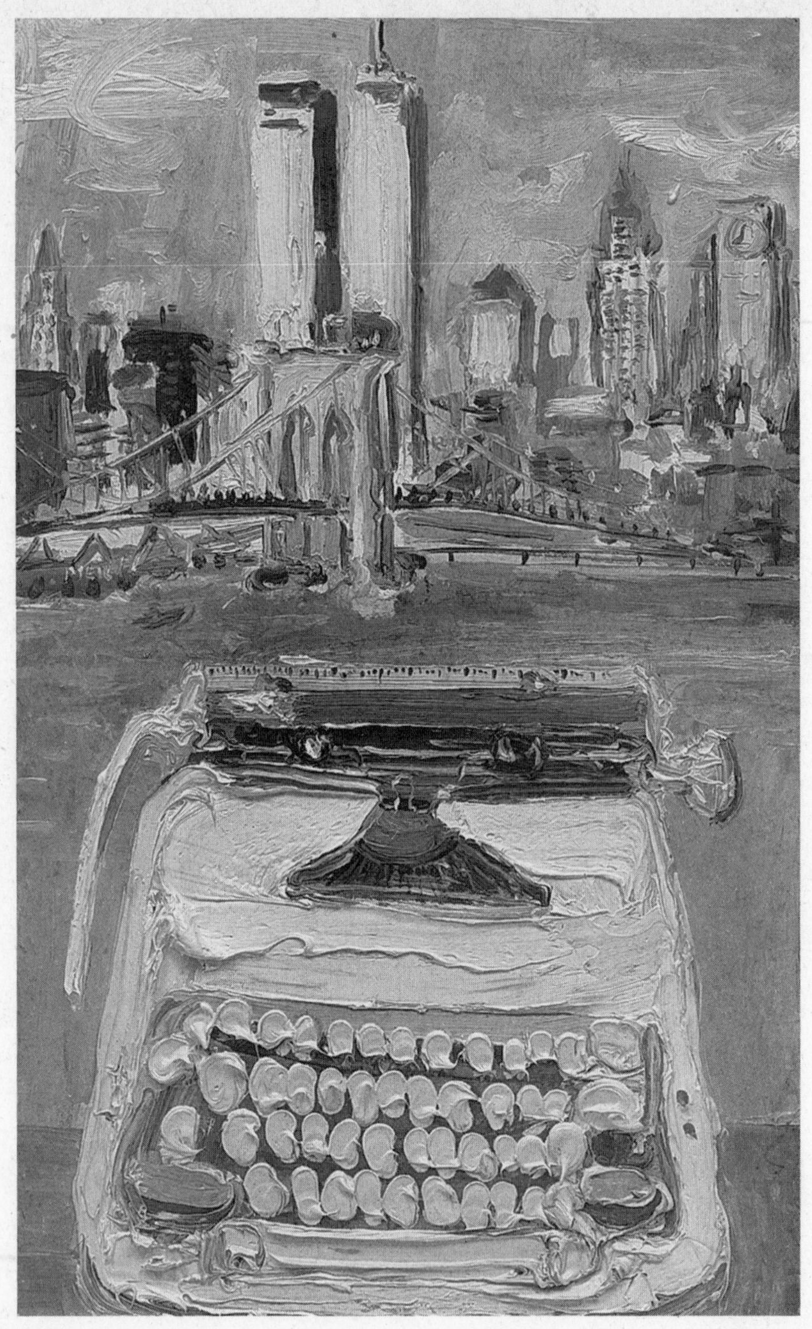

day and fell in love with a machine. There is no accounting for the passions of artists. The affair has lasted for several years now, and right from the beginning, I suspect that the feelings have been mutual.

Messer seldom goes anywhere without a sketchbook. He draws constantly, stabbing at the page with furious, rapid strokes, looking up from his pad every other second to squint at the person or object before him, and whenever you sit down to a meal with him, you do so with the understanding that you are also posing for your portrait. We have been through this routine so many times in the past seven or eight years that I no longer think about it.

I remember pointing out the typewriter to him the first time he visited, but I can't remember what he said. A day or two after that, he came back to the house. I wasn't around that afternoon, but he asked my wife if he could go downstairs to my work room and have another look at the typewriter. God knows what he did down there, but I have never doubted that the typewriter spoke to him. In due course, I believe he even managed to persuade it to bare its soul.

He has been back several times since, and each visit has produced a fresh wave of paintings, drawings, and photographs. Sam has taken possession of my typewriter, and little by little he has turned an inanimate object into a being with a personality and a presence in the world. The typewriter has moods and desires now, it expresses dark angers and exuberant joys, and trapped within its gray, metallic body, you would almost swear that you could hear the beating of a heart.

I have to admit that I find all this unsettling. The paintings are brilliantly done, and I am proud of my typewriter for proving itself to be such a worthy subject, but at the same time Messer has forced me to look at my old companion in a new way. I am still in the process of adjustment, but whenever I look at one of these paintings now (there are two of them hanging on my living room wall), I have trouble thinking of my typewriter as an *it*. Slowly but surely, the *it* has turned into a *him*.

We have been together for more than a quarter of a century now. Everywhere I have gone, the typewriter has gone with me. We have lived in Manhattan, in upstate New York, and in Brooklyn. We have traveled together to California and to Maine, to Minnesota and to Massachusetts, to Vermont and to France. In that time, I have written with hundreds of pencils and pens. I have owned several cars, several refrigerators, and have occupied several apartments and houses. I have worn out dozens of pairs of shoes, have given up on scores of sweaters and jackets, have lost or abandoned watches, alarm clocks, and umbrellas. Everything breaks, everything wears out, everything loses its purpose in the end, but the typewriter is still with me. It is the only object I own today that I owned twenty-six years ago. In another few months, it will have been with me for exactly half my life.

Battered and obsolete, a relic from an age that is quickly passing from memory, the damn thing has never given out on me. Even as I recall the nine thousand four hundred days we have spent together, it is sitting in front of me now, stuttering forth its old familiar music. We are in Connecticut for the weekend. It is summer, and the morning outside the window is hot and green and beautiful. The typewriter is on the kitchen table, and my hands are on the typewriter. Letter by letter, I have watched it write these words.

July 2, 2000

NORTHERN LIGHTS

Pages for Kafka

on the fiftieth anniversary of his death

He wanders toward the promised land. That is to say: he moves from one place to another, and dreams continually of stopping. And because this desire to stop is what haunts him, is what counts most for him, he does not stop. He wanders. That is to say: without the slightest hope of ever going anywhere.

He is never going anywhere. And yet he is always going. Invisible to himself, he gives himself up to the drift of his own body, as if he could follow the trail of what refuses to lead him. And by the blindness of the way he has chosen, against himself, in spite of himself, with its veerings, detours, and circlings back, his step, always one step in front of nowhere, invents the road he has taken. It is his road, and his alone. And yet on this road he is never free. For all he has left behind still anchors him to his starting place, makes him regret ever having taken the first step, robs him of all assurance in the rightness of departure. And the farther he travels from his starting place, the greater his doubt grows. His doubt goes with him, like breath, like his breathing between each step — fitful, oppressive — so that no true rhythm, no one pace, can be held. And the farther his doubt goes with him, the nearer he feels to the source of that doubt, so that in the end it is the sheer distance between him and what he has left behind that allows him to see what is behind him: what he is not and might have been. But this thought brings him neither solace nor hope. For the fact remains that he has left all this behind, and in all these things, now consigned to absence, to the longing born of absence, he might once have found himself, fulfilled himself, by following the one law given to him, to remain, and which he now transgresses, by leaving.

All this conspires against him, so that at each moment, even as he continues on his way, he feels he must turn his eyes from the distance that lies before him, like a lure, to the movement of his feet, appearing and disappearing below him, to the road itself, its dust, the stones that clutter its way, the sound of his feet clattering upon them, and he obeys this feeling, as though it were a penance, and he, who would have married the distance before him, becomes, against himself, in spite of himself, the intimate of all that is near. Whatever he can touch, he lingers over, examines, describes with a patience that at each moment exhausts him, overwhelms him, so that even as he goes on, he calls this going into question, and questions each step he is about to take. He who lives for an encounter with the unseen becomes the instrument of the seen: he who would quarry the earth becomes the spokesman of its surfaces, the surveyor of its shades.

Whatever he does, then, he does for the sole purpose of subverting himself, of undermining his strength. If it is a matter of going on, he will do everything in his power not to go on. And yet he will go on. For even though he lingers, he is incapable of rooting himself. No pause conjures a place. But this, too, he knows. For what he wants is what he does not want. And if his journey has any end, it will only be by finding himself, in the end, where he began.

He wanders. On a road that is not a road, on an earth that is not his earth, an exile in his own body. Whatever is given to him, he will refuse. Whatever is spread before him, he will turn his back on. He will refuse, the better to hunger for what he has denied himself. For to enter the promised land is to despair of ever coming near it. Therefore, he holds everything away from him, at arm's length, at life's length, and comes closest to arriving when farthest from his destination. And yet he goes on. And from one step to the next he finds nothing but himself. Not even himself, but the shadow of what he will become. For in the least stone touched, he recognizes a fragment of the promised land. Not even the promised land, but its shadow. And between shadow and shadow lives light. And not just any light, but this light, the light that grows inside him, unendingly, as he goes along his way.

1974

The Death of Sir Walter Raleigh

The Tower is stone and the solitude of stone. It is the skull of a man around the body of a man—and its quick is thought. But no thought will ever reach the other side of the wall. And the wall will not crumble, even against the hammer of a man's eye. For the eyes are blind, and if they see, it is only because they have learned to see where no light is. There is nothing here but thought, and there is nothing. The man is a stone that breathes, and he will die. The only thing that waits for him is death.

The subject is therefore life and death. And the subject is death. Whether the man who lives will have truly lived until the moment of his death, or whether death is no more than the moment at which life stops. This is an argument of act, and therefore an act which rebuts the argument of any word. For we will never manage to say what we want to say, and whatever is said will be said in the knowledge of this failure. All this is speculation.

One thing is sure: this man will die. The Tower is impervious, and the depth of stone has no limit. But thought nevertheless determines its own boundaries, and the man who thinks can now and then surpass himself, even when there is nowhere to go. He can reduce himself to a stone, or he can write the history of the world. Where no possibility exists, everything becomes possible again.

Therefore Raleigh. Or life lived as a suicide pact with oneself. And whether or not there is an art—if one can call it art—of living. Take everything away from a man, and this man will continue to exist. If he has been able to live, he will be able to die. And when there is nothing left, he will know how to face the wall.

It is death. And we say "death," as if we meant to say the thing we cannot know. And yet we know, and we know that we know. For we hold this knowledge to be irrefutable. It is a question for which no answer comes, and it will lead us to many questions that in their turn will lead us back to the thing we cannot know. We may well ask, then, what we will ask. For the subject is not only life and death. It is death, and it is life.

At each moment there is the possibility of what is not. And from each thought, an opposite thought is born. From death, he will see an image of life. And from one place, there will be the boon of another place. America. And at the limit of thought, where the new world nullifies the old, a place is invented to take the place of death. He has already touched its shores, and its image will haunt him to the very end. It is Paradise, it is the Garden before the Fall, and it gives birth to a thought that ranges farther than the grasp of any man. And this man will die. And not only will he die–he will be murdered. An axe will cut off his head.

This is how it begins. And this is how it ends. We all know that we will die. And if there is any truth we live with, it is that we die. But we may well ask the question of how and when, and we may well begin to ask ourselves if chance is not the only god. The Christian says not, and the suicide says not. Each of them says he can choose, and each of them does choose, by faith, or the lack of it. But what of the man who neither believes nor does not believe? He will throw himself into life, live life to the fullest of life, and then come to his end. For death is a very wall, and beyond this wall no one can pass. We will not ask, therefore, whether or not one can choose. One can choose and one cannot. It depends on whom and on why. To begin, then, we must find a place where we are alone and nevertheless together, that is to say, the place where we end. There is the wall, and there is the truth we confront. The question is: at what moment does one begin to see the wall?

Consider the facts. Thirteen years in the Tower, and then the final voyage to the West. Whether or not he was guilty (and he was not) has no bearing on the facts. Thirteen years in the Tower, and a man will begin to learn what solitude is. He will learn that he is nothing more than a body, and he will learn that he is nothing more than a mind, and he will learn that he is nothing. He can breathe, he can walk, he can speak, he can read, he can write, he can sleep. He can count the stones. He can be a stone that breathes, or he can write the history of the world. But at each moment he is the captive of others, and his will is no longer his own. Only his thoughts belong to him, and he is as alone with them as he is alone with the shadow he has become. But he lives. And not only does he live—he lives to the fullest that his confines will permit. And beyond them. For an image of death will nevertheless goad him into finding life. And yet, nothing has changed. For the only thing that waits for him is death.

But this is not all. And the facts must be considered still further. For the day comes when he is allowed to leave the Tower. He has been freed, but he is nevertheless not free. A full pardon will be granted only on the condition that he accomplish something that is flatly impossible to accomplish. Already the victim of the basest political intrigue, the butt of justice gone berserk, he will have his last fling and create his most magnificent failure as a sadistic entertainment for his captors. Once called the Fox, he is now like a mouse in the jaws of a cat. The King instructs him: go where the Spanish have rightful claim, rob them of their gold, and do not antagonize them or incite them to retaliation. Any other man would have laughed. Accused of having conspired with the Spanish thirteen years ago and put into the Tower as a result, he is now told to do a thing in such terms that they invalidate the very charge for which he was found guilty in the first place. But he does not laugh.

One must assume that he knew what he was doing. Either he thought that he could do what he set out to do, or the lure of the new world was so strong that he simply could not resist. In any case, it hardly matters now. Everything that could go wrong for him did go wrong, and from the very beginning the voyage was a disaster. After thirteen years of solitude, it is not easy to return to the world of men, and even less so when one is old. And he is an old man now, more than sixty, and the prison reveries in which he had seen his thoughts turn into the most glorious deeds now turn to dust before his eyes. The crew rebels against him, no gold can be found, the Spanish are hostile. Worst of all: his son is killed.

Take everything away from a man, and that man will continue to exist. But the everything of one man is not that of another, and even the strongest of men will have within himself a place of supreme vulnerability. For Raleigh, this place is occupied by his son, who is at once the emblem of his greatest strength and the seed of his undoing. To all things outward, the boy will bring doom, and though he is a child of love, he remains the living proof of lust—the wild heat of a man willing to risk everything to answer the call of his body. But this lust is nevertheless love, and such a love as seldom speaks more purely of a man's worth. For one does not cavort with a lady of the Queen unless one is ready to destroy one's position, one's honor, one's name. These women are the Queen's person, and no man, not even the most favored man, can approach or possess without royal consent. And yet, he shows no signs of contrition; he makes good on all he has done. For disgrace need not bring shame. He loves the woman, he will continue to love her, she will become the very substance of his life. And in this first, prophetic exile, his son is born.

The boy grows. And he grows wild. The father can do no more than dote and fret, prescribe warnings, be warmed by the fire of his flesh and blood. He writes an extraordinary poem of admonition to the boy, at once an ode to chance and a raging against the inevitable, telling him that if he does not mend his ways he will wind up at the end of a rope, and the boy sallies off to Paris with Ben Jonson on a colossal binge. There is nothing the father can do. It is all a question of waiting. When he is at last allowed to leave the Tower, he takes the boy along with him. He needs the comfort of his son, and he needs to feel himself the father. But the boy is murdered in the jungle. Not only does he come to the end his father had predicted for him, but the father himself has become the unwitting executioner of his own son.

And the death of the son is the death of the father. For this man will die. The journey has failed, the thought of grace does not even enter his head. England means the axe—and the gloating triumph of the King. The very wall has been reached. And yet, he goes back. To a place where the only thing that waits for him is death. He goes back when everything tells him to run for life—or to die by his own hand. For if nothing else, one can always choose one's moment. But he goes back. And the question therefore is: why cross an entire ocean only to keep an appointment with death?

We may well speak of madness, as others have. Or we may well speak of courage. But it hardly matters what we speak. For it is here that words begin to fail. And if we ever manage to say what we want to say, it will nevertheless be said in the knowledge of this failure. All this, therefore, is speculation.

If there is such a thing as an art of living, then the man who lives life as an art will have a sense of his own beginning and his own end. And beyond that, he will know that his end is in his beginning, and that each breath he draws can only bring him nearer to that end. He will live, but he will also die. For no work remains unfinished, even the one that has been abandoned.

Most men abandon their lives. They live until they do not live, and we call this death. For death is a very wall. A man dies, and therefore he no longer lives. But this does not mean it is death. For death is only in the seeing of death, and in the living of death. And we may truly say that only the man who lives his life to the fullest of life will be able to see his own death. And we may truly say what we will say. For it is here that words begin to fail.

Each man approaches the wall. One man turns his back, and in the end he is struck from behind. Another goes blind at the very thought of it and spends his life groping ahead in fear. And another sees it from the very beginning, and though his fear is no less, he will teach himself to face it, and go through life with open eyes. Every act will count; even to the last act, because nothing will matter to him anymore. He will live because he is able to die. And he will touch the very wall.

Therefore Raleigh. Or the art of living as the art of death. Therefore England—and therefore the axe. For the subject is not only life and death. It is death. And it is life. And we may truly say what we will say.

1975

Northern Lights

The paintings of Jean-Paul Riopelle

PROGRESS OF THE SOUL

At the limit of a man, the earth will disappear. And each thing seen of earth will be lost in the man who comes to this place. His eyes will open on earth, and whiteness will engulf the man. For this is the limit of earth — and therefore a place where no man can be.

Nowhere. As if this were a beginning. For even here, where the land escapes all witness, a landscape will emerge. That is to say, there is never nothing where a man has come, even in a place where all has disappeared. For he cannot be anywhere until he is nowhere, and from the moment he begins to lose his bearings, he will find where he is.

Therefore, he goes to the limit of earth, even as he stands in the midst of life. And if he stands in this place, it is only by virtue of a desire to be here, at the limit of himself, as if this limit were the core of another, more secret beginning of the world. He will meet himself in his own disappearance, and in this absence he will discover the earth — even at the limit of earth.

THE BODY'S SPACE

There is no need, then, except the need to be here. As if he, too, could cross into life and take his stand among the things that stand among him: a single thing, even the least thing, of all the things he is not. There is this desire, and it is inalienable. As if, by opening his eyes, he might find himself in the world.

A forest. And within that forest, a tree. And upon that tree, a leaf. A single leaf, turning in the wind. This leaf, and nothing else. The thing to be seen.

To be seen: as if he could be here. But the eye has never been enough. It cannot merely see, nor can it tell him how to see. For when a single leaf turns, it is the entire forest that turns around it. And he who turns around himself.

He wants to see what is. But no thing, not even the least thing, has ever stood still for him. For a leaf is not only a leaf: it is the earth, it is

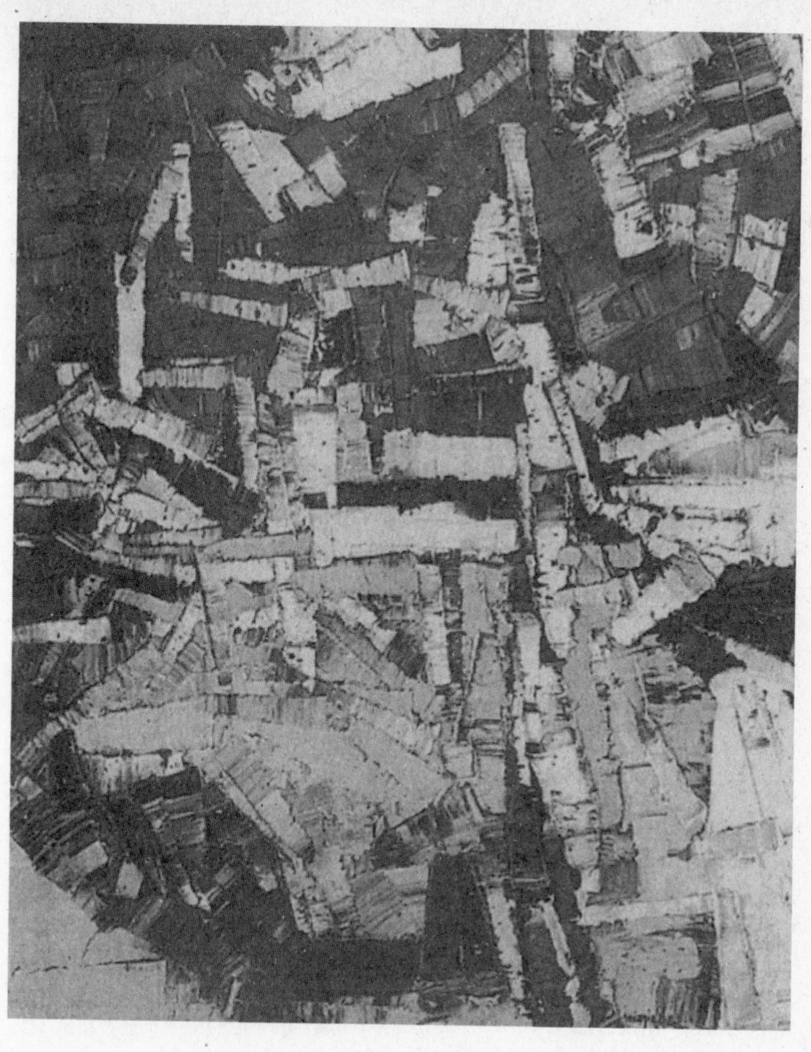

the sky, it is the tree it hangs from in the light of any given hour. But it is also a leaf. That is to say, it is what moves.

It is not enough, then, simply for him to open his eyes. If he is to see, he must begin by moving toward the thing that moves. For seeing is a process that engages the entire body. And though he begins as a witness of the thing he is not, once the first step has been taken, he becomes a participant in a motion that knows no boundaries between self and object.

Distances: what the quickness of the eye discovers, the body must then follow into experience. There is this distance to be crossed, and each time it is a new distance, a different space that opens before the eye. For no two leaves are alike. Therefore, he must feel his feet on the earth: and learn, with a patience that is the instinct of breath and blood, that this same earth is the destiny of the leaf as well.

DISAPPEARANCE

He begins at the beginning. And each time he begins, it is as if he had never lived before. Painting: or the desire to vanish in the act of seeing. That is to say, to see the thing that is, and each time to see it for the first time, as if it were the last time that he would ever see.

At the limit of himself: the pursuit of the nearly-nothing. To breathe in the whiteness of the farthest north. And all that is lost, to be born again from this emptiness in the place where desire carries him, and dismembers him, and scatters him back into earth.

For when he is here, he is nowhere. And time does not exist for him. He will suffer no duration, no continuity, no history: time is merely an alternation between being and not being, and at the moment he begins to feel time passing within him, he knows that he is no longer alive. The self flares up in an image of itself, and the body traces a movement it has traced a thousand times before. This is the curse of memory, or the separation of the body from the world.

If he is to begin, then, he must carry himself to a place beyond memory. Once a gesture has been repeated, once a road has been discovered, the act of living becomes a kind of death. The body must empty itself of the world in order to find the world, and each thing must be made to disappear before it can be seen. The impossible is that which allows him to breathe, and if there is life in him, it is only because he is willing to risk his life.

Therefore, he goes to the limit of himself. And at the moment he no longer knows where he is, the world can begin for him again. But there is no way of knowing this in advance, no way of predicting this miracle, and between each lapse, in each void of waiting, there is terror. And not only terror, but the death of the world in himself.

THE ENDS OF THE EARTH

Lassitude and fear. The endless beginning of time in the body of a man. Blindness, in the midst of life; blindness, in the solitude of a single body. Nothing happens. Or rather, everything begins to be nothing. And the world is so far from him that in each thing he sees of the world, he finds nothing but himself.

Emptiness and immobility, for as long as it takes to kill him. Here, in the midst of life, where the very density of things seems to suffocate the possibility of life, or here, in the place where memory inhabits him. There is no choice but to leave. To lock his door behind him and set out from himself, even to the ends of the earth.

The forest. Or a lapse in the heart of time, as if there were a place where a man could stand. Whiteness opens before him, and if he sees it, it will not be with the eye of a painter, but with the body of a man struggling for life. Gradually, all is forgotten, but not through any act of will: a man can discover the world only because he must — and for the simple reason that his life depends on it.

Seeing, therefore, as a way of being in the world. And knowledge as a force that rises from within. For after being nowhere at all, he will eventually find himself so near to the things he is not that he will almost be within them.

Relations. That is to say, the forest. He begins with a single leaf: the thing to be seen. And because there is one thing, there can be everything. But before there is anything at all, there must be desire, and the joy of a desire that propels him toward his very limit. For in this place, everything connects; and he, too, is part of this process. Therefore, he must move. And as he moves, he will begin to discover where he is.

NATURE

No painting captures the spirit of natural plentitude more truly than this one. Because this painter understands that the body is what sees, that there can be no seeing without motion, he is able to carry himself across the greatest distances — and come to a place of nearness and intimacy, where each thing can be set free to be what it is.

To look at one of these paintings is to enter it: to be whirled into a field of forces that is composed not only of things, but of the motion of things — of their dislocation and their harmony. For this is a man who knows the forest, and the almost inhuman energy to be found in these canvases does not speak of an abstract program to become one-with-nature, but rather, more basically, of a tangible need to be present, as if life could be lived only in the fullness of this desire. As a consequence, this work does not merely re-present the natural landscape. It is a record of an encounter, a process of penetration and mutual dependence, and, as such, a portrait of a man at the limit of himself.

This is a painter who paints in the same way that he breathes. He has never sought merely to create beautiful objects, but rather, in the act of painting, to make life possible for himself. For this reason, he has always avoided facile solutions, and whenever he has found his work becoming automatic, he has stopped work altogether — for as long as it takes for him to unmemorize his work, to block his means of access to the canvas. In effect, each burst of activity is a new beginning, the fruit of a period of unlearning the art of painting — during which time he has allowed himself to discover the world once again. His is an art of both knowledge and innocence, and the perpetual freshness of his work derives from the fact that painting is not something that he does and then divorces from himself, but a necessary struggle to gain hold of his own life and place himself in the world. It is the very substance of the man.

1976

CRITICAL ESSAYS

The Art of Hunger

> What is important, it seems to me, is not so much to defend a culture whose existence has never kept a man from going hungry, as to extract, from what is called culture, ideas whose compelling force is identical with that of hunger.
>
> Antonin Artaud

A young man comes to a city. He has no name, no home, no work: he has come to the city to write. He writes. Or, more exactly, he does not write. He starves to the point of death.

The city is Christiania (Oslo); the year is 1890. The young man wanders through the streets: the city is a labyrinth of hunger, and all his days are the same. He writes unsolicited articles for a local paper. He worries about his rent, his disintegrating clothes, the difficulty of finding his next meal. He suffers. He nearly goes mad. He is never more than one step from collapse.

Still, he writes. Now and then he manages to sell an article, to find a temporary reprieve from his misery. But he is too weak to write steadily and can rarely finish the pieces he has begun. Among his abortive works are an essay entitled "Crimes of the Future," a philosophical tract on the freedom of the will, an allegory about a bookstore fire (the books are brains), and a play set in the Middle Ages, "The Sign of the Cross." The process is inescapable: he must eat in order to write. But if he does not write, he will not eat. And if he cannot eat, he cannot write. He cannot write.

He writes. He does not write. He wanders through the streets of the city. He talks to himself in public. He frightens people away from him. When, by chance, he comes into some money, he gives it away. He is evicted from his room. He eats, and then throws everything up. At one point, he has a brief flirtation with a girl, but nothing comes of it except humiliation. He hungers. He curses the world. He does not die. In the end, for no apparent reason, he signs on board a ship and leaves the city.

These are the bare bones of Knut Hamsun's first novel, *Hunger*. It is a work devoid of plot, action, and — but for the narrator — character. By nineteenth-century standards, it is a work in which nothing happens. The radical subjectivity of the narrator effectively eliminates the basic concerns of the traditional novel. Similar to the hero's plan to make an "invisible detour" when he came to the problem of space and time in one of his essays, Hamsun manages to dispense with historical time, the basic organizing principle of nineteenth-century fiction. He gives us an account only of the hero's worst struggles with hunger. Other, less difficult times, in which his hunger has been appeased — even though they might last as long as a week — are passed off in one or two sentences. Historical time is obliterated in favor of inner duration. With only an arbitrary beginning and an arbitrary ending, the novel faithfully records the vagaries of the narrator's mind, following each thought from its mysterious inception through all its meanderings, until it dissipates and the next thought begins. What happens is allowed to happen.

This novel cannot even claim to have a redeeming social value. Although *Hunger* puts us in the jaws of misery, it offers no analysis of that misery, contains no call to political action. Hamsun, who turned fascist in his old age during the Second World War, never concerned himself with the problems of class injustice, and his narrator-hero, like Dostoevsky's Raskolnikov, is not so much an underdog as a monster of intellectual arrogance. Pity plays no part in *Hunger*. The hero suffers, but only because he has chosen to suffer. Hamsun's art is such that he rigorously prevents us from feeling any compassion for his character. From the very beginning, it is made clear that the hero need not starve. Solutions exist, if not in the city, then at least in departure. But buoyed by an obsessive, suicidal pride, the young man's actions continually betray a scorn for his own best interests.

> I began running so as to punish myself, left street after street behind me, pushed myself on with inward jeers, and screeched silently and furiously at myself whenever I felt like stopping. With the help of these exertions I ended up along Pile Street. When I finally did stop, almost weeping with anger that I couldn't run any farther, my whole body trembled, and I threw myself down on a house stoop. "Not so fast!" I said. And to torture myself right, I stood up again and forced myself to stand there, laughing at myself and gloating over my own fatigue. Finally, after a few minutes I nodded and so gave myself permission to sit down; however, I chose the most uncomfortable spot on the stoop.*

He seeks out what is most difficult in himself, courting pain and

* All quotations are from the Robert Bly translation, Farrar, Straus, and Giroux, 1967.

adversity in the same way other men seek out pleasure. He goes hungry, not because he has to, but from some inner compulsion, as if to wage a hunger strike against himself. Before the book begins, before the reader has been made the privileged witness of his fate, the hero's course of action has been fixed. A process is already in motion, and although the hero cannot control it, that does not mean he is unaware of what he is doing.

> I was conscious all the time that I was following mad whims without being able to do anything about it . . . Despite my alienation from myself at that moment, and even though I was nothing but a battleground for invisible forces, I was aware of every detail of what was going on around me.

Having withdrawn into a nearly perfect solitude, he has become both the subject and object of his own experiment. Hunger is the means by which this split takes place, the catalyst, so to speak, of altered consciousness.

> I had noticed very clearly that every time I went hungry a little too long it was as though my brains simply ran quietly out of my head and left me empty. My head became light and floating, I could no longer feel its weight upon my shoulders . . .

If it is an experiment, however, it has nothing to do with the scientific method. There are no controls, no stable points of reference — only variables. Nor can this separation of mind and body be reduced to a philosophical abstraction. We are not in the realm of ideas here. It is a physical state, brought into being under conditions of extreme duress. Mind and body have been weakened; the hero has lost control over both his thoughts and actions. And yet he persists in trying to control his destiny. This is the paradox, the game of circular logic that is played out through the pages of the book. It is an impossible situation for the hero. For he has willfully brought himself to the brink of danger. To give up starving would not mean victory, it would simply mean that the game was over. He wants to survive, but only on his own terms: survival that will bring him face to face with death.

He fasts. But not in the way a Christian would fast. He is not denying earthly life in anticipation of heavenly life; he is simply refusing to live the life he has been given. And the longer he goes on with his fast, the more death intrudes itself upon his life. He approaches death, creeps toward the edge of the abyss, and once there, clings to it, unable to move either forward or backward. Hunger, which opens the void, does not have the power to seal it up. A brief moment of Pascalian terror has been transformed into a permanent condition.

His fast, then, is a contradiction. To persist in it would mean death, and with death the fast would end. He must therefore stay alive, but only to the extent that it keeps him on the point of death. The idea of ending is resisted in the interests of maintaining the constant possibility of the end. Because his fasting neither posits a goal nor offers a promise of redemption, its contradiction must remain unresolved. As such, it is an image of despair, generated by the same self-consuming passion as the sickness unto death. The soul, in its despair, seeks to devour itself, and because it cannot — precisely because it despairs — sinks further into despair.

Unlike a religious art, in which self-debasement can play an ultimately cleansing role (the meditative poetry of the seventeenth century, for example), hunger only simulates the dialectic of salvation. In Fulke Greville's poem, "Down in the depth of mine iniquity," the poet is able to look into a "fatal mirror of transgression" which "shows man as fruit of his degeneration," but he knows that this is only the first step in a two-fold process, for it is in this mirror that Christ is revealed "for the same sins dying / And from that hell I feared, to free me, come . . ." In Hamsun's novel, however, once the depths have been sounded, the mirror of meditation remains empty.

He remains at the bottom, and no God will come to rescue the young man. He cannot even depend on the props of social convention to keep him standing. He is rootless, without friends, denuded of objects. Order has disappeared for him; everything has become random. His actions are inspired by nothing but whim and ungovernable urge, the weary frustration of anarchic discontent. He pawns his waistcoat in order to give alms to a beggar, hires a carriage in search of a fictitious acquaintance, knocks on strangers' doors, and repeatedly asks the time of passing policemen, for the single reason that he fancies to do so. He does not revel in these actions, however. They remain profoundly disquieting for him. Furiously trying to stabilize his life, to put an end to his wanderings, find a room, and settle down to his writing, he is thwarted by the fast he has set in motion. Once it starts, hunger does not release its progenitor-victim until its lesson has been made unforgettable. The hero is seized against his will by a force of his own making and is compelled to respond to its demands.

He loses everything — even himself. Reach the bottom of a Godless hell, and identity disappears. It is no accident that Hamsun's hero has no name: as time goes on, he is truly shorn of his self. What names he chooses to give himself are all inventions, summoned forth on the spur of the moment. He cannot say who he is because he does not know. His name is a lie, and with this lie the reality of his world vanishes.

He peers into the darkness hunger has created for him, and what he finds is a void of language. Reality has become a confusion of thingless names and nameless things for him. The connection between self and world has been broken.

> I remained for a while looking into the dark — this dense substance of darkness that had no bottom, which I couldn't understand. My thoughts could not grasp such a thing. It seemed to be a dark beyond all measurement, and I felt its presence weigh me down. I closed my eyes and took to singing half aloud and rocking myself back and forth on the cot to amuse myself, but it did no good. The dark had captured my brain and gave me not an instant of peace. What if I myself became dissolved into the dark, turned into it?

At the precise moment that he is in the greatest fear of losing possession of himself, he suddenly imagines that he has invented a new word: *Kubooa* — a word in no language, a word with no meaning.

> I had arrived at the joyful insanity hunger was: I was empty and free of pain, and my thoughts no longer had any check.

He tries to think of a meaning for his word but can only come up with what it doesn't mean, which is neither "God," nor the "Tivoli Gardens," nor "cattle show," nor "padlock," nor "sunrise," nor "emigration," nor "tobacco factory," nor "yarn."

> No, the word was actually intended to mean something spiritual, a feeling, a state of mind — if only I could understand it? And I thought and thought to find something spiritual.

But he does not succeed. Voices, not his own, begin to intrude, to confuse him, and he sinks deeper into chaos. After a violent fit, in which he imagines himself to be dying, all goes still, with no sounds but those of his own voice, rolling back from the wall.

This episode is perhaps the most painful in the book. But it is only one of many examples of the hero's language disease. Throughout the narrative, his pranks most often take the form of lies. Retrieving his lost pencil from a pawn shop (he had accidentally left it in the pocket of a vest he had sold), he tells the proprietor that it was with this very pencil that he had written his three-volume treatise on Philosophical

Consciousness. An insignificant pencil, he admits, but he has a sentimental attachment to it. To an old man on a park bench he recites the fantastic story of a Mr. Happolati, the inventor of the electric prayer book. Asking a store clerk to wrap his last possession, a tattered green blanket that he is too ashamed to carry around exposed to view, he explains that it is not really the blanket he wants wrapped, but the pair of priceless vases he has folded inside the blanket. Not even the girl he courts is immune from this sort of fiction. He invents a name for her, a name that pleases him for its beauty, and he refuses to call her by anything else.

These lies have a meaning beyond the jests of the moment. In the realm of language the lie has the same relationship to truth that evil has to good in the realm of morals. That is the convention, and it works if we believe in it. But Hamsun's hero no longer believes in anything. Lies and truths are as one to him. Hunger has led him into the darkness, and there is no turning back.

This equation of language and morals becomes the gist of the final episode in *Hunger*.

> My brain grew clearer, I understood that I was close to total collapse. I put my hands against the wall and shoved to push myself away from it. The street was still dancing around. I began to hiccup from fury, and struggled with every bit of energy against my collapse, fought a really stout battle not to fall down. I didn't want to fall, I wanted to die standing. A wholesale grocer's cart came by and I saw it was filled with potatoes, but out of fury, from sheer obstinacy, I decided that they were not potatoes at all, they were cabbages, and I swore violent oaths that they were cabbages. I heard my own words very well, and I took the oath again and again on this lie, and swore deliberately just to have the delightful satisfaction of committing such clear perjury. I became drunk over this superb sin, I lifted three fingers in the air and swore with trembling lips in the name of the Father, the Son, and the Holy Ghost that they were cabbages.

And that is the end of it. There are only two possibilities left for the hero now: live or die; and he chooses to live. He has said no to society, no to God, no to his own words. Later that same day he leaves the city. There is no longer any need to continue the fast. Its work has been done.

Hunger: or a portrait of the artist as a young man. But it is an apprenticeship that has little in common with the early struggles of other writers. Hamsun's hero is no Stephen Dedalus, and there is hardly a word in *Hunger* about aesthetic theory. The world of art has been translated into the world of the body — and the original text has been abandoned.

Hunger is not a metaphor; it is the very crux of the problem itself. If others, such as Rimbaud, with his program for the voluntary derangement of the senses, have turned the body into an aesthetic principle in its own right, Hamsun's hero steadfastly rejects the opportunity to use his deficiencies to his own advantage. He is weak, he has lost control over his thoughts, and yet he continues to strive for lucidity in his writing. But hunger affects his prose in the same way it affects his life. Although he is willing to sacrifice everything for his art, even submit to the worst forms of debasement and misery, all he has really done is make it impossible for himself to write. You cannot write on an empty stomach, no matter how hard you try. But it would be wrong to dismiss the hero of *Hunger* as a fool or a madman. In spite of the evidence, he knows what he is doing. He does not want to succeed. He wants to fail.

Something new is happening here, some new thought about the nature of art is being proposed in *Hunger*. It is first of all an art that is indistinguishable from the life of the artist who makes it. That is not to say an art of autobiographical excess, but rather, an art that is the direct expression of the effort to express itself. In other words, an art of hunger: an art of need, of necessity, of desire. Certainty yields to doubt, form gives way to process. There can be no arbitrary imposition of order, and yet, more than ever, there is the obligation to achieve clarity. It is an art that begins with the knowledge that there are no right answers. For that reason, it becomes essential to ask the right questions. One finds them by living them. To quote Samuel Beckett:

> What I am saying does not mean that there will henceforth be no form in art. It only means that there will be a new form, and that this form will be of such a type that it admits the chaos and does not try to say that the chaos is really something else . . . To find a form that accommodates the mess, that is the task of the artist now.*

Hamsun gives the portrait of this artist in the first stages of his development. But it is in Kafka's story, *A Hunger Artist*, that the aesthetics of hunger receives its most meticulous elaboration. Here the contradictions of the fast conducted by Hamsun's hero — and the artistic impasse it leads to — are joined in a parable that deals with an artist whose art consists in fasting. The hunger artist is at once an artist and not an artist. Though he wants his performances to be admired, he insists that they

* From an interview with Tom Driver, "Beckett at the Madeleine," in *The Columbia University Forum*, Summer 1961.

shouldn't be admired, because they have nothing to do with art. He has chosen to fast only because he could never find any food that he liked. His performances are therefore not spectacles for the amusement of others, but the unravelling of a private despair that he has permitted others to watch.

Like Hamsun's hero, the hunger artist has lost control over himself. Beyond the theatrical device of sitting in his cage, his art in no way differs from his life, even what his life would have been had he not become a performer. He is not trying to please anyone. In fact, his performances cannot even be understood or appreciated.

> No one could possibly watch the hunger artist continuously, day and night, and so no one could produce firsthand evidence that the fast had really been rigorous and continuous; only the artist himself could know that; he was therefore bound to be the sole completely satisfied spectator of his own fast.

This is not the classic story of the misunderstood artist, however. For the very nature of the fast resists comprehension. Knowing itself from the outset to be an impossibility, and condemning itself to certain failure, it is a process that moves asymptotically toward death, destined to reach neither fruition nor destruction. In Kafka's story, the hunger artist dies, but only because he forsakes his art, abandoning the restrictions that had been imposed on him by his manager. The hunger artist goes too far. But that is the risk, the danger inherent in any act of art: you must be willing to give your life.

In the end, the art of hunger can be described as an existential art. It is a way of looking death in the face, and by death I mean death as we live it today: without God, without hope of salvation. Death as the abrupt and absurd end of life.

I do not believe that we have come any farther than this. It is even possible that we have been here much longer than we are willing to admit. In all this time, however, only a few artists have been able to recognize it. It takes courage, and not many of us would be willing to risk everything for nothing. But that is what happens in *Hunger*, a novel written in 1890. Hamsun's character systematically unburdens himself of every belief in every system, and in the end, by means of the hunger he has inflicted upon himself, he arrives at nothing. There is nothing to keep him going — and yet he keeps on going. He walks straight into the twentieth century.

1970

New York Babel

In the preface to his novel *Le Bleu du Ciel,* Georges Bataille makes an important distinction between books that are written for the sake of experiment and books that are born of necessity. Literature, Bataille argues, is an essentially disruptive force, a presence confronted in "fear and trembling" that is capable of revealing to us the truth of life and its *excessive* possibilities. Literature is not a continuum, but a series of dislocations, and the books that mean most to us in the end are usually those that ran counter to the idea of literature that prevailed at the time they were written. Bataille speaks of "a moment of rage" as the kindling spark of all great works: it cannot be summoned by an act of will, and its source is always extra-literary. "How can we linger," he says, "over books we feel the author was not compelled to write?" Self-conscious experimentation is generally the result of a real longing to break down the barriers of literary convention. But most avant-garde works do not survive; in spite of themselves, they remain prisoners of the very conventions they try to destroy. The poetry of Futurism, for example, which made such a commotion in its day, is hardly read by anyone now except scholars and historians of the period. On the other hand, certain writers who played little or no part in the literary life around them — Kafka, for example — have gradually come to be recognized as essential. The work that revives our sense of literature, that gives us a new feeling for what literature can be, is the work that changes our life. It often seems improbable, as if it had come from nowhere, and because it stands so ruthlessly outside the norm, we have no choice but to create a new place for it.

Le Schizo et les Langues by Louis Wolfson* is such a book. It is not only improbable, but totally unlike anything that has come before it. To say that it is a work written in the margins of literature is not enough: its place, properly speaking, is in the margins of language itself. Written in French by an American, it has little meaning unless it is considered an American book: and yet, for reasons that will be made clear, it is also a book that excludes all possibility of translation. It hovers somewhere in

* Published by Editions Gallimard in 1971. Preface by Gilles Deleuze.

the limbo between the two languages, and nothing will ever be able to rescue it from this precarious existence. For what we are presented with here is not simply the case of a writer who has chosen to write in a foreign language. The author of this book has written in French precisely because he had no choice. It is the result of brute necessity, and the book itself is nothing less than an act of survival.

Louis Wolfson is a schizophrenic. He was born in 1931 and lives in New York. For want of a better description, I would call his book a kind of third-person autobiography, a memoir of the present, in which he records the facts of his disease and the utterly bizarre method he has devised for dealing with it. Referring to himself as "the schizophrenic student of languages," "the mentally ill student," "the demented student of idioms," Wolfson uses a narrative style that partakes of both the dryness of a clinical report and the inventiveness of fiction. Nowhere in the text is there even the slightest trace of delirium or "madness": every passage is lucid, forthright, objective. As we read along, wandering through the labyrinth of the author's obsessions, we come to feel with him, to identify with him, in the same way we identify with the eccentricities and torments of Kirilov, or Molloy.

Wolfson's problem is the English language, which has become intolerably painful to him, and which he refuses either to speak or listen to. He has been in and out of mental institutions for over ten years, steadfastly resisting all cooperation with the doctors, and now, at the time he is writing the book (the late sixties), he is living in the cramped lower-middle-class apartment of his mother and stepfather. He spends his days sitting at his desk studying foreign languages — principally French, German, Russian, and Hebrew — and protecting himself against any possible assault of English by keeping his fingers stuck in his ears, or listening to foreign language broadcasts on his transistor radio with two earplugs, or keeping a finger in one ear and an earplug in the other. In spite of these precautions, however, there are times when he is not able to ward off the intrusion of English — when his mother, for example, bursts into his room shrieking something to him in her loud and high-pitched voice. It becomes clear to the student that he cannot drown out English by simply translating it into another language. Converting an English word into its foreign equivalent leaves the English word intact; it has not been destroyed, but only put to the side, and is still there waiting to menace him.

The system that he develops in answer to this problem is complex, but not difficult to follow once one has become familiar with it, since it is based on a consistent set of rules. Drawing on the several languages he has studied, he becomes able to transform English words and phrases into phonetic combinations of foreign letters, syllables, and words that form new linguistic entities, which not only resemble the English in meaning, but in sound as well. His descriptions of these verbal acrobatics are highly detailed, often taking up as many as ten pages, but perhaps the end result of one of the simpler examples will give some idea of the process. The sentence, "Don't trip over the wire!" is changed in the following manner: "Don't" becomes the German "Tu'nicht," "trip" becomes the first four letters of the French "trébucher," "over" becomes the German "über," "the" becomes the Hebrew "èth hé," and "wire" becomes the German "zwirn," the middle three letters of which correspond to the first three letters of the English word: "Tu'nicht tréb über èth hé zwirn." At the end of this passage, exhausted but gratified by his efforts, Wolfson writes: "If the schizophrenic did not experience a feeling of joy as a result of his having found, that day, these foreign words to annihilate yet another word of his mother tongue (for perhaps, in fact, he was incapable of this sentiment), he certainly felt much less miserable than usual, at least for a while."*

The book, however, is far more than just a catalogue of these transformations. They are at the core of the work, and in some sense define its purpose, but the real substance is elsewhere, in the human situation and the daily life that envelop Wolfson's preoccupation with language. There are few books that have given a more immediate feeling of what it is like to live in New York and to wander through the streets of the city. Wolfson's eye for detail is excruciatingly precise, and each nuance of his observations — whether it be the prison-like atmosphere of the Forty-Second Street Public Library reading room, the anxieties of a high school dance, the Times Square prostitute scene, or a conversation with his father on a bench in a city park — is rendered with attentiveness and authority. A strange movement of objectification is continually at work, and much of the fascination of the prose is a result of this distancing, which acts as a kind of lure, always drawing us toward what is written. By treating himself in the third person, Wolfson is able to create a space between himself and himself, to prove to himself that he exists. The French language serves much the same function. By looking out on his

* My translation.

world through a different lens, by punning his world — which is immured in English — into a different language, he is able to see it with new eyes, in a way that is less oppressive to him, as if, to some slight degree, he were able to have an effect upon it.

His powers of evocation are devastating, and in his toneless, deadpan style, he manages to present a portrait of life among the Jewish poor that is so horrendously comical and vivid that it stands comparison with the early passages of Celine's *Death on the Installment Plan*. There seems to be no question that Wolfson knows what he is doing. His aims are not aesthetic ones, but in his patient determination to record everything, to set down the facts as accurately as possible, he has exposed the true absurdity of his situation, which he is often able to respond to with an ironical sense of detachment and whimsy.

His parents were divorced when he was four or five years old. His father has spent most of his life on the periphery of the world, without work, living in cheap hotels, idling away his time in cafeterias smoking cigars. He claims that his marriage took place "with a cat in the bag," since it was not until later that he learned his wife had a glass eye. When she eventually remarried, her second husband disappeared after the wedding with her diamond ring — only to be tracked down by her and thrown into jail the moment he stepped off a plane a thousand miles away. His release was granted only on the condition that he go back to his wife.

The mother is the dominant, suffocating presence of the book, and when Wolfson speaks of his "langue maternelle," it is clear that his abhorrence of English is in direct relation to his abhorrence of his mother. She is a grotesque character, a monster of vulgarity, who ridicules her son's language studies, insists on speaking to him in English, and perseveres in doing exactly the opposite of what would make his life bearable. She spends much of her spare time playing popular songs on an electric organ, with the volume turned up full blast. Sitting over his books, his fingers stuck in his ears, the student sees the lampshade on his desk begin to rattle, to feel the whole room vibrate in rhythm to the piece, and as soon as the deafening music penetrates him, he automatically thinks of the English lyrics of the songs, which drives him into a fury of despair. (Half a chapter is devoted to his linguistic transformation of the words to *Good Night Ladies*). But Wolfson never really judges her. He only describes. And if he allows himself an occasional smirk of understatement, it would seem to be his right.

"Naturally, her optical weakness seemed in no way to interfere with the capacity of her speech organs (perhaps it was even the reverse), and she would speak, at least for the most part, in a very high and very shrill voice, even though she was positively able to whisper over the telephone when she wanted to arrange secretly for her son's entrance into the psychiatric hospital, that is to say, without his knowledge."

Beyond the constant threat of English posed by his mother (who is the very embodiment of the language for him), the student suffers from her in her role as provider. Throughout the book, his linguistic activities are counterpointed by his obsession with food, eating, and the possible contamination of his food. He oscillates between a violent disgust at the thought of eating, as if it were a basic contradiction of his language work, and terrifying orgies of gluttony that leave him sick for hours afterward. Each time he enters the kitchen, he arms himself with a foreign book, repeats aloud certain foreign phrases he has been memorizing, and forces himself to avoid reading the English labels on the packages and cans of food. Reciting one of the phrases over and over again, like a magical incantation to keep away evil spirits, he tears open the first package that comes to hand — containing the food that is easiest to eat, which is usually the least nutritional — and begins to stuff the food into his mouth, all the while making sure that it does not touch his lips, which he feels must be infested with the eggs and larvae of parasites. After such bouts, he is filled with self-recriminations and guilt. As Gilles Deleuze suggests in his preface to the book, "His guilt is no less great when he has eaten than when he has heard his mother speak. It is the same guilt."

This is the point, I feel, at which Wolfson's private nightmare locks with certain universal questions about language. There is a fundamental connection between speaking and eating, and by the very excessiveness of Wolfson's experience, we are able to see how profound this relationship is. Speech is a strangeness, an anomaly, a biologically secondary function of the mouth, and myths about language are often linked to the idea of food. Adam is granted the power of naming the creatures of Paradise and is later expelled for having eaten of the Tree of Knowledge. Mystics fast in order to prepare themselves to receive the word of God. The body of Christ, the word made flesh, is eaten in holy communion. It is as if the life-serving function of the mouth, its role in eating, had been transferred to speech, for it is language that creates us and defines us as human beings. Wolfson's fear of eating, the guilt he feels over his escapades of self-indulgence, are an acknowledgement of his betrayal of the task he has set for himself: that of discovering a language he can live with. To eat is a compromise, since it sustains him within the context of an already discredited and unacceptable world.

In the end, Wolfson's search is undertaken in the hope of one day being able to speak English again — a hope that flickers now and then through the pages of the book. The invention of his system of transformations, the writing of the book itself, are part of a slow progression beyond the hermetic agony of his disease. By refusing to allow anyone to impose a cure on him, by forcing himself to confront his own problems, to live through them alone, he senses in himself a dawning awareness of the possibility of living among others — of being able to break free from his one-man language and enter a language of men.

The book he has created from this struggle is difficult to define, but it should not be dismissed as a therapeutic exercise, as yet another document of mental illness to be filed on the shelves of medical libraries. Gallimard, it seems to me, has made a serious error in bringing out *Le Schizo et les Langues* as part of a series on psychoanalysis. By giving the book a label, they have somehow tried to tame the rebellion that gives the book its extraordinary force, to soften "the moment of rage" that everywhere informs Wolfson's writing.

On the other hand, even if we avoid the trap of considering this work as nothing more than a case history, we should still hesitate to judge it by established literary standards and to look for parallels with other literary works. Wolfson's method, in some sense, does resemble the elaborate word play in *Finnegans Wake* and in the novels of Raymond Roussel, but to insist on this resemblance would be to miss the point of the book. Louis Wolfson stands outside literature as we know it, and to do him justice we must read him on his own terms. For it is only in this way that we will be able to discover his book for what it is: one of those rare works that can change our perception of the world.

1974

Dada Bones

Of all the movements of the early avant-garde, Dada is the one that continues to say the most to us. Although its life was short — beginning in 1916 with the nightly spectacles at the Cabaret Voltaire in Zurich and ending effectively, if not officially, in 1922 with the riotous demonstrations in Paris against Tristan Tzara's play, *Le Coeur à gaz* — its spirit has not quite passed into the remoteness of history. Even now, more than fifty years later, not a season goes by without some new book or exhibition about Dada, and it is with more than academic interest that we continue to investigate the questions it raised. For Dada's questions remain our questions, and when we speak of the relationship between art and society, of art versus action and art as action, we cannot help but turn to Dada as a source and as an example. We want to know about it not only for itself, but because we feel that it will help us toward an understanding of our own, present moment.

The diaries of Hugo Ball are a good place to begin. Ball, a key figure in the founding of Dada, was also the first defector from the Dada movement, and his record of the years between 1914 and 1921 is an extremely valuable document.* *Flight Out of Time* was originally published in Germany in 1927, shortly before Ball's death from stomach cancer at the age of forty-one, and it consists of passages that Ball extracted from his journals and edited with clear and partisan hindsight. It is not so much a self-portrait as an account of his inner progress, a spiritual and intellectual reckoning, and it moves from entry to entry in a rigorously dialectical manner. Although there are few biographical details, the sheer adventure of the thought is enough to hold us. For Ball was an incisive thinker; as a participant in early Dada, he is perhaps our finest witness to the Zurich group, and because Dada marked only one stage in his complex development, our view of it through his eyes gives us a kind of perspective we have not had before.

Hugo Ball was a man of his time, and to an extraordinary degree his

* *Flight Out of Time: A Dada Diary*, edited by John Elderfield and translated by Ann Raimes (Viking Press, 1975).

life seems to embody the passions and contradictions of European society during the first quarter of this century. Student of Nietzsche's work; stage manager and playwright for the Expressionist theatre; left-wing journalist; vaudeville pianist; poet; novelist; author of works on Bakunin, the German Intelligentsia, early Christianity, and the writings of Hermann Hesse; convert to Catholicism: he seemed, at one moment or another, to have touched on nearly all the political and artistic preoccupations of the age. And yet, despite his many activities, Ball's attitudes and interests were remarkably consistent throughout his life, and in the end his entire career can be seen as a concerted, even feverish attempt to ground his existence in a fundamental truth, in a single, absolute reality. Too much an artist to be a philosopher, too much a philosopher to be an artist, too concerned with the fate of the world to think only in terms of personal salvation, and yet too inward to be an effective activist, Ball struggled toward solutions that could somehow answer both his inner and outer needs, and even in the deepest solitude he never saw himself as separate from the society around him. He was a man for whom everything came with great difficulty, whose sense of himself was never fixed, and whose moral integrity made him capable of brashly idealistic gestures totally out of keeping with his delicate nature. We have only to examine the famous photograph of Ball reciting a sound poem at the Cabaret Voltaire to understand this. He is dressed in an absurd costume that makes him look like a cross between the Tin Man and a demented bishop, and he stares out from under a high witch doctor's hat with an expression on his face of overwhelming terror. It is an unforgettable expression, and in this one image of him we have what amounts to a parable of his character, a perfect rendering of inside confronting outside, of darkness meeting darkness.

In the Prologue to *Flight Out of Time* Ball presents the reader with a cultural autopsy that sets the tone for all that follows: "The world and society in 1913 looked like this: life is completely confined and shackled . . . The most burning question day and night is this: is there anywhere a force that is strong enough and above all vital enough to put an end to this state of affairs?" Elsewhere, in his 1917 lecture on Kandinsky, he states these ideas with even greater urgency: "A thousand-year-old culture disintegrates. There are no columns and no supports, no foundations anymore — they have all been blown up . . . The meaning of the world has disappeared." These feelings are not new to us. They confirm our sense of the European intellectual climate around the time of the

First World War, and echo much of what we now take for granted as having formed the modern sensibility. What is unexpected, however, is what Ball says a little further on in the Prologue: "It might seem as if philosophy had been taken over by the artists; as if the new impulses were coming from them; as if they were the prophets of rebirth. When we said Kandinsky and Picasso, we meant not painters, but priests; not craftsmen, but creators of new worlds and new paradises." Dreams of total regeneration could exist side by side with the blackest pessimism, and for Ball there was no contradiction in this: both attitudes were part of a single approach. Art was not a way of turning from the problems of the world, it was a way of directly solving these problems. During his most difficult years, it was this faith that sustained Ball, from his early work in the theater — "Only the theater is capable of creating the new society" — to his Kandinsky-influenced formulation of "the union of all artistic mediums and forces," and beyond, to his Dada activities in Zurich.

The seriousness of these considerations, as elaborated in the diaries, helps to dispel several myths about the beginnings of Dada, above all the idea of Dada as little more than the sophomoric rantings of a group of young draft-dodgers, a kind of willful Marx Brothers zaniness. There was, of course, much that was plainly silly in the Cabaret performances, but for Ball this buffoonery was a means to an end, a necessary catharsis: "Perfect skepticism makes perfect freedom possible . . . One can almost say that when belief in an object or a cause comes to an end, this object or cause returns to chaos and becomes common property. But perhaps it is necessary to have resolutely, forcibly produced chaos and thus a complete withdrawal of faith before an entirely new edifice can be built up on a changed basis of belief." To understand Dada, then, at least in this early phase, we must see it as a vestige of old humanistic ideals, a reassertion of individual dignity in a mechanical age of standardization, as a simultaneous expression of despair and hope. Ball's particular contribution to the Cabaret performances, his sound poems, or "poems without words," bears this out. Although he cast aside ordinary language, he had no intention of destroying language itself. In his almost mystical desire to recover what he felt to be a prelapsarian speech, Ball saw in this new, purely emotive form of poetry a way of capturing the magical essences of words. "In these phonetic poems we totally renounce the language that journalism has abused and corrupted. We must return to the innermost alchemy of the word. . . ."

Ball retreated from Zurich only seven months after the opening of the Cabaret Voltaire, partly from exhaustion, and partly from disenchantment with the way Dada was developing. His conflict was principally with Tzara, whose ambition was to turn Dada into one of the many movements of the international avant-garde. As John Elderfield summarizes in his introduction to Ball's diary: "And once away he felt he discerned a certain 'Dada hubris' in what they had been doing. He had believed they were eschewing conventional morality to elevate themselves as new men, that they had welcomed irrationalism as a way toward the 'supernatural', that sensationalism was the best method of destroying the academic. He came to doubt all this — he had become ashamed of the confusion and eclecticism of the cabaret — and saw isolation from the age as a surer and more honest path toward these personal goals. . . ." Several months later, however, Ball returned to Zurich to take part in the events of the Galerie Dada and to deliver his important lecture on Kandinsky, but within a short while he was again feuding with Tzara, and this time the break was final.

In July 1917, under Tzara's direction, Dada was officially launched as a movement, complete with its own publication, manifestos, and promotion campaign. Tzara was a tireless organizer, a true avant-gardist in the style of Marinetti, and eventually, with the help of Picabia and Serner, he led Dada far from the original ideas of the Cabaret Voltaire, away from what Elderfield correctly calls "the earlier equilibrium of construction-negation" into the bravura of anti-art. A few years later there was a further split in the movement, and Dada divided itself into two factions: the German group, led by Huelsenbeck, George Grosz, and the Herzefelde brothers, which was predominantly political in approach, and Tzara's group, which moved to Paris in 1920, and which championed the aesthetic anarchism that ultimately developed into Surrealism.

If Tzara gave Dada its identity, he also robbed it of the moral purpose it had aspired to under Ball. By turning it into a doctrine, by garnishing it with a set of programmatic ideals, Tzara led Dada into self-contradiction and impotence. What for Ball had been a true cry from the heart against all systems of thought and action became one organization among others. The stance of anti-art, which opened the way for endless provocations and attacks, was essentially an inauthentic idea. For art opposed to art is nevertheless art; you can't have it both ways at once. As Tzara wrote in one of his manifestos: "The true Dadaists are against

Dada." The impossibility of establishing this as dogma is obvious, and Ball, who had the foresight to realize this contradiction quite early, left as soon as he saw signs of Dada becoming a movement. For the others, however, Dada became a kind of bluff that was pushed to further and further extremes. But the real motivation was gone, and when Dada finally died, it was not so much from the battle it had fought as from its own inertia.

Ball's position, on the other hand, seems no less valid today than it did in 1917. Of what we have come to realize were several different periods and divergent tendencies in Dada, the moment of Ball's participation, as I see it, remains the moment of Dada's greatest strength, the period that speaks most persuasively to us today. This is perhaps a heretical view. But when we consider how Dada exhausted itself under Tzara, how it succumbed to the decadent system of exchange in the bourgeois art world, provoking the very audience whose favor it was courting, this branch of Dada must be seen as a symptom of art's essential weakness under modern capitalism — locked in the invisible cage of what Marcuse has called "repressive tolerance." But because Ball never treated Dada as an end in itself, he remained flexible, and was able to use Dada as an instrument for reaching higher goals, for producing a genuine critique of the age. Dada, for Ball, was merely the name for a kind of radical doubt, a way of sweeping aside all existing ideologies and moving on to an examination of the world around him. As such, the energy of Dada can never be used up: it is an idea whose time is always the present.

Ball's eventual return to the Catholicism of his childhood in 1921 is not really as strange as it may seem. It represents no true shift in his thinking, and in many ways can be seen as simply a further step in his development. Had he lived longer, there is no reason to believe that he would not have undergone further metamorphosis. As it is, we discover in his diaries a continual overlapping of ideas and concerns, so that even during the Dada period, for example, there are repeated references to Christianity ("I do not know if we will go beyond Wilde and Baudelaire in spite of all our efforts; or if we will not just remain romantics. There are probably other ways of achieving the miracle and other ways of opposition too — asceticism, for example, the church") and during the time of his most serious Catholicism there is a preoccupation with mystical language that clearly resembles the sound poem theories of his Dada period. As he remarks in one of his last entries, in 1921: "The socialist, the aesthete, the monk: all three agree that modern bourgeois education must be destroyed. The new ideal will take its new elements from all three." Ball's short life was a constant straining toward a synthesis of these different points of view. If we regard him today as an important figure, it is not because he managed to discover a solution, but because he was able to state the problems with such clarity. In his intellectual courage, in the fervor of his confrontation with the world, Hugo Ball stands out as one of the exemplary spirits of the age.

1975

Truth, Beauty, Silence

Laura Riding was still in her thirties when she published her 477-page *Collected Poems* in 1938. At an age when most poets are just beginning to come into their own, she had already reached full maturity, and the list of her accomplishments in literature up to that time is impressive: nine volumes of poetry, several collections of critical essays and fiction, a long novel, and the founding of a small publishing house, the Seizin Press. As early as 1924, soon after her graduation from Cornell, *The Fugitive* had called her "the discovery of the year, a new figure in American poetry," and later, in Europe, during the period of her intimate and stormy relationship with Robert Graves, she became an important force of the international avant-garde. Young Auden was apparently so influenced by her poems that Graves felt obliged to write him a letter reprimanding him for his blatant Laura Riding imitations, and the method of close textual criticism developed in *A Survey of Modernist Poetry* (written in collaboration with Graves) directly inspired Empson's *Seven Types of Ambiguity*. Then, after 1938, nothing. No more poems, no more stories, no more essays. As time went on, Laura Riding's name was almost totally forgotten, and to a new generation of poets and writers it was as if she had never existed.

She was not heard from again until 1962, when she agreed to give a reading of some of her poems for a BBC broadcast and to deliver a few remarks about the philosophical and linguistic reasons for her break with poetry. Since then, there have been several appearances in print, and now, most recently, the publication of two books: a selection of her poems, which is prefaced by a further discussion of her attitude toward poetry, and *The Telling*, a prose work which she has described as a "personal evangel." Clearly, Laura Riding is back. Although she has written no poems since 1938, her new work in *The Telling* is intimately connected with her earlier writings, and in spite of her long public silence, her career is of a single piece. Laura Riding and Laura (Riding) Jackson — the married name she now uses — are in many ways mirror images of one another. Each has attempted to realize a kind of universal truth in language, a way of speaking that would somehow reveal to us our essential humanness — "a linguistically ordained ideal, every degree of fulfillment of which is a degree of express fulfillment of the hope comprehended in being, in its comprehending us within it, as human" — and if this ambition seems at times to be rather grandiosely stated, it has nevertheless been constant. The only thing that has changed is the method. Up to 1938, Laura Riding was convinced that poetry was the best way to achieve this goal. Since then, she has revised her opinion, and has not only given up poetry, but now sees it as one of the prime obstacles on this path toward linguistic truth.

When we turn to her own poetry, what is above all striking is its consistency of purpose and manner. From the very beginning, it seems, Laura Riding knew where she was going, and her poems ask to be read not as isolated lyrics, but as interconnecting parts of an enormous poetic project.

> We must learn better
> What we are and are not.
> We are not the wind.
> We are not every vagrant mood that tempts
> Our minds to giddy homelessness.
> We must distinguish better
> Between ourselves and strangers.
> There is much that we are not.
> There is much that is not.
> There is much that we have not to be.

(from "The Why of the Wind")

This is essential Riding: the abstract level of discourse, the insistence upon confronting ultimate questions, the tendency toward moral exhortation, the quickness and cleanness of thought, the unexpected juxtapositions of words, as in the phrase "giddy homelessness." The physical world is hardly present here, and when it is mentioned, it appears only as metaphor, as a kind of linguistic shorthand for indicating ideas and mental processes. The wind, for example, is not a real wind, but a way of expressing what is changeable, a reference to the idea of flux, and we feel its impact only as an idea. The poem itself proceeds as an argument rather than as a statement of feeling or an evocation of personal experience, and its movement is toward generalization, toward the utterance of what the poet takes to be a fundamental truth.

"We are not the wind." In other words, we are what does not change. For Laura Riding, this is the given of her project; it cannot be proved, but nevertheless it operates as the informing principle of her work as a whole. In poem after poem we witness her trying somehow to peel back the skin of the world in order to find some absolute and unassailable place of permanence, and because the poems are rarely grounded in a physical perception of that world, they tend, strangely, to exist in an almost purely emotional climate, created by the fervor of this metaphysical quest. And yet, in spite of the high seriousness of the poems, there are moments of sharp wit that remind us of Emily Dickinson:

Then follows a description
Of an interval called death
By the living.
But I shall speak of it
As of a brief illness.
For it lasted only
From being not ill
To being not ill.
It came about by chance—
I met God.
"What," he said, "you already?"
"What," I said, "you still?"

(from "Then Follows," in *Collected Poems*)

In the beginning, it is difficult to take the full measure of these poems, to understand the particular kinds of problems they are trying to deal with. Laura Riding gives us almost nothing to see, and this absence of imagery and sensuous detail, of any true *surface,* is at first baffling. We feel as though we had been blinded. But this is intentional on her part, and it plays an important role in the themes she develops. She does not so much want to see as to consider the notion of what is seeable.

You have pretended to be seeing.
I have pretended that you saw.
So came we by such eyes—
And within mystery to have language.

*

There was no sight to see.

That which is to be seen is no sight.
You made it a sight to see.
It is no sight, and this was the cause.

Now, having seen, let our eyes close
And a dark blessing pass among us—
A quick-slow blessing to have seen
And said and done no worse or better.

(from "Benedictory")

The only thing that seems to be present here is the poet's voice, and it is only gradually, as we "let our eyes close," that we begin to listen to this voice with special care, to become extremely sensitive to its nuances. Malebranche said that attention is the natural prayer of the soul. In her best poems, I think, Laura Riding coaxes us into a state of rapt listening, *into* a voice to which we give our complete attention, so that we, as readers, become participants in the unfolding of the poem. The voice is not so much speaking out loud as thinking, following the complex process of thought, and in such a way that it is almost immediately internalized by us. Few poets have ever been able to manipulate abstractions so persuasively. Having been stripped of ornament, reduced to their bare essentials, the poems emerge as a kind of rhetoric, a system of pure argument that works in the manner of music, generating an interaction of themes and counter-themes, and giving the same formal pleasure that music gives.

And talk in talk like time in time vanishes.
Ringing changes on dumb supposition,
Conversation succeeds conversation,
Until there's nothing left to talk about
Except truth, the perennial monologue,
And no talker to dispute it but itself.

(from "The Talking World")

These strengths, however, can also be weaknesses. For in order to sustain the high degree of intellectual precision necessary to the success of the poems, Laura Riding has been forced to engage in a kind of poetic brinkmanship, and she has often lost more than she has won. Eventually, we come to realize that the reasons for her break with poetry are implicit in the poems themselves. No matter how much we might admire her work, we sense that there is something missing in it, that it is not really capable of expressing the full range of experience it claims to be expressing. The source of this lack, paradoxically, lies in her conception of language, which in many ways is at odds with the very idea of poetry:

Come, words, away from mouths,
Away from tongues in mouths
And reckless hearts in tongues
And mouths in cautious heads—
Come, words, away to where
The meaning is not thickened
With the voice's fretting substance . . .

(from "Come, Words, Away")

This is a self-defeating desire. If anything, poetry is precisely that way of using language which forces words to remain *in* the mouth, the way by which we can most fully experience and understand "the voice's fretting substance." There is something too glacial in Laura Riding's approach to gain our sympathy. If the truth in language she is seeking is a human truth, it would seem to be contradictory to want this truth at the expense of what is human. But in trying to deny speech its physical properties — in refusing to acknowledge that speech is an imperfect tool of imperfect creatures — this seems to be exactly what she is doing.

In the 1938 preface to the *Collected Poems*, at the moment of her most passionate adherence to poetry, we can see this desire for transcendence as the motivating force behind her work. "I am going to give you," she writes, "poems written for all the reasons of poetry — poems which are also a record of how, by gradual integration of the reasons of poetry, existence in poetry becomes more real than existence in time — more real because more good, more good because more true." Thirty years later, she uses almost the same terms to justify her equally passionate opposition to poetry: "To a poet the mere making of a poem can seem to solve the problem of truth . . . But only a problem of art is solved in poetry. Art, whose honesty must work through artifice, cannot avoid cheating truth. Poetic art cheats truth to further and finer degrees than art of any other kind because the spoken word is its exclusive medium. . . ."

For all their loftiness and intensity, these statements remain curiously vague. For the truth that is referred to is never really defined, except as something beyond time, beyond art, beyond the senses. Such talk seems to set us afloat in a vast realm of Platonic idealism, and it is difficult for us to know where we are. At the same time, we are unconvinced. Neither statement is very believable to us as a statement about poetry, because, at heart, neither one *is* about poetry. Laura Riding is clearly interested in problems that extend beyond the scope of poetry, and by dwelling on these problems *as if* they were poetry's exclusive concerns, she only confuses the issue. She did not renounce poetry because of any objective inadequacy in poetry itself — for it is no more or less adequate than any other human activity — but because poetry as she conceived of it was no longer capable of saying what she wanted to say. She now feels that she had "reached poetry's limit." But what really happened, it would seem, is that she had reached her own limit in poetry.

It is appropriate, then, that her work since 1938 has been largely devoted to a more general investigation of language, and when we come to *The Telling* we find a deeper discussion of many of the same questions she had tried to formulate in her poetry. The book, which fits into no established literary category, is positively Talmudic in structure. "The Telling" itself is a short text of less than fifty pages, divided into numbered paragraphs, originally written for an issue of the magazine *Chelsea* in 1967. To this "core-text" which is written in a dense, highly abstract prose almost totally devoid of outside references, she has added a series of commentaries, commentaries on commentaries, notes, and addenda, which flesh out many of the earlier conclusions and treat of various literary, political, and philosophical matters. It is an astonishing display of a consciousness confronting and examining itself. Based on the idea that "the human utmost is marked out in a linguistic utmost," she pursues an ideal of "humanly perfect word-use" (as opposed to "artistically perfect word-use"), by which she aims to uncover the essential nature of being. Again, or rather still, she is straining toward absolutes, toward an unshakable and unified vision of the world: ". . . the nature of our being is not to be known as we know the weather, which is by the sense of the momentary. Weather is all change, while our being, in its human nature, is all constancy . . . it is to be known only by the sense of the constant." Although Laura (Riding) Jackson has put her former poet self in parentheses, she looks upon *The Telling* as the successful continuation of her efforts as a poet: "To speak as I speak in it, say such things as I say in it, was part of my hope as a poet."

The first paragraph of *The Telling* sets forth the substance of the problem that she confronts in the rest of the book:

> There is something to be told about us for the telling of which we all wait. In our unwilling ignorance we hurry to listen to stories of old human life, new human life, fancied human life, avid of something to while away the time of unanswered curiosity. We know we are explainable, and not explained. Many of the lesser things concerning us have been told but the greater things have not been told; and nothing can fill their place. Whatever we learn of what is not ourselves, but ours to know, being of our universal world, will likewise leave the emptiness an emptiness. Until the missing story of ourselves is told, nothing besides told can suffice us: we shall go on quietly craving it.

What immediately strikes us here is the brilliance of the writing itself. The quiet urgency and strong, cadenced phrasing entice us to go on listening. It seems that we are about to be told something radically different from anything we have ever been told before, and of such fundamental importance that it would be in our best interests to pay careful attention to what follows. "We know we are explainable, and not explained." In the subsequent paragraphs we are shown why the various human disciplines — science, religion, philosophy, history, poetry — have not and cannot explain us. Suddenly, everything has been swept aside; the way seems to have been cleared for a totally fresh approach to things. And yet, when she reaches the point of offering her own explanations, we are once again presented with the mysterious and unbelievable Platonism we had encountered before. It seems, finally, as if she were rejecting the myth-making tendencies of previous thought only in order to present another myth of her own devising — a myth of memory, a faith in the capacity of human beings to remember a time of wholeness that preceded the existence of individual selves. "May our Manyness become All-embracing. May we see in one another the All that was once All-One re-become One." And elsewhere: "Yes, I think we remember our creation! — have the memory of it in us, to know. Through the memory of it we apprehend that there was a Before-time of being from which being passed into what would be us." The problem is not that we doubt this belief of hers. We feel, in fact, that she is trying to report back to us about a genuine mystical experience; what is hard for us to accept is that she assumes this experience to be accessible to everyone. Perhaps it is. But we have no way of knowing — and would have no way of proving it even if we did. Laura (Riding) Jackson speaks of this purely personal experience in rigorous and objective terms, and as a result mingles two kinds of incompatible discourse. Her private perceptions have been projected on to the world at large, so that when she looks out on that world she thinks she sees a confirmation of her findings. But there is no distinction made between what is asserted as fact and what is verifiable as fact. As a consequence, there is no common ground established with us, and we find no place where we would want to stand with her in her beliefs.

In spite of this, however, it would be wrong simply to dismiss the book. If *The Telling* ultimately fails to carry out its promises, it is still valuable to us for the exceptional quality of its prose and the innovations of its form. The sheer immensity of its ambitions makes it an exciting work, even when it is most irritating. More importantly, it is crucial to us for what it reveals — retroactively — about Laura Riding's earlier work as a poet. For, in the end, it is as a poet that she will be read and remembered. Whatever objections we might want to raise about her approach to poetry in general, it would be difficult not to recognize her as a poet of importance. We need not be in agreement with her to admire her.

Roses are buds, and beautiful,
One petal leaning toward adventure.
Roses are full, all petals forward,
Beauty and power indistinguishable.
Roses are blown, startled with life,
Death young in their faces.
Then comes the halt, and recumbence, and failing.
But none says, "A rose is dead."
But men die: it is said, it is seen.
For a man is a long, late adventure;
His budding is a purpose,
His fullness more purpose,
His blowing a renewal,
His death, a cramped spilling
Of rash measure and miles.
To the roses no tears:
Which flee before the race is called.
And to man no mercy but his will:

That he has had his will, and is done.
The mercy of truth — it is to be truth.

(from "The Last Covenant")

In one of the supplementary chapters of *The Telling*, "Extracts From Communications," she speaks of the relationship between the writer and his work in a way that seems to express her aspirations as a poet. "If what you write is true, it will not be so because of what you are as a writer but because of what you are as a being. There can be no literary equivalent to truth. If, in writing, truth is the quality of what is said, told, this is not a literary achievement: it is a simple human achievement." This is not very far from the spirit of Ben Jonson's assertion that only a good man is capable of writing a good poem. It is an idea that stands at one extreme of our literary consciousness, and it places poetry within an essentially moral framework. As a poet, Laura Riding followed this principle until she reached what she felt to be "a crisis-point at which division between craft and creed reveals itself to be absolute." In the making of poems, she concluded, the demands of art would always outweigh the demands of truth.

Beauty and truth. It is the old question, come back to haunt us. Laura Riding sacrificed here poetic career in a choice between the two. But whether she has really answered the question, as she appears to think she has, is open to debate. What we do have are the poems she left behind her, and it is not surprising, perhaps, that we are drawn to them most of all for their beauty. We cannot call Laura Riding a neglected poet, since she was the cause of her own neglect. But after more than thirty years of absence, these poems strike us with all the force of a rediscovery.

1975

From Cakes to Stones

A note on Beckett's French

Mercier and Camier was the first of Samuel Beckett's novels to be written in French. Completed in 1946, and withheld from publication until 1970, it is also the last of his longer works to have been translated into English. Such a long delay would seem to indicate that Beckett is not overly fond of the work. Had he not been given the Nobel prize in 1969, in fact, it seems likely that *Mercier and Camier* would not have been published at all. This reluctance on Beckett's part is somewhat puzzling, for if *Mercier and Camier* is clearly a transitional work, at once harking back to *Murphy* and *Watt* and looking forward to the masterpieces of the early fifties, it is nevertheless a brilliant work, with its own particular strengths and charms, unduplicated in any of Beckett's six other novels. Even at his not quite best, Beckett remains Beckett, and reading him is like reading no one else.

Mercier and Camier are two men of indeterminate middle age who decide to leave everything behind them and set off on a journey. Like Flaubert's Bouvard and Pécuchet, like Laurel and Hardy, like the other "pseudo couples" in Beckett's work, they are not so much separate characters as two elements of a tandem reality, and neither one could exist without the other. The purpose of their journey is never stated, nor is their destination ever made clear. "They had consulted together at length, before embarking on this journey, weighing with all the calm at their command what benefits they might hope from it, what ills apprehend, maintaining turn about the dark side and the rosy. The only certitude they gained from these debates was that of not lightly launching out, into the unknown." Beckett, the master of the comma, manages in these few sentences to cancel out any possibility of a goal. Quite simply, Mercier and Camier agree to meet, they meet (after painful confusion), and set off. That they never really get anywhere, only twice, in fact, cross the town limits, in no way impedes the progress of the book. For the book is not about what Mercier and Camier do; it is about what they are.

Nothing happens. Or, more precisely, what happens is what does not happen. Armed with the vaudeville props of umbrella, sack, and raincoat, the two heroes meander through the town and the surrounding countryside, encountering various objects and personages: they pause frequently and at length in an assortment of bars and public places; they consort with a warm-hearted prostitute named Helen; they kill a policeman; they gradually lose their few possessions and drift apart. These are the outward events, all precisely told, with wit, elegance, and pathos, and interspersed with some beautiful descriptive passages ("The sea is not far, just visible beyond the valleys disappearing eastward, pale plinth as pale as the pale wall of sky"). But the real substance of the book lies in the conversations between Mercier and Camier:

> If we have nothing to say, said Camier, let us say nothing.
> We have things to say, said Mercier.
> Then why can't we say them? said Camier.
> We can't, said Mercier.
> Then let us be silent, said Camier.
> But we try, said Mercier.

In a celebrated passage of *Talking about Dante*, Mandelstam wrote: "The *Inferno* and especially the *Purgatorio* glorify the human gait, the measure and rhythm of walking, the foot and its shape . . . In Dante philosophy and poetry are forever on the move, forever on their feet. Even standing still is a variety of accumulated motion; making a place for people to stand and talk takes as much trouble as scaling an Alp." Beckett, who is one of the finest readers of Dante, has learned these lessons with utter thoroughness. Almost uncannily, the prose of *Mercier and Camier* moves along at a walking pace, and after a while one begins to have the distinct impression that somewhere, buried deep within the words, a silent metronome is beating out the rhythms of Mercier and Camier's perambulations. The pauses, the hiatuses, the sudden shifts of conversation and description do not break this rhythm, but rather take place under its influence (which has already been firmly established), so that their effect is not one of disruption but of counterpoint and fulfillment. A mysterious stillness seems to envelop each sentence in the book, a kind of gravity, or calm, so that between each sentence the reader feels the passing of time, the footsteps that continue to move, even when nothing is said. "Sitting at the bar they discoursed of this and that, brokenly, as was their custom. They spoke, fell silent, listened to each other, stopped listening, each as he fancied or as bidden from within."

This notion of time, of course, is directly related to the notion of *timing*, and it seems no accident that *Mercier and Camier* immediately precedes *Waiting for Godot* in Beckett's oeuvre. In some sense, it can be seen as a warm-up for the play. The music-hall banter, which was perfected in the dramatic works, is already present in the novel:

> What will it be? said the barman.
> When we need you we'll tell you, said Camier.
> What will it be? said the barman.
> The same as before, said Mercier.
> You haven't been served, said the barman.
> The same as this gentleman, said Mercier.
> The barman looked at Camier's empty glass.
> I forget what it was, he said.
> I too, said Camier.
> I never knew, said Mercier.

But whereas *Waiting for Godot* is sustained by the implicit drama of Godot's absence — an absence that commands the scene as powerfully as any presence — *Mercier and Camier* progresses in a void. From one moment to the next, it is impossible to foresee what will happen. The action, which is not buoyed by any tension or intrigue, seems to take place against a background of nearly total silence, and whatever is said is said at the very moment there is nothing left to say. Rain dominates the book, from the first paragraph to the last sentence ("And in the dark he could hear better too, he could hear the sounds the long day had kept from him, human murmurs for example, and the rain on the water") — an endless Irish rain, which is accorded the status of a metaphysical idea, and which creates an atmosphere that hovers between boredom and anguish, between bitterness and jocularity. As in the play, tears are shed, but more from a knowledge of the futility of tears than from any need to purge oneself of grief. Likewise, laughter is merely what happens when tears have been spent. All goes on, slowly waning in the hush of time, and unlike Vladimir and Estragon, Mercier and Camier must endure without any hope of redemption.

The key word in all this, I feel, is dispossession. Beckett, who begins with little, ends with even less. The movement in each of his works is toward a kind of unburdening, by which he leads us to the limits of experience — to a place where aesthetic and moral judgments become inseparable. This is the itinerary of the characters in his books, and it has also been his own progress as a writer. From the lush, convoluted, and jaunty prose of *More Pricks than Kicks* (1934) to the desolate spareness of *The Lost Ones* (1970), he has gradually cut closer and closer to the bone. His decision thirty years ago to write in French was undoubtedly the crucial event in this progress. This was an almost inconceivable act. But again, Beckett is not like other writers. Before truly coming into his own, he had to leave behind what came most easily to him, struggle against his own facility as a stylist. Beyond Dickens and Joyce, there is perhaps no English writer of the past hundred years who has equalled Beckett's early prose for vigor and intelligence; the language of *Murphy*, for example, is so packed that the novel has the density of a short lyric poem. By switching to French (a language, as Beckett has remarked, that "has no style"), he willingly began all over again. *Mercier and Camier* stands at the very beginning of this new life, and it is interesting to note that in this English translation Beckett has cut out nearly a fifth of the original text. Phrases, sentences, entire passages have been discarded, and what we have been given is really an editing job as well as a translation. This tampering, however, is not difficult to understand. Too many echoes, too many ornate and clever flourishes from the past remain, and though a considerable amount of superb material has been lost, Beckett apparently did not think it good enough to keep.

In spite of this, or perhaps because of this, *Mercier and Camier* comes close to being a flawless work. As with all of Beckett's self-translations, this version is not so much a literal translation of the original as a re-creation, a "repatriation" of the book into English. However stripped his style in French may be, there is always a little extra something added to the English renderings, some slight twist of diction or nuance, some unexpected word falling at just the right moment, that reminds us that English is nevertheless Beckett's home.

> George, said Camier, five sandwiches, four wrapped and one on the side. You see, he said, turning graciously to Mr Conaire, I think of everything. For the one I eat here will give me the strength to get back with the four others.
>
> Sophistry, said Mr Conaire. You set off with your five, wrapped, feel faint, open up, take one out, eat, recuperate, push on with the others.
>
> For all response Camier began to eat.
>
> You'll spoil him, said Mr Conaire. Yesterday cakes, today sandwiches, tomorrow crusts, and Thursday stones.
>
> Mustard, said Camier.

There is a crispness to this that outdoes the French. "Sophistry" for "raisonnement du clerc," "crusts" for "pain sec," and the assonance with 'mustard' in the next sentence give a neatness and economy to the exchange that is even more satisfying than the original. Everything has been pared down to a minimum; not a syllable is out of place.

We move from cakes to stones, and from page to page Beckett builds a world out of almost nothing. Mercier and Camier set out on a journey and do not go anywhere. But at each step of the way, we want to be exactly where they are. How Beckett manages this is something of a mystery. But as in all his work, less is more.

1975

The Poetry of Exile

A Jew, born in Romania, who wrote in German and lived in France. Victim of the Second World War, survivor of the death camps, suicide before he was fifty. Paul Celan was a poet of exile, an outsider even to the language of his own poems, and if his life was exemplary in its pain, a paradigm of the destruction and dislocation of midcentury Europe, his poetry is defiantly idiosyncratic, always and absolutely his own. In Germany, he is considered the equal of Rilke and Trakl, the heir to Hölderlin's metaphysical lyricism, and elsewhere his work is held in similar esteem, prompting statements such as George Steiner's recent remark that Celan is "almost certainly the major European poet of the period after 1945." At the same time, Celan is an exceedingly difficult poet, both dense and obscure. He demands so much of a reader, and in his later work his utterances are so gnomic, that it is nearly impossible to make full sense of him, even after many readings. Fiercely intelligent, propelled by a dizzying linguistic force, Celan's poems seem to explode on the page, and encountering them for the first time is a memorable event. It is to feel the same strangeness and excitement that one feels in discovering the work of Hopkins, or Emily Dickinson.

Czernovitz, Bukovina, where Celan was born as Paul Anczel in 1920, was a multilingual area that had once been part of the Habsburg Empire. In 1940, after the Hitler-Stalin pact, it was annexed by the Soviet Union, in the following year occupied by Nazi troops, and in 1943 retaken by the Russians. Celan's parents were deported to a concentration camp in 1942 and did not return; Celan, who managed to escape, was put in a labor camp until December 1943. In 1945 he went to Bucharest, where he worked as a translator and publisher's reader, then moved to Vienna in 1947, and finally, in 1948, settled permanently in Paris, where he married and became a teacher of German literature at the Ecole Normale Supérieure. His output comprises seven books of poetry and translations of more than two dozen foreign poets, including Mandelstam, Ungaretti, Pessoa, Rimbaud, Valéry, Char, du Bouchet, and Dupin.

Celan came to poetry rather late, and his first poems were not published until he was almost thirty. All his work, therefore, was written after the Holocaust, and his poems are everywhere informed by its memory. The unspeakable yields a poetry that continually threatens to overwhelm the limits of what can be spoken. For Celan forgot nothing, forgave nothing. The death of his parents and his own experiences during the war are recurrent and obsessive themes that run through all his work.

> With names, watered
> by every exile.
> With names and seeds,
> with names dipped
> into all
> the calyxes that are full of your
> regal blood, man, — into all
> the calyxes of the great
> ghetto-rose, from which
> you look at us, immortal with so many
> deaths died on morning errands.

(from "Crowned Out . . .", 1963, trans. by Michael Hamburger)

Even after the war, Celan's life remained an unstable one. He suffered acutely from feelings of persecution, which led to repeated breakdowns in his later years — and eventually to his suicide in 1970, when he drowned himself in the Seine. An incessant writer who produced hundreds of poems during his relatively short writing life, Celan poured all his grief and anger into his work. There is no poetry more furious than his, no poetry so purely inspired by bitterness. Celan never stopped confronting the dragon of the past, and in the end it swallowed him up.

"Todesfugue" (Death Fugue) is not Celan's best poem, but it is unquestionably his most famous poem — the work that made his reputation. Coming as it did in the late forties, only a few years after the end of the war — and in striking contrast to Adorno's rather fatuous remark about the "barbarity" of writing poems after Auschwitz — "Todesfugue" had a considerable impact among German readers, both for its direct mention of the concentration camps and for the terrible beauty of its form. The poem is literally a fugue composed of words, and its pounding, rhythmical repetitions and variations mark off a terrain no less circumscribed, no less closed in on itself than a prison surrounded by barbed wire. Covering slightly less than two pages, it begins and ends with the following stanzas:

Black milk of dawn we drink it at dusk
we drink it at noon and at daybreak we drink it at night
we drink and drink
we are digging a grave in the air there's room for us all
A man lives in the house he plays with the serpents he
  writes
he writes when it darkens to Germany your golden hair
  Margarete
he writes it and steps outside and the stars all aglisten
  he whistles for his hounds
he whistles for his Jews he has them dig a grave in the
  earth
he commands us to play for the dance

*

Black milk of dawn we drink you at night
we drink you at noon death is a master from Germany
we drink you at dusk and at daybreak we drink and we
  drink you
death is a master from Germany his eye is blue
he shoots you with bullets of lead his aim is true
a man lives in the house your golden hair Margarete
he sets his hounds on us he gives us a grave in the air
he plays with the serpents and dreams death is a master
  from Germany
your golden hair Margarete
your ashen hair Shulamite

(trans. by Joachim Neugroschel)

In spite of the poem's great control and the formal sublimation of an impossibly emotional theme, "Todesfugue" is one of Celan's most explicit works. In the sixties, he even turned against it, refusing permission to have it reprinted in more anthologies because he felt that his poetry had progressed to a stage where "Todesfugue" was too obvious and superficially realistic. With this in mind, however, one does discover in this poem elements common to much of Celan's work: the taut energy of the language, the objectification of private anguish, the unusual distancing effected between feeling and image. As Celan himself expressed it in an early commentary on his poems: "What matters for this language . . . is precision. It does not transfigure, does not 'poetize', it names and composes, it tries to measure out the sphere of the given and the possible."

This notion of the possible is central to Celan. It is the way by which one can begin to enter his conception of the poem, his vision of reality. For the seeming paradox of another of his statements — "Reality is not. It must be searched for and won" — can lead to confusion unless one has already understood the aspiration for the real that informs Celan's poetry. Celan is not advocating a retreat into subjectivity or the construction of an imaginary universe. Rather, he is staking out the distance over which the poem must travel and defining the ambiguity of a world in which all values have been subverted.

Speak—
But keep yes and no unsplit,
And give your say this meaning:
give it the shade.

Give it shade enough,
give it as much
as you know has been dealt out between
midday and midday and midnight.

Look around:
look how it all leaps alive—
where death is! Alive!
He speaks truly who speaks the shade.

(from "Speak, You Also," trans. by Michael Hamburger)

In a public address delivered in the city of Bremen in 1958 after being awarded an important literary prize, Celan spoke of language as the one thing that had remained intact for him after the war, even though it had to pass through "the thousand darknesses of death-bringing speech." "In this language," Celan said — and by this he meant German, the language of the Nazis and the language of his poems — "I have tried to write poetry, in order to acquire a perspective of reality for myself." He then compared the poem to a message in a bottle — thrown out to sea in the hope that it will one day wash up to land, "perhaps on the shore of the heart." "Poems," he continued, "even in this sense are under way: they are heading toward something. Toward what? Toward some open place that can be inhabited, toward a thou which can be addressed, perhaps toward a reality which can be addressed."

The poem, then, is not a transcription of an already known world, but a process of discovery, and the act of writing for Celan is one that demands personal risks. Celan did not write solely in order to express himself, but to orient himself within his own life and take his stand in the world, and it is this feeling of necessity that communicates itself to a reader. These poems are more than literary artifacts. They are a means of staying alive.

In a 1946 essay on Van Gogh, Meyer Schapiro refers to the notion of realism in a way that could also apply to Celan. "I do not mean realism in the repugnant, narrow sense that it has acquired today," Professor Schapiro writes, ". . . but rather the sentiment that external reality is an object of strong desire or need, as a possession and potential means of fulfillment of the striving human being, and is therefore the necessary ground of art." Then, quoting a phrase from one of Van Gogh's letters — "I'm terrified of getting away from the possible . . ." — he observes: "Struggling against the perspective that diminishes an individual object before his eyes, he renders it larger than life. The loading of the pigment is in part a reflex of this attitude, a frantic effort to preserve in the image of things their tangible matter and to create something equally solid and concrete on the canvas."

Celan, whose life and attitude toward his art closely parallel Van Gogh's, used language in a way that is not unlike the way Van Gogh used paints, and their work is surprisingly similar in spirit.* Neither Van Gogh's stroke nor Celan's syntax is strictly representational, for in the eyes of each the "objective" world is interlocked with his perception of it. There is no reality that can be posited without the simultaneous effort to penetrate it, and the work of art as an ongoing process bears witness to this desire. Just as Van Gogh's painted objects acquire a concreteness "as real as reality," Celan handles words as if they had the density of objects, and he endows them with a substantiality that enables them to become a part of the world, his world — and not simply its mirror.

*Celan makes reference to Van Gogh in several of his poems, and the kinship between the poet and painter is indeed quite strong: both began as artists in their late twenties after having lived through experiences that marked them deeply for the rest of their lives; both produced work prolifically, at a furious pace, as if depending on the work for their very survival; both underwent debilitating mental crises that led to confinement; both committed suicide, foreigners in France.

Celan's poems resist straightforward exegesis. They are not linear progressions, moving from word to word, from point A to point B. Rather, they present themselves to a reader as intricate networks of semantic densities. Interlingual puns, oblique personal references, intentional misquotations, bizarre neologisms: these are the sinews that bind Celan's poems together. It is not possible to keep up with him, to follow his drift at every step along the way. One is guided more by a sense of tone and intention than by textual scrutiny. Celan does not speak explicitly, but he never fails to make himself clear. There is nothing random in his work, no gratuitous elements to obscure the perception of the poem. One reads with one's skin, as if by osmosis, unconsciously absorbing nuances, overtones, syntactical twists, which in themselves are as much the meaning of the poem as its analytic content. Celan's method of composition is not unlike that of Joyce in *Finnegans Wake*. But if Joyce's art was one of accumulation and expansion — a spiral whirling into infinity — Celan's poetry is continually collapsing into itself, negating its very premises, again and again arriving at zero. We are in the world of the absurd, but we have been led there by a mind that refuses to acquiesce to it.

Consider the following poem, "Largo," one of Celan's later poems — and a typical example of the difficulty a reader faces in tackling Celan.* In Michael Hamburger's translation it reads:

You of the same mind, moor-wandering near one:

more-than-
death-
sized we lie
together, autumn
crocuses, the timeless, teems
under our breathing eyelids,
the pair of blackbirds hangs
beside us, under
our whitely drifting
companions up there, our

meta-
stases.

* I am grateful to Katharine Washburn, a scrupulous reader and translator of Celan, for help in deciphering the German text of this poem and suggesting possible references.

The German text, however, reveals things that necessarily elude the grasp of translation:

> Gleichsinnige du, heidegängerisch Nahe:
> über-
> sterbens-
> gross liegen
> wir beieinander, die Zeit-
> lose wimmelt
> dir unter den atmenden Lidern,
> Das Amselpaar hängt
> neben uns, unter
> unsern gemeinsam droben mit-
> ziehenden weissen
>
> Meta-
> stasen.

In the first line, *heidegängerisch* is an inescapable allusion to Heidegger — whose thinking was in many ways close to Celan's, but who, as a pro-Nazi, stood on the side of the murderers. Celan visited Heidegger in the sixties, and although it is not known what they said to each other, one can assume that they discussed Heidegger's position during the war. The reference to Heidegger in the poem is underscored by the use of some of the central words from his philosophical writings: *Nahe, Zeit*, etc. This is Celan's way: he does not mention anything directly, but weaves his meanings into the fabric of the language, creating a space for the invisible, in the same way that thought accompanies us as we move through a landscape.

Further along, in the third stanza, there are the two blackbirds (stock figures in fairy tales, who speak in riddles and bring bad tidings). In the German one reads *Amsel* — which echoes the sound of Celan's own name, Anczel. At the same time, there is an evocation of Günter Grass's novel, *Dog Years*, which chronicles the love-hate relationship between a Jew and a Nazi during the war. The Jewish character in the story is named Amsel, and throughout the book — to quote George Steiner again — "there is a deadly pastiche of the metaphysical jargon of Heidegger."

Toward the end of the poem, the presence of "our whitely drifting / companions up there" is a reference to the Jewish victims of the Holocaust: the smoke of the bodies burned in crematoria. From early poems such as "Todesfugue" ("he gives us a grave in the air") to later poems such as "Largo," the Jewish dead in Celan's work inhabit the air, are the very substance we are condemned to breathe: souls turned into smoke, into dust, into nothing at all — "our / meta- / stases."

Celan's preoccupation with the Holocaust goes beyond mere history, however. It is the primal moment, the first cause and last effect of an entire cosmology. Celan is essentially a religious poet, and although he speaks with the voice of one forsaken by God, he never abandons the struggle to make sense of what has no sense, to come to grips with his own Jewishness. Negation, blasphemy, and irony take the place of devotion; the forms of righteousness are mimicked; Biblical phrases are turned around, subverted, made to speak against themselves. But in so doing, Celan draws nearer to the source of his despair, the absence that lives in the heart of all things. Much has been said about Celan's "negative theology." It is most fully expressed in the opening stanzas of "Psalm":

No One kneads us anew from earth and clay,
no one addresses our dust.
No One.

Laudeamus te, No One.
For your sake would we
bloom forth:
unto
You.

Nothing
were we, and are we and
will be, all abloom:
this Nothing's, this
no-man's-rose.

(trans. by Katharine Washburn)

In the last decade of his life, Celan gradually refined his work to a point where he began to enter new and uncharted territory. The long lines and ample breath of the early poems give way to an elliptical, almost panting style in which words are broken up into their component syllables, unorthodox word-clusters are invented, and the reductionist natural vocabulary of the first books is inundated by references to science, technology, and political events. These short, usually untitled poems move along by lightning-quick flashes of intuition, and their message, as Michael Hamburger aptly puts it, "is at once more urgent and more reticent." One feels both a shrinking and an expansion in them, as if, by traveling to the inmost recesses of himself, Celan had somehow vanished, joining with the greater forces beyond him — and at the same time sinking more deeply into his isolation.

Thread-suns
over the gray-black wasteland.
A tree-
high thought
strikes the note of light: there are
still songs to sing beyond
mankind.

(trans. by Joachim Neugroschel)

In poems such as this one, Celan has set the stakes so high that he must surpass himself in order to keep even with himself — and push his life into the void in order to cling to his identity. It is an impossible struggle, doomed from the start to disaster. For poetry cannot save the soul or retrieve a lost world. It simply asserts the given. In the end, it seems, Celan's desolation became too great to be borne, as if, in some sense, the world were no longer there for him. And when nothing was left, there could be no more words.

You were my death:
you I could hold
when all fell away from me.

(trans. by Michael Hamburger)

1975

Innocence and Memory

From his earliest important poems, written in the trenches of the First World War, to the last poems of his old age, Giuseppe Ungaretti's work is a long record of confrontations with death. Cryptic in utterance, narrow in rage, and built on an imagery that is drawn exclusively from the natural world, Ungaretti's poetry nevertheless manages to avoid the predictable, and in spite of the limitations of his manner, he leaves an impression of almost boundless energy and invention. No word in Ungaretti's work is ever used lightly — "When I find/in this my silence/a word/it is dug into my life/like an abyss" — and the strength of his poetry comes precisely from this restraint. For a man who wrote for more than fifty years, Ungaretti published remarkably little before he died in 1970, and his collected poems amount to no more than a couple of hundred pages. Like Mallarmé before him (though in ways that are very different), Ungaretti's poetic source is silence, and in one form or another, all his work is an expression of the inexhaustible difficulty of expression itself. Reading him, one feels that he has only grudgingly allowed his words to appear on the page, that even the strongest words are in constant danger of annihilation.

Born in 1888, Ungaretti belonged to a celebrated generation of modern writers that included Pound, Joyce, Kafka, Trakl, and Pessoa. Like theirs, his importance is measured not only by his own achievement but by its effect on the history of the literature of his language. Before Ungaretti, there was no modern Italian poetry. When his first book, *Il Porto Sepolto (The Buried Port)*, appeared in 1916 in an edition of eighty copies, it seemed to have dropped from the sky, to be without precedent. These short, fragmented poems, at times hardly more ample than notes or inscriptions, announced a definitive break with the late-nineteenth-century conventions that still dominated Italian poetry. The horrible realities of the war demanded a new kind of expression, and for Ungaretti, who at that time was just finishing his poetic apprenticeship, the front was a training ground that taught the futility of all compromise.

Watch
Cima Quattro, December 23, 1915

One whole night
thrust down beside
a slaughtered comrade
his snarling
mouth
turned to the full moon
the bloating
of his hands
entering
my silence
I have written
letters full of love

Never have I held
so
fast to life*

If the brevity and hardness of his first poems seemed violent in comparison to most Italian poetry of the period, Ungaretti was no poetic rebel, and his work showed none of the spirit of self-conscious sabotage that characterized the Futurists and other avant-garde groups. His break with the past was not a renunciation of literary tradition, but a way of affirming his connection with a more distant and vital past than the one represented by his immediate predecessors. He simply cleared the ground that lay between him and what he felt to be his true sources, and like all original artists, he created his own tradition. In later years, this led him to extensive critical work, as well as translations of numerous foreign poets, including Gongora, Shakespeare, Racine, Blake, and Mallarmé.

Ungaretti's need to invent this poetic past for himself can perhaps be attributed to the unusual circumstances of his early life. By the twin accidents of his birthplace and the nature of his education, he was freed from many of the constraints of a pure Italian upbringing, and though he came from old Tuscan peasant stock, he did not set foot in Italy until he was twenty-four. His father, originally from Lucca, had emigrated to Egypt to work on the construction of the Suez Canal, and by the time of

* All quotations are translated by Allen Mandelbaum and appear in his *Selected Poems of Giuseppe Ungaretti*, published by Cornell University Press in 1975.

Ungaretti's birth he had become the proprietor of a bakery in the Arab quarter of Moharrem Bay in Alexandria. Ungaretti attended French schools, and his first real encounter with Europe took place a year before the war, in Paris, where he met Picasso, Braque, De Chirico, Max Jacob, and became close friends with Apollinaire. (In 1918, transferred to Paris at the time of the Armistice, he arrived at Apollinaire's house with the latter's favorite Italian cigars just moments after his death.) Apart from serving in the Italian army, Ungaretti did not live in Italy until 1921 — long after he had found his direction as a poet. Ungaretti was a cultural hybrid, and elements of his varied past are continually mixed into his work. Nowhere is this more concisely expressed than in "I fiumi" ("The Rivers")(1916), a long poem that concludes:

I have gone over
the seasons
of my life

These are
my rivers

This is the Serchio
from whose waters have drawn
perhaps two thousand years
of my farming people
and my father and my mother

This is the Nile
that saw me
born and growing
burning with unknowing
on its broad plains

This is the Seine
and in its troubled flow
I was remingled and remade
and came to know myself

These are my rivers
counted in the Isonzo

This is my nostalgia
as it appears

in each river
now it is night
now my life seems to me
a corolla
of shadows

In early poems such as this one, Ungaretti manages to capture the past in the shape of an eternal present. Time exists, not as duration so much as accumulation, a gathering of discrete moments that can be revived and made to emerge in the nearness of the present. *Innocence and Memory* — the title given to the French edition of Ungaretti's essays — are the two contradictory aspirations embedded in his poetry, and all his work can be seen as a constant effort to renew the self without destroying its past. What concerns Ungaretti most is the search for spiritual self-definition, a way of discovering his own essence beyond the grip of time. It is a drama played out between the forces of permanence and impermanence, and its basic fact is human mortality. As in the war poem, "Watch," the sense of life for Ungaretti is experienced most fully in confronting death, and in a commentary on another of his poems, he describes this process as ". . . the knowing of being out of non-being, being out of the null, Pascalian knowing of being out of the null. Horrid consciousness."

If this poetry can be described as basically religious in nature, the sensibility that informs the poems is never monkish, and denial of the flesh is never offered as a solution to spiritual problems. It is, in fact, the conflict between the spiritual and the physical that sustains the poems and gives them their life. Ungaretti is a man of contradictions, a "man of pain," as he calls himself in one of his poems, but also a man of great passions and desires, who at times seems locked in "the glare of promiscuity," and who is able to write of ". . . the mare of your loins/Plunging you in agony/Into my singing arms." His obsession with death, therefore, does not derive from morbid self-pity or a search for other-worldliness, but from an almost savage will to live, and Ungaretti's robust sensuality, his firm adherence to the world of physical things, makes his poems tense with conflict between the irreconcilable powers of love and vanity.

In his later work, beginning with the second major collection, *Sentimento del Tempo (Sentiment of Time)* (1919–35), the distance between the present and the past grows, in the end becoming a chasm that is almost impossible to cross, either by an act of will or an act of grace. As with Pascal, as with Leopardi, the perception of the void translates itself into the central metaphor of an unappeasable agony in the face of an indifferent universe, and if Ungaretti's conversion to Catholicism in the late twenties is to be understood, it must be seen in the light of this "horrid consciousness." "La Pietà" (1928), the long poem that most clearly marks Ungaretti's conversion, is also one of his bleakest works, and it contains these lines, which can be read as a gloss on the particular nature of Ungaretti's anguish:

You have banished me from life.

And will you banish me from death?

Perhaps man is unworthy even of hope.

Dry, too, the fountain of remorse?

What matters sin
If it no longer leads to purity?

The flesh can scarcely remember
That once it was strong.

Worn out and wild — the soul.

God, look upon our weakness.

We want a certainty.

Not satisfied to remain on safe ground, without the comfort of a "certainty," he continually goads himself to the edge of the abyss, threatening himself with the image of his own extinction. But rather than inducing him to succumb to despair, these acts of metaphysical risk seem to be the source of an enduring strength. In poems such as "The Premeditated Death," a sequence that serves as the hub to the whole of *Sentimento del Tempo*, and nearly all the poems in his following collection, *Il Dolore (The Grief)* (1936–47) — most notably the powerful poem written on the death of his young son, "You Shattered" — Ungaretti's determination to situate himself at the extremes of his own consciousness is paradoxically what allows him to cure himself of the fear of these limits.

By the force and precision of his meditative insight, Ungaretti manages to transcend what in a lesser poet would amount to little more than an inventory of private griefs and fears: the poems stand as objects beyond the self for the very reason that the self within them is not treated as an example of all selves or the self in general. At all times one feels the presence of the man himself in the work. As Allen Mandelbaum notes in the preface to his translations: "Ungaretti's I is grave and slow, intensive rather than far-ranging; and his longing gains its drama precisely because that I is not a random center of desperations, but a *soma* bound by weight, by earthly measure, a hard, resisting, substantial object, not wished but willed, not dreamt-upon but 'excavated'."

In the poems of his later years, Ungaretti's work comes to an astonishing culmination in the single image of the promised land. It is the promised land of both Aeneas and the Bible, of both Rome and the desert, and the personal and historical overtones of these final major poems — "Canzone," "Choruses Describing the States of Mind of Dido," "Recitative of Palinurus," and "Final Choruses for the Promised Land," — refer back to all of Ungaretti's previous work, as if to give it its final meaning. The return to a Virgilian setting represents a kind of poetic homecoming for him at the end of his career, just as the desert revives the landscape of his youth, only to leave him in a last and permanent exile:

> We cross the desert with remnants
> Of some earlier image in mind,
>
> That is all a living man
> Knows of the promised land.

Written between 1952 and 1960, the "Final Choruses" were published in *Il Taccuino del Vecchio (The Old Man's Notebook)*, and they reformulate all the essential themes of his work. Ungaretti's universe remains the same, and in a language that differs very little from that of his earliest poems, he prepares himself for his death — his real death, the last death possible for him:

> The kite hawk grips me in his azure talons
> And, at the apex of the sun,
> Lets me fall on the sand
> As food for ravens.
>
> I shall no longer bear mud on my shoulders,
> The fire will find me clean,

The cackling beaks
The stinking jaws of jackals.

Then as he searches with his stick
Through the sand, the bedouin
Will point out
A white, white bone.

1976

Book of the Dead

During the past few years, no French writer has received more serious critical attention and praise than Edmond Jabès. Maurice Blanchot, Emmanuel Levinas, and Jean Starobinski have all written extensively and enthusiastically about his work, and Jacques Derrida has remarked, flatly and without self-consciousness, that "in the last ten years nothing has been written in France that does not have its precedent somewhere in the texts of Jabès." Beginning with the first volume of *Le Livre des Questions*, which was published in 1963, and continuing on through the other volumes in the series,* Jabès has created a new and mysterious kind of literary work — as dazzling as it is difficult to define. Neither novel nor poem, neither essay nor play, *The Book of Questions* is a combination of all these forms, a mosaic of fragments, aphorisms, dialogues, songs, and commentaries that endlessly move around the central question of the book: how to speak what cannot be spoken. The question is the Jewish Holocaust, but it is also the question of literature itself. By a startling leap of the imagination, Jabès treats them as one and the same:

> I talked to you about the difficulty of being Jewish, which is the same as the difficulty of writing. For Judaism and writing are but the same waiting, the same hope, the same wearing out.

The son of wealthy Egyptian Jews, Jabès was born in 1912 and grew up in the French-speaking community of Cairo. His earliest literary friendships were with Max Jacob, Paul Eluard, and René Char, and in the forties and fifties he published several small books of poetry which were later collected in *Je bâtis ma demeure* (1959). Up to that point, his reputation as a poet was solid, but because he lived outside France, he was not very well known.

* *Le Livre de Yukel* (1964), *Le Retour au Livre* (1965), *Yaël* (1967), *Elya* (1969), *Aély* (1972), *El, ou le dernier livre* (1973), which are followed by three volumes of *Le Livre des Resemblances*. Four books are available in English, all of them admirably translated by Rosmarie Waldrop: *The Book of Questions, The Book of Yukel, Return to the Book* (Wesleyan University Press), and *Elya* (Tree Books).

The Suez Crisis of 1956 changed everything for Jabès, both in his life and in his work. Forced by Nasser's regime to leave Egypt and resettle in France — consequently losing his home and all his possessions — he experienced for the first time the burden of being Jewish. Until then, his Jewishness had been nothing more than a cultural fact, a contingent element of his life. But now that he had been made to suffer for no other reason than that he was a Jew, he had become the Other, and this sudden sense of exile was transformed into a basic, metaphysical self-description.

Difficult years followed. Jabès took a job in Paris and was forced to do most of his writing on the Metro to and from work. When, not long after his arrival, his collected poems were published by Gallimard, the book was not so much an announcement of things to come as a way of marking the boundaries between his new life and what was now an irretrievable past. Jabès began studying Jewish texts — the Talmud, the Kabbala — and though this reading did not initiate a return to the religious precepts of Judaism, it did provide a way for Jabès to affirm his ties with Jewish history and thought. More than the primary source of the Torah, it was the writings and rabbinical commentaries of the Diaspora that moved Jabès, and he began to see in these books a strength particular to the Jews, one that translated itself, almost literally, into a mode of survival. In the long interval between exile and the coming of the Messiah, the people of God had become the people of the Book. For Jabès, this meant that the Book had taken on all the weight and importance of a homeland.

> The Jewish world is based on written law, on a logic of words one cannot deny. So the country of the Jews is on the scale of their world, because it is a book . . . The Jew's fatherland is a sacred text amid the commentaries it has given rise to . . .

At the core of *The Book of Questions* there is a story — the separation of two young lovers, Sarah and Yukel, during the time of the Nazi deportations. Yukel is a writer — described as the "witness" — who serves as Jabès's alter ego and whose words are often indistinguishable from his; Sarah is a young woman who is shipped to a concentration camp and who returns insane. But the story is never really told, and it in no way resembles a traditional narrative. Rather, it is alluded to, commented on, and now and then allowed to burst forth in the passionate and obsessive love letters exchanged between Sarah and Yukel — which seem to come from nowhere, like disembodied voices, articulating what Jabès calls "the collective scream . . . the everlasting scream."

> *Sarah:* I wrote you. I write you. I wrote you. I write you. I take refuge in my words, the words my pen weeps. As long as I am speaking, as long as I am writing, my pain is less keen. I join with each syllable to the point of being but a body of consonants, a soul of vowels. Is it magic? I write his name, and it becomes the man I love . . .

And Yukel, toward the end of the book:

> And I read in you, through your dress and your skin, through your flesh and your blood. I read, Sarah, that you were mine through every word of our language, through all the wounds of our race. I read, as one reads the Bible, our history and the story which could only be yours and mine.

This story, which is the "central text" of the book, is submitted to extensive and elusive commentaries in Talmudic fashion. One of Jabès's most original strokes is the invention of the imaginary rabbis who engage in those conversations and interpret the text with their sayings and poems. Their remarks, which most often refer to the problem of writing the book and the nature of the Word, are elliptical, metaphorical, and set in motion a beautiful and elaborate counterpoint with the rest of the work.

> "He is a Jew," said Reb Tolba. "He is leaning against a wall, watching the clouds go by."
>
> "The Jew has no use for clouds," replied Reb Jale. "He is counting the steps between him and his life."

Because the story of Sarah and Yukel is not fully told, because, as Jabès implies, it *cannot* be told, the commentaries are in some sense an investigation of a text that has not been written. Like the hidden God of classic Jewish theology, the text exists only by virtue of its absence.

> "I know you, Lord, in the measure that I do not know you. For you are He who comes."
>
> Reb Lod

What happens in *The Book of Questions*, then, is the writing of *The Book of Questions* — or rather, the attempt to write it, a process that the reader is allowed to witness in all its gropings and hesitations. Like the narrator in Beckett's *The Unnamable*, who is cursed by "the inability to speak [and] the inability to be silent," Jabès's narrative goes nowhere but around and around itself. As Maurice Blanchot has observed in his excellent essay on Jabès: "The writing . . . must be accomplished in the act of interrupting itself." A typical page in *The Book of Questions* mirrors this sense of difficulty: isolated statements and paragraphs are separated by white spaces, then broken by parenthetical remarks, by italicized passages and italics within parentheses, so that the reader's eye can never grow accustomed to a single, unbroken visual field. One reads the book by fits and starts — just as it was written.

At the same time, the book is highly structured, almost architectural in its design. Carefully divided into four parts, "At the Threshold of the Book," "And You Shall Be in the Book," "The Book of the Absent," and "The Book of the Living," it is treated by Jabès as if it were a physical place, and once we cross its threshold we pass into a kind of enchanted realm, an imaginary world that has been held in suspended animation. As Sarah writes at one point: "I no longer know where I am. I know. I am nowhere. Here." Mythical in its dimensions, the book for Jabès is a place where the past and the present meet and dissolve into each other. There seems nothing strange about the fact that ancient rabbis can converse with a contemporary writer, that images of stunning beauty can stand beside descriptions of the greatest devastation, or that the visionary and the commonplace can coexist on the same page. From the very beginning, when the reader encounters the writer at the threshold of the book, we know that we are entering a space unlike any other.

"What is going on behind this door?"
"A book is shedding its leaves."
"What is the story of the book?"
"Becoming aware of a scream."
"I saw rabbis go in."
"They are privileged readers. They come in small groups to give us their comments."
"Have they read the book?"
"They are reading it."
"Did they happen by for the fun of it?"
"They foresaw the book. They are prepared to encounter it."
"Do they know the characters?"
"They know our martyrs."
"Where is the book set?"
"In the book."
"What are you?"
"I am the keeper of the house."
"Where do you come from?"
"I have wandered . . ."

The book "begins with difficulty — the difficulty of being and writing — and ends with difficulty." It gives no answers. Nor can any answers ever be given — for the precise reason that the "Jew," as one of the imaginary rabbis states, "answers every question with another question." Jabès conveys these ideas with a wit and eloquence that often evoke the logical hairsplitting — *pilpul* — of the Talmud. But he never deludes himself into believing that his words are anything more than "grains of sand" thrown to the wind. At the heart of the book there is nothingness.

> "Our hope is for knowledge," said Reb Mendel. But not all his disciples were of his opinion.
>
> "We have first to agree on the sense you give to the word 'knowledge', " said the oldest of them.
>
> "Knowledge means questioning," answered Reb Mendel.
>
> "What will we get out of these questions? What will we get out of all the answers which only lead to more questions, since questions are born of unsatisfactory answers?" asked the second disciple.
>
> "The promise of a new question," replied Reb Mendel.
>
> "There will be a moment," the oldest disciple continued, "when we will have to stop interrogating. Either because there will be no answer possible, or because we will not be able to formulate any further questions. So why should we begin?"
>
> "You see," said Reb Mendel, "at the end of an argument, there is always a decisive question unsettled."
>
> "Questioning means taking the road to despair," continued the second disciple. "We will never know what we are trying to learn."

Although Jabès's imagery and sources are for the most part derived from Judaism, *The Book of Questions* is not a Jewish work in the same way that one can speak of *Paradise Lost* as a Christian work. While Jabès is, to my knowledge, the first modern poet consciously to assimilate the forms and idiosyncrasies of Jewish thought, his relationship to Jewish teaching is emotional and metaphorical rather than one of strict adherence. The Book is his central image — but it is not only the Book of the Jews (the spirals of commentary around commentary in the Midrash), but an allusion to Mallarmé's ideal Book as well (the Book that contains the world, endlessly folding in upon itself). Finally, Jabès's work must be considered as part of the on-going French poetic tradition that began in the late nineteenth century. What Jabès has done is to fuse this tradition with a certain type of Jewish discourse, and he has done so with such conviction that the marriage between the two is almost imperceptible. *The Book of Questions* came into being because Jabès found himself as a writer in the act of discovering himself as a Jew. Similar in spirit to an idea expressed by Marina Tsvetaeva — "In this most Christian of worlds / all poets are Jews" — this equation is located at the exact center of Jabès's work, is the kernel from which everything else springs. To Jabès, nothing can be written about the Holocaust unless writing itself is first put into question. If language is to be pushed to the limit, then the writer must condemn himself to an exile of doubt, to a desert of uncertainty. What he must do, in effect, is create a poetics of absence. The dead cannot be brought back to life. But they can be heard, and their voices live in the Book.

1976

Reznikoff ×2

1. THE DECISIVE MOMENT

Charles Reznikoff is a poet of the eye. To cross the threshold of his work is to penetrate the prehistory of matter, to find oneself exposed to a world in which language has not yet been invented. Seeing, in his poetry, always comes before speech. Each poetic utterance is an emanation of the eye, a transcription of the visible into the brute, undeciphered code of being. The act of writing, therefore, is not so much an ordering of the real as a discovery of it. It is a process by which one places oneself between things and the names of things, a way of standing watch in this interval of silence and allowing things to be seen — as if for the first time — and henceforth to be given their names. The poet, who is the first man to be born, is also the last. He is Adam, but he is also the end of all generations: the mute heir of the builders of Babel. For it is he who must learn to speak from his eye — and cure himself of seeing with his mouth.

The poem, then, not as a telling, but as a taking hold. The world can never be assumed to exist. It comes into being only in the act of moving towards it. *Esse est percipii*: no American poet has ever adhered so faithfully to the Berkeleyan formula as Reznikoff. It is more than just the guiding principle of his work — it is *embedded* in the work, and it contains all the force of a moral dogma. To read Reznikoff is to understand that nothing can be taken for granted: we do not find ourselves in the midst of an already established world, we do not, as if by preordained birthright, automatically take possession of our surroundings. Each moment, each thing, must be earned, wrested away from the confusion of inert matter by a steadiness of gaze, a purity of perception so intense that the effort, in itself, takes on the value of a religious act. The slate has been wiped clean. It is up to the poet to write his own book.

Tiny poems, many of them barely a sentence long, make up the core of Reznikoff's work. Although his total output includes fiction, biography, drama, long narrative poems, historical meditations, and book-length documentary poems, these short lyrics are the Ur-texts of Reznikoff's imagination: everything else follows from them. Notable for their precision and simplicity, they also run counter to normal assumptions about what a poem should aspire to be. Consider these three examples:

> *April*
> The stiff lines of the twigs
> blurred by buds.
>
> *Moonlit Night*
> The trees' shadows lie in black pools in the lawns.
>
> *The Bridge*
> In a cloud bones of steel.

The point is that there is no point. At least not in any traditional sense. These poems are not trying to drum home universal truths, to impress the reader with the skill of their making, or to invoke the ambiguities of human experience. Their aim, quite simply, is clarity. Of seeing and of speaking. And yet, the unsettling modesty of these poems should not blind us to the boldness of their ambition. For even in these tiniest of poems, the gist of Reznikoff's poetics is there. It is as much an ethics of the poetic moment as it is a theory of writing, and its message never varies in any of Reznikoff's work: the poem is always more than just a construction of words. Art, then, for the sake of something — which means that art is almost an incidental by-product of the effort to make it. The poem, in all instances, must be an effort to perceive, must be a moving *outward*. It is less a mode of expressing the world than it is a way of being in the world. Merleau-Ponty's account of contemplation in *The Phenomenology of Perception* is a nearly exact description of the process that takes place in a Reznikoff poem:

> . . . when I contemplate an object with the sole intention of watching it exist and unfold its riches before my eyes, then it ceases to be an allusion to a general type, and I become aware that each perception, and not merely that of sights which I am discovering for the first time, re-enacts on its own account the birth of intelligence and has some element of creative genius about it: in order that I may recognize the tree as a tree, it is necessary that, beneath this familiar meaning, the momentary arrangement of the visible scene should begin all over again, as on the very first day of the vegetable kingdom, to outline the individual idea of this tree.

Imagism, yes. But only as a source, not as a method. There is no desire on Reznikoff's part to use the image as a medium for transcendence, to make it quiver ineffably in some ethereal realm of the spirit. The progress from symbolism to imagism to objectivism is more a series of short-circuits than a direct lineage. What Reznikoff learned from the Imagists was the value — the force — of the image in itself, unadorned by the claims of the ego. The poem, in Reznikoff's hands, is an act of image-ing rather than of imagining. Its impulse is away from metaphor and into the tangible, a desire to take hold of what is rather than what is merely possible. A poem fit to the measure of the perceived world, neither larger than this world nor smaller than it. "I see something," Reznikoff stated in a 1968 interview with L. S. Dembo, "and I put it down as I see it. In the treatment of it, I abstain from comment. Now, if I've done something that moves me — if I've portrayed the object well — somebody will come along and also be moved, and somebody else will come along and say, 'What the devil is this?' And maybe they're both right."

If the poet's primary obligation is to see, there is a similar though less obvious injunction upon the poet — the duty of not being seen. The Reznikoff equation, which weds seeing to invisibility, cannot be made except by renunciation. In order to see, the poet must make himself invisible. He must disappear, efface himself in anonymity.

> I like the sound of the street—
> but I, apart and alone,
> beside an open window
> and behind a closed door.
>
> *
>
> I am alone—
> and glad to be alone;
> I do not like people who walk about
> so late; who walk slowly after midnight
> through the leaves fallen on the sidewalks.
> I do not like
> my own face
> in the little mirrors of the slot-machines
> before the closed stores.

It seems no accident that most Reznikoff poems are rooted in the city. For only in the modern city can the one who sees remain unseen, take his stand in space and yet remain transparent. Even as he becomes a part of the landscape he has entered, he continues to be an outsider. Therefore, objectivist. That is to say — to create a world around oneself by seeing as a stranger would. What counts is the thing itself, and the thing that is seen can come to life only when the one who sees it has disappeared. There can never be any movement toward possession. Seeing is the effort to create presence: to possess a thing would be to make it vanish.

And yet, it is *as if* each act of seeing were an attempt to establish a link between the one who sees and the thing that is seen. *As if* the eye were the means by which the stranger could find his place in the world he has been exiled to. For the building of a world is above all the building and recognition of relations. To discover a thing and isolate it in its singularity is only a beginning, a first step. The world is not merely an accumulation, it is a process — and each time the eye enters this world, it partakes in the life of all the disparate things that pass before it. While objectivity is the premise, subjectivity is the tacit organizer. As soon as there is more than one thing, there is memory, and because of memory, there is language: what is born in the eye, and nevertheless beyond it. In which, and out of which, the poem.

In his 1968 interview with Dembo, Reznikoff went on to say: "The world is very large, I think, and I certainly can't testify to the whole of it. I can only testify to my own feelings; I can only say what I saw and heard, and I try to say it as well as I can. And if your conclusion is that what I saw and heard makes you feel the way I did, then the poem is successful."

New York was Reznikoff's home. It was a city he knew as intimately as a woodcutter knows his forest, and in his prime he would walk between ten and twenty miles a day, from Brooklyn to Riverdale and back. Few poets have ever had such a deep feeling for city life, and in dozens of brief poems Reznikoff captures the strange and transitory beauties of the urban landscape.

> This smoky winter morning—
> do not despise the green jewel among the twigs
> because it is a traffic light.

*

> Feast, you who cross the bridge
> this cold twilight
> on these honeycombs of light, the buildings of Manhattan.

*

Rails in the subway,
what did you know of happiness
when you were ore in the earth;
now the electric lights shine upon you.

But Reznikoff's attention is focused on more than just the objects to be found in the city. He is equally interested in the people who fill the streets of New York, and no encounter, however brief, is too slight to escape his notice, too banal to become a source of epiphany. These two examples, from among many possibilities:

I was walking along Forty-Second Street as night was falling.
On the other side of the street was Bryant Park.
Walking behind me were two men
and I could hear some of their conversation:
"What you must do," one of them was saying to his companion,
"is to decide on what you want to do
and then stick to it. Stick to it!
And you are sure to succeed finally."

I turned to look at the speaker giving such good advice
and was not surprised to see that he was old,
But his companion
to whom the advice was given so earnestly,
was just as old;
and just then the great clock on top of a building across the park

began to shine.

*

The tramp with torn shoes
and clothing dirty and wrinkled—
dirty hands and face—
takes a comb out of his pocket
and carefully combs his hair.

The feeling that emerges from these glimpses of city life is roughly equivalent to what one feels when looking at a photograph. Cartier-Bresson's "decisive moment" is perhaps the crucial idea to remember in this context. The important thing is readiness: you cannot walk out into the street with the expectation of writing a poem or taking a picture, and yet you must be prepared to do so whenever the opportunity presents itself. Because the "work" can come into being only when it has been given to you by the world, you must be constantly looking at the world, constantly doing the work that will lead to a poem, even if no poem comes of it. Reznikoff walks through the city — not, as most poets do, with "his head in the clouds," but with his eyes open, his mind open, his energies concentrated on entering the life around him. Entering it precisely because he is apart from it. And therefore this paradox, lodged in the heart of the poem: to posit the reality of this world, and then to cross into it, even as you find yourself barred at all its gates. The poet as solitary wanderer, as man in the crowd, as faceless scribe. Poetry as an art of loneliness.

It is more than just loneliness, however. It is exile, and a way of coming to terms with exile that somehow, for better or worse, manages to leave the condition of exile intact. Reznikoff was not only an outsider by temperament, nurturing those aspects of himself that would tend to maintain his sense of isolation, he was also born into a state of *otherness*, and as a Jew, as the son of immigrant Jews in America, whatever idea of community he had was always ethnic rather than national (his dream as a poet was to go across the country on foot, stopping at synagogues along the way to give readings of his work in exchange for food and lodging). If his poems about the city — his American poems, so to speak — dwell on the surfaces of things, on the skin of everyday life, it is in his poems about Jewish identity that he allows himself a certain measure of lyrical freedom, allows himself to become a singer of songs.

> Let other people come as streams
> that overflow a valley
> and leave dead bodies, uprooted trees and fields of sand:
> we Jews are as dew,
> on every blade of grass,
> trodden under foot today
> and here tomorrow morning.

And yet, in spite of this deep solidarity with the Jewish past, Reznikoff never deludes himself into thinking that he can overcome the essential solitude of his condition simply by affirming his Jewishness. For not only has he been exiled, he has been exiled twice — as a Jew, and from Judaism as well.

How difficult for me is Hebrew:
even the Hebrew for *mother*, for *bread*, for *sun*
is foreign. How far I have been exiled, Zion.

*

The Hebrew of your poets, Zion,
is like oil upon a burn,
cool as oil;
after work,
the smell in the street at night
of the hedge in flower.
Like Solomon,
I have married and married the speech of strangers;
none are like you, Shulamite.

It is a precarious position, to say the least. Neither fully assimilated nor fully unassimilated, Reznikoff occupies the unstable middle ground between two worlds and is never able to claim either one as his own. Nevertheless, and no doubt precisely because of this ambiguity, it is an extremely fertile ground — leading some to consider him primarily as a Jewish poet (whatever that term might mean) and others to look on him as quintessentially American poet (whatever *that* term might mean). And yet it is safe to say, I think, that in the end both statements are true — or else that neither one is true, which probably amounts to the same thing. Reznikoff's poems are what Reznikoff is: the poems of an American Jew, or, if you will, of a hyphenated American, a Jewish-American, with the two terms standing not so much on equal footing as combining to form a third and wholly different term: the condition of being in two places at the same time, or, quite simply, the condition of being nowhere.

We have only to go on the evidence. In the two volumes of *Complete Poems* (1918–75), recently published by Black Sparrow Press, there are a surprising number of poems on Jewish themes. Poems not only about Jewish immigrant life in New York, but also long narratives on various episodes from ancient and modern Jewish history. A list of some of these titles will give a fair idea of some of Reznikoff's concerns: "King David," "Jeremiah in the Stocks: An Arrangement of the Prophecies," "The Synagogue Defeated: Anno 1096," "Palestine under the Romans," "The Fifth Book of the Maccabees," "Jews in Babylonia." In all, these poems cover more than 100 pages of the approximately 350 pages in the two volumes — or nearly a third of his total output. Given the nature of the poems he is best known for — the spare city lyrics, transcriptions of immediate sensual data — it is strange that he should have devoted so much of his writing life to works whose inspiration comes from *books*. Reznikoff, the least pretentious of all poets, never shows any inclination toward the scholarly acrobatics of some of his contemporaries — Pound, for example, or Olson — and yet, curiously, much of his writing is a direct response to, almost a translation of, his reading. By a further twist, these poems that treat of apparently remote subjects are among his most personal works.

To be schematic for a moment, a simplified explanation would be as follows: America is Reznikoff's present, Judaism is his past. The act of immersing himself in Jewish history is finally no different for him than the act of stepping out into the streets of New York. In both cases, it is an attempt to come to terms with what he is. The past, however, cannot be directly perceived: it can only be experienced through books. When Reznikoff writes about King David, therefore, or Moses, or any other Biblical figure, he is in effect writing about himself. Even in his most light-hearted moments, this preoccupation with his ancestors is always with him.

God and Messenger

The pavement barren
as the mountain
on which God spoke to Moses—
suddenly in the street
shining against my legs
the bumper of a motor car.

The point is that Reznikoff the Jew and Reznikoff the American cannot be separated from one another. Each aspect of his work must be read in relation to the *oeuvre* as a whole, for in the end each point of view inhabits all the others.

The tree in the twilit street—
the pods hang from its bare symmetrical branches
motionless—
but if, like God, a century were to us
the twinkling of an eye,
we should see the frenzy of growth.

Which is to say: the eye is not adequate. Not even the seen can be truly seen. The human perspective, which continually thrusts us into a place where "only the narrow present is alive," is an exile from eternity, an exclusion from the fullness of human possibility. That Reznikoff, who insists so strenuously in all his work on this human perspective, should at the same time be aware of its limits, gives his work a reflexive quality, an element of self-doubt that permeates even the most straightforward lyric. For all his apparent simplicity, Reznikoff is by no means a primitive. A reductionist, perhaps, but a highly sophisticated one — who, as an adroit craftsman, always manages to make us forget that each poem is the product (as he put it in one work) of "hunger silence, and sweat."

There is, however, a bridge between time and eternity in Reznikoff's work, a link between God and man, in the precise place where man is forced to abstain most vigorously from the demands of the self: in the idea of the Law. The Law in the Jewish sense of the word and, by extension, in the English sense. *Testimony* is a work in which reading has become the equivalent of seeing: "Note: All that follows is based on the law reports of the several states." What Reznikoff has observed, has brought to life, is the word, the language of men. So that the act of witness has become synonymous with the act of creation — and the shouldering of its burden. "Now suppose in a court of law," Reznikoff told Dembo in their interview, "you are testifying in a negligence case. You cannot get up on the stand and say, 'The man was negligent.' That's a conclusion of fact. What you'd be compelled to say is how the man acted. Did he stop before he crossed the street? Did he look? The judges of whether he is negligent or not are the jury in that case and the judges of what you say as a poet are the readers. That is, there is an analogy between testimony in the courts and the testimony of a poet."

Trained as a lawyer (though he never practiced) and for many years a researcher for a legal encyclopedia, Reznikoff used the workings of the law not only as a description of the poetic process, but also, more basically, as an aesthetic ideal. In his long autobiographical poem, *Early History of a Writer*, he explains how the study of the law helped to discipline him as a poet:

> I saw that I could use the expensive machinery
> that had cost me four years of hard work at law
> and which I had thought useless for my writing:
> prying sentences open to look at the exact meaning;

weighing words to choose only those that had meat for my purpose
and throwing the rest away as empty shells.
I, too, could scrutinize every word and phrase
as if in a document or the opinion of a judge
and listen, as well, for tones and overtones,
leaving only the pithy, the necessary, the clear and plain.

Testimony: The United States (1885–1915) Recitative is perhaps Reznikoff's most important achievement as a poet. A quietly astonishing work, so deceptive in its making that it would be easy to misread it as a document rather than as a piece of art, it is at once a kaleidoscopic vision of American life and the ultimate test of Reznikoff's poetic principles. Composed of small, self-contained fragments, each the distillation of an actual court case, the overall effect is nevertheless extremely coherent. Reznikoff has no lesson to teach, no axe to grind, no ideology to defend: he merely wants to present the facts. For example:

At the time of their marriage
Andrew was worth about fifty thousand dollars;
Polly had nothing.
"He has gone up to the mine,
and I wish to God he would fall down
and break his neck.
I just hate him.
I just shiver when he touches me."

"Andy, I am going to write a letter that may seem
hardhearted:
you know that I do not love you
as I should
and I know that I never can.
Don't you think it best
to give me a divorce?
If you do,
I will not have to sell the house in Denver
that you gave me,
and I will give you back the ranch in Delta.
After we are divorced,
if you care for me and I care for you,
we will marry again. Polly."

*

Jessie was eleven years old, though some said fourteen,
and had the care of a child
just beginning to walk—
and suddenly pulled off the child's diaper
and sat the child in some hot ashes
where she had been cooking ash cakes;
the child screamed
and she smacked it on the jaw.

It would be difficult for a poet to make himself more invisible than Reznikoff does in this book. To find a comparable approach to the real, one would have to go back to the great prose writers of the turn of the century. As in Chekhov or in early Joyce, the desire is to allow events to speak for themselves, to choose the exact detail that will say everything and thereby allow as much as possible to remain unsaid. This kind of restraint paradoxically requires an openness of spirit that is available to very few: an ability to accept the given, to remain a witness of human behavior and not succumb to the temptation of becoming a judge.

The success of *Testimony* becomes all the more striking when placed beside *Holocaust*, a far less satisfying work that is based on many of the same techniques. Using as his sources the US Government publication, *Trials of the Criminals before the Nuremberg Tribunal*, and the records of the Eichmann trial in Jerusalem, Reznikoff attempts to deal with Germany's annihilation of the Jews in the same dispassionate, documentary style with which he had explored the human dramas buried in American court records. The problem, I think, is one of magnitude. Reznikoff is a master of the everyday; he understands the seriousness of small events and has an uncanny sympathy with the lives of ordinary people. In a work such as *Testimony* he is able to present us with the facts in a way that simultaneously makes us understand them; the two gestures are inseparable. In the case of *Holocaust*, however, we all know the facts in advance. The Holocaust, which is precisely the unknowable, the unthinkable, requires a treatment beyond the facts in order for us to be able to understand it — assuming that such a thing is even possible. Similar in approach to a 1960s play by Peter Weiss, *The Investigation*, Reznikoff's poem rigorously refuses to pass judgment on any of the atrocities it describes. But this is nevertheless a false objectivity, for the poem is not saying to the reader, "decide for yourself," it is saying that the decision has already been made and that the only way we can deal with these things is to remove them from their inherently emotional setting. The problem is that we cannot remove them. This setting is a necessary starting point.

Holocaust is instructive, however, in that it shows us the limits of Reznikoff's work. I do not mean shortcomings — but limits, those things that set off and describe a space, that create a world. Reznikoff is essentially a poet of *naming*. One does not have the sense of a poetry immersed in language but rather of something that takes place before language and comes to fruition at the precise moment language has been discovered — and it yields a style that is pristine, fastidious, almost stiff in its effort to say exactly what it means to say. If any one word can be used to describe Reznikoff's work, it would be humility — toward language and also toward himself.

> I am afraid
> because of the foolishness
> I have spoken.
> I must diet
> on silence;
> strengthen myself
> with quiet.

It could not have been an easy life for Reznikoff. Throughout the many years he devoted to writing poetry (his first poems were published in 1918, when he was twenty-four, and he went on publishing until his death in early 1976), he suffered from a neglect so total it was almost scandalous. Forced to bring out most of his books in private editions (many of them printed by himself), he also had to fight the constant pressures of making a living.

> After I had worked all day at what I earn my living
> I was tired. Now my own work has lost another day,
> I thought, but began slowly,
> and slowly my strength came back to me.
> Surely, the tide comes in twice a day.

It was not until he was in his late sixties that Reznikoff began to receive some measure of recognition. New Directions published a book of his selected poems, *By The Waters of Manhattan*, which was followed a few years later by the first volume of *Testimony*. But in spite of the success of these two books — and a growing audience for his works —

New Directions saw fit to drop Reznikoff from its list of authors. More years passed. Then, in 1974, Black Sparrow Press brought out *By The Well of Living & Seeing: New & Selected Poems 1918–1973*. More importantly, it committed itself to the long overdue project of putting all of Reznikoff's work back into print. Under the intelligent and sensitive editing of Seamus Cooney, the sequence so far includes the two volumes of *Complete Poems, Holocaust, The Manner Music* (a posthumous novel), the first two volumes of *Testimony*, and will go on to include more volumes of *Testimony* and a book of *Collected Plays*.

If Reznikoff lived his life in obscurity, there was never the slightest trace of resentment in his work. He was too proud for that, too busy with the work itself to be overly concerned with its fate in the world. Even if people are slow to listen to someone who speaks quietly, he knew that eventually he would be heard.

Te Deum

Not because of victories
I sing,
having none,
but for the common sunshine,
the breeze,
the largess of the spring.
Not for victory
but for the day's work done
as well as I was able;
not for a seat upon the dais
but at the common table.

1974; 1976; 1978

2. "IT REMINDS ME OF SOMETHING THAT ONCE HAPPENED TO MY MOTHER . . ."

In 1974, I was invited by Anthony Rudolf to contribute an article to the London magazine, *European Judaism,* for an issue celebrating Charles Reznikoff's eightieth birthday. I had been living in France for the past four years, and the little piece I sent in on Reznikoff's work was the first thing I wrote after coming back to America. It seemed like a fitting way to mark my return.

I moved into an apartment on Riverside Drive in late summer. After finishing the article, I discovered that Reznikoff lived very near by—on West End Avenue—and sent him a copy of the manuscript, along with a letter asking him if it would be possible for us to meet. Several weeks went by without a response.

On a Sunday in early October I was to be married. The ceremony was scheduled to take place in the apartment at around noon. At eleven o'clock, just moments before the guests were due to arrive, the telephone rang and an unfamiliar voice asked to speak to me. "This is Charles Reznikoff," the voice said, in a sing-song tone, looping ironically and with evident good humor. I was, of course, pleased and flattered by the call, but I explained that it would be impossible for me to talk just now. I was about to be married, and I was in no condition to form a coherent sentence. Reznikoff was highly amused by this and burst out laughing. "I never called a man on his wedding day before!" he said. "Mazel tov, mazel tov!" We arranged to meet the following week at his apartment. Then I hung up the phone and marched off to the altar.

Reznikoff's apartment was on the twenty-second floor of a large building complex, with a broad, uncluttered view of the Hudson and sunlight pouring through the windows. I arrived in the middle of the day, and with a somewhat stale crumb cake set before me and numerous cups of coffee to drink, I wound up staying three or four hours. The visit made such an impression on me that even now, almost a decade later, it is entirely present inside me.

I have met some good story-tellers in my life, but Reznikoff was the champion. Some of his stories that day went on for thirty or forty minutes, and no matter how far he seemed to drift from the point he was supposedly trying to make, he was in complete control. He had the patience that is necessary to the telling of a good story—and the ability to savor the least detail that cropped up along the way. What at first seemed to be an endless series of digressions, a kind of aimless wandering, turned out to be the elaborate and systematic construction of a circle. For example: why did you come back to New York after living in Hollywood? There followed a myriad of little incidents: meeting the brother of a certain man on a park bench, the color of someone's eyes, an economic crisis in some country. Fifteen minutes later, just when I was beginning to feel hopelessly lost—and convinced that Reznikoff was lost, too—he would begin a slow return to his starting point. Then, with great clarity and conviction, he would announce: "So that's why I left Hollywood." In retrospect, it all made perfect sense.

I heard stories about his childhood, his aborted career in journalism, his law studies, his work for his parents as a jobber of hats and how he would write poems on a bench at Macy's while waiting his turn to show the store buyer his samples. There were also stories about his walks—in particular, his journey from New York to Cape Cod (on foot!), which he undertook when he was well past sixty. The important thing, he explained, was not to walk too fast. Only by forcing himself to keep to a pace of less than two miles per hour could he be sure to see everything he wanted to see.

On my visit that day, I brought along for him a copy of my first book of poems, *Unearth*, which had just been published. This evoked a story from Reznikoff that strikes me as significant, especially in the light of the terrible neglect his work suffered for so many years. His first book, he told me, had been published in 1918 by Samuel Roth (who would later become famous for pirating *Ulysses* and his role in the 1933 court case over Joyce's book). The leading American poet of the day was Edwin Arlington Robinson, and Reznikoff had sent him a copy of the book, hoping for some sign of encouragement from the great man. One afternoon Reznikoff was visiting Roth in his bookstore, and Robinson walked in. Roth went over to greet him, and Reznikoff, standing in the back corner of the shop, witnessed the following scene. Roth proudly gestured to the copies of Reznikoff's book that were on display and asked Robinson if he had read the work of this fine young poet. "Yeah, I read the book," said Robinson in a gruff, hostile voice, "and I thought it was garbage."

"And so," said Reznikoff to me in 1974, "I never got to meet Edwin Arlington Robinson."

It was not until I was putting on my coat and getting ready to leave that Reznikoff said anything about the piece I had sent him. It had been composed in an extremely dense and cryptic style, wrestling with issues that Reznikoff himself had probably never consciously thought about, and I had no idea what his reaction would be. His silence about it during our long conversation led me to suspect that he had not liked it.

"About your article," he said, almost off-handedly. "It reminds me of something that once happened to my mother. A stranger walked up to her on the street one day and very kindly and graciously complimented her on her beautiful hair. Now, you must understand that my mother had never prided herself on her hair and did not consider it to be one of her better features. But, on the strength of that stranger's remark, she spent the rest of the day in front of her mirror, preening and primping and admiring her hair. That's exactly what your article did to me. I stood in front of the mirror for the whole afternoon and admired myself."

Several weeks later, I received a letter from Reznikoff about my book. It was filled with praise, and the numerous quotations from the poems convinced me that he was in earnest—that he had actually sat down and read the book. Nothing could have meant more to me.

A few years after Reznikoff's death, a letter came to me from La Jolla, written by a friend who works in the American Poetry Archive at the University of California library—where Reznikoff's papers had recently been sold. In going through the material, my friend told me, he had come across Reznikoff's copy of *Unearth*. Astonishingly, the book was filled with numerous small notations in the margins, as well as stress marks that Reznikoff had made throughout the poems in an effort to scan them correctly and understand their rhythms. Helpless to do or say anything, I thanked him from the other side of the grave.

Wherever Edwin Arlington Robinson might be now, one can be sure that his accommodations aren't half as good as Charles Reznikoff's.

1983

The Bartlebooth Follies

Georges Perec died in 1982 at the age of forty-six, leaving behind a dozen books and a brilliant reputation. In the words of Italo Calvino, he was "one of the most singular literary personalities in the world, a writer who resembled absolutely no one else." It has taken a while for us to catch on, but now that his major work has at last been translated into English — *Life: A User's Manual* (1978) — it will be impossible for us to think of contemporary French writing in the same way again.

Born into a Jewish family from Poland that emigrated to France in the 1920s, Perec lost his father in the German invasion of 1940 and his mother to the concentration camps in 1943. "I have no memories of childhood," he would later write. His literary career began early, and by the age of nineteen he was already publishing critical notes in the *NRF* and *Les Lettres Nouvelles*. His first novel, *Les Choses*, was awarded the Prix Renadot for 1965, and from then until his death he published approximately one book a year.

Given his tragic family history, it is perhaps surprising to learn that Perec was essentially a comic writer. For the last fifteen years of his life, in fact, he was an active member of Oulipo, a strange literary society founded by Raymond Queneau and the mathematician François le Lionnais. This Workshop for Potential Literature (*Ouvroir de Littérature Potentielle*) proposes all kinds of madcap operations to writers: the S-7 method (rewriting famous poems by replacing each word with the seventh word that follows it in the dictionary), the Lipogram (eliminating the use of one or more letters in a text), acrostics, palindromes, permutations, anagrams, and numerous other "literary constraints." As one of the leading lights of this group, Perec once wrote an entire novel of more than 200 pages without using the letter "e"; this novel was followed by another in which "e" is the only vowel that appears. Verbal gymnastics of this sort seemed to come naturally to him. In addition to his literary work, he produced a notoriously difficult weekly crossword puzzle for the news magazine *Le Point*.

To read Georges Perec one must be ready to abandon oneself to a spirit of play. His books are studded with intellectual traps, allusions and secret systems, and if they are not necessarily profound (in the sense that Tolstoy and Mann are profound), they are prodigiously entertaining (in the sense that Lewis Carroll and Laurence Sterne are entertaining). In Chapter Two of "Life," for example, Perec refers to "the score of a famous American melody, 'Gertrude of Wyoming,' by Arthur Stanley Jefferson." By pure chance, I happened to know that Arthur Stanley Jefferson was the real name of the comedian Stan Laurel, but just because I caught this allusion does not mean there weren't a thousand others that escaped me.

For the mathematically inclined, there are magic squares and chess moves to be discovered in this novel, but the fact that I was unable to find them did not diminish my enjoyment of the book. Those who have read a great deal will no doubt recognize passages that quote directly or indirectly from other writers — Kafka, Agatha Christie, Melville, Freud, Rabelais, Nabokov, Jules Verne and a host of others — but failure to recognize them should not be considered a handicap. Like Jorge Luis Borges, Georges Perec had a mind that was a storehouse of curious bits of knowledge and awesome erudition, and half the time the reader can't be sure if he is being conned or enlightened. In the long run, it probably doesn't matter. What draws one into this book is not Perec's cleverness, but the deftness and clarity of his style, a flow of language that manages to sustain one's interest through endless lists, catalogues, and descriptions. Perec had an uncanny gift for articulating the nuances of the material world, and in his hands even a worm-eaten table can become an object of fascination. "It was after he had done this that he thought of dissolving what was left of the original wood so as to disclose the fabulous aborescence within, this exact record of the worms' life inside the wooden mass: a static, mineral accumulation of all the movements that had constituted their blind existence, their undeviating single-mindedness, their obstinate itineraries; the faithful materialisation of all they had eaten and digested as they forced from their dense surroundings the invisible elements needed for their survival, the explicit, visible, immeasurably disturbing image of the endless progressions that had reduced the hardest of woods to an impalpable network of crumbling galleries."

Life: A User's Manual is constructed in the manner of a vast jigsaw puzzle. Perec takes a single apartment building in Paris, and in ninety-nine short chapters (along with a Preamble and an Epilogue) proceeds to give a meticulous description of each and every room as well as the life stories of all the inhabitants, both past and present. Ostensibly, we are watching the creation of a painting by Serge Valène, an old artist who has lived in the building for fifty-five years. "It was in the final months of his life that the artist Serge Valène conceived the idea of a painting that would reassemble his entire existence: everything his memory had recorded, all the sensations that had swept over him, all his fantasies, his passions, his hates would be recorded on canvas, a compendium of minute parts of which the sum would be his life."

What emerges is a series of self-contained but interconnecting stories. They are all briskly told, and they run the gamut from the bizarre to the realistic. There are tales of murder and revenge, tales of intellectual obsessions, humorous tales of social satire, and (almost unexpectedly) a number of stories of great psychological penetration. For the most part, Perec's microcosm is peopled with a motley assortment of oddballs, impassioned collectors, antiquarians, miniaturists, and half-baked scholars. If anyone can be called the central character in this shifting, kaleidoscopic work, it would have to be Percival Bartlebooth, an eccentric English millionaire whose insane and useless fifty-year project serves as an emblem for the book as a whole. Realizing as a young man that his wealth has doomed him to a life of boredom, he undertakes to study the art of watercolor from Serge Valène for a period of ten years. Although he has no aptitude whatsoever for painting, he eventually reaches a satisfactory level of competence. Then, in the company of a servant, he sets out on a twenty-year voyage around the world with the sole intention of painting watercolors of five hundred different harbors and seaports. As soon as one of these pictures is finished, he sends it to a man in Paris by the name of Gaspard Winckler, who also lives in the building. Winckler is an expert puzzle-maker whom Bartlebooth has hired to turn the watercolors into 750-piece jigsaw puzzles. One by one, the puzzles are made over the twenty-year period and stored in wooden boxes. Bartlebooth returns from his travels, settles back into his apartment, and methodically goes about putting the puzzles together in chronological order. By means of an elaborate chemical process that has been designed for the purpose at hand, the borders of the puzzle pieces are glued together in such a way that the seams are no longer visible, thus restoring the watercolor to its original integrity. The watercolor, good as new, is then removed from its wooden backing and sent back to the place where it was executed twenty years earlier. There, by prearrangement, it is dipped into a detergent solution that eliminates all traces of the painting, leaving Bartlebooth with a clean and unmarked sheet of paper. In other words, he is left with nothing, the same thing he started with. The project, however, does not quite go according to plan. Winckler has made the puzzles too difficult, and Bartlebooth does not live long enough to finish all five hundred of them. As Perec writes in the last paragraph of the ninety-ninth chapter: "It is the twenty-third of June nineteen hundred and seventy-five, and it is eight o'clock in the evening. Seated at his jigsaw puzzle, Bartlebooth has just died. On the tablecloth, somewhere in the crepuscular sky of the four hundred and thirty-ninth puzzle, the black hole of the sole piece not yet filled in has the almost perfect shape of an X. But the ironical thing, which could have been foreseen long ago, is that the piece the dead man holds between his fingers is shaped like a W."

Like many of the other stores in *Life*, Bartlebooth's weird saga can be read as a parable (of sorts) about the efforts of the human mind to impose an arbitrary order on the world. Again and again, Perec's characters are swindled, hoaxed, and thwarted in their schemes, and if there is a darker side to this book, it is perhaps to be found in this emphasis on the inevitability of failure. Even a self-annihilating project such as Bartlebooth's cannot be completed, and when we learn in the Epilogue that Valène's enormous painting (which for all intents and purposes is the book we have just been reading) has come no farther than a preliminary sketch, we realize that Perec does not exempt himself from the follies of his characters. It is this sense of self-mockery that turns a potentially daunting novel into a hospitable work, a book that for all its high-jinx and japery finally wins us over with the warmth of its human understanding.

1987

PREFACES

Jacques Dupin

It is not easy to come to terms with Jacques Dupin's poetry. Uncompromisingly hermetic in attitude and rigorously concise in utterance, it does not demand of us a reading so much as an absorption. For the nature of the poem has undergone a metamorphosis, and in order to meet it on its own ground, we must change the nature of our expectations. The poem is no longer a record of feelings, a song, or a meditation. Rather, it is the field in mental space in which a struggle is permitted to unfold: between the destruction of the poem and the quest for the possible poem — for the poem can be born only when all chances for its life have been destroyed. Dupin's work is the progeny of this contradiction, existing within the narrowest of confines, like an invisible seed lodged in the core of stone. The struggle is not a simple either/or conflict between this and that, either destroy or create, either speak or be silent — it is a matter of destroying in order to create, and of maintaining a silent vigil within the word until the last living moment, when the word begins to crumble from the pressure that has been placed upon it.

That which I see, and do not speak of, frightens me. What I speak of, and do not know, delivers me. Do not deliver me.

Dupin has accepted these difficulties deliberately, choosing poverty and the astringencies of denial in place of facility. Because his purpose is not to subjugate his surroundings by means of some vain notion of mastery, but to harmonize with them, to enter into relation with them, and finally, to live within them, the poetic operation becomes a process whereby he unburdens himself of his garments, his tools, and his possessions, in order to assume, in nakedness, the fullness of being. In this sense, the poem is a kind of spiritual purification. But if a monk can fashion a worldly poverty for himself in the knowledge that it will draw him nearer to his God, Dupin is not able to give himself such assurances. He takes on the distress of what is around him as a way of ending his separation from it, but there is no sign to lead him, and nothing to guarantee him salvation. Yet, in spite of this austerity, or perhaps because of it, his work holds an uncommon richness. This stems at least in part from the fact that all his poems are grounded in a landscape, firmly rooted in the palpability of the real. The problems he confronts are never posed as abstractions, but present themselves in and through this landscape, and in the end cannot be separated from it. The universe he brings forth is an alchemical itinerary through the elements, the transfiguration of the seemingly indivisible by means of the word. Similar in spirit to the cosmic correspondences revealed in the pre-Socratic fragments, it is a universe in which speech and metaphor are synonymous. Dupin has not made nature his object, he carries it within him, and when he finally speaks, it is with the force of what he already contains. Like Rilke, he finds himself in what is around him. His voice does more than conjure the presences of things, it gives them the power of speech as well. But whereas Rilke is usually passive in his relation to things — attempting to isolate the thing and penetrate its essence in transcendent stillness — Dupin is active, seeing things in their interconnectedness, as perpetually changing.

To shatter, to retake, and thus, to rebuild. In the forest we are closer to the woodcutter than to the solitary wanderer. No innocent contemplation. No high forests crossed by sunlight and the songs of birds, but their hidden future: cords of wood. Everything is given to us, but for violence, to be forced open, to be almost destroyed — to destroy us.

The solitary wanderer is Dupin himself, and each poem emerges as an account of his movements through the terrain he has staked out for himself. Dominated by stone, mountain, farm implements, and fire, the geography is cruel, built of the barest materials, and human presence can never be taken for granted in it. It must be won. Generated by a desire to join what forbids him a place and to find a dwelling within it, the Dupin poem is always on the other side: the limit of the human step, the fruit of a terrestrial harrowing. Above all, it is trial. Where all is silence, where all seems to exclude him, he can never be sure where his steps are taking him, and the poem can never be hunted systematically. It comes to life suddenly and without warning, in unexpected places and by unknown means. Between each flash there is patience, and in the end it is this that quickens the landscape — the tenacity to endure in it — even if it offers us nothing. *At the limit of strength a naked word.*

The poem is created only in choosing the most difficult path. Every advantage must be suppressed and every ruse discarded in the interests of reaching this limit — an endless series of destructions, in order to come to a point at which the poem can no longer be destroyed. For the poetic word is essentially the creative word, and yet, nevertheless, a word among others, burdened by the weight of habit and layers of dead skin that must be stripped away before it can regain its true function. Violence is demanded, and Dupin is equal to it. But the struggle is pursued for an end beyond violence — that of finding a habitable space. As often as not, he will fail, and even if he does not, success will bear its own disquiet. *The torch which lights the abyss, which seals it up, is itself an abyss.*

The strength that Dupin speaks of is not the strength of transcendence, but of immanence and realization. The gods have vanished, and there can be no question of pretending to recover the divine *logos*. Faced with an unknowable world, poetry can do no more than create what already exists. But that is already saying a great deal. For if things can be recovered from the edge of absence, there is the chance, in so doing, of giving them back to men.

1971

André du Bouchet

. . . this irreducible sign — deutungslos *— . . . a word beyond grasping, Cassandra's word, a word from which no lesson is to be drawn, a word, each time, and every time, spoken to say nothing . . .*

Hölderlin aujourd'hui (*lecture delivered March 1970 in Stuttgart to commemorate the 200th anniversary of Hölderlin's birth*)

(*this joy . . . that is born of nothing . . .*)

Qui n'est pas tourné vers nous (1972)

Born of the deepest silences, and condemned to life without hope of life (*I found myself / free / and without hope*), the poetry of André du Bouchet stands, in the end, as an act of survival. Beginning with nothing, and ending with nothing but the truth of its own struggle, du Bouchet's work is the record of an obsessive, wholly ruthless attempt to gain access to the self. It is a project filled with uncertainty, silence, and resistance, and there is no contemporary poetry, perhaps, that lends itself more reluctantly to gloss. To read du Bouchet is to undergo a process of dislocation: here, we discover, is not here, and the body, even the physical presence within the poems, is no longer in possession of itself — but moving, as if into the distance, where it seeks to find itself against the inevitability of its own disappearance (*. . . and the silence that claims us, like a vast field.*) "Here" is the limit we come to. To be in the poem, from this moment on, is to be nowhere.

A body in space. And the poem, as self-evident as this body. In space: that is to say, this void, this nowhere between sky and earth, rediscovered with each step that is taken. For wherever we are, the world is not. And wherever we go, we find ourselves moving in advance of ourselves — as if where the world would be. The distance, which allows the world to appear, is also that which separates us from the world, and though the body will endlessly move through this space, as if in the hope of abolishing it, the process begins again with each step taken. We move toward an infinitely receding point, a destination that can never be reached, and in the end, this going, in itself, will become a goal, so that the mere fact of moving onward will be a way of being in the world, even as the world remains beyond us. There is no hope in this, but neither is there despair. For what du Bouchet manages to maintain, almost uncannily, is a nostalgia for a possible future, even as he knows it will never come to pass. And from this dreadful knowledge, there is nevertheless a kind of joy, a joy . . . that is born of nothing.

Du Bouchet's work, however, will seem difficult to many readers approaching it for the first time. Stripped of metaphor, almost devoid of imagery, and generated by a syntax of abrupt, paratactic brevity, his poems have done away with nearly all the props that students of poetry are taught to look for — the very difficulties that poetry has always seemed to rely on — and this sudden opening of distances, in spite of the lessons buried in such earlier poets as Hölderlin, Leopardi, and Mallarmé, will seem baffling, even frightening. In the world of French poetry, however, du Bouchet has performed an act of linguistic surgery no less important than the one performed by William Carlos Williams in America, and against the rhetorical inflation that is the curse of French writing, his intensely understated poems have all the freshness of natural objects. His work, which was first published in the early fifties, became a model for a whole generation of postwar poets, and there are few young poets in France today who do not show the mark of his influence. What on first or second reading might seem to be an almost fragile sensibility gradually emerges as a vision of the greatest force and purity. For the poems themselves cannot be truly felt until one has penetrated the strength of the silence that lies at their source. It is a silence equal to the strength of any word.

1973

Black on White

Recent paintings by David Reed

The hand of the painter has rarely instructed us in the ways of the hand. When we look at a painting, we see an accumulation of gestures, the layering and shaping of materials, the longing of the inanimate to take on life. But we do not see the hand itself. Like the God of the deists, it seems to have withdrawn from its own creation, or vanished into the density of the world it has made. It does not matter whether the painting is figurative or abstract: we confront the work as an object, and, as such, the surface remains independent of the will behind it.

In David Reed's new paintings, this has been reversed. Suddenly, the hand has been made visible to us, and in each horizontal stroke applied to the canvas, we are able to see that hand with such precision that it actually seems to be *moving*. Faithful only to itself, to the demands of the movement it brings forth, the hand is no longer a means to an end, but the substance of the object it creates. For each stroke we are given here is unique: there is no backtracking, no modeling, no pause. The hand moves across the surface in a single, unbroken gesture, and once this gesture has been completed, it is inviolate. The finished work is not a representation of this process — it is the process itself, and it asks to be *read* rather than simply observed. Composed of a series of rung-like strokes that descend the length of the canvas, each of these paintings resembles a vast poem without words. Our eyes follow its movement in the same way we follow a poem down a page, and just as the line in a poem is a unit of breath, so the line in the painting is a unit of gesture. The language of these works is the language of the body.

Some people will probably try to see them as examples of minimal art. But that would be a mistake. Minimal art is an art of control, aiming at the rigorous ordering of visual information, while Reed's paintings are conceived in a way that sabotages the idea of a preordained result. It is this high degree of spontaneity within a consciously limited framework that produces such a harmonious coupling of intellectual and physical energies in his work. No two paintings are or can be exactly alike, even though each painting begins at the same point, with the same fundamental premises. For no matter how regular or

controlled the gesture may be, its field of action is unstable, and in the end it is chance that governs the result. Because the white background is still wet when the horizontal strokes are applied, the painting can never be fully calculated in advance, and the image is always at the mercy of gravity. In some sense, then, each painting is born from a conflict between opposing forces. The horizontal stroke tries to impose an order upon the chaos of the background, and is deformed by it as the white paint settles. It would surely be stretching matters to interpret this as a parable of man against nature. And yet, because these paintings evolve in time, and because our reading of them necessarily leads us back through their whole history, we are able to re-enact this conflict whenever we come into their presence. What remains is the drama: and we begin to understand that, fundamentally, these works are the statement of that drama.

In the last sentence of Maurice Blanchot's novel, *Death Sentence*, the nameless narrator writes: "And even more, let him try to imagine the hand that has written these pages: and if he is able to see it, then perhaps reading will become a serious task for him." David Reed's new work is an expression of this same desire in the realm of painting. By allowing us to imagine his hand, by allowing us to *see* his hand, he has exposed us to the serious task of seeing: how we see and what we see, and how what we see in a painting is different from what we see anywhere else. It has taken considerable courage to do this. For it pushes the artist out from the shadows, leaving him with nowhere to stand but in the painting itself. And in order for us to look at one of these works, we have no choice but to go in there with him.

1975

Twentieth-Century French Poetry

I

French and English constitute a single language.

Wallace Stevens

This much is certain: If not for the arrival of William and his armies on English soil in 1066, the English language as we know it would never have come into being. For the next three hundred years French was the language spoken at the English court, and it was not until the end of the Hundred Years' War that it became clear, once and for all, that France and England were not to become a single country. Even John Gower, one of the first to write in the English vernacular, composed a large portion of his work in French, and Chaucer, the greatest of the early English poets, devoted much of his creative energy to a translation of *Le Roman de la rose* and found his first models in the work of the Frenchman Guillaume de Machaut. It is not simply that French must be considered an "influence" on the development of English language and literature; French is a part of English, an irreducible element of its genetic make up.

Early English literature is replete with evidence of this symbiosis, and it would not be difficult to compile a lengthy catalogue of borrowings, homages and thefts. William Caxton, for instance, who introduced the printing press in England in 1477, was an amateur translator of medieval French works, and many of the first books printed in Britain were English versions of French romances and tales of chivalry. For the printers who worked under Caxton, translation was a normal and accepted part of their duties, and even the most popular English work to be published by Caxton, Thomas Malory's *Morte d'Arthur*, was itself a ransacking of Arthurian legends from French sources: Malory warns the reader no less than fifty-six times during the course of his narrative that the "French book" is his guide.

In the next century, when English came fully into its own as a language and a literature, both Wyatt and Surrey — two of the most brilliant pioneers of English verse — found inspiration in the work of Clément Marot, and Spenser, the major poet of the next generation, not only took the title of his *Shepheardes Calender* from Marot, but two sections of the work are direct imitations of that same poet. More importantly, Spenser's attempt at the age of seventeen to translate Joachim du Bellay (*The Visions of Bellay*) is the first sonnet sequence to be produced in English. His later revision of that work and translation of another du Bellay sequence, *Ruines of Rome*, were published in 1591 and stand among the great works of the period. Spenser, however, is not alone in showing the mark of the French. Nearly all the Elizabethan sonnet writers took sustenance from the Pléiade poets, and some of them — Daniel, Lodge, Chapman — went so far as to pass off translations of French poets as their own work. Outside the realm of poetry, the impact of Florio's translation of Montaigne's essays on Shakespeare has been well documented, and a good case could be made for establishing the link between Rabelais and Thomas Nashe, whose 1594 prose narrative, *The Unfortunate Traveler*, is generally considered to be the first novel written in the English language.

On the more familiar terrain of modern literature, French has continued to exert a powerful influence on English. In spite of the wonderfully ludicrous remark by Southey that poetry is as impossible in French as it is in Chinese, English and American poetry of the past hundred years would be inconceivable without the French. Beginning with Swinburne's 1862 article in *The Spectator* on Baudelaire's *Les Fleurs du Mal* and the first translations of Baudelaire's poetry into English in 1869 and 1870, modern British and American poets have continued to look to France for new ideas. Saintsbury's article in an 1875 issue of *The Fortnightly Review* is exemplary. "It was not merely admiration of Baudelaire which was to be persuaded to English readers," he wrote, "but also imitation of him which, at least with equal earnestness, was to be urged on English writers."

Throughout the 1870s and 1880s, largely inspired by Théodore de Banville, many English poets began experimenting with French verse forms (ballades, lays, virelays and rondeaux), and the "art for art's sake" ideas propounded by Gautier were an important source for the Pre-Raphaelite movement in England. By the 1890s, with the advent of *The Yellow Book* and the Decadents, the influence of the French Symbolists became widespread. In 1893, for example, Mallarmé was invited to lecture at Oxford, a sign of the esteem he commanded in English eyes.

It is also true that little of substance was produced in English as a result of French influences during this period, but the way was prepared for the discoveries of two young American poets, Pound and

Eliot, in the first decade of the new century. Each came upon the French independently, and each was inspired to write a kind of poetry that had not been seen before in English. Eliot would later write that "... the kind of poetry I needed, to teach me the use of my own voice, did not exist in England at all, and was only to be found in France." As for Pound, he stated flatly that "practically the whole development of the English verse-art has been achieved by steals from the French."

The English and American poets who formed the Imagist group in the years just prior to World War I were the first to engage in a *critical* reading of French poetry, with the aim not so much of imitating the French as of rejuvenating poetry in English. More or less neglected poets in France, such as Corbière and Laforgue, were accorded major status. F. S. Flint's 1912 article in *The Poetry Review* (London) and Ezra Pound's 1913 article in *Poetry* (Chicago) did much to promote this new reading of the French. Independent of the Imagists, Wilfred Owen spent several years in France before the war and was in close contact with Laurent Tailhade, a poet admired by Pound and his circle. Eliot's reading of the French poets began as early as 1908, while he was still a student at Harvard. Just two years later he was in Paris, reading Claudel and Gide and attending Bergson's lectures at the Collège de France.

By the time of the Armory show in 1913, the most radical tendencies in French art and writing had made their way to New York, finding a home with Alfred Stieglitz and his gallery at 291 Fifth Avenue. Many of the names associated with American and European modernism became part of this Paris-New York connection: Joseph Stella, Marsden Hartley, Arthur Dove, Charles Demuth, William Carlos Williams, Man Ray, Alfred Kreymborg, Marius de Zayas, Walter C. Arensberg, Mina Loy, Francis Picabia and Marcel Duchamp. Under the influence of Cubism and Dada, of Apollinaire and the Futurism of Marinetti, numerous magazines carried the message of modernism to American readers: *291, The Blind Man, Rongwrong, Broom, New York Dada,* and *The Little Review,* which was born in Chicago in 1914, lived in New York from 1917 to 1927, and died in Paris in 1929. To read the list of *The Little Review*'s contributors is to understand the degree to which French poetry had permeated the American scene. In addition to work by Pound, Eliot, Yeats and Ford Madox Ford, as well as its most celebrated contribution, James Joyce's *Ulysses,* the magazine published Breton, Éluard, Tzara, Péret, Reverdy, Crevel, Aragon and Soupault.

Beginning with Gertrude Stein, who arrived in Paris well before

World War I, the story of American writers in Paris during the twenties and thirties is almost identical to the story of American writing itself. Hemingway, Fitzgerald, Faulkner, Sherwood Anderson, Djuna Barnes, Kay Boyle, e e cummings, Hart Crane, Archibald MacLeish, Malcolm Cowley, John Dos Passos, Katherine Anne Porter, Laura Riding, Thornton Wilder, Williams, Pound, Eliot, Glenway Wescott, Henry Miller, Harry Crosby, Langston Hughes, James T. Farrell, Anäis Nin, Nathanael West, George Oppen — all of these and others either visited or lived in Paris. The experience of those years has so thoroughly saturated American consciousness that the image of the starving young writer serving his apprenticeship in Paris has become one of our enduring literary myths.

It would be absurd to assume that each of these writers was directly influenced by the French. But it would be just as absurd to assume that they went to Paris only because it was a cheap place to live. In the most serious and energetic magazine of the period, *transition*, American and French writers were published side by side, and the dynamics of this exchange led to what has probably been the most fruitful period in our literature. Nor does absence from Paris necessarily preclude an interest in things French. The most Francophilic of all our poets, Wallace Stevens, never set foot in France.

Since the twenties, American and British poets have been steadily translating their French counterparts — not simply as a literary exercise, but as an act of discovery and passion. Consider, for example, these words from John Dos Passos's preface to his translations of Cendrars in 1930: ". . . A young man just starting to read verse in the year 1930 would have a hard time finding out that this method of putting words together has only recently passed through a period of virility, intense experimentation and meaning in everyday life. . . . For the sake of this hypothetical young man and for the confusion of Humanists, stuffed shirts in editorial chairs, anthology compilers and prize poets, sonnet writers and readers of bookchats, I think it has been worth while to attempt to turn these alive informal personal everyday poems of Cendrars' into English . . ." Or T. S. Eliot, introducing his translation of *Anabasis* by Saint-John Perse that same year: "I believe that this is a piece of writing of the same importance as the later work of James Joyce, as valuable as *Anna Livia Plurabelle*. And this is a high estimate indeed." Or Kenneth Rexroth, in the preface to his translations of Reverdy in 1969: "Of all the modern poets in Western European languages Reverdy has certainly been the leading influence on my own work — incomparably more than anyone in English or American — and I have known and loved his work since I first read *Les Épaves du ciel* as a young boy."

As the list of translators included in this book shows, many of the most important contemporary American and British poets have tried their hand at translating the French, among them Pound, Williams, Eliot, Stevens, Beckett, MacNeice, Spender, Ashbery, Blackburn, Bly, Kinnell, Levertov, Merwin, Wright, Tomlinson, Wilbur — to mention just some of the most familiar names. It would be difficult to imagine their work had they not been touched in some way by the French. And it would be even more difficult to imagine the poetry of our own language if these poets had not been a part of it. In a sense, then, this anthology is as much about American and British poetry as it is about French poetry. Its purpose is not only to present the work of French poets in French, but to offer translations of that work as our own poets have re-imagined and re-presented it. As such, it can be read as a chapter in our own poetic history.

II

The French tradition and the English tradition in this epoch are at opposite poles to each other. French poetry is more radical, more total. In an absolute and exemplary way it has assumed the heritage of European Romanticism, a romanticism which begins with William Blake and the German romantics like Novalis, and via Baudelaire and the Symbolists culminates in twentieth-century French poetry, notably Surrealism. It is a poetry where the world becomes writing and language becomes the double of the world.

Octavio Paz

On the other hand, this much is also certain: If there has been a steady interest in French poetry for the past hundred years on the part of British and American poets, enthusiasm for the French has often been tempered by a certain wariness, even hostility, to literary and intellectual practices in France. This has been more true of the British than the Americans, but, nevertheless, the American literary establishment remains strongly Anglophilic in orientation. One has only to compare the dominant trends in philosophy, literary criticism, or novel-writing, to realize the enormous gulf between the two cultures.

Many of these differences reside in the disparities between the two languages. Although English is in large part derived from French, it still holds fast to its Anglo-Saxon origins. Against the gravity and substantiality to be found in the work of our greatest poets (Milton, say, or Emily Dickinson), which embodies an awareness of the contrast between the thick emphasis of Anglo-Saxon and the nimble conceptuality of French/Latin — and to play one repeatedly against the other — French poetry often seems almost weightless to us, to be composed of ethereal puffs of lyricism and little else. French is necessarily a thinner medium than English. But that does not mean it is weaker. If English writing has staked out as its territory the world of tangibility, of concrete presence, of surface accident, French literary language has largely been a language of essences. Whereas Shakespeare, for example, names more than five hundred flowers in his plays, Racine adheres to the single word "flower". In all, the French dramatist's vocabulary consists of roughly fifteen hundred words, while the word count in Shakespeare's plays runs upward of twenty-five thousand. The contrast, as Lytton Strachey noted, is between "comprehension" and "concentration." "Racine's great aim," Strachey wrote, "was to produce, not an extraordinary nor a complex work of art, but a flawless one; he wished to be all matter and no impertinence. His conception of a drama was of something swift, inevitable; an action taken at the crisis, with no redundancies however interesting, no complications however suggestive, no irrelevances however beautiful — but plain, intense, vigorous, and splendid with nothing but its own essential force." More recently, the poet Yves Bonnefoy has described English as a "mirror" and French as a "sphere," the one Aristotelian in its acceptance of the given, the other Platonic in its readiness to hypothesize "a different reality, a different realm."

Samuel Beckett, who has spent the greater part of his life writing in both languages, translating his own work from French into English and from English into French, is no doubt our most reliable witness to the capacities and limitations of the two languages. In one of his letters from the mid-fifties, he complained about the difficulty he was having in translating *Fin de partie* (*Endgame*) into English. The line Clov addresses to Hamm, "Il n'y a plus de roues de bicyclette" was a particular problem. In French, Beckett contended, the line conveyed the meaning that bicycle wheels as a category had ceased to exist, that there were no more bicycle wheels in the world. The English equivalent, however, "There are no more bicycle wheels," meant simply that there were no more bicycle wheels available, that no bicycle wheels could be found in the place where they happened to be. A world of difference is embedded here beneath apparent similarity. Just as the Eskimos have more than twenty words for snow (a frequently cited example), which means they are able to experience snow in ways far more nuanced and elaborate than we are — literally to see things we cannot see — the French live inside their language in ways that are somewhat at odds with the way we live inside English. There is no judgment of any kind attached to this remark. If bad French poetry tends to drift off into almost mechanical abstractions, bad English and American poetry has tended to be too earthbound and leaden, sinking into triviality and inconsequence. Between the two bads there is probably little to choose from. But it is helpful to remember that a good French poem is not necessarily the same thing as a good English poem.

The French have had their Academy for more than three hundred years. It is an institution that at once expresses and helps to perpetuate a notion of literature far more grandiose than anything we have ever known in England or America. As an official point of view, it has had the effect of removing the literary from the realm of the everyday, whereas English and American writers have generally been more at home in the flux of the quotidian. But because they have an established tradition to react against, French poets — paradoxically — have tended to be more rebellious than their British and American counterparts. The pressures of conformity have had the net result of producing a vigorous anti-tradition, which in many ways has actually usurped the established tradition as the major current in French literature. Beginning with Villon and Rabelais, continuing on through Rousseau, Baudelaire, Rimbaud, and the cult of the *poète maudit*, and then on into the twentieth century with Apollinaire, the Dada movement, and the Surrealists, the French have systematically and defiantly attacked the accepted notions of their own culture — primarily because they have been secure in their knowledge that this culture exists. The lessons of this anti-tradition have been so thoroughly assimilated that today they are more or less taken for granted.

By contrast, the great interest shown by Pound and Eliot in French poetry (and, in Pound's case, the poetry of other languages as well) can be read not so much as an attack on Anglo-American culture as an effort to create a tradition, to manufacture a past that would somehow fill the vacuum of American newness. The impulse was essentially conservative in nature. With Pound, it degenerated into Fascist rantings; with Eliot, into Anglican pieties and an obsession with the notion of Culture. It would be wrong, however, to set up a simple dichotomy between radicalism and conservatism, and to put all things French in the first category and all things English and American in the second. The most subversive and innovative elements of our literature have frequently surfaced in the unlikeliest places and have then been absorbed into the culture at large. Nursery rhymes, which form an essential part of every English-speaking child's early education, do not exist as such in France. Nor do the great works of Victorian children's literature (Lewis Carroll, George Macdonald) have any equivalent in French. As for America, it has always had its own, homegrown Dada spirit, which has continued to exist as a natural force, without any need of manifestoes or theoretical foundations. The films of Buster Keaton and W.C. Fields, the skits of Ring Lardner, the drawings of Rube Goldberg surely match the corrosive exuberance of anything done in France during the same period. As Man Ray (a native American) wrote to Tristan Tzara from New York in 1921 about spreading the Dada movement to America: "Cher Tzara — Dada cannot live in New York. All New York is Dada, and will not tolerate a rival . . ."

Nor should one assume that twentieth-century French poetry is sitting out there as a convenient, self-contained entity. Far from being a unified body of work that resides neatly within the borders of France, French poetry of this century is various, tumultuous and contradictory. There is no typical case — only a horde of exceptions. For the fact is, a great number of the most original and influential poets were either born in other countries or spent a substantial part of their lives abroad. Apollinaire was born in Rome of mixed Polish and Italian parentage; Milosz was Lithuanian; Segalen spent his most productive years in China; Cendrars was born in Switzerland, composed his first major poem in New York, and until he was over fifty rarely stayed in France long enough to collect his mail; Saint-John Perse was born in Guadeloupe, worked for many years in Asia as a diplomat and lived almost exclusively in Washington, D.C. from 1941 until his death in 1975; Supervielle was from Uruguay and for most of his life divided his time between Montevideo and Paris; Tzara was born in Rumania and came to Paris by way of the Dada adventures at the Cabaret Voltaire in Zurich, where he frequently played chess with Lenin; Jabès was born in Cairo and lived in Egypt until he was forty-five; Césaire is from

Martinique; du Bouchet is part American and was educated at Amherst and Harvard; and nearly all the younger poets in this book have stayed for extended periods in either England or America. The stereotypical view of the French poet as a creature of Paris, as a xenophobic purveyor of French values, simply does not hold. The more intimately one becomes involved with the work of these poets, the more reluctant one becomes to make any generalizations about them. In the end, the only thing that can be said with any certainty is that they all write in French.

An anthology, therefore, is a kind of trap, tending to thwart our access to the poems even as it makes them available to us. By gathering the work of so many poets in one volume, the temptation is to consider the poets as a group, to drown them as individuals in the great pot of literature. Thus, even before it is read, the anthology becomes a kind of cultural dinner, a smattering of national dishes served up on a platter for popular consumption, as if to say, "Here is French poetry. Eat it. It's good for you." To approach poetry in that way is to miss the point entirely — for it allows one to avoid looking squarely at the poem on the page. And that, after all, is the reader's primary obligation. One must resist the notion of treating an anthology as the last word on its subject. It is no more than a first word, a threshold opening on to a new space.

III

In the end you are weary of this ancient world.

Guillaume Apollinaire

The logical place to begin this book is with Apollinaire. Although he is neither the first-born of the poets included nor the first to have written in a consciously modern idiom, he, more than any other artist of his time, seems to embody the aesthetic aspirations of the early part of the century. In his poetry, which ranges from graceful love lyrics to bold experiments, from rhyme to free verse to "shape" poems, he manifests a new sensibility, at once indebted to the forms of the past and enthusiastically at home in the world of automobiles, airplanes and movies. As the tireless promoter of the Cubist painters, he was the figure around whom many of the best artists and writers gathered, and poets such as Jacob, Cendrars and Reverdy formed an important part of his circle. The work of these three, along with Apollinaire's, has frequently been described as Cubist. While there are vast differences among them, both in methods and tone, they nevertheless share a certain point of view, especially in the epistemogolical foundations of the work. Simultaneity, juxtaposition, an acute feeling for the jaggedness of the real — these are traits to be found in all four, and each exploits them to different poetic ends.

Cendrars, at once more abrasive and voluptuous than Apollinaire, observed that "everything around me moves," and his work oscillates between the two solutions implicit in this statement: on the one hand, the ebullient jangle of sensations in works such as *Nineteen Elastic Poems*, and on the other the snapshot realism of his travel poems (originally entitled *Kodak* but changed, under pressure from the film company of the same name, to *Documentaires*) — as if each of these poems was the record of a single moment, lasting no longer than it takes to click the shutter of a camera. With Jacob, whose most enduring work is contained in his 1917 collection of prose poems, *The Dice Cup*, the impulse is toward an anti-lyrical comedy. His language is continually erupting into playfulness (puns, parody, satire) and takes its greatest delight in unmasking the deceptions of appearances: Nothing is ever what it seems to be, everything is subject to metamorphosis, and change always occurs unexpectedly, with lightning swiftness.

Reverdy, by contrast, uses many of these same principles, but with far more somber objectives. Here an accumulation of fragments is synthesized into an entirely new approach to the poetic image. "The image is a pure creation of the mind," wrote Reverdy in 1918. "It cannot be born from a comparison but from a juxtaposition of two more or less distant realities. The more the relationship between the two juxtaposed realities is both distant and true, the stronger the image will be — the greater its emotional power and poetic reality." Reverdy's strange landscapes, which combine an intense inwardness with a proliferation of sensual data, bear in them the signs of a continual search for an impossible totality. Almost mystical in their effect, his poems are nevertheless anchored in the minutiae of the everyday world; in their quiet, at times monotone music, the poet seems to evaporate, to vanish into the haunted country he has created. The result is at once beautiful and disquieting — as if Reverdy had emptied the space of the poem in order to let the reader inhabit it.

A similar atmosphere is sometimes produced by the prose poems of Fargue, whose work predates that of any other poet included here.

Fargue is the supreme modern poet of Paris, and fully half his writings are about the city itself. In his delicate, lyrical configurations of memory and perception, which retain an echo of their Symbolist predecessors, there is an attentiveness to detail combined with a rigorous subjectivity that transforms the city into an immense interior landscape. The poem of witness is at the same time a poem of remembrance, as if, in the solitary act of seeing, the world were reflected back to its solitary source and then, once more, reflected outward as vision. With Larbaud, a close friend of Fargue's, one also finds a hint of the late nineteenth century. A. O. Barnabooth, the supposed author of Larbaud's finest book of poems (in the first edition of 1908 Larbaud's name was intentionally left off the title page), is a rich South American of twenty-four, a naturalized citizen of New York, an orphan, a world traveler, a highly sensitive and melancholy young man — a more sympathetic and humorous version of the traditional dandy hero. As Larbaud later explained, he wanted to invent a poet "sensitive to the diversity of races, people, and countries; who could find the exotic everywhere . . .; witty and 'international,' one, in a word, capable of writing like Whitman but in a light vein, and of supplying that note of comic, joyous irresponsibility which is lacking in Whitman." As in the poems of Apollinaire and Cendrars, Larbaud-Barnabooth expresses an almost euphoric delight in the sensations of travel: "I experienced for the first time all the joy of living / In a compartment of the Nord-Express . . ." Of Barnabooth André Gide wrote: "I love his haste, his cynicism, his gluttony. These poems, dated from here and there, and everywhere, are as thirst-making as a wine list . . . In this particular book, each picture of sensation, no matter how correct or dubious it may be, is made valid by the speed with which it is supplanted."

The work of Saint-John Perse also bears a definite resemblance to that of Whitman — both in the nature of his stanza and in the rolling, cumulative force of his long syntactic breaths. If Larbaud in some sense domesticates Whitman, Saint-John Perse carries him beyond universalism into a quest for great cosmic harmonies. The voice of the poet is mythical in its scope, as if, with its thunderous and sumptuous rhetoric, it had come into being for the sole purpose of conquering the world. Unlike most of the poets of his generation, who made their peace with temporality and used the notion of change as the premise of their work, Saint-John Perse's poems are quickened by an almost Platonic urge to seek out the eternal. In this respect, Milosz also stands to the side of his contemporaries. A student of the mystics and the alchemists, Milosz combines Catholicism and cabalism with what Kenneth Rexroth has described as "apocalyptic sensualism," and his work draws much of its inspiration from numerological treatment of names, transpositions of letters, anagrammatic and acronymic combinations, and other linguistic practices of the occult. But, as with the poems of Yeats, the poetry itself transcends the restrictions of its sources, displaying, as John Peck has commented, "an obsessive range of feeling, in which personal melancholy is also melancholy for a crepuscular era, that long hour before first light 'when the shadows decompose.' "

Another poet who resists categorization is Segalen. Like Larbaud, who wrote his poems through an invented persona; like Pound, whose translations stand curiously among his best and most personal works, Segalen carried this impulse toward self-effacement one step further and wrote behind the mask of another culture. The poems to be found in *Stèles* are neither translations nor imitations, but French poems written by a French poet *as if he were Chinese*. There is no attempt to deceive on Segalen's part; he never pretended these poems were anything other than original works. What at first reading might appear to be a kind of literary exoticism on closer scrutiny holds up as a poetry of solid, universal interest. By freeing himself from the limitations of his own culture, by circumventing his own historical moment, Segalen was able to explore a much wider territory — to discover, in some sense, that part of himself that was a poet.

In many ways, the case of Jouve is no less unusual. A follower of the Symbolists as a young man, Jouve published a number of books of poetry between 1912 and 1923. What he described as a "moral, spiritual, and aesthetic crisis" in 1924 led him to break with all his early work, which he never allowed to be republished. Over the next forty years he produced a voluminous body of writing — his collected poems run well over a thousand pages. Deeply Christian in outlook, Jouve is primarily concerned with the question of sexuality, both as transgression and as creative force — "the beautiful power of human eroticism" — and his poetry is the first in France to have made use of the methods of Freudian psychoanalysis. It is a poetry without predecessors and without followers. If his work was somewhat forgotten during the period dominated by the Surrealists — which meant that recognition of Jouve's achievement was delayed for almost a generation — he is now widely considered to be one of the major poets of the half-century.

Supervielle was also influenced by the Symbolists as a young man, and of all the poets of his generation he is perhaps the most purely lyrical. A poet of space, of the natural world, Supervielle writes from a position of supreme innocence. "To dream is to forget the materiality of one's body," he wrote in 1951, "and to confuse to some degree the outer and the inner world . . . People are sometimes surprised over my marvelling at the world. This arises as much from the permanency of my dreams as from my bad memory. Both lead me from surprise to surprise, and force me to be amazed at everything."

It is this sense of amazement, perhaps, that best describes the work of these first eleven poets, all of whom began writing before World War I. The poets of the next generation, however, who came of age during the war itself, were denied the possibility of such innocent optimism. The war was not simply a conflict between armies, but a profound crisis of values that transformed European consciousness, and the younger poets, while having absorbed the lessons of Apollinaire and his contemporaries, were compelled to respond to this crisis in ways that were without precedent. As Hugo Ball, one of the founders of Dada, noted in his diary in 1917: "A thousand-year-old culture disintegrates. There are no columns and no supports, no foundations anymore — they have all been blown up . . . The meaning of the world has disappeared."

The Dada movement, which began in Zurich in 1916, was the most radical response to this sense of spiritual collapse. In the face of a discredited culture, the Dadaists challenged every assumption and ridiculed every belief of that culture. As artists, they attacked the notion of art itself, transforming their rage into a kind of subversive doubt, filled with caustic humor and willful self-contradiction. "The true Dadaists are against Dada," wrote Tzara in one of his manifestoes. The point was never to take anything at face value and never to take anything too seriously — especially oneself. The Socratic ironies of Marcel Duchamp's art are perhaps the purest expression of this attitude. In the realm of poetry, Tzara was no less sly or rambunctious. This is his recipe for writing a Dada poem: "Take a newspaper. Take a pair of scissors. Select an article as long as you want your poem to be. Cut out the article. Then carefully cut out each of the words that form this article and put them in a bag. Shake gently. Then take out each scrap, one after the other. Conscientiously copy them in the order they left the bag. The poem will resemble you. And there you are, an infinitely original writer, with a charming sensibility, beyond the understanding of the vulgar." If this is a poetry of chance, it should not be confused with the aesthetics of aleatory composition. Tzara's proposed method is an assault on the sanctity of Poetry, and it does not attempt to elevate itself to the status of an artistic ideal. Its function is purely negative. This is anti-art in its earliest incarnation, the "anti-philosophy of spontaneous acrobatics."

Tzara moved to Paris in 1919, introducing Dada to the French scene. Breton, Aragon, Éluard and Soupault all became participants in the movement. Inevitably, it did not last more than a few years. An art of total negation cannot survive, for its destructiveness must ultimately include itself. It was by drawing on the ideas and attitudes of Dada, however, that Surrealism became possible. "Surrealism is pure psychic automatism," Breton wrote in his first manifesto of 1924, "whose intention is to express, verbally, in writing, or by other means, the real process of thought and thought's dictation, in the absence of all control exercised by reason and outside all aesthetic or moral preoccupations. Surrealism rests on the belief in the superior reality of certain previously neglected forms of association; in the omnipotence of dream, and in the disinterested play of thought."

Like Dada, Surrealism did not offer itself as an aesthetic movement. Equating Rimbaud's cry to change life with Marx's injunction to change the world, the Surrealists sought to push poetry, in Walter Benjamin's phrase, "to the utmost limits of possibility." The attempt was to demystify art, to blur the distinctions between life and art, and to use the methods of art to explore the possibilities of human freedom. To quote Walter Benjamin again, from his prescient essay on the Surrealists published in 1929: "Since Bakunin, Europe has lacked a radical concept of freedom. The Surrealists have one. They are the first to liquidate the liberal-moral-humanistic ideal of freedom, because they are convinced that 'freedom, which on this earth can only be bought with a thousand of the hardest sacrifices, must be enjoyed unrestrictedly in its fullness, without any kind of programmatic calculation, as long as it lasts.' " For this reason, Surrealism associated itself closely with the politics of revolution (one of its magazines was even entitled *Surrealism in the Service of the Revolution*), flirting continually with the Communist Party and playing the role of fellow traveler during the era of the Popular Front — although refusing to submerge its identity in that of pure politics. Constant disputes over principles marked the history of the Surrealists, with Breton holding the middle ground between the activist and aesthetic wings of the group, frequently shifting positions in an effort to maintain a consistent program for Surrealism. Of all the poets associated with the movement, only Péret remained faithful to Breton over the long term. Soupault, by nature averse to the notion of literary movements, lost interest by 1927. Both Artaud and Desnos were excommunicated in 1929 — Artaud for opposing Surrealism's interest in politics and Desnos for supposedly compromising his integrity by working as a journalist. Aragon, Tzara and Éluard all joined the Communist Party in the thirties. Queneau and Prévert parted amicably after a brief association. Daumal, whose work was recognized by Breton as sharing the preoccupations of the Surrealists, declined an invitation to join the group. Char, ten or twelve years younger than most of the original members, was an early adherent but later broke with the movement and went on to do his best work during and after the war. Ponge's connection was peripheral, and Michaux, in some sense the most Surrealist of all French poets, never had anything to do with the group.

This same confusion exists when one examines the work of these poets. If "pure psychic automatism" is the underlying principle of Surrealist composition, only Péret seems to have stuck to it rigorously in the writing of his poems. Interestingly, his work is the least resonant of all the Surrealists — notable more for its comic effects than for any uncovering of the "convulsive beauty" that Breton envisaged as the goal of Surrealist writing. Even in Breton's poetry, with its abrupt shifts and unexpected associations, there is an undercurrent of consistent rhetoric that makes the poems cohere as densely reasoned objects of thought. With Tzara as well, automatism serves almost as a rhetorical device. It is a method of discovery, not an end in itself. In his best work — especially the long, multifaceted *Approximate Man* — a torrent of images organizes itself into a nearly systematic argument by means of repetition and variation, propelling itself forward in the manner of a musical composition.

Soupault, on the other hand, is clearly a conscious craftsman. While limited in range, his poetry displays a charm and a humility absent in the work of the other Surrealists. He is a poet of intimacy and pathos, at times strangely reminiscent of Verlaine, and if his poems have none of the flamboyance to be found in Tzara and Breton, they are more immediately accessible, more purely lyrical. By the same token, Desnos is a poet of plain speech, whose work often achieves a stunning lyrical intensity. His output extends from early experiments with language (dexterous, often dazzling exercises in word play) to free-verse love poems of great poignancy to longer, narrative poems and works in traditional forms. In an essay published just one year before his death, Desnos described his work as an effort "to fuse popular language, even the most colloquial, with an inexpressible 'atmosphere'; with a vital use of imagery, so as to annex for ourselves those domains which . . . remain incompatible with that fiendish, plaguing poetic dignity which endlessly oozes from tongues . . ."

With Éluard, arguably the greatest of the Surrealist poets, the love poem is accorded metaphysical status. His language, as limpid as anything to be found in Ronsard, is built on syntactic structures of extreme simplicity. Éluard uses the idea of love in his work to mirror the poetic process itself — as a way both to escape the world and to understand it. It is that irrational part of man which weds the inner to the outer, rooted in the physical and yet transcending matter, creating that uniquely human place in which man can discover his freedom. These same themes are present in Éluard's later work, particularly the poems written during the German Occupation, in which this notion of freedom is carried from the realm of the individual to that of an entire people.

If Éluard's work can be read as a continuous whole, Aragon's career as a poet divides into two distinct periods. Perhaps the most militant and provocative of the French Dadaists, he also played a leading role in the development of Surrealism and, after Breton, was the group's most active theorist. Attacked by Breton in the early thirties for the increasingly propagandist tone of his poetry, Aragon withdrew from the movement and joined the Communist Party. It was not until the war that he returned to the writing of poetry — and in a manner that bears almost no relation to his earlier work. His Resistance poems brought him national fame, and they are distinguished by their force and eloquence, but in their methods they are highly traditional, composed for the most part in alexandrines and rhyming stanzas.

Although Artaud was an early participant in Surrealism (for a time he even headed The Central Bureau for Surrealist Research) and although a number of his most important works were written during that period, he is a writer who stands so defiantly outside the traditional norms of literature that it is useless to label his work in any way. Properly speaking, Artaud is not a poet at all, and yet he has probably had a greater influence on the poets who came after him than any other writer of his generation. "Where others present their works," he wrote, "I claim to do no more than show my mind." His aim as a writer was never to create aesthetic objects — works that could be detached from their creator — but to record the state of mental and physical struggle in which "words rot at the unconscious summons of the brain." There is no division in Artaud between life and writing — and life not in the sense of biography, of external events, but life as it is lived in the intimacy of the body, of the blood that flows through one's veins. As such, Artaud is a kind of Ur-poet, whose work describes the processes of thought and feeling before the advent of language, before the possibility of speech. It is at once a cry of suffering and a challenge to all our assumptions about the purpose of literature.

In a totally different way from Artaud, Ponge also commands a unique place among the writers of his generation. He is a writer of supremely classical values, and his work — most of it has been written in prose — is pristine in its clarity, highly sensitive to nuance and the etymological origins of words, which Ponge has described as the "semantical thickness" of language. Ponge has invented a new kind of writing, a poetry of the object that is at the same time a method of contemplation. Minutely detailed in its descriptions, and everywhere infused with a fine ironic humor, his work proceeds as though the object being examined did not exist as a word. The primary act of the poet, therefore, becomes the act of seeing, as if no one had ever seen the thing before, so that the object might have "the good fortune to be born into words."

Like Ponge, who has frequently resisted the efforts of critics to classify him as a poet, Michaux is a writer whose work escapes the strictures of genre. Floating freely between prose and verse, his texts have a spontaneous, almost haphazard quality that sets them against the pretensions and platitudes of high art. No French writer has ever given greater rein to the play of his imagination. Much of his best writing is set in imaginary countries and reads as a bizarre kind of anthropology of inner states. Although often compared to Kafka, Michaux does not resemble the author of Kafka's novels and stories so much as the Kafka of the notebooks and parables. As with Artaud, there is an urgency of process in Michaux's writing, a sense of personal risk and necessity in the act of composition. In an early statement about his poetry he declared: "I write with transport and for myself. a) sometimes to liberate myself from an intolerable tension or from a no less painful abandonment. b) sometimes for an imaginary companion, for a kind of alter ego whom I would honestly like to keep up-to-date on an extraordinary transition in me or in the world, which I, ordinarily forgetful, all at once believe I rediscover in, so to speak, its virginity. c) deliberately to shake the congealed and established, to invent . . . Readers trouble me. I write, if you like, for the unknown reader."

An equal independence of approach is present in Daumal, a serious student of Eastern religions, whose poems deal obsessively with the rift between spiritual and physical life. "The Absurd is the purest and most basic form of metaphysical existence," he wrote, and in his dense, visionary work, the illusions of appearance fall away only to be transformed into further illusions. "The poems are haunted by a . . . consciousness of impending death," Michael Benedikt has commented, "seen as the poet's long-lost 'double'; and also by a personification of death as a sort of sinister mother, an exacting being avaricious in her search for beings to extinguish — but only so as to place upon them perversely the burden of further metamorphoses."

Daumal is considered one of the chief precursors of the "College of Pataphysics," a mock-secret literary organization inspired by Alfred Jarry that included both Queneau and Prévert among its members. Humor is the guiding principle in the work of these two poets. With Queneau, it is a linguistic humor, based on intricate word plays, parody, feigned stupidity and slang. In his well-known prose work of 1947, for example, *Exercices de style*, the same mundane event is given in ninety-nine different versions, each one written in a different style, each one presented from a different point of view. In discussing Queneau in *Writing Degree Zero*, Roland Barthes describes this style as "white writing" — in which literature, for the first time, has openly become a problem and question of language. If Queneau is an intellectual poet, Prévert, who also adheres closely to the patterns of ordinary speech in his work, is without question a popular poet — even a populist poet. Since World War II, no one has had a wider audience in France, and many of Prévert's works have been turned into highly successful songs. Anticlerical, antimilitaristic, rebellious in political attitude and extolling a rather sentimentalized form of love between man and woman, Prévert represents one of the more felicitous marriages between poetry and mass culture, and beyond the charm of his work, it is valuable as an indicator of popular French taste.

Although Surrealism continues to exist as a literary movement, the period of its greatest influence and most important creations came to an end by the beginning of World War II. Of the second-generation

Surrealists — or those poets who found inspiration in its methods — Césaire stands out as the most notable example. One of the first black writers to be recognized in France, founder of the *négritude* movement — which asserts the uniqueness and dignity of black culture and consciousness — Césaire, a native of Martinique, was championed by Breton, who discovered his work in the late thirties. As the South African poet Mazisi Kunene has written about Césaire: "Surrealism was for him a logical instrument with which to smash the restrictive forms of language which sanctified rationalized bourgeois values. The breaking up of language patterns coincided with his own desire to smash colonialism and all oppressive forms." More vividly perhaps than in the work of the Surrealists of France, Césaire's poetry embodies the twin aspirations of political and aesthetic revolution, and in such a way that they are inseparably joined.

For many of the poets who began writing in the thirties, however, Surrealism was never a temptation. Follain, for example, whose work has proved to be particularly amenable to American taste (of all recent French poets, he is the one who has been most frequently translated), is a poet of the everyday, and in his short, exquisitely crafted works one finds an examination of the object no less serious and challenging than Ponge's. At the same time, Follain is largely a poet of memory ("In the fields / of his eternal childhood / the poet wanders / wanting to forget nothing"), and his evocations of the world as seen through a child's eyes bear within them a shimmering, epiphanic quality of psychological truth. A similar kind of realism and attention to surface detail is also to be found in Guillevic. Materialist in his approach to the world, unrhetorical in his methods, Guillevic has also created a world of objects — but one in which the object is nevertheless problematical, a reality to be penetrated, to be striven for, but which is not necessarily given. Frénaud, on the other hand, although often grouped together with Follain and Guillevic, is a far more romantic poet than his two contemporaries. Effusive in his language, metaphysical in his concerns, he has been compared at times to the Existentialists in his insistence that man's world is a creation of man himself. Despairing of certainty (*There Is No Paradise*, reads the title of one of his collections), Frénaud's work draws its force not so much from a recognition of the absurd as from the attempt to find a basis for positive values within the absurd itself.

If World War I was the crucial event that marked the poetry of the twenties and thirties, World War II was no less decisive in determining the kind of poetry written in France during the late forties and fifties. The military defeat of 1940 and the Nazi Occupation that followed were among the darkest moments in French history. The country had been devastated both emotionally and economically. In the context of this disarray, the mature poetry of René Char came as a revelation. Aphoristic, fragmented, closely allied to the thought of Heraclitus and the pre-Socratics, Char's poetry is at once a lyrical summoning of natural correspondences and a meditation on the poetic process itself. Austere in its settings (for the most part the landscape is that of Char's native Provence) and roughly textured in its language, this is a poetry that does not attempt to record or evoke feelings so much as it seeks to embody the ongoing struggle of words to ground themselves in the world. Char writes from a position of deep existential commitment (he was an important field leader in the Resistance), and his work is permeated with a sense of new beginnings, of a necessary search to rescue life from the ruins.

The best poets of the immediate postwar generation share many of these same preoccupations. Bonnefoy, du Bouchet, Jaccottet, Giroux and Dupin, all born within four years of one another, manifest in their work a vigilant hermeticism that is characterized by a consciously reduced range of imagery, great syntactical inventiveness and a refusal to ask anything but essential questions. Bonnefoy, the most classical and philosophically oriented of the five, has largely been concerned in his work with tracking the reality that haunts "the abyss of concealed appearances." "Poetry does not interest itself in the shape of the world itself," he once remarked, "but in the world that this universe will become. Poetry speaks only of presences — or absences." Du Bouchet, by contrast, is a poet who shuns every temptation toward abstraction. His work, which is perhaps the most radical adventure in recent French poetry, is based on a rigorous attentiveness to phenomenological detail. Stripped of metaphor, almost devoid of imagery, and generated by a language of abrupt, paratactic brevity, his poems move through an almost barren landscape, a speaking "I" continually in search of itself. A du Bouchet page is the mirror of this journey, each one dominated by white space, the few words present as if emerging from a silence that will inevitably claim them again.

Of these poets, it is undoubtedly Dupin whose work holds the greatest verbal richness. Tightly sprung, calling upon an imagery that seethes with hidden violence, his poems are dazzling in both their energy and their anguish. "In this infinite unanimous dissonance," he writes, in a poem entitled "Lichens," "each ear of corn, each drop of blood, speaks its language and goes its way. The torch, which lights the abyss, which seals it up, is itself an abyss." Far gentler in approach are both Jaccottet and Giroux. Jaccottet's short nature poems, which in certain ways adhere to the aesthetics of Imagism, have an Oriental stillness about them that can flare at any moment into the brightness of epiphany. "For us living more and more surrounded by intellectual schemas and masks," Jaccottet has written, "and suffocating in the prison they erect around us, the poet's eye is the battering ram that knocks down these walls and gives back to us, if only for an instant, the real; and with the real, a possibility of life." Giroux, a poet of great lyrical gifts, died prematurely in 1973 and published only one book during his lifetime. The short poems in that volume are quiet, deeply meditated works about the nature of poetic reality, explorations of the space between the world and words, and they have had a considerable impact on the work of many of today's younger poets.

This hermeticism, however, is by no means present in the work of all the poets of the postwar period. Dadelsen, for example, is an effusive poet, monologic and varied in tone, who frequently launches into slang. There have been a number of distinguished Catholic poets in France during the twentieth century (La Tour du Pin, Emmanuel, Jean-Claude Renard and Mambrino are recent examples), but it is perhaps Dadelsen, less well known than the others, who in his tormented search for God best represents the limits and perils of religious consciousness. Marteau, on the other hand, draws much of his imagery from myth, and although his preoccupations often overlap with those of, say, Bonnefoy or Dupin, his work is less self-reflective than theirs, dwelling not so much on the struggles and paradoxes of expression as on uncovering the presence of archetypal forces in the world.

Of the new work that began to appear in the early sixties, the books of Jabès are the most notable. Since 1963, when *The Book of Questions* was published, Jabès has brought out ten volumes in a remarkable series of works, prompting comments such as Jacques Derrida's statement that "in the last ten years nothing has been written in France that does not have its precedent somewhere in the texts of Jabès." Jabès, an Egyptian Jew who published a number of books of poetry in the forties and fifties, has emerged as a writer of the first rank with his more recent work — all of it written in France after his expulsion from Cairo during the Suez crisis. These books are almost impossible to define. Neither novels nor poems, neither essays nor plays, they are a combination of all these forms, a mosaic of fragments, aphorisms, dialogues, songs and commentaries that endlessly move around the central question posed by each book: How to speak what cannot be spoken. The question is the Holocaust, but it is also the question of literature itself. By a startling leap of the imagination, Jabès treats them as one and the same: "I have talked to you about the difficulty of being Jewish, which is the same as the difficulty of writing. For Judaism and writing are but the same waiting, the same hope, the same wearing out."

This determination to carry poetry into uncharted territory, to break down the standard distinctions between prose and verse, is perhaps the most striking characteristic of the younger generation of poets today. In Deguy, for example, poetry can be made from just about anything at all, and his work draws on a broad range of material: from the technical language of science to the abstractions of philosophy to elaborate play on linguistic constructions. In Roubaud, the quest for new forms has led to books of highly intricate structures (one of his volumes, Σ, is based on the permutations of the Japanese game of go), and these invented shapes are exploited with great deftness, serving not as ends in themselves but as a means of ordering the fragments they encompass, of putting the various pieces in a larger context and investing them with a coherence they would not possess on their own.

Pleynet and Roche, two poets closely connected with the well-known review *Tel Quel*, have each carried the notion of antipoetry to a position of extreme combativeness. Pleynet's jocular, and at the same time deadly serious "Ars Poetica" of 1964, is a good example of this attitude. "I. ONE CANNOT KNOW HOW TO WRITE WITHOUT KNOWING WHY. II. THE AUTHOR OF THIS ARS POETICA DOES NOT KNOW HOW TO WRITE BUT HE WRITES. III. THE QUESTION 'HOW TO WRITE' ANSWERS THE QUESTION 'WHY WRITE' AND THE QUESTION 'WHAT IS WRITING'. IV. A QUESTION IS AN ANSWER." Roche's approach is perhaps even more disruptive of conventional assumptions about literature. "Poetry is inadmissible. Besides, it does not exist," he has written. And elsewhere: ". . . the logic of modern writing demands that one should take a vigorous hand in promoting the death agonies of [this] symbolist, outmoded ideology. Writing can only symbolize what it is in its functioning, in its 'society', within the frame of its utilization. It must stick to that."

This is not to say, however, that short, lyric poems do not continue to be written in France. Delahaye and Denis, both still in their thirties, have created substantial bodies of work in this more familiar mode — mining a landscape that had first been mapped out by du Bouchet and Dupin. On the other hand, many of the younger poets, having absorbed and transmuted the questions raised by their predecessors, are now producing a kind of work that is both original and demanding in its insistence upon the textuality of the written word. Although there are significant differences among Albiach, Royet-Journoud, Daive, Hocquard and Veinstein, in one fundamental aspect of their work they share a common point of view. Their medium as writers is neither the individual poem nor even the sequence of poems, but the book. As Royet-Journoud stated in a recent interview: "My books consist only of a single text, the genre of which cannot be defined. . . . It's a *book* that I write, and I feel that the notion of genre obscures the book as such." This is as true of Daive's highly charged, psycho-erotic work, Hocquard's graceful and ironic narratives of memory, and Veinstein's minimal theaters of the creative process as it is of Royet-Journoud's obsessive "detective stories" of language. Most strikingly, this approach to composition can be found in Albiach's 1971 volume, *État*, undoubtedly the major work to be published thus far by a member of this younger generation. As Keith Waldrop has written: "The poem — it is a single piece — does not progress by images . . . or by plot. . . . The argument, if it were given, might include the following propositions: 1) everyday language is dependent on logic, but 2) in fiction, there is no necessity that any particular word should follow any other, so 3) it is possible at least to imagine a free choice, a syntax generated by desire. *État* is the 'epic' . . . of this imagination. To state such an argument . . . would be to renounce the whole project. But what is presented is not a series of emotions . . . the poem is composed mindfully; and if Anne-Marie Albiach rejects rationality, she quite obviously writes with full intelligence . . ."

IV

. . . with the conviction that, in the end, translating is madness.

Maurice Blanchot

As I was about to embark on the project of editing this anthology, a friend gave me a piece of valuable advice. Jonathan Griffin, who served as British cultural attaché in Paris after the war, and has translated several books by De Gaulle, as well as poets ranging from Rimbaud to Pessoa, has been around long enough to know more about such things than I do. Every anthology, he said, has two types of readers: the critics, who judge the book by what is *not* included in it, and the general readers, who read the book for what it actually contains. He advised me to keep this second group uppermost in my thoughts. The critics, after all, are in business to criticize, and they are familiar with the material anyway. The important thing to remember is that most people will be reading the majority of these poets for the first time. They are the ones who will get the most out of the anthology.

During the two years it has taken for me to put this book together, I have often reminded myself of these words. Frequently, however, it has been difficult to take them to heart, since I myself am all too aware of what has not been included. My original plan for the anthology was to represent the work of almost a hundred poets. In addition to more familiar kinds of writing, I had wanted to use a number of eccentric works, provide examples of concrete and sound poetry, include several collaborative poems and, in a few instances, offer variant translations when more than one good version of a poem was available. As work progressed, it became apparent that this would not be possible. I was faced with the unhappy situation of trying to fit an elephant into a cage designed for a fox. Reluctantly, I changed my approach to the book. If my choice was between offering a smattering of poems by many poets or substantial selections of work by a reduced number of poets, there did not seem to be much doubt that the second solution was wiser and more coherent. Instead of imagining everything I would like to see in the anthology, I tried to think of the poets it would be inconceivable *not* to include. In this way, I gradually whittled the list down to forty-eight. These were difficult decisions for me, and though I stand by my final selection, it is with regret for those I was not able to include.*

There are no doubt some who will also wonder about certain other exclusions. In order to keep the book focused on poetry of the

* Among them are the following: Pierre Albert-Birot, Jean Cocteau, Raymond Roussel, Jean Arp, Francis Picabia, Arthur Cravan, Michel Leiris, Georges Bataille, Léopold Senghor, André Pieyre de Mandiargues, Jacques Audiberti, Jean Tardieu, Georges Schéhadé, Pierre Emmanuel, Joyce Mansour, Patrice de la Tour du Pin, René Guy Cadou, Henri Pichette, Christian Dotremont, Olivier Larronde, Henri Thomas, Jean Grosjean, Jean Tortel, Jean Laude, Pierre Torreilles, Jean-Claude Renard, Jean Joubert,

twentieth century, I decided on a fixed cutoff point to determine where the anthology should begin. The crucial year for my purposes turned out to be 1876: Any poet born before that year would not be considered. This allowed me, in good conscience, to forgo the problem posed by poets such as Valéry, Claudel, Jammes and Péguy, all of whom began writing in the late nineteenth century and went on writing well into the twentieth. Although their work overlaps chronologically with many of the poets in the book, it seems to belong in spirit to an earlier time. By the same token, 1876 was a convenient date for allowing me to include certain poets whose work is essential to the project — Fargue, Jacob and Milosz in particular.

As for the English versions of the poems, I have used already existing translations whenever possible. My motive has been to underscore the involvement, over the past fifty years, of American and British poets in the work of their French counterparts, and since there is abundant material to choose from (some of it hidden away in old magazines and out-of-print books, some of it readily available), there seemed to be no need to begin my search elsewhere. My greatest pleasure in putting this book together has been in rescuing a number of superb translations from the obscurity of library shelves and microfilm rooms: Nancy Cunard's Aragon, John Dos Passos' Cendrars, Paul Bowles's Ponge, and the translations by Eugene and Maria Jolas (the editors of *transition*), to mention just a few. Also to be noted are the translations that previously existed only in manuscript. Paul Blackburn's translations of Apollinaire, for example, were discovered among his papers after his death, and are published here for the first time.

Only in cases where translations did not exist or where the available translations seemed inadequate did I commission fresh translations. In each of these instances (Richard Wilbur's version of Apollinaire's "Le Pont Mirabeau," Lydia Davis's Fargue, Robert Kelly's Roubaud, Anselm Hollo's Dadelsen, Michael Palmer's Hocquard, Rosmarie Waldrop's Veinstein, Geoffrey Young's Aragon), I have tried to arrange the marriage with care. My aim was to bring together compatible poets — so that the translator would be able to exploit his particular strengths

---

Jacques Réda, Armen Lubin, Jean Pérol, Jude Stéfan, Marc Alyn, Jacqueline Risset, Michel Butor, Jean Pierre Faye, Alain Jouffroy, George Perros, Armand Robin, Boris Vian, Jean Mambrino, Lorand Gaspar, Georges Badin, Pierre Oster, Bernard Nöel, Claude Vigée, Joseph Gugliemi, Daniel Blanchard, Michel Couturier, Claude Esteban, Alain Sueid, Mathieu Bénézet.

as a poet in rendering the original into English. The results of this matchmaking have been uniformly satisfying. Richard Wilbur's "Mirabeau Bridge," for instance, strikes me as the first acceptable version of this important poem we have had in English, the only translation that comes close to re-creating the subtle music of the original.

In general, I have followed no consistent policy about translation in making my choices. A few of the translations are hardly more than adaptations, although the vast majority are quite faithful to the originals. Translating poetry is at best an art of approximation, and there are no fixed rules to follow in deciding what works or does not. It is largely a matter of instinct, of ear, of common sense. Whenever I was faced with a choice between literalness and poetry, I did not hesitate to choose poetry. It seemed more important to me to give those readers who have no French a true sense of each poem *as a poem* than to strive for word-by-word exactness. The experience of a poem resides not only in each of its words, but in the interactions among those words — the music, the silences, the shapes — and if a reader is not somehow given the chance to enter the totality of that experience, he will remain cut off from the spirit of the original. It is for this reason, it seems to me, that poems should be translated by poets.

1981

Mallarmé's Son

Mallarmé's second child, Anatole, was born on July 16, 1871, when the poet was twenty-nine. The boy's arrival came at a moment of great financial stress and upheaval for the family. Mallarmé was in the process of negotiating a move from Avignon to Paris, and arrangements were not finally settled until late November, when the family installed itself at 29 rue de Moscou and Mallarmé began teaching at the Lycée Fontanes.

Mme Mallarmé's pregnancy had been extremely difficult, and in the first months of his life Anatole's health was so fragile that it seemed unlikely he would survive. "I took him out for a walk on Thursday," Mme Mallarmé wrote to her husband on October 7. "It seemed to me that his fine little face was getting back some of its color . . . I left him very sad and discouraged, and even afraid that I would not see him anymore, but it's up to God now, since the doctor can't do anything more, but how sad to have so little hope of seeing this dear little person recover."

Anatole's health, however, did improve. Two years later, in 1873, he reappears in the family correspondence in a series of letters from Germany, where Mallarmé's wife had taken the children to meet her father. "The little one is like a blossoming flower," she wrote to Mallarmé. "Tole loves his grandfather, he does not want to leave him, and when he is gone, he looks for him all over the house." In that same letter, nine-year-old Geneviève added: "Anatole asks for papa all the time." Two years later, on a second trip to Germany, there is further evidence of Anatole's robust health, for after receiving a letter from his wife, Mallarmé wrote proudly to his friend Cladel: "Anatole showers stones and punches on the little Germans who come back to attack him in a group." The following year, 1876, Mallarmé was absent from Paris for a few days and received this anecdote from his wife: "Totol is a bad little boy. He did not notice you were gone the night you left; it was only when I put him to bed that he looked everywhere for you to say good-night. Yesterday he did not ask for you, but this morning the poor little fellow looked all over the house for you; he even pulled back the covers on your bed, thinking he would find you there." In August of that same year, during another of Mallarmé's brief absences from the family, Geneviève wrote to her father to thank him for sending her presents and then remarked: "Tole wants you to bring him back a whale."

Beyond these few references to Anatole in the Mallarmé family letters, there are several mentions of him in C. L. Lefèvre-Roujon's introduction to the *Correspondance inédite de Stephane Mallarmé et Henry Roujon* — in particular, three little incidents that give some idea of the boy's lively personality. In the first, a stranger saw Anatole attending to his father's boat and asked him, "What is your boat called?" Anatole answered with great conviction, "My boat isn't called anything. Do you give a name to a carriage?" On another occasion, Anatole was taking a walk through the Fountainebleau forest with Mallarmé. "He loved the Fountainebleau forest and would often go there with Stéphane. . . . [One day], running down a path, he came upon a very pretty woman, politely stepped to the side, looked her over from top to bottom and, out of admiration, winked his eye at her, clicked his tongue, and then, this homage to beauty having been made, continued on his child's promenade." Finally, Lefèvre-Roujon reports the following: One day Mme Mallarmé boarded a Paris bus with Anatole and put the child on her lap in order to economize on the extra fare. As the bus jolted along, Anatole fell into a kind of trance, watching a gray-haired priest beside him who was reading his breviary. He asked him sweetly: "Monsieur l'abbée, would you allow me to kiss you?" The priest, surprised and touched, answered: "But of course, my little friend." Anatole leaned over and kissed him. Then, in the suavest voice possible, he commanded: "And now, kiss mama!"

In the spring of 1879, several months before his eighth birthday, Anatole became seriously ill. The disease, diagnosed as child's rheumatism, was further complicated by an enlarged heart. The illness first attacked his feet and knees, and then, when the symptoms had apparently cleared up, his ankles, wrists, and shoulders. Mallarmé considered himself largely responsible for the child's suffering, feeling that he had given the boy "bad blood" through a hereditary weakness. At the age of seventeen, he had suffered terribly from rheumatic pain, with high fevers and violent headaches, and throughout his life rheumatism would remain a chronic problem.

In April, Mallarmé went off to the country for a few days with Geneviève. His wife wrote: "He's been a good boy, the poor little martyr, and from time to time asks me to dry his tears. He asks me often to tell little papa that he would like to write to him, but he can't move his little wrists." Three days later, the pain had shifted from Anatole's hand to his legs, and he was able to write a few words: "I think of you always. If you knew, my dear Little Father, how my knees hurt."

Over the following months, things took a turn for the better. By August, the improvement had been considerable. On the tenth, Mallarmé wrote to Robert de Montesquiou, a recently made friend who had formed a special attachment to Anatole, to thank him for sending the child a parrot. "I believe that your delicious little animal . . . has distracted the illness of our patient, who is now allowed to go to the country. . . . Have you heard from where you are . . . all the cries of joy from our invalid, who never takes his eyes . . . away from the marvelous princess held captive in her marvelous palace, who is called Sémiramas because of the stone gardens she seems to reflect? I like to think that this satisfaction of an old and improbable desire has had something to do with the struggle of the boy's health to come back; to say nothing . . . of the secret influence of the precious stone that darts out continually from the cage's inhabitant on the child. . . . How charming and friendly you have been, you who are so busy with so much, during this recent time; and it is more than a pleasure for me to announce to you, before anyone else, that I feel all our worries will soon be over."

In this state of optimism, Anatole was taken by the family to Valvins in the country. After several days, however, his condition deteriorated drastically, and he nearly died. On August 22, Mallarmé wrote to his close friend Henry Roujon:

"I hardly dare to give any news because there are moments in this war between life and death that our poor little adored one is waging when I allow myself to hope, and repent of a too sad letter written the moment before, as of some messenger of bad tidings I myself have dispatched. I know nothing anymore and see nothing anymore . . . so much have I observed with conflicting emotions. The doctor, while continuing the Paris treatment, seems to act as though he were dealing with a condemned person who can only be comforted; and persists, when I follow him to the door, in not giving a glimmer of hope. The dear boy eats and sleep a little; breathes. Everything his organs could do to fight the heart problem they have done; after another enormous attack, that is the benefit he draws from the country. But the disease, the terrible disease, seems to have set in irremediably. If you lift the blanket, you see a belly so swollen you can't look at it!

"There it is. I do not speak to you of my pain; no matter where my thought tries to lead it, this pain recoils from seeing itself worsen! But what does suffering matter, even suffering like that: the horrible thing is . . . the misfortune in itself that this little being might vanish. . . . I confess that it is too much for me; I cannot bring myself to face this idea.

"When my wife looks at the darling, she seems to see a serious illness and nothing more; I must not rob her of the courage she has found to care for the child in this quietude. I am alone here then with the hatchet blow of the doctor's verdict."

A letter from Mallarmé to Montesquiou on September 9 offers further details: "Unfortunately, after several days [in the country], everything . . . grew dark: we have been through the cruelest hours our darling invalid has caused us, for the symptoms we thought had disappeared forever have returned; they are taking hold now. The old improvements were a sham. . . . I am too tormented and too taken up with our poor little boy to do anything literary, except to jot down a few rapid notes. . . . *Tole* speaks of you, and even amuses himself in the morning by fondly imitating your voice. The parrot, whose auroral belly seems to catch fire with a whole orient of spices, is looking right now at the forest with one eye and at the bed with the other, like a thwarted desire for an excursion by her little master."

By late September there had been no improvement, and Mallarmé now centered his hopes on a return to Paris. On the twenty-fifth, he wrote to his oldest friend, Henri Cazalis: "The evening before your beautiful present came, the poor darling, for the second time since his illness began, was nearly taken from us. Three successive fainting fits in the afternoon did not, thank heaven, carry him off. . . . The belly disturbs us, as filled with water as ever. . . . The country has given us everything we could ask of it, assuming it could give us anything, milk, air, and peaceful surroundings for the invalid. We have only one idea now, to leave for a consultation with Doctor Peter. . . . I tell myself it is impossible that a great medical specialist cannot take advantage of the forces nature opposes so generously to a terrible disease. . . ."

After the return to Paris, there are two further letters about Anatole — both dated October 6. The first was to the English writer John Payne: "This is the reason for my long silence. . . . At Easter, already six hideous months ago, my son was attacked by rheumatism, which after a false convalescence has thrown itself on his poor heart with incredible violence, and holds him between life and death. The poor friend has twice almost been taken from us. . . . You can judge of our pain, knowing how much I live inside my family; then this child, so charming and exquisite, had captivated me to the point that I still include him in all my future projects and in my dearest dreams. . . ."

The other letter was to Montesquiou. "Thanks to immense precautions, everything went well [on the return to Paris] . . . but the darling paid for it with several bad days that drained his tiny energy. He is prey to a horrible and inexplicable nervous cough . . . it shakes him for a whole day and a whole night. . . . — Yes, I am quite beside myself, like someone on whom a terrible and endless wind is blowing. All-night vigils, contradictory emotions of hope and sudden fear, have supplanted all thought of repose. . . . My sick little boy smiles at you from his bed, like a white flower remembering the vanished sun."

After writing these two letters, Mallarmé went to the post office to mail them. Anatole died before his father managed to return home.

*

The 202 fragments that follow belonged to Mme E. Bonniot, the Mallarmé heir, and were deciphered, edited, and published in a scrupulously prepared volume by the literary scholar and critic Jean-Pierre Richard in 1961. In the preface to his book — which includes a lengthy study of the fragments — he describes his feelings on being handed the soft red box that contained Mallarmé's notes. On the one hand: exaltation. On the other hand: wariness. Although he was deeply moved by the fragments, he was uncertain whether publication was appropriate, given the intensely private nature of the work. He concluded, however, that anything that could enhance our understanding of Mallarmé would be valuable. "And if these phrases are no more than sighs," he wrote, "that makes them all the more precious to us. It seemed to me that the very nakedness of these notes . . . made their distribution desirable. It was useful in fact to prove once again to what extent the famous Mallarméan serenity was based on the impulses of a very vivid sensibility, at times even quite close to frenzy and delirium. . . . Nor was it irrelevant to show, by means of a precise example, how this impersonality, this vaunted objectivity, was in reality connected to the most subjective upheavals of a life."

A close reading of the fragments will clearly show that they are no more than notes for a possible work: a long poem in four parts with a series of very specific themes. That Mallarmé projected such a work and then abandoned it is indicated in a memoir written by Geneviève that was published in a 1926 issue of the *N.R.F.*: "In 1879, we had the immense sorrow of losing my little brother, an exquisite child of eight. I was quite young then, but the deep and silent pain I felt in my father made an unforgettable impression on me: 'Hugo,' he said, 'was happy to have been able to speak (about the death of his daughter); for me, it's impossible.' "

As they stand now, the notes are a kind of ur-text, the raw data of the poetic process. Although they seem to resemble poems on the page, they should not be confused with poetry per se. Nevertheless, more than one hundred years after they were written, they are perhaps closer to what we today consider possible in poetry than at the time of their composition. For here we find a language of immediate contact, a syntax of abrupt, lightning shifts that still manages to maintain a sense, and in their brevity, the sparse presence of their words, we are given a rare and early example of isolate words able to span the enormous mental spaces that lie between them — as if intelligible links could be created by the brute force of each word or phrase, so densely charged that these tiny particles of language could somehow leap out of themselves and catch hold of the succeeding cliff-edge of thought. Unlike Mallarmé's finished poems, these fragments have a startlingly unmediated quality. Faithful not to the demands of art but to the jostling movement of thought — and with a speed and precision that astonish — these notes seem to emerge from such an interior place, it is as though we could hear the crackling of the wires in Mallarmé's brain, experience each synapse of thought as a physical sensation. If these fragments cannot be read as a work of art, neither, I think, should they be treated simply as a scholarly appendage to Mallarmé's collected writings. For, in spite of everything, the Anatole notes do carry the force of poetry, and in the end they achieve a stunning wholeness. They are a work in their own right — but one that cannot be categorized, one that does not fit into any preexistent literary form.

The subject matter of the fragments requires little comment. In general, Mallarmé's motivation seems to have been the following: feeling himself responsible for the disease that led to Anatole's death, for not giving his son a body strong enough to withstand the blows of life, he would take it upon himself to give the boy the one indomitable thing he was capable of giving: his thought. He would transmute Anatole into words and thereby prolong his life. He would, *literally*, resurrect him, since the work of building a tomb — a tomb of poetry — would obliterate the presence of death. For Mallarmé, death is the consciousness of death, not the physical act of dying. Because Anatole was too young to understand his fate (a theme that occurs repeatedly throughout the fragments), it was as though he had not yet died. He was still alive in his father, and it was only when Mallarmé himself died that the boy would die as well. This is one of the most moving accounts of a man trying to come to grips with modern death — that is to say, death without God, death without hope of salvation — and it reveals the secret meaning of Mallarmé's entire aesthetic: the elevation of art to the stature of religion. Here, however, the work could not be written. In this time of crisis even art failed Mallarmé.

It strikes me that the effect of the Anatole fragments is quite close to the feeling created by Rembrandt's last portrait of his son, Titus. Bearing in mind the radiant and adoring series of canvases the artist made of the boy throughout his childhood, it is almost impossible for us to look at that last painting: the dying Titus, barely twenty years old, his face so ravaged by disease that he looks like an old man. It is important to imagine what Rembrandt must have felt as he painted that portrait; to imagine him staring into the face of his dying son and being able to keep his hand steady enough to put what he saw onto the canvas. If fully imagined, the act becomes almost unthinkable.

In the natural order of things, fathers do not bury their sons. The death of a child is the ultimate horror of every parent, an outrage against all we believe we can expect of life, little though it is. For everything, at that point, is taken away from us. Unlike Ben Jonson, who could lament the fact of his fatherhood as an impediment to understanding that his son had reached "the state he should envie," Mallarmé could find no support for himself, only an abyss, no consolation, except in the plan to write about his son — which, in the end, he could not bring himself to do. The work died along with Anatole. It is all the more moving to us, all the more important, for having been left unfinished.

1982

On the High Wire

The first time I saw Philippe Petit was in 1971. I was in Paris, walking down the Boulevard Montparnasse, when I came upon a large circle of people standing silently on the sidewalk. It seemed clear that something was happening inside that circle, and I wanted to know what it was. I elbowed my way past several onlookers, stood on my toes, and caught sight of a smallish young man in the center. Everything he wore was black: his shoes, his pants, his shirt, even the battered silk top hat he wore on his head. The hair jutting out from under the hat was a light red-blond, and the face below it was so pale, so devoid of color, that at first I thought he was in whiteface.

The young man juggled, rode a unicycle, performed little magic tricks. He juggled rubber balls, wooden clubs, and burning torches, both standing on the ground and sitting on his one-wheeler, moving from one thing to the next without interruption. To my surprise, he did all this in silence. A chalk circle had been drawn on the sidewalk, and scrupulously keeping any of the spectators from entering that space — with a persuasive mime's gesture — he went through his performance with such ferocity and intelligence that it was impossible to stop watching.

Unlike other street performers, he did not play to the crowd. Rather, it was somehow as though he had allowed the audience to share in the workings of his thoughts, had made us privy to some deep, inarticulate obsession within him. Yet there was nothing overtly personal about what he did. Everything was revealed metaphorically, as if at one remove, through the medium of the performance. His juggling was precise and self-involved, like some conversation he was holding with himself. He elaborated the most complex combinations, intricate mathematical patterns, arabesques of nonsensical beauty, while at the same time keeping his gestures as simple as possible. Through it all, he managed to radiate a hypnotic charm, oscillating somewhere between demon and clown. No one said a word. It was as though his silence were a command for others to be silent as well. The crowd watched, and after the performance was over, everyone put money in the hat. I realized that I had never seen anything like it before.

The next time I saw Philippe Petit was several weeks later. It was late at night — perhaps one or two in the morning — and I was walking along a quai of the Seine not far from Nôtre-Dame. Suddenly, across the street, I spotted several young people moving quickly through the darkness. They were carrying ropes, cables, tools, and heavy satchels. Curious as ever, I kept pace with them from my side of the street and recognized one of them as the juggler from the Boulevard Montparnasse. I knew immediately that something was going to happen. But I could not begin to imagine what it was.

The next day, on the front page of the *International Herald Tribune*, I got my answer. A young man had strung a wire between the towers of Nôtre-Dame Cathedral and walked and juggled and danced on it for three hours, astounding the crowds of people below. No one knew how he had rigged up his wire nor how he had managed to elude the attention of the authorities. Upon returning to the ground, he had been arrested, charged with disturbing the peace and sundry other offenses. It was in this article that I first learned his name: Philippe Petit. There was not the slightest doubt in my mind that he and the juggler were the same person.

This Nôtre-Dame escapade made a deep impression on me, and I continued to think about it over the years that followed. Each time I walked past Nôtre-Dame, I kept seeing the photograph that had been published in the newspaper: an almost invisible wire stretched between the enormous towers of the cathedral, and there, right in the middle, as if suspended magically in space, the tiniest of human figures, a dot of life against the sky. It was impossible for me not to add this remembered image to the actual cathedral before my eyes, as if this old monument of Paris, built so long ago to the glory of God, had been transformed into something else. But what? It was difficult for me to say. Into something more human, perhaps. As though its stones now bore the mark of a man. And yet, there was no real mark. I had made the mark with my own mind, and it existed only in memory. And yet, the evidence was irrefutable: my perception of Paris had changed. I no longer saw it in the same way.

It is, of course, an extraordinary thing to walk on a wire so high off the ground. To see someone do this triggers an almost palpable excitement in us. In fact, given the necessary courage and skill, there are probably very few people who would not want to do it themselves. And yet, the art of high-wire walking has never been taken very seriously.

Because wire walking generally takes place in the circus, it is automatically assigned marginal status. The circus, after all, is for children, and what do children know about art? We grownups have more important things to think about. There is the art of music, the art of painting, the art of sculpture, the art of poetry, the art of prose, the art of theater, the art of dancing, the art of cooking, the art of living. But the art of high-wire walking? The very term seems laughable. If people stop to think about the high-wire at all, they usually categorize it as some minor form of athletics.

There is, too, the problem of showmanship. I mean the crazy stunts, the vulgar self-promotion, the hunger for publicity that is everywhere around us. We live in an age when people seem willing to do anything for a little attention. And the public accepts this, granting notoriety or fame to anyone brave enough or foolish enough to make the effort. As a general rule, the more dangerous the stunt, the greater the recognition. Cross the ocean in a bathtub, vault forty burning barrels on a motorcycle, dive into the East River from the top of the Brooklyn Bridge, and you are sure to get your name in the newspapers, maybe even an interview on a talk show. The idiocy of these antics is obvious. I'd much rather spend my time watching my son ride his bicycle, training wheels and all.

Danger, however, is an inherent part of high-wire walking. When a man walks on a wire two inches off the ground, we do not respond in the same way as when he walks on a wire two hundred feet off the ground. But danger is only half of it. Unlike the stuntman, whose performance is calculated to emphasize every hair-raising risk, to keep his audience panting with dread and an almost sadistic anticipation of disaster, the good high-wire walker strives to make his audience forget the dangers, to lure it away from thoughts of death by the beauty of what he does on the wire itself. Working under the greatest possible constraints, on a stage no more than an inch across, the high-wire walker's job is to create a sensation of limitless freedom. Juggler, dancer, acrobat, he performs in the sky what other men are content to perform on the ground. The desire is at once far-fetched and perfectly natural, and the appeal of it, finally, is its utter uselessness. No art, it seems to me, so clearly emphasizes the deep aesthetic impulse inside us all. Each time we see a man walk on the wire, a part of us is up there with him. Unlike performances in the other arts, the experience of the high wire is direct, unmediated, simple, and it requires no explanation whatsoever. The art is the thing itself, a life in its most naked delineation. And if there is beauty in this, it is because of the beauty we feel inside ourselves.

There was another element of the Nôtre-Dame spectacle that moved me: the fact that it was clandestine. With the thoroughness of a bank robber preparing a heist, Philippe had gone about his business in silence. No press conferences, no publicity, no posters. The purity of it was impressive. For what could he possibly hope to gain? If the wire had snapped, if the installation had been faulty, he would have died. On the other hand, what did success bring? Certainly he did not earn any money from the venture. He did not even try to capitalize on his brief moment of glory. When all was said and done, the only tangible result was a short stay in a Paris jail.

Why did he do it, then? For no other reason, I believe, than to dazzle the world with what he could do. Having seen his stark and haunting juggling performance on the street, I sensed intuitively that his motives were not those of other men — not even those of other artists. With an ambition and an arrogance fit to the measure of the sky, and placing on himself the most stringent internal demands, he wanted, simply, to do what he was capable of doing.

After living in France for four years, I returned to New York in July of 1974. For a long time I had heard nothing about Philippe Petit, but the memory of what had happened in Paris was still fresh, a permanent part of my inner mythology. Then, just one month after my return, Philippe was in the news again — this time in New York, with his now-famous walk between the towers of the World Trade Center. It was good to know that Philippe was still dreaming his dreams, and it made me feel that I had chosen the right moment to come home. New York is a more generous city than Paris, and the people here responded enthusiastically to what he had done. As with the aftermath of the Nôtre-Dame adventure, however, Philippe kept faith with his vision. He did not try to cash in on his new celebrity; he managed to resist the honky-tonk temptations America is all too willing to offer. No books were published, no films were made, no entrepreneur took hold of him for packaging. The fact that the World Trade Center did not make him rich was almost as remarkable as the event itself. But the proof of this was there for all New Yorkers to see: Philippe continued to make his living by juggling in the streets.

The streets were his first theater, and he still takes his performances there as seriously as his work on the wire. It all started very early for him. Born into a middle-class French family in 1949, he taught himself magic at the age of six, juggling at the age of twelve, and high-wire walking a few years later. In the meantime, while immersing himself in such varied activities as horseback riding, rock-climbing, art, and carpentry, he managed to get himself expelled from nine schools. At sixteen, he began a period of incessant travels all over the world, performing as a street juggler in Western Europe, Russia, India, Australia, and the United States. "I learned to live by my wits," he has said of those years. "I offered juggling shows everywhere, for everyone — traveling around like a troubadour with my old leather sack. I learned to escape the police on my unicycle. I got hungry like a wolf; I learned how to control my life."

But it is on the high-wire that Philippe has concentrated his most important ambitions. In 1973, just two years after the Nôtre-Dame walk, he did another renegade performance in Sydney, Australia: stretching his wire between the northern pylons of the Harbour Bridge, the largest steel arch bridge in the world. Following the World Trade Center Walk in 1974, he crossed the Great Falls of Paterson, New Jersey, appeared on television for a walk between the spires of the Cathedral in Laon, France, and also crossed the Superdome in New Orleans before 80,000 people. This last performance took place just nine months after a forty-foot fall from an inclined wire, from which he suffered several broken ribs, a collapsed lung, a shattered hip, and a smashed pancreas.

Philippe has also worked in the circus. For one year he was a featured attraction with Ringling Brothers Barnum and Bailey, and from time to time he has served as a guest performer with The Big Apple Circus in New York. But the traditional circus has never been the right place for Philippe's talents, and he knows it. He is too solitary and unconventional an artist to fit comfortably into the strictures of the commercial big top. Far more important to him are his plans for the future: to walk across Niagara Falls; to walk from the top of the Sydney Opera House to the top of the Harbour Bridge — an inclined walk of more than half a mile. As he himself explains it: "To talk about records or risks is to miss the point. All my life I have looked for the most amazing places to cross — mountains, waterfalls, buildings. And if the most beautiful walks also happen to be the longest or most dangerous — that's fine. But I didn't look for that in the first place. What interests me is the performance, the show, the beautiful gesture."

When I finally met Philippe in 1980, I realized that all my feelings about him had been correct. This was not a daredevil or a stuntman, but a singular artist who could talk about his work with intelligence and humor. As he said to me that day, he did not want people to think of him as just another "dumb acrobat." He talked about some of the things he had written — poems, narratives of his Nôtre-Dame and World Trade Center adventures, film scripts, a small book on high-wire walking — and I said that I would be interested in seeing them. Several days later, I received a bulky package of manuscripts in the mail. A covering note explained that these writings had been rejected by eighteen different publishers in France and America. I did not consider this to be an obstacle. I told Philippe that I would do all I could to find him a publisher and also promised to serve as translator if necessary. Given the pleasure I had received from his performances on the street and wire, it seemed the least I could do.

On the High-Wire is in my opinion a remarkable book. Not only is it the first study of high-wire walking ever written, but it is also a personal testament. One learns from it both the art and the science of wire walking, the lyricism and the technical demands of the craft. At the same time, it should not be misconstrued as a "how to" book or an instruction manual. High-wire walking cannot really be taught: it is something you learn by yourself. And certainly a book would be the last place to turn if you were truly serious about doing it.

The book, then, is a kind of parable, a spiritual journey in the form of a treatise. Through it all, one feels the presence of Philippe himself: it is his wire, his art, his personality that inform the entire discourse. No one else, finally, has a place in it. This is perhaps the most important lesson to be learned from the treatise: the high-wire is an art of solitude, a way of coming to grips with one's life in the darkest, most secret corner of the self. When read carefully, the book is transformed into the story of a quest, an exemplary tale of one man's search for perfection. As such, it has more to do with the inner life than the high-wire. It seems to me that anyone who has ever tried to do something well, anyone who has ever made personal sacrifices for an art or an idea, will have no trouble understanding what it is about.

Until two months ago, I had never seen Philippe perform on the high-wire outdoors. A performance or two in the circus, and of course films and photographs of his exploits, but no outdoor walk in the flesh. I finally got my chance during the recent inauguration ceremony at the Cathedral of Saint John the Divine in New York. After a hiatus of several decades, construction was about to begin again on the cathedral's tower. As a kind of homage to the wire walkers of the Middle Ages — the *joglar* from the period of the great French cathedrals — Philippe had conceived of the idea of stretching a steel cable from the top of a tall apartment building on Amsterdam Avenue to the top of the Cathedral across the street — an inclined walk of several hundred yards. He would go from one end to the other and then present the Bishop of New York with a silver trowel, which would be used to lay the symbolic first stone of the tower.

The preliminary speeches lasted a long time. One after the other, dignitaries got up and spoke about the Cathedral and the historic moment that was about to take place. Clergymen, city officials, former Secretary of State Cyrus Vance — all of them made speeches. A large crowd had gathered in the street, mostly school children and neighborhood people, and it was clear that the majority of them had come to see Philippe. As the speeches droned on, there was a good deal of talking and restlessness in the crowd. The late September weather was threatening: a raw, pale gray sky; the wind beginning to rise; rain clouds gathering in the distance. Everyone was impatient. If the speeches went on any longer, perhaps the walk would have to be canceled.

Fortunately, the weather held, and at last Philippe's turn came. The area below the cable had to be cleared of people, which meant that those who a moment before had held center stage were now pushed to the side with the rest of us. The democracy of it pleased me. By chance, I found myself standing shoulder to shoulder with Cyrus Vance on the steps of the Cathedral. I, in my beat-up leather jacket, and he in his impeccable blue suit. But that didn't seem to matter. He was just as excited as I was. I realized later that at any other time I might have been tongue-tied to be standing next to such an important person. But none of that even occurred to me then. We talked about the high-wire and the dangers Philippe would have to face. He seemed to be genuinely in awe of the whole thing and kept looking up at the wire — as I did, as did the hundreds of children around us. It was then that I understood the most important aspect of the high wire: it reduces us all to our common humanity. A Secretary of state, a poet, a child: we became equal in each other's eyes, and therefore a part of each other.

A brass band played a Renaissance fanfare from some invisible place behind the Cathedral facade, and Philippe emerged from the roof of the building on the other side of the street. He was dressed in a white satin medieval costume, the silver trowel hanging from a sash at his side. He saluted the crowd with a graceful, bravura gesture, took hold of his balancing-pole firmly in his two hands, and began his slow ascent along the wire. Step by step, I felt myself walking up there with him, and gradually those heights seemed to become habitable, human, filled with happiness. He slid down to one knee and acknowledged the crowd again; he balanced on one foot; he moved deliberately and majestically, exuding confidence. Then, suddenly, he came to a spot on the wire far enough away from his starting-point that my eyes lost contact with all surrounding references: the apartment building, the street, the other people. He was almost directly overhead now, and as I leaned backward to take in the spectacle, I could see no more than the wire, Philippe, and the sky. There was nothing else. A white body against a nearly white sky, as if free. The purity of that image burned itself into my mind and is still there today, wholly present.

From beginning to end, I did not once think that he might fall. Risk, fear of death, catastrophe: these were not part of the performance. Philippe had assumed full responsibility for his own life, and I sensed that nothing could possibly shake that resolve. High-wire walking is not an art of death, but an art of life—and life lived to the very extreme of life. Which is to say, life that does not hide from death, but stares it straight in the face. Each time he sets foot on the wire, Philippe takes hold of that life and lives it in all its exhilarating immediacy, in all its joy.

May he live to be a hundred.

1982

Translator's Note

This is one of the saddest stories I know. If not for a minor miracle that occurred twenty years after the fact, I doubt that I would have been able to summon the courage to tell it.

It begins in 1972. I was living in Paris at the time, and because of my friendship with the poet Jacques Dupin (whose work I had translated), I was a faithful reader of *L'Éphémère*, a literary magazine financed by the Galerie Maeght. Jacques was a member of the editorial board—along with Yves Bonnefoy, André du Bouchet, Michel Leiris, and, until his death in 1970, Paul Celan. The magazine came out four times a year, and with a group like that responsible for its contents, the work published in *L'Éphémère* was always of the highest quality.

The twentieth and final issue appeared in the spring, and among the usual contributions from well-known poets and writers, there was an essay by an anthropologist named Pierre Clastres, "De l'Un sans le Multiple" ("Of the One Without the Many"). Just seven pages long, it made an immediate and lasting impression on me. Not only was the piece intelligent, provocative, and tightly argued, it was beautifully written. Clastres's prose seemed to combine a poet's temperament with a philosopher's depth of mind, and I was moved by its directness and humanity, its utter lack of pretension. On the strength of those seven pages, I realized that I had discovered a writer whose work I would be following for a long time to come.

When I asked Jacques who this person was, he explained that Clastres had studied with Claude Lévi-Strauss, was still under forty, and was considered to be the most promising member of the new generation of anthropologists in France. He had done his fieldwork in the jungles of South America, living among the most primitive stone-age tribes in Paraguay and Venezuela, and a book about those experiences was about to be published. When *Chronique des Indiens Guayaki* appeared a short time later, I went out and bought myself a copy.

It is, I believe, nearly impossible not to love this book. The care and patience with which it is written, the incisiveness of its observations, its humor, its intellectual rigor, its compassion—all these qualities reinforce one another to make it an important, memorable work. The *Chronicle* is not some dry academic study of "life among the savages," not some report from an alien world in which the reporter neglects to take his own presence into account. It is the true story of a man's experiences, and it asks nothing but the most essential questions: how is information communicated to an anthropologist, what kinds of transactions take place between one culture and another, under what circumstances might secrets be kept? In delineating this unknown civilization for us, Clastres writes with the cunning of a good novelist. His attention to detail is scrupulous and exacting; his ability to synthesize his thoughts into bold, coherent statements is often breathtaking. He is that rare scholar who does not hesitate to write in the first person, and the result is not just a portrait of the people he is studying, but a portrait of himself.

I moved back to New York in the summer of 1974, and for several years after that I tried to earn my living as a translator. It was a difficult struggle, and most of the time I was barely able to keep my head above water. Because I had to take whatever I could get, I often found myself accepting assignments to work on books that had little or no value. I wanted to translate good books, to be involved in projects that felt worthy, that would do more than just put bread on the table. *Chronicle of the Guayaki Indians* was at the top of my list, and again and again I proposed it to the various American publishers I worked for. After countless rejections, I finally found someone who was interested. I can't remember exactly when this was. Late 1975 or early 1976, I think, but I could be off by half a year or so. In any case, the publishing company was new, just getting off the ground, and all the preliminary indications looked good. Excellent editors, contracts for a number of outstanding books, a willingness to take risks. Not long before that, Clastres and I had begun exchanging letters, and when I wrote to tell him the news, he was just as thrilled as I was.

Translating the *Chronicle* was a thoroughly enjoyable experience for me, and after my labors were done, my attachment to the book was just as ardent as ever. I turned in the manuscript to the publisher, the translation was approved, and then, just when everything seemed to have been brought to a successful conclusion, the troubles started.

It seems that the publishing company was not as solvent as the world had been led to believe. Even worse, the publisher himself was a good deal less honest in his handling of money than he should have been. I know this for a fact because the money that was supposed to pay for my translation had been covered by a grant to the company by the CNRS (the French National Scientific Research Center), but when I asked for my money, the publisher hemmed and hawed and promised that I would have it in due course. The only explanation was that he had already spent the funds on something else.

I was desperately poor in those days, and waiting to be paid simply wasn't an option for me. It was the difference between eating and not eating, between paying the rent and not paying the rent. I called the publisher every day for the next several weeks, but he kept putting me off, kept coming up with different excuses. At last, unable to hold out any longer, I went to the office in person and demanded that he pay me on the spot. He started in with another excuse, but this time I held my ground and declared that I wouldn't leave until he had written out a check to me for the full amount. I don't think I went so far as to threaten him, but I might have. I was boiling with anger, and I can remember thinking that if all else failed, I was prepared to punch him in the face. It never came to that, but what I did do was back him into a corner, and at that moment I could see that he was beginning to grow scared. He finally understood that I meant business. And right then and there, he opened the drawer of his desk, pulled out his checkbook, and gave me my money.

In retrospect, I consider this to be one of my lowest moments, a dismal chapter in my career as a human being, and I am not at all proud of how I acted. But I was broke, and I had done the work, and I deserved to be paid. To prove how hard up I was during those years, I will mention just one appalling fact. I never made a copy of the manuscript. I couldn't afford to xerox the translation, and since I assumed it was in safe hands, the only copy in the world was the original typescript sitting in the publisher's office. This fact, this stupid oversight, this poverty-stricken way of doing business would come back to haunt me. It was entirely my fault, and it turned a small misfortune into a full-blown disaster.

For the time being, however, we seemed to be back on track. Once the unpleasantness about my fee was settled, the publisher behaved as if he had every intention of bringing out the book. The manuscript was sent to a typesetter, I corrected the proofs and returned them to the publisher—again neglecting to make a copy. It hardly seemed important, after all, since production was well under way by now. The book had been announced in the catalogue, and publication was set for the winter of 1977–1978.

Then, just months before *Chronicle of the Guayaki Indians* was supposed to appear, news came that Pierre Clastres had been killed in a car accident. According to the story I was told, he had been driving somewhere in France when he lost control of the wheel and skidded over the edge of a mountain. We had never met. Given that he was only forty-three when he died, I had assumed there would be ample opportunities in the future. We had written a number of warm letters to each other, had become friends through our correspondence, and were looking forward to the time when we would at last be able to sit down together and talk. The strangeness and unpredictability of the world prevented that conversation from taking place. Even now, all these years later, I still feel it as a great loss.

Nineteen seventy-eight came and went, and *Chronicle of the Guayaki Indians* did not appear. Another year slipped by, and then another year, and still there was no book.

By 1981, the publishing company was on its last legs. The editor I had originally worked with was long gone, and it was difficult for me to find out any information. That year, or perhaps the year after that, or perhaps even the year after that (it all blurs in my mind now), the company finally went under. Someone called to tell me that the rights to the book had been sold to another publisher. I called the publisher, and they told me yes, they were planning to bring out the book. Another year went by, and nothing happened. I called again, and the person I had talked to the previous year no longer worked for the company. I talked to someone else, and that person told me that the company had no plans to publish *Chronicle of the Guayaki Indians*. I asked for the manuscript back, but no one could find it. No one had even heard of it. For all intents and purposes, it was as if the translation had never existed.

For the next dozen years, that was where the matter stood. Pierre Clastres was dead, my translation had disappeared, and the entire project had collapsed into a black hole of oblivion. This past summer (1996), I finished writing a book entitled *Hand to Mouth*, an autobiographical essay about money. I was planning to include this story in the narrative (because of my failure to make a copy of the manuscript, because of the scene with the publisher in his office), but when the moment came to tell it, I lost heart and couldn't bring myself to put the words down on paper. It was all too sad, I felt, and I couldn't see any purpose in recounting such a bleak, miserable saga.

Then, two or three months after I finished my book, something extraordinary happened. About a year before, I had accepted an invitation to go to San Francisco to appear in the City Arts and Lectures Series at the Herbst Theatre. The event was scheduled for October 1996, and when the moment came, I climbed onto a plane and flew to San Francisco as promised. After my business onstage was finished, I was supposed to sit in the lobby and sign copies of my books. The Herbst is a large theater with many seats, and the line in the lobby was therefore quite long. Among all those people waiting for the dubious privilege of having me write my name in one of my novels, there was someone I recognized—a young man I had met once before, the friend of a friend. This young man happens to be a passionate collector of books, a bloodhound for first editions and rare, out-of-the-way items, the kind of bibliographic detective who will think nothing of spending an afternoon in a dusty cellar sifting through boxes of discarded books in the hope of finding one small treasure. He smiled, shook my hand, and then thrust a set of bound galleys at me. It had a red paper cover, and until that moment, I had never seen a copy of it before. "What's this?" he said. "I never heard of it." And there it was, suddenly sitting in my hands: the uncorrected proofs of my long-lost translation. In the big scheme of things, this probably wasn't such an astonishing event. For me, however, in my own little scheme of things, it was overwhelming. My hands started to tremble as I held the book. I was so stunned, so confused, that I was scarcely able to speak.

The proofs had been found in a remainder bin at a secondhand bookstore, and the young man had paid five dollars for them. As I look at them now, I note with a certain grim fascination that the pub date announced on the cover is April 1981. For a translation completed in 1976 or 1977, it was, truly, an agonizingly slow ordeal.

If Pierre Clastres were alive today, the discovery of this lost book would be a perfect happy ending. But he isn't alive, and the brief surge of joy and incredulity I experienced in the atrium of the Herbst Theatre has by now dissipated into a deep, mournful ache. How rotten that the world should pull such tricks on us. How rotten that a person with so much to offer the world should die so young.

Here, then, is my translation of Pierre Clastres's book, *Chronicle of the Guayaki Indians*. No matter that the world described in it has long since vanished, that the tiny group of people the author lived with in 1963 and 1964 has disappeared from the face of the earth. No matter that the author has vanished as well. The book he wrote is still with us, and the fact that you are holding that book in your hands now, dear reader, is nothing less than a victory, a small triumph against the crushing odds of fate. At least there is that to be thankful for. At least there is consolation in the thought that Pierre Clastres's book has survived.

1997

The National Story Project

I never intended to do this. The *National Story Project* came about by accident, and if not for a remark my wife made at the dinner table sixteen months ago, most of the pieces in this book never would have been written. It was May 1999, perhaps June, and earlier that day I had been interviewed on National Public Radio about my most recent novel. After we finished our conversation, Daniel Zwerdling, the host of *Weekend All Things Considered*, had asked me if I would be interested in becoming a regular contributor to the program. I couldn't even see his face when he asked the question. I was in the NPR studio on Second Avenue in New York, and he was in Washington, D.C., and for the past twenty or thirty minutes we had been talking to each other through microphones and headsets, aided by a technological marvel known as fiber optics. I asked him what he had in mind, and he said that he wasn't sure. Maybe I could come on the air every month or so and tell stories.

I wasn't interested. Doing my own work was difficult enough, and taking on a job that would force me to crank out stories on command was the last thing I needed. Just to be polite, however, I said that I would go home and think about it.

It was my wife, Siri, who turned the proposition on its head. That night, when I told her about NPR's curious offer, she immediately came up with a proposal that reversed the direction of my thoughts. In a matter of thirty seconds, no had become yes.

You don't have to write the stories yourself, she said. Get people to sit down and write their own stories. They could send them in to you, and then you could read the best ones on the radio. If enough people wrote in, it could turn into something extraordinary.

That was how the *National Story Project* was born. It was Siri's idea, and then I picked it up and started to run with it.

Sometime in late September, Zwerdling came to my house in Brooklyn with Rebecca Davis, one of the producers of *Weekend All Things Considered*, and we launched the idea of the project in the form of another interview. I told the listeners that I was looking for stories. The stories had to be true, and they had to be short, but there would be no restrictions as to subject matter or style. What interested me most, I said, were stories that defied our expectations about the world, anecdotes that revealed the mysterious and unknowable forces at work in our lives, in our family histories, in our minds and bodies, in our souls. In other words, true stories that sounded like fiction. I was talking about big things and small things, tragic things and comic things, any experience that felt important enough to set down on paper. They shouldn't worry if they had never written a story, I said. Everyone was bound to know some good ones, and if enough people answered the call to participate, we would inevitably begin to learn some surprising things about ourselves and each other. The spirit of the project was entirely democratic. All listeners were welcome to contribute, and I promised to read every story that came in. People would be exploring their own lives and experiences, but at the same time they would be part of a collective effort, something bigger than just themselves. With their help, I said, I was hoping to put together an archive of facts, a museum of American reality.

The interview was broadcast on the first Saturday in October, exactly one year ago today. Since that time, I have received more than four thousand submissions. This number is many times greater than what I had anticipated, and for the past twelve months I have been awash in manuscripts, floating madly in an ever expanding sea of paper. Some of the stories are written by hand; others are typed; still others are printed out from e-mails. Every month, I have scrambled to choose five or six of the best ones and turn them into a twenty-minute segment to be aired on *Weekend All Things Considered*. It has been singularly rewarding work, one of the most inspiring tasks I have ever undertaken. But it has had its difficult moments as well. On several occasions, when I have been particularly swamped with material, I have read sixty or seventy stories at a single sitting, and each time I have done that, I have stood up from the chair feeling pulverized, absolutely drained of energy. So many emotions to contend with, so many strangers camped out in the living room, so many voices coming at me from so many different directions. On those evenings, for the space of two or three hours, I have felt that the entire population of America has walked into my house. I didn't hear America singing. I heard it telling stories.

Yes, a number of rants and diatribes have been sent in by deranged people, but far fewer than I would have predicted. I have been exposed to groundbreaking revelations about the Kennedy assassination, subjected to several complex exegeses that link current events to verses from Scripture, and made privy to information pertaining to lawsuits against half a dozen corporations and government agencies. Some people have gone out of their way to provoke me and turn my stomach. Just last week, I received a submission from a man who signed his story "Cerberus" and gave his return address as "The Underworld 66666." In the story, he told about his days in Vietnam as a marine, ending with an account of how he and the other men in his company had roasted a stolen Vietnamese baby and eaten it around a campfire. He made it sound as though he were proud of what he had done. For all I know, the story could be true. But that doesn't mean I have any interest in presenting it on the radio.

On the other hand, some of the pieces from disturbed people have contained startling and arresting passages. Last fall, when the project was just getting under way, one came in from another Vietnam vet, a man serving a life sentence for murder in a penitentiary somewhere in the Midwest. He enclosed a handwritten affidavit that recounted the muddled story of how he came to commit his crime, and the last sentence of the document read, "I have never been perfect, but I am real." In some sense, that statement could stand as the credo of the *National Story Project*, the very principle behind this book. We have never been perfect, but we are real.

Of the four thousand stories I have read, most have been compelling enough to hold me until the last word. Most have been written with simple, straightforward conviction, and most have done honor to the people who sent them in. We all have inner lives. We all feel that we are part of the world and yet exiled from it. We all burn with the fires of our own existence. Words are needed to express what is in us, and again and again contributors have thanked me for giving them the chance to tell their stories, for "allowing the people to be heard." What the people have said is often astonishing. More than ever, I have come to appreciate how deeply and passionately most of us live within ourselves. Our attachments are ferocious. Our loves overwhelm us, define us, obliterate the boundaries between ourselves and others. Fully a third of the stories I have read are about families: parents and children, children and parents, husbands and wives, brothers and sisters, grandparents. For most of us, those are the people who fill up our world, and in story after story, both the dark ones and the humorous ones, I have been impressed by how clearly and forcefully these connections have been articulated.

A few high-school students sent in stories about hitting home runs and winning medals at track meets, but it was the rare adult who took advantage of the occasion to brag about his accomplishments. Hilarious blunders, wrenching coincidences, brushes with death, miraculous encounters, improbable ironies, premonitions, sorrows, pains, dreams—these were the subjects the contributors chose to write about. I learned that I am not alone in my belief that the more we understand of the world, the more elusive and confounding the world becomes. As one early contributor so eloquently put it, "I am left without an adequate definition of reality." If you aren't certain about things, if your mind is still open enough to question what you are seeing, you tend to look at the world with great care, and out of that watchfulness comes the possibility of seeing something that no one else has seen before. You have to be willing to admit that you don't have all the answers. If you think you do, you will never have anything important to say.

Incredible plots, unlikely turns, events that refuse to obey the laws of common sense. More often than not, our lives resemble the stuff of eighteenth-century novels. Just today, another batch of e-mails from NPR arrived at my door, and among the new submissions was this story from a woman who lives in San Diego, California. I quote from it not because it is unusual, but simply because it is the freshest piece of evidence at hand:

> I was adopted from an orphanage at the age of eight months. Less than a year later, my adoptive father died suddenly. I was raised by my widowed mother with three older adopted brothers. When you are adopted, there is a natural curiosity to know your birth family. By the time I was married and in my late twenties, I decided to start looking.
>
> I had been raised in Iowa, and sure enough, after a two-year search, I located my birth mother in Des Moines. We met and went to dinner. I asked her who my birth father was, and she gave me his name. I asked where he lived, and she said "San Diego," which was where I had been living for the last five years. I had moved to San Diego not knowing a soul—just knowing I wanted to be there.
>
> It ended up that I worked in the building next door to where my father worked. We often ate lunch at the same restaurant. We never told his wife of my existence, as I didn't really want to disrupt his life. He had always been a bit of a gadabout, however, and he always had a girlfriend on the side. He and his last girlfriend were "together" for fifteen-plus years, and she remained the source of my information about him.

Five years ago, my birth mother was dying of cancer in Iowa. Simultaneously, I received a call from my father's paramour that he had died of heart complications. I called my biological mother in the hospital in Iowa and told her of his death. She died that night. I received word that both of their funerals were held on the following Saturday at exactly the same hour—his at 11 A.M. in California and hers at 1 P.M. in Iowa.

•

After three or four months, I sensed that a book was going to be necessary to do justice to the project. Too many good stories were coming in, and it wasn't possible for me to present more than a fraction of the worthy submissions on the radio. Many of them were too long for the format we had established, and the ephemeral nature of the broadcasts (a lone, disembodied voice floating across the American airwaves for eighteen or twenty minutes every month) made me want to collect the most memorable ones and preserve them in written form. Radio is a powerful tool, and NPR reaches into almost every corner of the country, but you can't hold the words in your hands. A book is tangible, and once you put it down, you can return to the place where you left it and pick it up again.

This anthology contains 179 pieces—what I consider to be the best of the approximately four thousand works that have come in during the past year. But it is also a representative selection, a miniaturized version of the *National Story Project* as a whole. For every story about a dream or an animal or a missing object to be found in these pages, there were dozens of others that were submitted, dozens of others that could have been chosen. The book begins with a six-sentence tale about a chicken (the first story I read on the air last November) and ends with a wistful meditation on the role that radio plays in our lives. The author of that last piece, Ameni Rozsa, was moved to write her story while listening to one of the *National Story Project* broadcasts. I had been hoping to capture bits and fragments of American reality, but it had never occurred to me that the project itself could become a part of that reality, too.

This book has been written by people of all ages and from all walks of life. Among them are a postman, a merchant seaman, a trolley-bus driver, a gas-and-electric-meter reader, a restorer of player pianos, a crime-scene cleaner, a musician, a businessman, two priests, an inmate at a state correctional facility, several doctors, and assorted housewives, farmers, and ex-servicemen. The youngest contributor is barely twenty; the oldest is pushing ninety. Half of the writers are women; half are men. They live in cities, suburbs, and in rural areas, and they come from forty-two different states. In making my choices, I never once gave a thought to demographic balance. I selected the stories solely on the basis of merit: for their humanity, for their truth, for their charm. The numbers just fell out that way, and the results were determined by blind chance.

In an attempt to make some order out of this chaos of voices and contrasting styles, I have broken the stories into ten different categories. The section titles speak for themselves, but except for the fourth section, "Slapstick," which is made up entirely of comic stories, there is a wide range of material within each of the categories. Their contents run the gamut from farce to tragic drama, and for every act of cruelty and violence that one encounters in them, there is a countervailing act of kindness or generosity or love. The stories go back and forth, up and down, in and out, and after a while your head starts to spin. Turn the page from one contributor to the next and you are confronted by an entirely different person, an entirely different set of circumstances, an entirely different worldview. But difference is what this book is all about. There is some elegant and sophisticated writing in it, but there is also much that is crude and awkward. Only a small portion of it resembles anything that could qualify as "literature." It is something else, something raw and close to the bone, and whatever skills these authors might lack, most of their stories are unforgettable. It is difficult for me to imagine that anyone could read through this book from beginning to end without once shedding a tear, without once laughing out loud.

If I had to define what these stories were, I would call them dispatches, reports from the front lines of personal experience. They are about the private worlds of individual Americans, yet again and again one sees the inescapable marks of history on them, the intricate ways in which individual destinies are shaped by society at large. Some of the older contributors, looking back on events from their childhood and youth, are necessarily writing about the Depression and World War II. Other contributors, born in the middle of the century, continue to be haunted by the effects of the war in Vietnam. That conflict ended twenty-five years ago, and yet it lives on in us as a recurrent nightmare, a great wound in the national soul. Still other contributors, from several different generations, have written stories about the disease of American racism. This scourge has been with us for more than 350 years, and no matter how hard we struggle to eradicate it from our midst, a cure has yet to be found.

Other stories touch on AIDS, alcoholism, drug abuse, pornography, and guns. Social forces are forever impinging on the lives of these people, but not one of their stories sets out to document society per se. We know that Janet Zupan's father died in a prison camp in Vietnam in 1967, but that is not what her story is about. With a remarkable eye for visual detail, she tracks a single afternoon in the Mojave Desert as her father chases after his stubborn and recalcitrant horse, and knowing what we do about what will happen to her father just two years later, we read her account as a kind of memorial to him. Not a word about the war, and yet by indirection and an almost painterly focus on the moment before her, we sense that an entire era of American history is passing in front of our eyes.

Stan Benkoski's father's laugh. The slap to Carol Sherman-Jones's face. Little Mary Grace Dembeck dragging a Christmas tree through the streets of Brooklyn. John Keith's mother's missing wedding ring. John Flannelly's fingers stuck in the holes of a stainless-steel heating grate. Mel Singer wrestled to the floor by his own coat. Anna Thorson at the barn dance. Edith Riemer's bicycle. Marie Johnson watching a movie shot in the house where she lived as a girl. Ludlow Perry's encounter with the legless man. Catherine Austin Alexander looking out her window on West Seventy-fourth Street. Juliana C. Nash's walk through the snow. Dede Ryan's philosophical martini. Carolyn Brasher's regrets. Mary McCallum's father's dream. Earl Roberts's collar button. One by one, these stories leave a lasting impression on the mind. Even after you have read through all fifteen dozen of them, they continue to stay with you, and you find yourself remembering them in the same way that you remember a trenchant parable or a good joke. The images are clear, dense, and yet somehow weightless. And each one is small enough to fit inside your pocket. Like the snapshots we carry around of our own families.

October 3, 2000

A Little Anthology of Surrealist Poems

1968. I was twenty-one, a junior at Columbia, and these poems were among my first attempts at translation. Remember the times: the war in Vietnam, the clamor of politics on College Walk, a year of unending protests, the strike that shut down the university, sit-ins, riots, the arrest of 700 students (myself among them). In the light of that tumult (that questioning), the Surrealists were a major discovery for me: poets fighting against the conventions of poetry, poets dreaming of revolution, of how to change the world. Translation, then, was more than just a literary exercise. It was a first step toward breaking free of the shackles of myself, of overcoming my own ignorance. *You must change your life.* Perhaps, Back then, it was more a question of searching for a life, of trying to invent a life I could believe in. . . .

January 22, 2002

The Art of Worry

Art Spiegelman is a one-of-a-kind quardruple threat. He is an artist who draws and paints; a chameleon who can mimic and embellish upon any visual style he chooses; a writer who expresses himself in vivid, sharply turned sentences; and a provocateur with a flair for humor in its most savage and piercing incarnations. Mix those talents together, then put them in the service of a deep political conscience, and a man can make a considerable mark on the world. Which is precisely what Art Spiegelman has done for the past ten years at *The New Yorker*.

We know him best as the author of *Maus*, the brilliant two-volume narrative of his father's nightmare journey through the camps in the Second World War. Spiegelman showed himself to be an expert storyteller in that work, and no doubt that is how history will remember him: as the man who proved that comic books are not necessarily for children, that a complex tale can be told in a series of small rectangles filled with words and pictures—and attain the full emotional and intellectual power of great literature.

But there is another side to Spiegelman as well, one which has increasingly come to dominate his energies in the post-*Maus* years: the artist as social gadfly and critic, as commentator on current events. As Spiegelman's friend and admirer, I have always found it odd that he should have found a home for that aspect of his work at *The New Yorker*. The magazine was born in the Jazz Age and has been a fixture on the American scene for more than seventy-five years, rolling off the presses every week as the country has lived through wars, depressions, and violent upheavals, steadfastly maintaining a tone that is at once cool, sophisticated, and complacent. *The New Yorker* has published some excellent journalism over the years, but incisive and disturbing as many of those reports have been, the pages on which they appear have always been flanked by advertisements for luxury goods and Caribbean vacations, adorned with blithely amusing cartoons about the foibles of middle-class life. That is *The New Yorker* style. The world might be going to hell, but once we open the pages of our favorite weekly, we understand that hell is for other people. Nothing has changed for us—and nothing ever will. We are suave, tranquil, and urbane. Not to worry.

But Spiegelman wants to worry. That is his job. He has embraced worry as his life's calling, and he frets over every injustice he perceives in the world, froths diligently at the follies and stupidities of men in power, refuses to take things in his stride. Not without wit, of course, and not without his trademark comic touch—but still, the last thing anyone could call this man is complacent. Good for *The New Yorker*, then, for having had the wisdom to put him on its payroll. And good for Spiegelman for having reinvigorated the spirit of that stodgy bastion of good taste.

Contributing both to the inside and the outside of the magazine, he has produced approximately seventy works for *The New Yorker*, toiling under the reigns of two chief editors, Tina Brown and David Remnick. These works include single-page drawings and paintings (among them a bitter sendup of *Life is Beautiful*, a film that Spiegelman abhorred), extended articles on a variety of subjects presented in comic-book form (neo-Nazi hooliganism in Rostock, Germany; homages to Harvey Kurtzman, Maurice Sendak, and Charles Schultz; an attack on George W. Bush and the bogus elections of 2000; observations on pop culture as reflected in the behavior of his own children), and close to forty covers. The outside of a magazine is its most visible feature, the signature mark of its philosophy and editorial content, the dress it wears when it goes out in public. Until Spiegelman came along, *The New Yorker* had been famous—even hilariously famous—for the blandness of its cover art. Smug and subdued, confident in the loyalty of its wide readership, issue after issue would turn up on the newsstands sporting sedate autumn scenes, snowy winter landscapes, suburban lawns, and depopulated city streets—imagery so trite and insipid as to induce drowsiness in the eye of the beholder. Then, on February 15, 1993, for an issue that fortuitously coincided with Valentine's Day, Spiegelman's first cover appeared, and *The New Yorker* exploded into a new *New Yorker*, a magazine that suddenly found itself part of the contemporary world.

It was a bad time for the city. Crown Heights, an impoverished neighborhood in Brooklyn inhabited by African-Americans and Orthodox Jews, was on the brink of a racial war. A black child had been run over by a Jew, a Jew had been murdered in retaliation by an angry mob of blacks, and for many days running a fierce agitation dominated the streets, with threats of further violence from both camps. The mayor at the time, David Dinkins, was a decent man, but he was also a cautious man, and he lacked the political skill needed to step in quickly and defuse the crisis. (That failure probably cost him victory in the next election—which led to the harsh regime of Rudolph Giuliani, who served as mayor for the next eight years.) New York, for all its ethnic diversity, is a surprisingly tolerant city, and most people make an effort most of the time to get along with one another. But racial tensions exist, often smoldering in silence, occasionally erupting in isolated acts of brutality—but here was an entire neighborhood up in arms, and it was an ugly thing to witness, a stain on the democratic spirit of New York. That was when Spiegelman was heard from, the precise moment when he walked into the battle and offered his solution to the problem. *Kiss and make up*. His statement was that simple, that shocking, that powerful. An Orthodox Jew had his arms around a black woman, the black woman had her arms around the Orthodox Jew, their eyes were closed, and they were kissing. To round out the Valentine's Day theme, the background of the picture was solid red, and three little hearts floated within the squiggly border that framed the image. Spiegelman wasn't taking sides. As a Jew, he wasn't proposing to defend the Jewish community of Crown Heights; as a practitioner of no religion, he wasn't voicing his support of the African-American community that shared that same miserable patch of ground. He was speaking as a citizen of New York, a citizen of the world, and he was addressing both groups at the same time—which is to say, he was addressing all of us. No more hate, he said, no more intolerance, no more demonizing of the other. In pictorial form, the cover's message was identical to an idea expressed by W.H. Auden on the first day of World War II: *We must love one another or die*.

Since that remarkable debut, Spiegelman has continued to confound our expectations, consciously using his inventiveness as a destabilizing force, a weapon of surprise. He wants to keep us off balance, to catch us with our guard down, and to that end he approaches his subjects from numerous angles and with countless shadings of tone: mockery and whimsy, outrage and rebuke, even tenderness and laudatory affection. The heroic construction-worker mother breast-feeding her baby on the girder of a half-finished skyscraper; turkey-bombs falling on Afghanistan; Bill Clinton's groin surrounded by a sea of microphones; college diplomas that turn out to be help-wanted ads; the weirdo hipster family as emblem of cross-generational love and solidarity; the

spiegelman

crucified Easter bunny impaled on an IRS tax form; the Santa Claus and the rabbi with identical beards and bellies. Unafraid to court controversy, Spiegelman has offended many people over the years, and several of the covers he has prepared for *The New Yorker* have been deemed so incendiary by the editorial powers of the magazine that they have refused to run them. Beginning with the Valentine's Day cover of 1993, Spiegelman's work has inspired thousands of indignant letters, hundreds of canceled subscriptions and, in one very dramatic instance, a full-scale protest demonstration by members of the New York City Police Department in front of the *New Yorker* offices in Manhattan. That is the price one pays for speaking one's mind—for drawing one's mind. Spiegelman's tenure at *The New Yorker* has not always been an easy one, but his courage has been a steady source of encouragement to those of us who love our city and believe in the idea of New York as a place for everyone, as the central laboratory of human contradictions in our time.

Then came September 11, 2001. In the fire and smoke of three thousand incinerated bodies, a holocaust was visited upon us, and nine months later the city is still grieving over its dead. In the immediate aftermath of the attack, in the hours and days that followed that murderous morning, few of us were capable of thinking any coherent thoughts. The shock was too great, and as the smoke continued to hover over the city and we breathed in the vile smells of death and destruction, most of us shuffled around like sleepwalkers, numb and dazed, not good for anything. But *The New Yorker* had an issue to put out, and when they realized that someone would have to design a cover—the most important cover in their history, which would have to be produced in record time—they turned to Spiegelman.

That black-on-black issue of September 24 is, in my opinion, Spiegelman's masterpiece. In the face of absolute horror, one's inclination is to dispense with images altogether. Words often fail us at moments of extreme duress. The same is true of pictures. If I have not garbled the story Spiegelman told me during those days, I believe he originally resisted that iconoclastic impulse: to hand in a solid black cover to represent mourning, an absent image to stand as a mirror of the ineffable. Other ideas occurred to him. He tested them out, but one by one he rejected them, slowly pushing his mind toward darker and darker hues until, inevitably, he arrived at a deep, unmodulated black. But still that wasn't enough. He found it too mute, too facile, too resigned, but for want of any other solution, he almost capitulated.

Then, just as he was about to give up, he began thinking about some of the artists who had come before him, artists who had explored the implications of eliminating color from their paintings—in particular Ad Reinhardt and his black-on-black canvases from the sixties, those supremely abstract and minimal anti-images that had taken painting to the farthest edge of possibility. Spiegelman had found his direction. Not in silence—but in the sublime.

You have to look very closely at the picture before you notice the towers. They are there and not there, effaced and yet still present, shadows pulsing in oblivion, in memory, in the ghostly emanation of some tormented afterlife. When I saw the picture for the first time, I felt as if Spiegelman had placed a stethoscope on my chest and methodically registered every heartbeat that had shaken my body since September 11. Then my eyes filled up with tears. Tears for the dead. Tears for the living. Tears for the abominations we inflict on one another, for the cruelty and savagery of the whole stinking human race.

Then I thought: *We must love one another or die.*

June 2002

Invisible Joubert

Some writers live and die in the shadows, and they don't begin to live for us until after they are dead. Emily Dickinson published just three poems during her lifetime; Gerard Manley Hopkins published only one. Kafka kept his unfinished novels to himself, and if not for a promise broken by his friend Max Brod, they would have been burned. Christopher Smart's Bedlamite rant, *Jubilate Agno*, was composed in the early 1760s but didn't find its way into print until 1939.

Think of how many writers disappeared when the Library of Alexandria burned in 391 AD. Think of how many books were destroyed by the Catholic Church in the Middle Ages. For every miraculous resurrection, for every work saved from oblivion by free-thinkers like Petrarch and Boccaccio, one could enumerate hundreds of losses. Ralph Ellison worked for years on a follow-up novel to *Invisible Man*, then the manuscript burned in a fire. In a fit of madness, Gogol destroyed the second part of *Dead Souls*. What we know of the work of Heraclitus and Sappho exists only in fragments. In his later years Herman Melville was so thoroughly forgotten that most people thought he was dead when his obituary appeared in 1891. It wasn't until *Moby Dick* was discovered in a second-hand bookshop in 1920 that Melville came to be recognized as one of our essential novelists.

The afterlife of writers is precarious at best, and for those who fail to publish before they die—by choice, by happenstance, by sheer bad luck—the fate of their work is almost certain doom. The American poet Charles Reznikoff reported that his grandmother threw out every one of his grandfather's poems after he died—an entire life's work discarded with the trash. More recently, the young John Kennedy O'Toole committed suicide over his failure to find a publisher for his book. When the novel finally appeared, it was a critical success. Who knows how many unread masterpieces are hidden away in attics or moldering in cellars? Without someone to defend a dead writer's work, that work could just as well never have been written. Think of Osip Mandelstam, murdered by Stalin in 1938. If his widow, Nadezhda, had not committed the entire body of his work to memory, he would have been lost to us as a poet.

There are dozens of posthumous writers in the history of literature, but no case is stranger or more obscure than that of Joseph Joubert, a Frenchman who wrote in the last quarter of the eighteenth century and the first quarter of the nineteenth. Not only did he not publish a single word while he was alive, but the work he left behind escapes clear definition, which means that he has continued to exist as an almost invisible writer even after his discovery, acquiring a handful of ardent readers in every generation, but never fully emerging from the shadows that surrounded him when he was alive. Neither a poet nor a novelist, neither a philosopher nor an essayist, Joubert was a man of letters without portfolio whose work consists of a vast series of notebooks in which he wrote down his thoughts every day for more than forty years. All the entries are dated, but the notebooks cannot be construed as a traditional diary, since there are scarcely any personal remarks in it. Nor was Joubert a writer of maxims in the classcial French manner. He was something far more oblique and challenging: a writer who spent his whole life preparing himself for a work that never came to be written, a writer of the highest rank who paradoxically never produced a book. Joubert speaks in whispers, and one must draw very close to him to hear what he is saying.

He was born in Montignac (Dordogne) on May 7, 1754, the son of master surgeon Jean Joubert. The second of eight surviving children, Joubert completed his local education at the age of fourteen and was then sent to Toulouse to continue his studies. His father hoped that he would pursue a career in the law, but Joubert's interests lay in philosophy and the classics. After graduation, he taught for several years in the school where he had been a student and then returned to Montignac for two years, without professional plans or any apparent ambitions, already suffering from the poor health that would plague him throughout his life.

In May 1778, just after his twenty-fourth birthday, Joubert moved to Paris, where he took up residence at the Hôtel de Bordeaux on the rue des Francs-Bourgeois. He soon became a member of Diderot's circle, and through that association was brought into contact with the sculptor Pigalle and many other artists of the period. During those early years in Paris he also met Fontanes, who would remain his closest friend for the rest of his life. Both Joubert and Fontanes frequented the literary salon of the countess Fanny de Beauharnais (whose niece later married Bonaparte). Other members included Buffon, La Harpe, and Restif de la Bretonne.

In 1785, Fontanes and Joubert attempted to found a newsletter about Paris literary life for English subscribers, but the venture failed. That same year, Joubert entered into a liaison with the wife of Restif de la Bretonne, Agnès Lebègue, a woman fourteen years his senior. But by March 1786 the affair had ended—painfully for Joubert. Later that year, he made his first visit to the town of Villeneuve and met Victoire Moreau, who would become his wife in 1793. During this period Joubert read much and wrote little. He studied philosophy, music, and painting, but the various writing projects he began—an appreciation of Pigalle, an essay on the navigator Cook—were never completed. For the most part, it seems that Joubert watched the world around him, cultivated his friendships, and meditated. As time went on, he turned more and more to his notebooks as the place to develop his thoughts and explore his inner life. By the late 1780s and early 1790s, they had become a serious daily enterprise for him. At first, he looked upon his jottings as a way to prepare himself for a larger, more systematic work, a great book of philosophy that he dreamed he had it in him to write. As the years passed, however, and the project continued to elude him, he slowly came to realize that the notebooks were an end in themselves, eventually admitting that "these thoughts form not only the foundation of my work, but of my life."

Joubert had long been a supporter of revolutionary views, and when the Revolution came in 1789, he welcomed it enthusiastically. In late 1790, he was named Justice of the Peace in Montignac, a position that entailed great responsibilities and made him the leading citizen of the town. By all accounts, he fulfilled his tasks with vigilance and fairness and was widely respected for his work. But he soon became disillusioned with the increasingly violent nature of the Revolution. He declined to stand for reelection in 1792 and gradually withdrew from politics.

After his marriage in 1793, he retired to Villeneuve, from then on dividing his time between the country and Paris. Fontanes had gone into exile in London, where he met Chateaubriand. Eventually, upon their return to Paris, Joubert and these two younger men collaborated on the magazine *Mercure de France*. Joubert would later help Chateaubriand with many passages of *Le Génie du christianisme* and give him financial help in times of trouble. During the early years of the nineteenth century, Joubert was surrounded by many of the most successful men and women in France, deeply admired for his lucid ideas, his sharp critical intelligence, and his enormous talent for friendship.

When Joubert died in 1824 at the age of seventy, Chateaubriand, then Minister of Foreign Affairs, eulogized him in the *Journal des débats*:

> He was one of those men you loved for the delicacy of his feelings, the goodness of his soul, the evenness of his temper, the uniqueness of his character, the keenness and brilliance of his mind—a mind that was interested in everything and understood everything. No one has ever forgotten himself so thoroughly and been so concerned with the welfare of others.

Although Fontanes and Chateaubriand had both urged him to put together a book from his daily writings, Joubert resisted the temptation to publish. The first selection to appear in print, entitled *Pensées*, was compiled by Chateaubriand in 1838 and distributed privately among Joubert's friends. Other editions followed, eliciting sympathetic and passionate essays by such diverse figures as Saint-Beuve and Matthew Arnold, who compared Joubert favorably to Coleridge and remarked that "they both had from nature an ardent impulse for seeking the genuine truth on all matters they thought about, and an organ for finding it and recognising it when it was found." Those early editions all divided Joubert's writings into chapters with abstract headings such as "Truth," "Literature," "Family," "Society," and so on. It wasn't until 1938, in a two-volume work prepared by André Beaunier for Gallimard, that Joubert's writings were presented in the original order of their composition. I have drawn my selections for this book from the 900 tightly printed pages of Beaunier's scrupulous edition.

No more than a tenth of Joubert's work is included here. In choosing the entries, I have been guided above all by my own contemporary and idiosyncratic tastes, concentrating my attention on Joubert's aesthetic theories, his "imaginary physics," and passages of direct autobiographical significance. I have not included the lengthy reading notes that Joubert made during his study of various philosophers—Malebranche, Kant, Locke, and others—nor the frequent references to writers of his time, most of whom are unknown to us today. For convenience and economy, I have eliminated the dates that precede each entry.

I first discovered Joubert's work in 1971, through an essay written by Maurice Blanchot, "Joubert et l'espace." In it, Blanchot compares

Joubert to Mallarmé and makes a solid case for considering him to be the most modern writer of his period, the one who speaks most directly to us now. And indeed, the free-floating, questing nature of Joubert's mind, along with his concise and elegant style, has not grown old with the passage of time. Everything is mixed together in the notebooks, and reflections on literature and philosophy are scattered among observations about the weather, the landscape, and politics. Entries of unforgettable psychological insight ("Those who never back down love themselves more than they love the truth") alternate with brief, chilling comments on the turmoil around him ("Stacking the dead on top of one another"), which in turn are punctuated by sudden outbursts of levity ("They say that souls have no sex; of course they do"). The more you read Joubert, the more you want to go on reading him. He draws you in with his descretion and honesty, with his plain-spoken brilliance, with his quiet but utterly original way of looking at the world.

At the same time, it is easy to ignore Joubert. He doesn't point to himself or bang on loud rhetorical drums, and he isn't out to shock anyone with his ideas. Those of us who love his work guard him as a treasured secret, but in the 164 years since his writings were first made available to the public, he has scarcely caused a ripple in the world-at-large. This translation was first published by Jack Shoemaker of North Point Press in 1983, and the book failed to arouse anything but indifference on the part of American critics and readers. The book received just one review (in the *Boston Globe*), and sales amounted to something in the neighborhood of 800 copies. On the other hand, not long after the book was published, Joubert's relevance was brought home to me in a remarkable way. I gave a copy to one of my oldest friends, the painter David Reed. David had a friend who had recently landed in Bellevue after suffering a nervous breakdown, and when David went to visit him in the hospital, he left behind his copy of Joubert—on loan. Two or three weeks later, when the friend was finally released, he called David to apologize for not returning the book. After he had read it, he said, he had given it to another patient. That patient had passed it on to yet another patient, and little by little Joubert had made his way around the ward. Interest in the book became so keen that groups of patients would gather in the day room to read passages out loud to one another and discuss them. When David's friend asked for the book back, he was told that it no longer belonged to him. "It's our book," one of the patients said. "We need it." As far as I'm concerned, that is the most eloquent literary criticism I have ever heard, proof that the right book in the right place is medicine for the human soul.

As Joubert himself once put it in 1801: "A thought is a thing as real as a cannon ball."

August 11, 2002

Hawthorne at Home

Twenty Days with Julian & Little Bunny, by Papa is one of the least known works by a well-known writer in all of literature. Buried in the seventh folio of Hawthorne's *American Notebooks*—that massive, little-read tome of treasures and revelations—the fifty pages that comprise this brief, self-contained narrative were written in Lenox, Massachusetts, between July 28 and August 16, 1851. In June of the previous year, Hawthorne and his wife had moved to a small red farmhouse in the Berkshires with their two children, Una (born in 1844) and Julian (born in 1846). A third child, Rose, was born in May 1851. A couple of months later, accompanied by her two daughters and her older sister, Elizabeth Peabody, Sophia Hawthorne left Lenox to visit her parents in West Newton, just outside Boston. Remaining in the house were Hawthorne, the five-year-old Julian, Mrs. Peters (the cook and housekeeper), and a pet rabbit who eventually came to be known as Hindlegs. That evening, after putting Julian to bed, Hawthorne sat down and wrote the first chapter of his little saga. With no intention other than to record the doings in the household during his wife's absence, he had inadvertently embarked on something that no writer had ever attempted before him: a meticulous, blow-by-blow account of a man taking care of a young child by himself.

In some ways, the situation is reminiscent of the old folk tale about the farmer and his wife who swap chores for a day. There are many versions of the story, but the outcome is always the same. The man, who has either belittled the woman for not working as hard as he does or scolded her for not doing her work well, makes a complete botch of it when he dons an apron and assumes the role of domestic manager. Depending on which variant you read, he either sets fire to the kitchen or winds up dangling from a rope attached to the family cow, who, after a long chain of misadventures, has managed to get herself onto the roof of the house. In all versions, it is the wife who comes to the rescue. Calmly planting crops in a nearby field, she hears her husband's screams and runs back home to extricate him from his predicament before he burns the place down or breaks his neck.

Hawthorne didn't break his neck, but he clearly felt that he was on rocky ground, and the tone of *Twenty Days* is at once comic, self-deprecatory, and vaguely befuddled, shot through with what the grown-up Julian would later describe as his father's "humorous gravity." Readers familiar with the style of Hawthorne's stories and novels will be struck by the clarity and simplicity of expression in the *Notebooks*. The dark, brooding obsessions of his fiction produced a complex, often ornate density to his sentences, a refinement that sometimes bordered on the fussy or obscure, and some readers of his early tales (which were mostly published unsigned) mistakenly assumed that their author was a woman. Henry James, who wrote one of the first book-length studies of Hawthorne's work, learned much from this original and delicate prose, which was unique in its ability to join the intricacies of acute psychological observation with large moral and philosophical concerns. But James was not Hawthorne's only reader, and there are several other Hawthornes who have come down to us as well: Hawthorne the allegorist, Hawthorne the high Romantic fabulist, Hawthorne the chronicler of seventeenth-century colonial New England and, most notably, Hawthorne as reimagined by Borges—the precursor of Kafka. Hawthorne's fiction can be read profitably from any one of these angles, but there is yet another Hawthorne who has been more or less forgotten, neglected because of the magnitude of his other achievements: the private Hawthorne, the scribbler of anecdotes and impulsive thoughts, the workman of ideas, the meteorologist and depictor of landscapes, the traveler, the letter-writer, the historian of everyday life. The pages of the *American Notebooks* are so fresh, so vivid in their articulations, that Hawthorne emerges from them not as some venerable figure from the literary past, but as a contemporary, a man whose time is still the present.

Twenty Days was not the only occasion on which he wrote about his children. Once Una and Julian were old enough to talk, he seemed to take immense pleasure in jotting down some of their zanier utterances, and the notebooks are studded with entries such as these:

"I'm tired of all sings and want to slip into God. I'm tired of little Una Hawsorne." "Are you tired of Mamma?" "No." "But are you tired of Papa?" "No. I am tired of Dora, and tired of little Julian, and tired of little Una Hawsorne."

Una—"You hurt me a little."
Julian—"Well, I'll hurt you a big."

Julian—"Mamma, why is not dinner supper?"—Mamma—"Why is not a chair a table?"—Julian—"Because it's a teapot."

I said to Julian, 'Let me take off your bib'—and he taking no notice, I repeated it two or three times, each time louder than before. At last he bellowed—"Let me take off your Head!"

On Sunday, March 19, 1848, during the period when he was employed at the U.S. Custom House in Salem, Hawthorne spent the entire day recording the activities and antics of his two offspring—one just four and the other not quite two. It is a dizzying account of some nine pages that conscientiously takes note of every whim and twist of mood that occurred in the children over the course of eleven hours. Lacking the sentimental flourishes one might expect from a nineteenth-century parent, devoid of moralizing judgments or intrusive commentary, it stands as a remarkable portrait of the reality of childhood—which, on the strength of these passages, would seem to be eternal in its sameness.

Now Una offers her finger to Julian, and they march together, the little boy aping a manly measurement of stride. Now Una proposes to play Puss in the Corner; and there is a quick tatoo of little feet all over the floor. Julian utters a complaining cry about something or other—Una runs and kisses him. Una says, "Father—*this* morning, I am not going to be naughty at all." Now they are playing with India rubber balls. Julian tries to throw the ball into the air, but usually succeeds no farther than to drop it over his head. It rolls away—and he searches for it, inquiring—"where ball?". . . . Julian now falls into a reverie, for a little space—his mind seeming far away, lost in reminiscences; but what can they be about? Recollections of a pre-existence. Now, he sits in his little chair, his chunky little figure looking like an alderman in miniature. . . . Mamma is dressing little Una in her purple pelisse, to go out with Dora. Una promises to be a very good little girl, and mind Dora—and not run away, nor step in the mud. The little boy trudges round, repeating "Go!—go!"—intimating his desire to be taken out likewise. He runs to-and-fro across the room, with a marvellous swagger—of the ludicrousness of which he seems perfectly conscious; and when I laugh, he comes to my elbow and looks up in my face, with a most humorous response. . . . He climbs into a chair at my knee, and peeps at himself in the glass—now he looks curiously on the page as I write—now, he nearly tumbles down, and is at first frightened—but, seeing that I was likewise startled, pretends to tumble again, and then laughs in my face. Enter mamma with the milk. His sits on his mother's knee, gulping the milk with grunts and sighs of satisfaction—nor ceases till the cup is exhausted, once, and again, and again—and even then asks for more. On being undressed, he is taking an airbath—he enjoys the felicity of utter nakedness—running away from Mamma with cries of remonstrance, when she wishes to put on his night-gown. Now ensues a terrible catastrophe—not to be mentioned in our seemly history. . . . Enter Una—"Where is little Julian?" "He has gone out to walk." "No; but I mean where is the place of little Julian, that you've been writing about him." So I point to the page, at which she looks with all possible satisfaction; and stands watching the pen as it hurries forward. "I'll put the ink nearer to you," says she. "Father, are you going to write all this?" she adds, turning over the book. . . . I tell her that I am now writing about herself—"That's nice writing," says she. . . . Una now proposes to him to build a block house with her; so they set about it jointly; but it has scarcely risen above its foundation, before Julian tears it down. With unwearied patience, Una begins another. "Papa! 'Ouse!" cries Julian, pointing to two blocks which he has laid together. . . . They quit the blocks, and Julian again offers to climb the chair to the bookcase; and is again forbidden by me;—whereupon he cries—Una runs to kiss and comfort him—and then comes to me with a solemn remonstrance, of no small length; the burthen being, "Father, you should not speak so loudly to a little boy who is only half years old". . . . She comes and takes her place silently in my lap, resting her head on my shoulder. Julian has clambered into a chair at the window, and appears to observe and meditate; so that we have a very quiet interval, until he disturbs it by coming and pulling off her shoe. He seldom pretermits any mischief that his hand finds to do:—for instance, finding her bare knee, he has just taken occasion to pinch it with all his might . . .

Hawthorne repeated the exercise four days later, on Thursday, March twenty-third, and six times more in 1849, covering what would amount to another thirty pages in Centenary Edition of the *Notebooks*. Adding to his descriptions of his children's games and squabbles and inner storms, he sometimes paused to make a number of more generalized remarks about their personalities. Two small passages about Una are of particular interest, since she is usually taken to be the model on which he based the character of Pearl in *The Scarlet Letter*. From January 28, 1849: "Her beauty is the most flitting, transitory, most uncertain and unaccountable affair, that ever had a real existence; it beams out when nobody expects it, it has mysteriously passed away, when you think yourself sure of it;—if you glance sideways at her, you perhaps think it is illuminating her face, but, turning full round to enjoy it, it is gone again. . . . When really visible, it is rare and precious as the vision of an angel; it is a transfiguration—a grace, delicacy, an ethereal fineness, which, at once, in my secret soul, makes me give up all severe opinions that I may have begun to form respecting her. It is but fair to conclude that, on these occasions, we see her real soul; when she seems less lovely, we merely see something external. But, in truth, one manifestation belongs to her as much as another; for, before the establishment of principles, what is character but the series and succession of moods?" From July thirtieth of the same year: ". . . There is something that almost frightens me about the child—I know not whether elfish or angelic, but, at all events, supernatural. She steps so boldly into the midst of everything, shrinks from nothing, has such a comprehension of everything, seems at times to have but little delicacy, and anon shows that she possesses the finest essence of it; now so hard, now so tender; now so perfectly unreasonable, soon again so wise. In short, I now and then catch an aspect of her, in which I cannot believe her to be my own human child, but a spirit strangely mingled with good and evil, haunting the house where I dwell. The little boy is always the same child, and never varies in relation to me."

By the summer of 1851, Hawthorne was a seasoned observer of his own children, a veteran of family life. He was forty-seven years old and had been married for close to a decade. He couldn't have known it then, but nearly every important word of fiction he would ever publish had already been written. Behind him were the two editions of *Twice-Told Tales* (1837 and 1842), *Mosses from an Old Manse* (1846), and *The Snow-Image and Other Twice-Told Tales* (already finished and planned for publication in late 1851)—his entire output as a writer of short stories. His first two novels had been published in 1850 and 1851. *The Scarlet Letter* had turned "the obscurest man of letters in America" into one of the most respected and celebrated writers of his time, and *The House of the Seven Gables* had only strengthened his reputation, prompting many critics to call him the finest writer the Republic had yet produced. Years of solitary labor had at last won him public reward, and after two decades of scrambling to make ends meet, 1851 marked the first year that Hawthorne earned enough from his writing to be able to support his family. Nor was there any reason to think that his success would not continue. Throughout the spring and early summer, he had written *A Wonder Book for Girls and Boys*, finishing the preface on July fifteenth, just two weeks before Sophia's departure for West Newton, and he was already making plans for his next novel, *The Blithedale Romance*. Looking back on Hawthorne's career now, and knowing that he would be dead just thirteen years later (a few weeks short of his sixtieth birthday), that season in Lenox stands out as one of the happiest periods of his life, a moment of sublime equipoise and fulfillment. But it was nearly August now, and for many years Hawthorne had routinely suspended his literary work during the hot months. It was a time for loafing and reflection, in his opinion, a time for being outdoors, and he had always written as little as possible throughout the dog days of the New England summers. When he composed his little chronicle of the three weeks he spent with his son, he was not stealing time from other, more important projects. It was the only work he did, the only work he wanted to do.

The move to Lenox had been precipitated by Hawthorne's disastrous experiences in Salem in 1849. As he put it in a letter to his friend Horatio Bridge, he had come to dislike the town "so much that I hate to go into the streets or to have the people see me. Anywhere else, I shall at once be entirely another man." Appointed to the post of Surveyor in the Salem Custom House in 1846 (during the Democratic administration of James Polk), Hawthorne accomplished almost nothing as a writer during the three years he held this job. With the election of Whig candidate Zachary Taylor in 1848, Hawthorne was sacked when the new administration took office in March 1849—but not without raising a great noise in his own defense, which led to a highly publicized controversy about the practice of political patronage in America. At the precise moment when this struggle was being waged, Hawthorne's mother died after a short illness. The notebook entries from those days in late July are among the most wrenching, emotionally charged paragraphs in all of Hawthorne. "Louisa pointed to a chair near the bed; but I was moved to kneel down close to my mother, and take her hand. She knew me, but could only murmur a few indistinct words—among which I understood an injunction to take care of my sisters. Mrs. Dike left the chamber, and then I found the tears slowly gathering in my eyes. I tried to keep them down; but it would not be—I kept filling up, till, for a few moments, I shook with sobs. For a long time, I knelt there, holding her hand; and surely it is the darkest hour I have ever lived."

Ten days after his mother's death, Hawthorne lost his fight to save his job. Within days of his dismissal (perhaps even the same day, if family legend is to be believed), he began writing *The Scarlet Letter*, which was completed in six months. Under great financial strain during this period, his fortunes took a sudden, unexpected turn for the better just as plans were being made by the firm of Ticknor and Fields to publish the novel. By private, anonymous subscription, friends and supporters of Hawthorne (among them, most likely, Longfellow and Lowell) "who admire your genius and respect your character . . . [and to pay] the debt we owe you for what you have done for American literature" had raised the sum of five hundred dollars to help see Hawthorne through his difficulties. This windfall allowed Hawthorne to carry out his increasingly urgent desire to leave Salem, his hometown, and become "a citizen of somewhere else."

After a number of possibilities fell through (a farm in Manchester, New Hampshire, a house in Kittery, Maine), he and Sophia eventually settled on the red farmhouse in Lenox. It was, as Hawthorne put it to one of his former Custom House co-workers, "as red as the Scarlet Letter." Sophia was responsible for finding the place, which was situated on a larger property known as Highwood, currently being rented by the Tappan family. Mrs. Tappan, née Caroline Sturgis, was a friend of Sophia's, and it was she who offered the house to the Hawthornes—free of charge. Hawthorne, wary of the complications that might arise from living off the generosity of others, struck a bargain with Mr. Tappan to pay a nominal rent of seventy-five dollars for four years.

One would assume that he was satisfied with the arrangement, but that didn't stop him from grumbling about any number of petty annoyances. No sooner did the family settle into the house than Hawthorne came down with a bad cold, which confined him to bed for several days, and before long he was complaining in a letter to his sister Louisa that the farmhouse was "the most wretched little hovel that I ever put my head in." (Even the optimistic Sophia, who tended to see every adversity in the best possible light, admitted in a letter to her mother that is was "the smallest of ten-foot houses"—barely adequate for a family of four, let alone five.) If the house displeased Hawthorne, he had even harsher things to say about the landscape that surrounded it. Sixteen months after moving in, he wrote to his publisher, James T. Fields, that "I have staid here too long and constantly. To tell you a secret, I am sick to death of Berkshire, and hate to think of spending another winter here. . . . The air and climate do not agree with my health at all; and, for the first time since I was a boy, I have felt languid and dispirited, during almost my whole residence here. Oh that Providence would build me the merest little shanty, and make me out a rood or two of garden-ground, near the sea-coast." Two years later, long after he had moved away and resettled in Concord, he was still grinding the same axe, as shown in this passage from the introduction to *Tanglewood Tales* (a second volume of Greek myths for children): "But, to me, there is a peculiar, quiet charm in these broad meadows and gentle eminences. They are better than mountains, because they do not stamp and stereotype thoughts into the brain, and thus grow wearisome with the same strong impression, repeated day after day. A few summer weeks among mountains, a lifetime among green meadows and placid slopes, with outlines forever new, because continually fading out of the memory. Such would be my sober choice." It is ironic that the area around Lenox should still be referred to as "Tanglewood." The word was Hawthorne's invention and is now indelibly associated with the music festival that takes place there every year. For a man who hated the area and ran away from it after just eighteen months, he left his mark on it forever.

Still, it was the best moment of his life, whether he knew it or not. Solvent, successfully married to an intelligent and famously devoted woman, in the middle of the most prolific writing burst of his career, Hawthorne planted his vegetable garden, fed his chickens, and played with his children in the afternoon. The shyest and most reclusive of men, known for his habit of hiding behind rocks and trees to avoid talking to people he knew, Hawthorne largely kept to himself during his stint in the Berkshires, avoiding the social activities of the local gentry and appearing in town only to collect his mail at the post office and return home. Solitude was his natural element, and considering the circumstances of his life until his early thirties, it was remarkable that he had married at all. When you were a person whose ship-captain father had died in Surinam when you were four, when you had grown up with a remote and elusive mother who had lived in a state of permanent, isolated widowhood, when you had served what is probably the most stringent literary apprenticeship on record—locking yourself up in your room for twelve years in a house you had dubbed "Castle Dismal" and leaving Salem only in the summer to go on solitary rambles through the New England countryside—then perhaps the society of your immediate family was sufficient. Hawthorne had married late to a woman who had likewise married late, and in the twenty-two years they lived together, they were rarely apart. He called her Phoebe, Dove, Beloved, Dearissima, Ownest One. "Sometimes," he had written to her during their courtship in 1840, "during my solitary life in our old Salem house, it seemed to me as if I had only life enough to know that I was not alive; for I had no wife then to keep my heart warm. But, at length, you were revealed to me, in the shadow of a seclusion as deep as my own. I drew nearer and nearer to you, and opened my heart to you, and you came to me, and will remain forever, keeping my heart warm and renewing my life with your own. You only have taught me that I have a heart,—you only have thrown a light, deep downward and upward, into my soul. You only have revealed me to myself; for without your aid my best knowledge of myself would have been merely to know my own shadow,—to watch it flickering on the wall, and mistake its fantasies for my own real actions. Do you comprehend what you have done for me?"

They lived in isolation, but visitors nevertheless came (relatives, old friends), and they were in contact with several of their neighbors. One of them, who lived six miles down the road in Pittsfield, was Herman Melville, then thirty-one years old. Much has been written about the relationship between the two writers (some of it pertinent, some of it nonsense), but it is clear that Hawthorne opened up to the younger Melville with unaccustomed enthusiasm and took great pleasure in his company. As he wrote to his friend Bridge on August 7, 1850: "I met Melville, the other day, and liked him so much that I have asked him to spend a few days with me before leaving these parts." Melville had only been visiting the area at the time, but by October he was back, acquiring the property in Pittsfield he renamed Arrowhead and installing himself in the Berkshires as a fulltime resident. Over the next thirteen months, the two men talked, corresponded, and read each other's work, occasionally traveling the six miles between them to stay as a guest at the other's house. "Nothing pleases me more," Sophia wrote to her sister Elizabeth about the friendship between her husband and Melville (whom she playfully referred to as Mr. Omoo), "than to sit & hear this growing man dash his tumultuous waves of thought against Mr. Hawthorne's great, genial, comprehending silences. . . . Without doing anything on his own, except merely *being*, it is astonishing how people make him their innermost Father Confessor." For Melville, the encounter with Hawthorne and his writings marked a fundamental turn in his life. He had already begun his story about the white whale at the time of their first meeting (projected as a conventional high-seas adventure novel), but under Hawthorne's influence the book began to change and deepen and expand, transforming itself in an unabated frenzy of inspiration into the richest of all American novels, *Moby-Dick*. As everyone who has read the book knows, the first page reads: "In token of my admiration for his genius, this book is inscribed to Nathaniel Hawthorne." Even if Hawthorne had accomplished nothing else during his stay in Lenox, he unwittingly served as Melville's muse.

The lease was good for four years, but shortly after the completion of *Twenty Days* and Sophia's return from West Newton with Una and baby Rose, Hawthorne contrived to get himself into a dispute with his landlords over a trivial matter of boundaries. The issue revolved around the question of whether he and his family had the right to pick the fruits and berries from the trees and bushes on the property. In a long, hilariously acidic letter to Mrs. Tappan dated September 5, 1851, Hawthorne set forth his case, concluding with a rather nasty challenge: "At any rate, take what you want, and that speedily, or there will be little else than a parcel of rotten plums to dispute about." A gracious, conciliatory letter from Mr. Tappan the following day—which Sophia characterized to her sister as "noble and beautiful"—seemed to settle the matter once and for all, but by then Hawthorne had already made up his mind to move, and the family soon packed up their belongings and were gone from the house on November twenty-first.

Just one week earlier, on November fourteenth, Melville had received his first copies of *Moby-Dick*. That same day, he drove his wagon over to the red farmhouse and invited Hawthorne to a farewell dinner at Curtis's Hotel in Lenox, where he presented his friend with a copy of the book. Until then, Hawthorne had known nothing about the effusive dedication to him, and while there is no record of his reaction to this unexpected tribute to "his genius," one can only surmise that he was deeply moved. Moved enough, in any case, to begin reading the book immediately upon returning home, surrounded by the chaos of boxes and packing crates as his family prepared for their departure. He must have read the book quickly and intensely, for his letter of response reached Melville on the sixteenth. All but one of Hawthorne's letters to Melville have been lost, but numerous letters from Melville to Hawthorne have survived, and his answer to this one is among the most memorable and frequently quoted letters in all of American literature: ". . . A sense of unspeakable security is in me this moment, on account of your having understood the book. I have written a wicked book, and feel spotless as the lamb. Ineffable socialities are in me. I would sit down and dine with you and all the gods in old Rome's Pantheon. . . . Whence come you, Hawthorne? By what right do you drink from the flagon of my life? And when I put it to my lips—lo, they are yours and not mine. I feel that the Godhead is broken up like the bread at the Supper, and that we are the pieces. Hence this infinite fraternity of feeling. . . . I shall leave the world, I feel, with more satisfaction for having come to know you. Knowing you persuades me more than the Bible of our immortality."

Melville makes a couple of appearances in *Twenty Days with Julian &*

Little Bunny, but the gist of the piece is the little boy himself, the daily activities of father and son, the ephemeral nothings of domestic life. No dramas are reported, the routine is fairly monotonous, and in terms of content, one can hardly imagine a duller or more pedestrian undertaking. Hawthorne kept the diary for Sophia. It was written in a separate family notebook which they both used to record material about the children (and which the children had access to as well, sometimes adding drawings and infant scribbles of their own—and, in a few instances, even tracing their pencils directly over texts written by their parents). Hawthorne intended his wife to read the little work after her return from West Newton, and it appears that she did so at the earliest opportunity. Describing the trip home to Lenox in a letter to her mother three days later (August 19, 1851), Sophia wrote, ". . . Una was very tired, and her eyes looked as cavernous as Daniel Webster's till she saw the red house; and then she began to shout, and clap her hands for joy. Mr. Hawthorne came forth with a thousand welcomes in his eyes, and Julian leaped like a fountain, and was as impossible to hold fast. . . . I found that Mr. Hawthorne had written a minute account of his and Julian's life from the hour of our departure. He had a tea-party of New York gentlemen one day, and they took him and Julian a long drive; and they all had a picnic together, and did not get home till eight o'clock. Mr. Melville came with these gentlemen, and once before in my absence. Mr. Hawthorne also had a visit from a Quaker lady of Philadelphia, Elizabeth Lloyd, who came to see the author of "The Scarlet Letter." He said that it was a very pleasant call. Mr. [G.P.R.] James also came twice, once with a great part of his family, once in a storm. Julian's talk flowed like a babbling brook, he writes, the whole three weeks, through all his meditations and reading. They spent a great deal of time at the lakes, and put Nat's ship out to sea. . . . Sometimes Julian pensively yearned for mama, but was not once out of temper or unhappy. There is a charming history of poor little Bunny, who died the morning of the day we returned. It did not appear why he should die, unless he lapped water off the bathing-room floor. But he was found stark and stiff. Mrs. Peters was very smiling, and grimly glad to see me . . ."

After Hawthorne's death in 1864, Sophia was prevailed upon by James T. Fields, Hawthorne's publisher and also the editor of the *Atlantic Monthly*, to choose excerpts from her husband's notebooks for publication in the magazine. Passages appeared in twelve successive issues in 1866, but when it came to *Twenty Days with Julian & Little*

Bunny, which Fields was hoping to include, she hesitated, claiming that Julian would have to be consulted first. Her son apparently had no objections, but still Sophia was reluctant to give her consent, and after some further reflection she decided against printing the material, explaining to Fields that Hawthorne "would never have wished such an intimate domestic history to be made public, and I am astonished at myself that I ever thought of it." In 1884, when Julian published his own book, *Nathaniel Hawthorne and His Wife*, he included a number of extracts from *Twenty Days*, commenting that the three weeks he spent alone with his father "must have been weary work, sometimes, for Hawthorne, though for the little boy it was one uninterrupted succession of halcyon days." He mentions that a full version of the diary would make "as unique and quaint a little history as was ever seen," but it wasn't until 1932, when Randall Stewart put together the first scholarly edition of the *American Notebooks*, that *Twenty Days with Julian & Little Bunny* was finally made available to the public. Not as a separate book (as Julian had suggested) but as one section in a lengthy volume of 800 pages that spans the years 1835 to 1853.

Why publish it now as an independent work? Why should this small, uneventful piece of prose command our interest more than one hundred-fifty years after it was written? I wish I could mount a cogent defense on its behalf, make some dazzling, sophisticated argument that would prove its greatness, but if the piece is great, it is great only in miniature, great only because the writing, in and of itself, gives pleasure. *Twenty Days* is a humorous work by a notoriously melancholic man, and anyone who has ever spent an extended length of time in the company of a small child will surely respond to the accuracy and honesty of Hawthorne's account.

Una and Julian were raised in an unorthodox manner, even by the standards of mid-nineteenth-century Transcendentalist New England. Although they reached school-age during their time in Lenox, neither one was sent to school, and they spent their days at home with their mother, who took charge of their education and rarely allowed them to mingle with other children. The hermetic, Eden-like atmosphere that Hawthorne and Sophia tried to establish in Concord after their marriage apparently continued after they became parents. Writing to her mother from Lenox, Sophia eloquently delineated her philosophy of childrearing: ". . . Alas for those who counsel sternness and severity instead of love towards their young children! How little they are like God, how much they are like Solomon, whom I really believe many persons prefer to imitate, and think they do well. Infinite patience, infinite tenderness, infinite magnanimity,—no less will do, and we must practise them as far as finite power will allow. Above all, no parent should feel a *pride of power*. This, I doubt not, is the great stumbling-block, and it should never be indulged. From this comes the sharp rebuke, the cruel blow, the anger. A tender sorrow, a most sympathizing regret, alone should appear at the transgression of a child . . . Yet how immitigable is the judgment and treatment of these little misdemeanors often! When my children disobey, I am not personally aggrieved, and they see it, and find therefore that it is a disinterested desire that they should do right that induces me to insist. There is all the difference in the world between indulgence and tenderness."

Hawthorne, who acceded to his wife in all family and household matters, took a far less active role in raising the children. "If only papa wouldn't write, how nice it would be," Julian quoted Una as having declared one day, and according to him "their feeling about all their father's writings was, that he was being wasted in his study, when he might be with them, and there could be nothing in any books, whether his own or other authors', that could for a moment bear comparison with his actual companionship." When he finished working for the day, it seems that Hawthorne preferred acting as playmate with his children than as classic paternal figure. "Our father was a great tree-climber," Julian recalled, "and he was also fond of playing the magician. 'Hide your eyes!' he would say, and the next moment, from being there beside us on the moss, we would hear his voice descending from the sky, and behold! he swung among the topmost branches, showering down upon us a hail-storm of nuts." In her numerous letters and journal entries from that period, Sophia frequently noted glimpses of Hawthorne alone with the two children. "Mr. Hawthorne," she informed her mother, "has been lying down in the sunshine, slightly fleckered with the shadows of a tree, and Una and Julian have been making him look like the mighty Pan by covering his chin and breast with long grass-blades, that looked like a verdant, venerable beard." And again to her mother several days later: "Dear little harp-souled Una—whose love for her father grows more profound every day . . . was made quite unhappy because he did not go at the same time with her to the lake. His absence darkened all the sunshine to her; and when I asked her why she could not enjoy the walk as Julian did, she replied, 'Ah, *he* does not love papa as *I* do!'. . . .

After I put Julian to bed, I went out to the barn to see about the chickens, and she wished to go. There sat papa on the hay, and like a needle to a magnet she was drawn, and begged to see papa a little longer, and stay with him. Now she has come, weary enough; and after steeping her spirit in this rose and gold of twilight, she has gone to bed. With such a father, and such a scene before her eyes, and *with eyes to see*, what may we not hope of her? I heard her and Julian talking together about their father's smile, the other day—They had been speaking of some other person's smile—Mr. Tappan's, I believe; and presently Una said, 'But you know, Julian, that there is no smile like papa's!' 'Oh no,' replied Julian. 'Not like *papa's*!' " In 1904, many years after Una's early death at the age of thirty-three, Thomas Wentworth Higginson published a memorial piece about her in *The Outlook*, a popular magazine of the period. In it, he quoted her as once having said to him about her father: "He was capable of being the gayest person I ever saw. He was like a boy. Never was such a playmate as he in all the world."

All this lies behind the spirit of *Twenty Days with Julian & Little Bunny*. The Hawthornes were a consciously progressive family, and for the most part their treatment of their children corresponds to attitudes prevalent among the secular middle-class in America today. No harsh discipline, no physical punishment, no strident reprimands. Some people found the Hawthorne children obstreperous and unruly, but Sophia, ever inclined to see them as model creatures, happily reported in a letter to her mother that at a local torchlight festival "the children enjoyed themselves extremely, and behaved so beautifully that they won all hearts. They thought that there never was such a superb child as Julian, nor such a grace as Una. 'They are neither too shy, nor bold,' said Mrs. Field, 'but just right.' " What constitutes "just right," of course, is a matter of opinion. Hawthorne, who was always more rigorous in his observations than his wife—unable, by force of instinct and habit, to allow love to color his judgments—makes no bones about how annoying Julian's presence sometimes was to him. That theme is sounded on the first page of the diary, and it recurs repeatedly throughout the twenty days they spent together. The boy was a champion chatterbox, a pint-sized engine of logorrhea, and within hours of Sophia's departure, Hawthorne was already complaining that "it is impossible to write, read, think, or even to sleep (in the daytime) so constant are his appeals to me in one way or another." By the second evening, after remarking once again on the endless stream of babble that issued from

Julian's lips, Hawthorne put him to bed and added: "nor need I hesitate to say that I was glad to be rid of him—it being my first relief from his society during the whole day. This may be too much of a good thing." Five days later, on August third, he was again harping on the same subject: "Either I have less patience to-day than ordinary, or the little man makes larger demands upon it; but it really does seem as if he had baited me with more questions, references, and observations, than mortal father ought to be expected to endure." And again on August fifth: "He continues to pester me with his inquisitions. For instance, just now, while he is whittling with my jack-knife. 'Father, if you had bought all the jack-knives at the shop, what would you do for another, when you broke them all?' 'I would go somewhere else,' say I. But there is no stumping him. 'If you had bought all the jack-knives in the world, what would you do?' And here my patience gives way, and I entreat him not to trouble me with any more foolish questions. I really think it would do him good to spank him, apropos to this habit." And once again on August tenth: "Mercy on me, was ever man before so be-pelted with a child's talk as I am!"

These little bursts of irritation are precisely what give the text its charm—and its truth. No sane person can endure the company of a high-voltage child without an occasional meltdown, and Hawthorne's admissions of less-than-perfect calm turn the diary into something more than just a personal album of summer memories. There is sweetness in the text, to be sure, but it is never cloying (too much wit, too much bite), and because Hawthorne refrains from glossing over his own faults and downcast moments, he takes us beyond a strictly private space into something more universal, more human. Again and again, he curbs his temper whenever he is on the verge of losing it, and the talk of spanking the boy is no more than a passing impulse, a way of letting off steam with his pen instead of his hand. By and large, he shows remarkable forbearance in dealing with Julian, indulging the five-year-old in his whims and escapades and cockeyed discourses with steadfast equanimity, readily allowing that "he is such a genial and good-humored little man that there is certainly an enjoyment intermixed with all the annoyance." In spite of the difficulties and possible frustrations, Hawthorne was determined not to rein in his son too tightly. After the birth of Rose in May, Julian had been forced to tiptoe around the house and speak in whispers. Now, suddenly, he is permitted to "shout and squeal just as loud as I please," and the father sympathizes with the boy's craving for commotion. "He enjoys his freedom so greatly," Hawthorne writes on the second day, "that I do not mean to restrain him, whatever noise he makes."

Julian was not the only source of irritation, however. On July twenty-ninth, the wifeless husband unexpectedly exploded, blasting forth with a splenetic tirade on one of his constant obsessions: "This is a horrible, horrible, most hor-ri-ble climate; one knows not, for ten minutes together, whether he is too cool or too warm; but he is always one or the other; and the constant result is a miserable disturbance of the system. I detest it! I detest it!! I de-test it!!! I hate Berkshire with my whole soul, and would joyfully see its mountains laid flat." On August eighth, after an excursion with Melville and others to the Shaker community in nearby Hancock, he had nothing but the most vicious and cutting remarks to offer about the sect: ". . . all their miserable pretence of cleanliness and neatness is the thinnest superficiality . . . the Shakers are and must needs be a filthy set. And then their utter and systematic lack of privacy; their close junction of man with man [two men routinely slept in one small bed], and supervision of one man over another—it is hateful and disgusting to think of; and the sooner the sect is extinct the better . . ." Then, with a kind of gloating sarcasm, he applauds Julian for answering a call of nature during their visit and defecating on the property. "All through this outlandish village went our little man, happy and dancing, in excellent spirits; nor had he been there long before he desired to confer with himself—neither was I unwilling that he should bestow such a mark of his consideration (being the one of which they were most worthy) on the system and establishment of these foolish Shakers." Less severely, perhaps, but with a noticeable touch of disdain, he also had some unkind things to say about his neighbor and landlady, Caroline Tappan—a good month before the infamous fruit-tree controversy, which would suggest a prior antipathy, perhaps one of long standing. (Some biographers have speculated that she made a pass at Hawthorne during Sophia's absence—or at least would have been willing to do so if he had given her any encouragement.) Hawthorne and Julian had given the pet rabbit to the Tappans, thinking the animal might be happier in the larger house, but for various reasons (a threatening dog, mistreatment by the Tappans' young daughter) the new arrangement had not worked out. Mrs. Tappan came to Hawthorne and "spoke of giving him to little Marshall Butler, and suggested, moreover (in reply to something I said about putting him out of existence) that he might be turned out into the woods, to shift for himself. There is something characteristic in this idea; it shows the sort of sensitiveness, that finds the pain and misery of other people disagreeable, just as it would a bad scent, but is perfectly at ease once they are removed from her sphere. I suppose she would not for the world have killed Bunny, although she would have exposed him to the certainty of lingering starvation, without scruple or remorse."

Apart from these rare instances of pique and outrage, the atmosphere of *Twenty Days* is serene, measured, bucolic. Every morning, Hawthorne and Julian went to fetch milk at a neighboring farm; they engaged in "sham battles," collected the mail at the Lenox post office in the afternoon, and made frequent trips to the lake. On the way, they would "wage war with the thistles," which was Julian's favorite sport—pretending that the thistles were dragons and beating them heartily with sticks. They collected flowers, gathered currants, and picked green beans and summer squashes from the garden. Hawthorne built a makeshift boat for Julian, using a newspaper as a sail; a drowning cat was saved from a cistern; and during their visits to the lake, they variously fished, flung stones into the water, and dug in the sand. Hawthorne gave Julian a bath every morning and then wrestled with the task of trying to curl his hair, seldom with satisfactory results. There was a bed-wetting accident on August third, a painful wasp-sting on the fifth, a stomach ache and a headache to be attended to on the thirteenth and fourteenth, and an untimely loss of bladder control during a walk home on the sixth, which prompted Hawthorne to remark "I heard him squealing, while I was some distance behind; and approaching nearer I saw that he walked wide between the legs. Poor little man! His drawers were all a-sop." Even if he wasn't completely at home with the job, the father had little by little become the mother, and by August twelfth we understand how thoroughly Hawthorne had assumed this role when, for the first time in more than two weeks, he suddenly lost track of where Julian was. "After dinner, I sat down with a book . . . and he was absent in parts unknown, for the space of an hour. At last I began to think it time to look him up; for, now that I am alone with him, I have all his mother's anxieties, added to my own. So I went to the barn, and to the currant-bushes, and shouted around the house, without response, and finally sat down on the hay, not knowing which way to seek him. But by and by, he ran round the house, holding up his little fist, with a smiling phiz, and crying out that he had something very good for me."

Barring the excursion to the Shaker Village with Melville on August eighth, the pair stayed close to home, but that outing proved to be an exhilarating experience for the little boy, and Hawthorne is at his best in capturing his enthusiasm, in being able to see the event through his son's eyes. The group lost its way on the carriage-ride home, and by the time they passed through Lenox, "it was beyond twilight; indeed, but for the full moon, it would have been quite dark. The little man behaved himself still like an old traveller; but sometimes he looked round at me from the front seat (where he sat between Herman Melville and Evert Duyckinck) and smiled at me with a peculiar expression, and put back his hand to touch me. It was a method of establishing a sympathy in what doubtless appeared to him the wildest and unprecedentedest series of adventures that had ever befallen mortal travellers."

The next morning, Julian announced to Hawthorne that he loved Mr. Melville as much as his father, his mother, and Una, and based on the evidence of a short letter that Melville sent to Julian six months later (long after the Hawthornes had left the Berkshires), it would appear that this fondness was reciprocated. "I am very happy that I have a place in the heart of so fine a little fellow as you," he wrote, and then, after commenting on the heavy snow-drifts in the woods around Pittsfield, concluded with a warm valediction: "Remember me kindly to your good father, Master Julian, and Good Bye, and may Heaven always bless you, & may you be a good boy and become a great good man."

An earlier visit from Melville to Lenox on August first (his thirty-second birthday) provided Hawthorne with what were probably his most pleasurable hours during those three weeks of bachelor life. After stopping in at the post office with Julian that afternoon, he paused on the way home in a secluded spot to read his newspapers when "a cavalier on horseback came along the road, and saluted me in Spanish; to which I replied by touching my hat, and went on with the newspaper. But the cavalier renewing his salutation, I regarded him more attentively, and saw that it was Herman Melville!" The two men walked the mile to the red house together (with Julian, "highly pleased," sitting atop Melville's horse), and then, in what are probably the most frequently quoted sentences from the *American Notebooks*, Hawthorne continues: "After supper, I put Julian to bed; and Melville and I had a talk about time and eternity, things of this world and of the next, and books, and publishers, and all possible and impossible matters, that lasted pretty deep into the night; and if truth must be told, we smoked cigars even within the sacred precincts of the sitting-room. At last, he arose, and saddled his horse (whom we had put into the barn) and rode off for his own domicile; and I hastened to make the most of what little sleeping-time remained for me."

That was the one galvanizing moment in an otherwise torpid stretch of days. When he wasn't taking care of Julian, Hawthorne wrote letters, read Fourier as he prepared to begin *The Blithedale Romance*, and took a half-hearted stab at Thackeray's *Pendennis*. The diary includes many keenly written passages about the shifting light of the landscape (few novelists looked at nature as attentively as Hawthorne did) and a handful of droll and increasingly sympathetic descriptions of Hindlegs, the pet rabbit, who unfortunately expired as the chronicle was coming to an end. More and more, however, as his solitude dragged on, Hawthorne yearned for his wife to come home. By the beginning of the final week, that feeling had been turned into a constant ache. After putting Julian to bed on the evening of August tenth, he suddenly let himself go, breaking down in a rhapsodic gush of longing and allegiance. "Let me say outright, for once, that he is a sweet and lovely little boy, and worthy of all the love that I am capable of giving him. Thank God! God bless him! God bless Phoebe for giving him to me! God bless her as the best wife and mother in the world! God bless Una, whom I long to see again! God bless Little Rosebud! God bless me, for Phoebe's and all their sakes! No other man has so good a wife; nobody has better children. Would I were worthier of her and them!" The entry then concludes: "My evenings are all dreary, alone, and without books that I am in the mood to read; and this evening was like the rest. So I went to bed at about nine, and longed for Phoebe."

He was expecting her to return on the thirteenth, then on the fourteenth, then on the fifteenth, but various delays and missed communications put off Sophia's departure from West Newton until the sixteenth. Increasingly anxious and frustrated, Hawthorne nevertheless pushed on dutifully with the diary. On the very last day, during yet another visit to the lake with Julian, he sat down at the edge of the water with a magazine, and as he read, he was moved to make the following observation, which in some sense stands as a brief and inadvertent *ars poetica*, a precise description of the spirit and methodology of all his writing: ". . . the best way to get a vivid impression and feeling of a landscape, is to sit down before it and read, or become otherwise absorbed in thought; for then, when your eyes happen to be attracted to the landscape, you seem to catch Nature at unawares, and see her before she has time to change her aspect. The effect lasts but for a single instant, and passes away almost as soon as you are conscious of it; but it is real, for that moment. It is as if you could overhear and understand what the trees are whispering to one another; as if you caught a glimpse of a face unveiled, which veils itself from every wilful glance. The mystery is revealed, and after a breath or two, becomes just as much a mystery as before."

As with landscapes, so with people, especially little people in the flush of childhood. All is change with them, all is movement, and you can grasp their essence only "at unawares," at moments when you are not consciously looking for it. That is the beauty of Hawthorne's little piece of notebook-writing. Throughout all the drudgery and tedium of his constant companionship with the five-year-old boy, Hawthorne was able to glance at him often enough to capture something of his essence, to bring him to life in words. A century and a half later, we are still trying to discover our children, but these days we do it by taking snapshots and following them around with video cameras. But words are better, I think, if only because they don't fade with time. It takes more effort to write a truthful sentence than to focus a lens and push a button, of course, but words go deeper than pictures do—which can rarely record anything more than the surfaces of things, whether landscapes or the faces of children. In all but the best or luckiest photographs, the soul is missing. That is why *Twenty Days with Julian & Little Bunny* merits our attention. In his modest, deadpan way, Hawthorne managed to accomplish what every parent dreams of doing: to keep his child alive forever.

July *2002*

OCCASIONS

A Prayer for Salman Rushdie

When I sat down to write this morning, the first thing I did was think of Salman Rushdie. I have done this every morning for almost four and a half years, and by now it is an essential part of my daily routine. I pick up my pen, and before I begin to write, I think of my fellow novelist across the ocean. I pray that he will go on living another twenty-four hours. I pray that his English protectors will keep him hidden from the people who are out to murder him—the same people who have already killed one of his translators and wounded another. Most of all, I pray that a time will come when these prayers are no longer necessary, when Salman Rushdie will be as free to walk the streets of the world as I am.

I pray for this man every morning, but deep down, I know that I am also praying for myself. His life is in danger because he wrote a book. Writing books is my business as well, and I know that if not for the quirks of history and pure blind luck, I could be in his shoes. If not today, then perhaps tomorrow. We belong to the same club: a secret fraternity of solitaries, shut-ins, and cranks, men and women who spend the better part of our time locked up in little rooms struggling to put words on a page. It is a strange way to live one's life, and only a person who had no choice in the matter would choose it as a calling. It is too arduous, too underpaid, too full of disappointments to be fit for anyone else. Talents vary, ambitions vary, but any writer worth his salt will tell you the same thing: To write a work of fiction, one must be free to say what one has to say. I have exercised that freedom with every word I have written—and so has Salman Rushdie. That is what makes us brothers, and that is why his predicament is also mine.

I can't know how I would act in his place, but I can imagine it—or at least I can try to imagine it. In all honesty, I'm not sure I would be capable of the courage he has shown. The man's life is in ruins, and yet he has continued to do the thing he was born to do. Shunted from one safehouse to another, cut off from his son, surrounded by security police, he has continued to go to his desk every day and write. Knowing how difficult it is to do this even under the best of circumstances, I can only stand in awe of what he has accomplished. A novel; another novel in the works; a number of extraordinary essays and speeches defending the basic human right to free expression. All that is remarkable enough, but what truly astonishes me is that on top of this essential work, he has taken the time to review other people's books—in some cases even to write blurbs promoting the books of unknown authors. Is it possible for a man in his position to think of anyone but himself? Yes, apparently it is. But I wonder how many of us could do what he has done with our backs against that same wall.

Salman Rushdie is fighting for his life. The struggle has gone on for nearly half a decade, and we are no closer to a solution than when the *fatwa* was first announced. Like so many others, I wish there was something I could do to help. Frustration mounts, despair sets in, but given that I have neither the power nor the influence to affect the decisions of foreign governments, the most I can do is pray for him. He is carrying the burden for all of us, and I can no longer think of what I do without thinking of him. His plight has focused my concentration, has made me reexamine my beliefs, has taught me never to take the freedom I enjoy for granted. For all that, I owe him an immense debt of gratitude. I support Salman Rushdie in his struggle to win back his life, but the truth is that he has also supported me. I want to thank him for that. Every time I pick up my pen, I want to thank him.

1993

Appeal to the Governor of Pennsylvania

I am not here today to argue the pros and cons of the death penalty (I am fervently against it) nor to talk about the question of race relations in America (surely the central, burning issue of our culture) nor to get sidetracked into a discussion of free speech and first amendment rights. I simply want to address some words to the Honorable Thomas Ridge, Governor of Pennsylvania, who is the only person whose opinion counts anymore in the whole miserable and tragic case of Mumia Abu-Jamal.

As one American citizen to another, I would like the Governor to stop and consider the enormous power he has been given: the power to kill a man or to allow that man to go on living. Whatever the jury has decided about what Mumia Abu-Jamal did or didn't do, whatever laws might support the state of Pennsylvania's right to put Mumia Abu-Jamal to death, you have been designated by those same laws as the one person in that state with the authority to nullify the decision of the jury and save Mumia Abu-Jamal's life. That is because the law knows it isn't perfect. The law understands that it makes mistakes, that the men and women who carry out the law are imperfect creatures, and therefore the power to nullify the decisions of the law must be written into the law itself. In no instance is this more important than when the law proposes to take a man's life. That is why the appeals in such cases go directly to the governor—because the governor is assumed to be wise and just, even if the law isn't always wise and just.

Governor Ridge, you have been asked to take on the largest, most terrible task a man can be given: to decide another man's fate. Mumia Abu-Jamal's life is literally in your hands. Considering the enormous power and responsibility that have been thrust upon you, I take it for granted that you are intimately familiar with the facts of the case. Even I, an ordinary citizen with no power at all, have read endless amounts of material concerning the trial, and every report has indicated numerous irregularities and discrepancies with regard to jury selection, evidence, and the testimony of witnesses—enough for even the most cynical observer to conclude that there is far more than just a shadow of a doubt as to whether Mumia Abu-Jamal actually committed the crime he was accused of. And as long as there is a doubt, as long as a plausible argument can be made that Mumia Abu-Jamal did not do what he has been found guilty of doing, then it strikes me as monstrous that his life can be taken from him—monstrous and shameful, a sin against the laws of man and God.

Governor Ridge, we all want to live in a country we can be proud of. We all want to believe that America is a country in which there is, truly, justice for all. That is the single most important idea we have ever produced, and now it is your turn to uphold that principle and prove that America is indeed a great country worthy of the respect and admiration we want to give it. All eyes are on you, Governor Ridge. I am watching you, my fellow writers at PEN are watching you, tens of thousands of people around the world are watching you, and we are all praying that you will do what is wise and just.

Do us all proud, Governor. Save Mumia Abu-Jamal's life.

1995

The Best Substitute for War

When I was asked to write something about "the millennium," the first word that came to me was "Europe." The millennium is a European idea, after all, and it makes sense only if one refers to the European calendar, the Christian calendar. Most of the world keeps time by that calendar now, but go back a thousand years, and no one in Asia, Africa, or the Americas would have known what you were talking about if you had told him he was living in the year 1000AD. Europe is the only place on earth that has experienced this millennium from beginning to end, and when I cast about in my mind for a single, dominant image or idea that might sum up the past ten centuries of European history (when someone asks you to talk about "the millennium," you tend to take the long view), the word that kept coming back to me was "bloodshed." And by that I mean the metaphysics of violence: war, mass destruction, the slaughter of the innocent.

This is not to denigrate the glories of European culture and civilization. But in spite of Dante and Shakespeare, in spite of Vermeer and Goya, in spite of Chartres and the Declaration of the Rights of Man, it's a proven fact that scarcely a month has gone by in the past thousand years when one group of Europeans has not been intent on killing another group of Europeans. Country has fought against country (the Hundred Years War), alliances of countries have fought against other alliances of countries (the Thirty Years War), and the citizens of a single country have fought against each other (the French Religious Wars). When it comes to our own, much vaunted century of progress and enlightenment, just fill in the appropriate blanks. And lest anyone think the carnage has ended, he has only to open the paper and read about the current situation in former Yugoslavia. Not to speak of what has been happening in Northern Ireland for the past thirty years.

Mercifully, there has been peace among the major European powers since the end of World War II. For the first forty-five postwar years, that peace was tainted by another kind of war, but since the fall of the Berlin Wall and the breakup of the Soviet Union, the peace has held. This is unprecedented in European history. With a common currency on the horizon and passport-free borders already a reality, it looks as though the combatants have finally put down their arms. That doesn't mean they like each other, and it doesn't mean that nationalism is any less fervent than it used to be, but for once it seems that the Europeans have found a way to hate each other without hacking each other to pieces. This miracle goes by the name of soccer.

I don't want to exaggerate, but how else to interpret the facts? When France pulled off a surprise victory in the World Cup last summer, more than a million people gathered on the Champs-Elysées to celebrate. By all accounts, it was the largest demonstration of public happiness seen in Paris since the Liberation from the Germans in 1944.

One could only gape at the enormity of the event, the sheer excessiveness of the joy on display. It was just a sports victory, I kept telling myself, and yet there it was for everyone to see: on the same street in the same city, the same festive jubilation, the same outpouring of national pride that greeted General de Gaulle when he marched through the Arc de Triomphe fifty-four years earlier.

As I watched this scene on television, I thought of the title of a book I had read earlier in the decade: *The Soccer War*, by Ryszard Kapuściński. Was it possible that soccer had become a *substitute* for war?

Compared to American football, the European version seems rather tame, but the truth is that the history of soccer has always been steeped in violence. Legend or not, the first reference to football-playing in this millennium stems from an incident of war. In the year 1000 or thereabouts, the British were supposed to have celebrated their victory over an invading Danish chieftain by removing his head from his body and using it as a football. We don't have to believe that story, but verifiable documents confirm that by the 1100s Shrove Tuesdays were celebrated throughout England with massive football matches that pitted entire towns against one another. Five hundred players on a side. A field that could be up to several miles long. And games that lasted all day, with no fixed rules. It came to be known as "mob football," and the mayhem that resulted from these semi-organized brawls led to so many injuries, broken bones, and even deaths, that in 1314 Edward II issued an edict that banned the playing of football. "Forasmuch as there is great noise in the city, caused by hustling over large balls from which many evils might arise . . . we commend and forbid, on behalf of the King, on pain of imprisonment, such game to be used in the city in future."

Further bans were issued by Edward III, Richard II, and Henry IV.

These kings were not just disturbed by the violence of the sport, they were worried that too much "meddling in football" had cut into the time previously devoted to archery practice and that the kingdom would not be militarily prepared in the event of a foreign invasion. As far back as the first half of the millennium, then, the connection had already been made. War and football were two sides of the same coin.

With the development of firearms, archery ceased to be a required skill among soldiers, and by the late seventeenth century football was actively encouraged by Charles II. Standard rules were introduced in 1801, and as every schoolchild knows, Napoleon was defeated a decade and a half later "on the playing fields of Eton." After 1863, when the rules of present-day soccer were drawn up at Cambridge University, the game spread throughout Europe and the rest of the world. Since then, it has developed into the most popular and widely played sport in human history.

America seems to be the only country that has resisted its charms, but the importance of this game in Europe, its grip on the imagination of tens of millions of people living between Portugal and Poland, cannot be overestimated. Add together our interest in baseball, football, and basketball, then multiply by ten or twenty, and you begin to have an idea of the scope of the obsession. When you further consider that each country fields its own national team, and that these teams go head to head against each other in European and world tournaments, it isn't hard to imagine how the love of football and homeland can be turned into a cocktail for chauvinistic excess and the settling of ancient scores. No country in Europe has avoided invasion and humiliation by one or more of its neighbors during this millennium, and now, as we come to the end of these thousand years, it sometimes looks as though the entire history of the continent were being recapitulated on the soccer field. Holland versus Spain. England versus France. Poland versus Germany. An eerie memory of past antagonisms hovers over each game. Every time a goal is scored, one hears an echo of old victories and old defeats. Passions among the spectators run high. They wave their country's flag, they sing patriotic songs, they insult the supporters of the other team. Americans might look at these antics and think they're all in good fun, but they're not. They're serious business. But at least the mock battles waged by the surrogate armies in short pants do not threaten to increase the population of widows and fatherless children.

Yes, I am aware of the British football hooligans, and I know about the riots and injuries that occurred in several French cities during last year's World Cup. But these instances of extreme and violent behavior only reinforce my point. Soccer is a substitute for war. As long as countries square off against each other on the playing field, we will be able to count the casualties on the fingers of our two hands. A generation ago, they were tallied in the millions.

Does this mean that after a thousand years of bloodshed, Europe has finally found a peaceful way to settle its differences?

We'll see.

December 1, 1998

Reflections on a Cardboard Box

It's a cold and drizzly morning, eleven days before the end of the twentieth century. I am sitting in my house in Brooklyn, glad that I don't have to go out into that bleak December weather. I can sit here as long as I like, and even if I do go out at some point later in the day, I know that I will be able to return. Within a matter of minutes I will be warm and dry again.

I own this house. I bought it seven years ago by scraping together enough cash to cover one-fifth of the total price. The other 80 percent I borrowed from a bank. The bank has given me thirty years to pay off the loan, and every month I sit down and write them another check. After seven years, I have barely made a dent in the principal. The bank charges me for the service of holding the mortgage, and nearly every penny I have given them so far has gone toward reducing the interest I owe them. I don't complain. I'm happy to be spending this extra money (more than twice the amount of the loan) because it gives me a chance to live in this house. And I like it here. Especially on a raw and ugly morning like this one, I can think of no other place in the world where I'd rather be.

It costs me a lot of money to live here, but not as much as it would seem at first glance. When I pay my taxes in April, I'm allowed to deduct the entire amount I've spent on interest over the course of the year. It comes right off my income, no questions asked. The federal government does this for me, and I'm immensely grateful to them. Why shouldn't I be? It saves me thousands of dollars every year.

In other words, I accept welfare from the government. They have rigged things in such a way as to make it possible for a person like me to own a house. Everyone in the country agrees that this is a good idea, and not once have I heard of a congressman or a senator stepping forth to propose that this law be changed. In the past few years, welfare programs for the poor have been all but dismantled, but housing subsidies for the rich are still in place.

The next time you see a man living in a cardboard box, remember this.

The government encourages home ownership because it is good for business, good for the economy, good for public morale. It is also the universal dream, the American dream in its purest and most essential form. America measures itself as a civilization by this standard, and whenever we want to prove how successful we are, we begin by trotting out statistics which show that a greater percentage of our citizens own their own homes than anywhere else in the world. "Housing starts" is the key economic term, the bedrock indicator of our financial health. The more houses we build, the more money we will make, and the more money we make, the happier everyone will be.

And yet, as everyone knows, there are millions of people in this country who will never own a house, who struggle every month just to come up with the rent. We also know that there are many others who fall behind with the rent and are forced out onto the streets. We call them the homeless, but what we are really talking about is people who have no money. As with everything else in America, it comes down to a question of money.

A man does not live in a cardboard box because he wants to. He might be mentally deranged, he might be addicted to drugs, or he might be an alcoholic, but he is not in the box because he suffers from these problems. I have known dozens of madmen in my time, and many of them lived in beautiful houses. Show me the book in which it is written that an alcoholic is doomed to sleep on the sidewalk. He is just as likely to be driven around town by a chauffeur in a black hat. There is no cause and effect at work here. You live in a cardboard box because you can't afford to live anywhere else.

These are difficult days for the poor. We have entered a period of enormous prosperity, but as we rush down the highway of larger and larger profits, we forget that untold numbers of people are falling by the wayside. Wealth creates poverty. That is the secret equation of a free-market economy. We don't like to talk about it, but as the rich get richer and find themselves with greater and greater amounts of money to spend, prices have been going up. No one has to be told what has happened to the New York real estate market in the past several years. Housing costs have soared beyond what anyone would have thought possible just a short time ago. Even I, proud homeowner that I am, would not be able to afford my own house if I had to buy it today. For many others, the increases have spelled the difference between having a place to live and not having a place to live. For some people, it has been the difference between life and death.

Bad luck can hit any one of us at any time. It doesn't take much imagination to think of the various things that could do us in. Every person lives with the idea of his own destruction, and even the happiest and most successful person has some dark corner in his brain where horror stories are continually played out. You imagine that your house burns down. You imagine that you lose your job. You imagine that someone who depends on you comes down with an illness, and the medical bills wipe out your savings. Or else you gamble away your savings on a bad investment or a bad roll of the dice. Most of us are only one disaster away from genuine hardship. A series of disasters can ruin us. There are men and women wandering the streets of New York who were once in positions of apparent safety. They have college degrees. They held responsible jobs and supported their families. Now they have fallen on hard times, and who are we to think that such things couldn't happen to us?

For the past several months, a terrible debate has been poisoning the air of New York about what to do with *them*. What we should be talking about is what to do with ourselves. It is our city, after all, and what happens to them also happens to us. The poor are not monsters because they have no money. They are people who need help, and it doesn't help any of us to punish them for being poor. The new rules proposed by the current administration are not just cruel in my opinion, they don't make any sense. If you sleep on the street now, you will be arrested. If you go to a shelter, you will have to work for your bed. If you don't work, you will be thrown back onto the street—and there you will be arrested again. If you are a parent, and you don't comply with the work regulations, your children will be taken from you. The people who defend these ideas all profess to be devout, God-fearing men and women. They should know that every religion in the world insists on the importance of charity—not just as something to be encouraged, but as an obligation, as an essential part of one's relationship to God. Why has no one bothered to tell these people that they are hypocrites?

Meanwhile, it is getting later. Several hours have gone by since I sat down at my desk and began writing these words. I haven't stirred in all that time. The heat is rattling in the pipes, and the room is warm. Outside, the sky is dark, and the wind is lashing the rain against the side of the house. I have no answers, no advice to give, no suggestions. All I ask is that you think about the weather. And then, if you can, that you imagine yourself inside a cardboard box, doing your best to stay warm.

On a day like today, for example, eleven days before the end of the twentieth century, out in the cold and the clamor of the New York streets.

December 20, 1999

Random Notes—September 11, 2001—4:00 PM

Our fourteen-year-old daughter started high school today. For the first time in her life, she rode on the subway from Brooklyn to Manhattan—alone.

She will not be coming home tonight. The subways are no longer running in New York, and my wife and I have arranged for her to stay with friends on the Upper West Side.

Less than an hour after she passed under the World Trade Center, the Twin Towers crumbled to the ground.

From the top floor of our house, we can see the smoke filling the sky of the city. The wind is blowing toward Brooklyn today, and the smells of the fire have settled into every room of the house. A terrible, stinging odor: flaming plastic, electric wire, building materials.

My wife's sister, who lives in TriBeCa, just ten blocks north of what was once the World Trade Center, called to tell us about the screams she heard after the first tower collapsed. Friends of hers, who live on John Street, even closer to the site of the catastrophe, were evacuated by police after the door of their building was blown in by the impact. They walked north through the rubble and debris—which, they told her, contained human body parts.

After watching the news on television all morning, my wife and I went out for a walk in the neighborhood. Many people were wearing handkerchiefs over their faces. Some wore painters' masks. I stopped and talked to the man who cuts my hair, who was standing in front of his empty barber shop with an anguished look on his face. A few hours earlier, he said, the woman who owns the antique shop next door had been on the phone with her son-in-law—who had been trapped in his office on the 107th floor of the World Trade Center. Less than an hour after she spoke to him, the tower collapsed.

All day, as I have watched the horrific images on the television screen and looked at the smoke through the window, I have been thinking about my friend, the high-wire artist Philippe Petit, who walked between the towers of the World Trade Center in August 1974, just after construction of the buildings was completed. A small man dancing on a wire more than five hundred yards off the ground—an act of indelible beauty.

Today, that same spot has been turned into a place of death. It frightens me to contemplate how many people have been killed.

We all knew this could happen. We have been talking about the possibility for years, but now that the tragedy has struck, it's far worse than anyone ever imagined. The last foreign attack on American soil occurred in 1812. We have no precedent for what has happened today, and the consequences of this assault will no doubt be terrible. More violence, more death, more pain for everyone.

And so the twenty-first century finally begins.

September 11, 2001

Underground

Riding the subway at a busy time of day—morning rush hour, evening rush hour—and having the good luck to find a seat. Counting the number of newspapers not written in English, scanning the titles of books and watching people read (the mystery of it, the impossibility of entering another person's mind), listening in on conversations, sneaking a look at the baseball scores over someone's shoulder.

The thin men with their briefcases, the voluminous women with their Bibles and devotional pamphlets, the high school kids with their forty-pound textbooks. Trashy novels, comic books, Melville and Tolstoy, *How to Attain Inner Peace.*

Looking across the aisle at one's fellow passengers and studying their faces. Marveling at the variety of skin tones and features, floored by the singularity of each person's nose, each person's chin, exulting in the infinite shufflings of the human deck.

The panhandlers with their out-of-tune songs and tales of woe; the fractious harangues of born-again proselytizers; the deaf-mutes politely placing sign-language alphabet cards in your lap; the silent men who scuttle through the car selling umbrellas, tablecloths, and cheap wind-up toys.

The noise of the train, the speed of the train. The incomprehensible static that pours through the loudspeaker at each stop. The lurches, the sudden losses of balance, the impact of strangers crashing into one another. The delicate, altogether civilized art of minding one's own business.

And then, never for any apparent reason, the lights go out, the fans stop whirring, and everyone sits in silence, waiting for the train to start moving again. Never a word from anyone. Rarely even a sigh. My fellow New Yorkers sit in the dark, waiting with the patience of angels.

October 11, 2001

NYC = USA

Every day for a year, I read stories. The stories were short, true, and personal, and they were sent to me by men and women from all over America. On the first Saturday of every month, I would gather up some of my favorite ones and read them aloud on NPR's *Weekend All Things Considered*. We called the program the *National Story Project*, and in that year (October 1999 to October 2000) I received over 4000 submissions. They were written by country people and city people, by old people and young people, by people from all walks of life: farmers and priests, housewives and ex-soldiers, businessmen and doctors, postmen and meter readers, a restorer of player pianos, a trolley-bus driver, and several inmates at state correctional facilities.

Early on, I noticed a distinct and surprising trend. The only city that anyone ever wanted to talk about was New York. Not just New Yorkers, but people from every part of the country, some of whom had lived here in the past and regretted having moved away, some of whom had visited only once. In nearly every one of their stories, New York wasn't simply the backdrop for the events that were told, *it was the subject of the story itself.* Crazy New York, inspiring New York, fractious New York, ugly New York, beautiful New York, impossible New York—New York as the ultimate human spectacle of our time. America has had a tortured, even antagonistic relationship with our city over the years, but to an astonishing number of people from Michigan, Maine, and Nebraska, the five boroughs are a living embodiment of what the United States is all about: diversity, tolerance, and equality under the law. Alone among American cities, New York is more than just a place or an agglomeration of people. It is also an idea.

I believe that idea took hold in us when Emma Lazarus's poem was affixed to the pedestal of the Statue of Liberty. Bartholdi's gigantic effigy was originally intended as a monument to the principles of international republicanism, but "The New Colossus" reinvented the statue's purpose, turning Liberty into a welcoming mother, a symbol of hope to the outcasts and downtrodden of the world. New York has continued to represent the spirit of that message, and even today, 116 years after the unveiling of the statue, we still define ourselves as a city of immigrants. With 40 percent of our current population born in foreign countries, we are a cross-section of the entire world. It is a densely crowded ethnic hodge-podge, and the potential for chaos is enormous. No one would contend that we are not bedeviled by a multitude of problems, but when you think of what ethnic differences have done to cities like Sarajevo, Belfast, and Jerusalem, New York stands out as a shining example of civic peace and order.

The murderous attacks on the World Trade Center last September were rightly construed as an assault against the United States. New Yorkers felt that way, too, but it was our city that was bombed, and even as we wrestled to understand the hateful fanaticism that could lead to the deaths of 3000 innocent people, we experienced that day as a family tragedy. Most of us went into a state of intense mourning, and we dragged ourselves around in the days and months that followed engulfed by a sense of communal grief. It was that close to all of us, and I doubt there is a single New Yorker who doesn't know someone who didn't lose at least one friend or relative in the attack. Compute the numbers, and the results are staggering. Three thousand people in addition to their immediate families, their extended families, their friends, their neighbors, and their co-workers, and suddenly you're in the millions.

Last September 11 was one of the worst days in American history, but the dreadful cataclysm that occurred that morning was also an occasion for deep reflection, a time for all of us to stop and examine who we were and what we believed in. As it happened, I spent a good deal of time on the road last fall, co-hosting events with Jacki Lyden of NPR in connection with the release of the *National Story Project* anthology, *I Thought My Father Was God*. We traveled from Boston to San Francisco and points in between, and in each city contributors to the book read their stories in public to large and attentive audiences. I talked to scores of people on those trips, perhaps hundreds of people, and nearly every one of them told me the same thing. In the aftermath of September 11, they were reassessing the values of our country, trying to figure out what separated us from the people who had attacked us. Almost without exception, the single word they used was "democracy." That is the bedrock creed of American life: a belief in the dignity of the individual, a tolerant embrace of our cultural and religious differences. No matter how often we fail to live up to those ideals, that is America at its best—the very principles that are a constant, daily reality in New York.

It has been a year now. When the Bush administration launched its War on Terrorism by invading Afghanistan, we in New York were still busy counting our dead. We watched in horror as the smoking ruins of the towers were gradually cleared; we attended funerals with empty coffins; we wept. Even now, as the international situation turns ever more perilous, we are largely preoccupied with the debate over how to build a fitting memorial to the victims of the attack, trying to solve the problem of how to reconstruct that devastated area of our city. No one is sorry that the Taliban regime has been ousted from power, but when I talk to my fellow New Yorkers these days, I hear little but disappointment in what our government has been up to. Only a small minority of New Yorkers voted for George W. Bush, and most of us tend to look at his policies with suspicion. He simply isn't democratic enough for us. He and his cabinet have not encouraged open debate of the issues facing the country. With talk of an imminent invasion of Iraq now circulating in the press, increasing numbers of New Yorkers are becoming apprehensive. From the vantage point of Ground Zero, it looks like a global catastrophe in the making.

Not long ago, I received a poetry magazine in the mail with a cover that read: USA OUT OF NYC. Not everyone would want to go that far, but in the past several weeks I've heard a number of my friends talk with great earnestness and enthusiasm about the possibility of New York seceding from the Union and establishing itself as an independent city-state. That will never happen, of course, but I do have one practical suggestion. Since President Bush has repeatedly told us how much he dislikes Washington, why doesn't he come live in New York? We know that he has no great love for this place, but by moving to our city, he might learn something about the country he is trying to govern. He might learn, in spite of his reservations, that we are the true heartland.

July 31, 2002

References

THE INVENTION OF SOLITUDE. New York, Sun Books; 1982. Reprinted by Penguin USA; 1988.

HAND TO MOUTH. New York, Henry Holt; 1997.

TRUE STORIES. 'The Red Notebook' (*Granta*, 1993); 'Why Write?' (*The New Yorker*, 1995); 'Accident Report' (*Conjunctions*, 2000); 'It Don't Mean A Thing' (*Granta*, 2000). All four pieces were later collected in *The Red Notebook*. New York, New Directions; 2002.

GOTHAM HANDBOOK. In *Double Game*, by Sophie Calle. London, Violette; 1999.

THE STORY OF MY TYPEWRITER. New York, D.A.P.; 2002.

NORTHERN LIGHTS. 'Pages for Kafka' (*European Judaism*, 1974); 'The Death of Sir Walter Raleigh' (*Parenthèse*, 1975); 'Northern Lights' (Catalogue preface for Jean-Paul Riopelle exhibition, Galerie Maeght, Paris, 1976; *Derrière le miroir*, no. 218).

CRITICAL ESSAYS. 'The Art of Hunger' (*American Letters and Commentary*, 1988); 'New York Babel' (*The New York Review of Books*, 1975); 'Dada Bones' (*Mulch*, 1975); 'Truth, Beauty, Silence' (*The New York Review of Books*, 1975); 'From Cakes to Stones' (*Commentary*, 1975); 'The Poetry of Exile' (*Commentary*, 1976); 'Innocence and Memory' (*The New York Review of Books*, 1976); 'Book of the Dead' (*The New York Review of Books*, 1976); 'Reznikoff × 2' (*Parnassus*, 1979; in *Charles Reznikoff: Man and Poet*. Orano, Maine, National Poetry Foundation; 1984); 'The Bartlebooth Follies' (*The New York Times Book Review*, 1987).

PREFACES. 'Jacques Dupin' (*Fits and Starts: Selected Poems of Jacques Dupin*. New York, Living Hand; 1974); 'André du Bouchet' (*The Uninhabited: Selected Poems of André du Bouchet*. New York, Living Hand;

1976); 'Black on White' (Leaflet distributed at Susan Cauldwell Gallery, New York, for David Reed exhibition, 1975); 'Twentieth-Century French Poetry' (*The Random House Book of Twentieth-Century French Poetry*. New York, Random House; 1982); 'Mallarmé's Son' (*A Tomb for Anatole*, by Stéphane Mallarmé. San Francisco, North Point Press; 1983); 'On the High Wire' (*Traité du funambulisme*, by Philippe Petit. Arles [France], Actes Sud; 1997); 'Translator's Note' (*Chronicle of the Guayaki Indians*, by Pierre Clastres. New York, Zone Books; 1998); 'The National Story Project' (*I Thought My Father Was God and Other True Tales from NPR's National Story Project*. New York, Henry Holt; 2001); 'A Little Anthology of Surrealist Poems' (*A Little Anthology of Surrealist Poems*. Minneapolis, Rain Taxi; 2002. New preface for collection originally published in 1972); 'The Art of Worry' (Catalogue preface for Art Spiegelman exhibition, Nuage Gallery, Brescia [Italy], 2003); 'Invisible Joubert' (for reprint of *The Notebooks of Joseph Joubert*. New York, New York Review Books; forthcoming 2004. Book originally published by North Point Press, San Francisco; 1983); 'Hawthorne at Home' (*Nathaniel Hawthorne: Twenty Days with Julian & Little Bunny, by Papa*. New York, New York Review Books; 2003).

OCCASIONS. 'A Prayer for Salman Rushdie' (Op-ed piece: *The New York Times*; June 18, 1993); 'Appeal to the Governor of Pennsylvania' (Delivered at a press conference at the PEN American Center, New York, on July 28, 1995. Other participants included Dennis Brutus, Thulani Davis, Cornelius Eady, and William Styron); 'The Best Substitute for War' (*The New York Times Magazine*; April 1999. In response to the question: What is the best game of the millennium?); 'Reflections on a Cardboard Box' (Written at the request of the New York Coalition for the Homeless—for a brochure that was never published); 'Random Notes—September 11, 2001—4:00 PM' (Commissioned by *Die Zeit*; published September 13, 2001); 'Underground' (*The New York Times Magazine*; October 2001. In response to the question: Describe something about New York you love); 'NYC = USA' (Op-ed piece: *The New York Times*; September 9, 2002).